Foundations of Indian Contract Law

Foundations of Indian Contract Law

Edited by

KV KRISHNAPRASAD

Barrister, One Essex Court, London

NIRANJAN VENKATESAN

Barrister, One Essex Court, London

SHIVPRASAD SWAMINATHAN

Professor and Dean, Shiv Nadar School of Law, Shiv Nadar University, India

UMAKANTH VAROTTIL

Professor, Faculty of Law, National University of Singapore

OXFORD
UNIVERSITY PRESS

OXFORD
UNIVERSITY PRESS

Great Clarendon Street, Oxford, OX2 6DP,
United Kingdom

Oxford University Press is a department of the University of Oxford.
It furthers the University's objective of excellence in research, scholarship,
and education by publishing worldwide. Oxford is a registered trade mark of
Oxford University Press in the UK and in certain other countries

Published in the United States of America by Oxford University Press
198 Madison Avenue, New York, NY 10016, United States of America

British Library Cataloguing in Publication Data

Data available

Library of Congress Control Number: 2024936305

ISBN 9780198893752

DOI: 10.1093/9780191997211.001.0001

Printed and bound by
CPI Group (UK) Ltd, Croydon, CR0 4YY

MIX
Paper | Supporting
responsible forestry
FSC® C013604

Preface

The Indian Contract Act turned 150 in 2022. On any view, it has stood the test of time. This book has its origins in our perception that, nonetheless, Indian contract law has not received the scholarly attention that it warrants. In this, contract law in India is not alone. It is fair to say that, for many years, Indian legal literature has been dominated by public law rather than private law. Although the fact of this is beyond serious dispute, the reasons for it are not. One reason may be that the work of the higher courts in India tends to be dominated by public law. By contrast, for example, to the UK Supreme Court or the Singapore Court of Appeal, which tend to decide at least a few cases each year involving far-reaching and complex questions of private law, the Indian Supreme Court is best known for its public law jurisprudence. Indeed, it is difficult to think of any recent Indian Supreme Court decision in the field of private law (excluding arbitration) that has attracted anywhere near as much attention as some of its public law judgments.

This is not to say that Indian private law is unimportant. On the contrary, India is set to be the world's third biggest economy by 2030.[1] It is already home to very substantial commercial activity, and inherent in such activity is the need for mechanisms to resolve substantial commercial disputes. Many of the highest-value commercial disputes in India tend to be exported, most commonly to arbitration in Singapore or London and sometimes to the English courts. In such cases, of which some of us have professional experience, it is often necessary for a foreign court or arbitral tribunal to decide complex and controversial questions of Indian contract law (eg the distinction between a penalty and liquidated damages, the scope of the right to terminate for repudiatory breach, and the assessment of damages). In doing this, the first port of call tends to be standard textbooks on Indian contract law. However, valuable as those textbooks are, they do not always provide the answer, nor do they attempt to examine the foundational assumptions on which the Contract Act is based. Indeed, to our knowledge, there is no treatise that does so.

This gap in the literature has had two principal consequences.

The first is that scholarship examining the conceptual foundations of Indian contract law is rare, and an examination of the legislative history of particular provisions of the Contract Act is rarer still. As we hope this book demonstrates, such scholarship has valuable insights to offer as to the resolution of difficult questions of law that trouble the courts in modern litigation. One example suffices to illustrate the point. In English law, it is well-established that a wrongful termination of a contract may itself be

[1] S Sinha, 'India Set to Become 3rd Largest Economy by 2030, Says S&P Global', *The Hindu BusinessLine* (5 December 2023).

a repudiatory breach permitting the other party to treat the contract as discharged and sue for loss of bargain damages. This is why termination is a high-risk game: the price of getting it wrong is likely to be a substantial liability in damages. It would be surprising if the law were any different in India. On analysis, it is not, but what is perhaps surprising is the difficulty of arriving at that answer. It is not to be found in any express language in the Contract Act but instead in a (masterly) analysis of section 39 by the Full Bench of the Calcutta High Court (affirmed on appeal by the Privy Council) in 1939.[2] An analysis of the legislative history of section 39 reinforces that conclusion, but a busy practitioner does not have the luxury of exploring the intricacies of case law from the 1930s, still less the antecedents of section 39. An accessible account of that history is therefore likely to be valuable to practitioners and academics alike.

The second consequence is that India has largely been a bystander to the vigorous debates elsewhere in the common law world about contract law. This is mainly because the issues that are contentious in the common law world have largely not arisen in India. For example, there is virtually no Indian authority as to whether *The Achilleas*[3] is good law under the Contract Act, the test for the implication of terms,[4] the principles governing the interpretation of contracts,[5] the nature of and rationale for 'negotiating damages' awards,[6] or the nature of contractual estoppel[7] (and examples can, of course, be multiplied).

The purpose of this project is to address these gaps. This is why each chapter pays close attention to the legislative history of the relevant provision of the Contract Act, and none aims to survey every single Indian case in the area (probably an impossible exercise in any event). The result, we hope, is an overview of the foundational concepts of Indian contract law, derived from an analysis of what the legislator set out to achieve and the leading (but not all) authorities. Whether we have succeeded in that aim is for readers to judge.

When we embarked upon this project, the intention was that the book would be published to coincide with the 150th anniversary of the Contract Act. It was regrettably not possible to achieve this, largely because of the disruption caused by the COVID-19 pandemic. Happily, however, we were able to organise a conference (virtually, needless to say) in August 2020, which enabled each contributor to present their chapter. We are extremely grateful to the contributors for participating in this project. We are also grateful to Debaranjan Goswami, Vandita Khanna, Param Nayankumar Pandya, and Titiksha Mohanty, who assisted us greatly in preparing the draft chapters

[2] *International Film Co Ltd v Murlidhar Chatterjee* (1939) 44 CWN 11; *Muralidhar Chatterjee v International Film Co Ltd* (1943) 70 IA 35.

[3] [2008] UKHL 48, [2009] 1 AC 61.

[4] *Marks & Spencer plc v BNP Paribas Securities Services Trust Co (Jersey) Ltd* [2015] UKSC 72, [2016] AC 742.

[5] The finest modern account of these principles probably remains *Mannai Investment Co Ltd v Eagle Star Life Assurance Co Ltd* [1997] AC 749, 774–79 although other cases tend to be cited more frequently in practice.

[6] *One Step (Support) Ltd v Morris-Garner* [2018] UKSC 20, [2019] AC 649.

[7] *First Tower Trustees v CDS (Superstores International) Ltd* [2018] EWCA Civ 1396, [2019] 1 WLR 637.

for publication. We would also like to take this opportunity to thank Mindy Chen-Wishart, Arvind Datar, the Centre for Asian Legal Studies at the National University of Singapore, Jindal Global Law School, Melbourne University School of Law, the team at OUP, and the anonymous reviewers for their generous support (in different capacities) for this project.

KV Krishnaprasad
Niranjan Venkatesan
Shivprasad Swaminathan
Umakanth Varottil
31 December 2023

Contents

Table of Cases

Table of Legislation

INTERNATIONAL INSTRUMENTS

KENYA

MALAYSIA

MYANMAR

NEW ZEALAND

PAKISTAN

SINGAPORE

TANZANIA

UGANDA

UNITED KINGDOM

UNITED STATES

Abbreviations

AAEC	appreciable adverse effect on competition
ACA	Arbitration and Conciliation Act 1996
AOA	Articles of Association
CBI	Central Bank of India
CCA	Consumer Credit Act 1974
CIF	cost, insurance, and freight
CMA	Competition and Markets Authority
Contract Act	Indian Contract Act 1872
CPC	Code of Civil Procedure 1908
FEMA	Foreign Exchange Management Act 1999
FERA	Foreign Exchange Regulation Act 1973
HMGA	Hindu Minority and Guardianship Act 1956
IPC	Indian Penal Code 1860
LODR	Listing Obligations and Disclosure Requirements
Malaysian Act	Malaysian Contracts Act 1950
MTP Act	Major Ports Trust Act 1963
NYCC	New York Civil Code
OFT	Office of Fair Trading
RBI	Reserve Bank of India
RPA	Representation of the People Act 1951
SARFAESI Act	Securitisation and Reconstruction of Financial Assets and Enforcement of Security Interest Act 2002
SBI	State Bank of India
SEBI	Securities and Exchange Board of India
Singapore EA	Singapore Evidence Act
TDSAT	Telecom Disputes Settlement and Appellate Tribunal
TPA	Transfer of Property Act 1882
UCC	Uniform Commercial Code
UCTA	Unfair Contract Terms Act 1977
UNIDROIT	International Institute for the Unification of Private Law

Contributors

Aman Ahluwalia, Delhi High Court, India

TT Arvind, York Law School, University of York, United Kingdom <https://orcid.org/0000-0001-5468-3669> accessed 3 April 2024

Elise Bant, University of Western Australia, Perth, Australia; Melbourne Law School, University of Melbourne, Australia <https://orcid.org/0000-0003-2188-0521> accessed 3 April 2024

Katy Barnett, Melbourne Law School, University of Melbourne, Australia <https://orcid.org/0000-0001-6080-8296> accessed 3 April 2024

Hugh Beale KC (Hon), University of Warwick, Coventry, United Kingdom; Harris Manchester College, University of Oxford, United Kingdom

Divya Behl, Supreme Court of India and Delhi High Court, India

Nilima Bhadbhade, Former Associate Professor, ILS Law College, Pune, India

Chintan Chandrachud, Barrister, Brick Court Chambers, London, United Kingdom

May Fong Cheong, School of Private and Commercial Law, Faculty of Law & Justice, University of New South Wales, Sydney, Australia; Multimedia University, Melaka, Malaysia <https://orcid.org/0000-0002-9218-7516> accessed 3 April 2024

Wayne Courtney, National University of Singapore, Singapore <https://orcid.org/0000-0002-2360-2659> accessed 3 April 2024

Steven Elliott KC, Barrister, One Essex Court, London, United Kingdom

Nemika Jha, Jindal Global Law School, OP Jindal Global University, India

Vikramaditya S Khanna, University of Michigan Law School, Ann Arbor, United States <https://orcid.org/0000-0001-7779-613X> accessed 3 April 2024

KV Krishnaprasad, Barrister, One Essex Court, London, United Kingdom

Manasi Kumar, OP Jindal Global University, India <https://orcid.org/0000-0002-5027-4929> accessed 3 April 2024

Neel Maitra, Dechert LLP, United States

Poorna Mysoor, Lucy Cavendish College, University of Cambridge, United Kingdom <https://orcid.org/0000-0001-9710-9034> accessed 3 April 2024

Mihir Naniwadekar, Chambers of Mihir Naniwadekar, India

Shantanu Naravane, Herbert Smith Freehills LLP, London, United Kingdom

Nigam Nuggehalli, National Law School of India University, Bangalore, India

Jeannie Marie Paterson, Melbourne Law School, University of Melbourne, Australia

Gail Pearson, The Business School, University of Sydney, Australia

Thomas Sebastian, Barrister, Essex Court Chambers, London, United Kingdom

Veda Singh, Supreme Court of India and Delhi High Court, India

Ragini Surana, Max Planck Institute for Legal History and Legal Theory, Germany

Warren Swain, Faculty of Law, University of Auckland, New Zealand <https://orcid.org/0000-0002-6616-3481> accessed 3 April 2024

Shivprasad Swaminathan, Shiv Nadar School of Law, Shiv Nadar University, India

Zhong Xing Tan, Faculty of Law, National University of Singapore, Singapore

Stelios Tofaris, University of Cambridge, United Kingdom

Umakanth Varottil, Faculty of Law, National University of Singapore, Singapore <https://orcid.org/0000-0003-2468-1907> accessed 3 April 2024

Niranjan Venkatesan, Barrister, One Essex Court, London, United Kingdom

Goh Yihan, Supreme Court of Singapore, Singapore

PART I
GENERAL THEMES

1

History and Drafting of the Indian Contract Act 1872

Warren Swain

I. Introduction

One Bengal barrister would describe the Indian Contract Bill as 'a painful and cruel infliction'.[1] The passage of the legislation was certainly far from smooth. Members of the Third Indian Law Commission, who had drawn up the Bill, would end up resigning, partly over delays in seeing their recommendations enacted but also over attempts by the Indian legislature to change the content of their Bill. The response in a departmental memorandum was that their report was only four years old, whereas the Penal Code had taken more than two decades to be enacted.[2] This was more than just a characteristic bureaucratic reaction. It also reflected something more axiomatic: the enormous challenges that are faced by all codification projects—whether they are a comprehensive code or, as here, when they amount to the codification of a significant body of legal doctrine.

The Indian Contract Act 1872 (hereinafter 'the Contract Act') dates from a time when the British Raj was at the height of its prestige. Just a few years later, Queen Victoria would become Empress of India.[3] Yet, the story behind the drafting of the legislation is much more than a simple account of the exercise of power by a distant colonial power. India provides a good example of the way in which the British were prepared to adapt the common law for colonial conditions, at the same time also demonstrating the limits of that indulgence. Although the British Empire is a central component in the narrative, the Contract Act also fits within two wider nineteenth-century debates about the merits of codification and the structure of contract law.

[1] JB Money, Barrister to Assistant Secretary Bengal: 21 May1868 IOR L/PJ/5/15 (unfol).
[2] Some of the correspondence survives: IOR/L/P&J/5/438.
[3] Queen Victoria took a close interest in India; see M Taylor, *Empress: Queen Victoria and India* (Yale University Press 2018).

Warren Swain, *History and Drafting of the Indian Contract Act 1872* In: *Foundations of Indian Contract Law.* Edited by: KV Krishnaprasad, Niranjan Venkatesan, Shivprasad Swaminathan, and Umakanth Varottil, Oxford University Press. © Oxford University Press 2024.
DOI: 10.1093/9780191997211.003.0001

II. Law-Making in the British Empire

John Darwin, a leading historian of the British Empire, has observed that 'in histories of empire the sound and fury of the ideological battlefield are rarely absent for long'.[4] Niall Ferguson, who controversially challenged the negative portrayal of the British Empire, has said that 'we should not underestimate the benefits conferred by British law and administration'.[5] Even a writer whose views on the British Empire are much more negative has conceded that the common law brought some benefits to India.[6] The way that the common law applied across the British Empire varied enormously over time and place. Some of these differences were a reflection of local conditions.[7] But generally, by the mid-nineteenth century, as colonial legal systems became more legalistic, the law applied in the colonies grew closer to that which operated back in London. At the same time, each colony retained some local characteristics.[8] The situation in India was slightly different to that in other colonies because the British deliberately introduced extensive legislation that was intended to be a partial departure from English common law.[9]

The status of the common law in India was further complicated by the way that the country was run as a corporate state by the East India Company before 1858.[10] The Company operated its own courts.[11] As Stern notes, '[t]hese Company courts were designed first and foremost to maintain respect for government, from within and without, and satisfy the needs of inhabitants for both public order and the resolution of civil conflict'.[12] In one form or another, these courts survived into the nineteenth century.[13] By the 1780s, the power of the Company was beginning to be eroded and the Company would be placed under a Board of Control subordinate to Parliament.[14] The creation of a system of Charter courts was part of the process and further reduced the importance of the Company courts.

[4] J Darwin, *Unfinished Empire: The Global Expansion of Britain* (Penguin 2012) 6.

[5] N Ferguson, *Empire: How Britain Made the Modern World* (Penguin 2008) 369.

[6] S Tharoor, *Inglorious Empire: What the British Did to India* (Scribe 2018) 93–95.

[7] This pluralistic approach was common to other empires: L Benton and R Ross (eds), *Legal Pluralism and Empires, 1500–1850* (New York University Press 2013).

[8] For this analysis in relation to New Zealand, W Swain, 'The Great Britain of the South: The Law of Contract in Early Colonial New Zealand' (2020) 60 American Journal of Legal History 30. For Australia, see B Kercher, *An Unruly Child: A History of Law in Australia* (Allen & Unwin 1995) 67–81.

[9] The same was true of the Penal Code, which also departed from English law in important ways: KJM Smith, 'Macaulay's Utilitarian Indian Penal Code: An Illustration of the Accidental Function of Time, Place and Personalities in Law Making' in WM Gordon and TD Fergus (eds), *Legal History in the Making* (Hambledon Press 1991) 145, 153–60.

[10] For accounts see, W Dalrymple, *The Anarchy: The Relentless Rise of the East India Company* (Bloomsbury 2019); PJ Stern, *The Company–State Corporate Sovereignty and the Early Modern Foundations of the British Empire in India* (OUP 2011).

[11] Stern (n 10) 27–28. For an important recent study, see R Travers, *Empires of Complaints: Mughal Law and the Making of British India, 1765–1793* (CUP 2022).

[12] Stern (n 10) 28.

[13] For a detailed account of the court system, see MP Jain, *Indian Legal History* (University of Delhi Press 1956).

[14] TR Metcalf, *Ideologies of the Raj* (CUP 1994) 17. The process of emasculation of the East India Company began in 1773; see Dalrymple (n 10) 314.

Two principles underpinned the attitude of the British towards India in the late eighteenth century. The first of these was the description of India as a land of 'oriental despotism', which, some believed, could only be remedied by a wholesale introduction of English law.[15] The Governor General of Bengal, Warren Hastings, resisted this approach, arguing that India was an ancient civilization with its own system of laws, and this was the second element in the way that the British perceived the legal system.[16] This second idea was reflected in the enthusiastic way in which some of the British began to compile collections of Indian laws. The first of these works, NB Halhed's *A Code of Gentoo Laws*,[17] appeared in 1776. Another compilation, prepared by Sir William Jones, was an ambitious, comprehensive digest of Hindu and Islamic law.[18] Jones saw his project as on a par with Justinian's *Digest of Roman Law* in scale.[19] After his death, Jones's digest was completed by Henry Colebrooke.[20] However, despite attempts to collect and catalogue Indian laws, a deep tension between English law and local law persisted. Jones himself favoured the imposition of a procedural framework based on English law, at the same time believing that the substantive common law should not be transplanted wholesale into India.[21]

Different bodies of law, including contract law, had traditionally applied to different sections of the Indian population.[22] Writing in the 1780s, Edmund Burke, mindful of the recent loss of the American colony, saw this as a desirable state of affairs: 'Where thirty million are to be governed by a few thousand men, government must be established by consent, and must be congenial to feelings and to the habits of the people.'[23] The legislation that created a Supreme Court at Calcutta and two Recorders' courts at the other Presidency towns in Madras and Bombay brought those populations under the jurisdiction of English law.[24] It did not follow that these courts necessarily applied English law in all circumstances. The legislation explicitly provided that Muslim and Hindu residents were to be governed by their own law and usages in 'all matters of contract'.[25] But by the early nineteenth century, some British observers were sceptical that anything other than the English law was ever applied in these Charter courts, regardless of the religion of the litigants. In the 1820s, Sir Francis Macnaghten said that,

[15] BS Cohn, 'Law and the Colonial State in India' in J Starr and J Collier (eds), *History and Power in the Study of Law* (Cornell University Press 1989) 131, 141.

[16] ibid 141; Metcalf (n 14) 15.

[17] NB Halhed, *A Code of Gentoo Laws* (*sine nomine* 1776).

[18] For a life of Jones, see MJ Franklin, *Orientalist Jones Sir William Jones, Poet, Lawyer, and Linguist, 1746–1794* (OUP 2011).

[19] As with Justinian, a shorter *Institutes* was completed as well: W Jones, *Institutes of Hindu Law* (Brojendrolall Doss 1794). On Jones's vision, see D Ibbetson, 'Sir William Jones as a Comparative Lawyer' in A Murray (ed), *Sir William Jones 1746–94: A Commemoration* (OUP 1998) 17, 29.

[20] H Colebrooke, *A Digest of Hindu Law on Contracts and Successions* (Government Printer 1798). For Colebrooke's work on Indian law, see R Rocher and L Rocher, *The Making of Western Ideology* (Routledge 2012) 33–60.

[21] Ibbetson, 'Sir William Jones' (n 19) 26–27.

[22] BS Cohn, *Colonialism and Its Forms of Knowledge* (Princeton University Press 1996) ch 3; BS Cohn, 'From Indian Status to British Contract' (1961) 21 Journal of Economic History 613.

[23] PJ Marshall (ed), *The Writings and Speeches of Edmund Burke: India, Madras and Bengal 1774–1785*, vol V (OUP 2000) 141 .

[24] (1781) 21 Geo III c 70. This legislation is usually known as the Settlement Act or the Amending Act.

[25] ibid s 17.

in his experience, he 'never knew or heard of an instance in which the Supreme Court was called upon in a case of contract, to decide by Hindu laws and usages'.[26] William Macpherson noted, in 1860, that 'the privilege, if it can be so called is of little value' and explained that 'the English Law is generally found to supply just principles'.[27] A modern study suggests that English law was sometimes applied in contractual disputes in the Charter courts even when the parties were not Europeans.[28] Yet, this was far from a blanket rule of the kind suggested by Macnaghten. There are plenty of examples in which local law rather than English law was applied in contract cases, which include the application of laws of usury as well as the limitation rules.[29]

Outside the Presidency towns, the mofussil courts operated according to different principles.[30] Indigenous judges sat at the lowest levels. The English judges, who sat at higher levels, were civil servants with no more than a smattering of English legal training. They were unlikely to have been any more familiar with local rules than they were with English law and were assisted by indigenous law officers. In Henry Maine's opinion, this arrangement was unsatisfactory:

> [T]he inferior judges, when they were applying some half-remembered legal rule learnt in boyhood, or culling a proposition of law from a half-understood English text-book, no doubt honestly thought in many cases that they were following the rule prescribed for them, to decide 'by equity and good conscience' wherever no native law or usage was discoverable.[31]

'Equity and good conscience', when used in this context, amounted to something less carefully defined than English contract law or even the law applied in the English Court of Chancery. The phrase is best equated with a pragmatic common sense that allowed judges to apply a mixture of local law, English law, and vaguer notions of fairness and justice. It was the standard formula used in the lowest-level civil courts in England—the Courts of Conscience.[32] The same idea was also found in other colonial courts—notably the Court of Civil Jurisdiction in the early New South Wales colony.[33]

In 1861, a new structure was put in place with a High Court in each of the three Presidency towns. The new High Courts absorbed the jurisdiction of the Sudder courts, which had formerly acted as courts of appeal for the mofussil courts.[34] The

[26] F Macnaghten, *Considerations on the Hindoo Law, as it is Current in Bengal* (Mission Press 1824) 403.

[27] W Macpherson, *Outlines of the Law of Contracts as Administered in the Courts of British India* (RC Lepage 1860) vi.

[28] S Tofaris, 'A Historical Study of the Indian Contract Act 1872' (PhD thesis, University of Cambridge 2011) 5–87. See also MP Jain, 'The Indian Law of Contract before Its Codification' [1972] Journal of the Indian Law Institute 178, 180–83.

[29] Jain, 'The Indian Law of Contract' (n 28) 184–87. For further examples, see G Pearson, 'Consultation for a Code: Nineteenth-Century Consultation on the Proposed Commercial Laws' in N Jayaram (ed), *Interrogating Ideas, Institutions, and Processes: Essays in Memory of Satish Saberwall* (Orient Blackswan 2014) 115, 122.

[30] For these courts, see *Report of the Law Commissioners on the Judicial System of India* (1842) IOR/V/26/100/4.

[31] H Maine, *Village-Communities in East and West* (3rd edn, John Murray 1876) 299.

[32] These courts in large urban centres dispatched quick, informal justice; see M Finn, *The Character of Credit* (CUP 2003) 197–235.

[33] For an account of that court, see B Kercher, *Debt, Seduction and Other Disasters* (Federation Press 1996).

[34] Indian High Courts Act 1861 (24 & 25 Vict c 104).

Privy Council became a court of final appeal.[35] English trained lawyers also began to arrive in greater numbers.[36] Writing at this time, Macpherson stated that judges 'generally avoided any wide departure from its [the common law] principles except in cases affected by some of the special features of oriental life and transactions'.[37] In a minute for the Governor General's Council, Henry Maine argued that 'justice, equity and good conscience have of late years been much affected, as a fact, by the English law of contract'.[38] At the same time, it would be a mistake to conclude that by the mid-nineteenth century, Indian courts simply applied English law. In important respects there continued to be divergence between the law of contract as it applied to Muslims, Hindus, and Europeans.[39] Although the Act was intended to be secular and apply to all populations, these existing differences could not help but come to the fore during the drafting process.[40] Meanwhile, in England during this period, lawyers were debating the merits of codification—contract law was in a period of flux. Both of these events would have a significant impact on Indian contract law.

III. Codification in England in the Early Nineteenth Century

In 1830, the *Law Magazine* observed that '[c]odification . . . has become a dead letter in England'.[41] Jeremy Bentham had begun working on his complete code of the laws or 'pannomion' decades earlier, but the idea died with him, and his work was never finished.[42] Codification also met determined opposition from many lawyers. Edward Sugden, a future Lord Chancellor, reacted to a detailed proposal of James Humphreys for a code of English real property law[43] in extremely disparaging terms:

> In regard to the proposed Code generally, I must avow myself decidedly opposed to all codes. The laws owe much to the reverence which their antiquity inspires; and where, as in our case, they have in a succession of ages been adapted to the free institutions of the country, it were rash, as the Code proposes, to abolish them all by one declaration, and establish a new law. Time mellows and indeed forms laws.[44]

[35] Jain, *Indian Legal History* (n 13) 359–86.
[36] ibid 442; D Duman, *The English and Colonial Bars in the Nineteenth Century* (Croom Helm 1983) 130–34.
[37] Macpherson (n 27) viii.
[38] 'Statement of Objects and Reasons', 9 July 1867, *Copies of Papers Showing the Present Position of the Question of Contract Law for India* (1867–68) [239] PP vol xlix 86 (*Contract Law for India*).
[39] For an illustration from this period in the context of a dispute over a lien, see *Varden Seth Sam v Luckpathy Royjee Lallah* (1862) 9 Moo Ind App 307, 325–26.
[40] For example, in relation to the debate about the *nemo dat* rule, G Pearson, 'A Cattle Lifter's Bill: Nemo dat Rule and the Indian Contract Act' (2015) 89 Australian Law Journal 31, 40.
[41] Anon, 'Events of the Quarter' (1830) 4 Law Magazine 244.
[42] Albeit into the late nineteenth century there were some in England who still saw value in codification: S Amos, *A English Code, Its Difficulties and Modes of Overcoming Them* (Strahan 1873).
[43] J Humphreys, *Observations on the Actual State of the English Laws of Real Property with the Outline of a Code* (John Murray 1826). For details of the project, see B Rudden, 'A Code Too Soon: The 1826 Property Code of James Humphreys: English Rejection, American Reception, English Acceptance' in P Wallington and RM Merkin (eds), *Essays in Memory of FH Lawson* (Butterworths 1986) 101.
[44] EB Sugden, *A Letter to James Humphreys, Esq: On His Proposal to Repeal the Laws of Real Property and Substitute a New Code* (2nd edn, J & WT Clarke 1826) 5.

Although there was some piecemeal legislation on property law[45] and, later in the century, on bills of exchange, partnership, sale of goods, and marine insurance,[46] no general code of private law was ever enacted in England.

Whilst it was a struggle for those who favoured the idea to convince lawyers and the legislature of the benefits of codification in England, India was a different proposition. A number of those sympathetic to Bentham's philosophy ended up in positions of influence.[47] James Mill, the father of JS Mill, in his history of India, described Sir William Jones's *Institute* as

> [A] disorderly compilation of loose, vague, stupid or unintelligible quotations and maxims: selected arbitrarily from books of law, books of devotion, and books of poetry; attended with a commentary which only adds to the mass of absurdity and darkness; a farrago by which nothing is defined, nothing established.[48]

Mill regarded codification as a solution to the 'absurdity and darkness.'[49] Another admirer of Bentham, Thomas Macaulay, in a speech to Parliament in 1833, said that 'I believe that no country ever stood so much in need of a code of law as India, and I believe also that there never was a country in which the want might be so easily supplied.'[50] Macaulay, who became Law Member of the Indian Legislative Council in the mid-1830s, was in the ideal position to push for reform along utilitarian lines.[51] James Fitzjames Stephen,[52] who was also sympathetic to Benthamite ideas, would later occupy the same post and play an important role in the Contract Act. While some utilitarians even saw successful Indian codification as a means of reviving the idea in England,[53] the movement extended beyond a mere coalition of idealists. There was also pressure for law reform from lawyers and officials in India.[54] The circumstances were also propitious. Men like Macaulay were able to bring about radical reform because they could legislate in an authoritarian manner that would have been impossible in London.[55]

The first Indian Law Commission was appointed in 1833 and drafted a Penal Code.[56] Macaulay also pushed for the codification of the civil law by quoting from an Indian judge of his acquaintance on the state of commercial law: 'He told me that it was a mere

[45] S Anderson, 'Property' in W Cornish and others (eds), *The Oxford History of the Laws of England*, vol XII (1820–1914) Private Law (OUP 2010) 49–78.

[46] Lord Rodger, 'The Codification of Commercial Law in Victorian Britain' (1992) 108 Law Quarterly Review 570.

[47] E Stokes, *The English Utilitarians and India* (OUP 1959).

[48] J Mill, *The History of British India in 6 Volumes*, vol 5 (2nd edn, Baldwin, Cradock, and Joy 1820) 513.

[49] RE Sullivan, *Macaulay: The Tragedy of Power* (Harvard University Press 2009) 108.

[50] HC Deb 10 July 1833, vol 19, col 531.

[51] Sullivan (n 49) 137.

[52] KJM Smith, *James Fitzjames Stephen* (CUP 2002).

[53] Sullivan (n 49) 149.

[54] Whitley Stokes believed that the origins of the reform movement could be traced to correspondence in the 1820s between Sir Charles Metcalfe, a colonial governor, and the Judges of Bengal: W Stokes, *The Anglo-Indian Codes*, vol 1 (OUP 1887) x.

[55] B Wright, 'Macaulay's India Law Reforms and Labour in the British Empire' in S Dorsett and J McLaren (eds), *Legal Histories of the British Empire* (Routledge 2014) 281, 221.

[56] On the Penal Code generally, see G Rankin, *Background to Indian Law* (CUP 1946) 197–217.

lottery. He knew how he should himself decide. But he knew nothing more.'[57] Although resistance to codification in India was less fierce than in England, the fact that it took twenty years for the Penal Code to be enacted was a salutary lesson to any would-be codifiers.[58]

IV. The Third Indian Law Commission

The Third Indian Law Commission produced its report on contract law in 1866.[59] Three of the six members of the Commission were judges.[60] The Master of the Rolls, Sir John Romilly, who was a son of Bentham's friend Samuel Romilly, headed the list.[61] The second judge, Sir Edward Ryan, was the former Chief Justice of India and author of Ryan and Moody's law reports.[62] The third judge, Sir William James, was Vice Chancellor of the Court of Chancery at the time of the report and later a Lord Justice of Appeal. He took a special interest in India.[63] Of the remaining members of the Commission, there was a civil servant, Sir John Macleod, who had been a member of the Indian Law Commission since the beginning,[64] and two barristers, Robert Lowe, who would later become the Chancellor of the Exchequer and Home Secretary,[65] and John Henderson.[66] The secretary to the Commission, William Macpherson, was something of an expert on Indian contract law, which may have made him particularly influential. Six years earlier, he had published his *Outlines of the Law of Contracts as Administered in the Courts of British India*.[67]

V. The State of the Common Law of Contract Law in 1860

The mid-nineteenth century was a crucial period in the history of contract doctrine in England. In 1826, the legal writer Joseph Chitty had remarked that '[p]erhaps no branch of the jurisprudence of this country has of late years been more subject of judicial inquiry and decision than the Law of Contracts'.[68] Several things happened around

[57] HC Deb 10 July 1833, vol 19, col 532.

[58] Stokes, *The English Utilitarians* (n 47) 219–33.

[59] *The Report of the Indian Law Commissioners on the Subject of Contracts* (1867–68) PP HC, vol xlix.

[60] The Commission responsible for contract was appointed in 1864 when two members of the Third Commission, appointed in 1861 (J Willes and Sir William Earle) retired; see *Commissions and Appointments in India*, IOR/H/25.

[61] JA Hamilton and P Polden, 'Romilly, John' in BH Harrison (ed), *Oxford Dictionary of National Biography* (OUP 2004). Romilly was Master of the Rolls between 1851 and 1873.

[62] Ryan was Chief Justice between 1833 and 1843; see K Prior, 'Ryan, Sir Edward' in Harrison (n 61).

[63] He wrote a book on the history of India, which was edited by his daughter Mary Schwabe and published posthumously: W James, *The British in India* (Macmillan 1882).

[64] In a letter to his friend Thomas Ellis, Macaulay described Macleod as 'the cleverest man that I have found in India by many degrees': T Pinney (ed), *The Letters of Thomas Babington Macaulay*, vol III (CUP 1976) 201.

[65] J Winter, *Robert Lowe* (University of Toronto Press 1976).

[66] On his death, Henderson was replaced by Sir Robert Lush, a judge; see JA Hamilton and H Mooney, 'Lush, Sir Robert' in Harrison (n 61).

[67] Macpherson (n 27).

[68] J Chitty, *A Practical Treatise on the Law of Contracts* (S Sweet 1826) iii.

this time.[69] The most important of these events saw the old learning around the forms of action, which was rooted in the Middle Ages, replaced by a new substantive structure. By the late nineteenth century, something akin to a unified law of contract built around core principles and with a methodical order and structure was created. It has remained, largely unchanged, into modern times. The driving forces for this development are complex, but changes in the legal system were undoubtedly one factor. The boundary between questions of law and fact began to firm up and juries began to have a diminishing role. One consequence of these procedural developments was that legal doctrine came more clearly to the surface, having, in the past, been hidden behind pleadings and jury verdicts.

The main consequence of these changes was that judges needed to develop a body of substantive law. Fortunately, there was an off-the-peg theory that was suited to the task. Their inspiration was a slightly surprising one. It was founded in the work of the French jurist, Robert-Joseph Pothier, who published his *Traité des Obligations* in 1750. The book had not attracted much attention in England until decades later when an English translation by Sir William Evans appeared in 1806.[70] Evans's translation was serendipitous. It gave the book wider attention at an opportune time. At the heart of Pothier's will theory was a simple idea—that contracts were formed by a meeting of wills. One of the first writers to take up Pothier's ideas was the Anglo-Indian writer Henry Colebrooke.[71] More mainstream English writers, including Chitty, also embraced Pothier,[72] who also began to be cited by judges.[73]

Pothier's influence was greatest when the existing common law was silent or incomplete. But even here, for example in the development of an English doctrine of contractual mistake, 'English treatise writers did not accept Pothier's work . . . in its entirety: they were selective in their borrowing and they merged this with common law concerns, such as objectivity.'[74] English lawyers were engaged in a delicate blending exercise. By this time, there were already centuries of established doctrine to be taken into account. Prominent among these was the doctrine of consideration. This was too central to contract liability to be ignored; yet, to accept, as Pothier claimed, that contracts were formed by a meeting of wills would render the whole concept of consideration superfluous. English law reached a compromise which saw a gradual shift in the way that consideration was perceived and which left the doctrine looking less like an attempt to find a genuine exchange and more about whether an agreement was intended to have contractual effect.[75] The situation in India was different. Although English law was always likely to form a prominent part of any contract statute, the fact that the legislation

[69] For a detailed account, see W Swain, *The Law of Contract 1670–1870* (CUP 2015).

[70] RJ Pothier, *A Treatise on the Law of Obligations or Contracts* (W Evans tr, Strahan 1806).

[71] HT Colebrooke, *A Treatise on Obligations and Contracts* (H Colebrooke 1818).

[72] This shift can be seen by comparing the first edition of Chitty's contract treatise with the second edition: J Chitty, *A Practical Treatise on the Law of Contracts Not under Seal* (2nd edn, S Sweet 1834).

[73] B Rudden, 'Pothier et la common law' in J Monéger (ed), *Robert-Joseph Pothier. D'hier àujourd'hui* (Economica 2001) 91–101.

[74] C MacMillan, *Mistakes in Contract Law* (Hart 2010) 133.

[75] For an account of this process, see W Swain, 'The Changing Nature of the Doctrine of Consideration, 1750–1850' (2005) 26 Journal of Legal History 55.

was specially designed for a colony made it easier to depart from English law even in fundamental respects. This fact alone gave the Commission some degree of greater freedom, and they took advantage of it.

VI. Possible Influences on the Commission

Utilitarian philosophy was a significant influence on the whole scheme of codification in India. The sources of substantive law in the Contract Act are more varied. The Commission was quite explicit, in the introduction to its report, that it was willing to depart from English law.[76] Unsurprisingly, the provisions which diverged most from English law would become the most controversial in the whole scheme. The Commission admitted that it was prepared to borrow from civilian systems. Italy, France, and Germany were all mentioned on points of detail.[77] Civilian ideas were even more important in shaping the legislation than these references would suggest—they would form the basis of some of the underlying principles on which the legislation was constructed. This was evident from the draft Bill, clause 1 of which began with a definition of contract: 'A Contract is an agreement between parties whereby a party engages to do a thing or engages not to do a thing.' This statement closely resembles the definition of a contract that appears in the *Code Civil*[78] and Pothier's treatise.[79]

The definition of a contract as an agreement was hardly unfamiliar in England. The medieval action of covenant was, after all, based on agreement.[80] The novelty lay in the way that agreement was presented as the underlying principle of all contracts. The Will Theory was more than a single principle that contracts were a consequence of a meeting of wills; it informed the way that Pothier structured the whole subject. Although these ideas were perhaps even more evident in the final legislation, given the prominence afforded to the need for consent, the influence of Pothier's writing could be observed from the start. Clause 7 of the Bill was unadulterated Pothier: 'Where both parties to an engagement by contract are under a mistake as to a matter of fact essential to the engagement, the engagement is void.'[81] English law, by this stage, had not yet developed a substantive doctrine of contractual mistake, although Pothier's ideas on mistake can be traced in the writings of Henry Colebrooke and Stephen Leake.[82] It was left to writers of the next generation like Frederick Pollock and William Anson to build these principles into a comprehensive, well-worked-out law of contractual mistake.[83] That these writers did so was in spite of the fact that relevant English case law was thin

[76] *Contract Law for India* (n 38) 3.
[77] ibid 5, 6 in relation to the obligations around partnership and the discharge of a surety.
[78] *Code Civil*, Book 3, 3, 1§1101.
[79] Pothier (n 70) 1.1.1§1.
[80] For example, a year book case of 1321: H Cam, *Year Books of Edward II* (Selden Society 1969) 286.
[81] Macpherson (n 27) 8.
[82] Colebrooke, *A Treatise on Obligations and Contracts* (n 71); S Leake, *The Elements of the Law of Contracts* (Stevens & Sons 1867).
[83] F Pollock, *Principles of Contract at Law and in Equity* (Stevens & Sons 1876); W Anson, *Principles of the English Law of Contract* (Clarendon Press 1879).

on the ground. Significantly, the year before the Commission report, Blackburn J was forced to rely on Roman law in order to demonstrate that English law did not recognize a mistake as to quality.[84] The first illustration of contractual mistake in the draft Bill was based on the facts of *Couturier v Hastie*.[85] Yet, there was no need to reinterpret earlier authority such as this in order to promote a doctrine of mistake. The Commission was working from first principles, which meant that it was not inconvenienced in the same way as English writers were by the absence of authority. It also seems likely that the Commission was probably influenced by Macpherson on this issue, given that he had specifically praised Pothier's analysis on the subject of mistake.[86]

The Indian Law Commission was not the only body working on a contract code in the middle decades of the nineteenth century. In New York between the late 1850s and mid-1860s, David Dudley Field produced a comprehensive Civil Code, which was itself inspired by other sources including the French *Code Civil*, the Louisiana Civil Code, Pothier, and Justinian.[87] In the end, in the face of opposition from lawyers, the Civil Code was never enacted in New York,[88] although it was taken up in a few other American states.[89] The fact that Field adopted the standard civilian definition of contract ('a contract is an agreement to do or not to do a thing')[90] is less interesting than how consent was stated as an essential element of a contract and a key feature of the whole scheme.[91] One Indian respondent commenting on the Bill made the connection between the proposed legislation and Field's Code.[92] Yet, if anything, as Rankin has noted, the influence of the proposed New York Code was more pronounced in James Fitzjames Stephen's version of the Indian Contract Bill;[93] Stephen himself would note these parallels.[94]

VII. Departures from English Law in the Bill

The influence that civilian ideas had on the Commissioners meant that a key decision for them concerned what to do about the doctrine of consideration, which civilian systems lacked. Rather than abolish consideration, the Commission took an almost equally radical step of granting two major exceptions to the need for consideration in clause 10 of the Bill.[95] The first exception proposed to remove the requirement of

[84] *Kennedy v Panama, New Zealand and Australian Royal Mail Company* (1867) LR 2 QB 580.
[85] (1852) 8 Exch 40, (1853) 9 Exch 102, (1856) 5 HLC 673.
[86] Macpherson (n 27) xi.
[87] R Batiza, 'Sources of the Field Civil Code: The Civil Law Influences on a Common Law Code' (1986) 60 Tulane Law Review 799.
[88] M Lang, *Codification in the British Empire and America* (The Lawbook Exchange 2005) 146–48.
[89] ibid 149. Georgia, North and South Dakota, California, Montana, and Idaho adopted some of the provisions in Field's civil code.
[90] Part II, Title 1, Chapter 1 § 744.
[91] ibid § 745; Part II, Title 1, Chapter 3 § 750.
[92] IOR/L/PJ/5/15 (CD Field).
[93] Rankin (n 56) 100.
[94] IOR/L/PJ/5/15: J Fitzjames Stephen, 29 October 1871.
[95] See the much more limited exceptions in the final legislation in s 25 discussed in Section VIII below.

consideration where a contract was in writing and also registered. Minus the registration requirement, Lord Mansfield and Wilmot J had supported versions of a similar principle in the mid-eighteenth century, albeit that Lord Mansfield confined his remarks to commercial contracts.[96] However, this novel doctrine was extinguished in *Rann v Hughes* before it could be properly established.[97] Under the second exception, a promise—to compensate a person for doing something they were already legally bound to do or to pay (wholly or in part) a debt that was already legally owed—was binding even without consideration. Even in modern times, the English law does not recognize valid consideration in these situations, albeit practically there are usually easy enough ways to circumvent the restrictions.[98] The true importance of this exception would only become fully apparent nearly two decades after the report following *Foakes v Beer*,[99] in which the House of Lords reasserted the so-called rule in *Pinnel's Case*[100] by holding that a promise to pay a pre-existing debt was not good consideration. The Commission gave little by way of detailed justification for these changes. Rather, they reflect a willingness to facilitate the intentions of the parties in spite of the traditional formulations of consideration.

The original Bill diverged from the English law of the time in other ways as well. Several of these changes led to practical objections when the Bill was circulated for comment among lawyers and government officials in India. The overall reaction to the Bill was neither wholly favourable nor entirely consistent. This meant that while one Indian judge could argue that judges were left with too much discretion, another thought that they were left with too much.[101] A small number of provisions attracted the most comment. The Commission omitted an Indian equivalent of the Statute of Frauds, which, in England, required certain agreements to be in writing.[102] The omission was justified on the grounds that '[t]hose provisions are not of unquestionable expediency even in England; and we think that they are not suited to the habits and present condition of the people of India.'[103] One respondent claimed that the omission was likely to 'cause much baseless litigation', but this reform was less controversial than might have been expected, and it survived into the final legislation.[104] The rule in *Pinnel's Case* was abolished in the legislation by section 63.[105]

[96] *Pillans v Van Mierop* (1765) 3 Burr 1663.

[97] (1778) 4 Bro PC 27, 7 TR 350, LI MS Misc 130 f 74. For an analysis, see Swain, 'The Changing Nature of the Doctrine of Consideration' (n 75) 58–62.

[98] There is good consideration where there was something else with the promise to pay the debt or do what one is already bound to do. For example, a promise to pay the debt a day earlier or to do more than one was already bound to do amount to good consideration.

[99] (1884) 9 App Cas 605; M Lobban, 'Foakes v Beer' in C Mitchell and P Mitchell (eds), *Landmark Cases in the Law of Contract* (Hart 2008) 223–67.

[100] (1602) 5 Co Rep 117 a.

[101] IOR/L/PJ/5/15 (Belli); IOR/L/PJ/5/15 (West).

[102] (1677) 29 Car II c 3. For an account see AWB Simpson, *A History of the Common Law of Contract* (OUP 1987) 599–620.

[103] *Contract Law for India* (n 38) 3–4.

[104] IOR/L/PJ/15 (Pitt-Kennedy).

[105] Pollock drew attention to the Indian rule, which he regarded as superior to what he called the 'absurd paradox' of the English position: Pollock (n 83) 160.

The proposal to abolish the distinction between penalty and liquidated damages clauses was more contentious. Originally, equity prevented penalty clauses from being enforced. Later on, the common law would also strike down penalty clauses.[106] Various approaches to identifying a penalty were tried. By the time of the Commission report, the earlier test for determining the character of a clause—one supposedly based on the intentions of the parties but which was actually rather formulaic—had given way to an assessment of whether the stipulated sum was proportionate.[107] Abolishing the distinction between penalties and liquidated damages altogether simplified matters, although, as a judge in the Bombay Small Causes Court pointed out, it would also 'afford greater facilities to the grasping money lender to impose on the ignorant borrower'.[108] He was not the only critic; the measure was also described as a 'retrograde step',[109] one that caused 'grave apprehensions'[110] and was 'regrettable'.[111] Another judge of the Small Causes Court put the contrary argument based on freedom of contract:

> The penalty of a contract is, in my opinion, always intended, in fact as a device to ensure the punctual and exact performance of a contract; and whether it be in the nature of a punishment, or only by way of fixing definitely beforehand by mutual consent the amount of damage consequent on a breach appears to me to be wholly immaterial, so long as both parties with their eyes open have consented.[112]

Despite the intention of the drafters to abolish the distinction between penalties and liquidated damages, the Indian courts went on to reintroduce it.[113]

But it was the debate about two other clauses that really created tensions between the Commission and the Indian bureaucracy. The first proposal, that a bona fide purchaser took good title even when the seller had no good title to pass,[114] was contrary to the traditional common law rule of *nemo dat quod non habet*. The Commission conceded that 'the subject is difficult' but, in the end, concluded that if two innocent parties were to suffer, it should be the one who was deprived of the property in the first place as they are 'very often justly chargeable with remissness or negligence in the custody of the property'.[115]

[106] On the relationship between these jurisdictions, see PG Turner, '*Lex Sequitur Equitatem* Fusion and the Penalty Doctrine' in J Goldberg, H Smith, and PG Turner (eds), *Equity and Law Fusion and Fission* (CUP 2019) 254–79.
[107] M Lobban, 'Contract', in Cornish and others (n 45) 523–29.
[108] IOR/L/PJ/5/15 (Canoba). For similar remarks, see IOR/L/PJ/5/15 (Deputy Commissioner, Delhi), who argued that 'the people of this country need to be protected against the results of their own rashness in entering into over-reaching contracts'.
[109] IOR/L/PJ/5/15 (Coghlan).
[110] IOR/L/PJ/5/15 (Turner).
[111] IOR/L/PJ/5/15 (Rào).
[112] IOR/L/PJ/5/15 (Fagan).
[113] See cl 50 and the Contract Act, s 74. On this point, see S Swaminathan, 'Deinventing the Wheel: Liquidated Damages, Penalties and the Indian Contract Act' (2018) 6 Chinese Journal of Comparative Law 103; also TT Arvind, Chapter 17 of this volume.
[114] See cl 81.
[115] *Contract Law for India* (n 38) 4.

Some respondents argued that a reform of the traditional rule would encourage theft of cattle.[116] A select committee of the Indian legislature drew up its own Bill, which re-instated the *nemo dat* rule.[117] This decision caused a rift, placing the Duke of Argyll, the then Secretary of State for India, and the Indian Law Commissioners in conflict with the Governor General's Ruling Council in Calcutta.[118] Henry Maine, as the Legal Member of the Council, was placed in a difficult position.[119] In a defence of the Indian legislature in a minute in April 1868, a rather exasperated Maine stressed the need to take account of local conditions:

> I have striven to prevail on the Legislature to sanction the Commissioners' drafts with the minimum of change; and they will believe me when I say that, in making this effort, I have often had to contend against criticisms which were at least plausible, and to struggle with difficulties which however slightly they may be believed at home, are still real and substantial because they assume a form somewhat unlike that which impede legislation in England.[120]

A second proposal caused almost as many problems. In the original Bill, there was a series of clauses granting specific performance as a remedy in contract disputes.[121] The scope of specific performance largely mirrored the English position, and it could be granted for land or chattels.[122] One situation was excluded: when the agreement was to cultivate land in a particular manner or grow particular crops.[123] There was a good practical reason for this exception. Tensions between indigenous growers of indigo (the ryots) and European planters had caused civil unrest for decades.[124] On one side, the ryots argued that the planters were exploiting them; the planters, in response, said that the ryots, having received advanced payment, were refusing to perform their contracts and grow indigo. Maine addressed the issue in a number of minutes. He thought that issues around indigo planting 'no longer arise from a complicated system of contracts';[125] he also thought that specific performance should appear, if at all, in a code of procedure rather than substantive contract legislation.[126] The Governor General John Lawrence was in favour of the original proposal rather than Maine's amendment but

[116] IOR/L/PJ/5/15 (Fitzpatrick, Baden-Powell, Oliphant). For a detailed analysis of this issue see Pearson, 'A Cattle Lifter's Bill' (n 40).

[117] *Report of the Select Committee on the Bill to Define and Amend the Law Relating to Contracts* (1868) IOR/L/PG/5/15.

[118] For an outline of the dispute, see CP Ilbert, 'Indian Codification' (1889) 5 Law Quarterly Review 347, 350–52.

[119] For the life of Maine, see G Feaver, *From Status to Contract: A Biography of Sir Henry Maine 1822–1888* (Longmans 1969); R Cocks, *Sir Henry Maine: A Study in Victorian Jurisprudence* (CUP 2004). On his role as Law Member, see G Johnson, 'India and Henry Maine' in A Diamond (ed), *The Victorian Achievement of Sir Henry Maine* (CUP 1991) 376–88.

[120] H Maine, *Minutes by the Honourable Sir HS Maine (1862–69)* (Government of India 1890) 134.

[121] On the problems created around specific performance, see N Venkatesan, Chapter 18 of this volume.

[122] See cls 51–55.

[123] See cl 52.

[124] B Bling, *The Blue Mutiny: The Indigo Disturbances in Bengal 1859–1862* (University of Pennsylvania Press 1966).

[125] *Contract Law for India* (n 38) 92.

[126] ibid 94.

referred the matter to the Secretary of State, who, in turn, consulted the Commission, which remained unmoved by Maine's objections.[127]

By this stage, both sides had become increasingly intransigent. In the spring of 1870, the Indian government repeated its desire to include the *nemo dat* rule and was adamant that the Secretary of State should not impose a Bill on it when faced with objections from the Indian legislature.[128] The specific performance question remained unresolved. The Commission then resigned. Its final letter to the Secretary of State concluded, rather bitterly,

> We must repeat that no information which has reached the Commissioners does in our opinion explain the inaction of the legislature to which we advert in our former letter, and which we have been obliged to consider as systematic and persistent.[129]

Henry Maine also withdrew by returning to England in order to become the Corpus Professor of Jurisprudence at Oxford.[130] Now that the Commission was gone, the Secretary of State conceded defeat. Maine successfully lobbied for James Fitzjames Stephen to replace him.[131] Maine was sceptical about the Benthamite hue of the Third Commission.[132] Stephen had more sympathy with Benthamite ideas, but he was a pragmatist and, like Maine, also worried that some of the proposals did not reflect local conditions. In a letter to the Duke of Argyll, Stephens complained of having 'very little belief in the opinion that you can properly frame systems of . . . substantive law upon abstract principles as if they were mathematical theories at a distance from the places and people effected by them'.[133] With the resignation of the Commission, Stephen was left with a free hand to make changes to its Bill.

VIII. Stephen and the Final Legislation

Stephen had more room for manoeuvre than did Maine. He wrote, 'I am a sort of king in my own department for nobody interferes with me and I can bring in . . . pretty well whatever I choose.'[134] Stephen complained that the first part of the original Bill was 'arranged in a very obscure and confused manner', and he set about redrafting it.[135] Not everyone agreed that Stephen's version was superior. James Bryce complained that Stephen's 'capacity for the work of drafting was deemed not equal to his fondness for it'.[136] Pollock and Mulla were more specific in their criticism. They concluded that

[127] ibid 92–93, 96, 101–103.
[128] Ilbert, 'Indian Codification' (n 118) 350–52.
[129] ibid 352.
[130] Cocks (n 119) 95.
[131] Feaver (n 119) 106–107.
[132] ibid 101.
[133] Smith, *James Fitzjames Stephen* (n 52) 128.
[134] ibid.
[135] IOR/L/PJ/5/438.
[136] J Bryce, *Studies in History and Jurisprudence* (OUP 1901) 129.

allowing for all 'the drawbacks', the legislation was generally 'sound' and 'useful',[137] but they took particular exception to the first part of the Act, in which Stephen set out some definitions. This was said to be 'in a wholly different style and not altogether in harmony with the body of the work'.[138] Yet, in his English contract treatise, Pollock would praise the same part of the legislation on the basis that its 'completeness and accuracy ... are not likely, to be much improved upon for any practical purposes'.[139]

Criticisms of the definitional section aside, the order of the Act is undoubtedly odd. The first clause of the original Bill had defined a contract. This was the logical place for it, but it did not appear until section 10 in the Act, where its wording and position are significant: 'All agreements are contracts if they are made by the free consent of the parties competent to contract, for a lawful consideration and with a lawful object, and are not hereby expressly declared to be void.'

As with the original Bill, this definition of contract stresses that contracts are founded on an agreement. This accords with the Will Theory. The section, according to Pollock, was a 'concise and complete' version of the 'modern conception of contract'.[140] With the exception of the final phrase, this definition of a contract exactly mirrors that used in the Field Code.[141] Pollock and Mulla were highly critical of the way that the legislation in the final stages borrowed from Field and even went so far as to suggest that those sections should be removed.[142] The influence of Field did have one very significant impact on the way that the Act was drafted. It meant that, as in the Field Code, consent became a central pillar of the legislation: section 14 listed the situations in which free consent required for an enforceable contract was missing.[143] The way consent was used as a central organizing principle had other earlier precedents. Henry Colebrooke had written that it is of the 'essence of every contract, that the parties to be bound by it, should consent'.[144] Colebrooke had even used consent as a way of explaining factors vitiating a contract in the same manner as the Act.[145] Colebrooke was ahead of his time in this respect but, by the time Pollock published his treatise on contract in the 1870s, this sort of analysis had become standard.[146]

Consideration remained a requirement for a valid contract in the Act. The exceptions in the original Bill were restricted by the Act.[147] First, it was no longer sufficient for a contract to be valid without consideration because the agreement was in writing and registered. In addition to those requirements, the agreement had to be also one 'made on account of natural love and affection between the parties standing in a near

[137] F Pollock and D Mulla, *The Indian Contract Act with a Commentary, Critical and Explanatory* (OUP 1905) v.
[138] ibid.
[139] Pollock (n 83).
[140] ibid 116.
[141] Part II, I, I § 744–45.
[142] Pollock and Mulla (n 137) v.
[143] In the Field Code, this was Part II, I, III § 750–74. For further discussion on the influence of Field, see KV Krishnaprasad, Chapter 10 of this volume.
[144] Colebrooke, *A Treatise on Obligations and Contracts* (n 71) 43.
[145] For example, in relation to compulsion or duress, see ibid 49.
[146] In the introduction to his treatise, Pollock highlighted the way that consent was a central organizational element: Pollock (n 83) vii.
[147] See cl 10.

relation to each other'.[148] 'Natural love and affection' had not been accepted as a valid form of consideration in its own right since around 1580.[149] This made it a curious limitation device, but it had the effect of closing off a potentially broad exception of the sort contemplated in *Pillans v Van Mierop*.[150] As Pollock and Mulla also point out, the Act makes no provision for the use of a deed (a sealed instrument) as an alternative to consideration without the other conditions being present. This reflected a historical refusal of Indian law to accept the binding force of a contract entered into by deed; in this way, Indian contract law remained more restricted than English law.[151]

The second exception to the requirement of consideration allowed a promise to be enforced where it was to compensate for something already done or which the promisor was legally bound to do. This exception is a clear divergence from the English view of what constituted valid consideration.[152] This section of the Bill was nevertheless retained in the Act.[153] The third exception, however, was rewritten. It was no longer enough to merely promise to pay part or the whole of a debt, as was contemplated by the original Bill. It had to be a debt that the creditor could not have enforced as a result of the limitation rules. As a result, only promises to pay debts otherwise time-barred could be enforced in this way. Again, this is much narrower than the original exception, although it would encompass one of the categories that English law of the time treated as exceptional cases of enforceability—where an existing duty was barred by statute.[154]

As originally drafted, the Bill provided an opportunity to limit the importance of consideration significantly. However, the actual Act stepped back from this position. Pollock was uncritical of this part of the Act. Indeed, he would later on insist that it should be read as consistent with English consideration orthodoxy.[155] In fact, Pollock was generally very reluctant to criticize the doctrine of consideration publicly and, on occasion, even defended it, even if in private he was rather more doubtful of its merits.[156] The Act, albeit with several modifications, especially in relation to past consideration, accepted the standard English position on consideration. In this regard, it can be seen as a missed opportunity. Stephen was hardly the last person to suffer a failure of nerve. A recommendation of the English Law Revision Committee sixty years later to reintroduce the principle of *Pillans v Van Mierop* was never enacted.[157] By the

[148] Contract Act, s 25.

[149] DJ Ibbetson, 'Consideration and the Theory of Contract in Sixteenth Century Common Law' in J Barton (ed), *Towards a General Law of Contract* (Duncker and Humblot 1990) 67, 81.

[150] (1765) 3 Burr 1663.

[151] Pollock and Mulla (n 137) 129; *Kaleepershad Tewarree v Rajah Sahib Perhlad Sein* (1869) 12 Moo Ind App 310, 314.

[152] See Ibbetson, 'Consideration and the Theory of Contract' (n 149) 67, 78–79, 88–96. Early examples include *Sidenham v Worlington* (1585) 2 Leon 224; *Lowes v Haynes* (1616) HLS MS 112b, 270.

[153] Contract Act, s 25(2).

[154] Swain, 'The Changing Nature of the Doctrine of Consideration' (n 75) 69; *Roscorla v Thomas* (1842) 3 QB 234, 237.

[155] His assertion was not completely true; see S Swaminathan, 'Eclipsed by Orthodoxy: The Vanishing Point of Consideration and the Forgotten Ingenuity of the Indian Contract Act 1872' (2017) 12 Asian Journal of Comparative Law 141, 153.

[156] N Duxbury, *Frederick Pollock and the English Juristic Tradition* (OUP 2004) 203–05.

[157] Law Revision Committee, *Sixth Interim Report (Statute of Frauds and the Doctrine of Consideration)* Cmd 5449 (HMSO 1937).

time the Indian Law Commission came to reconsider the place of consideration post-independence, it would conclude that it was 'too firmly rooted in our concept of contract' to be overturned.[158]

The legislation diverged from English law in a number of other ways. In the appendices on the Indian legislation that he included in his treatise on English contract law, Pollock highlighted some of the key differences between the Act and the common law.[159] The two most controversial aspects of the original Bill would ultimately be resolved in favour of the position adopted by Maine and the Indian legislature. Specific performance would be contained in a separate statute just as Maine had wanted.[160] The Act also retained the *nemo dat* rule.[161] The Act, as it would be adopted, however, saw a significant blunting of the original proposals.

The Contract Act rationalized mistake in much the same way as the Bill had done. A mistake as to some essential fact rendered an agreement void.[162] Some of the English authorities could be explained in this way even if the law was not expressed with such neat exactitude. It was only after *Bell v Lever Brothers Ltd*[163]—which was, in many respects, an unsatisfactory authority—that the absence of consent became firmly established as a justification for a doctrine of contractual mistake. Mistake was not the only doctrine that was fluid in England at this time. *Taylor v Caldwell*[164] held that there was no action by lessees against the owner of a music hall on a contract of hire when the building had burnt down on the grounds that there was an implied condition that the property should continue to exist. This decision marked a move away from the harshness of the theory of absolute liability, as explained in *Paradine v Jane*.[165] English contemporaries saw *Taylor v Caldwell* as no more than an addition to the existing list of exceptions to the rule of absolute liability. It would only be perceived much later as the foundation of the modern law of frustration.[166] The Bill stated that a person who fails to perform a contract must pay compensation and gave an exception to absolute liability.[167] The illustration was based on the facts of *Taylor v Caldwell* itself, and the wording of the clause was not particularly broad in scope. The exception survived into the final Act, but section 56 went much further than English law of the time as well as the Bill by stating that impossibility or unlawfulness subsequent to the contract renders it void. In Pollock's view, 'simplicity is gained at the expense of a considerable departure from the principles of English law'.[168]

[158] MC Setalvad, *The Common Law in India* (Stevens & Sons 1960) 76–77; *13th Law Commission of India Report, Indian Contract Act 1872* (1958) <https://indianculture.gov.in/reports-proceedings/thirteenth-report-contract-act-1872> accessed 8 May 2024.

[159] Pollock (n 83).

[160] Specific Relief Act 1877.

[161] Contract Act, s 108.

[162] ibid s 20.

[163] [1932] AC 161. For a detailed discussion, see MacMillan, *Mistakes in Contract Law* (n 74) 270–78.

[164] (1863) 3 B & S 826. For a discussion, see C MacMillan, 'Taylor v Caldwell (1863)' in Mitchell and Mitchell (n 99) 167–203.

[165] (1647) Aleyn 26, 82 ER 897.

[166] MacMillan, *Mistakes in Contract Law* (n 74) 200–202.

[167] See cl 25.

[168] Pollock (n 83) 353.

There were other significant modifications to English contract in the Act. *Tweddle v Atkinson*[169] came to stand for the proposition that only those who are parties to a contract can bring a claim on it.[170] The rule in England in the absence of a deed had previously been expressed in the phrase 'consideration must move from the promisee'.[171] By the late nineteenth century, the parties-only rule had become the dominant form of the restriction, but this formula was not established as such when the legislation was drafted, at which point the consideration rule was still dominant.[172] It can then be supposed that the drafters of the legislation intended to remove the restriction as it then existed. The wording of the Act allowed for consideration from 'any other person'.[173] Nevertheless, over time, the privity rule came to be established in the Indian courts,[174] albeit that there are still situations in which someone else provides consideration for a party to the contract and renders the contract enforceable through that party.[175]

English law in the nineteenth century experienced difficulty in providing a justification for those obligations that modern lawyers regard as arising out of restitution or unjust enrichment. In the eighteenth century, Lord Mansfield had treated an action for money had and received as something close to an action in equity. This view had fallen out of favour by the nineteenth century.[176] Nineteenth-century lawyers were still to settle on an alternative. Pollock himself used the term quasi-contract and stressed that there was no true contract, only something analogous to one.[177] Chapter 5 of the Act grouped together a series of instances 'Of certain relations resembling those created by contract'. This part of the Act was rather more expansive at a time when English law was timid, with Pollock noting that '[t]he Indian Act provides for matters of this kind more simply in form and more comprehensively in substance than our present law'.[178]

IX. Conclusion

Roscoe Pound observed that the English are 'not instinctively averse to codification [as] is shown by the Anglo-Indian codes'.[179] The Contract Act was not extensive enough to be regarded as a law code in the civilian manner. Nor, because it changed the law, was it the equivalent of a restatement of either English or Indian contract law. At the same time, it went rather further than the more piecemeal statutory reform of contract that took place in England a few decades later.[180] In this respect, the legislation is difficult to

[169] (1861) 1 B & S 393, 30 LJQB 265, 4 LT 468.
[170] Pollock (n 83) 190–91.
[171] D Ibbetson and W Swain, 'Third Party Beneficiaries in English Law: From Dutton v Poole to Tweddle v Atkinson' in E Schrage (ed), *Ius quaesitum tertio* (Duncker and Humblot 2008) 190–213.
[172] ibid 212–13.
[173] Contract Act, s 2(d).
[174] S Swaminathan, 'The Great Indian Privity Trick: Hundred Years of Misunderstanding Nineteenth Century English Contract Law' (2016) 16 Oxford University Commonwealth Law Journal 160.
[175] *Chinnaya v Ramayya* (1882) 4 Mad 137.
[176] For an account, see W Swain, 'Moses v Macferlan (1760)' in Mitchell and Mitchell (n 99) 19–37.
[177] Pollock (n 83) 28–29.
[178] ibid 29.
[179] R Pound, *Interpretations of Legal History* (CUP 1923) 81.
[180] For example, in the Sale of Goods Act 1893, 56 & 57 Vict c 71.

characterize. The way it was drafted involved a delicate balance between the demands of doctrinal purity, on the one hand, and the need to accommodate local conditions, on the other. There were both intellectual and practical issues at stake when it came to drafting. The former was reflected in the way that the legislation drew on a diverse range of sources. This approach did not receive universal approval. Ilbert complained that '[m]any gobbets of undigested Field went out to India in the Contract Bill; too many of them still remain in the Contract Act'.[181] The practical aspect of the whole process centred around the problems of indigo farming and cattle theft.

It is easy enough to criticize certain parts of the final legislation. It was, after all, a compromise. At this point, a third factor comes into play, namely, the desire not to diverge too far from English contract law. Although both a wish to achieve drafting elegance and local conditions were relevant in the process, the current English law still provided the starting point. In this respect, Stephen was more cautious than the Commissioners. The provisions on consideration were a lost opportunity to reform the law of contract in a positive and lasting fashion. But perhaps the extraordinary thing is not that Stephen baulked at this measure but that the Commissioners contemplated it in the first place. The final legislation was still more than a mere carbon copy of English contract law.[182] It nevertheless possessed the kind of ordered and principled structure so beloved of treatise writers of the time but that was so difficult to achieve in a common law system.

[181] CP Ilbert, 'In Memoriam Sir James Stephen as a Legislator' (1894) 10 Law Quarterly Review 222, 222–23.

[182] There were a number of other less significant differences from English law, which are discussed in more detail elsewhere: RN Gooderson, 'English Contract Problems in Indian Code and Case Law' (1958) 16 Cambridge Law Journal 67.

2

Legislative Design and the Codification Project

Jeannie Marie Paterson and Elise Bant

I. Introduction

This project attests to the significance and longevity of the Indian Contract Act 1872 (hereinafter 'the Contract Act').[1] The history of the Contract Act is ably discussed by Warren Swain in Chapter 1 of this volume.[2] Swain draws attention to the size of the project, and the chapters in this book are testimony to that work. It is merely necessary to note here that the Contract Act was initiated to codify English contract law in a form appropriate for India.[3] Codification was intended to express, consolidate, and also improve on the existing law.[4] The Contract Act sets out general principles affecting the formation, performance, and consequences of breach of contracts and then the rules for particular contracts, indemnity and guarantee, bailment, agency, and partnership (although the rules on partnership and sale of goods were subsequently replaced with their own distinct acts).[5] The Contract Act replaced the earlier practice in India of courts drawing on a mix of the law and custom applicable to different sections of the population in deciding contract disputes.[6]

[1] See DRR Sethu, 'The History, Impact and Influence of the Indian Contract Act 1872' (2011) 28 Journal of Contract Law 31, 33 (also citing Pollock to the effect that 'the result, after allowing for all drawbacks, was a generally sound and useful one').

[2] See also S Tofaris, 'A Historical Study of the Indian Contract Act 1872' (PhD thesis, University of Cambridge 2011).

[3] See eg N Venkatesan, 'Specific and Agreed Remedies for Breach of Contract in Indian Law: A Code of English Law?' in M Chen-Wishart, A Loke, and B Ong (eds), *Studies in the Contract Laws of Asia I: Remedies for Breach of Contract* (OUP 2016) 59, 60.

[4] Preamble of the Contract Act: 'Whereas it is expedient to define and amend certain parts of the law relating to contracts'.

[5] Law Commission of India, *Report on Indian Contract Act 1872* (Law Com Report No 13, 1958) 3.

[6] J Minattur, 'The Indian Contract Act: Its Wanderlust and Warmer Climes' (1972) Journal of the Indian Law Institute 107, 108:

> Before the passing of the Contract Act, the British-Indian courts decided matters of contract by the customs of Hindus when the parties were Hindus, by those of Muslims when the parties were Muslims, and by those of the defendant where one of the parties was a Muslim and the other a Hindu.

See also A Chandra Patra, 'Historical Background of the Indian Contract Act 1872' (1962) 4 Journal of the Indian Law Institute 373, 379.

Jeannie Marie Paterson and Elise Bant, *Legislative Design and the Codification Project* In: *Foundations of Indian Contract Law.*
Edited by: KV Krishnaprasad, Niranjan Venkatesan, Shivprasad Swaminathan, and Umakanth Varottil, Oxford University Press.
 DOI: 10.1093/9780191997211.003.0002

The Contract Act is not a complete code dealing with the whole of the law relating to contracts.[7] It specifically covers some but not all major kinds of contract.[8] Nor is it exhaustive.[9] It does not contain any statement excluding judicial gap filling.[10] Moreover, in a common law system, courts will necessarily interpret and supplement the field of application of any statutory expression of the law. Courts have typically drawn on English law in this process.[11] The Contract Act is influenced by a number of sources: Benthamite ideals of universal law; aspirations to a 'civil code based on existing Hindu, Muslim and English law';[12] English contract law; and the civil law of Italy, France, and Germany.[13] Largely, it mirrors the English law of the time, but other influences have also introduced some, often surprising, variations.[14]

The Contract Act has proved influential as a statutory statement of law, being replicated in a number of former British colonies.[15] In England[16] and Australia,[17] by contrast, there has been little support for the codification of contract, despite the occasional expression of interest in this task.[18] The pattern, instead, has been of legislation applying to particular applications of private law, which overlays and interacts with contract law without restating its fundamental rules. Notable examples of this more limited model of contractual reform are the Sale of Goods Act 1893, the Consumer Rights Act 2015, and, in Australia, the Australian Consumer Law (2010).[19] Typically,

[7] Sethu (n 1) 40.

[8] See TT Arvind, Chapter 17 of this volume, section 3, noting that the Contract Act does not contain a separate regime for employment contracts.

[9] See F Pollock and DF Mulla, *The Indian Contract Act: With a Commentary, Critical and Explanatory* (Sweet & Maxwell 1909) 6.

[10] Contract Act, s 1 ('nothing herein contained shall affect . . . any incident of any contract . . . not inconsistent with the provisions of this Act').

[11] Sethu (n 1) 40, citing *Irrawaddy Flotilla Co Lyd v Bugwandas* (1891) 18 LR Indian Appeals 121, 129. See also MP Ram Mohan, P Murugavelu, G Ray, and K Parakh, 'The Doctrine of Frustration under Section 56 of the Indian Contract Act' (2020) 4 Indian Law Review 85.

[12] See G Pearson, 'The Resignation of the Third Indian Law Commission: Who Makes Law?' (2020) 41 Adelaide Law Review 575, 578.

[13] W Swain, Chapter 1 of this volume, section VI.

[14] Minattur (n 6) 109.

[15] For example, Bangladesh, Brunei, Burma, Malaysia, Sri Lanka, Singapore, Pakistan, parts of Africa, and the West Indies. See further Minattur (n 6) 107 ('The impact of the Indian Contract Act, like that of the *Dharmasastra* of old, has been great and widespread').

[16] The English and Scottish Law Commissions proposed codifying English contract law: H McGregor, *Contract Code Drawn Up on Behalf of the English Law Commission* (Giuffre Editore 1993). See generally HL MacQueen, 'Glory with Gloag or the Stake with Stair? TB Smith and the Scots Law of Contract' in E Reid and DL Carey Miller (eds), *A Mixed Legal System in Transition* (Edinburgh University Press 2005) 157–61; SM Waddams, 'Codification, Law Reform and Judicial Development' (1996) 9 Journal of Contract Law 192. See also the opposition to efforts to codify English contact law at the same time as the drafting of the Contract Act in W Swain, Chapter 1 of this volume, section III.

[17] Commonwealth of Australia, 'Improving Australia's Law and Justice Framework: A Discussion Paper to Explore the Scope for Reforming Australian Contract Law' (22 March 2012) <https://apo.org.au/sites/default/files/resource-files/2012-03/apo-nid28736.pdf> accessed 13 May 2023. For a discussion of this project, see J Eldridge, 'Contract Codification: Cautionary Lessons from Australia' (2019) 23 Edinburgh Law Review 204. See also Victorian Law Reform Commission, *An Australian Contract Code* (Discussion Paper No 27, 1992) (premised on the principle of unconscionability) discussed in A Stewart, 'What's Wrong with the Australian Law of Contract?' (2012) 29 Journal of Contract Law 74, 76.

[18] There have been further efforts to codify European contract law: O Lando and H Beale (eds), *Principles of European Contract Law Parts I and II* (Kluwer Law International 2000); O Lando, E Clive, A Prüm, and R Zimmermann (eds), *Principles of European Contract Law Part III* (Kluwer Law International 2003); C Von Bar and E Clive (eds), *Principles, Definitions and Model Rules of European Private Law: Draft Common Frame of Reference* (OUP 2010) 3; S Whittaker, 'A Framework of Principle for European Contract Law' (2009) 125 Law Quarterly Review 645.

[19] Here, compare the Indian Consumer Protection Act 2019.

the arguments in favour of more expansive codification of contract law focus on the role of a code in rationalising[20] and clarifying[21] the law. There are other arguments as well. A code may be used to tailor the law to local conditions[22] and also to make the law more accessible to lawyers and 'law-consumers'. A code makes the law accessible in ways that the common law, with its basis in judgment and precedent, is not.[23] Yet, these possible outcomes are also contested, with many arguing in particular that the supposed attractions of rationalising and clarifying the law through codification are overstated.[24] We consider that, at least partly, the success of codification also lies in the design of the legislation.

Legislative design refers to the way in which the statute is structured and expressed, including its balance between rules and principles, the degree to which it draws upon established legal concepts or language, and its use of examples. These features, although often overlooked in debates about codification, will have a significant impact on the extent to which a code achieves its stated goals. This chapter considers, in turn, the arguments about the attractions of a code and examines the key determinants of legislative design, with particular reference to the Contract Act. As we will see, the Indian experience with codification has much to offer for other jurisdictions seeking to engage with meaningful and effective contractual reform.

II. The Case for Codification

Arguments in favour of codifying a field of common law, such as the law of contract, are commonly premised on a number of overlapping values sought to be enhanced by the measure. These values prominently include rationality (or coherence), certainty, homogeneity, and accessibility.[25] At least the first three of these values were driving considerations for the Contract Act. The Contract Act was premised on the ambition to discern 'a systematic exposition and statement of law that could be more easily and consistently applied to resolve disputes between those who approached existing and newly established courts'.[26] Jain argues that the pre-existing law in India was seen to be 'bulky, uncertain, contradictory and inconsistent'.[27] Codification was

[20] AL Diamond, 'Codification of the Law of Contract' (1968) 31 Modern Law Review 361; HL MacQueen, 'Third Party Rights in Contract: A Case Study on Codifying and Not Codifying' in L Chen and CH van Rhee (eds), *Towards a Chinese Civil Code: Comparative and Historical Perspectives* (Martinus Nijhoff 2012) 309–31.

[21] J Eldridge, 'Contract Codification and Certainty' (2018) 35 Journal of Contract Law 146.

[22] G Pearson, 'Consultation for a Code: Nineteenth Century Consultation on the Proposed Commercial Laws' in N Jayaram (ed), *Ideas, Institutions, Processes: Essays in Memory of Satish Saberwal* (Orient BlackSwan 2015) 115–41.

[23] Diamond (n 20).

[24] Eldridge, 'Contract Codification and Certainty' (n 21); Eldridge, 'Contract Codification: Cautionary Lessons from Australia' (n 17); W Swain, 'Codification of Contract Law: Some Lessons from History' (2012) 3 University of Queensland Law Journal 39.

[25] M Doris, 'Promising Options, Dead Ends and the Reform of Australian Contract Law' (2014) 34 Legal Studies 24; D Svantesson 'Codifying Australia's Contract Law: Time for a Stocktake in the Common Law Factory' (2008) 20 Bond Law Review 92, 96.

[26] Pearson, 'Consultation for a Code' (n 22) 116.

[27] MP Jain, *Outlines of Indian Legal and Constitutional History* (6th edn, Wadhwa 2006) 392, quoted in Pearson, 'Consultation for a Code' (n 22) 123.

a way to resolve these concerns and introduce a law that was 'certain, coherent and definite'.[28]

1. Rationality

Thomas Babington Macaulay, chairman of the first Law Commission and responsible for the initial draft of the Contract Act, was strongly influenced by the utilitarian ideas of Jeremy Bentham.[29] Bentham promoted the value of a rational order in the law,[30] which was to be found in legislation. As described by Swain, for Bentham, the common law was 'a cause of "dark chaos" which could only be rectified by legislation'.[31] Pearson records that an ambition was for the Act to be 'scientific'.[32] This theme of rationality continues to inform many of the current debates around codifying contract law, namely that the law should be structured in a rational and logical form that is then capable of dealing effectively with the classes of problems to which it applies. It should resolve the complexities of the common law, typically riddled with exceptions to formal rules and inconsistency between different domains, with a more orderly scheme.[33] An example of this scientific search for order, identified by Steven Elliott KC and Divya Behl, is the schema of the Contract Act in dealing with rescission: '[t]hese innovations put the remedy on a sound modern footing'.[34]

The ambition of promoting, or attaining, coherence is, of course, more easily stated then achieved. As Diamond and Doris point out, it is difficult to consider codifying, and thus rationalising, one field of law without engaging at the boundaries with other fields.[35] A good example of this hurdle to a rational and coherent statement of contract law concerns misrepresentation,[36] which spans contract, tort, equity, and unjust enrichment.[37] But nonetheless, a codified law also offers the possibility of creating a rational and consistent relationship between different parts of the codified law and related fields of law. In this sense, codification acts as driver of law reform, pruning and reforming those areas of the common law that have become inconsistent or incoherent.[38] This ambition of codification in smoothing relationships between different fields of law

[28] ibid 549.

[29] CN Gregory, 'Bentham and the Codifiers' (1900) 13 Harvard Law Review 344; E Stokes, *The English Utilitarians and India* (OUP 1989) 219. See also W Swain, Chapter 1 of this volume, section III (noting that Jeremy Bentham began working on a complete code of the laws or 'pannomion' 'but the idea died with him and his work was never finished').

[30] See in HJ Randall, 'Jeremy Bentham' (1906) 22 Law Quarterly Review 311.

[31] Swain, 'Codification of Contract Law' (n 24) 41, citing D Lieberman, *The Province of Legislation Determined: Legal Theory in Eighteenth-Century Britain* (CUP 2002) 198.

[32] Pearson, 'The Resignation of the Third Indian Law Commission' (n 12) 589, citing Letter from Argyll, Secretary of State for India to Governor General of India (24 November 1870) BL IOR PP LVI 1876.

[33] ibid 2, noting this aspiration was raised by Commissioner Hayne in the Commonwealth of Australia, *Royal Commission into Misconduct in the Banking, Superannuation and Financial Services Industry: Final Report* (February 2019).

[34] S Elliott KC and D Behl, Chapter 19 of this volume, section I.

[35] Diamond (n 20) 383; Doris (n 25) 25.

[36] Diamond (n 20) 383.

[37] J Cartwright, *Misrepresentation, Mistake and Non-Disclosure* (5th edn, Sweet & Maxwell 2019) [1-03], [1-04].

[38] Diamond (n 20) 372–75.

may also be linked to ideas of the value of coherence, both within the common law and between common law and statute.[39]

There are, however, a number of brakes on this ideal of creating an entirely rational restatement of the law through codification that are very much evident in the Contract Act. In particular, the inherent immovability of a code combined with innate judicial conservatism may undermine its own aspirations. Unless drafted with a degree of leeway, a codified expression of the law itself can become quickly outdated. MacQueen notes that the common law method allows a degree of flexibility in the law that may not be achieved by codified rules or legislation.[40] The hallmark of the common law is that it evolves by decisions that illuminate particular applications of more general principles. The process imbues a certain conservatism but, equally, keeps the law attuned to evolving commercial practices.[41] A code, by contrast, is static: fixed at the point in time at which it was made. This can lead to it becoming static in the face of rules no longer thought appropriate or efficacious but which, nonetheless, represent too great a challenge to judicial ingenuity or tradition to be revised.[42] As we will see, legislative design presents means of moderating this inherent tendency to ossification. Where principles-based drafting is adopted, for example, a code may present and operate more like traditional common law,[43] although this may also have consequences for other aims of codification, such as clarity and predictability, to which we also return.[44]

It is, of course, possible to amend a statute. Chalmers himself commented, 'It is always easier to amend an Act than to alter common law. Legislation, too, is cheaper than litigation.'[45] But once legislation is enacted, it may be difficult to summon the interest and energy required of the legislature to reform that instrument,[46] at least in the absence of serious shortcomings.[47] The Contract Act itself contains such reform bottlenecks. For example, section 19 of the Contract Act provides that

> A party to a contract whose consent was caused by fraud or misrepresentation, may, if he thinks fit, insist that the contract shall be performed, and that he shall be put in the position in which he would have been if the representations made had been true.

[39] E Bant, 'Statute and Common Law: Interaction and Influence in Light of Principle of Coherence' (2015) 38 University of New South Wales Law Journal 367.

[40] MacQueen, 'Third Party Rights in Contract' (n 20).

[41] J Cartwright, 'The English Law of Contract: Time for Review?' (2009) 17 European Review of Private Law 155.

[42] MacQueen, 'Third Party Rights in Contract' (n 20) (discussing the doctrine of privity); Diamond (n 20) 880–81. See also P Finn, 'Internationalisation or Isolation: The Australian *cul de sac*? The Case of Contract Law' in E Bant and M Harding (eds), *Exploring Private Law* (CUP 2010) 41, 64.

[43] See below at section III.1.

[44] The Contract Act's use of illustrative examples is a particularly astute means of negotiating the delicate balancing act involved: discussed at section III.4 below.

[45] MDES Chalmers, 'Introduction to First Edition' in *Chalmers' Sale of Goods Act 1893* (1st edn, WM Clowes & Sons 1894) reprinted in vol 1 (3rd edn, 1870) [188], quoted in Diamond (n 20) 374.

[46] See F Pollock and DF Mulla, *The Indian Contract Act: With a Commentary, Critical and Explanatory* (2nd edn, Sweet & Maxwell 1909) preface (calling for urgent reform to certain sections).

[47] Diamond (n 20) 381; P Finn, 'Unity, Then Divergence: The Privy Council, the Common Law of England and the Common Laws of Canada, Australia and New Zealand' in A Robertson and M Tilbury (eds), *The Common Law of Obligations: Divergence and Unity* (Hart 2016) 37.

KV Krishnaprasad observes that the effect of this provision is 'to treat all false representations as enforceable promises whether or not they were contractual terms' and argues that the provision requires reconsideration.[48] Yet, this striking issue has yet to attract the attention of those engaged in reform or revision of the Act. Mihir Naniwadekar likewise notes continuing uncertainty over whether Indian law recognises the tripartite division of terms relevant to termination for breach from *Hong Kong Fir Shipping*.[49]

This risk of ossified statutory incoherence in the codification of general law is not, of course, unique to the Contract Act but applies across jurisdictions. A prime and pertinent example, also drawn from the contractual context, is the English Misrepresentation Act 1967, in particular section 2(1), which provides a right to damages for non-fraudulent misrepresentation. As is well known, the original legislative aim was to provide novel and ameliorative remedial options in cases of misrepresentations that induce entry into a contract. This objective was, however, immediately affected by developments at common law in the law of negligent misstatement.[50] Notwithstanding, its 'extraordinarily tortuous and obscure'[51] rules-based provision continues to operate alongside, and in contradiction to, the common law, actively undermining the broader rationality of the statute and its relationship with the general law operating in this field.[52] Again, principles of legislative design may be central in minimising such risks.

Judicial interpretation offers at least a partial solution to the problem of a code ossifying in the face of social or business developments.[53] Judicial reliance on the relevant general law in interpreting the codified law is inevitable and appropriate for a code operating in a common law context. This interpretive approach may operate to promote greater connection and coherence between the code and its surrounding general law or national context. For example, Gooderson discusses the Indian courts' approach to illegality[54] as applied to marriage brokaging contracts, which departed in several respects from the approach taken in England in order to accommodate local practices.[55] However, while it may offer some benefits of this kind, the common law interpretative method may also result in a constrained or subversive interpretation, in particular where the code's drafters sought to depart from pre-existing common law approaches but where courts are unwilling to acknowledge such a departure. Pollock, in 1909, observed a tendency in Indian courts to 'follow English authorities too literally'.[56]

[48] KV Krishnaprasad, Chapter 10 of this volume, section III.4.

[49] M Naniwadekar, Chapter 13 of this volume, section V.II.

[50] *Hedley Byrne & Co Ltd v Heller & Partners Ltd* [1964] AC 465 (HL).

[51] PS Atiyah and GH Treitel, 'Misrepresentation Act 1967' (1967) 30 Modern Law Review 369, 378.

[52] JM Paterson and E Bant, 'Misrepresentation, Misleading Conduct and Statute through the Lens of Form and Substance' in A Robertson and J Goudkamp (eds), *Form and Substance in Private Law* (Hart 2019) 401; cf *RBC Properties Pte Ltd v Defu Furniture Pte Ltd* [2014] SGCA 62, [2015] 1 SLR 997 [83]–[84] (Andrew Phang Boon Leong JA delivering the judgment of the court), which seeks to realign the statutory and general law principles.

[53] See G Calabresi, *A Common Law for the Age of Statutes* (Harvard University Press 1982) discussing Pomeroy's suggestion to treat the Field Code like the common law and thus ensure its ongoing relevance in JN Pomeroy, 'The True Method of Interpreting the Civil Code' (1884) 4 West Coast Reporter 109, 110.

[54] Contract Act, s 23. See also T Sebastian and A Ahluwalia, Chapter 11 of this volume.

[55] RN Gooderson, 'Turpitude and Title in England and India' (1958) 16 Cambridge Law Journal 199, 202–203, with other examples of Indian courts departing from English law in their interpretation of the illegality provision at 215.

[56] See Pollock and Mulla, *The Indian Contract Act* (2nd edn) (n 47) vii (preface).

Shivprasad Swaminathan argues that judges in India commonly went beyond drawing on the common law of England to interpret the Contract Act and instead used this body of law to override the legislative intent underlying the Act,[57] in particular interpreting language with a pre-existing meaning in the common law 'not on the terms in which it is defined in the code but on the terms in which it is understood in the antediluvian law that the code is replacing'.[58] The consequence is a failure to give effect to the statutory regime, with potentially stultifying consequences. Not only may the evident intention behind code provisions be disabled but also so might any potential for influence on evolving, cognate general law concepts.[59]

An example of this tension between the aspiration to reform and countervailing restrictions arising from judicial tendencies to interpret legislation in the light of the general law, combined with an imprudent use of language, may be found in section 74 of the Contract Act. The provision purports to address the position of sums payable under the contract and the common law doctrine of penalties. Shivprasad Swaminathan notes that the drafters of the Act had sought to avoid the distinction recognised in English law between penalties and liquidated damages by avoiding any use of these terms.[60] Moreover, there is no stated need to have regard to the loss likely to be suffered on breach. Instead, the code allows such sums 'named in the contract' to be *prima facie* payable,[61] and grants courts a discretion to scale down excessive amounts so as to award compensation that is reasonable.[62] Nonetheless, in applying section 74, Indian courts have relied on a test that asks whether an agreed contractual sum payable on breach is a 'genuine preestimate' of loss .[63] TT Arvind observes that this test 'relies heavily on the traditional common law approach'.[64] This effectively reinstates the common law rule against penalties.

Swaminathan posits that the Indian Court's approach reflects the influence of an 1899 amendment to the Act, drafted by Mackenzie Chalmers, the architect of the Sale of Goods Act, introduced an extension to section 74 of the Contract Act that used the catch-all phrase 'or . . . any other stipulation by way of penalty'. Swaminathan comments that this use of language 'turned out to be the Trojan horse that let in the liquidated damages/penalty distinction the drafters had been so keen on avoiding'.[65]

[57] S Swaminathan, 'De-inventing the Wheel: Liquidated Damages, Penalties and the Indian Contract Act, 1872' (2018) 6 Chinese Journal of Comparative Law 103, 125.

[58] ibid.

[59] Bant (n 40) 367.

[60] Swaminathan, 'De-inventing the Wheel' (n 58) 108, citing W Stokes, *Anglo-Indian Codes*, vol 1 (Clarendon Press 1888) 506.

[61] ibid 106–107.

[62] ibid 126.

[63] See TT Arvind, Chapter 17 of this volume, section II.1.

[64] ibid.

[65] Swaminathan, 'De-inventing the Wheel' (n 58) 125. See also 121ff, discussing the interpretation given to 'reasonable compensation' and S Swaminathan, 'The Will Theorist's Mailbox: Misunderstanding the Moment of Contract Formation in the Indian Contract Act, 1872' (2018) 39 Statute Law Review 14, discussing the courts' misinterpretation of the Contract Act, ss 4 and 5 dealing with the communication and withdrawal of acceptance of a contract offer.

2. Certainty

A second prominent aspiration in codifying a field of law is to promote certainty.[66] Eldridge explains that certainty relates to the 'confidence with which the content and scope of substantive legal principles can be stated'.[67] This is said to come from having a set of stable, ordered principles as the source of law, as opposed to the potentially chaotic exposition of the law developed through courts.[68] Certainty was undoubtedly a driving concern for the development of the Contract Act. Contract law in India was characterised at the time by numerous sources of uncertainty and confusion, including over the application of English law, different regional and religious customs, language barriers, and lack of legal and judicial expertise.[69] Macaulay said,

> I believe that no country ever stood so much in the need of a code of law as India . . . Uniformity when you can have it; diversity when you must have it; but in all cases certainty.[70]

The ambition to enhance and clarify the law of contract law is evident throughout in the Contract Act. Take, for example, the codification of contract damages:

> 73. Compensation of loss or damage caused by breach of contract
> When a contract has been broken, the party who suffers by such breach is entitled to receive, from the party who has broken the contract, compensation for any loss or damage caused to him thereby, which naturally arose in the usual course of things from such breach, or which the parties knew, when they made the contract, to be likely to result from the breach of it.

The provision is described by Katy Barnett as 'short and simple' in combining the principles of the measure of and limitations of damages.[71]

For many, the certainty of a code is an 'illusion'[72] or at least short lived. A code situated in a common law system will inevitably develop a surrounding suite of judicial interpretations of its provisons. There is a risk that this process will cloud the plain meaning apparent on the face of the statute and undermine the original aspiration of clarity and simplicity.[73] Even relatively simply expressed provisions require judicial

[66] See generally Eldridge, 'Contract Codification and Certainty' (n 21).
[67] ibid 148.
[68] See Stewart (n 17) 81 (calling for greater clarity in judicial pronouncements on contract law).
[69] See Pearson, 'The Resignation of the Third Indian Law Commission' (n 12) 580.
[70] See H Cowell and S Chandra Bagchi, *The History and Constitution of the Courts and Legislative Authority in India* (6th edn, Thacker, Spink and Co 1936) quoted in AS Sankhyan, 'Study of Dimensions of Principle of Frustration in Indian Contract Law System' (2016) 37 Journal of the Indian Law Institute 442, 443. See also Patra (n 6) 397.
[71] See K Barnett, Chapter 16 of this volume, section II.
[72] See Minattur (n 6) 115 ('Certainty of law is an illusion . . . India which entertains a general concept of illusion, of a boundless maya, may be inclined to be disillusioned in relation to this illusion').
[73] Eldridge, 'Contract Codification and Certainty' (n 21) 158.

interpretation. In the context of the Contract Act, Barnett, for example, notes the need to look beyond the illustrations for the meaning of 'loss or damage' to give content to section 73 of the Contract Act.[74]

It is important, however, not to overstate the uncertainty engendered by the interaction between the language and judicial interpretation of the provisions of a code. A well-drafted statute may still provide more certainty than the preceding law by clarifying the steps to be taken in the application of a doctrine and ruling out alternative approaches. This capacity is illustrated in the Indian context by the approach taken to parol evidence rule—a heavily contested topic in Australian and English law.[75] The Indian Evidence Act sections 73- 100 controls the evidence that may be admitted to interpret a contract.[76] Thus for example, section 94 of the Indian Evidence Act provides that

> When language used in a document is plain in itself and when it applies accurately to existing facts, evidence may not be given to show that it was not meant to apply to such facts.

As Goh Yihan observes, the need for fidelity to the provisions of the statute must be reconciled with developments in the general law on which the regime was based. [77] Modern English courts have shown greater proclivity to embrace context as a relevant consideration in the process of interpretation than the provisions of the Indian Evidence Act allows, reflecting as it does contract law of the 19th century. Goh Yihan emphasises that the correct approach is to start with the provisions of the Act, rather than any assumption about the way in which English general law would now apply.[78] Goh argues that Indian courts have, by and large, taken an approach that is consistent with the words of the Act by seeking ambiguity before looking to context in interpretation.[79] Arguably, this is not a substantial restriction of the use of context; as Australian courts have noted, ambiguity is not a high hurdle to scale.[80] But it is one that remains committed to the integrity and clarity of the Act.

Equally, however, the tendency, discussed under section II.1 above, of some judges to interpret concepts used in the Contract Act narrowly by reference to their traditional

[74] See K Barnett, Chapter 16 of this volume, section II. The same phrase is similarly central to, and undefined by, the remedial scheme for misleading conduct, unconscionable conduct, and the consumer guarantees under Australian consumer protection regimes: see E Bant and J Paterson, 'Limitations on Defendant Liability for Misleading or Deceptive Conduct under Statute: Some Insights from Negligent Misstatement' in K Barker, R Grantham, and W Swain (eds), *The Law of Misstatements: 50 Years on from Hedley Byrne v Heller* (Hart 2015) 159; E Bant and JM Paterson, 'Exploring the Boundaries of Compensation for Misleading Conduct: The Role of Restitution under the ACL' (2019) 41 Sydney Law Review 155.

[75] Compare *Investors Compensation Scheme Ltd v West Bromwich Building Society* [1997] UKHL 28, [1998] 1 WLR 896, 912–13 and *Mount Bruce Mining Pty Ltd v Wright Prospecting Pty Ltd* [2015] HCA 37, (2015) 256 CLR 104 [46].

[76] G Yihan, Chapter 3 of this volume.

[77] *Investors Compensation* (n 76) 912–13 (Lord Hoffmann). See also *Bank of Credit and Commerce International SA v Ali* [2001] UKHL 8, [2002] 1 AC 251 [39] (Lord Hoffmann).

[78] G Yihan, Chapter 3 of this volume, section III.1.

[79] ibid.

[80] See discussion in *Cherry v Steele-Park* [2017] NSWCA 295, (2017) 96 NSWLR 548 [71].

use in general law may have the effect of undermining the clarity that the Contract Act was intended to provide. An example of this phenomenon is found in the treatment of consideration. The definition of consideration in section 2(d) of the Contract Act provides that

> When, at the desire of the promisor, the promisee or any other person has done or abstained from doing, or does or abstains from doing, or promises to do or to abstain from doing, something, such act or abstinence or promise is called a consideration for the promise.

Shivprasad Swaminathan explains that the provision was 'designed to mark the vanishing point of consideration without having to formally abolish it'.[81] It avoids the references to benefit and detriment that are found in English formulations of consideration and recognises the role of reliance.[82] However, this more elegant and straightforward formulation was undermined as Indian courts superimposed the English doctrine over the Act's provisions.[83] Shivprasad Swaminathan further documents the parallel influence of English law on courts who have interpreted section 16 (undue influence) of the Contract Act more narrowly than the words of section 16(3), as amended in 1899, would appear to allow, so as to remove the possibility of relief on the basis of unconscionable conduct or contractual unfairness.[84] Pollock suggests, presciently, that this problem may be at least partly due to uncertainty as to whether fundamental notions of the common law have been modified 'by deliberate design or by accident in the execution'.[85]

3. Regional Adaption

A third aspiration, and at times criticism, of codified law lies in producing a comprehensive and uniform law applicable to the jurisdiction to which it applies.[86] This idea of a uniform body of law tailored for local environs was certainly a consideration

[81] S Swaminathan, 'Eclipsed by Orthodoxy: The Vanishing Point of Consideration and the Forgotten Ingenuity of the Indian Contract Act' (2017) 12 Asian Journal of Comparative Law 141, 141.
[82] ibid 144.
[83] ibid 145.
[84] See S Swaminathan and V Singh, Chapter 9 of this volume, section II.4 citing *Raja Balla Mal v Ahad Shah* (1919) 21 Bom LR 558 (PC). Also S Swaminathan, 'Contractual Unfairness: Another Way of Skinning the Cat' (2019) 3 Indian Law Review 299. See also TT Arvind, Chapter 17 of this volume, section I.1, discussing the Indian courts' use of s 23 (public policy) to respond to instances of unconscionability. Nevertheless, such a doctrine was read into the Contract Act in 1986 by the Supreme Court in *Central Indian Water Transport Corp v Brojo Nath Ganguly* AIR 1986 SC 1571, which held that a contract that was unconscionable would violate public policy, and hence be void under the Contract Act, s 23, which deals with contracts against public policy.
[85] See Pollock and Mulla, *The Indian Contract Act* (1st edn) (n 9) v (preface).
[86] On Singapore's search for 'autochthonous' law tailored for its local context, see A Phang, 'Constructing Theoretical Frameworks' (1988) 30 Malaya Law Review 211; A Phang, *The Development of Singapore Law: Historical and Socio-Legal Perspectives* (Butterworths 1990) 8–13 and, in the context of misleading conduct, A Phang, 'Critical Pressure Points in the Regulation of Silence in Misleading Conduct' in E Bant and JM Paterson (eds), *Misleading Silence* (Hart 2020) ch 2.

influencing the development of the Contract Act, albeit contested at times. Regional adaption presupposes opportunities for organic development and, through this, the scope for adjusting the law to local conditions and customs.[87] However, any willingness to defer to local conditions conflicts with the ideal of rationalism in codification, which, as it was understood at the time, drew on an assumption of universal 'scientific' principles.[88] Thus, Pearson observes that there was unresolved tension in the principles that were supposed to inform the drafting of the Contract Act, which envisaged that the Act would both express the ideals of the English law of contract and be adjusted to the circumstances of application in India. Indeed, Pearson notes that

> When two of the Second Law Commission proposed a complete code of substantive law for India based on English law—yet revised and reframed in accord with 'enlightened jurisprudence' and 'the customs and prejudices of the natives—two of the Commissioners rejected this as overly ambitious'.[89]

Swain argues that 'India provides a good example of the way in which the British were prepared to adapt the common law for colonial conditions, at the same time also demonstrating the limits of that indulgence'.[90] Some proposals made little headway, where they were thought to depart too far from the English law of contract.[91] The primacy of English law can be seen in the examples accompanying the sections of the Act, which typically concern the kind of hypotheticals that would inform English texts (albeit changed to accommodate Indian currency), being full of examples of contracts for horses and problems involving estates.[92]

Nonetheless, although the Contract Act may have been drawn from English contract law, some aspects were included as a response to local custom and conditions.[93] TT Arvind argues that the Contract Act was drafted in some core areas to depart from the existing common law not merely for reasons of certainty but also to provide a response sensitive to social concerns.[94] Notable divergences from English contract law of the period can be found in the absence of a requirement for writing (ie statute of frauds requirements),[95] the rules concerning communication of acceptance/

[87] Scholars and judges in Australia have similarly expressed an ambition of reconfiguring the common law for local conditions, particularly following emancipation from Privy Council oversight by the Australia Acts 1987 (Cth): see further A Mason, 'Australian Contract Law' (1988) 1 Journal of Contract Law 1; A Mason, 'Future Directions in Australian Law' (1987) 13 Monash University Law Review 149. See also P Finn, 'Common Law Divergences' (2013) 37 Monash University Law Review 509.

[88] Pearson, 'The Resignation of the Third Indian Law Commission' (n 12) 579 and 589.

[89] ibid 592, citing United Kingdom, *Second Report of Her Majesty's Commissioners Appointed to Consider the Reform of the Judicial Establishments, Judicial Procedure, and Laws of India* (Report No 2036, 1856) 11 and also 594.

[90] See W Swain, Chapter 1 of this volume, section I. But cf Sethu (n 1).

[91] See Patra (n 6) 397–99 (discussing unsuccessful proposals for ensuring one-sided contracts should not be enforced). See also Swaminathan, 'Contractual Unfairness' (n 86) 306 (discussing Chalmers's proposals for a fairness jurisdiction).

[92] See also section III.4 below.

[93] Minattur (n 6) 109; W Swain, Chapter 1 of this volume; Pearson, 'The Resignation of the Third Indian Law Commission' (n 12) 983; Sethu (n 1) 31.

[94] See TT Arvind, Chapter 17 of this volume, section III.

[95] See W Swain, Chapter 1 of this volume, section VII; Sethu (n 1) 36.

revocation,[96] certain rules around consideration,[97] minors' contracts,[98] and a judicial discretion over stipulated sums payable on breach (subsequently read down by courts to a more conventional approach).[99] A useful illustration for our purposes is found in sections 16 and 19 of the Contract Act, introduced in 1899, which define and provide for relief against undue influence respectively:

> 16. 'Undue influence' defined.—(1) A contract is said to be induced by 'undue influence' where the relations subsisting between the parties are such that one of the parties is in a position to dominate the will of the other and uses that position to obtain an unfair advantage over the other.
>
> (2) In particular and without prejudice to the generality of the foregoing principle, a person is deemed to be in a position to dominate the will of another—
> (a) where he holds a real or apparent authority over the other, or where he stands in a fiduciary relation to the other; or
> (b) where he makes a contract with a person whose mental capacity is temporarily or permanently affected by reason of age, illness, or mental or bodily distress.
>
> (3) Where a person who is in a position to dominate the will of another, enters into a contract with him, and the transaction appears, on the face of it or on the evidence adduced, to be unconscionable, the burden of proving that such contract was not induced by undue influence shall lie upon the person in a position to dominate the will of the other.

On its face, the provision does not replicate the English doctrine of undue influence. It does not acknowledge the presumption of influence[100] that English law recognises as arising in an established relationship of influence.[101] It does not address the related problem of undue pressure.[102] Nor does it separately address the equitable doctrine of unconscionable dealing. Nonetheless, section 16 has been used effectively in India to protect certain cohorts recognised as vulnerable to influence from pressure and exploitation: these include followers of spiritual leaders[103] and *pardanashin* women,[104]

[96] Minattur (n 6) 110. See further Swaminathan, 'The Will Theorist's Mailbox' (n 66).

[97] Minattur (n 6) 109; W Swain, Chapter 1 of this volume, section VII; Sethu (n 1) 37.

[98] Minattur (n 6) 109; Sethu (n 1) 56. See also the discussion of debates about the *nemo dat quod non habet* rule in G Pearson, 'A Cattle Lifter's Bill: Nemo dat Rule and the Indian Contract Act' (2015) 89 Australian Law Journal 31.

[99] See TT Arvind, Chapter 17 of this volume, section II.1.

[100] Notably, the confusing role of presumptions in this space has considerably hampered clarity and coherence in the English law of undue influence: see W Swadling, 'Undue Influence: Lessons from America?' in C Mitchell and W Swadling (eds), *The Restatement Third: Restitution and Unjust Enrichment* (Hart 2013) 111–31.

[101] Shivprasad Swaminathan notes that this is partly addressed through the Indian Evidence Act 1872, s 111: see S Swaminathan, Chapter 9 of this volume. See also ML Sarin, 'Contract Unconscionability in India' (1972) 14 Loyola of Los Angeles International and Comparative Law Review 569, 577.

[102] The relationship between undue influence, pressure, and the equitable doctrine of unconscionable dealing has been a continuing challenge to common law jurisdictions: see J Edelman and E Bant, *Unjust Enrichment* (2nd edn, Hart 2016) chs 9 and 10 and discussions in *Thorne v Kennedy* [2017] HCA 49, (2017) 263 CLR 85.

[103] *Manu Singh v Umadat Pande* 12 Indian LR (Allahabad HC) 523 (1890).

[104] *Tara Kumari v Chandra Mauleshwar* AIR 1931 PC 303.

who live a sheltered life and do not appear in public, a development we return to further below.[105]

Also important is section 19A of the Contract Act, which provides a power to set aside a contract induced by undue influence.

> 19A. Power to set aside contract induced by undue influence.—When consent to an agreement is caused by undue influence, the agreement is a contract voidable at the option of the party whose consent was so caused.
>
> Any such contract may be set aside either absolutely or, if the party who was entitled to avoid it has received any benefit thereunder, upon such terms and conditions as to the Court may seem just.

Notably, section 19A allows a partial reading down of the contract. This remedial response is not available under English law. The provision provides courts the option of a more circumspect response to a contract procured by undue influence than setting aside a contract entirely or rejecting such a remedy on grounds that the parties' positions cannot be precisely restored. Shivprasad Swaminathan points to the Illustration (b) for section 19A of the Contract Act, which provides that

> A, a money-lender, advances Rs. 100 to B, an agriculturist, and, by undue influence, induces B to execute a bond for Rs. 200 with interest at 6 per cent. per month. The Court may set the bond aside, ordering B to repay the Rs. 100 with such interest as may seem just.

The illustration confirms the radical proposition presented by the Contract Act that a court has the power to allow a loan with usurious interest to remain on foot, while adjusting the interest rate on grounds of undue influence, a response not available under English law.[106] A similarly broad discretion to shape appropriate remedies is found in the Australian Consumer Law.[107] As discussed further below, both reforms also reflect significantly greater domestic comfort in those jurisdictions with the concept of judicial discretion than typically found in English law.[108]

4. Accessibility

A fourth, though often less prominent, objective of codification is to make the particular body of law more accessible.[109] In principle, the consequence of making the law

[105] See section III.3 below.
[106] See S Swaminathan and V Singh, Chapter 9 of this volume, section II.3.
[107] See Australian Consumer Law, ss 237 and 243.
[108] P Finn, 'Commerce, the Common Law and Morality' (1989) 17 Monash University Law Review 87, 98. See also E Bant and JM Paterson, 'Evolution and Revolution: The Remedial Smorgasbord for Misleading Conduct in Australia' (2020) 14 Florida International University Law Review 25.
[109] See Diamond (n 20) 363–72; M Arden, 'Time for an English Commercial Code?' (1997) 56 Cambridge Law Journal 516, 532.

more rational and certain is that it should become more accessible to those who use it.[110] Accessibility as a driver of codification aims to assist those who are subject to the law, the 'law-consumer'.[111] It allows those law-consumers to find the law and also to understand its potential application to them. As Eldridge explains, '"accessibility" is a function not only of the ease with which legal sources can be accessed and understood, but also of the degree to which the law's "consumers" can confidently predict the outcome of adjudicative processes'.[112]

The view that law should be accessible in both of these senses has considerable historical support, as well as informing more modern reform movements and proposals.[113] Sir Frederick Pollock explained:

> Laws exist not for the scientific satisfaction of the legal mind, but for the convenience of lay people who sue and are sued. Now to say that law is for practical purposes more certain without a code than with one seems to me sheer paradox.[114]

This ambition has influenced the 'plain English' movement in legal and statutory drafting[115] and also the design of some modern statutes, which aspire to be both comprehensive and accessible.[116]

The ambition to make the law accessible to law-consumers also influenced the work of those responsible for the Contract Act. As already noted, at least some of the provisions were adopted for local conditions, and some of the examples included regionally specific elements. These features do not ensure accessibility but may be of assistance when combined with efforts to provide a rational structure and expression of the cognate provisions. Indeed, it may prompt more general engagement on the part of law-consumers with the law as a whole. Sir James Fitzjames Stephen, the law member of the government in India and responsible for preparing the Bill, was later to suggest that the various Indian codes were responsible for the interest in legal studies at Indian universities.[117]

Eldridge warns that the work done by codification in promoting accessibility in the law should not be overstated.[118] The motivation in drafting legislation will commonly be precision, as opposed to easy application. As we have seen above, knowing the legal principles is only the first step to resolving a dispute, and codified law in

[110] Recognising that parties such as consumers and small business also face practical hurdles to enforcing their rights in order to make use of codified law: see R Brownsword, 'After Brexit: Regulatory-Instrumentalism, Coherentism and the English Law of Contract' (2017) 34 Journal of Contract Law 139, 148 and 152.

[111] Diamond (n 20) 370, attributing this phrase to Llewellyn.

[112] Eldridge, 'Contract Codification and Certainty' (n 21) 158.

[113] L Spagnolo, BT Horrigan, and E Tetteh Laryea, 'Improving Australia's Law and Justice Framework: A Discussion Paper to Explore the Scope for Reforming Australian Contract Law' (22 March 2012) [3.6], discussed in Doris (n 25) 25.

[114] M De Wolfe Howe (ed), *The Pollock-Holmes Letters*, vol 1 (CUP 1942) 8, cited in Swain, 'Codification of Contract Law' (n 24) 44.

[115] R Grantham, 'To Whom Does Australian Corporate and Consumer Legislation Speak?' (2018) 37 University of Queensland Law Journal 57, 58.

[116] ibid (discussing Australia's corporations and consumer protection statutes).

[117] Gregory (n 29) 352.

[118] Eldridge, 'Contract Codification and Certainty' (n 21) 161.

a common law system will necessarily acquire a veneer of case law in treating and applying its provisions. But it may, at least, promote more effective planning. While the work of Stewart Macaulay and others have shown that business people—at least in manufacturing and related industries—do not rely heavily on contract law in contract dealings,[119] that is not equivalent to saying that contract law is irrelevant to their planning. Indeed, a number of writers have pointed to the commercial benefits of clear, minimalist rules underpinning business transacting.[120] On the other hand, consumers will require greater levels of protection in their dealings with business, given the inevitable information asymmetry and power imbalances, between these entities.[121] Here, there can develop a tension between contract law 'proper' and any statutory consumer protection regime, such as in the Indian Consumer Protection Act 2019, which needs not only to be accessible but also to provide substantive protection for consumer interests.[122]

Accessibility also assists legal practitioners for whom resolving difficult questions on complex areas of law may take considerable time, adding to the cost of legal advice to clients and also the quality of the advice obtained.[123] This was a driving consideration informing the development of the Contract Act. Access to resources was a pressing issue for lawyers in India at the time the Act was being drafted. Diamond observes, 'Where the legal profession is undermanned or non-existent, and where books are hard to get, a code supplies a pressing need.'[124] Beale observes that lawyers may have been the prime target audience of the Contract Act,[125] given it remained complex and possibly beyond the reach of many business people in India, still less ordinary citizens. Moreover, the ambition may have been to make the law more accessible not only to lawyers but also to decision-makers. Gail Pearson notes the prevailing distrust in India at the time of codification of the judgment of the local judiciary, many of whom were not qualified to practice law in the United Kingdom.[126] The value of an instructive role for the Contract Act is perhaps illustrated in the provisions setting out the law of mistake. This is a notoriously difficult field and yet is expressed with elegant simplicity in sections 20 and 22 of the Contract Act, described by KV Krishnaprasad as 'significantly ahead of English courts and commentators'.[127] KV Krishnaprasad is less complementary of the provisions dealing with misrepresentation in sections 17 and 18 of the Contract Act, concurring with Pollock in describing the regime being 'rather worse,

[119] S Macaulay, 'Non-Contractual Relations in Business: A Preliminary Study' (1963) 28 American Sociological Review 55.

[120] See J Morgan, *Contract Law Minimalism: A Formalist Restatement of Commercial Contract Law* (CUP 2013). See also J Gava, 'Taking Stewart Macaulay and Hugh Collins Seriously' (2016) 33 Journal of Contract Law 108.

[121] See eg MJ Radin, *Boilerplate: The Fine Print, Vanishing Rights, and the Rule of Law* (Princeton University Press 2013).

[122] See JM Paterson and E Bant, 'Contract and the Challenge of Consumer Protection Legislation' in TT Arvind and J Steele (eds), *Contract Law and the Legislature: Autonomy, Expectations, and the Making of Legal Doctrine* (Hart 2020) 79.

[123] Diamond (n 20) 368–69.

[124] ibid 362.

[125] See H Beale, Chapter 24 of this volume.

[126] Pearson, 'The Resignation of the Third Indian Law Commission' (n 12) 580. See also Patra (n 6) 384.

[127] See KV Krishnaprasad, Chapter 10 of this volume, section I.

if anything, than the average badness of the whole'.[128] That said, the explanation as to when 'silence' or a failure to speak may be fraudulent and the illustrations that accompany that explanation may be seen as pithy, useful, and accurate.[129]

III. Legislative Design

Section II identified how the themes of codification projects in general were also at play in the codification of Indian contract law in particular. We have also seen that the aspirations of the Contract Act have, in certain instances, been stymied by the infelicitous use of language and the preferences of judges in certain key instances to narrow the scope of the statute by reference to pre-existing law. The design choices made in drafting the statute (including reliance on terminology with a pre-existing meaning, the balance between rules and principles-based drafting, and the use of illustrations) will also play a significant role in the extent to which the statute is effective in achieving its ends. As Pollock commented in the first edition of the commentary on the Contract Act,

> Every written law which goes beyond mere regulation of details is a work of art; it can no more afford to dispense with unity of design and continuity of execution than a monumental building.[130]

This important and complex issue of legislative design merits further examination, to which we now turn.

1. Drafting Styles and Structure

The Contract Act did not set out to rewrite the law of contract. Rather, it expressed its core principles, in some instances striving to remove anomalies or inconsistencies and to adapt to local conditions. In this task, it was necessarily closely tethered to existing law. In many instances, the common law's influence, as we have seen, had a constricting tendency. But this is a necessary consequence of the decision not to start anew, so to speak, which would have been a much more radical proposition. But even providing a form of rational restatement of core principle is no easy task, as disagreements between the various drafters of the Contract Act, discussed by Swain, reveal.[131]

[128] Pollock and Mulla, *The Indian Contract Act* (1st edn) (n 9) v, quoted in KV Krishnaprasad, Chapter 10 of this volume, section I.

[129] See also M Bryan, 'Historical and Theoretical Perspectives on Silence and Deception in Private Law' in Bant and Paterson, *Misleading Silence* (n 88).

[130] Pollock and Mulla, *The Indian Contract Act* (1st edn) (n 9) vi (preface).

[131] See W Swain, Chapter 1 of this volume, section VII-VIII.

The process extended over some eleven years and was shaped by numerous hands and influences. The diverse intellectual influences on those who drafted the Act included, notably, Pothier but also the treatise on contract law produced by William Macpherson in 1960[132] and Dudley Field's draft civil code for New York of 1862,[133] the last particularly on fraud and misrepresentation, and itself influenced by the Louisiana Civil Code.[134] Numerous different drafters were involved,[135] a problem some commentators see as responsible for many of the 'internal incongruities' of the Contract Act.[136] Thus, KV Krishnaprasad tracks the deleterious influence on the Code's treatment of fraud and misrepresentation wielded by Pothier's will theory of contract,[137] alongside Field's Code and the pre-existing common law, objective theory of contract.[138]

2. Use of Language with a Pre-existing Meaning

Inevitably, the drafters of a code will draw upon terminology with an established meaning in the common law synthesised by the code. This use of language with established meaning acts as a direction to courts to draw upon those meanings in interpreting the code. As we have discussed, it may also have the effect of inviting courts to interpret provisions narrowly, by reference to historical common law connotations, rather than give effect to indications of a legislative intention to depart from the common law. Shivprasad Swaminathan suggests,

> Even a very clear definition of the term, short of specific traversal of specific connotations of the term, which seeks to disabuse any such association, cannot be a foolproof insurance against the antediluvian understanding of the term being brought over to understanding the term in the new code.[139]

We have already observed something of this trend in judicial interpretations of the Contract Act, such as in approaches to consideration,[140] undue influence,[141] and penalties.[142]

[132] W Macpherson, *Outlines of the Law of Contracts, as Administered in the Courts of British India* (1st edn, RC Lepage 1860).
[133] For its influence on the Contract Act, see KV Krishnaprasad, Chapter 10 of this volume, section II.
[134] Discussed in R Batiza, 'Sources of the Field Civil Code: The Civil Law Influences on a Common Law Code' (1986) 60 Tulane Law Review 799.
[135] See KV Krishnaprasad, Chapter 10 of this volume, section II.
[136] ibid section II quoting Pollock and Mulla, *The Indian Contract Act* (1st edn) (n 9) v.
[137] Beale suggests that the influence of Pothier generally may be to fill gaps in English doctrine: see H Beale, Chapter 24 of this volume, section II.1.
[138] See KV Krishnaprasad, Chapter 10 of this volume, section IV.1.
[139] Swaminathan, 'Eclipsed by Orthodoxy' (n 83) 164–65.
[140] See ibid; Minattur (n 6) 109; W Swain, Chapter 1 of this volume, section VIII; Sethu (n 1) 37.
[141] See n 101 above.
[142] See Swaminathan, 'De-inventing the Wheel' (n 58) 108, citing Stokes (n 61) 506.

3. Principles and Rules

Clearly, a code will, of necessity, include a combination of rule- and standard-based provisions. But it is important to be aware of the impact of different drafting techniques. These may present different risks to the goals of codification (including of rationality, certainty, and accessibility) and will provide different kinds of prompts for judges and decision-makers.[143] Thus, for example, rule-based drafting carries a veneer of certainty but may find itself lacking the required tools to address party needs or (as we saw earlier) fall out of step with extraneous developments in law, practice, and social norms. In a potential example of the former, Neel Maitra observes that section 11 of the Contract Act 'provides no catch-all or umbrella term' that may be used to support or protect vulnerable parties that fall outside the three enumerated categories of incapacity—minority, unsoundness of mind, and legal disqualification.[144] Instead, the more broadly framed principles of undue influence under section 16 have been able to be called into service for the benefit of exceptionally vulnerable parties, in particular, *pardanashin* women.[145]

So far as the latter drafting risk is concerned, the more prescriptive and exhaustive a rule, the less likely it will be able to evolve with changing circumstances. We gave earlier the salient example of the English Misrepresentation Act 1967.[146] Additional factors, such as judicial culture and styles of reasoning, may operate as countervailing (or, indeed, supportive) influences on legislative reforms, alongside statutory design.[147] But more substantive or purposive reasoning, employed by judges to ameliorate or expand rules-based drafting in order to meet changing broader contexts and needs, will necessarily confront, and may contradict, the formal language and structure of the provision. This may, in turn, undermine foundational ideas of statutory interpretation and the educative or expressive role of statutes.[148] Here, Maitra's discussion of the treatment of parties suffering from illiteracy and other significant vulnerabilities provides a powerful example of judicial sensitivity to the limits of purposive interpretation and, in that case, 'as a matter of judicial deference to the text of section 11'.[149] Maitra considers that the judicial preference for using undue influence is, in that light, correct.[150] We may add, moreover, that a response based on undue influence rather than lack of capacity is consistent with a recognition that the constraint on contracting rises from

[143] Paterson and Bant, 'Misrepresentation, Misleading Conduct and Statute' (n 53).
[144] N Maitra, Chapter 8 of this volume, section II.
[145] See section II.3 above and further discussion in Pollock and Mulla, *The Indian Contract Act* (2nd edn) (n 47) 80–83.
[146] See *Hedley Byrne* (n 51).
[147] In the context of the Misrepresentation Act, see *RBC Properties* (n 53) (Andrew Phang Boon Leong JA, delivering the judgment of the court); see also *Xia Zhengyan v Geng Changqing* [2015] SGCA 22, [2015] 3 SLR 732 [97].
[148] See Pollock and Mulla, *The Indian Contract Act* (2nd edn) (n 47) vii (preface).
[149] See N Maitra, Chapter 8 of this volume, section II.2.
[150] ibid.

societal influences rather than any innate inability to exercise legal capacity on the part of people in these cohorts.[151]

By contrast, standards-based drafting may appear to come at the cost of certainty, particularly in the early stages of application. We have noted earlier the open-ended language of 'loss or damage' employed in section 73 of the Contract Act, discussed further in Katy Barnett's chapter in this volume.[152] However, it is possible, and even likely, that this form of drafting will, in time, produce a flexible and substantive approach to adjudication, which allows the regime to adapt to new practices, circumstances, and developments in neighbouring general law contexts.[153] The end result may be both certain and coherent.

Nonetheless, to return to a theme raised earlier, even principles-based drafting will not necessarily be able to accommodate significant changes in the underlying legal or social context. Shivprasad Swaminathan argues that the provision for statutory relief on grounds of coercion in section 15 of the Contract Act is ill fitted to accommodate modern notions of duress, with the result that courts' 'attempts at accommodating within the ambit of the provision, forms of illegitimate pressure like economic duress, come across as tenuous and contrived'.[154] TT Arvind charts how, despite the apparently clear discretion awarded to the courts under section 74 of the Contract Act, courts have adopted doctrinal tests for responding to penalty clauses that are impede certainty and are 'also frequently over-interventionist'.[155]

4. Illustrations

As we have already noted, the Contract Act uniquely provides short illustrative examples of the intended application of the law for key provisions,[156] pre-empting the US Restatements of the 20th century. Neither the influential Field Code nor the Louisiana Code use illustrations. The Field Code gives case references but, presumably, these may have been thought inaccessible in the Indian context for the reasons already noted, pertaining to a general absence of legal texts and, in some contexts, legal training.[157] Illustrations are additionally found in the Indian Penal Code of 1860, the initial draft of which was also by Macaulay.[158] Indeed, Jain suggests that the unique use of illustrations

[151] See Y Maker and others, 'From Safety Nets to Support Networks: Beyond "Vulnerability" in Protection for Consumers with Cognitive Disabilities' (2018) 41 University of New South Wales Law Journal 818.

[152] See K Barnett, Chapter 16 of this volume.

[153] Shivprasad Swaminathan's analysis of the development of an unfairness jurisdiction under the Contract Act perhaps illustrates this potential: Swaminathan, 'Contractual Unfairness' (n 86).

[154] ibid.

[155] See TT Arvind, Chapter 17 of this volume, section I.

[156] E Bant and JM Paterson, 'Statutory Interpretation and The Critical Role of Soft Law Guidelines in Developing a Coherent Law of Remedies in Australia' in R Levy and others (eds), *New Directions for Law in Australia: Essays in Contemporary Law Reform* (ANU Press 2017) 301.

[157] See H Beale, Chapter 24 of this volume; Pearson, 'The Resignation of the Third Indian Law Commission (n 12) 580; Patra (n 6) 384.

[158] See further E Phillips, 'The Codification Enterprise: Principled Law Reform and the Indian Penal Code' (2017) Jersey & Guernsey Law Review 166.

across the Indian codes is referable to this draft undertaken by Macauley.[159] The First Law Commission charged with drafting the Contract Act explained the aim of the illustrations as follows:

> These illustrations will, we trust, greatly facilitate the understanding of law, and will at the same time often serve as a defence of law. In our definitions, we have often found ourselves under the necessity of sacrificing neatness and perspicuity to precision, and of using hard and awkward expressions which would convey our whole meaning and no more than our whole meaning. Such definitions standing by themselves would repel and perplex every reader . . . we hope that when each of these definitions is followed by a collection of cases falling under it, and of cases which, though at first sight they appear to fall under it, do not really fall under it, the definitions and the reasons which led the adoption of it will be readily understood.[160]

The illustrations therefore are intended to give direction where there may otherwise have been some doubt about the scope and application of the provisions and the sometimes terse statements of principle contained in them. Illustrations, therefore, have a considerable role to play in achieving codification objectives of certainty and accessibility. A good example is found in the illustrations on misrepresentation in sections 17 and 19 of the Contract Act. This is a complex field of contract law that draws on neighbouring doctrines from tort and equity. We have commented on criticisms of these examples,[161] but the illustrations may do some useful work in giving content to what nonetheless remain abstract concepts, particularly in the context of fraud and misrepresentation by omission, a notoriously difficult field. Unfortunately, this ambition for clarity may be somewhat stymied by the parochialism of the examples. These are drawn from common examples used by largely English jurists in unpicking the conundrums of misrepresentations and disclosure obligations,[162] with some, likely superficial, effort to tailor them to the circumstances existing in India.

Illustrations serve a dual purpose of linking the new code provisions to the rich body of pre-existing general law principles, while also operating to provide specific guidance to law-consumers, from the public to the judiciary, about their operation in practice. This dual operation reinforces the inevitable tendency of important legislative reforms of this kind to interact with their legal surrounds and history, as well as embracing a forward-looking perspective introducing reform to address inconsistencies or incoherence in that pre-existing law, with, as we have seen, varied success. Perhaps unsurprisingly, not all of the illustrations are successful. Wayne Courtney points to Illustration (c) of section 127 of the Contract Act, which not only fails to resolve the question of

[159] MP Jain, *Outlines of Indian Legal History* (NM Tripathi 1952) 486.

[160] House of Lords, 'Returns and Papers Relative to the Affairs of the East India Company', vol 4 (Sessional No 263, 30 June 1852) 27–28 <www.google.com.au/books/edition/Returns_and_Papers_Presented_to_the_Hous/YklDAAAAcAAJ?hl=en&gbpv> accessed 4 April 2024.

[161] See Pollock and Mulla, *The Indian Contract Act* (1st edn) (n 9) v.

[162] See also A Duggan, M Bryan, and F Hanks, *Contractual Non-disclosure: An Applied Study in Modern Contract Theory* (Longman Professional 1994).

whether past consideration is adequate for a guarantee but also notes that the illustration is itself tautological.[163]

IV. Conclusion

Attempts to codify a body of common law express an ideal of legislative design. They aim to produce a version of the law that is more rational, clear, and accessible than what went before. The chapters in this collection illustrate that while these goals may not have been fully achieved (and, moreover, may represent an ultimately impossible task), the Contract Act itself has largely stood the test of time. In that way, there is little doubt that it achieved one of the key aspirations of its drafters. Moreover, the Act provides a rich source of insight and lessons for other jurisdictions that share its goals. Importantly, these include jurisdictions that are yet to embrace the codification project. More generally, Contract Act points to the complex relationship between legislative design and its interpretation and operation. This relationship is interactive and dynamic and has an impact that goes, potentially, well beyond the immediate concerns of the particular statute.[164] The 'oil-and-water'[165] characterisation of general law and statute so ably criticised by Beatson appears, in this light, an impoverished one indeed.

[163] W Courtney, Chapter 20 of this volume, section III.1.ii.

[164] Finn, 'Unity, Then Divergence' (n 48) 47 and Finn, 'Commerce, the Common Law and Morality' (n 111). See also Bant and Paterson, 'Evolution and Revolution' (n 111).

[165] J Beatson, 'The Role of Statute in the Development of Common Law Doctrine' (2001) 117 Law Quarterly Review 247, 259.

3

Contractual Interpretation

*Goh Yihan**

I. Introduction

Contractual interpretation in India is also an exercise in statutory interpretation. This is because the Indian Evidence Act 1872 (hereinafter 'the Evidence Act'), derived from the work of Sir James Fitzjames Stephen in the 19th century,[1] limits the range of admissible evidence that can be used to interpret contracts. In this way, even though the Evidence Act does not lay down a substantive rule of interpretation, it indirectly affects how the Indian courts interpret contracts. However, since the Evidence Act was crafted in the 19th century with the explicit aim of fossilising the law of evidence at the time, modern courts have had to grapple with how to interpret the relevant provisions. Courts may have to choose between an interpretation that remains true to the law at the time of drafting or adopt an 'updating' interpretation to bring the modern contextual approach, which treats background facts (or the 'factual matrix') as being usually relevant, into operation.

Which is the correct interpretation of the Evidence Act, with its concomitant effect on contractual interpretation in India, will be the central question in this chapter. The answer affects not just India. Indeed, because the Evidence Act was adopted in many former British colonies, including Pakistan, Bangladesh, Sri Lanka, Burma, Malaysia, Singapore, Brunei, and parts of Africa and the West Indies,[2] its influence extends far beyond India. To answer this question, the chapter is divided into three main parts. First, it discusses the significance of the Evidence Act in relation to contractual interpretation and seeks to understand its basic approach towards the admission of evidence. Second, it considers the proper interpretation of the Evidence Act and discusses how that affects the approach towards contractual interpretation in India. Third, it considers the specific issue of the admissibility of prior negotiations and subsequent conduct under

* The views expressed in this chapter reflect the personal views of the author and not of the Supreme Court of Singapore. Much of the material for this chapter is based on my previous work on the same topic: Y Goh, 'Contractual Interpretation in Indian Evidence Act Jurisdictions: Compatibility with Modern Contextual Approach?' (2013) 13 Oxford University Commonwealth Law Journal 17. In addition, I would like to thank Carol Yap and Chong Fu Shan for their editorial assistance.

[1] The Indian Evidence Bill was considered and passed on 12 March 1872 in India by the thirteen members of the Viceroy's Legislative Council: see JD Heydon, 'The Origins of the Indian Evidence Act' (2010) 9 Oxford University Commonwealth Law Journal 1, 1–2.

[2] ibid 13.

Goh Yihan, *Contractual Interpretation* In: *Foundations of Indian Contract Law*. Edited by: KV Krishnaprasad, Niranjan Venkatesan, Shivprasad Swaminathan, and Umakanth Varottil, Oxford University Press. © Oxford University Press 2024.
DOI: 10.1093/9780191997211.003.0003

the Evidence Act to demonstrate the inherent tension between staying true to the structure of the Evidence Act and modern rules developed by the common law.

II. The Significance of the Evidence Act

1. Operation of the Evidence Act

In order to understand how the Evidence Act affects contractual interpretation in India, it is necessary to first consider its approach to the admission of evidence in general. The Evidence Act deals with this by way of two broad steps. The first concerns the facts that *may be proved*, which is covered by Part I.

The controlling provision, section 5, provides that evidence may be given of the existence or non-existence of every fact in issue or of any relevant fact, as defined by the Evidence Act. According to Stephen, facts may be related to rights and liabilities either by (a) constituting such a state of things that the existence of the disputed right or liability would be a legal inference from the fact (such facts are known as 'facts in issue') or (b) affecting the probability of the existence of facts in issue (known as 'relevant facts').[3] Only facts that come within these two definitions may be proved. This therefore affects the facts, and thereby the context, that may be considered when a contract is being interpreted.

Section 5 is elaborated upon by sections 7 and 9, which are set out below:

> 7 Facts which are the occasion, cause or effect, immediate or otherwise, of relevant facts, or facts in issue, or which constitute the state of things under which they happened, or which afforded an opportunity for their occurrence or transaction, are relevant.
>
> 9 Facts necessary to explain or introduce a fact in issue or relevant fact, or which support or rebut an inference suggested by a fact in issue or relevant fact, or which establish the identity of any thing or person whose identity is relevant, or fix the time or place at which any fact in issue or relevant fact happened, or which show the relation of parties by whom any such fact was transacted, are relevant in so far as they are necessary for that purpose.

These appear to be *prima facie* wide enough to make the 'factual matrix'—the focus of the modern contextual approach—relevant and hence provable under the Evidence Act. This is because, in the context of a dispute about contractual interpretation, the 'fact in issue' would be the meaning of the contractual words. The 'relevant fact[s]' would then be facts that can affect the probability of this 'fact in issue', pursuant to sections 7 and 9. In fact, Illustration (a) to section 9 provides that the state of *A*'s property and *A*'s

[3] JF Stephen, *An Introduction to the Indian Evidence Act: The Principles of Judicial Evidence* (2nd impression, Thacker, Spink & Co 1904) 12–13.

family at the date of an alleged will may be relevant facts to ascertain whether a given document is the will of *A*. This seems at least analogous to the relevant background information in contractual interpretation. The only way in which this might not be so is if they were expressly excluded by virtue of some other provision. Obviously, this does not mean that everything and anything is admissible. The general provision of section 5—that evidence can only be given of facts in issue or relevant facts and of nothing else—continues to control and limit the admissible evidence. The result is that relevance continues to be important but that one has to fall back on the very general test of relevance set out in Part I in deciding what facts a party can be allowed to prove and what facts a party cannot.

Once a fact is defined by the Evidence Act as provable, the second step prescribed by the Evidence Act concerns how that fact *is to be proved*. Part II of the Evidence Act provides that even if a fact is declared to be relevant by Part I, certain types of evidence (eg oral, as opposed to documentary, evidence) may not be adduced to prove such a fact if Part II excludes such evidence. The Evidence Act gives effect to this step by way of ten provisions.[4] These provisions mirror three distinct rules of the common law parol evidence rule,[5] which gives effect to the objective theory of contract.[6]

2. The Parol Evidence Rule

i. Evidence used to contradict, vary, add to, or subtract from the contract

There are two important aspects of the parol evidence rule in so far as contractual interpretation is concerned. The first is that parties who have reduced a contract to writing should be bound by the contract and nothing else. Over time, this aspect of the parol evidence rule became narrower so that only extrinsic evidence which 'add[s] to, vary or contradict' the written contract is excluded; all other evidence can be adduced to prove the terms of the contract. Furthermore, a good number of exceptions to the rule had been developed by the common law and incorporated into the Evidence Act.[7]

The starting point is to consider section 91, the 'proof by documentary evidence' provision, which provides that

> When the terms of a contract, or of a grant, or of any other disposition of property, have been reduced to the form of a document, and in all cases in which any matter is required by law to be reduced to the form of a document, no evidence shall be given in

[4] As the numberings of these provisions differ according to the jurisdiction concerned, they will be referred to in this chapter by reference to their purpose. Where a provision is reproduced, it will be from the Evidence Act rather than any of its derivative versions operative in other jurisdictions.

[5] Singapore Academy of Law, *Report of the Law Reform Committee on the Review of the Parol Evidence Rule* (2006) [13].

[6] See generally Law Commission, *Law of Contract: The Parol Evidence Rule* (Law Com No 154, 1986); DW McLauchlan, *The Parol Evidence Rule* (Professional Publications Ltd 1976).

[7] See eg Law Commission (n 6) and G McMeel, *The Construction of Contracts: Interpretation, Implication and Rectification* (2nd edn, OUP 2011) 411.

> proof of the terms of such contract, grant or other disposition of property, or of such matter, except the document itself, or secondary evidence of its contents in cases in which secondary evidence is admissible under the provisions [of this Act].

Section 91 of the Evidence Act relates to the exclusiveness of documentary evidence and is an aspect of the 'best evidence' rule.[8] It provides that where a contract has been reduced to a document, that document must be produced as proof, being the best evidence of the agreement reached between the parties. Thus, oral evidence is generally inadmissible to prove the agreement unless the relevant exceptions as provided by section 92 of the Evidence Act are satisfied. This section provides that

> When the terms of any such contract, grant or other disposition of property, or any matter required by law to be reduced to the form of a document, have been proved according to the last section, no evidence of any oral agreement or statement shall be admitted, as between the parties to any such instrument or their representatives in interest, for the purpose of contradicting, varying, adding to, or subtracting from, its terms [subject to provisos 1–6].

Thus seen, section 92 operates in tandem with section 91. Section 92 operates only where the contract (among other documents) has been proved under section 91. It is therefore based on the same principle that documentary evidence is superior to oral evidence such that no oral evidence is generally admissible to contradict, add to, or subtract from the terms of the contract proved by way of documentary evidence.[9] In this way, section 91 is said to deal with the exclusiveness of documentary evidence, whereas section 92 deals with the conclusiveness and inclusiveness of documentary evidence. Section 92 supplements section 91 by excluding extrinsic evidence that may be used to control its terms.[10]

Section 92 is, however, subject to six provisos, which largely replicate the exceptions to the parol evidence rule at common law. Under these provisos, parol evidence is exceptionally admissible to prove (1) any vitiating factor such as fraud or illegality, (2) a separate oral agreement that is not inconsistent with the terms of the written contract, (3) a separate oral agreement constituting a condition precedent to any obligation under the written contract, (4) a distinct subsequent oral agreement to rescind or modify the written contract,[11] (5) any usage or custom not expressly mentioned in the written contract (and not being inconsistent with its terms) but which is usually annexed to such contracts, and (6) any fact that shows the manner in which the language of a document is related to existing facts.

[8] Singapore Academy of Law (n 5) [31].

[9] ibid [39]. See also M Monir, *Principles and Digest of the Law of Evidence*, vol 1 (7th edn, University Book Agency 1989) 969.

[10] S Sarkar and VR Manohar, *Sarkar's Law of Evidence* (16th edn, LexisNexis Butterworths 2007) 1461.

[11] Except in cases in which such contract, grant, or disposition of property is by law required to be in writing or has been registered according to the law in force for the time being as to the registration of documents.

While provisos 1–5 largely replicate existing common law exceptions to the parol evidence rule, proviso 6 is different. Although it appears as an exception to section 92, it has been regarded as providing specifically for the admissibility of evidence used for contractual interpretation.[12] This view is supported by Stephen's *Digest*, in which Stephen viewed sections 91 and 92 collectively, under what he termed 'Article 90'.[13] However, Article 90, while including provisos 1–5,[14] did not contain proviso 6. Instead, proviso 6 was discussed separately under 'Article 91', which dealt with 'what evidence may be given for the interpretation of documents'.[15] Indeed, Stephen regarded that Articles 90 and 91 dealt with different matters: Article 91 dealt with the interpretation of documents by oral evidence, whereas Article 90 defined the cases in which documents are exclusive evidence.[16] Although arranged slightly differently in the Evidence Act, one view is that proviso 6 to section 92 should be treated separately from sections 91 and 92.[17] Rather, it is to be understood together with sections 93–100, to which I now turn.

ii. Evidence used to interpret the contract

The second aspect of the parol evidence rule relating to contractual interpretation is the specific prohibition against the admission of extrinsic evidence to interpret a contract unless there is a latent ambiguity to be cured. Thus, where there is patent ambiguity, extrinsic evidence cannot be used to interpret the contract.[18] This aspect of the parol evidence rule is derived from proviso 6 read with sections 93–100 of the Evidence Act. These sections together correspond to Stephen's 'Article 91', which, as mentioned earlier, concerned the admissibility of evidence used to interpret contracts.

These sections may be categorised into three distinct groups. The first group (comprising sections 93 and 94 of the Evidence Act) deals with situations where extrinsic evidence is *not* allowed to be used in interpreting contracts. The second group (comprising sections 95, 96, and 97 of the Evidence Act) deals with situations where extrinsic evidence is *allowed* to be used in interpreting contracts; these situations all concern latent ambiguities. Finally, the third group (comprising sections 98, 99, and 100 of the Evidence Act) deals with more technical matters and, unlike sections 93–97 of the Evidence Act, does not lay down general principles.

[12] See eg Sarkar and Manohar (n 10) 1538; V Kesava Rao, *Sir John Woodroffe & Syed Amir Ali's Law of Evidence* (18th edn, LexisNexis Butterworths 2009) 3711–12; R Ranchhoddas and DK Thakore, *Ratanlal and Dhirajlal's The Law of Evidence* (23rd edn, LexisNexis Butterworths 2010) 1148–49.

[13] See Stephen, *An Introduction to the Indian Evidence Act* (n 3) 88–89.

[14] ibid 88–89.

[15] See ibid 91–92.

[16] ibid 158. Indeed, the Law Commission of India, in their 69th and 185th Reports, which discussed various aspects of the Evidence Act, discussed 'the first five provisos' and 'the sixth proviso [ie proviso 6]' differently: see eg Law Commission of India, *Review of the Indian Evidence Act, 1872* (Law Com Report No 185, 2003) 441.

[17] See eg *Belapur Co v State Farming Corpn* AIR (1969) Bom 231 (Bom HC) [24]–[25]. It is also important to note that Stephen himself noted that art 91 differed from the six similar propositions in J Wigram, *Admission of Extrinsic Evidence in Aid of the Interpretation of Wills* (2nd edn, Charles Hunter 1835) only in its arrangement and form of expression: see Stephen, *An Introduction to the Indian Evidence Act* (n 3) 160–61.

[18] This aspect of the parol evidence rule is defunct at common law today: see eg McMeel (n 7) 166–68.

The starting point is thus the first group of provisions. In this regard, section 93 of the Evidence Act, is the 'patent ambiguity' provision. This section deals with the exclusion of evidence to explain or amend a document that is patently ambiguous. Section 93 provides that

> When the language used in a document is on its face ambiguous or defective, evidence may not be given of facts which would show its meaning or supply its defects.

Accordingly, no evidence may be given to cure patent ambiguity, which may arise either by the language used being uncertain (though intelligible) or so defective as to be meaningless. Section 93 is based on the old English cases of *Clayton v Lord Nugent*[19] and *Baylis v The Attorney General*,[20] which each correspond to the illustrations accompanying the section.[21] In *Clayton*, a card that supplied meaning to initials appearing in a will was held to be inadmissible because the initials were uncertain in meaning. In *Baylis*, evidence as to the testator's intention to fill in a blank was similarly held inadmissible because the blank was regarded as inherently defective.[22] More broadly, section 93 has been explained on the basis that it is impermissible to speculate what the parties meant when there is a patent ambiguity, with the result that the contract fails.[23]

Closely related to section 93, is section 94 of the Evidence Act, the 'plain language' provision. This provision provides that

> When language used in a document is plain in itself and when it applies accurately to existing facts, evidence may not be given to show that it was not meant to apply to such facts.

In contrast to section 93, which is concerned with outward ambiguity, section 94 is concerned with outward clarity. Such clarity arises because the language as used by the parties is 'plain' *and* applies accurately to existing facts. In such cases, no evidence may be admitted to provide an alternative meaning, that is, to explain that the contractual language was *not* meant to apply to such facts. Section 93 may thus be explained on the basis that, where the language used by the parties is outwardly clear as applied to facts, extrinsic evidence may not be adduced to contradict this meaning. This may be regarded as another way of characterising a situation 'where external circumstances do not create any doubt or difficulty as to the proper application of those words to claimants under the instrument'.[24] As Denman LCJ said in *Rickman v Carstairs*, '[t]he

[19] (1844) 13 K & W 200, 153 ER 83.
[20] (1741) 2 Atk 239, 26 ER 548.
[21] The second more than the first; however, see Stephen, *An Introduction to the Indian Evidence Act* (n 3) 92, 94, in which Stephen identifies these two cases as illustrating the equivalent of the 'patent ambiguity' provision.
[22] Cf *Price v Page* (1799) 4 Ves Jun 680, 31 ER 351; *Harrhy v Wall* (1817) 1 B & Ald 103, 106 ER 39.
[23] Sarkar and Manohar (n 10) 1552.
[24] See *Shore v Wilson* (1842) 9 Cl & F 355, 565; (1842) 8 ER 450, 532. See also D Seng, 'Another Clog on the Construction of Contracts? Parol Evidence Rule and Use of Extrinsic Evidence' [1997] Singapore Journal of Legal Studies 457, 488.

question . . . is not what was the intention of the parties, but what is the meaning of the words they have used'.[25]

Whereas sections 93 and 94 of the Evidence Act exclude the admission of evidence where there is either patent ambiguity or no ambiguity, the next three sections, which comprise the second group mentioned earlier, permit the admission of such evidence in the face of latent ambiguity. Such ambiguity 'arise[s] extrinsically in the application of an instrument of clear and definite intrinsic meaning to doubtful subject-matter'.[26] The rationale behind these sections is that, because such ambiguities arise from an extrinsic fact, extrinsic evidence must therefore be admissible to resolve the ambiguity.[27] Put in a different way, it is presupposed, in these situations, 'that the resources of construction, aided by all admissible extrinsic facts, have been first exhausted'.[28] It is after this threshold is passed that extrinsic evidence showing the person or thing that the language was intended to apply to is admitted.[29]

The Evidence Act covers the admission of extrinsic evidence in the face of a latent ambiguity in three sections. The first of these is section 95 of the Evidence Act, which concerns the situation where plain contractual language is rendered meaningless in reference to existing facts.[30] Section 95 is based on cases such as *Allgood v Blake*,[31] in which Blackburn J said that '[t]he general rule is to give the words their natural meaning unless, when applied to the subject matter . . . they produce . . . an absurdity'.[32] In that case, extrinsic evidence is admissible to give the words an alternative meaning.

Second, section 96 of the Evidence Act is a more specific application of section 95. It concerns an 'equivocation' or where the contractual language used might have been meant to apply to only one of several things that are each susceptible to the same description used. This section is based on[33] *Doe v Needs*,[34] in which evidence of the testator's statements of intention and circumstances were admissible to ascertain which of two 'George Gords' the testator meant.

Finally, section 97 of the Evidence Act, concerns the situation where the contractual language could apply partially to two sets of existing facts, but the whole does not apply correctly to either. Similar to the previous sections, section 97 is based on[35] several cases decided at the time the Evidence Act was drafted.[36] These cases stand for the

[25] (1833) 5 B & Ad 651, 663; 8 ER 931, 935.

[26] T Starkie, *A Practical Treatise of the Law of Evidence, and Digest of Proofs in Civil and Criminal Proceedings*, vol 3 (3rd edn, Stevens & Norton 1842) 755, 768.

[27] See eg *Doe d Chichester v Oxenden* (1816) 4 Dow 65, 92; 3 ER 1091, 1100.

[28] J Thayer, *A Preliminary Treatise on Evidence at the Common Law* (Rothman Reprints 1969) 455.

[29] Seng (n 24) 493.

[30] Cf *Zurich Insurance (Singapore) Pte Ltd v B-Gold Interior Design & Construction Pte Ltd* [2008] 3 SLR(R) 1029 (Sing CA) [79], in which the Court stated that this provision did not pertain to latent ambiguity since, after the context is considered, multiple meanings of the words in question do not exist; rather, the original language becomes meaningless, in the light of the surrounding circumstances, to convince the Court that such language could not be used in its 'plain' sense.

[31] (1873) LR 8 Ex 160.

[32] ibid 163 (Blackburn J).

[33] Stephen, *An Introduction to the Indian Evidence Act* (n 3) 93, 95.

[34] (1839) 2 M & W 129, 150 ER 698.

[35] Stephen, *An Introduction to the Indian Evidence Act* (n 3) 93–95.

[36] *Doe v Hiscocks* 5 M & W 363; *Ryall v Hannam* 10 Beav 35; *Stringer v Gardiner* (1859) 27 Beav 35, 54 ER 14.

proposition that evidence of surrounding circumstances may be admitted to show to which of two sets of existing facts the contract was meant to refer.

Sections 98, 99, and 100 of the Evidence Act comprise the third group of provisions. They relate mainly to technical matters. Section 98, the 'evidence as to meaning of illegible characters' provision, allows the admission of evidence from experts and such persons to explain illegible writing. Section 99 governs who may give evidence of an agreement varying terms of the written document. And finally, section 100 provides that the previous provisions do not apply to the construction of wills. This chapter does not focus on this group, which contain provisions of rather technical significance.

3. The Absence of Any Rule of Interpretation

So far, we have been concerned with evidentiary rules that control the extrinsic evidence that courts may consider in the interpretation of contracts. In contrast to these rules, it ought to be noted that the Evidence Act does not directly prescribe any substantive rules on the interpretation of contracts. Thus, the Evidence Act does not, for instance tell us how contracts are to be interpreted. This, therefore, does not encompass the modern contextual approach now widely accepted in many courts, including those in jurisdictions governed by derivatives of the Evidence Act. However, the Evidence Act affects this substantive question indirectly: by controlling the evidence, and hence the context, which courts can consider, the Evidence Act indirectly mandates how courts are to interpret contracts. If, for example, we accept that the Evidence Act limits the situations where extrinsic evidence can be considered, then it necessarily results in a more restrictive application of the modern contextual approach.

In summary, we have seen thus far that the Evidence Act adopts an approach that fossilises, to a certain degree, various aspects of the parol evidence rule as it appeared in the 19th century. It is largely concerned with two broad aspects of the parol evidence rule that are relevant to contractual interpretation: first, when evidence can be adduced to prove the terms of the contract (which are already rendered provable via Part I of the Evidence Act), and second, when evidence can be adduced to explain the terms of the contract so discerned. As regards the second aspect, the Evidence Act contains a series of provisions that sets out a detailed regime for the admissibility of evidence. The next question that arises is whether these provisions, together with their embedded ideas, are compatible with the modern contextual approach to contractual interpretation. This is the question to which we now turn.

III. The Appropriate Interpretation Approach Pursuant to the Evidence Act

Lord Hoffmann summarised the modern contextual approach to the interpretation of contracts in *Investors Compensation* by way of five points. The key point made is that '[i]nterpretation is the ascertainment of the meaning which the document would convey to a reasonable person having all the background knowledge which would reasonably have been available to the parties in the situation in which they were at the time of the contract'.[37] This is the essence of the modern contextual approach and posits that interpretation cannot occur in a vacuum but must be done by reference to all the relevant background information. This approach shifted the substantive rules governing the interpretative process from focusing on the meaning of the *words* used in the document to focusing on what would be understood as the meaning of the person *using* those words.

The Indian courts seem to have accepted the modern contextual approach. Thus, the Supreme Court in *Delta International v Shyam Sundar Ganeriwalla* referred to *The Interpretation of Contracts* by Kim Lewison:

> For the purpose of the construction of contracts, the intention of the parties is the meaning of the words they have used. There is no intention independent of that meaning. Where the words of a contract are capable of two meanings, one of which is lawful and the other unlawful, the former construction should be preferred.[38]

This suggests that where there are multiple possible meanings to the words contained in the contract, the court would compare the result of each meaning against what the contracting parties would have reasonably intended, having regard to their knowledge of the surrounding circumstances at the time when the contract was entered into. Similarly, the Supreme Court held, in *Bank of India v K Mohandas*, that 'the intention of the parties must be ascertained from the language they have used, considered in the light of the surrounding circumstances and the object of the contract. The nature and purpose of the contract is an important guide in ascertaining the intention of the parties.'[39]

More recently, in *Pubali Bank Limited v Nagreka Exports Limited*,[40] the High Court of Calcutta affirmed the approach taken by the UK Supreme Court in *Arnold v Britton*,[41] where Lord Neuberger (with whom Lord Sumption and Lord Hughes agreed) opined that there exist six prongs used to pierce through the wording in a contract: (a) the natural and ordinary meaning of the clause, (b) any other relevant provisions of the contract, (c) the overall purpose of the clause and the contract, (d) the facts and circumstances known or assumed by the parties at the time that the document was executed, and (e) commercial common sense, but (f) disregarding subjective evidence of any party's intentions. Following these principles, the Court in *Pubali* arrived at an 'objective, reasonable, contextualised and iterative interpretation'. But more broadly,

[37] [1998] 1 WLR 896 (HL) 912 (Lord Hoffmann).
[38] (1999) 3 MLJ 70 (SC) 79–80.
[39] [2009] 5 MLJ 807 (SC) 813.
[40] APD No 208 of 2015.
[41] [2015] AC 1619 [15].

this decision reflects the shifting of the manner of contractual interpretation from a literal method towards a more commercial approach.

1. The Evidence Act Does Not Preclude the Consideration of Context

Given that the Evidence Act does not absolutely disallow the consideration of extrinsic evidence, it may be said that it does not preclude the contextual approach. Indeed, it has been said that Lord Hoffmann's speech in *Investors Compensation* did not, perhaps, break any new ground but rather re-established old grounds, which date back to the time when the Evidence Act was drafted to codify the English law then.[42] Thus, since the 19th century or even earlier, the English courts had been emphasising the importance of interpreting contracts in their proper context.[43] This was done in contrast to a slavish adherence to the strict literal meaning of the contractual terms.[44] It is therefore unlikely that the Evidence Act—which was meant to enable English law to be more easily applicable via a complete code—was intended to supersede the contextual approach to interpretation.

What the Evidence Act did do was perhaps to restrict the reach of the contextual approach. As explained earlier, the Evidence Act does this by limiting the range of background information that a court can consider and adhering to certain default positions concerning the plain meaning of words as the criterion for admissibility. This raises the quite separate question of the *extent* to which the contextual approach applies pursuant to the Evidence Act. To answer this question, we turn to a document closely related to the Evidence Act, *viz* Stephen's *Digest*. In contrast to the Evidence Act, Stephen's *Digest* contained substantive rules of interpretation.[45] For example, Article 91 contains certain rules that govern how to interpret a document. Specifically, Article 91(1) provides that

> (1) Putting a construction upon a document means ascertaining the meaning of the signs or words made upon it, and their relation to facts.

However, this rule was not included in the Evidence Act. The exclusion of an interpretative approach in the Evidence Act may be taken as a *deliberate* departure from the approach prescribed by the *Digest*. As such, it may be said that the Evidence Act was never meant to give effect to a broad contextual approach, which is what the *Digest* arguably lays down. Indeed, at the most, the Evidence Act allows recourse to context via proviso 6 of section 92. To that extent, it *indirectly* supports a contextual approach. However, the modern contextual approach is not fully adopted by the Evidence Act. Indeed, the Evidence Act appears to subscribe to the notion that words have certain fixed or plain meanings.

[42] McMeel (n 7) 162.
[43] *Shore* (n 24) 521.
[44] HT Colebrooke, *Treatise on Obligations and Contracts* (Black, Kingsbury, Parbury, and Allen 1818) 65.
[45] See JF Stephen, *A Digest of the Law of Evidence* (1st edn, MacMillan and Co 1876).

Consider for example section 94, which provides that

> When language used in a document is plain in itself and when it applies accurately to existing facts, evidence may not be given to show that it was not meant to apply to such facts.

This clearly contemplates that language used in a document can be 'plain' and imposes a plain-meaning rule. Under this rule, evidence is not admissible to contradict the otherwise plain meaning of a contractual provision. This is consistent with the prevailing common law of the time. For example, Lord Halsbury, in *North E Ry Co v Hastings*,[46] said that words of a written instrument must be construed according to their natural meaning, and this principle is universally insisted upon.[47] Moreover, Article 91(2) of Stephen's *Digest* contains a plain-meaning rule. It provides that

> [E]vidence may not be given to show that common words, the meaning of which is plain, and which do not appear from the context to have been used in a peculiar sense, were in fact so used.

Section 94, which is reproduced above, is the closest counterpart to this formulation of the plain-meaning rule in the Evidence Act. It is also useful to compare the language of section 94 of the Evidence Act with Article 91(6) of Stephen's *Digest*, its closest equivalent. This Article provides as follows:

> (6) If the document has one distinct meaning in reference to surrounding circumstances, it must be construed accordingly, and evidence to show that the author intended to express some other meaning is not admissible.

Viewed this way, there may not be a significant distinction between the Evidence Act and the modern contextual approach in so far as the plain meaning of words is concerned. It is true that in *Investors Compensation*, Lord Hoffmann said that '[t]he meaning which a document (or any other utterance) would convey to a reasonable man is not the same thing as the meaning of its words'.[48] According to Lord Hoffmann, the meaning of words is the matter of dictionaries and grammar; this is a reference to the notion that words have fixed or plain meanings, which do not change with the context and which is not followed under the modern approach. Instead, the modern contextual approach suggests that words do not have such plain meanings and are susceptible to a variety of meanings, even to the extent that there is an outright departure from the fixed meaning of the word used. Indeed, an eminent commentator has described the modern approach as having abandoned the plain-meaning rule in favour

[46] (1900) AC 260, 263 (Halsbury LC).
[47] See also *Gibson v Minet* (1791) 1 Hy Bl 569, 616; 126 ER 326, 352; *Shore* (n 24) 485–87.
[48] *Investors Compensation* (n 37) 913 (Lord Hoffmann).

of an inference—which may be displaced by the context—that words are used in their natural, ordinary, or common signification.[49] In other words, there is limited fidelity to the plain meaning of the words. On the other hand, this is subject to the caveat that the courts 'do not easily accept that people have made linguistic mistakes, particularly in formal documents'.[50] This is similar to the approach in the Evidence Act, which presupposes that words have plain meaning, and which insists that there must be latent ambiguity before such meanings are displaced by the context. In summary, while both approaches subscribe to the notion that words have plain or fixed meanings, they acknowledge that this can be departed from where the context requires it.

2. A Limited Contextual Approach

It is clear, therefore, that while the Evidence Act allows for some extrinsic evidence to be admitted, this is primarily limited to situations where there is latent ambiguity. This question of *when* extrinsic evidence may be admitted in turn affects *what* kinds of evidence may be admitted. If this is in fact true, this would be in contrast to the modern contextual approach, which imposes fewer restrictions as to the admissible evidence. As Lord Hoffmann said in *Investors Compensation*,

> Subject to the requirement that it should have been reasonably available to the parties and to the exception to be mentioned next, it includes absolutely anything which would have affected the way in which the language of the document would have been understood by a reasonable man.[51]

Although Lord Hoffmann qualified the ambit of this statement in a later case,[52] the fact remains that the modern contextual approach allows for a greater range of admissible evidence than the Evidence Act when it comes to the interpretation of contracts. In contrast, as we have seen above, the Evidence Act restricts the range of admissible evidence primarily by recourse to the distinction between latent and patent ambiguities. The distinction between these two types of ambiguities originated from Lord Bacon's *Maximes*.[53] Although those maxims were originally formulated for pleadings, they have attained substantive effects of their own on the basis that 'a transaction of one "nature" cannot be overturned by anything of an inferior "nature"'.[54] While this was once also a restriction of the admissible evidence under the common law, that distinction

[49] DW MacLauchlan, 'Contract Formation, Contract Interpretation and Subsequent Conduct' (2006) 25 University of Queensland Law Journal 77, 92.
[50] *Investors Compensation* (n 37) 913 (Lord Hoffmann).
[51] ibid 912–13 (Lord Hoffmann).
[52] See *Bank of Credit and Commerce International SA v Ali* [2001] UKHL 8, [2002] 1 AC 251 [39] (Lord Hoffmann).
[53] F Bacon, *A Collection of Some Principal Rules and Maximes of the Common Lawes of England* (1st edn, 1630) 91.
[54] JH Wigmore, *A Treatise on the Anglo-American System of Evidence in Trials at Common Law*, vol IX (3rd edn, Little Brown and Company 1940) 88.

has largely been done away with in the present time.[55] The result is that the ambiguities restrict the range of admissible evidence under the Evidence Act,[56] although only for the specific purpose of explaining words. This is very clear on the face of the relevant provisions. For example, section 94 refers to extrinsic evidence being used to show that the words were 'not meant to apply to such [existing] facts'. Likewise, section 95, the first of the 'latent ambiguity' provisions, allows for extrinsic evidence to be 'given to show that it was used in a peculiar sense'. The common purpose contemplated is the use of extrinsic evidence to *explain* the words concerned.[57]

3. The Indian Courts' Approach

From the above, it is at least arguable that the modern contextual approach does not apply with full force in the Evidence Act. This is largely the approach taken in India, even if it has been said that not all the authorities speak with the same voice.[58] The predominant Indian approach is to treat proviso 6 of section 92 (the 'exclusion of oral evidence' provision) as a substantive provision of its own governing what evidence is admissible in aid of the interpretation of written documents such as contracts, with its operation being dictated by the next five provisions of the Evidence Act.[59] The collective effect of these provisions is well summarised by the Bombay High Court in *Ganpatrao Appaji v Bapit Bin Tukaram*:

> [W]here a document itself is a perfectly plain, straightforward document, no extrinsic evidence is required to show in what manner the language of the document is related to existing facts. There may be cases where such extrinsic evidence is required, and it will therefore be admitted. But it can only be in such cases where the terms of the documents themselves require explanation, and then, evidence can be led within the restrictions laid down [by the proviso 6].[60]

According to this reasoning, the modern contextual approach towards contractual interpretation is not denied and is, in fact, indirectly recognised.[61] However, it is only indirectly recognised because, as mentioned earlier, the Evidence Act does not

[55] Maybe even earlier: see eg *Colpoys v Colpoys* (1822) Jacob 451, 463; 37 ER 921, 925. See also *L Schuler AG v Wickman Machine Tool Sales Ltd* [1974] AC 235 (HL) 268 ('[T]he distinctions between patent ambiguities, latent ambiguities and equivocations as regards admissibility of extrinsic evidence are based on outmoded and highly technical and artificial rules and introduce absurd refinements').

[56] See eg FM Morgan, 'Extrinsic Evidence in the Evidence of Wills' (1860) 2 Juridical Society Papers 351, 378, in which the author noted that Lord Bacon's maxim was not intended to be a complete dissertation upon the use of extrinsic evidence in the juridical interpretation of legal instruments, and it was a maxim relating to pleadings, not to evidence. See also Seng (n 24) 485.

[57] See eg *Thomas v Thomas* (1796) 6 TR 671, 101 ER 764.

[58] *Zurich Insurance* (n 30) [115].

[59] See eg Sarkar and Manohar (n 10) 1539.

[60] (1920) ILR 64 Bom 710 [12].

[61] See eg *Govindram Mihamal v Chetumal Villardas* AIR (1970) Bom 251 (Bom HC) [9]; HK Saharay, *Dutt on Contract: The Indian Contract Act 1872* (10th edn, Eastern Law House 2006) 4, 22–24; RG Padia, *Pollock & Mulla: Indian Contract and Specific Relief Acts* (13th edn, LexisNexis Butterworths 2007) 273–74.

prescribe a substantive rule of contractual interpretation. What may be said at best is that the modern contextual approach is indirectly recognised because the ambit of admissible evidence in aid of interpretation is potentially large. This means that much of the context is potentially admissible, which is a lynchpin of the modern contextual approach.

However, as we have seen, the extent of the recognition of the modern contextual approach is limited by the terms of the Evidence Act. This much has been accepted by the Indian courts. To reiterate, if the language employed is ambiguous, the five provisions following the 'exclusion of oral evidence' provision would regulate the question of the admissibility of extrinsic evidence.[62] Specifically, proviso 6 admits extrinsic evidence only where there is latent ambiguity in the contract, of which there are several instances recognised in the Evidence Act.[63] Finally, where there is patent ambiguity, extrinsic evidence is inadmissible to interpret the contract in accordance with the 'patent ambiguity' provision.[64] Thus, as Lord Atkin observed in *Pakala Narayana Swami v R*, 'when the meaning of words is plain, it is not the duty of the courts to busy themselves with supposed intention.'[65] The presumption here is that the parties meant what they have written, that is, the plain meaning of the words. This limited (and indirect) recognition of the modern contextual approach, in line with the Evidence Act, was summarised by the Andhra Pradesh High Court relatively recently in *Pradeep Kumar v Mahaveer Pershad* by way of five points, the most pertinent of which is this:

> (5) in construing the document, the intention must be gathered from the document itself. However, if there is ambiguity in the language used in the document, it is

[62] See eg *Rani Mewa v Hulas* (1874) LR 1 IA 157 (PC) [4]; *Bhairon v Janki* (1897) 19 All 133 (All HC) [4]; *Balkishen Dass v Legge* (1899) LR 27 IA 58 (PC) [10]; *Jafar v Ranjit* (1899) ILR 21 All 4 (All HC) [7]; *Ganpatrao Apaji* (n 60) [11]; *Martand v Amritrao* AIR (1925) Bom 501 (Bom HC) [6]; *Chunchun Jha v Ebadat Ali* AIR (1954) SC 345 (India SC) [16]; *Belapur* (n 17) [24]–[25]; *Bhatt v VR Thakkar* AIR (1972) Bom 365 (Bom HC) [3]; cf *Baijnath v Vally Mahommed* AIR (1925) PC 75 (PC) [22] ('[The exclusion of oral evidence provision] merely prescribes a rule of evidence; it does not fetter the Court's power to arrive at the true meaning and effect of a transaction in the light of all the surrounding circumstances'); *Buddhu Shaw v Mongal Shaw* (1966) ILR 2 Cal 641 (Cal HC) [17], in which it was said,

> The principle behind the rule, which the sixth proviso embodies, appears to be that in suitable cases, such as where the 'haves' prey upon the want and misery of the 'have-nots', it is the duty of the Court to get at the truth by entering into evidence with the subject of finding out in what manner the document's language is related to the existing facts.

This is unlikely to be correct; proviso 6 does not confer a power to the court to go behind otherwise unambiguous language where it would be 'fair' to do so owing to the unequal statuses of the contracting parties.

[63] *The Chairman, Serajgunj Municipality v Chittagong Co Ltd* (1922) 72 Ind Cas 969 (Cal HC) [5]; *Basanti v Official Receiver* AIR (1936) Lah 508 (Lah HC) [3]; *Ram Narain v Manki* AIR (1954) Pat 562 (Pat HC) [15]–[16] (cf *Zurich Insurance* (n 30) [116]–[118]); *Chandra Sekhar v Mural Gope* AIR (1957) Pat 673 (Pat HC) [3]; *Firm Bolumal v Venkatachelapathi Rao* AIR (1959) AP 612 (Andh Prad HC) [8]; *Darshan Dass v Ganga Bux* AIR (1962) Pat 53 (Pat HC) [6]; *Ramprashad Sahu v Basantia* AIR (1925) Pat 729 (Pat HC) [11]; *Baleshwar v Lal Bahadur* AIR (1972) Pat 87 (Pat HC) [10]; *Pradeep Kumar v Mahaveer Pershad* AIR (2003) AP 107 (Andh Prad HC) [18]. The academic texts are united in adopting this approach: see Sarkar and Manohar (n 10) 1538–39; Rao (n 12) 3451, 3712; Ranchhoddas and Thakore (n 12) 1161.

[64] *Deojit v Pitambar* (1875) ILR 1 All 275 (All HC) [1]; *Keshavlal Lallubhai Patel v Lalbhai Trikumlal Mills Ltd* AIR (1958) SC 512 (India SC) [11].

[65] AIR (1939) PC 47 (PC) [10] (Atkin LJ), albeit in the context of interpreting a statute; however, Lord Atkin did agree that this principle extended to all written instruments.

> permissible to look to surrounding circumstances to gather the intention, such as user or possession and enjoyment.[66]

However, while the Evidence Act does not outwardly prescribe any substantive contractual interpretative approach,[67] what courts should not do is to import the entirety of the modern contextual approach into the Evidence Act. The interpretation of the Evidence Act, a piece of legislation written more than a century before *Investors Compensation*, should not be affected by the latter case and developments thereafter. Thus, while a Law Reform Committee formed by the Singapore Academy of Law has stated that 'a broader and more permissive application of [proviso 6] is to be preferred' as '[i]t accords with the modern approach to construction of contracts',[68] it is submitted that this starts on the wrong premise. As already mentioned, the interpretation of contracts in jurisdictions governed by the Evidence Act—including Singapore—starts with a prior interpretation of a statute. The ascertainment of the legislative intent should be the starting point, rather than whether a particular mode of contractual interpretation accords with a modern development. This is especially since the very purpose of a code is to preserve the legislative intent at a particular time, subject, of course, to a limited degree of flexibility.

IV. The Specific Admissibility of Prior Negotiations and Subsequent Conduct

1. Prior Negotiations

The admissibility of evidence under the modern contextual approach is subject to two prominent exceptions: both prior negotiations and subsequent conduct cannot be admitted to interpret the contract. According to Lord Hoffmann in *Investors Compensation*, '[t]he law makes this distinction for reasons of practical policy and, in this respect only, legal interpretation differs from the way we would interpret utterances in ordinary life'.[69] While the ambits of these exceptions has been reduced in recent times, they still block out a range of evidence that may be relevant in the interpretative exercise. The Indian courts seem to have accepted this exclusionary rule. The High Court of Madras in *PTC India Ltd v Tamil Nadu Electricity Board* affirmed the holding of Lord Wilberforce in *Prenn v Simmons* [1971] 1 WLR 1381 that

> [t]he reason for not admitting evidence of these exchanges is not a technical one or even mainly of convenience.... It is simply that such evidence is unhelpful. By the nature of things, where negotiations are difficult, the parties' positions, with each passing

[66] ibid [18].
[67] Neither the Indian Contract Act 1872 nor its equivalents prescribe an interpretative approach.
[68] Singapore Academy of Law (n 5) [125].
[69] *Investors Compensation* (n 37) 913 (Lord Hoffmann).

> letter are changing and until the final agreement, though converging, still different. It is only the final document which records a consensus. If the previous documents use different expressions, how does construction of those expressions, itself a doubtful process, help on the construction of the contractual words? If the same expressions are used, nothing is gained by looking back; indeed something may be lost since the relevant surrounding circumstances may be different. And at this stage there is no consensus of the parties to appeal to.[70]

The Court further stated that the exception to this principle lies only for recourse to misrepresentation. Pre-contractual correspondence may be looked at so as to ascertain whether the representations were made.

However, is this compatible with the Evidence Act? While the Evidence Act does not expressly prohibit recourse to evidence of prior negotiations, it still potentially excludes such evidence, along with other types of evidence, due to the distinction it draws between latent and patent ambiguities. Indeed, this was the position taken by the common law in the nineteenth century until certain cases at the turn of the 20th century, such as *Inglis v John Buttery Co*,[71] established the currency of an independent rule that excludes recourse to prior negotiations and subsequent conduct—a rule that has remained to the present day despite its questionable historical lineage. There is no special exclusion made by the Evidence Act towards prior negotiations or subsequent conduct: both may be admissible to interpret the contract provided that they do not infringe the rules pertaining to latent or patent ambiguities. However, the courts applying the Evidence Act still adopt the common law exclusionary rule against both types of extrinsic evidence, regardless of whether the contractual language is ambiguous or not.[72]

This may require reconsideration of whether the Evidence Act exhaustively sets out the situations in which evidence is admissible. In this regard, it is important that the Evidence Act has provided for the instances where extrinsic evidence (which can include prior negotiations) may (or may not) be admitted under sections 94–100 for the interpretation of a contract. As such, to apply a common law rule that justifies the exclusion of evidence of prior negotiations would be inconsistent with the Evidence Act. This argument is strengthened when one considers that evidence of prior negotiations was not treated apart from other types of evidence at the time the Evidence Act was enacted. Indeed, prior negotiations were, in fact, admissible to ascertain the aim and object of the contract as early as in 1835. In *Reay v Richardson*,[73] a previous conversation was held admissible to explain the motive that induced the plaintiff to enter into a compromise agreement with the defendant. Parke B held that the evidence of the conversation was not to add to or qualify the terms of the agreement but to show with what view the agreement was written.[74] In the words of a learned commentator, prior

[70] OP No 338 of 2014 [10].
[71] (1878) 3 App Cas 552 (HL).
[72] See eg *Belapur* (n 17) [23]; *Zurich Insurance* (n 30) [132].
[73] (1835) 150 Eng Rep 182.
[74] ibid 184.

negotiations were only excluded in that case on the principle that 'it is not permitted to interpret what has no need of interpretation'.[75] This rested upon the belief that words have fixed meanings, such that a party who has used clear and unambiguous language will be held to all that naturally follows from a direct and plain understanding of such language.[76] It was only when a term was susceptible to several meanings[77] that recourse could be had to the relevant context in order to discover the parties' true intentions.[78] The criterion, it bears repeating, used to be that of 'ambiguity' to determine whether extrinsic evidence of any kind can be admitted to interpret contracts.

Thus, since the Evidence Act[79] was intended to codify the English evidence law at that time,[80] it is likely that Stephen, the draftsman, intended to import these common law principles into the Evidence Act. If so, the recognition of the exclusionary rule, based as it is on a different rationale for excluding prior negotiations, would be inconsistent with the rationale of the Evidence Act, which provides for when extrinsic evidence may be admissible based on the criterion of 'ambiguity'. While the Evidence Act may be non-exhaustive, the very idea of separating prior negotiations as a species of evidence to be treated differently is inconsistent with the central criterion of 'ambiguity' that governs admissibility for all extrinsic evidence. This is not a situation involving the common law filling in a lacuna in the Evidence Act; rather, the Evidence Act has provided an approach with which the exclusionary rule is inconsistent. This is because the Evidence Act has spelt out the circumstances when prior negotiations can be admitted, and this is contrary to the common law prohibition against such evidence.

2. Subsequent Conduct

The same might be said of subsequent conduct.[81] The Indian courts have, in some cases, rejected the use of subsequent conduct in the interpretation of contracts, holding that evidence of the subsequent conduct of the parties is not relevant or admissible for the purposes of interpreting a written document.[82] However, in various cases, the courts in India have taken the opposite approach. In this regard, it is submitted that the correct approach is to allow evidence of subsequent conduct to be admitted as long as the central criterion of 'ambiguity' that governs admissibility for all extrinsic evidence is fulfilled.

To begin, if the use of subsequent conduct is really a question of admissibility and a rule of evidence, it is necessary to start our discussion by referring to the Evidence Act,

[75] Colebrooke (n 44) 66.

[76] ibid; J Chitty, *A Practical Treatise on the Law of Contracts Not under Seal and upon the Usual Defences of Actions Thereon* (Sweet Chancery Lane 1826) 20, citing 5 Vin Ab 510, 4 East 136.

[77] *Smith v Jeffryes* (1846) 153 Eng Rep 972, 972–973.

[78] Colebrooke (n 44) 67.

[79] More specifically, the Evidence Act: see Heydon (n 1) 1–2.

[80] See Stephen, *A Digest of the Law of Evidence* (n 45) 2.

[81] See G Yihan, 'Towards a Consistent Use of Subsequent Conduct in Singapore Contract Law' [2017] Journal of Business Law 387.

[82] See *Belapur* (n 17) [24].

which governs the range of evidence admissible. Unlike English evidence law which prescribes a broad criterion of 'relevance' to determine the admissibility of evidence, the Evidence Act operates more specifically through several related provisions. The general provision governing the admission of evidence is section 5, which provides as follows:

> Evidence may be given in any suit or proceeding of the existence or non-existence of every fact in issue and of such other facts as are hereinafter declared to be relevant, and of no others.

As Pinsler explains, there are two fundamental categories of admissible evidence under the Singapore Evidence Act (Singapore EA), which is, in material respects, substantially similar to the Evidence Act. These two categories are 'facts in issue', which are primary facts that concern liability and non-liability, and 'relevant facts', which are the related facts from which the facts in issue can be inferred.[83] Turning to the Indian context, these are evident from section 3 of the Evidence Act, which defines a 'fact in issue' as 'any fact from which, either by itself or in connection with other facts, the existence, non-existence, nature or extent of any right, liability, or disability, asserted or denied in any suit or proceeding, necessarily follows'. It also defines a fact as 'relevant' to another 'when the one is connected with the other in any of the ways referred to in the provisions of this Evidence Act relating to the relevancy of facts'. Thus, by way of illustration, if *A* brings an action for breach of contract against *B*, and *B* denies that the contract was ever formed, then the facts in issue will include whether the contract was ever formed, whether it was breached, and the loss suffered by *A*. A relevant fact may be *B*'s conduct after the contract was formed, from which the fact in issue concerning the formation of the contract may be inferred.

Of course, direct evidence of a fact in issue is always superior to circumstantial evidence of the same fact. However, direct evidence is not always available, and hence facts in issue tend to be proved by relying on 'relevant facts'.[84] Sections 6–16 of the Evidence Act define exhaustively what counts as a 'relevant fact' for the purpose of admission under section 5. Thus, as the Singapore Court of Appeal explained in *Lee Chez Kee v PP*, the Singapore EA adopts 'an inclusionary approach, stating what may be admitted in evidence'.[85] The key question for admissibility under Singapore evidence law is whether the evidence sought to be admitted satisfies any of the definitions of legal (not logical) relevancy as defined by the Singapore EA; if so, that fact is made admissible.[86] As the framework governing the admission of evidence under the Evidence Act is substantially similar to the Singapore EA, these comments are applicable to the Evidence Act as well.

[83] J Pinsler, *Evidence and the Litigation Process* (7th edn, LexisNexis 2020) [2.002], [2.005].
[84] ibid.
[85] [2008] 3 SLR(R) 447 [69].
[86] ibid.

Understood this way, there are a few questions that need to be answered as a matter of evidence law in our discussion relating to subsequent conduct. First of all, although subsequent conduct will almost never be direct evidence of a fact in issue, is it nonetheless a 'relevant' fact under the terms of the Evidence Act, rendering it admissible? Second, if subsequent conduct is indeed admissible, can the courts formulate common law rules restricting its admissibility?

The Evidence Act does, in fact, allow the admission of subsequent conduct. Section 8 provides as follows:

> The conduct of any party, or of any agent to any party, to any suit or proceeding, in reference to such suit or proceeding, or in reference to any fact in issue therein or relevant thereto, and the conduct of any person an offence against whom is the subject of any proceeding, is relevant, if such conduct influences or is influenced by any fact in issue or relevant fact, and whether it was previous or subsequent thereto.

Explanation 1 to section 8 provides that conduct does not include statements unless they accompany and explain acts. As Pinsler explains, section 8(2) of the Singapore EA, which is substantially similar to section 8 of the Evidence Act, 'admits evidence of the conduct of a party or his agent—including the conduct of a person accused in the proceedings—which is influenced by, or influences, any fact in issue or relevant issue'.[87] In Singapore, the courts are conscious that this is merely an inference and so do not regard evidence admitted under section 8(2) of the Singapore EA as conclusive. As the Singapore High Court stated in *Lewis Christine v PP*, a criminal case, 'conduct subsequent to the offence, without more, is not conclusive of prior guilt'.[88]

Indeed, most of the cases that have admitted evidence under section 8(2) of the Singapore EA have concerned criminal matters. Thus, in the Singapore case of *Krishna Jayaram v PP*,[89] it was held that evidence of an accused person arranging for a meeting to induce another person to change that person's statements to the investigation authorities was admissible as relevant subsequent conduct. In *Chanderasekaran v PP*,[90] evidence that a person accused of obtaining money in a dishonest fashion gave false explanations that the person obtained the money honestly may be admissible as subsequent conduct influenced by the facts in issue. Similarly, a person's attempt to escape from custody has been admitted as a relevant fact to support the inference that she had committed theft.[91] All of these cases have involved the admission of subsequent conduct to prove a prior fact, that is, the accused's guilt in relation to the alleged offence.

Although used primarily in criminal cases, it is clear that section 8 of the Evidence Act can apply to civil cases as well. Indeed, the section does not limit its application to only criminal cases but also refers to the conduct of any party or such party's agent

[87] Pinsler (n 83) [2.040].
[88] [2001] 2 SLR(R) 131 [29].
[89] [1989] 2 SLR(R) 21 [20].
[90] [1971] 1 MLJ 153.
[91] *Lewis Christine* (n 88).

in 'any suit or proceeding'. The key requirement under section 8 is that the conduct sought to be admitted 'influences or is influenced by any fact in issue or relevant fact'. Logically, subsequent conduct that is used to prove a prior fact can only ever 'be influenced' by the prior fact and so falls within this part of section 8. However, to be admissible, subsequent conduct must also be influenced by 'any fact in issue or relevant fact'. For instance, if we take a case where the meaning of a contract is a fact in issue, there is no reason why subsequent conduct cannot fall within section 8 as being 'influenced' by this fact in issue. Similarly, if the existence of a contract is a fact in issue, there is also no reason why subsequent conduct cannot be said to be 'influenced' so as to be admissible by section 8. Indeed, these examples are analogous to the criminal cases where subsequent conduct is admitted freely as a matter of course: in those cases, the accused's conduct subsequent to the alleged offence is admitted by section 8 to prove the fact in issue, which is whether the alleged offence was committed. There is no reason why the outcome should be different just because the case concerns a contractual claim rather than a criminal offence. Accordingly, it is submitted that the Evidence Act does, in fact, allow subsequent conduct to be admitted under section 8, even for contract cases.

Accordingly, to the extent that the Evidence Act does not enact any restrictions on the admissibility of subsequent conduct (indeed, it allows for an expansive admission of such evidence by section 8), the courts' pronouncements of a more restrictive use of subsequent conduct to determine a prior fact in contract law are inconsistent with section 8 of the Evidence Act. As such, those decisions should not be followed as they add an impermissible gloss to the express words of section 8.

There are Indian decisions that have accepted subsequent conduct along these arguments. In *Godhra Electricity Company v State of Gujarat*,[92] the Supreme Court accepted the fact that the conduct of the parties in rendering or receiving performance under the contract can be of assistance in interpreting the statements made by the parties themselves in the contract. The Court further opined that the conduct of the parties is a further expression by the parties of the meaning they had given and intended to give to the terms of the contracts previously made. As such, subsequent practice and conduct can, in certain circumstances, be taken into consideration where there is ambiguity as it throws light on the meaning of a term or a clause. Though subsequent statements cannot change the meaning of a word, phrase, or clause that is crystal clear from a plain reading of the same, in cases of ambiguity, extrinsic evidence in the shape of subsequent statements of both the parties and their conduct is admissible. On the facts of that case, subsequent conduct was admissible to determine the meaning of the terms where latent ambiguity arose. The Court in *Godhra Electricity Company* also considered the House of Lords decision of *Schuler AG v Wickman Ltd*,[93] which discusses the English position. In that case, Lord Wilberforce stated that extrinsic evidence of subsequent actions is not admissible for the construction of a written contract

[92] AIR 1975 SC 32.
[93] [1974] AC 235.

and that the parties' intentions must be ascertained, on legal principles of construction, from the words they have used.

The Court then stated that in the process of interpretation, the court can frequently get great assistance from interpreting statements made by the parties themselves or from their conduct in rendering or in receiving performance under it. There is no good reason why the courts should not give great weight to those further expressions by the parties, in view of the fact that they still have the same freedom of contract that they originally had. Parties can, by mutual agreement, make their own contracts; they can also, by mutual agreement, remake them. The Court referred to the US, French, Italian, and German courts, which have held that subsequent actions are admissible in guiding interpretation. The Court then reaffirmed its decision in *Abdulla Ahmed v Animendra Kissen Mitter*[94] regarding the general proposition that extrinsic evidence to determine the effect of an instrument is permissible where there remains doubt as to its true meaning and that evidence of the acts done under it is a guide to the intention of the parties, particularly where they are done shortly after the date of the instrument.

In *Union of India v Association of Unified Telecom*,[95] the Supreme Court reaffirmed the above propositions in *Godhra*. However, they expressed their concern that if evidence of subsequent conduct were admissible, it might have the result that a contract would mean one thing the day it was signed but would mean something else on a later date. The Court thus stated that if the meaning of the word is clear, extrinsic evidence is not admissible. It is only where there is latent ambiguity that extrinsic evidence of subsequent conduct should be admissible.

V. Conclusion

This chapter began by stating that contractual interpretation in India is a matter of statutory interpretation first and foremost. That process shows that the proper way to approach contractual interpretation in India is not to apply the predominant English approach without heed to the statutory framework provided by the Evidence Act but to apply it in a nuanced manner that is consistent with the statutory intent behind the Evidence Act, at least until it is amended to reflect any later development.

94 AIR 1950 SC 15.
95 2020 SCC OnLine SC 703.

4

Migration of the Indian Contract Act 1872

The Case of Malaysia

May Fong Cheong[*]

I. Introduction

This chapter traces the migration of the Indian Contract Act 1872 (hereinafter 'the Contract Act') to Malaysia. Like other British colonies that adopted the Contract Act, the Malaysian Contracts Act 1950 (the Malaysian Act)[1] is a product of a 'double legal transplant' modelled on the Contract Act, which, in turn, codified the then prevailing English common law and rules of equity on the law of contract. Except for the numbering of the statutory provisions and some modifications, the Malaysian Act is a copy of the Contract Act. Before embarking on the migration of the Contract Act to Malaysia, an overview of the countries where the Contract Act has been adopted[2] could help contextualise the case of Malaysia.

For a start, Pakistan[3] Bangladesh[4] and Burma (now Myanmar)[5] are not cases of 'migration' as they were once part of undivided India (Pakistan and Bangladesh until 1947, and Myanmar until 1937). The Act is now known as 'the Contract Act' and governs contractual obligations in these three countries. In contrast, another set of three African countries, Kenya,[6] Uganda[7] and Tanganyika (now Tanzania),[8] which once had copies of the Contract Act have now repealed it and adopted English common law in newly enacted statutes. Cyprus, with a mixed legal system, has its contract law—based on the Contract Act—placed in the Cypriot Civil Code.[9]

* I acknowledge the research assistance of Yoshita Sood and Joseph Jordan Black. All errors are mine.

1 (Revised 1974), Act 136.

2 See J Minatur, 'The Indian Contract Act: Its Wanderlust and Warmer Climes' (special issue) [1972] Journal of Indian Law Institute 107.

3 See T Soomro, *The Contract Law of Pakistan* (OUP 2015); M Lau, 'Introduction to the Pakistani Legal System, with Special Reference to the Law of Contract' [1994] Yearbook of Islamic and Middle Eastern Law 3.

4 See ME Haque, *Law of Contract* (3rd edn, Law Lyceum 2016); AB Siddique, *Law of Contract (including Partnership & Sale of Goods)* (Kamrul Book House 2017).

5 See A Briggs and A Burrows, *The Law of Contract in Myanmar* (OUP 2017).

6 See The Law of Contract 1961, CAP 23.

7 See the Contracts Act 2010; see also DJ Bakibinga, *Law of Contract in Uganda* (Fountain 2001).

8 See The Law of Contract Act 2019, CAP 345, which differed from the Contract Act only in certain details.

9 See ch 149; see also N Charalampidou, *Contract Law in Cyprus* (Kluwer Law International 2022).

May Fong Cheong, *Migration of the Indian Contract Act 1872* In: *Foundations of Indian Contract Law.* Edited by: KV Krishnaprasad, Niranjan Venkatesan, Shivprasad Swaminathan, and Umakanth Varottil, Oxford University Press. © Oxford University Press 2024. DOI: 10.1093/9780191997211.003.0004

In Asia, the state of Brunei has adopted the Contract Act. However, the migration of the Contract Act to Malaysia is particularly significant as Malaysian courts and academics have followed developments in Indian law—and Indian contract law has had a strong influence on the early development of Malaysian contract law. This provides important lessons in legal transplant.[10]

The 'double legal transplant' of the Malaysian Act is unique. It invites deliberation on the extent to which Malaysian contract law has been, and continues to be, influenced by developments in the United Kingdom and India. In tracing the migration of the Contract Act to Malaysia, the chapter pays close attention to the extent to which decisions of the Indian courts have been followed and, conversely, areas where Malaysian courts have diverged from the Indian position and indigenised Malaysian contract law.[11] In essence, the chapter traces the trajectories of the two contract codes and draws useful lessons from them. The analysis of Malaysian case law indicates a tension in the relationship between statute and the common law and, at the same time, reveals the creativity of the courts in adapting a statute enacted in 1872 to deal with the challenges of modern contracting.

The chapter proceeds in the following manner. Section I introduces the topic of the chapter on migration of the Contract Act to Malaysia and the 'double legal transplant' of the Malaysian Act. Section II sets out the legislative history and traces the migration of the Contract Act to Malayan shores in colonial times down to the present Malaysian legislation. Section III highlights two major themes arising from the transplantation of contract law from the Contract Act (and English law) to Malaysia by offering a comparative analysis of minors' contracts and stipulated sums by way of penalties.[12] The two major themes that permeate the chapter are the following. First, while the Malaysian Act is modelled on the Contract Act, Malaysian courts have continued to rely on English common law and rules of equity to interpret the Malaysian Act. Second, while Indian decisions were influential in the early development of the Malaysian Act, its influence has ebbed in subsequent years. As Malaysian jurisprudence developed, the courts, including the apex court,[13] applied local cases and only engaged to a limited extent with developments occurring in India. Section IV explains the reasons for the reduced dependency on Indian authorities despite the Malaysian Act being a near-verbatim copy of the Contract Act. In doing that, it adds to observations on Alan Watson's theory of the ease of legal transplant. In the case of the Malaysian Act's double legal transplant, there is a strong inclination to revert to the source jurisdiction,

[10] See MF Cheong, D Dhankar, and S Star, 'Legal Transplantation of Minors' Contracts in India and Malaysia: Weak Watson and a "Misfitted" Transplant' (2023) 23 Oxford University Commonwealth Law Journal 17.

[11] 'Indigenised' refers to how local courts 'develop a body of contract law consonant with the needs and circumstances of the country itself?': see A Phang, 'Contract Law at Century's End: Some Personal Reflections' (2000) 8 Asia Pacific Law Review 1, 2 in the context of its early usage in Singapore, a close neighbour and for a short duration, a part of Malaysia.

[12] On minors' contracts, see Cheong, Dhankar and Star (n 10). On penalties, see MF Cheong and PM Tan, 'The New Law on Penalties in Malaysia: The Impact of *Cubic Electronics* after *Cavendish Square*' (2023) 38 Journal of Contract Law 132.

[13] The apex court is the Federal Court, which was previously known as the Supreme Court prior to 24 June 1994. Appeals on civil matters to the Privy Council were abolished on 1 January 1985.

English law, rather than to the jurisprudence developed in the Contract Act. Section V concludes.

II. 'Double Legal Transplant': English Law, the Contract Act, and the Malaysian Act

The adoption of the Contract Act model—which, in turn, embedded to a great extent the then extant English law—for contract legislation in early Malaya was not unexpected. The relative ease of transplanting English common law of contract by Great Britain to India and Malaya[14] can be attributed to two reasons. First, the transplant arose from the exercise of British imperial powers on its colonies.[15] An English common law-based legal and judicial system was considered necessary to preserve British commercial interests in India[16] and the strategic trading posts in the Straits Settlements (Penang, Malacca, and Singapore).[17] Second, the commonality of contract principles in private law throughout the Western world facilitated the transfer of English contract law.[18]

India and Malaysia experienced a comparable history of being subjects of British trading interest followed by colonialism. A legal and judicial system was established and formalised through the Charters and Letter Patents.[19] In India, the Regulating Act 1773 established a Supreme Court of Judicature applying English law, including the law of contract, to English subjects and foreigners who lived under the East India Company's protection and natives of India who chose to appeal to the Company.[20] However, the uncertain application of broad principles of 'justice, equity and good conscience' by the regional courts resulted in confusion and inconsistency. Contractual disputes were frequently litigated in all parts of India and, as Jain described it, the state of the law 'was a mixed bag. It was partly English law, partly Hindu law and partly Muslim law.'[21] The

[14] See A Watson, 'Legal Transplants and Law Reform' (1976) 92 Law Quarterly Review 79, 84 (on the ease of legal transplant); A Watson, 'Comparative Law and Legal Change' (1978) 37 Cambridge Law Journal 313, 314 ('England's own common law became in its turn another great export; to the larger part of Canada and the United States, to Australia, New Zealand, India and elsewhere.')

[15] W Twining, 'Diffusion of Law: A Global Perspective' (2004) 36 Journal of Legal Pluralism and Unofficial Law 1; CR Burset, 'Why Didn't the Common Law Follow the Flag?' (2019) 105 Virginia Law Review 483, 501.

[16] GT Warner, HK Marten, and DE Muir, *The New Groundwork of British History* (Blackie & Son Limited 1943) 639; RJ Daniels, MJ Trebilcock, and LD Carson, 'The Legacy of Empire: The Common Law Inheritance and Commitments to Legality in Former British Colonies' (2011) 59 American Journal of Comparative Law 111, 164 (Britain holding imperial power adopted diverse approaches in colonial India 'to meet new economic, social and governance challenges.')

[17] R Emerson, *Malaysia: A Study in Direct and Indirect Rule* (2nd edn, University of Malaya Press 1979) 92–94.

[18] A Watson, *Legal Transplants: An Approach to Comparative Law* (2nd edn, University of Georgia Press 1993) 22.

[19] According to Sir James Stephen (differing from Morley), the common law of England was introduced into India by the Charter of 1726 and the English statute law of that year; this was affirmed by the Privy Council in *Advocate-General of Bengal v Ranee Surnomoye Dasee* (1863) 9 Moo IA 387, 426; see V Bose, 'The Migration of the Common Law' (1960) 76 Law Quarterly Review 39, 60.

[20] W Bolts, *Considerations on India Affairs; Particularly Respecting the Present State of Bengal and its Dependencies* (2nd edn, J Almon 1772) 76.

[21] MP Jain, 'The Law of Contract before Its Codification' (special edn) [1972] Journal of the Indian Law Institute 178, 199. See also CP Ilbert, *Government of India* (2nd edn, Clarendon Press 1907) 339: 'it became necessary to draw up for the guidance of untrained judges and magistrates a set of rules which they could understand, and

ultimate response and result was the codification of contract principles in the Contract Act, which, despite its chequered history,[22] was welcomed by British mercantile interests[23] and the local population.[24] The Contract Act remains the main source of contract law in India today.[25]

In the Straits Settlements in Malaya, the Charter of Justice of 1807[26] established a Court of Judicature Act in Penang. The Second Charter of Justice of 1826 extended Britain's jurisdiction to Singapore and Malacca. Due to their proximity to India, these settlements were administered as part of India, thus Indian legislation was applied until 1867,[27] followed by successive charters and ordinances for applying English law 'as far as the circumstances will admit'.[28] Besides the proximity, on a practical level, many judges and court officers at the Malay Peninsula who were tasked with the administration of justice in applying English common law, equity, and statutes had served as officers of the East India Company and acquired experience in India. As a result, there was a tendency for them to look towards Indian law when administrative needs called for it, which explains the adoption and almost wholesale transplant of Indian statutes (including the Contract Act)[29] to then Malaya.[30]

English principles of contract law (and commercial law) were applied to resolve contractual disputes in the Straits Settlements through the Civil Law Ordinance 1878.[31] In the Federated Malay States, contract enactments based on the Contract Act were passed in the states of Negeri Sembilan, Perak, and Selangor in 1899 and in Pahang in 1900.[32] In the Unfederated Malay States, the Contract Enactment 1899 was extended to Johor.[33] In Kedah, the Courts Enactment provided that the principles of law and equity in force for the time being in the Straits Settlement shall apply to matters of tort and contract.[34] In the remaining Unfederated Malay States (Perlis, Kelantan, and

which were adapted to the circumstances of the country.' quoted in Bose (n 19) 62. See also CP Ilbert, 'Indian Codification' (1889) 5 Law Quarterly Review 347.

[22] See G Pearson, 'The Resignation of The Third Indian Law Commission: Who Makes Law?' (2020) 41 Adelaide Law Review 575, 576.

[23] A Chandra Patra, 'Historical Background of The Indian Contract Act, 1872' (1962) 4 Journal of the Indian Law Institute 373, 395.

[24] W Stokes, *The Anglo-Indian Codes,* vol 1 (Clarendon Press 1887–88) xxi–xxii.

[25] The Constitution of India 1950, art 372(1) provides for the continuance of the existing law until it is 'altered, repealed or amended by a competent Legislature'.

[26] This was affirmed in *Ong Cheng Neo v Yeap Cheng Neo* (1872) LR 6 PC 381. See generally, SA Aziz, 'The Malaysian Legal System: The Roots, the Influence and the Future' (2009) 3 Malayan Law Journal xcii.

[27] See Emerson (n 17).

[28] JN Matson, 'The Common Law Abroad: English and Indigenous Laws in the British Commonwealth' (1993) 42 International and Comparative Law Quarterly 753, 762.

[29] Besides the Contract Act, India's most well-known codification exports, the Penal Code and the Criminal Procedure Code, continue to apply in Malaysia, with some modifications.

[30] RH Hickling, *Malaysian Law: An Introduction to the Concept of Law in Malaysia* (Pelanduk Publications 2001) 130–35; Minatur (n 2).

[31] Civil Law Ordinance 1878; see generally A Ibrahim, *Towards a History of Law in Malaysia and Singapore* (Dewan Bahasa and Pustaka 1992).

[32] LA Sheridan, *Malaya and Singapore, The Borneo Territories: The Development of Their Laws and Constitutions* (Stevens & Sons Limited 1961) 260.

[33] Courts Enactment 1914.

[34] Section 11, Courts Enactment (No 25); see V Sinnadurai, *Law of Contract* (3rd edn, LexisNexis Butterworths 2003) 9.

Trengganu), there was no formal extension, and English law was applied merely by the presence of the British and was judicially imported on reasons of uniformity.[35]

With the formation of the Federation of Malaya in 1948, the Contracts (Malay States) Ordinance 1950 was enacted. The Ordinance was a reproduction of, and replaced, the 1899 Enactment. It applied to the Federated and Unfederated Malay States except for Penang and Malacca, which continued to apply English law. Malaya obtained independence in 1957, and Malaysia was formed in 1963 with the admission of Sabah, Sarawak and Singapore (with Singapore subsequently separating in 1965). To harmonise the law, the Ordinance was revised and re-enacted in 1974 as the present Contracts Act 1950 (Revised 1974) and extended to Penang, Malacca, Sabah, and Sarawak.[36] These historical movements completed the formal migration of the Contract Act to Malaysia. There have been only two major amendments to the Malaysian Act: one to remove the partnerships provisions[37] and the other on scholarship agreements.[38] Section III examines and evaluates the degree to which Malaysian contract law has been impacted by the Contract Act and Indian law.

III. Migration of the Contract Act to Malaysia: Two Select Areas

This part highlights the major themes and challenges resulting from the migration of the Contract Act to Malaysia through a study of two select areas: (a) minors' contracts and (b) stipulated sums amounting to penalties. Both these subjects demonstrate the challenge in interpreting the provisions drafted in the Contract Act—the draft of which dates to 1866—and how they fail to meet adequately the needs of modern contracting in the twenty-first century. The trajectory of the Malaysian Act indicates two recurrent themes: first, even though the Malaysian Act is a near-verbatim copy of the Contract Act, the Malaysian courts are much more inclined to look to English law to interpret the Malaysian legislation. Second, the initial influence of Indian precedents has declined

[35] In *Engku Leh bin Engku Dris v Che Wok binte Awang Mat* (1949) 15 MLJ 61 (High Court), Murray Aynsley J stated,

> Although neither English Law nor the Contract Enactment of the Federated Malay States appear to be part of the law of Kelantan where there has been no legislation on the subject, we consider that where questions of public policy of this kind are concerned, there ought as far as possible, to be unity within the Malayan Union.

[36] The exceptional status of these four states following their relationship with Great Britain is reflected in the Civil Law Act 1956 (Revised 1972) Act 67, s 5, which governs the reception of English law post-independence. While s 3 provides for general reception of English law with a cut-off date of 7 April where English ceases to be binding and is only of persuasive authority, s 5(2) provides for continuing reception of English law in commercial matters for these four states.

[37] See the Partnership (Amendment) Act 1974, Act A240. The law governing partnership is now found in the Partnership Act 1961, Act 135; the Labuan Limited Partnerships and Limited Liability Partnerships Act 2010, Act 707; and the Limited Liability Partnership Act 2012, Act 743.

[38] See Contracts (Malay States) (Amendment) Act 1967, Act 18 of 1967 to include Exception 3 to s 29 following the decision in *Government of Malaysia v Thelma Fernandez* [1967] 1 MLJ 194 (High Court); see Contracts (Amendment) Act 1976, Act A329 to provide for the validity of scholarship agreements entered into by minors with the government of Malaysia in response to the decision of*Government of Malaysia v Gurcharan Singh* [1971] 1 MLJ 211 (High Court). See discussion corresponding to this case at n 47..

over time, and in the subsequent years, the Malaysian courts have only engaged to a limited extent with developments occurring in India.

1. Minors' Contracts

A study of the legal position of minors in India and Malaysia is relevant for an evaluation of legal transplantation and codification of the Contract Act.[39] Its importance is underscored by the unclear legislative drafting in the Contract Act, which requires that parties must be of the age of majority[40] in order to be competent to contract.[41] However, the Contract Act does not specifically set out the consequences of contracting with a minor.[42] The Privy Council, in 1903, decided, in *Mohori Bibee v Dharmodas Ghose* (*Mohori Bibee*),[43] that contracts with minors are *void ab initio*.[44] According to the Privy Council, an agreement involving minors cannot exist—even for the purpose of restitution of benefits under section 65 of the Contract Act, when such an agreement is being declared void—as minors are not competent to contract from the reading of sections 10 and 11 of the Contract Act. This position is in stark contrast with the English common law position, then and now, that contracts by minors are voidable and could be aside at the minor's option except in certain circumstances.[45]

Mohori Bibee has since been invoked as an 'axiom' by the Indian courts and a recent Supreme Court of India decision unquestioningly endorses it.[46] The position that minors' contracts are *void ab initio* has impacted Malaysian law. It resulted in an amendment to the Malaysian Act in 1976 to validate scholarship contracts entered into by persons below eighteen years with the government of Malaysia. This arose from the decision in *Government of Malaysia v Gurcharan Singh*,[47] which followed *Mohori Bibee* and held that the scholarship agreement entered by a minor with the government was *void ab initio*. However, the High Court held that the provision of professional and vocational training for the minor amounted to necessaries. Notwithstanding this,

[39] See Cheong, Dhankar, and Star (n 10).

[40] Section 11 of both the Contract Act and the Malaysian Act provides: 'Every person is competent to contract who is of the age of majority according to the law to which he is subject, and who is of sound mind, and is not disqualified from contracting by any law to which he is subject.' The age of majority in both India and Malaysia is eighteen years following the age of majority legislations.

[41] Section 10 of both the Contract Act and the Malaysian Act provides: 'All agreements are contracts if they are made by the free consent of parties competent to contract, for a lawful consideration and with a lawful object, and are not hereby expressly declared to be void.'

[42] See SN Upadhyay, 'Legal Consequences of a Minor's Agreement in India' (2014) 35 Business Law Review 136.

[43] (1903) 30 ILR Cal 539.

[44] See S Swaminathan and R Surana, 'Minors' Contracts: A Major Problem with the Indian Contract Act, 1872' (2021) 42 Statute Law Review 101, 101 ('the Privy Council's reading of the Act in *Mohori Bibee* is problematic, and its invention of the category of contracts *void ab initio* is unsupported by the Act.')

[45] RS Pandey, 'Minors' Agreement in the India and the U.K.—A Comparative Survey' (special issue) [1972] Journal of Indian Law Institute 205.

[46] *Mathai Mathai v Joseph Mary Alias Marykkutty Joseph* (2015) 5 SCC 622.

[47] *Government of Malaysia v Gurcharan Singh* (n 38).

the amendment to validate scholarship agreements signed by minors was passed a few months after this decision.[48]

The decision in *Mohori Bibee* is inapplicable to marriage contracts. In *Rajeswary v Balakrishnan*,[49] the High Court held that contracts of marriage entered by minors are valid on the basis that *Mohori Bibee* was concerned with business contracts. The Court cited the Indian case of *Fernandes v Gonsalves*[50] for the statement that marriage contracts in India are commonly made between minors and between an adult and a minor. Accordingly, it reasoned, it would not have been the intention of the legislature to deny a minor to a remedy for its breach. This decision must now be read with section 10 of the Law Reform (Marriage and Divorce) Act 1976,[51] which provides that marriages entered by persons below eighteen years of age (by either party) are void. However, a female over sixteen years old may apply for a licence to marry. *Rajeswary v Balakrishnan* remains good law for a claim for damages for breach of promise to marry.[52]

While statutory exceptions are available for minors in employment contracts[53] and insurance contracts,[54] the general legal position of minors following *Mohori Bibee* is unsatisfactory. The Privy Council's decision that the contract is *void ab initio* means that the minor and the contracting party have no contractual cause of action. Further, they are precluded from invoking restitutionary remedies under voidable contracts or void agreements in sections 64 or 65, respectively, of the Contract Act (sections 65 and 66 of the Malaysian Act).[55] While Malaysian courts have followed *Mohori Bibee* in holding contracts with minors *void ab initio*,[56] in *Leha Binte Jusoh v Awang Johari Bin*

[48] Contracts (Amendment) Act 1976, Act A329. See A Ibrahim, 'Legislative Digest on This Amendment Act' (1976) 1 Malayan Law Journal lxxxvi; IC Saxena, 'Scholarship Agreements in Malaysia: A New Deal' (1977) 2 Journal of Malaysian and Comparative Law 4.

[49] [1958] 3 MC 178 (High Court).

[50] (1924) ILR 48 Bom 673.

[51] Act 164. The Act is inapplicable to a Muslim or to any person who is married under Islamic law (s 3(3)) or to any native of Sabah or Sarawak or any aborigine of Peninsular Malaysia whose marriage or divorce is governed by native customary law or aboriginal custom (s 3(4)).

[52] See SK Chan, 'Minor's Capacity to Sue for Breach of Promise of Marriage—What Is Sauce for the Goose Is Not Sauce for the Gander: V. Rajaswary v. V. Balakrishnan' (1961) 2 University of Malaya Law Review 127.

[53] See the Children and Young Persons (Employment) Act 1966, Revised 1988, Act 350, which allows any child or young person to be employed and enter contracts of service. However, such a person cannot be an employer.

[54] See the Financial Services Act 2013, Act 758, s 128, sch 8, para 4(1)(2), which allows minors between the ages of ten and sixteen years (with the consent of their parent or guardian) to take up a life policy upon the minor's own life or upon the life of another in which the minor has an insurable interest. See R Che Hashim and FN Dusuki, 'Minors and their incapacity to contract: A revisit' (2023) 14 UUM Journal of Legal Studies 269 (this article provides commentaries on minors' contracts in relation to scholarship, insurance, employment and marriage, and online contracts.)

[55] However, restitution may be possible under the Indian Specific Relief Act 1963, s 33 (which repealed and replaced the Indian Specific Relief Act 1877). Section 33 specifically provides,

> Where a defendant successfully resist any suit on ground . . . (b) that the agreement sought to be enforced against him in the suit is void by reason of his not having been competent to contract under section 11 of the Indian Contract Act, 1872 (9 of 1872), the court may, if the defendant has received any benefit under the agreement from the other party, require him to restore, so far as may be, such benefit to that party, to the extent to which he or his estate has benefited thereby.

The Malaysian Specific Relief Act 1950 (Revised 1974) Act 137, s 40 (modelled on the Indian Specific Relief Act 1877) provides: 'On adjudging the cancellation of an instrument, the court may require the party to whom the relief is granted to make any compensation to the other party which justice may require.'

[56] Besides the cases above mentioned, see also *Tan Hee Juan By His Next Friend Tan See Bok v Teh Boon Keat Lai Soon* [1934] 3 MLJ 96 (High Court); *Kharil Anuar bin Muda v Sulong bin Muda* [2017] 6 MLJ 192 (High Court). See also *Mohd Ali Jahn bin Yusop Sahibjahn v Zaleha Bt Mat Zin* [1995] 1 CLJ 533 (High Court), which held the agreement was *void ab initio* without reference to *Mohori Bibee* (n 43); only Malaysian cases were referred to.

Hashim (*Leha Binte Jusoh*),[57] the apex court, the Federal Court, diverged from *Mohori Bibee* on the issue of remedies by making available to a minor a remedy under section 66 of the Malaysian Act (section 65 of the Contract Act) for a void agreement. In *Leha Binte Jusoh*, following *Mohori Bibee*, the Court refused the minor's application for specific performance of an agreement to purchase land as the contract was void. However, pursuant to section 66 of the Malaysian Act, the Court ordered the administratrix of the seller's estate to repay the full purchase price to the minor. The Court did not refer to the Privy Council decision in *Thakurain Harnath Kaur v Thakur Indar Bahadur* (*Harnath Kaur*),[58] which held that section 66 of the Malaysian Act (section 65 of the Contract Act) applied to agreements *void ab initio*, although the section provides for restitutionary relief 'when an agreement is discovered to be void, or when a contract becomes void'.[59]

The unsatisfactory position in *Mohori Bibee* on minors' lack of contractual capacity and remedies under the Contract Act (and the Malaysian Act) needs to be urgently addressed. The position in *Mohori Bibee*, decided more than a century ago, does not adequately address the needs of minors and persons who contract with them including contracting online and in the digital world,[60] and in the sport and entertainment industry[61] where minors have creatively applied their talents. Conversely, there is the challenge that minors are not liable for their actions despite a fraudulent misrepresentation of their age.[62] The extant Indian law, which is dominated by *Mohori Bibee*, fails to strike the correct balance between the underlying interests, namely, protecting the minor from rash decisions and allowing them access to plainly valuable goods and services and protecting those who genuinely deal with minors in good faith. This is an area where Indian law has been lagging behind, and adhering scrupulously to *Mohori Bibee* has led to suboptimal results.[63] While *Leha Binte Jusoh* has ameliorated the effects of *Mohori Bibee* to some extent, minors in Malaysia face similar challenges. Law reform is needed to improve the position of minors and persons contracting with minors in India and Malaysia.[64] In doing so, one would do

[57] [1978] 1 MLJ 202 (Federal Court).

[58] AIR 1922 PC 403.

[59] In an article published in 1978, Saxena observed the reference to case authorities in court decisions on s 66 (s 65 of the Contract Act) as follows:

> In Malaysia *Harnath Kaur* has been discussed in just a few cases ... [i]n the Privy Council cases, which went from Malaysia, *Harnath Kaur* was hardly discussed on the subject. In the Privy Council cases, however, which went from India, the theme of that case was echoed and re-echoed in case after case.

See IC Saxena, 'New Discoveries in Void Agreements: Restitution in India, Pakistan and Malaysia' (1978) 5 Journal of Malaysian and Comparative Law 105, 114, 159. See also discussion (n 104) below.

[60] See S Gangwar, 'Minors' Contracts in the Digital Age' (2022) 43 Liverpool Law Review 237.

[61] See S Star and D Dhankar, 'Major Differences in Minors' Contracts: A Comparative Analysis into the Validity of Contracts with Minors in the Sport and Entertainment Industry' (2022) 43 Liverpool Law Review 203.

[62] Minors are not estopped from pleading minority where there is a fraudulent misrepresentation of age where the other party was aware of the minors age (see *Mohori Bibee* at n 43) or even if the minor had induced the other party to enter into the agreement; see the Privy Council decision in *Khan Gul v Lakna Singh* AIR 1928 Lahore 609, which was followed in Malaysia in *R Natesan v K Thanaletcumi* [1952] MLJ 1 (High Court).

[63] See Swaminathan and Surana (n 44).

[64] See Cheong, Dhankar, and Star (n 10) 26.

well to look at Australian state legislations offering different models that could be considered.[65]

2. Stipulated Sums Amounting to Penalties

This topic is selected as a study on the migration of the Contract Act to Malaysia and, broadly, as a legal transplantation of English law to India and Malaysia due to its rich legislative history. Section 74 of the Contract Act (section 75 of Malaysian Act) was one of the most notable departures from English law as it sought to abolish the troublesome dichotomy in English law between liquidated damages and penalties.[66] Despite the express language of the statutory provision to reflect the abolition of the distinction, the Indian courts subsequently reverted to English's law distinction between penalties and liquidated damages. This unsatisfactory state of the law has somewhat influenced Malaysian law, although the greater challenge in Malaysia relates to the issue of proof.

Section 74 of the Contract Act, as it originally stood in 1872, provided that whenever parties stipulate that any sum is to be paid in case of breach, the court could award 'reasonable compensation not exceeding the amount so named'.[67] The section also provides that compensation is payable 'whether or not actual damage or loss is proved to have been caused thereby'. Indeed, this prompted Pollock and Mulla to note that this section 'cuts the most troublesome knot in the common law doctrine of damages'.[68] There was an amendment to the section in 1899,[69] but the point of this amendment was merely to make the section applicable to a wider array of cases than just stipulated sums. This extension was expressed in the phrase 'or any other stipulation by way of penalty'. However, the Supreme Court of India in a series of decisions (*Fateh Chand v Balkishen Das*,[70] *Maula Bux v Union of India* (*Maula Bux*),[71] *Oil & Natural Gas Corp Ltd v Saw Pipes Ltd*[72] and *Kailash Nath Associates v Delhi Development Authority*

[65] See eg the Minors (Property and Contracts) Act 1970 (NSW), which has been regarded as comprehensive. See DJ Harland, *The Law of Minors in Relation to Contracts and Property, An Analysis of the Minors (Property and Contracts) Act 1970* (Butterworths 1974).

[66] AC Banerjee, *English Law in India* (Abhinav Publications 1983) 186 (the complexities in the common law on penalties were already known at the time of the drafting of the Contract Act). See also similar view by Lord Neuberger and Lord Sumption (with whom Lord Carnwath agreed) in the UK Supreme Court case of *Cavendish Square Holding BV v Talal El Makdessi* and *ParkingEye Limited v Beavis* [2016] AC 1172, 1192; [2015] UKSC 67 [3].

[67] The Contract Act, s 74 reads,

> When a contract has been broken, if a sum is named in the contract as the amount to be paid in case of such breach, or *if the contract contains any other stipulation by way of penalty*, the party complaining of the breach is entitled, whether or not actual damage or loss is proved to have been caused thereby, to receive from the party who has broken the contract reasonable compensation not exceeding the amount so named *or, as the case may be, the penalty stipulated for* [emphasis added for additions brought about by the 1899 Amendment Act in India].

This provision is found in the Malaysian Act, s 75.

[68] RK Abichandan, *Pollock & Mulla Indian Contract and Specific Relief Acts*, vol 2 (11th edn, NM Tripathi Private Ltd 1994) 884.

[69] See the Indian Contract Act Amendment Act 1899. The additions brought by this amendment are italicised in setting out the provision of s 74 (see n 67 above).

[70] AIR 1963 SC 1405.

[71] [1969] 2 SCC 554.

[72] AIR 2003 SC 2629.

(*Kailash Nath*)[73]), interpreted section 74 as referring to a 'penalty' in the English sense. The Indian courts reverted to the English law distinction between liquidated damages and penalties and referred to the House of Lords guidelines in *Dunlop Pneumatic Tyre Co Ltd v New Garage & Motor Co Ltd* (*Dunlop Pneumatic Tyres*).[74] This ended up re-introducing the troublesome liquidated damages–penalty dichotomy that the drafters had sought to avoid.[75]

Early Indian cases proclaiming the 'cutting of the difficult knot' has been followed in Malaysia. In *SS Maniam v The State of Perak*,[76] Thomson J referred to *Bhai Panna Singh v Firm Bhai Arjun Singh—Bhajan Singh—Surjan Singh* (*Bhai Panna*).[77] However, the anomaly in the Indian cases reverting to the troublesome distinction between liquidated damages and penalties has also found its way in the Malaysian cases, including *Wearne Brothers (M) Ltd v Jackson* (*Wearne Brothers*),[78] which followed *Bhai Panna*. Here, one can see a clear trajectory of Indian law initially influencing Malaysian law in the early years of the migration of the Contract Act to Malaysia.

Besides the abolition of the distinction between liquidated damages and penalties, the Indian cases led the direction on the issue of proof. Despite the literal words in section 74 in the Contract Act 'whether or not actual damage or loss is proved to have been caused thereby', *Bhai Panna* held that '[t]he plaintiff must prove the damage they have suffered unless the sum named is a genuine pre estimate'.[79] In *Maula Bux*, Shah J interpreted the section as requiring damage or loss for its invocation, with the reasoning that it only dispenses with the proof to assess the compensation, not with the proof of actual damage or loss.[80] *Bhai Panna's* decision was followed in *Wearne Brothers* and subsequently by the Federal Court in a landmark case, *Selva Kumar a/l Murugiah v Thiagarajah a/l Retnasamy* (*Selva Kumar*),[81] which set out the (initial) Malaysian law on onus of proof in section 75 of the Malaysian Act (section 74 of the Contract Act). *Fateh Chand* and *Maula Bux* were also followed in *Selva Kumar*. This trend again signalled the strong influence of Indian authorities in the interpretation of the Malaysian Act.

The Federal Court in *Selva Kumar* held that section 75 of the Malaysian Act must be given a restricted meaning and that a plaintiff must prove actual damages or reasonable compensation in accordance with the principles in *Hadley v Baxendale*, and the failure to do so will result in a refusal of the court to award any damages. An exception applies

[73] [2015] 4 SCC 136.
[74] [1915] AC 79.
[75] See S Swaminathan, 'De-inventing the Wheel: Liquidated Damages, Penalties and the Indian Contract Act, 1872' (2018) 6 Chinese Journal of Comparative Law 103, 109–15. According to Swaminathan, in *Kailash Nath* (n 73), Nariman J introduced a trichotomy—'liquidated damages', 'other liquidated damages', and 'penalty'.
[76] [1957] 23 MLJ 75 (High Court).
[77] AIR 1929 PC 179.
[78] [1966] 2 MLJ 155 (High Court).
[79] *Bhai Panna* (n 77) 180.
[80] *Maula Bux* (n 71) 559.
[81] [1995] 1 MLJ 817 (Federal Court). For a discussion of this and other Malaysian cases on s 75, see MF Cheong and YH Lee, 'Specific Remedies and Money Awards in the Protection of the Performance Interest under Malaysian Contract Law' in M Chen-Wishart, A Loke and B Ong (eds), *Studies in the Contract Laws of Asia 1: Remedies for Breach of Contract* (OUP 2016) 325, 346-351.

for cases in which the court finds it difficult to assess loss.[82] In these cases, the court will grant substantial damages (subject to acap, not exceeding the sum contractually provided) that are reasonable and fair according to the court's good sense and fair play. The strict application of this principle has been followed in many cases and has caused challenges as the courts seek to provide exceptions to avoid the difficulties of parties having to prove actual loss.[83]

In a relatively recent development, in *Cavendish Square Holding BV v Talal El Makdessi* and *ParkingEye Limited v Beavis* (*Cavendish Square*),[84] English law has finally broken free of the troublesome dichotomy between liquidated damages and penalties. The UK Supreme Court, in *Cavendish Square*, has changed the law's treatment of penalties. While not overruling *Dunlop Pneumatic Tyres*, the Court provided new tests of legitimate interest and proportionality to determine the validity of penalty clauses. According to Lord Neuberger and Lord Sumption (with whom Lord Carnwath agreed), the true test is whether the impugned clause imposes a detriment on the contract-breaker which is out of all proportion to any legitimate interest of the innocent party.[85] This test has been considered as operating practically as a test of 'reasonableness' of stipulated sums.[86] Viewed in this light, *Cavendish Square* has now redefined the notion of penalties as a sum *in terrorem*, and the new test effectively renders otiose the notion of liquidated damages. However, Indian law continues to embrace English law's traditional distinction between liquidated damages and penalties. The development in English law has been embraced by the Malaysian apex court, which has now set the Malaysian position on the law of penalties quite apart from the Indian position.

In Malaysia, the 2016 decision in *Cubic Electronics Sdn Bhd v Mars Telecommunications Sdn Bhd* (*Cubic Electronics*)[87] brought a sea change to the law on penalties in Malaysia in three aspects. First, in a bold move, the Federal Court adopted the tests of legitimate interest and proportionality introduced by *Cavendish Square* to determine reasonable compensation in section 75 of the Malaysian Act (section 74 of the Contract Act). While not overruling *Selva Kumar*, the Court held that proof of actual loss is not the only way to determine reasonable compensation, although that may be a useful starting point. Second, the Court reformulated the rules on onus of proof.[88]

[82] This was applied in a building contract for delayed completion; see *Keen Builders Sdn Bhd v Utara Dua (Malaysia) Sdd Bhd (Samudra Malaysia) Sdn Bhd, Garnishee)* [1998] 2 CLJ Supp 256 (High Court).

[83] In many of cases that followed *Selva Kumar* (n 81), the liquidated damages clauses were not enforced for failing to bring proof of actual loss. A small number of cases declined to follow *Selva Kumar*, and in a number of cases, exceptions to *Selva Kumar* were recognised.

[84] [2016] AC 1172, [2015] UKSC 67.

[85] ibid [32].

[86] S Swaminathan, 'A Centennial Refurbishment of *Dunlop*'s Emporium of Contractual Concepts: *Cavendish Square Holding BV v Talal El Makdessi and ParkingEye Limited v Beavis* [2015] UKSC 67' (2016) 45 Common Law World Review 248, 254.

[87] [2019] 6 MLJ 15 (Federal Court). See Cheong and Tan (n 12).

[88] In *Cubic Electronics* (n 87) [70], Richard Malanjum CJ sets out the position as follows:

> The initial onus lies on the party seeking to enforce a damages clause under s 75 to adduce evidence that firstly, there was a breach of contract and that secondly, the contract contains a clause specifying a sum

Following *Cubic Electronics*, now an aggrieved party needs to only show a breach of contract by the defaulting party and the applicability of the liquidated damages clause. The plaintiff does not need to show that the amount claimed pursuant to the clause is reasonable. Once it has discharged its onus of proof, it is entitled to the sum named, and if there is any dispute as to what constitutes reasonable compensation, the onus of proof is shifted to the defaulting party to show that the liquidated damages clause is unreasonable. This may bring the position closer to the original intent of the drafters for section 74 of the Contract Act (section 75 of the Malaysian Act) to have a sliding scale to bring down the amount of compensation to a reasonable amount in cases where it was unreasonable.[89] This position differs sharply from *Selva Kumar*, where the defaulting party's liability is only established once the aggrieved party can prove its losses.

The third change relates to the issue of deposits. Before *Cubic Electronics*, the governing law was the Privy Council's decision in *Linggi Plantations Ltd v Jagatheesan*,[90] which held that section 75 of the Malaysian Act was inapplicable to true deposits. In an unprecedented move, *Cubic Electronics* held that the mutually exclusive view that the law relating to forfeiture of deposits and the law on penalties are distinct should no longer prevail. The Court relied on statements from *Cavendish*[91] and three cases of the Supreme Court of India, which overrode earlier Indian cases which previously held that section 74 of the Contract Act did not apply to deposits for due performance of a contract that are to be forfeited for breach.[92] The Court quoted parts of the judgments of *Maula Bux*,[93] which affirmed *Fateh Chand*. The Court also referred to *Kailash Nath*, which reiterates the Indian position that 'as earnest money is an amount to be paid in case of breach of contract and named in the contract as such, it would necessarily be covered by section 74'.[94]

The chronological developments in the law of penalties in section 75 of the Malaysian Act reflect the theme in this chapter of the early influence of Indian authorities on Malaysian law seen in *SS Maniam* and *Wearne Brothers*, which continued in *Selva Kumar*. In his personal reflections on the law of contract, Phang writes of the need to balance the autochthonous development of the law, at the same time meeting the challenges of globalisation. He argues that indigenisation can be developed simultaneously to accommodate doctrines from other jurisdictions, particularly in the areas of commercial law where uniformity is desirable.[95] It is submitted that the latest Federal Court decision in *Cubic Electronics* mirrors this movement in the Malaysian context. The decision in *Cubic Electronics* has significantly impacted the law on penalties under the Malaysian

to be paid upon breach. Once these two elements have been established, the innocent party is entitled to receive a sum not exceeding the amount stipulated in the contract irrespective of whether actual damage or loss is proven subject always to the defaulting party proving the unreasonableness of the damages clause including the sum stated therein, if any.

89 See Swaminathan, 'De-inventing the Wheel' (n 75) 114.
90 [1972] 1 MLJ 89.
91 *Cubic Electronics* (n 87) [44].
92 ibid [42], [43].
93 *Maula Bux* (n 71) 559: 'But if forfeiture is of the nature of penalty, Section 74 applies'.
94 *Kailash Nath* (n 73) [40].
95 Phang (n 11) 2–3.

Act.[96] The Federal Court's adoption of the UK Supreme Court decision in *Cavendish Square* enables the court to fill a gap in the existing law in view of the lack of guidance as to how to determine reasonable compensation in section 75 of the Malaysian Act. In India, as the Supreme Court of India has not had the opportunity to consider this important issue, the gap remains, particularly in the light of its reversion to the troublesome dichotomy highlighted by Swaminathan.[97] There has only been a small number of cases that have reached the Supreme Court of India.[98] There have been no decisions on the legitimate interest test, while the proportionality test was applied in *Electronics Corporation of Tamil Nadu Limited v ICMC Corporation Limited*,[99] which held that 'the sum stipulated bears a reasonable correlation to anticipated loss in as much as there is proportionality as between the extent of delay and the amount of LD [liquidated damages]'. Indian commentaries have supported the decision in *Cavendish Square*, as it gives effect to the intention of the parties to ascertain their legitimate interests, and have called for the Indian courts to 'adapt' the test to promote party autonomy.[100] Swaminathan is of the view that the new test of penalties propounded in *Cavendish Square* achieves a workable balance between party autonomy to agree on stipulated sums with the countervailing interest to protect weaker parties from potential abuse of such clauses.[101]

IV. Declining Dependency on Indian Authorities in Interpreting the Malaysian Act

The studies of the two areas of minors' contracts and stipulated sums amounting to penalties display the limits of dependency on Indian authorities despite the Malaysian Act's near-verbatim transcription of the Contract Act. It also shows the challenges of interpreting the Malaysian Act within a growing indigenisation of Malaysian contract law in light of developments occurring internationally. This is reflected in the Malaysian Federal Court decision in *Leha Binte Jusoh* in relation to minors' contract to provide a remedy via section 66 of the Malaysian Act (section 65 of the Contract Act), finding a way around *Mohori Bibee's* decision that the agreement was *void ab initio*—an approach that is in contrast with the one taken by the Indian Supreme Court in *Mathai Mathai*, which insisted on the strict adherence to *Mohori Bibee*. In relation to

[96] For commentaries, see SM Choong, 'The Supervisory Jurisdiction of the Courts in Regulating Secondary Obligations in Contracts' (2023) 3 Malayan Law Journal lxxviii; J Teng and K Kalairasu, 'Divergence and Convergence in the Law of Contractual Penalties and Liquidated Damages Clauses in England, Singapore and Malaysia' (2022) 43 Liverpool Law Review 451; SY Ng, 'Cubic Electronics: A Fresh Look or a Daze on Section 75 of the Contracts Act 1950' (2021) 3 Malayan Law Journal lxxxviii; CF Lim, 'Enforcement of Liquidated Damages—A Legal Conundrum Resolved?' [2019] (July) Journal of the Malaysian Judiciary 72.

[97] See Swaminathan, 'De-inventing the Wheel' (n 75).

[98] See *Dishnet Wireless Ltd v The Union of India* (2016) 1 TLR 10; *LIC Housing Finance Ltd v Commissioner of S T* 2019 SCC OnLine CESTAT 8290.

[99] 2020 SCC OnLine Mad 244.

[100] L Dasgupta, 'Legitimate Interest Test and Party Autonomy: Correcting the Discourse on Liquidated Damages within the Indian Contract Act 1872' (2022) 13 Indian Journal of Law and Justice 101, 113, 117; see also A Shiralkar, 'The Legitimate Test (UK) on the Enforceability of Liquidated Damages Clauses and Its Implications for Indian Law' (2021) 2 Supreme Court Cases J-37.

[101] See Swaminathan, 'A Centennial Refurbishment' (n 86).

stipulated sums amounting to penalties under section 75 of the Malaysian Act (section 74 of the Indian Act), the more recent Federal Court decision in *Cubic Electronics*, adopting the legitimate interest and proportionality tests of *Cavendish Square*, highlights the Malaysian courts' readiness to look to the original English source jurisdiction. This, it appears, is not merely a Malaysian experience. The tendency of the Indian courts, while construing the Contract Act and yet producing results that are virtually indistinguishable from English contract law, has been identified in three areas:[102] consideration, privity,[103] and stipulated sums.

Three related factors may explain why, over time, the Malaysian courts' dependence on Indian authorities in interpreting the Malaysian Act has declined[104] and, going forward, there is likely to be a greater movement away from the Indian case law and jurisprudence on the Contract Act. As evident from *Cubic Electronics*, the first main factor (which links to the other two factors) is the inclination of the Malaysian courts to look to the original source jurisdiction, English law, instead of the Indian jurisprudence that developed the codified English law in the Contract Act. This factor is related to the second factor with regards to the legal training of early Malayan (subsequently Malaysian) judges and senior counsels, who were primarily British trained. Post-independence, the continuing relationship with England made English law schools a popular destination for Malaysian students seeking a legal career. Thus, it is reasonable to expect that the judges (and the counsels) would be influenced by the English legal background from which they receive their formal training. Swaminathan, observing a similar Indian experience, attributes this to the 'tacit knowledge' acquired during the legal training and refers to the formative decades of the adjudication of cases under the Contract Act in the late nineteenth and early twentieth centuries wherein the Indian judiciary came from the ranks of English lawyers who had spent considerable time at the English bar.[105] In Malaysia, the early preponderance towards an overseas English legal education was in part due to the limited availability of places at local universities for legal education. The first Malaysian law school established at the University of Malaya in 1972 had an annual intake of fifty students. From 1978 onwards, this was increased to about 100 students and this figure has been steadily maintained through the years. The number of local law graduates has increased as more local law schools have become established. The judicial profile has also changed in recent years with more judges being graduates of local law schools.[106] This partly explains the growing

[102] S Swaminathan, 'Persistence of the "Codeless Myriad": The Indian Contract Act and a Puzzle Surrounding Common Law Codification' (2022) 44 Statute Law Review 1.

[103] S Swaminathan, 'The Great Indian Privity Trick: Hundred Years of Misunderstanding Nineteenth Century English Contract Law' (2016) 16 Oxford University Commonwealth Law Journal 160.

[104] See discussion (n 59) above on Saxena's observation that the Malaysian Federal Court in *Leha Binte Jusoh* (n 57) did not refer to *Harnath Kaur* in a decision on the Malaysian Act, s 66 (s 65 of the Contract Act).

[105] See Swaminathan, 'Persistence of the "Codeless Myriad"' (n 102) 15.

[106] See Keynote Address by The Right Honourable The Chief Justice of Malaysia Tun Tengku Maimun Binti Tuan Mat, 'Parallel Perspectives from Malaysia and the United Kingdom', 24 September 2021 (via Zoom). The current Chief Justice, The Right Honourable Tun Tengku Maimun Binti Tuan Mat who is an alumna of the Faculty of Law, University of Malaya stated: 'Today, many of our graduates still do qualify in England but we have since established numerous local law schools to produce our own home-grown graduates . . . Indeed, our alumi has achieved considerable feats . . . Even the Judiciary is proud to have within it graduates of the Faculty alumni throughout the Court hierarchy. The Top 4 senior-most judges are alumni as is the Chief Registrar of the Federal

indigenisation of Malaysian law and the declining influence of Indian law scholarship. Other external factors also impact on this matter. As an example, in the earlier years when the University of Malaya law school was established, it had the tradition of inviting professors of law from universities in India to teach in the law programs at the law school.[107] The declining reference to Indian case law in Malaysian cases is also attributable to the third factor—the general difficulty in accessing Indian case reports in the early years prior to the availability of online and digital copies. In the past, access to hard copies of Indian cases was limited, and the treatise by Pollock & Mulla on the *Indian Contract and Specific Relief Acts* was the main source of reference to Indian case law.

The extent to which the Contract Act and Indian decisions impact Malaysian contract law is also influenced by the question of whether parties can contract out of the Malaysian Act. The Privy Council in *Ooi Boon Leong v Citibank NA*[108] held that parties are free to contract out of the Malaysian Act unless the provisions expressly prohibit it.[109] Another matter relates to the adherence of English precedents and the reference to decisions of the courts in jurisdictions besides the United Kingdom and India. While the Civil Law Act 1956[110] provides that after the cut-off date of 7 April 1956, English common law and rules of equity are only of persuasive authority and are not binding on the Malaysian courts,[111] the preponderant practice has been to follow English cases, even after the cut-off date.[112] The inclination to refer to foreign sources, particularly from Commonwealth countries, is also attributable to the fact that the Malaysian Act (like the Contract Act) is regarded as not being exhaustive. While the Malaysian Act's preamble states that it is '[a]n act relating to contracts',[113] the Privy Council has held that the Malaysian Act is not a complete code, neither is it expressed to be a consolidating or

Court.' See: (https://www.kehakiman.gov.my/sites/default/files/documents/teks_ucapan/2021/SP2021.10.15.pdf (accessed 21 May 2024)).

[107] These included eminent professors including MP Jain, KB Rohatgi, H Chand and S Sharma, who each taught for many years at the Faculty of Law, University of Malaya.

[108] [1984] 1 MLJ 222, 226 (Lord Brightman).

[109] Cf a different view that the parties cannot contract out of the Malaysian Act unless the statute expressly allows for it; see RR Sethu, 'The History, Impact and Influence of the Indian Contracts Act 1872' (2011) 28 Journal of Contract Law 31, 45. There are, however, exceptions for legislations that are enacted to protect a certain class of the public, eg contracts provided in the Housing Developers (Control and Licensing Act) 1966 and regulations; see *SEA Housing Corporation Sdn Bhd v Lee Poh Choo* [1982] 2 MLJ 31, 34 (Federal Court); *Ang Ming Lee v Menteri Kesejahteraan Bandar, Perumahan dan Kerajaan Tempatan* [2020] 1 MLJ 281 [57] (High Court).

[110] See n 36 above.

[111] This has been affirmed by the highest court; see *Chung Khiaw Bank Ltd v Hotel Rasa Sayang Sdn Bhd* [1990] 1 MLJ 356, 361 (Federal Court) (Hashim Yeop Sani CJ (Malaya)) ('The development of the common law after 7 April 1956 . . . is entirely in the hands of the Courts of this country. We cannot just accept the development of the common law in England.') See also *Saad Marwi v Chan Huan Hwa* [2001] 3 CLJ 98, 114-15 (Court of Appeal) (Gopal Sri Ram JCA) ('The position is that after 1956, we are at liberty to fashion rules of common law and equity to suit our own needs and are not to treat ourselves as being bound hand and foot by English cases).

[112] See *Lori Malaysia Bhd v Arab-Malaysian Finance Bhd* [1999] 2 CLJ 997, 1015–16 (Federal Court). Edgar Joseph FCJ after agreeing with *Chung Khiaw Bank*, stated, 'But, having said that, we consider that the trend shown by the courts in Common Law countries to be slow in striking down commercial contracts on the ground of illegality is a sensible one, which we should follow thus incorporating it as part of our Common Law'.

[113] Cf the preamble in the Contract Act that the purpose of the Act is 'to define and amend certain parts of the law relating to contracts'.

amending statute.[114] This has allowed the Malaysian courts to refer to external sources, particularly when there is a lacuna in the statutory provisions.

The former Chief Justice of Malaysia, The Honourable Tun Dato' Seri Zaki Tun Azmi, has observed that, over time, Malaysian case law has become conspicuously 'variegated' in its approach and has engaged with case law from many other jurisdictions besides the United Kingdom.[115] In contract law, the Malaysian courts have followed the High Court of Australia's decision in *Walton Stores (Interstate) Ltd v Maher* (*Walton Stores*)[116] on promissory estoppel. In *Saad Marwi v Chan Huan Hwa*,[117] the Court of Appeal referred to cases from four jurisdictions to interpret section 16 of the Malaysian Act on undue influence and held that the wider doctrine of inequality of bargaining power applied in Malaysia. Besides cases from India,[118] the Court referred to English,[119] Australian,[120] and Canadian[121] cases on unconscionability. This case also shows the courts drawing upon wider and flexible notions of equity in interpreting statutory provisions in the Malaysian Act and highlights the tension as to the extent that Malaysian courts could manoeuvre new concepts within the codified framework inherited from the Contract Act. In *American International Assurance Co Ltd v Koh Yen Bee (F)*,[122] the High Court expressed doubts about *Saad Marwi*'s introduction of the doctrine of inequality of bargaining power in relation to undue influence. According to the Court, this would amount to 'legislating' on substantive law with retrospective effect since 'free consent' has been defined to recognise only coercion, undue influence, fraud, misrepresentation, and mistake. Similar issues arise about whether the definition of 'coercion' in section 15 of the Malaysian Act could encompass the common law doctrine of economic duress.[123]

The wider receptivity of Malaysian courts towards developments from other jurisdictions also impacts the influence of Indian law in interpreting the Malaysian Act. Besides Australia and Canada, Malaysian courts are also receptive to commercial law

[114] See *Ooi Boon Leong* (n 108) 224. A similar position was adopted by the Privy Council in relation to the Contract Act; see *Irrawaddy Flotilla Co Ltd v Bugwandass* (1891) 18 IA 121 and *Jwaladutt Pillani v Bansilal Motilal* (1929) 115 IC 707.

[115] The Hon Tun Dato' Seri Zaki Tun Azmi, 'The Common Law of Malaysia in the 21st Century' (2012) 24 Singapore Academy of Law Journal 1, 11.

[116] (1988) 184 CLR 387 (High Court of Australia). *Walton Stores* was followed in *Boustead Trading (1985) Sdn Bhd v Arab-Malaysian Bank Berhad* [1995] 3 MLJ 331; see MF Cheong, 'Estoppel in Boustead's Case: A Move Away from Reliance to Unconscionability' (1999) 26 Journal of Malaysian and Comparative Law 71. Justice Brennan's six elements in *Walton Stores* to establish an estoppel were adopted in Malaysia in *Bongsor Bina Sdn Bhd v* Malaysian *Building Society* (2014) 1 LNS 1174 (Court of Appeal); see A Trakic, 'Promissory Estoppel and Its Relevance to Malaysian Contract Law' (2018) 34 Journal of Contract Law 240, 254.

[117] See n 111.

[118] *Lakshminarayana v Singaravelu* AIR 1963 Mad 24; *Rangasami Gounder v Periamuthu Gounder* [1977] 1 Mad 231; *Manak Chand v Puran* AIR 1960 Madh Pras 253; *Davis v Maung Shwe Go* [1911] 38 IA 155.

[119] *Credit Lyonnais Bank Nederland NV v Burch* [1997] 1 All ER 144.

[120] *Commercial Bank of Australia v Amadio* [1983] 151 CLR 447 (High Court of Australia); *Westwill Pty Ltd v Heath* [1959] 52 SASR 46.

[121] *Paris v Machnick* [1972] 32 DLR 723, emphasising the flexibility of Canadian equity in the remedial field.

[122] [2004] 4 MLJ 301, 319 (Court of Appeal). See MF Cheong, 'A Malaysian Doctrine of Inequality of Bargaining Power after Saad Marwi?' [2005] 4 Malayan Law Journal i; see also a reprint of the article in KJ Tan and A Sharom (eds), *Developments in Singapore and Malaysian Law* (Marshall Cavendish Academic 2007) 89–105.

[123] See *Perlis Plantation Berhad v Mohammad Abdullah Ang* [1988] 1 CLJ 670, 676 (High Court) (VC George J) ('our Contract Act does not provide for any form of coercion other than as defined by section 15').

developments from neighbouring Singapore.[124] This wider receptivity has also extended beyond jurisdictions in the common law traditions and encompassed civil law concepts. In *Dream Property Sdn Bhd v Atlas Housing Sdn Bhd*,[125] in considering whether the plaintiff was unjustly enriched, the Federal Court preferred the civil law and mixed systems 'absence-of-basis' approach over the English law's application of 'unjust factors'.[126] Further, the Court did not refer to the provisions in 'Part VI Of Certain Relations Resembling Those Created by Contract' which provide for statutory restitutionary remedies[127] and, instead, recognised a separate common law cause of action for restitution. These developments, referring to wider sources of law outside of the Contract Act and adopting a more fluid interpretation of the Malaysian Act, have resulted in a reduced adherence to follow Indian case precedents compared to the earlier years in the history of the Malaysian Act.

V. Conclusion

This chapter, which evaluates the migration of contract law from India to Malaysia, from the Contract Act to the Malaysian Act, shows that the transfer of law is more complex than envisaged by Watson's theory of legal transplants. While Indian case law was highly influential in the early development of Malaysian contract law, its influence has gradually declined as the Malaysian courts refer to English law, the original source jurisdiction, and decisions from Commonwealth jurisdictions. When the transplantation involves a 'double legal transplant' and the immediate transplant source is statutory in nature (as in the Contract Act embodying English common law of contract), there could be an inclination of the receiving jurisdiction (as in the Malaysian Act) to revert directly to the original (English common law) source. This could result in a loss of the rich jurisprudence developed in the statutory language of the transplanted codified law.

At the same time, the chapter also reveals a process of indigenisation of contract law as the Malaysian courts develop the law to meet the needs and circumstances in Malaysia. There is also the continuing challenge for the courts to develop the law to relate to international developments and emergent technology and other 'disruptions' to contracting when applying the Malaysian Act, which was modelled on the Contract Act, an 1872 legislation embodying English law as it then was. This raises the important question of law reform to keep pace with the times and underscores the need for a full-scale review of the Malaysian Act.

[124] In *Perwira Habib Bank Malaysia Bhd v Syarikat Johor Tenggara Sdn Bhd* [1989] 2 MLJ 476, 478 (High Court), Gunn Chit Tuan J stated, 'I considered that courts in this country hearing commercial cases ought to follow the trend of authorities in the appellate tribunals of other Commonwealth countries such as the United Kingdom and the Republic of Singapore.'

[125] [2015] 2 MLJ 441 (Federal Court).

[126] See LW Tchung, 'Mapping Uncharted Waters: Restitution for Indirect Benefits under Section 71 of the Contracts Act 1950' [2021] Journal of the Malaysian Judiciary 187.

[127] See MF Cheong, 'Restitutionary Developments under Part VI, Malaysian Contracts Act 1950' (2005) 7 The Australian Journal of Asian Law 24.

PART II
CORE CONCEPTS

5

Formation

Stelios Tofaris

I. Introduction

Under the Indian Contract Act 1872 (hereinafter 'the Contract Act'), a contract is an *agreement enforceable by law.*[1] The first stage of formation of contract is to establish an *agreement.* The statutory framework provides that a proposal,[2] when accepted,[3] becomes a promise,[4] and every promise or set of promises is an agreement.[5] An agreement is a necessary but not sufficient condition of a contract. The second stage of formation of contract is to establish that the agreement is *enforceable by law.*[6] This occurs when the agreement is made by the free consent of parties who are competent to contract for a lawful consideration and with a lawful object, and it is not declared void by the Contract Act.[7]

This chapter is concerned with the first stage of formation of contract, that is, whether an agreement is reached. It seeks to explain the internal workings and analytical reach of the framework set in place by the Contract Act. In doing so, it considers the extent to which it is possible to analyse practical problems through the statutory framework in a manner that is coherent and capable of producing sound outcomes. This is particularly important in the light of changes in the methods of communication and contracting brought about by technological, economic, and social developments in the past 150 years.

Section II looks briefly at the drafting of the relevant sections for the purpose of uncovering their theoretical and doctrinal sources. Section III considers how intention is assessed in Indian contract law as a prelude to the examination of proposal and acceptance. Sections IV–VI analyse, respectively, the specifics of proposal, acceptance, and revocation, identifying some key questions. Section VII explores the limits of

[1] The Contract Act, s 2(h).
[2] ibid s 2(a).
[3] ibid s 2(b).
[4] ibid s 2(b).
[5] ibid s 2(e).
[6] If not, it is said to be void: ibid s 2(g).
[7] ibid s 10.

Stelios Tofaris, *Formation* In: *Foundations of Indian Contract Law.* Edited by: KV Krishnaprasad, Niranjan Venkatesan, Shivprasad Swaminathan, and Umakanth Varottil, Oxford University Press.
DOI: 10.1093/9780191997211.003.0005

proposal and acceptance. Section VIII concludes by considering whether any reforms are desirable and the form that these may take.

II. Drafting

1. General

The legislative history of the Contract Act proved contentious.[8] The resignation of the Indian Law Commission in 1870, following their disagreements with Henry Maine, the Indian government's law member, left his successor James Fitzjames Stephen 'practically & substantially . . . a sort of king in [his] own department',[9] able to pursue his bold legislative plans.

As regards the Contract Bill, Stephen was able to 'reap where others had sown'.[10] Having criticised the commissioners' draughtsmanship of the sections on the general principles of contract law,[11] Stephen reworked the existing draft in 1871–72 with the help of a select committee and his department's officials. Stephen introduced structural changes and added new sections under the influence of the Civil Code, which David Dudley Field drafted in 1862 for New York but which was never enacted there (hereinafter 'the Field Code').[12] His stated goal was to make the Act 'simpler and more intelligible'.[13]

Stephen's draftsmanship, however, was not without shortcomings. Much of the criticism has been directed at the use of the Field Code. This was described as the 'worst piece of codification ever produced' and the 'evil genius' of the Contract Act.[14] Yet, Stephen's own definitions were not always free from ambiguity and could diverge from ordinary meaning. For example, in relation to the definition of 'promise' in section 2(b), 'it is . . . difficult . . . to say, without doing some violence to language, that in the common affairs of life a promise is always an accepted proposal'.[15] What is more, Stephen had a tendency to over-define at the expense of clarity. This can be seen in sections 3–9 on proposal and acceptance, where Stephen's effort to define every relevant term in detail and then construct the general rules through cross-referencing created a doctrinal labyrinth.[16]

[8] S Tofaris, 'A Historical Study of the Indian Contract Act 1872' (PhD thesis, University of Cambridge 2011) 88–133.

[9] 'Letter from JF Stephen to GS Venables, 4 July 1870', Cambridge University Library (CUL) Ms Add 7349/12.

[10] JF Stephen, 'Codification in India and England' (1872) XVII *Fortnightly Review* 653.

[11] 'Note by Stephen on the Re-arrangement of the First Part of the Indian Contract Law, 29 October 1871', British Library (BL) Mss Eur F86/111.

[12] *The Civil Code of the State of New York* (Albany, Weed, Parsons & Co 1865) (hereinafter 'the Field Code').

[13] *Final Report of the Select Committee on the Bill to Define and Amend the Law Relating to Contracts, Sale of Moveables, Indemnity and Guarantee, Bailment, Agency and Partnership, 12 March 1872*, British Library (BL) IOR/L/PJ/5/15; National Archives of India (NAI), Legislative Department, A Proceedings, May 1872, No 612.

[14] F Pollock and DF Mulla, *The Indian Contract Act: With a Commentary, Critical and Explanatory* (2nd edn, Sweet & Maxwell 1909) vii, 164.

[15] ibid 13.

[16] See generally CP Ilbert, 'Sir James Fitzjames Stephen as a Legislator' (1894) 10 Law Quarterly Review 222.

2. Model of Formation of Contract

The Contract Act formulated a single law of contract by analysing common law and equity doctrines within a common framework. Most rules were taken from English law, although there were significant changes, partly to reflect local conditions and partly out of a desire to reform those rules. In its general tenor, the Contract Act emulated the classical model of contract law that was prevalent in England and was premised on the Will Theory. At the heart of this was the idea that contractual liability arose from the meeting of wills.[17] In this respect, the Contract Act treated contract as an agreement with consent elevated to a central concept of organisation; the validity of the contract was assessed, for the most part, by examining whether consent was 'free'. The alignment of the Contract Act with the Will Theory was the result of two factors beyond its general foundation in 19th-century English law: the involvement of the law commission's secretary, William Macpherson, in the drafting,[18] and the borrowing from the Field Code. Yet, the hold of the Will Theory over the Contract Act was by no means absolute. Doctrines that were incompatible with the Will Theory survived,[19] as did rules which undercut the parties' will.[20] Overall, no single overarching theory infused the Act.

This can be seen in the sections on formation of contract. The commission's draft adopted the doctrine of proposal and acceptance, which had, by that time, become firmly part of English law under the influence of the Will Theory.[21] According to the doctrine, an agreement is reached when a proposal is accepted. In the Will Theory, the doctrine demonstrated that a meeting of wills had occurred. In the commission's draft, the topic was covered in two sections. Clause 3 established that a proposal to enter a contract could be retracted or altered by the proposer at any time before it was accepted,[22] while clause 4 held that a proposal did not bind the proposer unless accepted within the time prescribed.[23]

Stephen found these unsatisfactory, so he sought to define the terms 'proposal', 'promise', 'agreement', and 'contract' with greater precision. The definitions were meant to reflect what Stephen believed to be the 'natural order'[24] of contract law.[25] In distinguishing between 'proposal' and 'promise' and in analysing 'promise' as an *accepted* proposal and 'agreement' as a promise, Stephen adopted the doctrine of proposal and acceptance. The Act's direct source seems to have been John Austin's explanation of

[17] DJ Ibbetson, *A Historical Introduction to the Law of Obligations* (OUP 1999) 220–44.

[18] In W Macpherson, *Outlines of the Law of Contracts as Administered in the Courts of British India* (RC Lepage and Co 1860), Macpherson borrowed heavily from George Spence (tr), *The Code Napoleon; Or, The French Civil Code* (Hunter 1824).

[19] See eg the Contract Act, ss 2(d), 25.

[20] See eg ibid s 74.

[21] AWB Simpson, 'Innovation in Nineteenth Century Contract Law' (1975) 91 Law Quarterly Review 247, 258–62.

[22] *Second Report of Indian Law Commissioners*, Parliamentary Papers (PP), House of Commons (HC), vol XLIX (1867–68) 607.

[23] ibid.

[24] *Final Report of the Select Committee* (n 13) [14].

[25] ibid [4].

'convention' or 'agreement'.[26] Austin asserted that a 'convention' or 'agreement' properly called 'consists of *a promise* (or mutual promises) *proffered and accepted*'[27] and that 'unless the promise be accepted . . . the promise is not a convention' but '*a pollicitation*'.[28] This was a civilian distinction, which had been discussed by English treatise-writers for almost a century.[29] The effect of this was to anchor the formation model in the Contract Act, at least superficially, in a meeting of minds: as Stephen wrote, if a proposal is accepted, the parties are 'at one'; they 'agree'.[30]

While the rules on formation of contract illustrate the influence of the Will Theory, they also expose the limits of that influence. Those limits are made clear in the sections on the communication, acceptance, and revocation of proposals, found in sections 3–9. In particular, the rules on the communication of dispatched acceptances (in sections 4–5) and dispatched revocations of proposals (in sections 4–6) were based on Stephen's assessment of the balance of convenience between the parties and contradicted the results generated by a faithful application of the Will Theory. This is a reminder that the Contract Act was no pure exercise in theory-based doctrinal formulation. Any adoption was incomplete and haphazard, modified by competing considerations (of policy or principle) and operating at a level of generality rather than generating, in any perfect sense, the theory's practical conclusions.

III. Objective Test of Intention

A person's intention is assessed objectively for the purpose of determining whether that person made a proposal or acceptance.[31] The focus is on apparent rather than actual intention. Accordingly, words or acts are interpreted as understood by the reasonable person. For example, the law determines whether a statement by *A* to *B* amounts to a proposal by asking whether a reasonable person would have understood *A*'s statement to signify a willingness to do something if *B* assented to that act.

The importation of the objective test into Indian law seems to have been the result of judicial borrowing from English law outside the Contract Act.[32] The Act makes no express reference to the test. This is not as surprising as it may appear to modern eyes: although the objective approach had long lineage in English law,[33] it did not come to the forefront of juristic thinking until the late 19th century, when it was primarily treated

[26] *Report on the Indian Contract Law, 7 February 1872*, British Library (BL) Mss Eur F86/111.
[27] J Austin, *The Province of Jurisprudence Determined* (2nd edn, J Murray 1861) 296.
[28] ibid 299.
[29] Simpson (n 21) 259–60.
[30] *Final Report of the Select Committee* (n 13) [4].
[31] RY Vardhan and C Narayan, *Pollock & Mulla's Indian Contract Act and Specific Relief Acts* (15th edn, LexisNexis 2017) 118, 329–30.
[32] See eg *ITC Limited v George Joseph Fernandes* (1989) 2 SCC 1 [21] (Saikia J); *Commissioner of Wealth Tax, Bhopal v Abdul Hussain Mulla Mohammad Ali* AIR 1988 SC 1417 [10] (Venkatachaliah J); cf N Nuggehalli, 'Contract Formation in India: Law and Practice' in M Chen-Wishart, A Loke, and S Vogenauer (eds), *Studies in the Contract Laws of Asia Vol II: Formation and Third Party Beneficiaries* (OUP 2017) 65.
[33] JM Perillo, 'The Origins of the Objective Theory of Contract Formation and Interpretation' (2000) 69 Fordham Law Review 427. A version of the test is found in the Field Code (n 12) s 814.

as a rule of evidence.[34] Nonetheless, the Contract Act's language is compatible with the objective test.[35]

The objective test protects a party's reasonable reliance on the other's apparent intention, even where that conflicts with the latter's actual intention. Although this can potentially undercut the parties' will, it enhances certainty, predictability, and commercial convenience.[36]

IV. Proposal

1. What Is a Proposal?

A proposal[37] is made 'when one person signifies to another his willingness to do or to abstain from doing anything, with a view to obtaining the assent of that other to such act or abstinence'.[38]

The analytical framework in section 2 makes clear the essence of proposal. A promise, and consequently an agreement, arises when a proposal is accepted. It follows that a proposal must be capable of acceptance and must require nothing other than an acceptance to be converted into a promise. This means that what is communicated by the person making the proposal must indicate the proposer's willingness to be bound as soon as the other person accepts. For example, *A* texts *B*, 'Do you want to buy my bicycle for ₹500?' and *B* replies, 'Yes, I do.' *A*'s text is a proposal, which *B* accepts.

2. Proposal and Invitation to Treat

A proposal is different from an invitation to treat. Although the Contract Act makes no mention of invitation to treat, the concept is analytically useful in explaining what a proposal is not and, by extension, what it is. As such, it features prominently in Indian case law.

An invitation to treat is an expression of willingness to negotiate, that is, an invitation to another to make a proposal. It differs from a proposal in that what is communicated is not intended to be automatically binding upon acceptance. It is an attempt to have further discussions with a view, potentially, to reaching an agreement at a later point.

Whether a statement, or an act, is a proposal or an invitation to treat depends primarily on the intention of the party making the statement, objectively assessed. This is

[34] M Lobban, 'Contract' in W Cornish and others (eds), *The Oxford History of the Laws of England, 1820–1914: Private Law*, vol XII (OUP 2010) 338–39.

[35] This illustrates that any alignment of the Contract Act with the Will Theory was incomplete. For the same in English law, see S Waddams, *Principle and Policy in Contract Law* (CUP 2011) ch 2.

[36] M Chen-Wishart, 'Contractual Mistake, Intention in Formation and Vitiation: The Oxymoron of *Smith v Hughes*' in J Neyers and others (eds), *Exploring Contract Law* (Hart 2009) 345–47.

[37] 'Proposal' is used synonymously with 'offer'.

[38] The Contract Act, s 2(a).

essentially a question of fact. The wording used by the party to describe their statement is relevant but not conclusive.[39] A statement described as a 'proposal' or 'offer' may turn out to be an invitation to treat.[40]

In the leading case *Bank of India v OP Swaranakar*,[41] the Supreme Court held that a voluntary retirement scheme floated by a bank to its employees was an invitation to treat and not a proposal. This was because the bank reserved the right to accept or reject an employee's application, meaning that it did not signify willingness to be bound when an employee applied. It was the employee's application that constituted the proposal.

A statement may be merely supplying information and not be open to acceptance, and thus not be a proposal. For example, *B* texts *A*, 'I would like to buy your bicycle; send me your lowest price.' *A* texts back, 'Lowest price, ₹100.' *B* replies, 'I agree to buy your bicycle for ₹100.' *A*'s text is an invitation to treat, not a proposal, as *A* does not evince an intention to be bound without further negotiations.[42]

Although the distinction between a proposal and an invitation to treat is sufficiently clear, drawing it is not always easy. In some common situations, the distinction turns on the application of general rules, guided by considerations of practical convenience, rather than a search for the parties' intention. Pollock and Mulla's observation that, in such situations, 'interpretation must be largely guided . . . by business usage and common sense'[43] remains as true today as a century ago when it was made. The general rules, however, are displaceable by evidence that the parties in question objectively intended something different.

A classic illustration is the display of goods with price in a shop.[44] This is generally viewed as an invitation to treat, that is, an invitation to the customer to make a proposal to the shopkeeper, which the shopkeeper can accept or reject. Otherwise, the shopkeeper would lose the freedom not to sell to a particular customer.

A second illustration is an advertisement, for example, of goods for sale. In general, this is an invitation to treat.[45] If the advertisement is a proposal, the owner may be obliged to supply the goods to everyone who expressed willingness to buy them, even if the owner runs out of stock. Furthermore, the owner may legitimately wish to check that the other party is able to perform their obligations (eg pay) before becoming bound. Nonetheless, an advertisement may be interpreted as a proposal if it demonstrates an intention to be bound.[46] This is more likely to occur where the acceptance takes the form of performance by act. In *Har Bhajan Lal v Har Charan Lal*,[47] a father issued a pamphlet, offering a reward of ₹500 to anybody who could trace his missing

[39] *Bank of India v OP Swaranakar* AIR 2003 SC 858 [48] (Sinha J).
[40] *Adikanda Biswal v Bhubaneswar Development Authority* AIR 2006 Ori 36.
[41] *OP Swaranakar* (n 39) (relying on *Gibson v Manchester City Council* [1979] 1 WLR 294 (HL)).
[42] *Col DI MacPherson v MN Appanna* AIR 1951 SC 184 (relying on *Harvey v Facey* [1893] AC 552 (PC)).
[43] Pollock and Mulla (n 14) 47.
[44] Where no price is attached, the display is clearly an invitation to treat.
[45] *Ghaziabad Development Authority v Union of India* AIR 2000 SC 2003.
[46] See eg *Adikanda Biswal* (n 40).
[47] *Har Bhajan Lal v Har Charan Lal* AIR 1925 All 539.

son and bring him home. This was held to be a proposal to the whole world capable of acceptance by any person who fulfilled the condition.

A third illustration concerns auctions. An advertisement that an auction will take place on a specific date is an invitation to treat, not a proposal to hold it.[48] When an auctioneer presents an item for sale at an auction and invites bids, the auctioneer makes an invitation to treat. A bid made in response is a proposal.[49] The highest bid represents the final proposal.[50] When the hammer falls, the auctioneer accepts the final proposal and is taken to have rejected all preceding proposals, that is, all lower bids.[51] This analysis appears to be true even if it was stated in advance that the item will be sold to the highest bidder.[52] In this respect, Indian law differs from English law, where holding an auction 'without reserve' (thereby suggesting that it will be sold to the highest bidder) is a proposal by the auctioneer to sell the item to the highest bidder.[53] The analysis in English law aims to protect the reasonable expectations of customers but fits uneasily with the framework of proposal and acceptance. For example, in cases where the item is withdrawn, it is difficult to identify the highest bidder to whom the obligation is owed, since a bid can be retracted or outbid before it is accepted. Indian courts have been mindful of this criticism in following a different path.[54]

The final illustration relates to tenders. As a general rule, a statement inviting tenders for the sale of goods or a project is an invitation to treat.[55] It indicates readiness to receive proposals. Those submitting tenders make proposals, and the person inviting the tenders can accept one of them or reject all.[56] Whether the same analysis persists where the invitation to tender states that the highest or most favourable tender will be accepted does not seem to have been resolved in Indian law.[57]

3. Communication of Proposal

To be effective, a proposal must be communicated.[58] This proposition is based on sections 3 and 4 of the Contract Act. By section 3, derived from the Field Code,[59] the communication of a proposal is 'deemed to be made by any act or omission of the party proposing . . . by which he intends to communicate such proposal, or which has the effect of communicating it'. This can be done by words or conduct.[60] For example, the

[48] *Vishal Builders (P) Ltd v Delhi Development Authority* (1977) ILR 1 Delhi 724.
[49] This can be withdrawn at any point before the auctioneer accepts: *Agra Bank v Hamlin* (1891) ILR 14 Mad 235; *Raghunandhan Reddy v State of Hyderabad* AIR 1963 AP 110.
[50] *The Rajah of Bobbili v Akella Suryanarayana Rao Garu* (1919) ILR 42 Mad 776, 782 (Ayyar J).
[51] ibid 780 (Oldfield J).
[52] *Vishal Builders* (n 48) [16] (Rohtagi J); cf *Abdul Aziz Khan v Municipal Committee* AIR 1924 Nag 227.
[53] *Warlow v Harrison* (1859) 120 ER 925; *Barry v Davies* [2000] 1 WLR 1962 (CA).
[54] *Joravarmull Champalal v Jeygopaldas Ghanshandas* (1922) ILR 45 Mad 799.
[55] See eg *Anil Kumar Srivastava v State of Uttar Pradesh* (2004) 8 SCC 671 [12] (Kapadia J).
[56] *UP State Electricity Board v Goel Electric Stores* AIR 1977 All 494.
[57] In English law, such an invitation is treated as an offer to sell to the highest bidder: *Harvela Investments Ltd v Royal Trust Co of Canada* [1986] AC 207 (HL).
[58] *Baroda Oil Cakes Traders v Parshottam Narayandas Bagulia* AIR 1954 Bom 491.
[59] Field Code (n 12) s 766.
[60] Cf the Contract Act, s 9.

display of a weighing machine at a railway station is a proposal, which is accepted when a person inserts a coin into the slot so long as that person is unable to get their money back. By section 4, 'the communication of a proposal is complete when it comes to the knowledge of the person to whom it is made'. It follows that a proposal sent by post, email, or text takes effect only when the other party becomes aware of it.[61]

V. Acceptance

An acceptance is made 'when the person to whom the proposal is made signifies his assent thereto'.[62] The effect of the acceptance is to convert the proposal into a promise.[63] For this to happen, the acceptance must be[64]

(1) absolute and unqualified;[65]
(2) expressed in some usual and reasonable manner, unless the proposal prescribes the manner in which it is to be accepted.[66]

1. Correspondence of Acceptance with Proposal

An acceptance is an unqualified expression of assent to the terms of the proposal.[67] It must therefore correspond unequivocally and unconditionally to the terms of the proposal.

A purported acceptance, which seeks to vary the terms of the proposal, is not an acceptance but a counter-proposal. For example, *A* proposes to sell *A*'s bicycle to *B* for ₹100. *B* replies by proposing to buy it for ₹80. *B*'s reply is a counter-proposal.

A counter-proposal constitutes a new proposal, which can be accepted or rejected.[68] It signifies rejection of the original proposal. But can the original proposal be subsequently accepted by the party making the counter-proposal? There seem to be two conflicting lines of authority in Indian law. The first holds that a counter-proposal kills off the original proposal, rendering it incapable of subsequent acceptance unless reinstated.[69] The second distinguishes between a counter-proposal that is rejected by the person making the original proposal (as in *Nihal Chand*), in which case the original proposal cannot be automatically revived, and a counter-proposal that has been withdrawn before the person making the original proposal has rejected it, in which case the

[61] See eg ibid s 4, Illustration (a).
[62] ibid s 2(b).
[63] ibid s 2(b).
[64] ibid s 7.
[65] Based on the Field Code (n 12) s 770.
[66] Based on ibid s 767.
[67] See eg *Mayawanti v Kaushalya Devi* (1990) 3 SCC 1.
[68] *Haji Mahomed Haji Jiva v E Spinner* (1900) ILR 24 Bom 510, 523 (Jenkins CJ).
[69] *Nihal Chand v Amar Nash* AIR 1926 Lah 645 (relying on *Hyde v Wrench* (1840) 3 Beav 334).

original proposal stands unrejected and can be accepted as long as the acceptance is made within a reasonable time.[70] This is problematic. First, the aim of the law is to protect the reasonable expectations of the person making the original proposal, who may act in reliance on the counter-proposal, for example, by selling to someone else. Where the original proposer does not respond to the counter-proposal, it is difficult to infer an intention to keep the original proposal open. Second, under *Govindam*, the question is whether the time taken by the counter-proposer to change their mind and accept the original proposal is reasonable. This is more likely to lead to uncertainty.

The issue is best analysed by reference to the parties' intention, objectively assessed. The starting point should be that a counter-proposal terminates the original proposal and, with it, the power of the counter-proposer to accept it. This, however, is subject to the proposer, in the original proposal, or the counter-proposer, in the counter-proposal, reasonably manifesting an intention to the contrary.[71]

A counter-proposal must be distinguished from an enquiry. This typically takes the form of a request for information or clarification about available terms. An enquiry does not terminate the original proposal.[72] The distinction is therefore significant, and yet it is often a fine one to draw. It ultimately rests on the parties' intention. In general, a statement is an enquiry if it does not include words that in any way reject the proposal or put forward a firm counter-proposal.

2. Acceptance without Knowledge of the Proposal

A valid acceptance must be made in response to a known proposal. Put differently, a proposal cannot be accepted by someone with no knowledge of the existence of the proposal.[73] Although this is recognised as a cardinal principle of Indian law, it is not expressly stated in the Contract Act and is based on *Lalman Shukla v Gauri Dutt*.[74] As an authority for the proposition, however, the decision is less strong than typically accepted.

In *Lalman Shukla*, the defendant sent the plaintiff, one of his servants, to search for his nephew, who went missing. He subsequently issued handbills offering a reward of ₹501 to anyone who found the boy. The plaintiff found him, but it is unclear whether he was aware of the offer of reward when he did so. He argued that the handbills were sent to him at the place of search. The trial judge found that the offer of reward was made after he left. The High Court rejected that conclusion but found

[70] *M Govindam v Gulabchand Rawatmull* (1956) ILR 1 Cal 164.

[71] M Furmston, GJ Tolhurst, and E Mik, *Contract Formation: Law and Practice* (2nd edn, OUP 2016) [3.23]–[3.25].

[72] *Moolji Jaitha v Seth Kirodimal* AIR 1961 Ker 21; *UP State Electricity Board* (n 56).

[73] Vardhan and Narayan (n 31) 130.

[74] *Lalman Shukla v Gauri Dutt* (1913) 40 ALJ 489, applied in *Manish Kumar Sinha v M/O Home Affairs* OA No 1037/2019 (Central Administrative Tribunal, Hyderabad Bench); cf *Ganesh R v State of Tamil Nadu* MANU/TN/2911/2021 [14] (Banerjee CJ).

for the defendant on the separate ground of consideration.[75] Contrary to the explanation in standard textbooks,[76] the authority for the proposition lies not in the outcome or reasoning of the decision but in Banerji J's *obiter* comments that 'there can be no acceptance unless there is a knowledge of the offer. Motive is not essential but knowledge and intention are.'[77]

3. Appropriate Mode of Acceptance

Unless the method of acceptance is stipulated in the proposal, any words or conduct which objectively signify an unqualified expression of assent to the terms of the proposal are enough.

i. Acceptance by words or conduct

Acceptance can be made by words, oral or written. This gives rise to an 'express' promise.[78] Acceptance can also be made by conduct,[79] in which case the resulting promise is said to be 'implied'.[80]

ii. Acceptance by silence

According to section 3 of the Contract Act, an acceptance is deemed to be communicated by any act or omission by which the acceptor intends to communicate such acceptance or which has the effect of communicating it.[81] A literal reading might suggest that silence, as an omission of the acceptor, can be an adequate mode of acceptance.[82] Nonetheless, under the influence of English law, Indian courts have held, as a general rule, that silence cannot constitute acceptance.[83] Where, for example, *A* proposes to sell *A*'s bicycle to *B* for ₹100, stating that *A* would consider the bicycle sold to *B* if *A* does not hear from *B*, and *B* does not respond, there is no acceptance.

The general rule is warranted. First, it would be unfair to expect the person to whom the proposal is made to spend time and incur expenses to avoid the imposition of unsolicited contractual obligations. Second, silence is generally ambiguous, making it hard to infer from it an intention to accept.

The rule, however, is subject to exceptions. Silence may lead to acceptance where it is coupled with conduct which indicates that the person to whom the proposal is made

[75] *Lalman Shukla* (n 74) 493.
[76] A Singh, *Contract and Specific Relief* (10th edn, Eastern Book Company 2010) 10.
[77] *Lalman Shukla* (n 74) 492–93.
[78] The Contract Act, s 9.
[79] ibid ss 3, 7–9.
[80] ibid s 9.
[81] Based on the Field Code (n 12) s 766.
[82] This would be subject to the Contract Act, s 4.
[83] For cases applying *Felthouse v Bindley* (1862) 11 CB (NS) 869, see eg *Haji Mahomed Haji Jiva* (n 68); *Hindusthan Co-Operative Insurance Society v Shyam Sunder* AIR 1952 Cal 691. For other cases, see eg *Bhagwandas Govardhandas Kedia v Girdharilal Pashottamdas* AIR 1966 SC 543; *Viswesardas Gokuldas v BK Narayan Singh* AIR 1969 SC 1157.

intends to accept the proposal.[84] Silence can also amount to acceptance where there has been a prior agreement or course of dealing between the parties in the context of which it is possible to infer an intention to accept from silence.[85]

A question arises whether an exception should be recognised whenever it is the offeree who is claiming to have accepted by silence.[86] Given that the rule's aim is primarily to protect the offeree, it is arguable that it should not apply to protect a proposer who has invited acceptance by silence. The problem is that this may allow the offeree to assert or deny acceptance depending on how the contract turns out for the offeree. To counter this, it is contended that the law should recognise an exception only where an offeree who has been silent has acted in reliance on the proposal and is able to provide some evidence that the offeree accepted the proposal.

iii. Prescribed manner of acceptance

A proposer can prescribe the manner in which the proposal is to be accepted.[87] Where acceptance is not made in the prescribed manner, the proposer may insist, within a reasonable time, that the proposal is accepted in the prescribed manner. If the proposer fails to so insist, the proposer is deemed to have accepted the acceptance.[88]

4. Communication and Timing of Acceptance

The moment at which a proposal is accepted is critical. It determines not only when a promise—and therefore an agreement—is formed but also where it is formed, which can have practical consequences, for example, on jurisdiction and tax liability. The issue is primarily regulated by section 4 of the Contract Act, which provides that the communication of an acceptance is complete

> as against the proposer, when it is put in a course of transmission to him, so as to be out of the power of the acceptor;
>
> as against the acceptor, when it comes to the knowledge of the proposer.

Section 5 further states,

> An acceptance may be revoked at any time before the communication of the acceptance is complete as against the acceptor, but not afterwards.

As a general rule, acceptance of the proposal must be communicated to the proposer, and an acceptance is communicated to the proposer when it comes to the proposer's

[84] See eg *Bharat Petroleum Corporation Ltd v The Great Eastern Shipping Co Ltd* AIR 2008 SC 357.
[85] *Gaddarmal Hiralal v Chandrabhan Agarwal* AIR 1968 All 292.
[86] C Miller, 'Felthouse v Bindley Revisited' (1972) 35 Modern Law Review 489.
[87] The Contract Act, s 7(2).
[88] ibid.

knowledge. At that moment, an agreement is concluded. The general rule is subject to exceptions. One is where the acceptance is by performance of the conditions in the proposal.[89]

Another is where the acceptance is by expression of agreement and the acceptance is non-instantaneous; that is, there is a delay between transmission and reception of the acceptance. The classic example is acceptance by post. This was at the centre of contractual thinking in the 19th century and was clearly behind section 4. This dictates that the acceptance takes effects as against the proposer when the letter is posted and as against the acceptor when the letter comes to the knowledge of the proposer.

The orthodox understanding of section 4 and the accompanying section 5 has four elements. First, the agreement is concluded when acceptance of the proposal is put into a course of transmission to the proposer, that is, when the letter of acceptance is posted.[90] In this way, section 4 embraces the core of the English 'postal rule'.[91] Second, the proposer cannot revoke the proposal at any point after acceptance has been posted. Third, the risk of either a delay or loss of the letter of acceptance is on the proposer;[92] this is on the ground that the agreement is concluded when the letter is posted. Fourth, the acceptor can revoke the acceptance after the acceptor has posted it so long as the revocation reaches the proposer before the letter of acceptance.

Thus understood, the position in Indian law has attracted criticism. It has been argued that the operation of the relevant sections has 'an air of unreality' where the posted acceptance is lost and the proposer, who does not know of the acceptance, is bound, whereas the acceptor, who has posted it, is not.[93] A more fundamental criticism is that the orthodox position gravely misunderstands the operation of sections 4 and 5.[94] Properly understood, the sections prevent the proposer from being able to revoke the proposal once the acceptance has been posted but do not establish that the agreement is concluded at the moment of posting. Instead, the agreement is concluded when the posted acceptance comes to the knowledge of the proposer. Swaminathan supports this by noting that the relevant sections are based on the Scottish case *Dunmore v Alexander*,[95] which accepts both that an offeror's revocation of the offer is ineffective after the acceptance is posted and that the conclusion of the agreement depends on the arrival of the posted acceptance at the offeror's place.

Sections 4 and 5 were drafted by Stephen. His formulation did not follow the Field Code;[96] it was probably guided by (what was then) recent English authority and his view of where the balance of convenience lay. The seeds for that formulation were

[89] See section V.5 below.
[90] *Bhagwandas Goverdhandas Kedia* (n 83).
[91] ibid [10] (Shah J). For the same, see Pollock and Mulla (n 14) 31.
[92] *JK Enterprises v State of Madhya Pradesh* AIR 1997 MP 68.
[93] RN Gooderson, 'English Contract Problems in Indian Code and Case Law' (1958) 16 Cambridge Law Journal 67, 71; PH Winfield, 'Some Aspects of Offer and Acceptance' (1939) 55 Law Quarterly Review 499, 505.
[94] S Swaminathan, 'The Will Theorist's Mailbox: Misunderstanding the Moment of Contract Formation in the Indian Contract Act, 1872' (2018) 39 Statute Law Review 14.
[95] *Dunmore v Alexander* (1830) 9 S 190. In this, Swaminathan follows Pollock and Mulla (n 14) 33, though, unlike him, they embrace the orthodox understanding of the relevant sections.
[96] Field Code (n 12) s 768 held that the contract was complete as soon as a letter of acceptance was put into the post office.

planted by the law commission. The explanation to clause 3 in their draft provided that a proposal is accepted when acceptance is posted so long as no revocation of the acceptance reaches the proposer before or at the same time as the posted acceptance reaches the proposer.[97] The reference to the simultaneous arrival of the posted acceptance and its revocation might suggest that the commission was aware of *Dunmore v Alexander* as that was what the case ultimately decided. However, it is also true that the position in English law was far from settled. While a line of authority applied the postal rule,[98] other cases adopted a more ambivalent position. For example, in *Potter v Sanders*,[99] Wigram VC suggested that the posting of a letter of acceptance concluded the contract, unless its progress had been interrupted. The law commission's chairman, Lord Romilly MR, was counsel in the case and, in the years immediately after the publication of the commission's draft, became a leading voice from the bench against the application of the postal rule.[100] Whether Romilly's invisible hand was responsible for the provisions in the commission's draft is impossible to tell.

At the time of Stephen's redrafting, the latest word on the matter in English law was *British and American Telegraph Co v Colson*.[101] Kelly CB held that where a letter of acceptance was posted, the proposer was only bound when the letter was received by the proposer, unless the non-receipt was the proposer's fault.[102] He further held that when the letter was received, it was retrospectively effective from the moment it was posted.[103] Stephen's thinking, laid bare in an article he published after his return to England, was along the same lines.[104] Stephen enumerated rules that 'any authority competent' would lay down to 'dispose of very nearly all the questions' raised with respect to posted acceptances. The rules unsurprisingly echoed the language used in the Contract Act. According to those rules, a posted acceptance was complete as against the proposer 'as soon as the letter of acceptance is posted, if the letter of acceptance reaches the proposer'. If the letter was lost without either party's fault, 'the proposal shall be deemed to have been refused'; that is, no agreement was formed. If the letter was delayed without either party's fault, the proposal ought to be deemed to be accepted when the letter was posted, unless the delay was so long as to be equivalent to its loss. If the loss or delay was due to the acceptor's fault, the acceptor ought to be responsible for it. Finally, the acceptance could be withdrawn before or when the acceptance reached the proposer, but the proposer was not affected until the withdrawal came to the proposer's knowledge.[105] Stephen thought that to reach the desired result,

[97] *Second Report of Indian Law Commissioners* (n 22) 607.
[98] *Adams v Lindsell* (1818) 1 B & Ald 681; *Dunlop v Higgins* (1848) 1 HL Cas 381 (HL).
[99] *Potter v Sanders* (1846) 6 Hare 1.
[100] *Re Constantinople and Alexandria Hotel Co, Finucane's Case* (1869) 17 WR 813; *Re Constantinople and Alexandria Hotel Co, Reidpath's Case* (1870) LR 11 Eq 86; cf *In re National Savings Bank Association, Hebb's Case* (1867) LR 4 Eq 9. See further S Gardner, 'Trashing with Trollope: A Deconstruction of the Postal Rules in Contract' (1992) 12 Oxford Journal of Legal Studies 170.
[101] *British and American Telegraph Co v Colson* (1871) LR 6 Ex 108. See also *Re Imperial Land Co of Marseilles, Townsend's Case* (1871) LR 13 Eq 155.
[102] *British and American Telegraph Co* (n 101) 111.
[103] ibid 116. *Colson* was disapproved and the postal rule affirmed in *Re Imperial Land Co of Marseilles, Harris's Case* (1872) LR 7 Ch App 587; *Household Fire and Carriage Accident Insurance v Grant* (1879) 4 Ex D 216.
[104] JF Stephen, 'Law and Science', *Pall Mall Gazette* (18 November 1874) 4.
[105] ibid 5.

it was necessary to explain away part of *Dunlop v Higgins* and to supply missing links in *Colson*.[106] It is not far-fetched to suggest that Stephen's explanation of his thinking makes explicit what is left implicit in the Contract Act. If this is so, it becomes clear that Stephen's understanding of the relevant provisions goes against their orthodox understanding in Indian law influentially supported, among others, by Pollock and Mulla.[107]

The reasons why Stephen adopted this position are also made clear in the article. This was based on the balance of convenience between the two parties. According to Stephen,

> if a man gets no answer to a proposal after waiting for a reasonable time, he naturally concludes that it is declined, and he can take no precautions against the loss of another man's letter. It would be very hard . . . to bind him by a letter which he had not received . . . [W]hen a man accepts a proposal by post he has ready and simple ways of learning whether his letter has been received in due course, and by sending it in duplicate or by using the telegraph he can render its loss practically impossible or immaterial. The consequence, therefore, should fall upon him if the letter is lost.[108]

Overall, Swaminathan's explanation of the operation of sections 4 and 5 is closer to the understanding of their draftsman. The Contract Act was not intended to embrace the postal rule. Accordingly, under the Act, a posted acceptance should not conclude an agreement when it is posted but, instead, when it is delivered. This means that if the letter never arrives, there should be no agreement. Although the Contract Act makes no mention of this, it is submitted that this is what was intended. The true effect of the moment of posting an acceptance is to prevent the proposer from being able to revoke the proposal.

This is analytically more convincing than the orthodox understanding. It explains logically why a posted acceptance can be withdrawn if the withdrawal reaches the proposer before or at the same time as the posted acceptance. To the contrary, the rule in the Contract Act is difficult to align with the postal rule without analytical violence.

This analysis is also preferable on policy grounds. Many of the justifications given for the postal rule have now been discredited.[109] The issue is ultimately one of commercial convenience. Both the favoured analysis and the postal rule protect the offeree from the risk that the proposer will revoke the proposal after the offeree sent the acceptance; the difference relates to the risk that the letter gets lost. It is contended that, in such a case, the balance of convenience rests in favour of placing the risk on the offeree.[110]

Three situations warrant further examination. The first is where there is instantaneous communication while the parties negotiate in each other's presence. No delay

[106] ibid 5.
[107] Pollock and Mulla (n 14).
[108] Stephen, 'Law and Science' (n 104) 5.
[109] M Chen-Wishart, *Contract Law* (7th edn, OUP 2022) 73–75.
[110] International Institute for the Unification of Private Law (UNIDROIT) Principles of International Commercial Contracts, art 2.1.6(2); Scottish Law Commission, *Report on Review of Contract Law* (2018) (Scot Law Com No 252) 4.86–4.90.

exists between transmitting and receiving the acceptance, and the parties can readily detect and remedy any failure of communication. In such a case, acceptance takes effect when it comes to the knowledge of the proposer.[111]

The second situation is where there is instantaneous communication, but the parties are not in each other's presence, for example, when they negotiate by telephone. In *Bhagwandas Goverdhandas Kedia v Girdharilal Parshottamdas*,[112] the Supreme Court was asked to decide the place where the contract was formed, as that would determine which court had jurisdiction to hear the dispute. The acceptor was in Khamgaon when he accepted by telephone, while the proposer was in Ahmedabad. Relying on Denning LJ's judgment in *Entores Ltd v Miles Far East Corporation*,[113] Shah and Wanchoo JJ in the majority held that telephonic communications were essentially instantaneous communications, like face-to-face communications, and as such were governed by the general rule; section 4 of the Contract Act did not apply. They further held that there were no reasons of expedience to justify its application: failures of communication in telephonic conversations tend to be instantly detectable and easily remediable. It followed that the agreement was concluded when the acceptance was communicated to the proposer at Ahmedabad, meaning that the Court there had jurisdiction. It is submitted that the Court reached the right decision for the wrong reason: section 4 does apply, but, properly understood, it supports the Court's conclusion.[114]

The third situation is where there is one-way instantaneous method of communication, that is, where there is no simultaneous communication. In this case, the message arrives almost instantaneously, but the recipient does not necessarily access the message instantaneously. Examples include using a telex, fax, or email. Indian courts have applied *Bhagwandas Goverdhandas* and held that acceptances in the form of a telex[115] or fax[116] are completed when received by the proposer. A similar idea seems to apply to emails.[117] In turn, this gives rise to questions as to what constitutes receipt. It is suggested that the same analysis should be adopted as for revocation of proposals.[118]

5. Acceptance by Performance of Conditions

A proposal may be accepted by performing the conditions in the proposal.[119] The relevant section was lifted almost verbatim from the Field Code.[120] It sets in place what

[111] Vardhan and Narayan (n 31) 132, relying on *Firm Kanhaiyalal v Dineshchandra* AIR 1959 MP 234. This is in line with the analysis of section 4 adopted here.
[112] *Bhagwandas Goverdhandas Kedia* (n 83).
[113] *Entores Ltd v Miles Far East Corporation* [1955] 2 QB 327 (CA).
[114] Swaminathan (n 94) 25.
[115] *Triveni Oil Field Service Ltd v Oil and Natural Gas Commission* AIR 2006 Del 331.
[116] *Quadricon Pvt Ltd v Bajararang Alloys Ltd* AIR 2008 Bom 88.
[117] *PR Transport Agency v Union of India* AIR 2006 All 23; *Trimex International FZE Ltd Dubai v Vedanta Aluminium Ltd, India* (2010) 3 SCC 1 [10]. Electronic contracts are subject to the Information Technology Act 2000. See, in particular, ss 10A, 13.
[118] See section VI below.
[119] The Contract Act, s 8.
[120] Field Code (n 12) s 769.

other common law jurisdictions commonly refer to as a 'unilateral' contract, under which only one party has outstanding obligations. The classic illustration is a proposal to pay someone if that person does a specific act; the doing of the act constitutes the acceptance. For example, *A* proposes to give a reward to anyone who finds and returns *A*'s lost bicycle. *B* finds and returns the bicycle to *A*. *B* has accepted *A*'s proposal and is entitled to the reward.[121] Section 8 is to be read alongside section 7,[122] meaning that the offeree's conduct must be such that it signifies that the offeree's acceptance is unequivocal and without reservation.[123]

Given that acceptance is made by performing the stipulated act, there is no need for communication beyond the performance of that act. This is because the proposer has impliedly waived the need for express communication of the acceptance.[124]

The main difficulty in these cases lies in determining when the proposal can be revoked, which, in turn, depends on when the proposal can be said to be accepted. Suppose *A* proposes to pay *B* ₹500 if *B* runs and finishes the Indian marathon. Can *A* revoke *A*'s proposal when *B* has almost completed the marathon on the basis that *B* has not fully performed the conditions in the proposal? It is arguably unjust for the law to allow this where *B* is willing and able to run the whole distance.[125] The injustice is found in *B*'s reliance, which *A* induced, and the potential that *A* might derive a benefit free of charge from *B*'s partial performance.

The Contract Act does not define 'performance of the conditions of a proposal'. Therefore it is unclear whether complete performance is required or partial performance is adequate. The Indian Law Commission suggested revising the Act in line with the recommendation put forward by the English Law Revision Committee in 1937.[126] According to this, the proposal constitutes a contract as soon as the offeree has entered upon the performance of the stipulated act, unless the proposal contains an express or implied term that it can be revoked before the act's completion.[127] Under this, *B* accepts *A*'s proposal by starting to run the marathon, but *B* is not entitled to the ₹500 unless and until *B* finishes it. This is not without problems. First, an act of partial performance might not always be sufficiently unequivocal to constitute acceptance. Second, it would be hard to work out commencement where the offeree is asked to abstain from doing something.

A different approach is to hold that the proposal is accepted upon completion of the performance, but the proposer is under an implied obligation not to revoke the proposal once the offeree has commenced performance.[128] Under this, *B* accepts *A*'s

[121] See eg *Har Bhajan Lal* (n 47).
[122] *Union of India v Babulal Uttamchand Bhandari* AIR 1968 Bom 294 [9].
[123] *Bhagwati Prasad Pawan Kumar v Union of India* (2006) 5 SCC 311.
[124] *The State of Bihar v Bengal Chemical and Pharmaceutical Works Ltd* AIR 1954 Pat 14; *Hindusthan Co-Operative Insurance Society v Shyam Sunder* (n 83), citing with approval *Carlill v Carbolic Smoke Ball Co Ltd* [1893] 1 QB 256 (CA) 269–70 (Bowen LJ).
[125] HW Ballantine, 'Acceptance of Offers for Unilateral Contracts by Partial Performance of Service Requested' (1921) 5 Minnesota Law Review 94. For the opposite view, see *Mobil Oil Australia Ltd v Lyndel Nominees Pty Ltd* (1998) FCA 205, 224.
[126] Law Revision Committee, *6th Interim Report* (Cmd 5449, 1937) [39].
[127] Law Commission (India), *Contract Act 1872* (Law Com R No 13, 1958) [32]; *Errington v Errington* [1952] 1 KB 290 (CA); *Soulsbury v Soulsbury* [2007] EWCA Civ 949.
[128] *Daulia v Four Millbank Nominees* [1978] Ch 231 (CA).

proposal when *B* finishes the marathon, but once *B* has started running, *A* has an implied obligation not to revoke the proposal. The approach draws a distinction between full acceptance, which gives rise to an agreement, and a more limited acceptance, which prevents revocation of the proposal. While it requires a somewhat complicated analysis, this arguably provides the most satisfactory solution.

VI. Revocation of Proposal

A party denying the existence of a contract may argue that, although there was a valid proposal, it ceased to exist by the time that it was purported to be accepted. Revocation of proposals is regulated by sections 5 and 6 of the Contract Act. Section 5 deals with the *timing* of the revocation. It provides that 'a proposal may be revoked at any time before the communication of its acceptance is complete against the proposer, but not afterwards'.[129] This means a proposal can be revoked before the offeree accepts or despatches the acceptance. For example, where *A* proposes to sell *A*'s car to *B* and *B* accepts the proposal by a letter sent by post, *A* may revoke *A*'s proposal at any time before *B* posts a letter of acceptance.[130]

Section 6 deals with the *method* of revocation.[131] It provides that a proposal is revoked:

(1) by the communication of notice of revocation by the proposer to the other party;
(2) by the lapse of the time prescribed in such proposal for its acceptance, or, if no time is so prescribed, by the lapse of a reasonable time, without communication of the acceptance;
(3) by the failure of the acceptor to fulfil a condition precedent to acceptance; or
(4) by the death or insanity of the proposer, if the fact of his death or insanity comes to the knowledge of the acceptor before acceptance.

As to what constitutes communication of notice of revocation in section 6(1), section 4 provides that 'the communication of a revocation is complete

> as against the person who makes it, when it is put into a course of transmission to the person to whom it is made, so as to be out of the power of the person who makes it; as against the person to whom it is made, when it comes to his knowledge.

[129] Copied from the Field Code (n 12) s 771.
[130] The Contract Act, s 5 (illustration).
[131] Copied from the Field Code (n 12) s 772.

This establishes that an offeree cannot accept a proposal if the revocation of the proposal has come to the offeree's knowledge. The cumulative effect of sections 4–6 has been held to be that a proposal is revoked if the revocation comes to the offeree's knowledge before or at the moment when the offeree has despatched the acceptance.[132]

The position might, in truth, be more complicated. The Act seems to suggest that the proposer is bound by the revocation, in the sense that the proposer cannot claim there is an agreement, when the proposer posts a letter revoking the proposal. The decision to give some effect to revocation on dispatch appears to be traceable to the Field Code.[133] For Will Theorists like Pothier, there was no contract where an offer was withdrawn without communication before it was accepted because the consent necessary to form an agreement was lacking.[134] Pothier pursued the consent-based reasoning to its rational conclusion. The Contract Act did not: the refusal to rule that uncommunicated revocation was absolutely effective (binding both parties) signified the limits of any influence that the Will Theory had.

Difficult questions can potentially arise in respect of the communication of notice of revocation. What if, for example, a fax revoking the proposal arrives on the offeree's fax machine, but the offeree fails to read it? Or a message is left in the voicemail, but the offeree does not listen to it? Read literally, section 4 seems to require nothing short of knowledge by the offeree, meaning that the revocation does not take effect against the offeree. Such a conclusion is problematic where the proposer acts reasonably in communicating a notice of revocation, and the full responsibility for failure to become aware of it lies with the offeree. It is submitted that where the offeree is solely responsible for not receiving or becoming aware of the revocation, the offeree should be precluded from denying that the revocation has been communicated. This would require interpreting 'knowledge' in section 4 in a way that goes beyond its literal meaning to encompass 'constructive knowledge', that is, cases where the offeree should have known about the notice of revocation.[135] Similarly, in cases where the proposal is made to the public at large (eg an offer of reward), it should be sufficient for the proposer to take reasonable steps to bring the revocation of the proposal to the notice of the persons to whom it was addressed, for example, by communicating the revocation in the same way as the initial proposal. Again, this would require an expansive interpretation of 'knowledge' in section 4.

[132] *Firm Kanhaiya Lal* (n 111); *Sadhoo Lal Motilal v State of Madhya Pradesh* AIR 1972 All 137.

[133] Field Code (n 12) ss 772, 768. In the 1860s and 70s, English law seemed open to revocation being effective at posting: *Hebb's Case* (n 100); *Townsend's Case* (n 101). This was reversed in *Byrne & Co v Leon Van Tienhoven & Co* (1880) 5 CPD 344.

[134] RJ Pothier, *Treatise on the Contract of Sale* (LS Cushing tr, Charles Little and James Brown 1839) 18–19. This was subject to the offeror's liability to indemnify the offeree who relied on the offer.

[135] Cf *Entores* (n 113); *Brinkibon Ltd v Stahag Stahl* [1983] 2 AC 34 (HL).

VII. The Limits of Proposal and Acceptance

1. General Position

In *Deep Chandra v Ruknuddaula Shamsher Jang Nawab Mohammad Sajjad Ali Khan*,[136] Seth J stated, 'the theory of "offer and acceptance" has received statutory recognition in this country, so that, every contract must originate in a proposal and every transaction to be recognised as a contract must, in its ultimate analysis, resolve itself into a proposal and its acceptance'. This suggests that the framework of proposal and acceptance enshrined in the Contract Act is of universal application, and Indian courts must determine whether a contract is formed by fitting the varying factual circumstances within it.[137]

The framework's aim is to determine whether there is *consensus* between the parties that may lead to a contract. As a creation of late-18th- and 19th-century thinking, it was a legal response to contemporary realities. Contract-making practices have changed significantly in the past two centuries. One reason is the emergence of standard-form contracts, whose use pre-dated the Contract Act but has exploded since.[138] Another is the expansion in the variety of goods and services that form the subject matter of contracts and the development and commercial use of technology, such as the Internet. The increased complexity with which contracts are now made and communicated has led judges and commentators to acknowledge that the analysis of agreement through proposal and acceptance can sometimes be artificial and 'forced'.[139] Indeed, it would be naïve to expect every real-life transaction to be perfectly accommodated within proposal and acceptance. Life is complex, and transactions in the real world do not follow, *pace* James Fitzjames Stephen, a 'natural order'.

Nevertheless, the framework of proposal and acceptance found in the Contract Act remains sound. The framework can accommodate most forms of contract making with tolerable clarity. It provides a degree of certainty as lawyers can determine, without much difficulty, its basic rules and can advise parties with confidence.[140] This is so even if specific rules within that framework need to be revisited. At the same time, the framework should be applied flexibly and as the main, not exclusive, way of establishing a contract.[141] The Contract Act should not be viewed as an obstacle to this. The Act was

[136] *Deep Chandra v Ruknuddaula Shamsher Jang Nawab Mohammad Sajjad Ali Khan* AIR 1951 All 93 [24], cited in eg *Bhagwati Enterprises v Rajasthan State Road Transport Corporation* AIR 2006 Raj 233 [13] (Sharma J).

[137] There *may* be situations where Indian courts can analyse formation of contract without recourse to this framework. For discussion of the English case of *Clarke v Earl of Dunraven (The Satanita)* [1897] AC 59 (HL), in which this was arguably done, see *Dharam Dass Hiralal v Manik Lal Kanhaiya Lal* MANU/MP/0208/1955; *State of Bihar v Inderchand Jain* AIR 1968 Pat 171 [6]; cf A Pathak, *Contract Law* (OUP 2011) 100.

[138] O Prausnitz, *The Standardization of Commercial Contracts in English and Continental Law* (Sweet & Maxwell 1937); JN Adams, 'The Standardization of Commercial Contracts, or the Contractualization of Standard Forms' (1978) 7 Anglo-American Law Review 136.

[139] *New Zealand Shipping v AM Satterthwaite and Co Ltd (The Eurymedon)* [1975] AC 154 (PC) 167 (Lord Wilberforce).

[140] J Morgan, *Contract Law Minimalism* (CUP 2013) 222; cf SJ Bayern, 'Offer and Acceptance in Modern Contract Law: A Needless Concept' (2015) 103 California Law Review 67.

[141] See also Vardhan and Narayan (n 31) 34–36.

never intended to be a complete code, and there are many areas in which the courts have developed the law either by applying the Act's provisions flexibly or operating outside it.

2. 'Battle of Forms'

Questions about the limits of proposal and acceptance arise acutely in the context of the 'battle of forms'. Businesses commonly use standard-form contracts to set out the general terms upon which they wish to transact. Such pre-printed terms are often in conflict with those of other businesses. A 'battle of forms' arises when two businesses purport to make a contract by an exchange of conflicting proposals contained in their own standard terms. For example, *A* offers to buy goods from *B* on a form that includes *A*'s standard terms. *B* confirms the sale on a form that includes *B*'s standard terms and delivers the goods. *A*'s standard terms vary materially from those of *B*. Has a contract been formed and, if so, on what terms?

The answer rests on the application of the rules of proposal and acceptance in the Contract Act. In a 'battle-of-forms' scenario, the courts must be able to find a proposal by one party that is unequivocally accepted by the other. If they can, an agreement will be formed on the terms set out in the last proposal; if they cannot, there will be no agreement. This is called the 'last-shot' approach because the party who makes the last proposal typically wins: given that there is no correspondence in the documents exchanged between the parties, the last document will usually be regarded as a proposal accepted by the conduct of the other party when it acts in accordance with that document.

The analysis of the 'battle of forms' through the framework of proposal and acceptance can generate arbitrary results and may not reflect the reasonable expectations of *both* parties. It may also fail to correspond to commercial reality and how parties act in practice.[142] This prompted Lord Denning MR, in his minority judgment in *Butler Machine Tool Co Ltd v Ex-Cell-O Corporation (England) Ltd*,[143] to adopt an alternative approach under which the courts determine, first, whether a contract is formed by examining if there is agreement on 'all material facts', and second, the terms of the contract by considering the documents as a whole and, if necessary, by 'reasonable implication'.[144] Lord Denning's approach, however, has been rejected by English courts on the grounds that it undermines commercial certainty and undercuts party autonomy.[145]

While Indian courts have not considered the issue at length, the position is analogous to English law by virtue of the operation of the Contract Act.[146] An approach

[142] R Rawlings, 'The Battle of Forms' (1979) 42 Modern Law Review 715.
[143] *Butler Machine Tool Co Ltd v Ex-Cell-O Corporation (England) Ltd* [1979] 1 WLR 401 (CA).
[144] See also UNIDROIT Principles of International Commercial Contracts, arts 2.1.1, 2.1.22; US Uniform Commercial Code, §2-207.
[145] *Gibson* (n 41).
[146] Cf S Khanderia, 'International Approaches as Plausible Solutions to Resolve the Battle of Forms under the Indian Law of Contract' (2019) 8 Global Journal of Comparative Law 1.

based on proposal and acceptance is defensible but should not be applied in an excessively rigid way. Where the documents exchanged between the parties and their overall conduct clearly indicate that they intended their relationship to be governed by other terms, those terms should be given effect.[147]

VIII. Conclusion

The enactment of the Contract Act in 1872 by the legislative council was a cause for celebration. The Act was hailed as 'the most lucid, simple, sound and workable law of contract, so far as it goes, which exists in any country and in any tongue'.[148] The judgement of writers, however, has mostly been different. In his monumental work on Anglo-Indian codification, Whitley Stokes reserved some of his harsher words for the Contract Act. Its provisions, he wrote, 'are so incomplete and sometimes so inaccurately worded that the time seems to have come for repealing the Act, and re-enacting it with . . . amendments in arrangement, wording and substance'.[149]

Notwithstanding its limitations, the Contract Act has stood the test of time. In many respects, this is a significant feat. As a product of its own times, the Contract Act embodied the values of classical contract law. These are evident in the rules on formation of contract. In the past century-and-a-half, however, there have been considerable changes in the methods of contracting and communicating. These have placed the rules in the Contract Act under pressure. Indian contract law has coped through a process of flexible application of the rules and external supplementation, mostly by rules of English law, at the hands of the courts. The process of adaptation has not been without problems. The assumption that the Contract Act reflected English law is not always safe. Nor are assumptions about the contemporary state of English law, which was often more fluid than it later appeared. At the same time, the supplanted rules were primarily concerned with protecting the reasonable expectations of the parties, rather than ensuring their meeting of mind. This was no insurmountable problem as many of the Contract Act's rules did the same: the Act had no all-embracing theory. All in all, the Contract Act has proved to be a far-sighted statute. At the age of 150, it remains a living instrument: a text of the past alive in the present, serving the needs of a people that is as diverse—geographically, religiously, socially, and economically—as when the Act was enacted. This is indeed a cause for celebration.

The future is likely to increase the pressure on the rules in the Act. If anything, the methods of contracting and communicating will continue to change rapidly. Indian law will have to deal with difficult questions that will inevitably arise. One approach is to revisit the Act, in the light of its history, and examine afresh whether it provides

147 See eg *Tekdata Interconnections Ltd v Amphenol Ltd* [2009] EWCA Civ 1209.

148 'Meeting of 9 April 1872', Abstracts of the Proceedings of the Council of the Governor General of India, Assembled for the Purpose of Making Laws and Regulations, vol 11, 1872 (Robinson) 359, British Library (BL) IOR/V/9/12.

149 W Stokes, *The Anglo-Indian Codes* (Clarendon Press 1887) 534.

an answer. This has been suggested in respect of dispatched acceptances. A second approach is to adopt a flexible and creative reading of the Act's provisions.[150] This would be profitable in respect of the communication of the revocation of proposal and the 'battle of forms'. Nonetheless, there are limits to how far the Act's language can apply. A third approach, therefore, is to seek solutions outside it. This is aided by the fact that the Act was never intended to be a complete code, providing an answer to every eventuality.[151] Solutions of this type can take the form of judicial law-making or separate legislation. These offer a way of dealing with revocation of proposals which are accepted by performance of conditions or when an agreement can be reached without the use of proposal and acceptance. A fourth approach is to revise the Contract Act. This would facilitate its comprehensiveness and strengthen its position as the doctrinal pivot for the future development of Indian contract law. It would also be in line with the intention of those who drafted the Act.[152] 'To suppose', Stephen wrote, 'that any code will go on by itself for ever is like supposing that a railway can be built which will not want repairs.'[153]

[150] A Briggs and A Burrows, *The Law of Contract in Myanmar* (OUP 2017) 44.
[151] The Contract Act, Preamble; *Irrawaddy Flotilla Co v Bugwan Das* (1891) LR 18 IA 121 (PC) [11] (Macnaghten J).
[152] *First Report of Indian Law Commissioners*, PP, HC, vol 16 (1864) 367.
[153] Stephen, 'Codification in India and England' (n 10) 668. See further, 'Recommendation of the Civil Justice Committee' (1925), National Archives of India (NAI) Home Department, Judicial Proceedings Nos 296/I-41/25; Law Commission (India) (n 127).

6

Consideration

*Nigam Nuggehalli and Ragini Surana**

I. Introduction

In the law of contract, the term 'consideration' is used to designate the price or value exchanged under the contract.[1] The doctrine of consideration enjoys a pride of place in the common law of contract and sets it apart from its civilian counterpart.[2] The doctrine of consideration has also been highly contentious. Attempts to abolish it can be traced all the way back to Lord Mansfield.[3] However, along with the doctrines of offer and acceptance, consideration continues to form a part of the 'indivisible trinity' that come together in the idea of a bargain.[4] Consideration is also an integral part of the contract law of India.[5] Under section 10 of the Indian Contract Act 1872 (hereinafter 'the Contract Act') in order to be enforceable, an agreement must be made for lawful consideration. Consideration is also framed as a negative requirement for the validity of an agreement. Section 25 of the Contract Act declares any agreement without consideration void. Section 2(d) of the Act defines consideration as under

> (d) When, at the desire of the promisor, the promisee or any other person has done or abstained from doing, or does or abstains from doing, or promises to do or to abstain from doing, something, such act or abstinence or promise is called a consideration for the promise.

* The authors would like to thank Abhinav Shankarraman (JGLS) for his excellent research assistance. We would also like to thank Shivprasad Swaminathan for his detailed comments on earlier drafts of the chapter. All errors remain our own.

[1] H Beale and others (eds), *Chitty on Contracts*, vol I (34th edn, Sweet & Maxwell 2021) 480 (hereinafter *Chitty*).

[2] H Beale and others (eds), *Cases, Material and Text on Contract Law* (Hart 2019) 344; A von Mehren, 'Civil Law Analogues to Consideration' (1959) 72 Harvard Law Review 1009.

[3] *Pillans & Rose v Van Mierop & Hopkins* (1765) 3 Burr 1663; R Wright, 'Ought the Doctrine of Consideration to Be Abolished from the Common Law?' (1936) 49 Harvard Law Review 1225; JA Phang, 'Consideration at the Crossroads' (1991) 107 Law Quarterly Review 21.

[4] CJ Hamson, 'The Reform of Consideration' (1938) 54 Law Quarterly Review 233, 234.

[5] N Nuggehalli, 'Contract Formation in India: Law and Practice' in M Chen-Wishart and others (eds), *Studies in the Contract Laws of Asia Vol II: Formation and Third Party Beneficiaries* (OUP 2017) 64.

Nigam Nuggehalli and Ragini Surana, *Consideration* In: *Foundations of Indian Contract Law.* Edited by: KV Krishnaprasad, Niranjan Venkatesan, Shivprasad Swaminathan, and Umakanth Varottil, Oxford University Press. © Oxford University Press 2024.
DOI: 10.1093/9780191997211.003.0006

Traditionally, in English law, in order to be seen as consideration, an act or promise must be such that it amounts to a 'benefit' to one and a 'detriment' to the other.[6] The 'benefit' and 'detriment' in this formulation refer to the same act or promise viewed from the perspective of the promisor and the promisee.[7] Sometimes, this formula is reduced to requiring only a 'detriment' to one without requiring a corresponding benefit to the other.[8] However, courts have also found valid consideration where one party receives a benefit without a corresponding detriment to the other.[9] This conception of consideration as corresponding benefit and detriment is also the one adopted by Indian courts to define consideration.[10] Although a closer look at the definition under section 2(d) shows the absence of the terms 'benefit', 'detriment', or their equivalent in defining consideration, Indian courts and commentators have adopted them along with the traditional definition.[11] Thus, as per the latest edition of *Pollock and Mulla*, '[c]onsideration for a promise may consist in either some benefit conferred on the promisor, or detriment suffered by the promisee, or both'. This move has been criticized by those who argue that the Indian statute's departure from English law was aimed at abolishing the difficulties associated with the doctrine; and that the definition under section 2(d) therefore corresponds with the wider, more subjective notion of consideration that prevailed in courts of equity.[12] However, this innovation has largely been ignored in India, and courts have adopted the traditional 'benefit'/'detriment' formula.[13] Similarly, although the requirement that consideration be 'valuable in the eyes of law' does not find explicit mention in the Contract Act, Indian courts have read it into the definition of consideration.[14] Also significant are the Indian Law Commission's comments that the idea of 'legal value' is inherent to the concept of consideration.[15] A landmark case in this regard is that of *Curie v Misa*, where it was held that forbearance to sue on a valid claim would be good consideration.[16] In coming to this conclusion, the House of Lords held that

[6] *Curie v Misa* (1875–76) LR 1 App Cas 554 (Lush J).

[7] E Peel (ed), *Treitel on the Law of Contract* (14th edn, Sweet & Maxwell 2015) 1056 (hereinafter *Treitel on the Law of Contract*).

[8] The formulation is usually attributed to Christopher Columbus Langdell: JB Ames, 'Two Theories of Consideration I' (1899) 12 Harvard Law Review 515. For its application in India, see RY Vardhan and others (eds), *Pollock and Mulla: The Indian Contract Act, 1872* (16th edn, Lexis Nexis 2022) 49 (hereinafter *Pollock and Mulla* (16th edn)) 51; *Kulasekaraperumal v Pathakutty Thalevanar* [1961] AIR Mad 405 (Madras High Court).

[9] *Chitty* (n 1) 480; *Treitel on the Law of Contract* (n 7) 1057; *O'Sullivan v Management Agency & Music Ltd* [1985] QB 428, 459.

[10] *Pollock and Mulla* (16th edn) (n 8); *Suresh v Ganesh* [2017] 6 AIR Bom 442 (Bombay High Court) (monetary benefit or sacrifice in kind); *Chidamber Iyer v PS Renga Iyer* [1966] 1 SCR 168 (Supreme Court of India).

[11] *Pollock and Mulla* (16th edn) (n 8) 51.

[12] S Swaminathan, 'Eclipsed by Orthodoxy: The Vanishing Point of Consideration and the Forgotten Ingenuity of the Indian Contract Act 1872' (2017) 12 Asian Journal of Comparative Law 141, 156.

[13] ibid 153.

[14] *Chidamber Iyer* (n 10); *Swarampudi Nagaratnamba v Kunuku Ramayya* [1968] AIR SC 253 (Supreme Court of India); *Kulasekaraperumal* (n 8).

[15] *13th Law Commission of India Report, Indian Contract Act 1872* (1958) <https://cdnbbsr.s3waas.gov.in/s3ca0daec69b5adc880fb464895726dbdf/uploads/2022/08/2022080532.pdf> accessed 16 October 2023.

[16] *Curie* (n 6) (House of Lords); *Pollock and Mulla* (16th edn) (n 8) 50.

> The giving time is only one of many kinds of what the law calls consideration. A valuable consideration, in the sense of the law, may consist either in some right, interest, profit, or benefit accruing to the one party, or some forbearance, detriment, loss, or responsibility, given, suffered, or undertaken by the other.[17]

An exchange of promises or mutual promises are always good consideration for each other.[18] Perhaps the most common example of this is the contract of guarantee.[19] The decision of *Curie v Misa* was relied upon by the Supreme Court of India in the case of *Chidamber Iyer v PS Renga Iyer*.[20] The Court held that the promisee (a family-run charitable trust), by refraining from enforcing its rights under the family settlement deed, had provided valuable consideration for the payment. It must also be noted that Indian courts have adopted the requirement that consideration must be real, although it is not necessary that it should be adequate.[21] These rules are discussed in greater detail in section III below.

There exist both 'formal' and 'substantive' justifications for the doctrine. The formal justification focuses on its evidentiary and cautionary function.[22] The presence of consideration ensures that only those bargains that have been seriously considered by the parties are enforced by courts.[23] A corollary to the evidentiary role that consideration plays in a legal system is that often contracts that meet certain formal requirements are exempt from the requirement of consideration.[24] It was this line of reasoning that Lord Mansfield used in his favour to justify abolishing the requirement of consideration for contracts in writing entered into by merchants.[25] However, this was overturned by the House of Lords[26] The drafters of the Indian statute also attempted to incorporate this rule into the Contract Act, although it did not make its way into the final version.[27] Fragments of the abolished rule survive in section 25(1) of the Contract Act, whereby contracts made out of natural love and affection are exempt from the requirement of consideration if they are in writing and have been registered.[28] The 'substantive' justification put forth in favour of the doctrine points to the role that it has in ensuring reciprocity of exchange.[29] Consideration represents the legal system's values

[17] (1875) 10 LR Exch 153, 162 (House of Lords); the decision of *Curie v Misa* (n 6) was adopted by the Supreme Court of India in the case of *Chidamber Iyer* (n 10).

[18] *Pollock and Mulla* (16th edn) (n 8); *Firm Gopal Company v Firm Hazarilal Company* [1963] AIR MP 37 (Madhya Pradesh High Court).

[19] *Haigh v Brooks* (1840) 10 A&E 323 (Exchequer Chamber). In the Contract Act, contracts of guarantee are dealt with by the Contract Act, s 222 and therefore this question does not arise.

[20] *Chidamber Iyer* (n 10); *Munnalal v Duklo* [1924] AIR Nag 149 (Nagpur Judicial Commissioner's Court).

[21] *Kulasekaraperumal* (n 8).

[22] von Mehren (n 2) 1016–17.

[23] L Fuller, 'Consideration and Form' (1941) 41 Columbia Law Review 799, 800–801; PS Atiyah, 'Consideration: A Restatement' in PS Atiyah, *Essays on Contract* (OUP 1990) 194, 241.

[24] *Treitel on the Law of Contract* (n 7) 1054, 1267 (Promises in deeds).

[25] *Pillans & Rose* (n 3); DJ Ibbetson, *A Historical Introduction to the Law of Obligations* (OUP 1999) 205–206.

[26] (1778) 2 ER 18.

[27] Clause 10, Exception I, Law Commission for India, *Second Report of the Indian Law Commissioners on the Substantive Laws of India* (Parliamentary Papers, House of Commons 1866) 8–9; Swaminathan (n 12) 142.

[28] Contract Act, s 25(1).

[29] *Treitel on the Law of Contract* (n 7) 1054; Atiyah (n 23) 205; M Chen-Wishart, 'In Defence of Consideration' (2013) 13 Oxford Journal of Legal Studies 209.

in terms of the bargains it believes are worth enforcing. Thus, the existence of the doctrine signals a legal system's belief that the receiver of a purely one-sided promise or a gratuitous promise does not have as compelling a reason warranting the law's interference.[30] Others see within the doctrine of consideration the courts' normative decision regarding which promises should be enforced by a legal system.[31] An interest in ensuring reciprocity also informs the requirement that consideration must be 'something of value in the eyes of the law'.[32]

The Contract Act begins with a statement that it is a legislation that both defines and amends the English law of contract.[33] Indian courts generally look to their English counterparts in order to interpret as well as fill in gaps left by the Act.[34] It is for this reason that we begin our analysis of consideration in Indian contract law by noting how the Contract Act interacts with English common law.

II. Historical Background and Indian Beginnings

The common law history of the doctrine of consideration has given rise to as much debate as its continued existence.[35] Most of the rules that form a part of the doctrine, and are discussed below, have been traced to its development between 1580 and 1600.[36] In its initial manifestation, consideration set out the inducement or motive of the transaction.[37] Absent a well-formed law of contract, consideration not only explained the motive behind the undertaking but also determined whether an action would lie for its breach.[38] As the 17th and 18th centuries progressed, a model of contract that focused on the element of consensus over exchange emerged.[39]

It is only in the 19th century that we find the concept that forms a part of the modern law of contract.[40] This branch of the law underwent a systemization of its doctrines under the auspices of the 'Will Theory' of contract. The Will Theory, as expounded in works of continental jurists such as Robert Joseph Pothier, theorized contracts as expressions of parties' wills, which should be respected by the law. The theory was at odds with the doctrine of consideration, which ostensibly saw reason for enforcement in the

[30] On other kinds of limits on enforceability, see von Mehren (n 2).

[31] Atiyah (n 23) 193–94; Chen-Wishart, 'In Defence of Consideration' (n 29).

[32] *Treitel on the Law of Contract* (n 7) 1054; *Thomas v Thomas* (1842) 2 QB 851, 859 (Queen's Bench).

[33] The Preamble to the Contract Act states 'Whereas it is expedient to define and amend certain parts of the law relating to contracts'.

[34] *Irrawaddy Flotilla Co v Bhagwandas* (1891) 18 ILR Cal 620 (Privy Council); *Naresh Chandra Guha v Ram Chandra Samanta* [1951] AIR Cal 93 (Calcutta High Court).

[35] JH Baker, 'Origins of the "Doctrine" of Consideration' in M Arnold and others (eds), *On the Laws and Customs of England: Essays in Honour of SE Thorne* (University of North Carolina Press 1981) 336–37.

[36] ibid 341–50.

[37] AWB Simpson, *A History of the Common Law of Contract: The Rise of the Action of Assumpsit* (Clarendon Press 1975) 320–21.

[38] Baker (n 35) 342.

[39] Ibbetson (n 25) 202–203.

[40] AWB Simpson, 'Innovations in Nineteenth Century Contract Law' (1975) 91 Law Quarterly Review 247; Ibbetson (n 25) ch 12; W Swain, *Contract 1670–1870* (CUP 2015) ch 8; M Horwitz, 'The Historical Foundation of Modern Contract Law' (1974) 87 Harvard Law Review 917; P Hamburger, 'The Development of Nineteenth-Century Consensus Theory of Contract' (1989) 7 Law and History Review 241.

exchange between the parties.[41] This resulted in some discontent felt by English lawyers with the doctrine of consideration.[42] It was under the influence of the Will Theory that the Contract Act was drafted.[43] Although, in their report, the drafters of the Act recorded an intention to get rid of the doctrine of consideration, this intention was not carried out in the final draft of the statute.[44] A commitment to the Will Theory remains in the capacious terms in which section 2(d) of the Act defines consideration.[45]

In England, the problem of consideration was referred to the Law Revision Committee, led by Lord Wright, whose report appeared in 1937.[46] Following Mansfield's proposal, the Committee recommended making all contracts in writing enforceable, even when they were not made for valuable consideration.[47] The recommendations of the Law Revision Committee were not, however, given effect. In 1958, when the Indian Law Commission undertook the task of revising the Contract Act, it also took into account the recommendations made by the Law Revision Committee as well as the criticism of the doctrine put forth by both English and US commentators.[48] However, like the English Committee, it felt unable to recommend complete abolition of the doctrine.[49] Instead, it recommended adding more exceptions to those already existing under section 25 of the Act to avoid certain particularly anomalous situations,[50] namely, those where there is detrimental reliance on a promise that lacks consideration.

III. Scope of the Doctrine

In what follows, we discuss the scope of the doctrine in terms of some basic rules.

1. Adequacy

Although consideration must be 'valuable' in the eyes of law, it need not be substantial, adequate, or equivalent to the value exchanged.[51] In other words, courts do not compare the value of the things exchanged in order to determine the validity of a transaction. This is to avoid entering into an enquiry regarding the subjective motives behind the transaction.[52] Nor is it important that the consideration in question cannot be easily

[41] Swaminathan (n 12) 146.
[42] Swain, *Contract 1670–1870* (n 40) 186.
[43] W Swain, 'Contract Codification and the English: Some Observations from the Indian Contract Act 1872' in J Devenney and M Kenny (eds), *The Transformation of European Private Law: Harmonisation, Consolidation, Codification or Chaos?* (CUP 2013) 192; Swaminathan (n 12) 146–47.
[44] *Second Report of the Indian Law Commissioners on the Substantive Laws of India* (n 27) 4, 8.
[45] Swaminathan (n 12) 152.
[46] Law Revision Committee, *Sixth Interim Report: Statute of Frauds and the Doctrine of Consideration* (Cmd 5449 1937) (hereinafter *Sixth Interim Report*).
[47] *Pillans & Rose* (n 3); *Sixth Interim Report* (n 46) 18.
[48] *13th Law Commission of India Report* (n 15) 4–8.
[49] *Sixth Interim Report* (n 46) 17–18.
[50] *13th Law Commission of India Report* (n 15) 6.
[51] *Chitty* (n 1) 488–96; *Treitel on the Law of Contract* (n 7) 1054; *Thomas* (n 32).
[52] *Haigh* (n 19).

converted to an ascertainable amount of money. Thus, used chocolate wrappers to be returned to the manufacturer in order to claim a prize were held to constitute adequate consideration.[53] As discussed earlier, even forbearance or abstinence from doing something will be good consideration. Thus, where an acceptor of a bill of exchange was allowed time in order to procure a replacement bill, it was held that the trouble of suspending legal action was sufficient consideration.[54] Baron Parke observed that 'it is not for us to estimate whether the bargain was a good one or not'.[55] The fact that the law does not look into the value of the consideration exchanged has prompted commentators to conclude that the law is not as committed to ensuring an exchange as the existence of a doctrine of consideration would suggest.[56]

The second part of the Explanation to the provision shows that the rule regarding non-interference is not absolute. A significant disparity between the values exchanged may create a presumption regarding the unfairness of the transaction.[57] This rule has been reproduced under section 25 of the Contract Act. As per Explanation 2 of said provision,

> An agreement to which the consent of the promisor is freely given is not void merely because the consideration is inadequate; but the inadequacy of the consideration may be taken into account by the Court in determining the question whether the consent of the promisor was freely given.

However, in order to impugn the transaction, the element of coercion, undue influence, or fraud must be separately alleged and proven. In keeping with this principle, the Supreme Court in *Dharampal v State of UP* held that, in the absence of an allegation of fraud, it would not interfere in a sale of shares by the company under liquidation merely on the grounds of inadequacy of price.[58]

Great disparity in the values exchanged may also affect how the court uses its discretionary powers. Thus, the equitable relief of specific performance may be refused if there is a large disparity between the values exchanged. Where land valued at ₹9 lakhs was sold for ₹1.5 lakhs, although no fraud could be proven, the Court refused to grant specific performance of the agreement to sell and awarded monetary compensation instead,[59] although specific relief would not be denied on the mere grounds of an escalation in price of the property after the contract was made.[60] In another case, the Court

[53] *Chappell v Nestle* [1960] AC 87 (House of Lords).
[54] *Moss v Hall* (1850) 5 Ex 46 (Exchequer Chamber).
[55] ibid 49 (Exchequer Chamber).
[56] Atiyah (n 23) 192–93; The debate is explored in greater detail in Nuggehalli (n 5) 77.
[57] Contract Act, s 25, explanation 2; *Pollock and Mulla* (16th edn) (n 8) 65–66, 465–66; *Chitty* (n 1) 494; *Treitel on the Law of Contract* (n 7) 1074; *Thomas* (n 32) 1056–63; SM Waddams, 'Unconscionability in Contracts' (1976) 39 Modern Law Review 369, 388.
[58] *Alote Estate v RB Seth Hiralal Kalyanmal* [1970] 1 SCC 425 (Supreme Court of India); cf Insolvency and Bankruptcy Code 2016, s 45 (India).
[59] *Surendra Singh v Sanjeev* (2018) 6 Allahabad Weekly Cases 5470 (Allahabad High Court); *Jayakantham v Abaykumar* [2017] 5 SCC 178 (Supreme Court of India).
[60] *Ramathal v Maruthathal* [2018] AIR SC 340 (Supreme Court of India).

was willing to disregard a strict application of the parol evidence rule under section 92 of the Indian Evidence Act in cases where consideration seemed inadequate. Thus, where the Court found that the consideration recorded in the deed was 'grossly inadequate', it allowed evidence of additional consideration to be proved.[61]

Finally, courts may look into the adequacy of the consideration where it seems as if the transaction is designed to evade an existing statutory or legal rule. For example, the prohibition on individual members of a Hindu Undivided Family from alienating their share by way of gift cannot be overcome by providing inadequate consideration for the transaction.[62] However, where the Court found that the transferee had incurred actual detriment in terms of a promise to pay existing debts, as well as maintaining the transferor's mother, the transfer was enforceable.[63] Sometimes, a statute may itself impose restrictions on dispositions made either gratuitously or for a nominal consideration. For example, under the Gift Tax Act 1958, 'consideration' was read to mean 'adequate' consideration.[64] Thus, transfers for inadequate consideration would be considered gifts in cases where the tax authorities believed that the value of the property at the date of the transfer significantly exceeded the value of the consideration exchanged.[65]

2. Consideration Must Not Be Illusory

As discussed earlier, in order to be valid, consideration must have 'value' in the eyes of the law. A corollary to this is the rule that consideration must not be illusory.[66] These phrases address several issues. First, consideration must have some economic value. Thus, feelings of 'love and affection' or any 'spiritual benefit' one may receive do not amount to valid consideration for a transaction.[67] These are better described as the 'motive' behind the transaction and are therefore considered to be different from consideration.[68] Thus, section 25 imposes the additional requirement of registration for cases where consideration for the promise is the love and affection existing between parties.[69] This rule does not imply a value equal to the promise or performance being exchanged.[70] As discussed earlier, relinquishment of a doubtful claim, when made in good faith, is valuable consideration.[71] An example of consideration that is illusory

[61] *Srimati Kasturi Bai v Ramlal Pandey* (1961–62) 66 CWN 8 (Calcutta High Court).
[62] *Rottalla Runganatham Chetty v Pulicat Ramasami Chetty* (1903) 27 ILR Mad 162 (Madras High Court).
[63] *Kulasekaraperumal* (n 8).
[64] *Keshub Mahindra v Commissioner of Gift-Tax* (1968) 70 ITR Bom 1 (Bombay High Court).
[65] ibid.
[66] *Pollock and Mulla* (16th edn) (n 8) 63; *Treitel on the Law of Contract* (n 7) 1088; *Thomas* (n 32) (consideration is different from motive).
[67] *Sonia Bhatia v State of UP* [1981] 2 SCC 585 (Supreme Court of India); *Sakuntala v State of Haryana* [1979] AIR SC 843 (Supreme Court of India); *Thomas* (n 32).
[68] *Subhash Chandra v Nagar Mahapalika* [1984] AIR All 228 (Allahabad High Court); *Debi Saran Koiri v Nandalal Chubey* [1929] AIR Pat 591 (High Court of Patna).
[69] Contract Act, s 25(1).
[70] See the discussion on Adequacy in section III.1 above.
[71] *Ranganayakamma v KS Prakash* [2008] 15 SCC 673 (Supreme Court of India).

can be found in a passage from the decision of the Madras High Court in the case of *Muthukaruppa Mudali v Pi Mu Kathappudayan*:

> For instance, if B asks his friend A to take Rs. 5 from A's left-hand pocket and put it into A's right-hand pocket and A accordingly transfers the money from his left-hand pocket into his right-hand pocket, A suffers no detriment at all by complying with that request of B. It would be against common sense to hold that A's above act at B's request will be good consideration for B's signing a promissory note in favour of A for Rs. 1000.[72]

Sometimes, arrangements that seem gratuitous may be found to have been made for good consideration. This was found to be the case for 'complimentary' parking services provided by a hotel.[73] The Supreme Court of India found that while no direct fees was paid for the parking service, the high tariffs charged by the hotel for rooms, food, and beverage would suffice as a detriment to the customer. Further, provision of such a service was beneficial to the hotel because it could have the effect of attracting more customers.[74] They therefore found that the contract of bailment between the hotel and its customers was not gratuitous but made for valid consideration.

The phrase 'nominal consideration' has been used to describe situations where the amount specified is so small that it is clearly only made to circumvent the requirement of consideration.[75] These typically involve situations where the question of whether there is consideration is mixed up with questions regarding the adequacy of consideration.[76] Therefore, it becomes important to distinguish between nominal consideration and consideration that is merely inadequate or even grossly inadequate.[77] The fact that the value of the property sold far exceeds the value of the consideration given for it does not, in itself, make the consideration 'nominal'.[78] In *John Tinson v Surjeet Malhan*, the Supreme Court of India held that the consideration of Re 1 did not amount to valuable consideration under the Act.[79] The case has been criticized by the current editors of *Pollock and Mulla* as being wrongly decided and ignoring the provisions of the Act.[80]

[72] *Muthukaruppa Mudali v Pi Mu Kathappudayan* (1914) 27 MLJ 249 (Madras High Court); Nuggehalli (n 5) 77.
[73] *Taj Mahal Hotel v United India Insurance* (2020) AIR SC 597 (Supreme Court of India).
[74] ibid [18.7].
[75] *Chitty* (n 1) 492; *Treitel on the Law of Contract* (n 7) 1071–73.
[76] *Chitty* (n 1) 493; *Treitel on the Law of Contract* (n 7) 1071–73.
[77] *Midland Bank Trust v Green* [1981] AC 513 (House of Lords).
[78] *Westminster City Council v Duke of Westminster* (1991) 23 HLR 174.
[79] [1997] AIR SC 1411 (Supreme Court of India).
[80] *Pollock and Mulla* (16th edn) (n 8) 66.

3. Pre-existing Legal Duty Rule

For an act or forbearance to amount to a 'benefit' or 'detriment' for the purposes of the doctrine of consideration, its performance must not be already legally due.[81] Thus, one of the limitations imposed by the doctrine of consideration on the enforceability of arrangements entered into by consenting parties is that the law does not enforce agreements to do what one was already bound to do by law or contract. This is sometimes called the 'pre-existing duty' rule.[82] It is believed that since the party in question is already bound by law to perform a certain act, its performance does not accrue to the 'benefit' of the promisor; nor does the subsequent promise or performance of an existing legal duty add to the 'detriment' of the promisee.[83] The resulting act or promise is therefore neither a 'benefit' nor a 'detriment' to either of the parties. The Indian Law Commission was of the view that the pre-existing duty rule did not apply in India because of the provisions of section 62 of the Act.[84] A similar conclusion was reached by Andrew Burrows and Adrian Briggs when analysing the same provision of the Contract Act of Myanmar.[85] Indian courts have, nevertheless, applied the pre-existing duty rule in some situations.

In order to understand the extent of the rule and subsequent qualifications to its scope imposed by courts, we distinguish the cases based on the nature of the pre-existing duty. The categories considered are (a) where the new promise is for performance already owed to the promisee under an existing contract, (b) where the new promise of performance is to do something already owed to a third-party under a contract with them, and (c) a promise to perform a duty the promisor is bound by law to perform.

i. Duty owed to promisor

The strictest application of the pre-existing duty rule is to be found in cases where the original duty is already owed by the promisee to the promisor under a prior contract between the parties.[86] A classic statement of this rule can be found in Sir Frederick Pollock's *Principles of Contract*:

> neither the promise to do a thing nor the actual doing of it will be a good consideration if it is a thing which the party is already bound to do either by the general law or by a subsisting contract with the other party.[87]

[81] *Chitty* (n 1) 510; *Treitel on the Law of Contract* (n 7) 1106; FMB Reynolds and GH Treitel, 'Consideration for the Modification of Contracts' (1965) 7 Malaya Law Review 1.
[82] *Treitel on the Law of Contract* (n 7) 1106; *Pollock and Mulla* (16th edn) (n 8) 66.
[83] *Chitty* (n 1) 510; *Treitel on the Law of Contract* (n 7) 1106; *Pollock and Mulla* (16th edn) (n 8) 66.
[84] *13th Law Commission of India Report* (n 15) 8.
[85] Myanmar Contract Act 1872; A Briggs and A Burrows, *The Law of Contract in Myanmar* (OUP 2017) 166.
[86] *Chitty* (n 1) 513; *Treitel on the Law of Contract* (n 7) 1111–15.
[87] F Pollock, *Principles of Contract* (10th edn, Stevens & Sons 1936) cited in *Firm Gopal Company* (n 18).

Application of the pre-existing duty rule often comes up in situations where there has been what can be described as a 'one-sided' modification of the contract. Its origins have been traced to the case of *Stilk v Myrick*.[88] The case involved a variation to the original agreement between crew members and the captain of a ship, whereby the latter agreed to pay a higher rate of wages for the continuing crew members to complete the voyage when a few crew members deserted. The Court rejected the claim for additional wages because it found that the subsequent promise was without consideration. The crew members did not incur any detriment in addition to their existing obligation under the original hire contract. The pre-existing duty rule has come under sharp criticism.[89] The rule's critics often point out that the decision in *Stilk v Myrick* was perhaps motivated by the desire of the Court to deter similar negotiations at the performance stage, an issue that can be addressed today by the doctrine of economic duress.[90] The dissatisfaction with the pre-existing duty rule has reflected in calls for law reform in England.[91]

Despite calls for its abolition,[92] the pre-existing duty rule continued to be legal orthodoxy in the United Kingdom until as late as 1980.[93] The 1989 decision of the Court of Appeal in *William v Roffey Brothers* has significantly diluted its scope.[94] The case involved a contract for carpentry services. However, the carpenters ran into financial difficulty and realized they would not be able to finish. To ensure timely completion, the contractor offered to pay an amount in addition to the original price agreed. However, they later refused to pay the additional amount, claiming that since the promise was in exchange for something the carpenters were already bound to provide, there was no consideration for the promise to pay the additional amount. The Court of Appeal took the view that *Stilk v Myrick* was outdated and no longer protected the concerns it had once addressed, that is, economic duress.[95] According to the Court, the 'benefit' a party derives from a transaction may not always be valuable in the eyes of law, as was the case for promises to perform a pre-existing duty. However, such renegotiation may involve a 'practical' or factual benefit to the promisee in the form of some commercial advantage. By relying on the idea of a 'factual' rather than a legal benefit, the Court avoided having to overturn established authority.

The decision in *William v Roffey Brothers* has been questioned by a differently constituted Court of Appeal,[96] as well as in Supreme Court dicta.[97] The basis of the doubts raised is the opinion of the House of Lords in *Foakes v Beer*,[98] which is seen

[88] (1809) 2 Camp 317 (King's Bench); *Chitty* (n 1) 513; *Treitel on the Law of Contract* (n 7) 1106.
[89] *Sixth Interim Report* (n 46) 22; *Chitty* (n 1) 513–14; *Treitel on the Law of Contract* (n 7) 1272.
[90] *Chitty* (n 1) 513–14, 518; *Treitel on the Law of Contract* (n 7) 1113–14; *Pao On v Law Yiu Long* [1980] AC 614 (Privy Council); Reynolds and Treitel (n 81) 5.
[91] *Sixth Interim Report* (n 46); R Halson, 'Opportunism, Economic Duress and Contractual Modifications' (1991) 107 Law Quarterly Review 649.
[92] *Sixth Interim Report* (n 46) 18–22.
[93] *Pao On* (n 90).
[94] *William v Roffey Brothers* [1989] 1 QB 1 (Court of Appeal).
[95] ibid; cf M Chen-Wishart, 'A Bird in Hand: Consideration and Contractual Modification' in A Burrows and E Peel (eds), *Contract: Formation and Parties* (OUP 2010) 89, 110–111.
[96] *In re Selectmove Ltd* [1995] 1 WLR 474 (Court of Appeal).
[97] *MWB Business Exchange Ltd v Rock Advertising Ltd* [2018] UKSC 24, [2019] AC 119, 131.
[98] (1884) 9 App Cas 605 (House of Lords).

as specifically opposing the inclusion of a practical benefit as good consideration.[99] It remains open to Indian courts to take a broader view on the basis of the decision in *William v Roffey Bros.*[100] The current editors of *Pollock and Mulla* argue that the 'practical benefit' rule allows a party to rely on their own breach to establish consideration.[101] Other commentators argue that the subjective idea of consideration found in section 2(d) avoids the difficulty altogether.[102] An Indian analogue to *Stilk v Myrick* can be found in *Lalman v Gauri Dutt.*[103] The promisee sought to claim a public reward offered by his employer to locate his missing nephew. Rejecting the employee's claim, the Court found that the promisee was already under an obligation under the employment agreement to exert himself to find the missing nephew and, hence, the promise to reward him for it was unenforceable for want of consideration. An agreement whereby an advocate was to receive fees in addition to that provided under a *vakalatnama* was without consideration.[104] This is because the new agreement was for services already due under the *vakalatnama.* Similarly, a subsequent agreement to reduce the rate of interest on the original loan, where made without additional consideration, could not be enforced.[105]

ii. Duty owed to third party

An important qualification to the pre-existing duty rule has been carved out in cases where the promise is made to a third party to do something that the promisor is already liable to do under a separate contract with another person.[106] Where the pre-existing duty is due under a contract with another person, the subsequent promise brings into existence a contract with valid consideration.[107] Identifying the jurisprudential basis for this exception to the pre-existing duty rule has not been straightforward, and scholars of eminence such as William Anson have highlighted some of its difficulties.[108] The subsequent promise is taken to impose on the promisee an additional detriment as they are now open to additional liability in the form of a suit from the third party in addition to the duty that they previously owed. It also provides the new promisor with a benefit they never enjoyed, that is, the right to directly enforce a promise.[109]

It is believed that some articulation of the exception can be found as early as 1600 in *Slade's Case.*[110] However, the widely regarded landmark cases on the point are *Shadwell*

[99] *MWB Business Exchange Ltd* (n 97).
[100] Nuggehalli (n 5) 81.
[101] *Pollock and Mulla* (16th edn) (n 8) 68.
[102] Swaminathan (n 12) 152.
[103] [1913] 40 ALJ 489 (Allahabad High Court).
[104] *Ramchandra Chintaman v Kalu Raju* (1878) 2 ILR Bom 362 (Bombay High Court).
[105] *Rudra Pratap Singh v Ballabh Das* [1948] AIR Oudh152 (High Court of Oudh).
[106] *Chitty* (n 1) 513–14; *Treitel on the Law of Contract* (n 7) 1113–14; *Pollock and Mulla* (16th edn) (n 8) 67.
[107] *Firm Gopal Company* (n 18).
[108] WR Anson, *Principles of the English Law of Contracts* (8th edn, Macmillan & Co 1895) 109–11; cf JB Ames, 'Two Theories of Consideration II' (1899) 13 Harvard Law Review 29, 31; For a full account of the debate, see AG Davis, 'Promises to Perform an Existing Duty' (1937) 6 Cambridge Law Journal 202.
[109] *New Zealand Shipping v AM Satterthwaite & Company Limited* (*The Eurymedon*) [1974] UKPC 4, 8 (Privy Council).
[110] 3 Bulst 1 (Exchequer Chamber); Ames, 'Two Theories of Consideration I' (n 8).

v Shadwell[111] and *Scotson v Pegg*.[112] In the latter, the defendant had purchased coal from *B*, who was to receive said coal from the plaintiff under a separate sales contract. In order to fulfil its obligation to supply the coal, *B* asked the defendant to take the coal from the plaintiff.[113] When the plaintiff failed to deliver the coal, the defendant offered an additional amount in order to get the expected delivery. However, once the coal was delivered, the defendant refused to pay the additional amount on the grounds that there was no consideration for its agreement with the plaintiff. The Court found that the delivery of the coal amounted to a benefit to the defendant regardless of the fact that the plaintiff was already bound to do so under its contract with *B*. This is because it ensured unconditional delivery to the defendant without a dispute regarding its rights under their respective contracts or the risk of bankruptcy of the parties involved.[114] Modern authority for this rule can be found in the Privy Council's decisions in the cases of *New Zealand Shipping v AM Satterthwaite*[115] and *Pao On v Lau Yiu Long*.[116]

This qualification to the pre-existing duty rule was adopted by Indian courts in the case of *Firm Gopal Company v Firm Hazarilal Company*.[117] The plaintiff had entered into a contract for the purchase of cloth from the defendant's principal. The defendant had also signed the original sales contract as guarantee brokers. Later, the plaintiff refused to take delivery of the full amount under the contract on account of a drastic fall in the price of cloth. In response, the defendant gave it the option of paying a certain sum of money to exit the contract. However, it later contended that the offer to exercise this option lacked consideration and would not be enforced against it. In coming to this conclusion, the High Court of Madhya Pradesh relied on the decision in *Scotson v Pegg* as well as the writings of English authors such as Fredrick Pollock and William Anson.[118]

iii. Public duty/duty imposed by law

Where the pre-existing duty consists of a public duty or a duty imposed by law, a subsequent promise to perform the duty will lack consideration as the promisor is already bound to perform the act.[119] Thus, an agreement by a public officer to perform their duty is invalid for lack of consideration.[120] A common example of this aspect of the rule is an agreement to remunerate someone for the inconvenience incurred as a result of them acting as a witness in court proceedings.[121] Duties imposed by the personal law of the parties, such as maintenance of children, will also be taken into account when

[111] (1860) 9 CB (NS) 159 (Common Pleas).
[112] *Scotson v Pegg* (1861) 6 H&N 295 (Court of Exchequer).
[113] ibid.
[114] ibid 299–300.
[115] *New Zealand Shipping* (n 109).
[116] [1979] UKPC 17 (Privy Council).
[117] *Firm Gopal Company* (n 18).
[118] ibid.
[119] *Chitty* (n 1) 511; *Treitel on the Law of Contract* (n 7) 1107.
[120] *Wathen v Sandys* (1811) 2 Camp 640 (Assize); *Morris v Burdett* (1808) 1 Camp 218 (Assize).
[121] *Chitty* (n 1) 511; *Collins v Godefroy* (1831) 1 B&Ad 950 (King's Bench); *P Sashannah Chetti v P Ramasamy Chetti* (1868) 4 Mad HC Rep 7 (Madras High Court).

determining whether a pre-existing duty exists.[122] Indian courts have taken a different position when it comes to consideration for these kinds of arrangements.[123] In relation to such arrangements, the Supreme Court has held, on multiple occasions, that the mutual adjustment of rights as well as the settlement of disputes was valid consideration.[124] Generally, a wider conception of benefit and detriment is adopted when assessing the consideration for family settlements.[125]

4. *Pinnel's Rule*

According to *Pinnel's rule*, an agreement to accept payment of a lesser sum on a larger debt is without consideration.[126] The rule can be traced back to the case of *Pinnel v Cole*[127] and was adopted into modern English contract law by the House of Lords in *Foakes v Beer*.[128] It is closely related to the pre-existing duty rule.[129] The common law's approach here can be seen as somewhat pedantic and technical because, while it takes the view that it is not possible for an arithmetically lesser sum to be a satisfaction to the plaintiff for a greater sum, it also allows for the gift of a horse, hawk, or robe and the like to be regarded as good consideration. The problem brought up in this case, similar to that discussed under the pre-existing duty rule, is whether fresh consideration is required to vary the terms of a contract. In these cases, however, the term sought to be varied is regarding what constitutes performance sufficient to discharge the contract.

Like the pre-existing duty rule, this rule has also been subject to criticism.[130] Lord Blackburn, in *Foakes v Beer*, pointed out that a creditor may, in fact, acquire a 'practical' benefit from accepting a smaller sum in having received a part of the sum and avoiding the risk of the debtor's possible bankruptcy. Section 63 of the Contract Act abolishes *Pinnel's rule* for Indian contracts.[131] As per section 63,

> **Promisee may dispense with or remit performance of promisee**—Every promisee may dispense with or remit, wholly or in part, the performance of the promisee made to him, or may extend the time for such performance, or may accept instead of it any satisfaction which he thinks fit.

[122] *Ward v Byham* [1956] 1 WLR 496 (Court of Appeal); *Williams v Williams* [1957] 1 WLR 148, 151–53 (Court of Appeal).

[123] *Sukha v Ninni* (1966) AIR Raj 163 (Rajasthan High Court); *Vennangot Anuradha Samir v Vennangot Mohandas Samir* [2015] 16 SCC 596 (Supreme Court of India).

[124] *Ram Charan Das v Girja Nandini Devi* [1965] 3 SCR 841(Supreme Court of India); *Kale v Deputy Director of Consolidation* [1976] 3 SCR 202 (Supreme Court of India); *Maturi Pullaiah v Maturi Narasimham* (1966) AIR SC 1836 (Supreme Court of India).

[125] *Pollock and Mulla* (16th edn) (n 8) 62.

[126] *Chitty* (n 1) 558; *Treitel on the Law of Contract* (n 7) 1185.

[127] [1602] 5 Co Rep 117 (Common Pleas).

[128] *Foakes* (n 98).

[129] *Chitty* (n 1) 558; *Treitel on the Law of Contract* (n 7) 1184.

[130] *Treitel on the Law of Contract* (n 7) 1246–47; *Collier v Wright* [2007] EWCA (Civ) 1329 [3]–[5] (Court of Appeal).

[131] Ames, 'Two Theories of Consideration I' (n 8) 525; Swaminathan (n 12) 152; Swain, 'Contract Codification and the English' (n 43).

The absence of the requirement of consideration is noteworthy and signifies the intention of the drafters of the Act to abolish the requirement when it came to discharge of agreements.[132] In this regard, the Supreme Court of India has held that 'accord and satisfaction' refers to discharge of a contract by substituted performance.[133] The agreement whereby the original obligation is discharged is called 'accord', and the discharge of the substituted obligation by its performance is called 'satisfaction'.[134] Whether the payment of a certain sum amounts to satisfaction is a question of fact that is decided based on the surrounding circumstances.[135] At the time the Act was enacted, Indian commentators were quick to point out that section 63 had the effect of dispensing the requirement of consideration for variation of contracts.[136] However, the significance of the abolition of *Pinnel's rule* in India is diluted by a qualification read into section 63 by Indian courts.[137] According to this qualification, section 63 abolishes the requirement of consideration where the party actually dispenses with performance under the original contract. However, it has no application where the dispensation is to happen in the future. Thus, a promise to dispense with the requirement of full performance must be supported by consideration.[138] This 'dilution' of section 63 seems unwarranted in light of the broad language used by the legislature for both sections 62 and 63. This view is supported by the *Report of the Indian Law Commission*[139] as well as High Court decisions that adopt an alternative interpretation of the provision.[140]

Although often discussed in relation to the doctrine of consideration, because of the operation of the pre-existing duty rule, the rules dealing with variation of contracts are actually rules regarding discharge. The Contract Act reflects this by putting these rules in the chapter dealing with performance of contracts rather than their formation. One of the ways that a contract can be 'discharged' is by both parties agreeing to dissolve the agreement.[141] Often, the agreement to rescind or vary will 'generate' its own consideration in terms of a change in the rights and liabilities of the parties under the contract.[142] Under English law, in cases where a wholly executory contract is rescinded and neither party is in breach, the benefit and the detriment for both can be found in the agreement by the other to not enforce their rights under the original contract.[143] However, where the new agreement only involves one party giving up its rights, the agreement fails to generate its own consideration and must be supported by additional

[132] *Pollock and Mulla* (16th edn) (n 8) 751.
[133] *National Insurance Company v Boghara Polyfab* [2009] 1 SCC 267 [27] (Supreme Court of India).
[134] ibid.
[135] *Shyamnagar Tin Factory v Snow White Food Product* [1965] AIR Cal 541 (Calcutta High Court); *Digambar Das v Harendra Narain Pande* (1914) 20 CLJ 112 (Calcutta High Court) affirmed in *Citi Bank v Standard Chartered Bank* [2004] 1 SCC 12 (Supreme Court of India); *Pollock and Mulla* (16th edn) (n 8) 753.
[136] F Pollock and D Mulla, *The Indian Contract Act, With a Commentary, Critical and Explanatory* (2nd edn, Sweet & Maxwell 1909) 272.
[137] Nuggehalli (n 5) 82.
[138] *Mirriyala China Subbaraidu v Kallarsu Mahadeva Rao* [1965] AIR AP 171 (Andhra Pradesh High Court); *Ramaswami v Rudrappa* (1939) AIR Mad 688 (Madras High Court).
[139] *13th Law Commission of India Report* (n 15) 78.
[140] *Jitendra Chandra Banerjee v SN Roy* (1943) AIR Cal 181 (Calcutta High Court).
[141] *Chitty* (n 1) 522; *Treitel on the Law of Contract* (n 7) 1184.
[142] *Treitel on the Law of Contract* (n 7) 1181–82 (rescission), 1186 (variation).
[143] ibid 1256–58.

consideration.[144] Here, it may be useful to consider the statute's provision on novation and variation. The provision is as under

> **62. Effect of novation, rescission, and alteration of contract.**—If the parties to a contract agree to substitute a new contract for it, or to rescind or alter it, the original contract, need not be performed.

It is believed that while section 62 applies to variation affecting the rights and liabilities of both parties to the agreement, section 63 applies in situations where the variation has the effect of reducing one person's liability under the original agreement.[145] In this regard, it is also believed that section 63 embodies the doctrine of waiver.[146] By permitting remission or waiver of performance in this way, Indian law requires neither consideration nor an agreement to constitute waiver.[147]

5. Firm Offer Rule

A 'firm offer' refers to a stipulation in the offer allowing the offeree a specific amount of time to reply.[148] In order to be valid, such a stipulation must be supported by consideration.[149] Where the promisor stipulates that the offer is open for a certain period of time and there is consideration to support the stipulation, the offer becomes irrevocable. Failure to keep the offer open for the period stipulated entitles the promisee to sue for breach of the option.[150]

In 2003, in the case *State Bank of India v OP Swarnakar*, the Supreme Court of India affirmed the applicability of the rule to Indian law.[151] The case concerned a retirement scheme advertised by the appellant banks. Under the said scheme, employees who chose to retire early were entitled to additional gratuity. Some employees who had applied under the scheme sought to withdraw their application. The Court found that the retirement scheme circulated by the bank amounted to an invitation to offer. Consequently it held that absent consideration, the employees were not bound by their offer, that is, their application to be considered for voluntary early retirement.

The rule has also been independently upheld by Indian High Courts.[152] In *Manickam Chettiar v Madras City Municipal Corp*, the appellant was the highest bidder for the rights to charge an entry fee at a swimming pool owned by the respondent

[144] ibid 1182–83.
[145] *Mirriyala China Subbaraidu* (n 138).
[146] *Pollock and Mulla* (16th edn) (n 8) 753.
[147] *Chrisomar Corp v MJR Steels* [2018] 16 SCC 117 (Supreme Court of India); *Treitel on the Law of Contract* (n 7) 1134.
[148] *Chitty* (n 1) 609; *Treitel on the Law of Contract* (n 7) 1256–58.
[149] *Chitty* (n 1) 609; *Treitel on the Law of Contract* (n 7) 1256–58; *Pitt v PHH Asset Management Ltd* [1994] 1 WLR 327 (lock-out agreements).
[150] *Bank of India v OP Swarnakar* [2003] 2 SCC 721 (Supreme Court of India).
[151] ibid.
[152] ibid; *T Linga Gowder v State of Madras* [1971] AIR Mad 28 (Madras High Court); *Somasundaran Pillai v Provincial Govt of Madras* [1947] AIR Mad 365 (Madras High Court).

corporation.[153] The corporation contended that the appellant failed to provide security as per the terms of the offer and forfeited its deposit. The appellant contended that it withdrew its offer before the acceptance was sent by the corporation. More importantly, it argued that absent any consideration flowing from the corporation to the appellant, it was not liable to keep the bid open.[154] The Madras High Court found in favour of the appellant on both counts.

The 'firm offer' rule has been criticized in both England[155] and India.[156] The 1958 report of the Law Commission of India opined that the 'firm offer' rule was a necessary implication of sections 5(2) and 6 of the Contract Act.[157] The Law Commission recommended that, in keeping with findings of the UK Law Revision Committee, the rule be abolished in India as well by adding an exception to section 25 of the Act. Absent legislative action fifty years after the recommendation was made, perhaps it is possible for change to come through judicial action.[158]

6. Past Consideration Rule

Past consideration has been defined as a promise given in exchange for an act or forbearance that took place before the promise and was done without the promise in mind.[159] Under English law, past consideration is not enough to form a valid contract.[160] An exception to this rule exists with regard to actions that were done at the request of the promisor, although the promise was only made once the act was completed.[161] Indian law, on the other hand, does not adopt the past consideration rule. Section 25(2) of the Act creates an exception in favour of promises to compensate for past voluntary conduct:

> (2) it is a promise to compensate, wholly or in part, a person who has already voluntarily done something for the promisor, or something which the promisor was legally compellable to do;

Indian courts and commentators have stressed the importance of the voluntary nature of the initial action in order to fall within the ambit of this provision.[162] A good

[153] (1976) ILR Mad 31 (Madras High Court).
[154] ibid 39–45.
[155] *Treitel on the Law of Contract* (n 7) 1259–60.
[156] *Pollock and Mulla* (16th edn) (n 8) 120.
[157] *13th Law Commission of India Report* (n 15) 8. For a contrary view, see Swaminathan (n 12) 145.
[158] In this regard, see the interpretation proposed by Swaminathan (n 12) 162 to the effect that under the terms of s 2(d), so long as there is reliance on such a promise, it should be enforceable without consideration in the English sense of the term.
[159] *Chitty* (n 1) 496; *Treitel on the Law of Contract* (n 7) 1076–78.
[160] *Chitty* (n 1) 496–97; *Treitel on the Law of Contract* (n 7) 1076–78; *Eastwood v Kenyon* (1840) 11 A&A 438 (Queen's Bench).
[161] *Chitty* (n 1) 498; *Treitel on the Law of Contract* (n 7) 1079–82; *Lampleigh v Brathwait* [1615] 80 ER 255 (King's Bench).
[162] *Pollock and Mulla* (16th edn) (n 8) 456–57; *Kalipada Das v Durgadas Roy* [1923] AIR Cal 677 (High Court of Calcutta).

illustration of the principle can be found in the case of *Kalipada Das v Durgadas Roy*.[163] The case involved a contract for performance of legal services that failed to meet the formalities required of such a contract. Since the original contract was unenforceable, the plaintiff argued that promissory notes given in pursuance of the contract had the effect of creating a fresh contract. The new contract was one whereby the defendant agreed to compensate the plaintiff for past services. However, the Court held that since the services were rendered pursuant to an agreement, they could not be characterized as voluntary. Similarly, where the act in question, setting up a market, was done at the behest of a third party instead of the defendant in the suit, and was therefore not completely 'voluntary', it was held that section 25(2) did not apply.[164]

It is important to distinguish between 'past' and 'executed' consideration.[165] Where, instead of a promise, consideration consists of an act performed at the time that the contract is formed, it is referred to as 'executed' consideration.[166] A good example of executed consideration can be found in cases where the promisor offers a reward for a lost pet or item.[167] In such cases, for a valid contract to exist, the other party already has to have performed the act of finding the lost thing. Consideration for such a promise can only be performance, that is, executed consideration. The phrase 'has done or abstained from doing' under section 2(d) of the Contract Act refers to executed consideration because it refers to performance that is already rendered but still done at the desire of the promisor. Thus, where the written agreement relied on in court was drawn up after services under it had been rendered, it was held that the agreement could not be challenged on the basis of lack of consideration. Oddly, this situation was described as an agreement with 'past consideration'.[168]

IV. Promissory Estoppel

The modern doctrine of promissory estoppel was originally conceived as a way of circumventing *Pinnel's rule* in English law. In *Central London Property Trust v High Trees*, the question before the Court was whether a landlord should be allowed to go back on their promise to accept lower rents during war time in variation of the terms of a long-term lease, and claim arrears.[169] The promise to accept rent lower than that specified in the agreement, without additional consideration for it, was not enforceable.[170] However, Lord Denning relied upon the doctrine of promissory estoppel and induced

[163] *Kalipada Das* (n 162).
[164] *Durga Prasad v Baldeo* (1880) 3 ILR All 222 (Allahabad High Court).
[165] The two are equated by the current editors of *Pollock and Mulla* (16th edn) (n 8) 57 but distinguished at ibid 456.
[166] Anson (n 108) 15–16.
[167] *Carlill v Carbolic Smoke Ball Co* [1892] EWCA Civ 1.
[168] *EID Parry v SAE India* (1987) 100 LW 1069 (Madras High Court).
[169] *Central London Property Trust v High Trees* [1947] KB 130 (Court of Appeal).
[170] *Foakes v Beer* [1884] UKHL 1 (House of Lords); *Jorden v Money* (1854) 5 HLC 185 (House of Lords).

reliance to argue that it would be wrong to go back on a promise seriously made, especially if it had been acted on by the person to whom it was made.[171]

A similar hardship caused by the doctrine of consideration was faced by Indian courts in relation to donative or charitable promises.[172] In order to remedy this situation, the Law Commission of India recommended adding another exception to those already existing under section 25 of the Contract Act.[173] The addition proposed to do away with the requirement of consideration in cases where the promise had been relied on.[174] While one can find the principle of induced reliance pressed into service by Indian courts in relation to donative charitable promises,[175] the principle of promissory estoppel has taken a different path.

The principle was borrowed by the Supreme Court of India in the case of *Motilal Padampat v State of Uttar Pradesh*.[176] The appellant alleged that it was in reliance of the state governments promising tax exemptions to developing industries that it had set up its factory in Uttar Pradesh. Besides advertisements in popular newspapers, the appellant had received assurances from the Director of Industries of the state government confirming exemption from all taxes for the first three years of operation. The Court found that, under Indian law, the doctrine of promissory estoppel afforded the plaintiff a cause of action; that is,. it could be used as a sword and not just a shield.[177] In practice, the doctrine's application has been restricted to cases against the state. There was some doubt cast on this in *Jeet Ram v State of Haryana*,[178] but ultimately, the issue was settled in favour of holding governmental bodies accountable using the doctrine of promissory estoppel.[179] This also prompted the Law Commission of India to assess the state of the law on promissory estoppel. In its report, the Commission concluded that a claim based on promissory estoppel could be brought against a governmental authority so long as the suit concerned an act of said authority outside its powers as an instrumentality of the state.[180] It was also of the opinion that, in light of the equitable nature of the doctrine, it should be allowed to be used as a sword as well as a shield.[181]

Promissory estoppel is now recognized as a well-established doctrine of administrative law in India, although its label is of contractual provenance.[182] It represents a principle evolved by equity to avoid injustice and, though commonly named promissory

[171] *Central London Property Trust* (n 169) 134 (King's Bench).
[172] *Lakshmana Swami Mudaliar v LIC* (1963) AIR SC 1185 (Supreme Court of India) (holding that such cases would not have any valuable consideration).
[173] *13th Law Commission of India Report* (n 15) 77.
[174] ibid.
[175] *Nair Service Society v Krishna Pillai Kunjukrishna* [1964] AIR Ker 265 (Kerala High Court); cf Swaminathan (n 12) 156–60 (Swaminathan argues that the terms of s 2(d) are 'capacious' enough to cover cases of induced reliance).
[176] [1979] 2 SCC 409 (Supreme Court of India).
[177] ibid [19] citing *Ganges Manufacturing v Sourujmull* (1880) 5 ILR Cal 669; *Municipal Corporation of Bombay v Secretary of State* (1905) 29 ILR Bom 580.
[178] [1980] 3 SCR 689 (Supreme Court of India).
[179] *Union of India v Godfrey Philips India* (1985) 4 SCC 369 (Supreme Court of India); *Kasinka Trading v Union of India* (1995) 1 SCC 274 (Supreme Court of India).
[180] *108th Law Commission of India Report on Promissory Estoppel* (1984) <https://cdnbbsr.s3waas.gov.in/s3ca0daec69b5adc880fb464895726dbdf/uploads/2022/08/2022080842.pdf> accessed 16 October 2023.
[181] ibid.
[182] *Union of India v Godfrey Philips* (n 179).

estoppel, it is neither in the realm of contract nor in the realm of estoppel. The basis of this doctrine is the interposition of equity, which has always, true to its form, stepped in to mitigate the rigour of strict law. Important limitations apply to the use of the doctrine of promissory estoppel against the state. This was recognized in the case of *Motilal* itself. There can be no promissory estoppel against the legislature in the exercise of its legislative functions. Nor can the government or public authority be debarred from enforcing statutory prohibitions.[183] In addition, the doctrine cannot be invoked against the government or public authority if the promise or representation is contrary to law or against public interest or ultra vires the authority.[184]

Recently, the Supreme Court of India, in *State of Jharkhand v Bhramputra Metallics*,[185] pointed out that there is an error in conflating the doctrine of 'promissory estoppel', a contract law doctrine applicable to promises made without consideration, and the doctrine of 'legitimate expectations', a doctrine of public law applicable to representations made by the government. According to Chandrachud J (as he then was), the conflation of the two doctrines has the effect of diluting the effect of both, which adversely affects trade and investment in the country generally.[186] In differentiating between the doctrines, the Court relied on a portion of a concurring opinion of Justice HL Gokhale in *Monnet Ispat and Energy Ltd v Union of India*.[187]

In summary, while the doctrine of promissory estoppel bases itself on a promise, which another has acted on to their prejudice, the doctrine of legitimate expectation primarily concerns itself with the reasonableness and fairness of state action. In conformity with these decisions, courts now examine claims involving governmental representation under the doctrine of 'legitimate expectations'.[188]

[183] *Union of India v Indo-Afghan Agencies* [1968] AIR SC 718 (Supreme Court of India); *Century Spinning v Ulhasnagar Municipal Council* [1971] AIR SC 1021 (Supreme Court of India).
[184] *Vasantkumar Radhakisan Vora v The Board of Trustees of the Port of Bombay* (1991) 1 SCC 76 (Supreme Court of India).
[185] (2020) SCC OnLine SC 968 (Supreme Court of India).
[186] ibid [41] citing MP Jain and SN Jain, *Principles of Administrative Law* (7th edn, EBC 2013).
[187] *Monnet Ispat and Energy Ltd v Union of India* (2012) 11 SCC 1 (Supreme Court of India).
[188] *Indian Ex-Servicemen Movement v Union of India* (2022) 7 SCC 323 (Supreme Court of India).

7
Parties and Assignment

Shantanu Naravane

I. Introduction: Privity and the Three Questions

Privity of contract, notwithstanding doubts as to its true nature[1] and its continued relevance,[2] continues to be one of the pillars of English contract law. Although it presents itself in various guises, at its core, the doctrine deals with two questions:

The Benefit Question: whether a contract can confer rights on a person who is not party to it.

The Burden Question: whether a contract can impose obligations on (or restrict the rights of) a person who is not party to it.

Indian law accepts the common law's starting position, which is to answer both these questions in the negative.[3] While its position under Indian law may rest on weak foundations,[4] the strength of the edifice built through repeated judicial affirmation arguably puts privity of contract into a rarefied category of Indian private law principles that may be considered fundamental. Further, notwithstanding the Law Commission of India's recommendations in its *13th Report*,[5] the statutory exception created in English law by the Contracts (Rights of Third Parties) Act 1999 has, as yet, no parallel in India.

Intricately intertwined with the Benefit Question is a third question, which is also relevant when discussing privity in a contractual context:

The Consideration Question: whether the consideration under a contract may be provided by a person who is not party to the contract.

[1] Lord Denning MR, for instance, suggested in *Beswick v Beswick* [1966] Ch 538, 557 that 'at bottom [privity] is only a rule of procedure. It goes to the form of remedy, not to the underlying right.' A similar sentiment was also expressed by the Calcutta High Court in *Debnarayan Dutt v Chunilal Ghose* (1914) ILR 41 Cal 137, [3].

[2] It has been suggested, for instance, that there is 'no doctrinal, logical or policy reason' for the rule: Steyn LJ in *Darlington BC v Wiltshier Northern Ltd* [1995] 1 WLR 68, 76. In England, the Contracts (Rights of Third Parties) Act 1999 has also created 'a general and wide-ranging exception to' the doctrine of privity: Law Commission, *Report on Privity of Contract: Contracts for the Benefit of Third Parties* (Law Com No 242, 1996).

[3] *Dunlop Pneumatic Tyre v Selfridge* [1915] AC 847.

[4] See S Swaminathan, 'The Great Indian Privity Trick: Hundred Years of Misunderstanding Nineteenth Century English Contract Law' (2016) 16 Oxford University Commonwealth Law Journal 160.

[5] *13th Law Commission of India Report, Indian Contract Act 1882* (1958) 11 <https://cdnbbsr.s3waas.gov.in/s3ca0daec69b5adc880fb464895726dbdf/uploads/2022/08/2022080532.pdf> accessed 3 November 2023.

Shantanu Naravane, *Parties and Assignment* In: *Foundations of Indian Contract Law*. Edited by: KV Krishnaprasad, Niranjan Venkatesan, Shivprasad Swaminathan, and Umakanth Varottil, Oxford University Press. © Oxford University Press 2024.
DOI: 10.1093/9780191997211.003.0007

The common law's answer to the Consideration Question is also a largely unqualified 'No',[6] and this rule may be referred to as privity of *consideration*. However, in this respect, Indian law marks a departure from the common law.[7] Section 2(d) of the Indian Contract Act 1872 (hereinafter 'the Contract Act') reads,

> When, at the desire of the promisor, *the promisee or any other person* has done or abstained from doing, or does or abstains from doing, or promises to do or to abstain from doing, something, such act or abstinence or promise is called a consideration for the promise (emphasis added).

In other words, if *A* enters into a contract with *B* pursuant to which *A* agrees to deliver a crate of apples to *B* in consideration for *C* paying the market price to *A*, *B* may not enforce this contract under English law but may do so under Indian law.

On one view, privity of contract and privity of consideration are fundamentally distinct concepts. Privity of contract deals with the effect of a contract on third parties. Privity of consideration, instead, covers what role, if any, third parties may play in the formation of a contract. However, it is equally possible to adopt the position that privity of contract is just a description of the consequence which follows from applying privity of consideration. The privity-of-contract rule, on this alternative view, would be better framed as being that a third party cannot sue on a contract *because* they have not provided consideration.[8]

As a historical matter, the doctrine of privity of consideration pre-dates, and is in fact the genesis of, the doctrine of privity of contract.[9] However, the precise point at which the two doctrines began their independent existence is far from clear. *Tweddle v Atkinson*[10] is often considered the turning point in establishing privity of contract in English law. However, the judgments in *Tweddle* strongly suggest that the decision was, in fact, based on privity of consideration and not privity of contract.[11] There is also little evidence that *Tweddle* was immediately recognised as having given birth to an independent doctrine. *Tweddle* only began being interpreted as authority for a separate privity-of-contract doctrine towards the end of the nineteenth century and early in the twentieth century. The independent existence of the two doctrines was eventually

[6] *Charnock v Liverpool Corporation* [1968] 1 WLR 1498 is an interesting example of a case where this rule was tested.

[7] The definition of consideration in the Contract Act also departs from English law in treating past consideration as valid: F Pollock and D Mulla, *The Indian Contract Act, With a Commentary, Critical and Explanatory* (2nd edn, Sweet & Maxwell 1909) 21. There is also some disagreement as to whether the definition intentionally marks a departure from the requirement in the common law for the consideration to have some 'value' (compare ibid 25 with W Stokes, *Anglo-Indian Codes*, vol 1 (Clarendon Press 1888) 497. The contrary argument is to be found in S Swaminathan, 'Eclipsed by Orthodoxy: The Vanishing Point of Consideration and the Forgotten Ingenuity of the Indian Contract Act, 1872' (2017) 12 Asian Journal of Comparative Law 141.

[8] R Flannigan, 'Privity—The End of an Era (Error)' (1987) 103 Law Quarterly Review 564, 568.

[9] R Merkin, 'Historical Introduction to the Law of Privity' in R Merkin (ed), *Privity of Contract* (Routledge 2000); Swaminathan, 'The Great Indian Privity Trick' (n 4).

[10] *Tweddle v Atkinson* (1861) 1 B&S 393.

[11] PS Atiyah, *The Rise and Fall of Freedom of Contract* (Clarendon Press 1979) 413–14; Flannigan (n 8).

established conclusively more than fifty years after *Tweddle* by Viscount Haldane LC in *Dunlop Pneumatic Tyre v Selfridge*.[12]

The Contract Act does not expressly deal with the question of who may enforce a contract. As such, privity of contract is not expressly dealt with by the Contract Act. What it does do is disapply privity of consideration. Since English law recognises both privity of contract and privity of consideration, the precise relationship between them is of little practical significance under English law. However, since the Contract Act expressly disapplies privity of consideration, in the first few decades after the enactment of the Contract Act, an important question Indian courts grappled with was the impact on privity of contract under Indian law of disapplying the doctrine of privity of consideration.

It is important to note, in this context, that the Contract Act was being drafted in the period when the privity of contract was in the process of separating from privity of consideration under English law and well before it was firmly established as an independent doctrine in *Dunlop Pneumatic Tyre*. As has been pointed out by Shivprasad Swaminathan,[13] the Contract Act had been substantially drafted by 1866, and the definition of 'consideration' in section 2(d) did not change materially between then and the final version of the Contract Act in 1872. Consequently, there is a strong argument that by disapplying the privity of consideration through section 2(d), the drafters of the Contract Act also intended to disapply privity of contract under Indian law.[14]

A few Indian cases decided soon after the enactment of the Contract Act did take the view that the privity of contract was not recognised under Indian law.[15] However, with the exception of a passing reference made by Jenkins CJ in *Debnarayan Dutt v Chunnilal Ghose*,[16] none of these decisions placed much reliance on this argument drawing on the evolution of privity under English law. Instead, the judges who held that privity of contract did not apply in India seem to have been motivated either by the practical considerations of doing justice between parties[17] or cited the lack of a distinction between the common law and equity in India as the basis on which to reject the privity doctrine.[18] As a result, there is little to no judicial recognition in India of the argument that section 2(d) was intended to disapply privity of contract in India.

On the other hand, the argument that section 2(d) should be limited to the privity of consideration alone, which is separate to the privity of contract, was articulated by Pollock and Mulla, the leading commentary on the Contract Act.[19] Pollock and Mulla went further and argued that the definition of 'promisor' and 'promise' in section 2(c), taken together with the definitions of 'offer' and 'acceptance' in sections 2(a) and 2(b),

[12] *Dunlop* (n 3).
[13] Swaminathan, 'The Great Indian Privity Trick' (n 4).
[14] ibid; A Briggs and A Burrows, *The Law of Contract in Myanmar* (OUP 2017) 144.
[15] *Debnarayan Dutt* (n 1); *Khirodbehari Dutt v Mangobinda* [1934] AIR Cal 682; *Areti Singarayya v Areti Subbaya* (1924) 20 Law Weekly 721; *Dwarika Nath v Priyanath* (1916) 36 Ind Cas 792; *Ramaswami Aiyar v Deivasigamani Pillai* (1922) 43 MLJ 129.
[16] *Debnarayan Dutt* (n 1).
[17] *Areti Singarayya* (n 15).
[18] *Debnarayan Dutt* (n 1); *Khirodbehari Dutt* (n 15); *Dwarika Nath* (n 15).
[19] Pollock and Mulla (n 7) 19.

clearly incorporated the privity of contract into Indian law. However, a combined reading of these provisions merely sets out that

(1) a person signifying to another their willingness to do or to abstain from doing anything is the promisor, and is said to make a proposal;
(2) when the person to whom the proposal is made assents to it, the proposal is accepted, turning the proposal into a promise, with the person accepting the proposal being the promisee.

While these definitions shed light on the meaning of 'promisor' and 'promisee' and indicate that the making and acceptance of a promise is a bilateral act, they do nothing to suggest that a promise, once made, may only be enforced by the promisee. Nor is any such suggestion made by section 2(e) ('Every promise and every set of promises, forming the consideration for each other, is an agreement')[20] or section 2(h) ('An agreement enforceable by law is a contract'). The only implicit suggestion may be derived from section 2(i) ('An agreement which is enforceable by law at the option of one or more of the parties thereto, but not at the option of the other or others, is a voidable contract'), which could be read as proceeding on the unstated assumption that only parties to a contract may enforce it. In any event, it is amply clear that the Contract Act provides little textual support for the argument that only parties a contract were entitled to enforce it under Indian law.

However, notwithstanding the tenuous foundations of Pollock and Mulla's argument, it gained widespread judicial support in India through the first half of the twentieth century. By 1936, the High Courts of Madras,[21] Bombay,[22] and Calcutta[23] had each held that the Contract Act preserves the privity of contract, and eventually, this position was firmly established within a century of the Contract Act's enactment by the Supreme Court decision in *MC Chacko*, which observed: 'It is settled law that a person not a party to a contract cannot, subject to certain well recognised exceptions, enforce the terms of the contract.'[24]

II. 'Exceptions' to Privity of Contract

It has been said, with some justification, that there are no true common law 'exceptions' to the doctrine of privity of contract.[25] Instead, the situations that are commonly

[20] Which Lord Wilberforce relies on with no explanation in *Kepong Prospecting v Schmidt* [1968] AC 810, a decision of the Privy Council in an appeal from Malaysia, which had the same definition of 'consideration' as the Contract Act.

[21] *Iswaram Pillai v Sonivaveru Taragan* [1914] AIR Mad 701; *Subbu Chetty v Arunachalam Chettiar* (1930) 31 Law Weekly 371.

[22] *Shankar Vishvanath v Umabai* (1913) 37 ILR Bom 471.

[23] *Krishna Lal Sadhu v Pramila Bala Dasi* (1928) 32 CWN 634; *Adhar Chandra Mondal v Dalgobinda* (1936) 67 Ind Cas 604.

[24] *MC Chacko v State Bank of Travancore* AIR 1970 SC 500.

[25] *Trident General Insurance v McNiece* (1988) 165 CLR 107.

referred to as 'exceptions' are typically better explained as either instances where privity between two parties is deemed to exist in law even though they are not counterparties to the contract (such as collateral contracts, implied contracts, or agency) or where legal institutions other than contract law are used to enable the enforcement of rights (such as the law of tort, the creation of a trust, or the assignment of a contractual right).[26] Although a detailed examination of all the so-called exceptions is beyond the scope of this chapter, a couple of the relevant exemptions are discussed below, before a detailed examination of the assignment of contractual rights in the remainder of the chapter.

1. Collateral Contracts

The archetypal situation in which a collateral contract arises is where two parties (*A* and *B*), enter into a contract, accompanied by one of them (say, *B*) entering into another contract with a third party (*C*) relating to the subject matter of the first contract. A representation or undertaking made by *C* to *B* in relation to the second contract could, in certain situations, be considered to form the basis of a collateral contract between *A* and *C*.[27]

Collateral contracts could, on one view, be considered to enable a person (*A*) to enforce a contractual representation or undertaking to which s/he is not party. However, they are not truly an exception to privity of contract. The basis for the claim by *A* in the scenario outlined above is that there is, in fact, a contractual relationship between *A* and *C*. This is supported by the fact that, for a collateral contract to have arisen, it is necessary to establish the existence of contractual intention[28] and consideration.[29]

Collateral contracts, as a concept, have been recognised in India,[30] with the Delhi High Court observing, in *New Bank of India*,

> When the shop-keeper sells goods to the consumer and hands over to him the guarantee given by the manufacturer in respect of the goods, the buyer of the goods can claim that a collateral contract between him and the manufacturer may be implied if and only if the guarantee of the manufacturer ensures [*sic*?], for the benefit of the buyer of the goods. Since a guarantee will have no other meaning except for the benefit of the buyer such collateral contracts have been implied between the buyers and the manufacturers.[31]

[26] The exception relating to covenants running with land also falls into this latter category and is now statutorily recognised under English law (Law of Property Act 1925, ss 78, 79) and Indian law (Transfer of Property Act 1882, s 40).

[27] *Shanklin Pier Ltd v Detel Products Ltd* [1951] 2 KB 854.

[28] *Independent Broadcasting Authority v EMI Electronics* (1980) 14 Build LR 1.

[29] *Shanklin Pier Ltd* (n 27). However, it is worth noting that in India, since consideration can be provided by the promisee or any other person, the sorts of difficulties that arise in a case like *Charnock* (n 6) would not arise; see M Furmston and GJ Tolhurst, *Privity of Contract* (OUP 2015) 53.

[30] *Nandganj Sihori Sugar v Badri Nath Dixit* 1991 AIR 1525.

[31] *New Bank of India v Union of India* ILR 1977 Delhi 672. Although it should be noted that the observations about collateral contracts were *obiter*, with the decision actually turning on the question of whether the power of attorney authorises the assignee of the creditor to recover from the original debtor.

2. Implied Contracts

In addition to collateral contracts, Indian courts have been willing to imply the existence of a contract in certain other circumstances, thereby creating legally enforceable rights or obligations between parties to the primary contract and a third party. In English law, there is precedent for such a contractual relationship being implied, often on a quasi-agency basis, where a party to a contract containing an exemption clause seeks to rely on the clause in a claim brought against it by a third party.[32]

Indian courts, however, have been more willing to imply contractual relationships in a wider range of cases. The apogee of this line of reasoning is probably the Delhi High Court decision in *Utair Aviation*,[33] where the Court observed,

> there may be cases, where there is no privity existing at the first place but, the party may by acknowledgement or by his conduct, can proceed to create such privity with the said third party . . . The said privity can be created by way of conduct also either express or implied and the court has to see in those cases as to whether actually the party can be said to be a complete stranger to a contract or where the plea is taken only to defeat the claims of the party . . . it becomes clear that any case where one party is made aware about the relationship of the other party with that of a stranger and the said party proceeds to contract out only with other party in question, knowing fully well the participation and role of the said stranger, further, it corresponds with the said third party/stranger, and conduct suggests kind of relationship, then there can be said to be a nexus or a privity which can be said to have been created by virtue of conduct.

This line of reasoning, especially when combined with the Supreme Court's suggestion in *Kushalbhai Mahojibhai*[34] that there may be circumstances where a presumption of privity could be raised from the circumstances, could well materially dilute the application of the privity of contract doctrine in India.[35] Further, the reasoning adopted by the Court has also led leading Indian law commentaries to suggest that acknowledgement, conduct, or estoppel is an independent exception to the privity of contract doctrine in India.[36]

[32] See E Peel (ed), *Treital on the Law of Contract* (14th edn, Sweet & Maxwell 2015) 752–54 (hereinafter *Treitel on the Law of Contract*).

[33] *Utair Aviation v Jagson Airlines* [2012] 129 DRJ 630. For a detailed critical analysis of the decision, see S Swaminathan 'In Search of a Mythical Exception to Privity of Contract in Indian Law' (2016) 43 Journal of Malaysian & Comparative Law 53.

[34] *Kushalbhai Mahojibhai Patel v A Firm of Mohmadhussain Rahimbux* AIR 1981 SC 977. Here, the plaintiff had supplied goods to the defendant and the defendant had issued cheques to the plaintiff. The Supreme Court held that this raised a presumption that there was privity of contract between the parties and the onus of proof shifted to the defendant to prove that the supply of goods was, in fact, pursuant to a contract entered into with a different entity.

[35] It is worth noting that the Delhi High Court in *Utair Aviation* (n 33) came very close to taking the view that the privity of contract doctrine should be substantially diluted in India.

[36] A Singh, *Law of Contract and Specific Relief* (12th edn, Eastern Book Company 2019) 123; RY Vardhan and C Narayan (eds), *Pollock & Mulla: The Indian Contract Act 1872* (15th edn, LexisNexis 2017) 107. See Swaminathan,

It is submitted that while there may be circumstances where an Indian court may imply the existence of a contract, the observations in *Utair Aviation* overstate the situations in which this may be acceptable. Where a third party is seeking to enforce the terms of a contract, the factual circumstances need to be examined carefully to assess whether there is, in fact, some contractual nexus between the third party and the promisor under the contract. The establishment of such a nexus would require the typical ingredients of a contract to be established on the facts. Contrary to the suggestion in *Utair Aviation*, the desire to 'do complete justice between the parties'[37] should not be a substitute for the factual existence of a contractual nexus between the third party and the obligor under the contract.[38]

3. Trusts and Marriage Settlements

Trusts have long been recognised as an 'exception' to the privity of contract, and the recognition of a trust was one of the principal means by which equity sought to ameliorate the perceived injustices arising from a strict application of the common law doctrine of privity. The existence of a clear intention to hold the promise for the benefit of a third party (and not merely for the third party to benefit from the contract) is a requirement for the creation of a trust. The mere fact that a contract requires a party to do an act for the benefit of a third party does not make the third party a *cestui que* trust.[39] It is not necessary to use the word 'trust', and the existence of the intention is a matter of the legal effect of the words and conduct of the parties.

The application of the trust exception was recognised under Indian law by the Privy Council in *Khwaja Muhammad Khan v Hussaini Begum*[40] and has thereafter been recognised by the Supreme Court in *MC Chacko*[41] and widely applied in India.[42] However, as is the case under English law, the requirements for the creation of the trust need to have been satisfied in order for the exception to be available.[43] The mere fact

'In Search of a Mythical Exception' (n 33), for a detailed analysis on the limited support offered by the other cases cited by these commentaries in favour of this additional exception.

[37] *Utair Aviation* (n 33).

[38] A final, albeit important, point to note is that this implied contract analysis is conceptually distinct to the operation of the Contract Act, s 70, which provides, 'Where a person lawfully does anything for another person, or delivers anything to him, not intending to do so gratuitously, and such other person enjoys the benefit thereof, the latter is bound to make compensation to the former in respect of, or to restore, the thing so done or delivered.' Section 70 is the statutory basis of a claim for restitution or unjust enrichment in India, and by its very nature, it applies where there is no contractual relationship in existence.

[39] *Re Empress Engineering Co* (1880) 16 Ch D 125 (Jessel MR); *Vandepitte v Preferred Accident Insurance Corporation of New York* [1933] AC 70.

[40] (1910) 37 IA 152.

[41] *MC Chacko* (n 24).

[42] *Sri Rajah Inuganti Kasturamma v Chelikani Venkatasurayya Garu* AIR 1916 Mad 65; *Deb Narain Dutt v Ram Sadhan Mandal* AIR 1914 Cal 129; *Snow White Food Product Pvt Ltd v Sohanlal Bagla* AIR 1964 Cal 209; *Narayani Devi v Tagore Commercial Corporation* AIR 1973 Cal 401.

[43] The Indian Trust Act 1882, s 6 states that

> a trust is created when the author of the trust indicates with reasonable certainty by any words or acts (a) an intention on his part to create thereby a trust, (b) the purpose of the trust, (c) the beneficiary, and (d) the trust-property, and (unless the trust is declared by will or the author of the trust is himself to be the trustee) transfers the trust-property to the trustee.

that a contract is for the benefit of a third party does not give the third party an equitable interest in it.[44] In the words of the Supreme Court in *Motilal Chhadami Lal Jain v Commissioner Of Income Tax*,[45] where the settlor is the same as the trustee, the creation of a trust requires that there be 'a declaration of trust, using language which, taken in connection with his acts, shows a clear intention on his part to divest himself of all beneficial interest in it and to exercise dominion and control over it exclusively in the character of a trustee'.

It is also worth noting, in this context, that section 15(c) of the Specific Relief Act 1963 creates a specific statutory exception to the privity of contract, enabling beneficiaries of a settlement on a marriage, or a compromise of doubtful rights between members of the same family, to enforce such a contract. This exception had been recognised by Indian courts even prior to its statutory enactment,[46] with the relevant decisions indicating strongly that the doctrinal basis of the exception was akin to the trust exception.[47]

4. Assignment

As noted earlier, privity of contract deals with the questions of whether a contract itself can confer rights on a person who is not party to it and whether it can impose obligations or curtail the rights of a person who is not party to it. On that view, it is perhaps not entirely accurate to describe assignment as 'a clear exception'[48] to the doctrine of privity.[49] Indeed, the assignment of contractual rights results in a third party to a contract having rights against the promisor under the contract. However, these rights are not conferred on the third party by the contract itself. They emanate from the transfer to the third party, by the promisee under the contract, of rights that the contract conferred on the promisee. The rights of the third party owe their existence to the act of assignment rather than to the original contract itself.[50]

This distinction is more than merely an intellectual exercise and forms the basis of much of the law on the assignment of contractual rights. Since assignment is based on the transfer of contractual rights by one person to another, it can only be permitted where the rights are capable of being transferred. Since the act of transfer is bilateral as between the assignor and the assignee, it gives right to independent rights and obligations as between them.[51] Since the assigned rights may be exercised by a person

[44] *Jnan Chandra Mukherjee v Manoranjan Mitra* AIR 1942 Cal 251; *United Commercial Bank Ltd v Okara Grain Buyers Syndicate* AIR 1968 SC 1115.

[45] 1991 SCR (2) 237.

[46] *Shuppu Ammal v K Subramaniam* (1909) ILR 33 Mad 238; *Arumuga Gounden v Chinnammal* (1911) 21 MLJ 918; *Tirumulu Subbu Chetti v Arunachalam Chettiar* AIR 1930 Mad 382; *Dan Kuer v Sarla Devi* (1946) 2 MLJ 420.

[47] *Veeramma v Appayya* AIR 1957 AP 965, [21].

[48] *Treitel on the Law of Contract* (n 32) 760.

[49] G Tolhurst, *The Assignment of Contractual Rights* (2nd edn, Bloomsbury 2016) 59.

[50] As Cozens-Hardy LJ explained in *Fitzroy v Cave* [1905] 2 KB 364, it was precisely because equity characterised contractual rights as property, and common law instead treated assignment as enabling a third party to bring a claim to enforce the performance of a contractual obligation owed to the original promisee, that assignments were upheld in equity and were considered to fall foul of the rules against maintenance at common law.

[51] See Tolhurst (n 49) 389.

different to whom they were conferred by the promisor under the contract, such exercise as against the promisor is, in some ways, conditional on the promisor having had notice of the transfer. This analysis of assignment as being based on contractual rights being transferred from one person to another is also why the contract (if any) under which the assignment takes effect cannot be considered to have imposed obligations on a third party to the assignment contract, that is, the promisor under the original contract.[52] This is because the obligations of the third party/assignor arise not from the contract of assignment but from the original contract—the assignment merely transfers these pre-existing obligations from one person to another.

Common law did not recognise the assignment of contractual rights as conferring any rights on the assignee vis-à-vis the obligor under the original contract.[53] Such assignment was, however, recognised by equity.[54] If the rights being assigned were equitable in nature, the assignee could sue in the assignee's own name (provided the assignor did not retain any interest in the subject matter),[55] but if the right was a legal right, the assignee had to sue in the assignor's name (and equity would compel the assignor to permit the assignee to do so).[56]

The position at common law was amended by section 25(6) of the Judicature Act 1873 (hereinafter 'the Judicature Act'), which was substantially re-enacted by section 136 of the Law of Property Act 1925. Under section 136, the assignment of contractual rights is now recognised in English law by statute if three conditions are satisfied:

(1) the assignment must be absolute,
(2) it must be in writing under the hand of the assignor,
(3) express notice in writing thereof must be given to the debtor or trustee.

The statutory regime set out above did not 'forbid or destroy equitable assignments or impair their efficacy in the slightest degree'.[57] Consequently, an assignment that fails to comply with the statutory requirements of section 136 is not necessarily invalid, and it may take effect as an equitable assignment.

Interestingly, the codification of private law in India was underway at around the same time as the enactment of the Judicature Act. The Contract Act does not contain any provisions on the assignment of contractual rights. This is likely because the assignment of contractual rights proceeds on the basis of these rights being 'property'. Instead, the primary statutory framework governing the assignment of contractual

[52] J Edelman and S Elliott, 'Two Conceptions of Equitable Assignment' (2015) 131 Law Quarterly Review 228; CH Tham, 'The Nature of Equitable Assignment and Anti-Assignment Clauses' in J Neyers et al (eds), *Exploring Contract Law* (Hart 2009) 283.
[53] It did, however, recognise the existence of rights as between the assignor and assignee: *Gerrard v Lewis* (1867) LR 2 CP 305.
[54] *Treitel on the Law of Contract* (n 32) 800.
[55] *Cator v Croydon Canal Co* (1841) 4 Y&C Ex 405.
[56] *Treitel on the Law of Contract* (n 32) 800–801.
[57] *Brandt's Sons & Co v Dunlop Rubber Co* [1905] AC 454, 462.

rights in India is the Transfer of Property Act 1882 (hereinafter 'the TPA').[58] However, the TPA only establishes an exhaustive framework for the assignment of contractual rights that qualify as 'actionable claims' as defined in the TPA. In addition, the TPA also prohibits the assignment of certain types of contractual rights. However, contractual rights that are not actionable claims remain assignable under Indian law, subject only to the prohibitions on assignment set out in the TPA.

III. Contractual Rights and Actionable Claims: An Imperfect Fit

The TPA recognises an 'actionable claim' as a type of transferable property.[59] The transferee of an actionable claim is entitled to sue in their own name without obtaining the transferor's consent and without making the transferee a party to the claim.[60] Consequently, to the extent a contractual right is an actionable claim, it may be assigned pursuant to the TPA.

When the TPA was enacted in 1882, it defined an actionable claim as 'a claim which the civil courts recognise as grounds for affording relief'.[61] In 1900, the definition was amended, seemingly to confine it to a narrower range of cases,[62] to read as follows: 'a claim to any debt . . . or to any beneficial interest in moveable property not in the possession, either actual or constructive, of the claimant, which the civil courts recognise as affording grounds for relief'.[63] As a result, a contractual right can be an actionable claim under the TPA only if it is either a debt or a beneficial interest in moveable property. Both categories require careful analysis.

The TPA does not define the word 'debt'. The authorities indicate that it includes any ascertained sum, by contrast to unliquidated damages or claims for compensation, which require ascertainment or assessment.[64] A debt may be due and owing or it may be payable in the future; however, it must be due in order to be assignable.[65] So, if *A*

[58] The assignment of certain specific types of contractual rights is subject to separate statutory regimes (eg railway receipts, negotiable instruments, shares, intellectual property, non-performing assets, among others). This chapter deals only with those contractual rights that are not subject to such other statutory frameworks.

[59] TPA, ch VIII. It is important to note that there is considerable Indian case law on the meaning of 'actionable claims' for the purposes of tax legislation. However, no uniform definition of 'actionable claim' is used for these purposes, and it does not necessarily align with the definition in the TPA. Accordingly, this discussion is limited to an analysis of the definition in the TPA and does not examine broader jurisprudence on the meaning of this term in other contexts.

[60] ibid s 130(2).

[61] ibid s 130 as originally enacted: see *70th Law Commission of India Report, The Transfer of Property Act 1882* (1977) 47 <https://cdnbbsr.s3waas.gov.in/s3ca0daec69b5adc880fb464895726dbdf/uploads/2022/09/2022090983.pdf> accessed 3 November 2023.

[62] It is worth noting, however, that although the original definition of an 'actionable claim' was wider, the provision corresponding to the current TPA, s 130 (which provides for the transfer of actionable claims) only referred to the transfer of debts or beneficial interests in moveable property. As a result, it is unlikely that the applicability of the TPA to the assignment of contractual rights was narrowed in any material respect by amending the definition of 'actionable claim'.

[63] TPA, s 3.

[64] *Economic Transport Organization v Charan Spinning Mills* (2010) 4 SCC 114; *Union of India v Raman Iron Foundry* (1974) 2 SCC 231.

[65] *Subramanian v Arunachalam* (1902) ILR 25 Mad 603; *Bhancharam Majumdar v Adyanath Bhatacharjee* (1909) ILR 36 Cal 936.

promises to pay an agreed sum within a month of *B* delivering certain goods, a debt arises upon the delivery of the goods by *B*, even though the payment is due only at a future date. However, it is apparent that this does not exhaust the wide range of rights that may arise under a contract. For instance, although *B* has, prior to delivering the goods, a contractual right to receive payment following delivery, this contractual right would not be a debt. Similarly, if the terms of the contract required advance payment, *A* would, upon making that payment, be entitled to receive the goods from *B*, but this contractual right would obviously not be a debt either.

A contractual right that is not a debt can be an actionable claim only if it is a 'beneficial interest in moveable property'. Again, the TPA does not define this phrase. The reference to 'beneficial interest'[66] appears to be an attempt to distinguish between title to moveable property[67] and a claim to such moveable property, with only the latter being an actionable claim transferable under the TPA.[68] This suggests that of the universe of contractual rights, only those rights upon which claims to moveable property may be founded are 'beneficial interest in moveable property'. Other contractual rights (eg the right to repurchase land or a right to receive a service) are not and, therefore, would not be actionable claims.

The leading decision on the meaning of this phrase is *Jaffer Meher Ali v Budge Budge Jute Mills*.[69] Budge Budge Jute Mills had agreed to deliver a certain quantity of gunny-bags to Karim. Karim assigned the benefit of this contract to Ali. The mill refused to perform its obligations under the contract and challenged its assignability. The Calcutta High Court rejected this challenge.[70] Sale J observed that 'the right to claim the benefit of the contract, or, in other words, the right on certain conditions to call for delivery of the goods mentioned in the contract, constitutes a "beneficial interest in moveable property"'.[71] It was therefore an actionable claim capable of assignment under the TPA. On appeal, the Full Bench of the Calcutta High Court agreed, observing that '[t]he plaintiff himself has shewn that it was an actionable claim within the meaning of section 3 of the Transfer of Property Act . . . on the footing that there was property under the contract, which the assignor could pass to the assignee'.[72]

Therefore, it is clear that *Jaffer Meher Ali* held only those contractual rights that entitle the beneficiary to call for moveable goods to be 'beneficial interest in moveable property'. It did not hold that all contractual rights are 'beneficial interest in moveable property'. However, there is some authority to the contrary.

In *Deoji v Union of India*,[73] Tambe J observed that: 'rights under a contract are beneficial interest in moveable properties . . . [the] right to benefit of a contract therefore falls

[66] Notwithstanding the use of the term 'beneficial interest', there is no suggestion in the TPA's legislative history, subsequent case law, or academic commentary that this was intended to refer only to trusts of moveable property.
[67] Which would not be an actionable claim and would instead be transferable in India under the Sale of Goods Act 1930: see Sale of Goods Act, s 2(7), which expressly excludes actionable claims from the definition of 'goods'.
[68] For an authority drawing this distinction, see *Nathu Gangaram v Hansraj Morarji* (1907) 9 Bom LR 119.
[69] *Jaffer Meher Ali v Budge Budge Jute Mills* (1906) ILR 33 Cal 702.
[70] Although Ali's claim failed on other grounds, which are not relevant to the present discussion.
[71] *Jaffer Meher Ali* (n 69).
[72] ibid.
[73] *Shah Mulji Deoji v Union of India* AIR 1957 Nag 31.

within the definition of "actionable claim"'. Similarly, the Law Commission suggests, relying on *Jaffer Meher Ali*, that 'the right to claim the benefit of a contract is a beneficial interest in moveable property'.[74] That view is also endorsed by the leading commentary on the TPA.[75]

This wide interpretation of 'beneficial interest in moveable property' may have been influenced by a desire to ensure that contractual rights are generally assignable under Indian law and to accommodate cases that have upheld the assignability of contractual rights which clearly do not found a claim to moveable property.[76] This desire is apparent, for example, in *Deoji* itself. Tambe J relied on *Jaffer Meher Ali*, one decision of the Privy Council,[77] and two High Court decisions[78] in support of his construction. *Jaffer Meher Ali* and one of the High Court decisions[79] do not assist because they were both concerned with the purchaser's right under a contract for the sale of goods and did not bear upon whether other contractual rights are beneficial interests in moveable property. The Privy Council decision[80] and the other High Court decision[81] are more important, since they were concerned with contractual rights to immoveable property (land). While both cases did hold that such contractual rights are assignable, they did so on the basis that the benefit of a contract is generally assignable under Indian law and not that such contractual rights constitute an actionable claim under the TPA. Indeed, neither decision makes any reference to the TPA. They do not therefore support the wider interpretation of 'beneficial interest in moveable property' for which Tambe J cites them. They are, instead, authority for the proposition that contractual rights that are not actionable claims may be assignable otherwise than in accordance with the TPA.[82] Tambe J also relied on English authority, the decision of the House of Lords in *Tolhurst v Associated Portland Cement Manufacturers*.[83] *Tolhurst* is obviously of no relevance to the meaning of 'actionable claim' or 'beneficial interest in moveable property' under Indian law. However, the key to understanding Tambe J's reliance on *Tolhurst* may lie in Lord Macnaghten's observation in that case (which is quoted by Tambe J)[84] that 'as a general rule the benefit of a contract is

[74] *13th Law Commission of India Report* (n 5) 48.

[75] PP Saxena, *Mulla on the Transfer of Property Act* (13th edn, LexisNexis 2018) 1115.

[76] For example, the right to repurchase immoveable property has been held to be assignable by the Supreme Court, the Privy Council, and the Bombay High Court: *TM Balakrishna Mudaliar v M Satyanarayana Rao* AIR 1993 SC 2449; *Sakalaguna Nayudu v Chinna Munuswami Nayakar* AIR 1928 PC 174; *Vishweshwar v Durgappa* AIR 1946 Bom 339; *Sinnakaruppa v Karuppuswami* AIR 1965 Mad 506. Similarly, pre-emption rights in respect of land and buildings have been held to be assignable by the Calcutta High Court: *Ram Baran Prosad v Ram Mohit Hazra* AIR 1961 Cal 152.

[77] *Sakalaguna Nayudu* (n 76).

[78] *Hunsraj v Nathu* 9 Bom LR 838; *Seth Bhabhootmal v Moolchand* AIR 1943 Nag 266.

[79] *Hunsraj* (n 78).

[80] *Sakalaguna Nayudu* (n 76).

[81] *Seth Bhabhootmal* (n 78).

[82] In addition to the cases cited in n 18 above, where contractual rights relating to immoveable property were held to be assignable without any reference to the TPA, there are also several cases pre-dating the TPA which held that contractual rights are generally assignable under Indian law: *Kadarbacha Sahib v Rangaswami Nayak* (1864) MHCR 150; *Kanhaiya Lal v Domingo* (1875) ILR 1 All 732; *Anonymous v Muttusamiya Pillai* (1864) MHCR 140; *Kristna Chetti v Balarama Chetti* (1864) MHCR 139; *Jagabhai Lallubhai v Rustamji Nasarwanji* (1885) ILR 9 Bom 311 (decided prior to the TPA being applicable in Bombay). Also see Stokes (n 7) 498. Nothing in the TPA's legislative history indicates that the TPA was intended to alter this position.

[83] *Tolhurst v Associated Portland Cement Manufacturers* [1903] AC 414 (HL).

[84] *Shah Mulji Deoji* (n 73) [90].

assignable'[85] under English law. This lends further support to the suggestion that Tambe J was interpreting 'beneficial interest in moveable property' widely primarily with a view to replicating in Indian law this general assignability of contractual rights. However, since contractual rights are assignable even where they are not actionable claims,[86] this was, with respect, misconceived and unnecessary.

An alternative explanation for the wide interpretation of *Jaffer Meher Ali* is that it is based on an apparent misreading of the relevant portion of Sale J's judgment. As set out above, after considering the sale of goods contract with which he was concerned, Sale J observed that 'the right to claim the benefit of *the* contract' was a beneficial interest in moveable property. However, Tambe J in *Deoji*,[87] the Law Commission,[88] and Mulla,[89] when referring to this quote, refer to 'the benefit of a contract' instead of 'the contract'. This seemingly minor but crucial distinction significantly, and incorrectly, broadens the scope of what *Jaffer Meher Ali* actually decided. It is also inconsistent with the definition of 'actionable claim' under the TPA.[90]

In summary, an 'actionable claim' under the TPA includes only certain categories of contractual rights, namely, debts and contractual rights upon which a claim to moveable property may be founded. Subject to the specific statutory prohibitions set out in the TPA,[91] all other contractual rights may be assigned otherwise than in accordance with the TPA.[92]

IV. Assigning Actionable Claims

Section 130(1) of the TPA provides that '[t]he transfer of an actionable claim . . . shall be effected *only* by the execution of an instrument in writing signed by the transferor' (emphasis added).

It follows from the use of the word 'only' that the TPA 'provides an exclusive procedure for transferring actionable claims'.[93] However, the Supreme Court's decision in

[85] *Tolhurst* (n 83) 420.

[86] There are observations in one High Court decision that could be read as suggesting that if a contractual right is not an 'actionable claim', it can be nothing else but a 'mere right to sue', which is not assignable pursuant to the TPA, s 6: *Abu Mohamed v SC Chunder* (1909) ILR 36 Cal 345. However, the right in question in that case was, in fact, a mere right to sue and, consequently, was clearly unassignable. Any broader observations as to whether all contractual rights that are not actionable claims would necessarily be mere rights to sue are accordingly *obiter*.

[87] *Shah Mulji Deoji* (n 73) [91].

[88] *13th Law Commission of India Report* (n 5) 48.

[89] Saxena (n 75) 1115.

[90] The Law Commission acknowledges that 'the position regarding benefits under contract is not evident from the definition [of an actionable claim] as it now stands' and recommends that the definition should be amended to expressly include all rights arising under a contract (Law Commission (n 3) 47, 51). This suggests that the Law Commission agrees that 'actionable claim', as currently defined, does not include all contractual rights, but incorrectly interprets *Jaffer Meher Ali* as necessitating a different conclusion.

[91] See eg the TPA, s 6, which prohibits the transfer of a 'mere right to sue'. The principal statutory prohibitions in the TPA that are relevant to the assignment of contractual rights are discussed in section VI below.

[92] See section V below for a discussion of the requirements applicable to such 'non-statutory' assignments.

[93] Law Commission (n 3) 669. See also *Jugalkishore Saraf v Raw Cotton* AIR 1966 SC 376; *Mulraj Khatau v Vishwanath* ILR 37 Bom 198 (PC); *Sadasook Ramprotap v Hoare Miller* 80 Ind Cas 632; *Champabai Manilal Shah v Anandrao Ramchandra Patil* 1993 (3) Bom CR 305.

Bharat Nidhi v Takhatmal[94] appears to suggest that actionable claims may be assigned otherwise than in accordance with the TPA. As this would be a clear departure from the language of section 130(1), it warrants closer examination.

In *Bharat Nidhi*, a bank agreed to finance the execution of certain contracts awarded to the promisee. The promisee executed an irrevocable power of attorney in the bank's favour (making the bank an assignee), under which it acquired the right to receive any sums payable to the promisee by the promisor (the Indian government) for the execution of those contracts. In due course, the promisee invoiced the promisor, but with an endorsement instructing the promisor to pay the invoiced amount to the assignee. However, prior to payment, the amount due under the invoice was attached by Takhatmal in execution of a judgment he had obtained against the promisor. The Supreme Court was therefore required to consider the competing claims of Takhatmal (claiming through the promisee pursuant to the attachment) and the assignee.

The Court upheld the bank's claim as an assignee. It observed that '[w]here a document does not amount to a transfer within section 130 it may apart from and independently of the section operate as an equitable assignment of the actionable claim'.[95] Some textbooks rely on this observation to suggest that 'a transfer of actionable claims may be recognised even if it is not in compliance with section 130'.[96] However, upon closer inspection, *Bharat Nidhi* provides very limited support for this far-reaching proposition.

For one thing, previous decisions of the Privy Council[97] and the Supreme Court[98] clearly indicate that actionable claims are transferable only in accordance with the TPA. The Court in *Bharat Nidhi* did not refer to these cases or suggest in any way that it intended to depart from prior precedent.[99] Further, the Court's observations about assigning actionable claims other than in accordance with the TPA were, in fact, unnecessary. *First*, the power of attorney, coupled with the endorsed bill, would appear to have satisfied the procedural requirements of the TPA. Such arrangements had previously been considered sufficient for the purposes of the TPA,[100] and it is not obvious why they were not in *Bharat Nidhi*. *Second*, it is apparent from the judgment that *Bharat Nidhi* was concerned with the assignment of a future debt,[101] which is not an actionable claim at all.[102] Therefore, the facts in *Bharat Nidhi* fell squarely within the

[94] *Bharat Nidhi v Takhatmal* AIR 1969 SC 313.
[95] ibid [5].
[96] Saxena (n 75) 1122.
[97] *Mulraj Khatau* (n 93).
[98] *Jugalkishore Saraf* (n 93).
[99] In fact, although *Bharat Nidhi* does not cite *Jugalkishore Saraf*, it does rely on the Supreme Court's decision in *Loonkaran Sethiya*, which derives its support almost entirely from *Jugalkishore Saraf*: *Loonkaran Sethiya v State Bank of Jaipur* AIR 1969 SC 73. This makes it all the more unlikely that the Court in *Bharat Nidhi* intended to depart from *Jugalkishore Saraf*.
[100] *Tripura Modern Bank v Nawadwip Chandra* 49 CWN 494; *Alkash Ali Khalifa v Nath Bank* (Gauhati High Court, 14 July 1950).
[101] The amount owed by the Government to Malhotra was not a debt due as at the date of the power of attorney but only came into existence at a future date. Acknowledging this, Bachawat J cited the decision of the House of Lords in *Tailby v Official Receiver* (1888) 13 App Cas 523 (HL) and observed that 'In the present case, the power of attorney authorised [the bank] to receive all monies due or to become due to Malhotra in respect of pending or future contracts with the government authorities . . . when the debt due to Malhotra came into existence, he specifically appropriated it for payment to [the bank]': *Bharat Nidhi* (n 94) [6].
[102] See the discussion in section I on the meaning of the word 'debt' for the purposes of the TPA.

principle formulated in *Jugalkishore Saraf* that the assignment of 'future property' is not governed by the TPA.

Consequently, the better reading of *Bharat Nidhi* is that it reaffirms prior precedent on the assignment of contractual rights that are not actionable claims. It is not authority for the proposition that actionable claims may be transferred otherwise than in accordance with the TPA. As contractual rights that are actionable claims may only be transferred in accordance with the TPA, any such assignment needs to satisfy the procedural requirements set out in Part VIII of the TPA.

V. Assigning Contractual Rights That Are Not Actionable Claims

Prior to the TPA, the assignability of contractual rights was a relatively settled matter under Indian law.[103] The one potential disagreement was whether the assignee could sue in its own name or whether the assignee was required to sue in the name of the assignor (which was the view of the Calcutta High Court in *Rajnarain Bose v Universal Life Assurance*).[104] However, the better view appears to be that prior to the TPA, an assignee was not required to bring its claim in the name of the assignor.[105]

Given the position in India prior to the enactment of the TPA, and the fact that the TPA only legislated for the transfer of 'actionable claims', it follows that contractual rights that are not actionable claims remain assignable in India following the enactment of the TPA (subject to the prohibitions on assignment in section 6 of the TPA).[106] This proposition is supported by several cases enforcing the assignment of contractual rights without any reliance on the TPA.[107]

In addition, there is also considerable authority on the availability of 'equitable assignments' in India.[108] As previously discussed, the concept of equitable assignment arose under English law in response to the common law's prohibition of assignment. It owes its existence to the historical split in England between courts of common law and equity. As such, given that no such split has ever existed in India and that Indian law has always recognised, and continues to recognise, the assignment of contractual rights (whether under the TPA or otherwise), there appears to be neither a doctrinal basis nor a practical need to import equitable assignments into Indian law.[109] Instead, the better

[103] *Kanhaiya Lal* (n 82); *Kadarbacha Sabir* (n 82); *Anonymous v Muttusamiya Pillai* (n 82); *Kritna Chetti v Balarama Chetti* (1864) MHCR 139; *Jagabhai Lallubhai* (n 82) (decided prior to the TPA being applicable in Bombay). Also see Stokes (n 7) 498.

[104] (1881) ILR 7 Cal 594.

[105] H Shephard and K Brown, *Commentaries on the Transfer of Property Act, 1882* (4th edn, Higginbotham 1899) 417; Stokes (n 7) 498.

[106] The proposition that s 6 imposes limitations on the general assignability of contractual rights in India has also been accepted by the *70th Law Commission of India Report* (n 61) 50.

[107] *TM Balakrishna Mudaliar* (n 76); *Sakalaguna Nyudu* (n 76); *Vishweshwar* (n 76); *Sinnakaruppa* (n 76); *Ram Baran Prosad* (n 76). There are stray statements to the contrary in a couple of High Court decisions (see *Abu Mohamed* (n 86) and *Ibrahim Isaphai v Union of India*, AIR 1966 Guj 6). However, a better explanation of these decisions is that they were concerned merely with the assignment of a 'mere right to sue', which is subject to the prohibition on assignment under the TPA, s 6.

[108] *Jugalkishore Saraf* (n 93); *Loonkaran Sethiya v State Bank of Jaipur* AIR 1969 SC 73; *Bharat Nidhi* (n 94).

[109] *Kanhaiya Lal* (n 82); *Kadarbacha Sabir* (n 82). See also W Swain, Chapter 1 of this volume, section **.

reading of these decisions is that they merely reaffirm the non-statutory assignment of contractual rights that are not actionable claims under Indian law.

VI. Contractual Rights and Liabilities That May Not Be Assigned

As previously discussed, the assignment of contractual rights is based on them being considered transferable property. Therefore, any such assignment is subject to restrictions on the transfer of property under Indian law. Section 6 of the TPA sets out the kinds of property that may not be transferred, two of which merit closer examination in this context.

1. Personal Rights

Under English law, the benefit of a contract is only assignable 'where it can make no difference to the person on whom the obligation lies to which of two persons he is to discharge it'.[110] This is a question of construction and must be judicially determined on objective grounds.[111] A materially similar exception has been recognised in India, in cases where the contract 'has been induced by personal qualifications or considerations as regards the parties to it'.[112] The assignment of contractual rights may also be prohibited by the terms of the contract itself,[113] and such a prohibition would normally render the assignment void or inoperative.[114] This principle has also been recognised by the Indian Supreme Court.[115] In both the situations discussed above, the underlying principle is the same—if, on its true construction, a contract creates rights that are for the benefit of only the parties to the contract, these rights are incapable of being assigned. This principle is also codified in section 6(d) of the TPA, which provides that 'all interest in property restricted in its enjoyment to the owner personally cannot be transferred by him'.

2. A 'Mere' Right to Sue

Under English law, a bare right of action cannot be assigned.[116] This principle owes its origins to the rules relating to champerty and maintenance and, arguably, to the fact that, prior to the Judicature Act, claims by assignees of legal choses in action had to be

110 *Tolhurst* (n 83) 668; affirmed [1903] AC 414.
111 *Fitzroy* (n 50).
112 *Jaffer Meher Ali* (n 69).
113 *Linden Gardens Trust Ltd v Lenesta Sludge Disposal Ltd* [1994] 1 AC 85.
114 YK Liew, *Guest on the Law of Assignment* (3rd edn, Sweet & Maxwell 2018) 103.
115 *Khardah v Raymon* AIR 1962 SC 1810.
116 *Prosser v Edmonds* 1 Y & C Exch 481.

brought in the name of the assignor.[117] Consequently, while a right of action may be assigned if it is incidental or ancillary to the transfer of a property right or interest, a bare right of action, or the mere right to litigate cannot be transferred.[118] This principle has been statutorily recognised in India through section 6(e) of the TPA, which provides that a 'mere right to sue' is not transferable.[119] The Law Commission of India has noted that the use of the word 'mere' is 'crucial',[120] and that 'it was never the law, and it is not the law, that the transfer of a right to sue is totally prohibited'.[121]

A right to sue may therefore be assigned if it is incidental or ancillary to a property right or interest that is also being assigned (and even if it is not necessarily a right to recover the property interest being transferred).[122] Over time, English law also recognised a wider exception to the non-assignability of rights to sue—cases where the assignee has a genuine commercial interest in taking the assignment and enforcing it for his/her own benefit.[123] In such cases, the assignment may be of a right that is not strictly 'incidental or ancillary' to property. However, the assignment is permitted based on the assignee's genuine commercial interest in the enforcement of the right (which interest exists independently of the assignment of the right to sue)[124] and, therefore, does not 'savour of maintenance'.[125] Since this exception operates independently to the 'incidental to property' exception, there is potentially a question as to whether this additional exception may be transported into Indian law.

On the face of it, where a 'right to sue' is the only right being transferred, it is difficult to reconcile this with the prohibition in section 6(e) on the basis of the assignee's genuine commercial interest in enforcing the right. However, a literal application of section 6(e) would, in these cases, be at odds with its purported purpose. The Supreme Court has observed that

> The reason behind the rule is that a bare right of action for damages is not assignable because the law will not recognise any transaction which may savour of maintenance of champerty. It is only when there is some interest in the subject matter that a transaction can be saved from the imputation of maintenance. That interest must exist apart from the assignment and to that extent must be independent of it.[126]

[117] A Tettenborn, 'Assignment of Rights to Compensation' [2007] Lloyd's Maritime and Commercial Law Quarterly 392, 402.

[118] *Williams v Protheroe* (1829) 5 Bing 309; *Dawson v Great Northern & City Railway* [1905] 1 KB 260; *Ellis v Torrington* [1920] 1 KB 399.

[119] *Jai Narain Pande v Kishun Dutta Misra* (1924) ILR 3 PAT 575.

[120] *70th Law Commission of India Report* (n 61) 67.

[121] ibid.

[122] *Susai Lazar Villanarayya v Ramaswami Naidu* AIR 1933 Mad 710; *Benumetcha Gangaraju v Veluri Gopala Krishnamurthi* AIR 1957 AP 190; *Pusuluri Varahaswami v Mantena Ramachandra Raju* (1913) 24 MLJ 298. This principle was recognised in England even before the drafting of the TPA: *Williams* (n 118).

[123] *Martell v Consett Iron* [1955] Ch 363; *Trendtex Trading Corp v Credit Suisse* [1982] AC 679.

[124] An example of this being an insurer taking an assignment of the right of action from the insured to further enhance the interest it already had by way of subrogation: *Compania Colombiana de Seguros v Pacific Steam Navigation Co* [1965] 1 QB 101.

[125] *Trendtex Trading Corp* (n 123).

[126] *Union of India v Sri Sarada Mills* AIR 1973 SC 281.

There is also a certain irony in interpreting section 6(e) more widely than it is in England, given that the doctrine of champerty and maintenance has not been adopted in India.[127] Therefore, much can be said in favour of the proposition that

> the doctrine of champerty and maintenance not having been fully adopted in this country, Section 6(e) of the Transfer of Property Act should not be extended beyond that it was intended to prohibit . . . a rule originating with a view to preserve another should not be held as having been infringed where the principal rule is not being broken.[128]

There are also a few old High Court cases that have upheld litigation financing agreements, where only the right to sue was being transferred but in circumstances where there was a legitimate purpose to the transfer. In *Abdool Hakim*,[129] the Calcutta High Court observed that Indian courts are

> untrammelled . . . by any laws regarding maintenance and champerty [and] what has to be considered in such cases is whether the transaction is merely the acquisition of an interest in the subject of litigation bona fide entered into, or whether it is an unfair or illegitimate transaction got up for the purpose merely of spoil, or of litigation disturbing the peace of families and carried on from a corrupt and improper motive.

This test was also followed by the Bombay High Court in *Tara Chand v Suklal*[130] to uphold the enforceability of a litigation funding contract. Admittedly, neither of these cases was required to consider section 6(e)—*Abdool Hakim* was decided before the TPA came into force and *Tara Chand* was decided before the TPA was applicable in Bombay.[131] However, absent any suggestion that section 6(e) was intended to depart from the then prevailing Indian law position,[132] section 6(e) should be interpreted as permitting the assignment of rights of action in cases where the assignee has a 'genuine commercial interest' in its enforcement.

There are also a few other scenarios that do not permit an easy solution on a literal reading of section 6(e).

When a continuing executory contract is assigned (eg a crate of apples is to be delivered every month), does the assignment of the contract also amount to an assignment of the right to sue in respect of past breaches? The position here is conceptually different to cases where a claim is brought for *mesne* profits in respect of land that has

[127] *Coomar Coondoo v Chunder Canto Mookerjee* 4 IA 23 (G).
[128] *Benumetcha Gangaraju* (n 122).
[129] *Abdool Hakim v Doorga Proshad Banerjee* (1880) ILR 5 Cal 4.
[130] *Tara Chand v Suklal* (1888) ILR 12 Bom 559.
[131] The TPA was extended to the then province of Bombay by a notification of 1 January 1893. See *70th Law Commission of India Report* (n 61) 50.
[132] *Abdool Hakim* (n 129) and *Tara Chand* (n 130) derived their support from the Privy Council's observations in *Chedambar Chetty v Renga Krishna* LR 1 Ind App 241.

been transferred. However, it is difficult to see a policy reason why the assignee of such an executory contract should be denied the right to claim damages for past breaches.[133]

What if the contract is for a single delivery of a crate of apples by a specified date, which has been missed, but the assignee is willing to extend the delivery date with retrospective effect and has no reason to believe that the vendor will not be able to deliver the apples by the extended date? Is this truly a case where a 'mere' right to sue has been transferred?

Finally, what about where a set of contracts is transferred (eg on the acquisition of an entire business or undertaking), some of which have been breached? Does the fact that the only right remaining under the breached contracts is a right to sue mean that those contracts cannot be assigned?[134] What policy objective would this be in aid of?

In each of these cases, the appropriate solution cannot be found in the language of section 6(e). This is because section 6(e) sought to codify a principle into Indian law rather than a prescriptive rule.[135] Consequently, in each of these cases, an Indian court should consider whether, in light of all the circumstances surrounding the assignment, the transfer of the right to sue may be said to further a legitimate interest of the assignee or whether the assignment in question 'savours of maintenance'.

3. Contractual Obligations and Liabilities

As a general rule, unless the contract or statute provides otherwise, liabilities or obligations under a contract cannot be assigned.[136] As Greg Tolhurst points out, the doctrinal explanation for this rule lies in assignment being conceptualised as the transfer of a property right.[137]

The Supreme Court in *Khardah*[138] effectively restated the English law prohibition on the assignment of liabilities and observed: 'As a rule obligations under a contract cannot be assigned except with the consent of the promisee, and when such consent is given, it is really a novation resulting in substitution of liabilities.' Neither in the case of novation nor vicarious performance is the obligation under the original contract transferred to a third party.

[133] On very similar facts, the Calcutta High Court in *Abu Mohamed* (n 86) held that the assignee could not bring a claim for damages suffered due to the breach on the basis that this was the assignment of a mere right to sue. However, it is difficult to reconcile this decision with the other dicta quoted above, which lend support to a more restrictive application of s 6(e). It is also worth noting that one of the three judges in *Abu Mohamed* (Fletcher J) commented that while he did not dissent, he felt 'very considerable doubt that the Statute meant to limit the right of a person to assign his right under a contract by the fact that the other party to the contract had broken it'.

[134] It is worth noting, in this context, the judgment of the Madras High Court in *Halonix Technologies v Cema Electric Lighting Products* (Madras High Court, 3 November 2023), which suggests that such a transfer would be upheld.

[135] Elise Bant and Jeannie Paterson, Chapter 2 of this volume, section **.

[136] *Tolhurst* (n 83).

[137] Tolhurst (n 49) 302.

[138] *Khardah* (n 115).

Further, the principle that liabilities under a contract cannot generally be assigned also appears to have been statutorily recognised by section 37 of the Contract Act, which states,

> The parties to a contract must either perform, or offer to perform, their respective promises, unless such performance is dispensed with or excused under the provisions of this Act, or of any other law.

8

Incapacity and Its Consequences

Neel Maitra[*]

I. An Introduction and a Note on Scope

This chapter discusses the capacity of parties to contract under the Indian Contract Act 1872 (hereinafter 'the Contract Act') and the judicial treatment of agreements with the incapacitated. In section I, the chapter briefly reviews the categories of incapacity under the Contract Act. Section II examines the consequences of incapacity for the agreement, specifically the voidness or voidability of such agreements, while section III reviews some remedies for an agreement entered with, or by, an incapacitated individual, followed by some concluding observations.

The current state of the Indian law on incapacity under the Contract Act is unsatisfactory in many respects, and courts and commentators have often been unsparing in their criticisms. This chapter attempts to capture some of the principal objections to the law as it stands, but moving beyond, it aims to show that 'incapacity' is an umbrella term for two types of disparate situations. Denying a person capacity to contract may serve varying social or economic policies, and the differing outcomes of such situations cannot be considered parts of a single consistent whole.[1] Attempts to infer the consequences of a contract with one type of incapacitated person by reference to other categories of incapacity risks producing anomalous or untenable outcomes.

* The views expressed in this chapter do not reflect the view of Wilson Sonsini Goodrich & Rosati, or any of the partners thereof. I would like to thank Niranjan Venkatesan for his careful review of earlier drafts and insightful comments and Ananth Padmanabhan for his invaluable research suggestions and assistance. All errors remain my own.

[1] Readers may question why the chapter confines itself entirely to the contractual capacity of natural persons. This focus may seem unduly restrictive given the volume of writing and case law on corporate contractual capacity. In contrast, one commentary notes, 'In modern commercial law, the problems which arise when agreements are made by children are rarely encountered . . .The problems which arise when an adult who is "of unsound mind" makes an agreement are similarly rare': see A Briggs and A Burrows, *The Law of Contract in Myanmar* (OUP 2017) 54. At least two reasons may justify the exclusion of corporate contractual capacity from this chapter. First, this volume is on the Contract Act, rather than contract law more generally. Corporate capacity to contract may more properly be governed by the company legislation or principles developed by the courts. Second, corporate capacity to contract stems from, and significantly overlaps with, the law of agency, which is beyond the scope of this chapter. Without disagreeing that cases on contracts by minors or persons of unsound mind are vanishingly rare, it is this rarity that gives landmark cases their longevity and, perversely, their ability to develop or distort doctrine over decades. The relative paucity of cases preserves a stagnant breeding ground for rebarbative outcomes.

Neel Maitra, *Incapacity and Its Consequences* In: *Foundations of Indian Contract Law.* Edited by: KV Krishnaprasad, Niranjan Venkatesan, Shivprasad Swaminathan, and Umakanth Varottil, Oxford University Press. © Oxford University Press 2024.
DOI: 10.1093/9780191997211.003.0008

For the purposes of this chapter, references to contracts by minors should be taken to refer to contracts by minors who are not represented by guardians.[2] References to contracts by persons of unsound mind should be taken to refer to contracts by only those of such persons who are not represented by nominated representatives appointed under the Mental Healthcare Act 2017.[3]

II. The Categories of Incapacity

Section 10 of the Contract Act states that 'All agreements are contracts if they are made by the free consent of parties competent to contract, for a lawful consideration and with a lawful object, and are not hereby expressly declared to be void.' Section 11 of the Contract Act states that 'Every person is competent to contract who is of the age of majority according to the law to which he is subject, and who is of sound mind and is not disqualified from contracting by any law to which he is subject.' No provision of the Act expressly provides for the consequences of agreements entered into by persons who lack capacity to contract.

Section 11 denies contractual capacity to three classes of persons: those below the age of majority according to the law to which they are subject; those not of sound mind; and perhaps most intriguingly, those disqualified from contracting by any law to which they are subject. Several judgments under the Act (as well as one prominent commentary) use the confusing term 'inherent incapacity' to refer to the categories of incapacity covered by section 11.[4] In a pragmatic sense, 'inherent incapacity' might refer to an incapacity that is immutable or incurable at the incapacitated party's will. For example, the minor can take no steps to remedy their minority other than to wait until majority is attained, and the lunatic is unable to regain their sanity at will. The term is, however, imprecise, and potentially misleading because while lunacy and minority may be considered inherent conditions, it is difficult to consider a disqualification imposed by law in the same way. Further, while lunacy may be an inherent condition, section 11 refers to soundness of mind, and an unsound mind is not necessarily an inherent condition

[2] Minors may, of course, validly enter into contract if they are represented by guardians. The Hindu Minority and Guardianship Act 1956 (HMGA) s 6 specifies natural guardians for minors, and s 9 permits the appointment of testamentary guardians; see HMGA, ss 6 and 9. The HMGA, ss 8 and 9(5) empower natural and testamentary guardians, respectively, to do all acts that are necessary or reasonable and proper for the benefit of the minor or for the realisation, protection, or benefit of the minor's estate, although the guardian cannot bind the minor by a personal covenant. Notably, however, s 8 prohibits guardians from disposing of or encumbering the immovable property of minors in certain ways, except with court permission, and expressly requires courts to only permit such transactions in case of necessity or for an evident advantage to the minor; see HMGA, ss 8 and 9(5). The Guardians and Wards Act 1890 provides for court-appointed guardians irrespective of the religion of the minor, and subjects such guardians to similar restrictions; see Guardian and Wards Act1890, ss 7 and 29.

[3] Every person who is not a minor shall have a right to appoint a nominated representative; see Mental Healthcare Act 2017, s 14(1). Minors of unsound mind are represented by their legal guardians; see Mental Healthcare Act 2017, s 15(1). In the absence of a nomination, certain persons are deemed to be the nominated representative; see Mental Healthcare Act 2017, s 14(4).

[4] See eg *Ram Nagina Singh v Governor General in Council* AIR 1952 Cal 306; *Dharmeswar Kalita v Union of India* AIR 1955 Assam 86; RY Vardhan and C Narayan (eds), *Pollock & Mulla: The Indian Contract and Specific Relief Acts* (15th edn, LexisNexis 2017).

in the sense of being immutable. The second illustration to section 12 of the Contract Act describes two conditions—a fevered delirium and drunkenness—that cannot be considered inherent, although they may result in an unsound mind for the purposes of contracting.

Not all incapacities are alike, and not all incapacities are inherent. The categories of incapacity enumerated by section 11 are not united by a single common thread. Two distinct types of incapacity are apparent from the three categories enumerated in section 11. The first type of incapacity covers the first two categories enumerated in section 11 and relates to those whom the law presumes to be incapable of contracting—that is, minors and those of unsound mind. The second type of incapacity covers those persons whom the law deprives of the power to contract by imposing a disqualification. The first type of incapacity serves to protect classes of vulnerable persons from exploitation and, perhaps secondarily, to protect market transactions from the disruptions that could arise from contracting with the incapacitated.[5] The second type of incapacity, arising from disqualifications, may serve disparate underlying policy objectives of varying importance. The first type of incapacity philosophically resembles a factor that vitiates consent and operates as an irrebuttable presumption that certain classes of persons cannot give free and fair consent. The second type of incapacity deprives otherwise competent persons of the ability to contract, not necessarily because they are vulnerable or easily exploited but to serve contextual policy goals, such as judicial independence or administrative transparency. These two types of incapacity are therefore qualitatively different, and it follows that the legal consequences that turn on each type of incapacity may differ. Sections II and III of this chapter develop this theme, but each type of incapacity is first considered in greater detail.

1. Minority

Unlike the other two categories in section 11 of the Contract Act, the question of whether a contract party is a minor appears to be an entirely objective determination. This is especially so following the passage of the Indian Majority Act 1875 (the 'Majority Act'). Section 3 of the Majority Act states that every person domiciled in India shall attain the age of majority on their completing the age of eighteen years.[6] This seems straightforward, but even this seemingly objective question of minority status is not without its interpretive wrinkles.

Section 11 of the Contract Act speaks of capacity not in terms of a single universal age of majority but in terms of the age of majority according to the law to which the

[5] S Deakin, *Capacitas: Contract Law and the Institutional Preconditions of a Market Economy* (Hart 2009).

[6] The Act was amended in 1999 to lower the age of majority from twenty-one to eighteen. Before its amendment, the age of majority for contracting was not uniform. In general, persons attained majority at eighteen. However, a minor of whose person, or property, or both a guardian had been appointed by the court, or of whose person or property the superintendence was assumed by a Court of Wards before the age of eighteen years, attained majority on completing twenty-one years. If a guardian had been appointed for a minor by the court, an agreement made by the minor before completing twenty-one years of age was void.

contracting party is subject. If the contracting party is domiciled in India, section 3 of the Majority Act would treat that party as a minor if they were eighteen or older. But what of a party not domiciled in India who enters into a contract governed by the Act?[7] Presumably, the law of domicile would determine the age of majority, but this does not necessarily follow from the phrase 'according to the law to which he is subject', and cases on the point have produced different results.

In 1906, Sir Ernest Trevelyan, formerly a judge of the Calcutta High Court, took the view in a treatise that the majority status of persons not domiciled in India would be determined by the law of their domicile.[8] The decision in *Rohilkhand and Kumaun Bank v Row*[9] provides a useful discussion of the contemporary English law on the question,[10] noting that it was not entirely clear that capacity was necessarily governed by the law of a person's domicile but pointing out that it would be anomalous if a person were treated as being a major for the purposes of contracting in India and then treated as having reverted to minority upon their return to their domicile.[11]

At least one case has taken the view that it is the *lex loci contractus* that should govern questions of capacity to enter 'ordinary mercantile contracts'.[12] There, the Madras High Court observed that 'though at one time the preponderance of authority was in favour of applying the law of domicile as regards the capacity to enter into contracts *vide Cooper v. Cooper* . . . still as to ordinary mercantile contracts the preponderance now seems to be the other way' (internal citations omitted). Although it is unclear what agreements would be covered by the term 'ordinary mercantile contracts', there is certainly an argument to be made for using the law of the place of contract to determine contractual capacity. It could create great commercial confusion if a person who seemingly has capacity to contract under the *lex loci contractus* could resile from an agreement because that person is a minor under the law of their domicile. But conversely,

[7] The standard approach appears to be in *Kashiba v Shripat Narshiv* (1895–96) ILR 19–20 Bom 466, in which a widow was found to be a minor, based upon her domicile in British India, and therefore not liable upon a bond that had been executed in the erstwhile princely state of Kolhapur.

[8] EJ Trevelyan, *The Law Relating to Minors as Administered in the Provinces Subject to the High Courts of British India* (3rd edn, W Thacker & Co 1906) 13, citing, in support of his view, the decision in *Rohilkhand and Kumaun Bank v Row* 1884 7 All 490 (holding that the question of majority status was to be determined by the law of the non-Indian person's domicile).

[9] *Rohilkhand* (n 8).

[10] The decision cited, among other things, Story's commentary on conflict of laws, noting that while foreign jurists generally stated that the law of the person's domicile ought to apply to questions of capacity, American and English commentators disagreed. The decision also noted that commentators such as Dicey and Westlake expressed uncertainty on the question and cited a decision of the House of Lords suggesting that the law of the domicile should govern questions of capacity; see *Udny v Udny* (1869) LR 1 HL 441; *Rohilkhand* (n 8) 496. Although it was not cited in *Rohilkhand*, the House of Lords' decision in *Cooper v Cooper* ((1888) 13 App Cas 88) also considered whether capacity should be governed by the law of the domicile (albeit in the context of a marriage), and Lord Macnaghten opined that though the question was 'not finally settled, the preponderance of opinion here, as well as broad, seems to be in favour of the law of the domicile'. A few years later, in *Lachmi Narain v Fateh Bahadur Singh* (1902) 25 All 195, the Allahabad High Court applied the law of the domicile to determine contractual capacity, noting that it was 'a well-established principle in England that the personal incapacity of a person to contract depends on the law of the place where the contracting party is domiciled'.

[11] *Rohilkhand* (n 8) 499.

[12] *TNS Firm v VPS Muhammad Hussain* (1933) 65 MLJ 458. There, one of the defendants in a suit for recovery of a loan pleaded that he was a minor under the law of Ceylon, the place of contract, although he was not a minor under the law of India, his domicile. The Madras High Court agreed that he was a minor for the purposes of the contract, on the ground that questions of capacity to enter into mercantile contracts were governed by the law of the place of contract, rather than the law of the domicile.

this argument may support the case for applying the law of the domicile to questions of capacity by placing the burden on contract parties to thoroughly investigate the background of any counterparties of questionable contractual capacity.[13] Further, if questions of capacity were governed by the *lex loci contractus*, the unscrupulous selection of a governing law could frustrate the domicile's ability to protect minors from the consequences of contracting.

Even if it were assumed that the law of the domicile governs the question of capacity, a reference to a foreign law may become even more complex where *renvoi* applies—for example, where the law of the foreigner's domicile treats the proper age of majority as being governed by the *lex loci contractus* or by reference to some other legal system.[14] However, this question does not appear to have been discussed in the decisions rendered thus far.

Another related point of interest may be the distinction between the first and third categories of section 11 of the Contract Act. While the first part of section 11 speaks of a person 'who is of the age of majority according to *the* law to which he is subject', the third part of section 11 speaks of a person who 'is not disqualified from contracting by *any* law to which he is subject' (emphases added). The distinction suggests that while majority is to be determined with reference to a single objectively applicable law, a contractual disqualification could be founded in any applicable legal system, irrespective of whether the parties have chosen it to govern their contract or whether it is the law of their respective domiciles. Again, there appear to be no cases that have addressed the distinction, and prior drafts of the Act have not discussed this difference in language, but the text of the provision reinforces the notion that the question of majority must be settled by reference to a single applicable legal system.

[13] This discussion of the competing claims of the law of the domicile and the *lex loci contractus* omits a third possibility, raised in *Nachiappa Chettiar v Muthu Karuppan Chettiar* AIR 1946 Mad 398. Although that case did not involve a minor, it considered the contractual capacity of an individual to dispose of immovable property held by a joint family and concluded that the capacity to alienate an immovable must be governed by the *lex situs*. If this rule holds good for transfers of immovable property by non-Indian minors, then, even if the law of the domicile ordinarily applies to questions of contractual capacity, the capacity to transfer property would instead be governed by the *lex situs*.

[14] One commentary takes the view that 'The doctrine of *renvoi* does not form part of the conflicts resolution process in India': see VC Govindaraj, *The Conflict of Laws in India: Inter-Territorial and Inter-Personal Conflict* (OUP 2011) 36–37. This questionable conclusion seems to be based on the Supreme Court's decision in *National Thermal Power Corporation v Singer Company* AIR 1993 SC 998. While *Singer* does appear to support the equally questionable proposition that there should be no room for *renvoi* where there is an express or implied choice of law, it does not necessarily follow that *renvoi* has no role to play in questions relating to contractual capacity. The view in *Singer* has been followed by other courts. See eg *Bhanu Constructions Company v Andhra Pradesh State Electricity Board* 1997 (6) ALT 328. This case may be going too far to definitively conclude that *renvoi* has no place in Indian law. However, even if Indian courts may resort to *renvoi*, it is unclear how they would do so, and under what conditions, for example, whether Indian courts would, or should follow partial or total *renvoi*. Accordingly, it is speculative to discuss how an Indian court would discuss a question of *renvoi* relating to capacity in the absence of any applicable case law.

2. Unsoundness of Mind

Individuals may sometimes misunderstand the consequences of, or the obligations under, their agreements. In extreme cases, parties to an agreement may not even recognise that they are entering into a contract. Indeed, the illiterate wage-labourer or farmer duped by a moneylender or landlord is a common plot element in Bollywood.[15] Are cases where one party is illiterate, unfamiliar with the language of the contract, or simply a very poor bargainer cases of incapacity under section 11 of the Contract Act? Or are they more properly treated as cases of contracts that should be voidable for the absence of free consent for some other ground under section 19 of the Contract Act? Or are they valid contracts? The unsatisfactory answer must be that it depends on the circumstances, but a few points on the boundaries of incapacity for unsoundness of mind may be worth noting here.

Unlike the other two categories of incapacity enumerated in section 11 of the Contract Act, the idea of a 'sound mind' is described further under the Act. Section 12 of the Contract Act states that 'A person is said to be of sound mind for the purpose of making a contract, if, at the time when he makes it, he is capable of understanding it and of forming a rational judgement as to its effect upon his interests.' Thus, in contract law, as in criminal law, the law's concept of a sound mind may not completely conform to that of medicine or psychiatry. What the text of section 12 appears to require for contract formation is not that the parties actually understand and appreciate the terms, merely that they be capable of doing so.

The cases on section 12 also seem to agree that what is required is an inability to understand, typically arising from some physical or mental infirmity, rather than the mere failure to do so. For example, in *Durga Bakhsh Singh v Mirza Muhammad Ali Beg*, the Privy Council noted that the mortgagor whose conduct was in question may have been blind, old, and 'helpless' but that none of these conditions amounted to lunacy.[16] Similarly, in *Kanhaiyalal v Harsing Laxman Wanjari*,[17] the Bombay High Court observed that what section 12 requires for a finding of unsoundness of mind is the inability to understand the business concerned and its implications, as opposed to 'mere weakness of mind'. What this entails is a factual, contextual determination of an inability to understand the consequences of one's actions, rather than the application of a uniform legal standard.

These inevitably contextual judicial determinations of soundness of mind have often been accompanied by broad statements that obscure the underlying doctrine. There are, for example, judicial pronouncements that unsoundness of mind is 'not a total deprivation of reason but an inability from defect of perception, memory and judgment to do the act in question or to understand its nature and

[15] For two prominent examples, see *Do Bigha Zamin* (1953) and *Mother India* (1957).
[16] (1904) 31 IA 235.
[17] AIR 1944 Ngp 232.

consequences'[18] so that it can be difficult to determine precisely where an unsound mind ranks on the continuum of mental impairment. In general, however, the case law on section 12 suggests that the provision protects those who are incapable of forming a judgment as to their own interests,[19] rather than those who are poorly educated or poorly advised.

The question of what an unsound mind is is distinct from what constitutes proof of an unsound mind for the purposes of section 12 of the Contract Act. In *Sona Bala Bora v Jyotirindra Bhattacharjee*,[20] which concerned the transfer of property by a person alleged to be of unsound mind, the transferor would threaten to dispossess his family whenever he sank into depression. The Supreme Court noted that medical or expert evidence need not be adduced to prove an unsound mind[21] and that it is enough to show that the contracting party's conduct was not in keeping with his character and that it could not be explained on any reasonable basis. The Court therefore concluded that the transfer of property in question, which could not be otherwise explained by a need for money or continuing strain in family relationships, was not 'in accord with natural and normal affection'.[22] The decision suggests that all section 12 requires as proof of unsoundness of mind are acts that are abnormal or irrational when viewed within a person's usual course of conduct. Thus, the inability to form a judgement as to one's interests may be inferred from an abnormal course of conduct, although this is not the only means by which to prove unsoundness of mind.

How should we distinguish the inability to judge one's interests from the effects of illiteracy or an unfamiliarity with commercial transactions? Many retail investors are, today, sold complex financial products whose consequences they may only dimly comprehend. It would be difficult to contend, however, that such contracts are vitiated by the incapacity of one of the contract parties, although claims of fraud may credibly be raised in some cases. The bulk of the case law suggests that unsoundness of mind may be something less than medical lunacy and must be something more than mere illiteracy, unfamiliarity with commercial contexts, or weak bargaining. The prevailing judicial understanding of an unsound mind has sometimes shaded into other areas where free consent is vitiated, most notably cases of undue influence. The Privy Council and at least one High Court have taken the view that questions of undue influence and of incapacity by reason of unsoundness of mind involve 'totally different issues', but it is not evident why the distinction is necessarily clear in all cases.[23]

[18] *Sona Bala Bora v Jyotirindra Bhattacharjee* (2005) 4 SCC 501, citing the definition from *Black's Law Dictionary*. The Court clarified that a person need not be a lunatic to be of unsound mind—it is sufficient that that person is incapable of judging the consequences of their acts.

[19] *Indar Singh v Parmeshwardhari Singh* AIR 1957 Pat 491, 493 (where the incapacity arose from a 'congenital' unsoundness of mind).

[20] *Sona Bala Bora* (n 18).

[21] Note, however, that where there is medical evidence as to the soundness of mind, a contrary judicial determination does not appear to be possible; see *Kanhaiyalal* (n 17).

[22] *Sona Bala* (n 18).

[23] *Sayad Muhammad v Fatteh Muhammad* (1894) 22 IA 4, 12; *Ram Sunder Saha v Kali Narain Sen Choudhury* AIR 1927 Cal 889. The statement does not appear to have been discussed at any length, but the first edition of Pollock and Mulla takes the same view, although it cites only the same cases in support; see F Pollock and DF Mulla, *The Indian Contract Act: With a Commentary, Critical and Explanatory* (1st edn, Sweet & Maxwell 1905) 55.

Besides the three enumerated categories of incapacity (minority, unsoundness of mind and legal disqualification), section 11 of the Contract Act provides no other catch-all or umbrella term. Indian courts have therefore had no textual support to recognise new categories of incapacity if they do not qualify as cases of unsoundness of mind. Courts confronted with cases involving parties perceived to be exceptionally vulnerable, such as the *parda nashin* woman or the illiterate, have little basis in the language of section 11 to treat such parties as incapacitated. As a result, in a number of cases, Indian courts have sought to use the doctrine of undue influence to extend protection to parties who cannot be considered to be incapacitated under section 11. For example, in the case of the *parda nashin* woman, courts in colonial India recognised a presumption of undue influence[24] in a number of cases that featured either the involvement of a close confidante, adviser, or fiduciary of the *parda nashin* or a transaction that was seemingly suspect on its face.[25] Cases of illiteracy under the Act have often been similarly decided.[26] These outcomes seem correct not only as a matter of judicial deference to the text of section 11 but also in terms of section 12's requirement as to the capability to comprehend rather than actual comprehension.

3. Legal Disqualification

Even persons of sound mind who have attained the age of majority are not capable of entering into contracts if they are disqualified from doing so by any law to which they are subject. The Third Indian Law Commission's *Second Report on the Substantive Law for India*,[27] which contains an earlier draft of the Contract Act, shows that this third category relating to disqualifications was a later addition. The draft in the Law Commission's Second Report stated, in section 2, only that 'Every person who is of the age of majority according to the law to which he is subject, and who is of sound mind, may enter into a contract.'[28]

This third category under section 11 is formulated not in terms of prohibitions upon certain types of contracts but of 'disqualifications' upon contract parties. The term conveys something distinct from section 23 of the Contract Act, which identifies situations where the consideration or object of an agreement is unlawful. An agreement

[24] *Mohamad Baksh Khan v Hosseini Bibi* (1888) 15 IA 81, 96. But see the judgment of Sinha J in *Indar Singh* (n 19), which seems to equate *parda nashin* ladies with persons of unsound mind as deserving similar protection. This view appears to be an outlier.

[25] For a more detailed treatment of cases relating to *parda nashin* women, see Sk E Uddin Ahmed, 'Purdah Norms and the British Courts in Colonial India,' (2016) 77 Proceedings of the Indian History Congress 504; W Rattigan, 'The Parda Nashin Woman and Her Protection by British Courts of Justice' (1901) 3 Journal of the Society of Comparative Legislation 252. Over time, however, the presumption of undue influence based on certain surrounding circumstances seems to have given way to a generalised presumption of undue influence in all transactions with *parda nashin* women. See eg the judgment of Subba Rao J in *Kharbuja Kuer v Jangbahadur Rai* 1963 AIR 1203. The burden appears to be upon the person who seeks to sustain a document executed by a *parda nashin* woman that she executed it understanding the nature of the transaction.

[26] *Agadhei Malikani v Abhimanyu Mallik* ILR 1968 Cut 576; *Gajraj Pasayat v Debraj Pasayat* MANU/OR/0230/2018.

[27] Third Indian Law Commission, *Second Report on the Substantive Law for India* (31 July 1866) 6.

[28] ibid 7.

to commit robbery, for example, has an unlawful object, but it would distort the text to suggest that the would-be robbers are 'disqualified' by the Indian Penal Code, 1860 from entering into the agreement.

The use of the phrase 'disqualified from contracting by any law to which he is subject' suggests a prohibition or restriction placed on a person (who would otherwise be competent to contract under the Act), by virtue of the person's official position, for example, or because of some other attribute or status, such as their nationality or domicile. One such instance may be found in section 136 of the Transfer of Property Act 1882, which states that 'No judge, legal practitioner or officer connected with any court of justice shall buy or traffic in, or stipulate for, or agree to receive any share of, or interest in, any actionable claim.'[29] While the provision is phrased as a prohibition upon the person who holds one or more of the offices identified, as well as a ban on a particular types of contracts, the ban on entering into such contract flows only from the position held by the person—that is, the position is a pre-requisite for the provision to apply. Rule 16 to the Second Schedule to the Income Tax Act 1961 provides another example of a legal disqualification. That rule, which forms part of the procedure for the recovery of taxes due under the Act, states that once a notice has been served on a tax defaulter, 'the defaulter or his representative in interest shall not be competent to mortgage, charge, lease or otherwise deal with any property belonging to him except with the permission of the Tax Recovery Officer'. Here, it is a person's status as a defaulter served with notice that disqualifies the defaulter from entering into certain types of contracts.[30] These seemingly semantic distinctions between disqualifications upon persons and prohibitions upon certain contracts may pose some questions in terms of section 24 of the Act, which renders void contracts for unlawful ends. The distinction and its consequences are discussed further in section II.

Another ambiguity posed by the section 11's third category of incapacity is the ambit of the term 'law' in the phrase 'disqualified from contracting by any law to which he is subject'. The term 'law' is not defined under the Contract Act, and it is unclear whether it has, or should have the same meaning as the term 'Indian law' under the General Clauses Act 1897. Does the term 'law' in section 11 refer only to an enactment or an instrument that has the force of law in India, or any part thereof, or can it apply more broadly to any restriction legally enforceable in India, including those created by contractual arrangements? At least one court has suggested that the former definition applies, although this seems to have been in the nature of *obiter dicta*.[31] No Indian court appears to have considered whether a disqualification imposed by a foreign law would result in incapacity to contract under section 11, but the question must arise whenever a non-Indian person contracts under the Act. If, as discussed above, questions of

[29] See Transfer of Property Act 1882, s 136.

[30] See eg *Sri Sivalaya Advances v Tax Recovery Officer* (Madras High Court, 28 February 2018).

[31] *Dharmeswar Kalita* (n 4). Whitley Stokes, in his *The Anglo-Indian Codes*, takes the view that 'law', at least as used in s 23 of the Act, refers to a legislative enactment. No authority is cited in support of this proposition; see W Stokes, *The Anglo Indian Codes*, vol I (Clarendon 1887) 559.

capacity are governed by the law of one's domicile, disqualifications imposed by the law of the domicile would likely serve to incapacitate, since section 11 speaks in broad terms of a person 'disqualified from contracting by *any* law to which he is subject' (emphasis added).

III. The Consequences of Incapacity

1. Voidness and Voidability

The Contract Act does not expressly address the legal status of agreements entered into with, or by, parties lacking capacity. Section 19 of the Contract Act states that agreements without free consent are voidable but that provision speaks only of agreements where consent is procured by fraud, coercion, or misrepresentation. Section 20 of the Contract Act states that contracts where both parties are mistaken as to an essential fact or facts are void, but this is unlikely to be relevant to the cases where at least one of the parties is not mistaken or unaware as to the existence of an incapacity—which may be the majority of cases. In fact, section 22 expressly addresses this situation by stating that a contract is not voidable merely because it was caused by one of the parties to it being under a mistake as to a matter of fact. Where a person contracts with a minor or lunatic, believing their counterpart to have contractual capacity, the contract is not voidable solely on the basis of that unilateral mistake.

Before ascertaining the legal status of an agreement entered into by an incapacitated party, one might ask whether all forms of incapacity should lead to the same legal outcome. The policy considerations that relate to agreements with lunatics or minors may not apply to agreements with the legally disqualified. Indian courts have not usually taken section 11 as a single directive. Instead, judicial pronouncements have usually specifically discussed the status of minors' contracts, or contracts with the mentally unsound, rather than section 11 generally. It may also be useful to distinguish between two distinct, though related issues—first, the legal status of agreements with incapacitated persons; and second, the relief, if any, for such agreements. It may be logical to assume that the disposition of the second issue flows from the first, but the case law has not always taken this approach.

A few decisions dominate all discussions on the legal status of agreements with the incapacitated—perhaps none more so than the Privy Council's judgment in *Mohori Bibee v Dharmodas Ghose*.[32] This decision, which has been severely criticised,[33] nevertheless exerts influence in the highest judicial quarters, as shown by a recent approving reference to *Mohori Bibee* by the Supreme Court in *Mathai Mathai v Mary Joseph*.[34]

[32] (1902) 30 IA 114.

[33] For a recent and very thorough critical examination of *Mohori Bibee* (n 32) and the problems it creates, see S Swaminathan and R Surana, 'Minors' Contracts: A Major Problem with the Indian Contract Act, 1872' (2018) XX Statute Law Review 1.

[34] (2015) 5 SCC 622.

In *Mohori Bibee*, the estate of a money lender sought to recover a loan made to a minor against a mortgage. The Privy Council observed that although 'the general current of decision in India' treated the 'contracts of infants' as voidable, there had also been 'vigorous protests' to the contrary.[35] In the Privy Council's view, this apparent lack of consensus among Indian courts entitled their Lordships to 'consider themselves at liberty to act on their own view of the law'. Thus liberated, the Privy Council held that because minors lacked the capacity to contract under the Contract Act, their contracts never came into existence and were necessarily void rather than voidable. The proposition that the contract had never come into existence led the Privy Council to conclude that no restoration of any advantage received by the contract parties was required under section 65 of the Contract Act.[36]

The infirmities of *Mohori Bibee* range across statute, precedent, and policy. First, as sections 19[37] and 19A[38] of the Contract Act suggest, the absence of free consent does not necessarily make a contract void *ab initio*, and there is nothing in sections10 or 11 of the Contract Act to suggest that a minor's contract is necessarily void. There is no reason why a party's minority or unsoundness of mind is somehow a qualitatively worse defect in contract formation than fraud, coercion, misrepresentation, or undue influence. The incapacity of minors and the mentally unsound therefore ought not lead to qualitatively different contract outcomes.

Second, despite the Privy Council's observations, it is not clear that there had been 'vigorous protests' in the Indian courts against treating minors' contracts as voidable rather than void. Few decisions, if any, seem to evidence such protest, and none of them seem very vigorous. For example, in *Saraswati Debya v Mahamed Arif*,[39] the Calcutta High Court observed that its precedents on Hindu personal law had treated minors' contracts as voidable at the minor's instance and that this position had not been changed by the enactment of the Contract Act.[40]

[35] *Mohori Bibee* (n 32) 5. No decisions were cited in the judgment, either as evidence of the 'general current' for voidability or of the 'vigorous protests' against it.

[36] ibid 7–8.

[37] The first sentence of the Contract Act, s 19 states that 'When consent to an agreement is caused by coercion, fraud or misrepresentation, the agreement is a contract voidable at the option of the party whose consent was so caused.'

[38] The first sentence the Contract Act, s 19A states that 'When consent to an agreement is caused by undue influence, the agreement is a contract voidable at the option of the party whose consent was so caused.'

[39] (1891) ILR 18 Cal 259.

[40] In support of its decision, the Court cited *Sashi Bhushan Dutt v Jadu Nath Dutt* (1885) ILR 11 Cal 552, which expressly noted that Indian law and English law on the point were alike and that '[a] contract entered into with a minor is only voidable at the option of the minor'. In *Saraswati Debya* (n 39), the Court also cited the decisions in *Rennie v Gunga Narain Chowdhry* (1865) 3 WR 10; *Hari Ram v Jitan Ram* (1869) 3 Bom LR (AC) 426; *Boiddonath Dey v Ram Kishore Dey* (1870) 13 WR 166; *Doorga Churn Saha v Ram Narain Doss* (1870) 13 WR 172, but these appear to have been decisions on the Hindu personal law rather than the Act. See also *Hanmant Lakshman v Jayarao Nasinha* (1889) ILR 13 Bom 50 (a very brief decision, which does not discuss its reasoning, holding that a minor who had executed a bond could be sued upon it) and the observations of Stuart, CJ on the ability of a minor to enter into a mortgage in *Behari Lal v Beni Lal* 3 All 408. By contrast, *Fatima Bibi v Debnauth Shah* (1893) ILR 20 Cal 508 is the rare case which seems to have taken the view that minors' contracts were void rather than voidable, but this observation seems to have been in the nature of *obiter dicta* as it had no bearing upon the decision. On the continuation of English common law doctrines after the passage of the Act, the Privy Council's decision in *Bugwandas v The Irrawaddy Flotilla Company* observed that the Act 'does not profess to be a complete code dealing with the law relating to contracts. It purports to do no more than to define and amend certain parts of that law.' The decision went on to state that 'It is scarcely conceivable that [the Act] could have been intended to sweep away the common law by a side wind': (1891) 18 ILR Cal 620, 629–30.

Third, the decision in *Mohori Bibee* appears unworkable because it automatically renders void all minors' contracts so that everyday commerce is seriously threatened. Minors should not have to be represented by guardians to undertake quotidian transactions of little value or significance. Nor are there strong policy concerns that would suggest that an absolute bar on contracts made by minors unrepresented by guardians is desirable, especially when such contracts may be advantageous to the minor.

It is also notable that the Guardian and Wards Act 1890, which took effect well before *Mohori Bibee*, prohibits dispositions or encumbrances of minors' immovable property by guardians acting without court approval but only makes such transactions voidable at the instance of any other person affected thereby, including the minor.[41] It seems odd that the minor can effectively ratify the act of a third party but not the minor's own.

These difficulties of law and policy notwithstanding, *Mohori Bibee* has received judicial deference, if only sometimes grudgingly. Several High Courts sought to finesse their way past the absolutism of *Mohori Bibee* by enforcing contracts in cases where the minor, as the promisee, had performed his obligations in their entirety and was suing for performance by the other party.[42] This doctrine could not help minors who were promisors[43] or minors who had only partly performed their obligations,[44] but it certainly blunted the application of the sweeping rule in *Mohori Bibee* in favour of what may have appeared to be a class of sympathetic defendants.

Dexterous though this judicial manoeuvre may have been, it has not survived the Supreme Court's decision in *Mathai Mathai v Joseph Mary*. Holding a mortgage deed in favour of an unrepresented minor invalid, the Court observed that while many decisions had held that a minor could be a mortgagee as it was in the minor's interests, this was 'an erroneous application of the law keeping in mind the decision of the Privy Council in *Mohori Bibee*'s case'.[45]

Mathai Mathai thus seems to revive *Mohori Bibee* to its full potency, so that every contract by a minor is void *ab initio*, irrespective of the benefits conferred on the minor, the minor's performance of its obligations, and the minor's desire to enforce performance. It is less clear what the impact of *Mathai Mathai* is on the ability to recover advantages or benefits conferred on the minor, but if *Mohori Bibee* is taken to be entirely correct, no recovery should ever be possible because no contract ever existed. Perhaps most worryingly, *Mohori Bibee* did not permit even a restitutionary claim under section 65 of the Act, although it is unclear whether this bar on recovery was confined to

[41] See Guardian and Wards Act 1890, s 30. See also the HMGA, s 8(3), which makes such transactions voidable at the instance of the minor or any person claiming under the minor.

[42] Swaminathan and Surana trace the origins of this judicial manoeuvre to the Transfer of Property Act 1882, s 7, which requires only the transferor of property to have contractual capacity and does not expressly require this of the transferee. Although the courts have likened these cases to 'unilateral contracts', the authors suggest that the doctrine's 'conceptual foundations may be questionable', given that the cases all involved contracts with obligations due from both sides: Swaminathan and Surana (n 33) 5–7.

[43] *Navakoti Narayana Chetty v Loyalinga Chetty* (1910) 33 ILR Mad 312; *Munni Kunwar v Madan Gopal* (1916) 38 ILR All 62.

[44] *Pramila Balidas v Jogeshwar* AIR 1918 Pat 626, 627; *Raj Rani v Prem Adib* AIR 1949 Bom 215.

[45] *Pramila Balidas* (n 44) 634–35.

the particular circumstances in that case, where the lender had proceeded with clear knowledge of the borrower's incapacity. This is clearly an untenable situation, and High Courts and the subordinate judiciary may continue to find ways to escape its full rigour, although the net effect may be the creation of inconsistent contractual doctrines unmoored in precedent.[46] The discussion in section III suggests that Indian courts have not interpreted *Mohori Bibee* to bar recovery so uniformly.

The situation in respect of agreements with the mentally unsound seems very similar to the position in *Mohori Bibee*. In *Monosseh Jacob Monosseh v Shapurji Hormusji Harver*,[47] the Bombay High Court referred to *Mohori Bibee* for the proposition that a contract by a person of unsound mind was void *ab initio*, although it affirmed the validity of the mortgage in question. Not long thereafter, the Madras High Court referred to *Mohori Bibee* to conclude that the defendant could not rely on a sale deed executed during a period of lunacy to prove his title.[48] Other High Courts have also followed the view that an agreement with a person of unsound mind is void *ab initio*.[49] These decisions diverged from the English common law, which had traditionally treated contracts by a person of unsound mind as voidable at that person's instance if two conditions were met. First, the person had to show that he or she did not know what he or she was doing; and second that the person with whom he or she contracted 'knew him to be so insane as not to be capable of understanding what he was about'.[50]

The current unsatisfactory position is therefore that agreements with unrepresented minors and persons of unsound mind are void *ab initio*, rather than merely voidable at their instance. For the reasons discussed earlier, it seems preferable that these be regarded as contracts voidable at the instance of the minor or mentally impaired person. However, although these categories of incapacity dominate the case law under section 11, it is necessary to also consider contracts made by persons incapacitated by a legal disqualification. The relatively few cases that deal with this third category expose the difference in policies that may underlie the types of incapacity described in section 11 of the Contract Act.

It seems plainly correct that an agreement entered into by a person legally disqualified from doing so must be void *ab initio*, rather than voidable at the instance of either

[46] See the Indian Supreme Court order in *Gopal Prasad v Bihar School Examination Board* [2020] 11 SCR170. This decision serves as a recent example where *Mohori Bibee* (n 32) was effectively ignored, despite its seeming relevance. There, a two-judge bench of the Supreme Court was unable to agree on whether the point at which a government employee was mandatorily required to retire should be determined based on the employee's age or the duration of his employment. Justice Rastogi noted that the employee had been a minor at the time when he began his employment, and therefore took the view that employment could not have legally commenced until the employee reached the age of majority. In contrast, Justice Indira Banerjee stated that the employee's status as a minor at the time of entering employment was 'inconsequential', asserting that the contract had effectively been ratified by the employee upon attaining majority. Irrespective of the merits of Justice Banerjee's view that the minor's contract of employment was effectively voidable rather than void *ab initio*, her judgment makes no mention of *Mohori Bibee* (n 32) or *Mathai Mathai* (n 34) and the doctrinal difficulties they may pose.

[47] (1908) 10 Bom LR 1004.

[48] *Machaima v Usman Beari* (1907) 17 Mad LJ 78.

[49] *Amina Bibi v Saiyid Yusuf* AIR 1922 All 449; *Indar Singh* (n 19); *Johri v Mahila Draupti* AIR 1991 MP 340.

[50] *Imperial Loan Co v Stone* (1892) 1 QB 599, 601. That rule has been developed further by the decision in *Hart v O'Connor* [1985] 2 All ER 880, but these more recent developments do not appear to have been adopted by the Indian High Courts as yet.

party.[51] While contractual incapacity for minors and the mentally unsound ostensibly serves to protect vulnerable persons, statutory disqualifications from contracting may serve varying policy goals, such as preserving the integrity of the judicial process,[52] restraining tax defaulters from hindering recovery of unpaid taxes,[53] or guarding against conflicts of interest in the administrative process.[54] It would be unacceptable to permit parties to contractually nullify legislation in furtherance of such policies. Further, in several cases relating to legal disqualifications, the statute expressly declared the contract void *ab initio*, thus putting the matter beyond doubt.[55]

Cases of legal disqualification are thus different from other cases of incapacity under the Act for a number of reasons. First, they typically involve legislative goals other than the protection of a vulnerable class of persons. Second, and as a result of the first difference, the fact that a contract may be advantageous to the incapacitated party cannot be a sufficient reason for allowing the contract to stand. Third, many statutes that impose a legal disqualification also expressly state that the contract made by a disqualified person will be void. This is unlike the Contract Act, which does not expressly provide for the voidness of contracts entered into by incapacitated persons. Even if the statute does not expressly state that contracts by disqualified persons are void, such voidness would have to be inferred from the mandatory nature of the statute and the policy goals it was enacted to further. Further, if contracts by legally disqualified persons were treated as voidable for some reason, this would be a difficult result to square with section 24 of the Contract Act, which states that contracts for unlawful objects are void. The overall effect might be chaotic, with litigants resorting to semantic sleights-of-hand to varyingly contend either that it was a contracting party that was disqualified or that the contract was for an unlawful end.

The debate regarding the voidness or voidability of contracts entered into by persons subject to different types of incapacity serve to underline again that incapacity is not a uniform type of legal defect in contract formation. Rather, the determination as to whether a contract is void *ab initio* or merely voidable for incapacity ought to depend on the type of incapacity in question. Yet, the profoundly problematic precedent in *Mohori Bibee* stands in the way of a more nuanced understanding of incapacity and its consequences, particularly the recovery of benefits conferred.

[51] *Lachmi Narain* (n 10); *Shah Jethalal Lalchand v Darbar Shri Amarwala Laxmanwala* AIR 1953 Sau 177. The latter case, however, is complicated by the fact that the contract in question was executed by a person who was not only subject to a legal disqualification but also a minor at the time of execution.

[52] See eg The Transfer of Property Act 1882, s 136.

[53] *DS Senthilvel v Tax Recovery Officer* MANU/TN/2308/2018.

[54] See eg The Indian Forest Act 1927, s 75; The Patents Act 1970, s 75.

[55] See eg *Shah Jethalal Lalchand* (n 51), in which the statute in question stated that the owners of certain types of estates would be incompetent to enter into any contract involving them or their estates in any pecuniary liability, and that if such contract were made, it would be void. See also *Lal Chandradwaj Deo v Lal Artraran Deo* AIR 1936 Ngp 15; but see *DS Senthilvel* (n 53) for an example of a case where voidness was inferred from the statute.

IV. Remedies

One reason *Mohori Bibee* may have survived as long as it has, may be because its holding that all minors' contracts are void *ab initio* has not been matched by a corresponding bar on all recoveries from such contracts.[56] Indian courts have instead usually weighed the asymmetries of information between the contract parties in determining recovery—an approach that may have softened the impact of *Mohori Bibee*.

In *Mohori Bibee*, the Privy Council barred recovery under section 65 of the Contract Act because no contract had ever come into being. This effectively ignores the text of section 65 of the Contract Act, which applies to 'agreements' rather than 'contracts', so that recoveries should be possible even for contracts void *ab initio*, that is, for agreements that are not legally enforceable.[57] But section 65's phrase 'discovered to be void' suggests that to avail of the provision, neither party should have known that the agreement was void at the time of entry.[58] Thus, section 65 cannot be used by plaintiffs who knew of their counterpart's incapacity. More inequitably, the text of section 65 would appear to bar recovery even to the unwitting plaintiff who advanced money to an incapacitated party who knew of their own incapacity, but courts and the Law Commission appear to have taken the view that returning benefits conferred in such cases is consistent with *Mohori Bibee*, since it restores the parties to the *status quo*.[59]

Restricting recovery under section 65 of the Contract Act to cases where neither party knew of the incapacity is consistent with the facts in *Mohori Bibee*, where the lender knew of, and had made efforts to get around, the borrower's minor status.[60] The courts, and the drafters of the Specific Relief Act 1963 have also considered whether the consequences of misrepresentations by minors should be the same as in situations where a person knowingly contracts with an incapacitated party. Should recovery be barred in both cases? Or should the misrepresenting minor and the knowing counterparty be dealt with asymmetrically?

The Law Commission of India sought to provide for differing outcomes for these two situations by recommending an amendment to permit recovery under section 65 of the Contract Act where the minor misrepresented the minor's status as an adult, while continuing to bar recovery where the counterparty knew of the other's incapacity at the time of contracting.[61] This would have read down the phrase 'discovered to be

[56] The discussion in this section is premised on the Privy Council's ruling that all contracts with minors are necessarily void *ab initio*, a position with which this chapter disagrees. If, however, a future bench of the Indian Supreme Court was to hold that contracts with minors and the mentally unsound are voidable, rather than void, then plaintiffs would likely seek their remedy under the Contract Act, s 64 besides any remedies under the Specific Relief Act 1963.

[57] Swaminathan and Surana (n 33) 11.

[58] Stokes (n 31) 583. See also *Harnath Kuar v Inder Bahadur Singh* AIR 1922 PC 403, 405; *Anand Mohan v Gour Mohan* AIR 1923 PC 189, 191; *Hans Raj v Dehra Dun MT Co* AIR 1923 PC 63, 66; *Kuju Collieries v Jharkhand Mines* AIR 1974 SC 1892. However, the marginal note to s 65 appears to suggest that s 65 applies more broadly to all void contracts, not just those 'discovered to be void'; see Briggs and Burrows (n 1) 223.

[59] Law Commission of India, *Report on Indian Contract Act 1872* (Law Com Report No 13, 1958) 20; *Ajudhia Prasad v Chandan Lal* AIR 1937 All 610 (618).

[60] *Mohori Bibee* (n 32), 2.

[61] Law Commission of India, *Report on Indian Contract Act 1872* (n 59) 39.

void' in section 65 to bar recovery only by parties who proceeded with knowledge of an incapacity. The move to formally amend section 65 did not fructify, but the provision today is understood to bar recovery where the party seeking to recover knew of the incapacity at the time of contracting.[62]

1. Remedies under the Specific Relief Act

Plaintiffs frustrated by the limitations of section 65 of the Contract Act sought relief under sections 39 and 41 of the Specific Relief Act of 1887, which permitted the cancellation of void instruments and compensation upon cancellation, respectively.[63] The text of these provisions did not incorporate the *in pari delicto* principle so that knowledge of an incapacity at the time of contracting did not bar recovery. However, section 41 only empowered courts to require compensation by the party who successfully sought cancellation—a defendant who successfully resisted suit on the ground that the instrument was void was left unable to recover. The effect of sections 39 and 41 of the 1887 Act was combined in section 33 of the Specific Relief Act 1963 of 1963, but section 33[64] expanded section 41 to permit courts to require compensation by a defendant who successfully resisted a suit on the grounds of voidness of the instrument.

On its face, section 33 of the Specific Relief Act 1963 permits the courts to move beyond *Mohori Bibee*'s holding that no recovery is possible for a contract with a minor because it is void *ab initio*. However, section 33 is couched in permissive terms and

[62] In *Amolakchand Seth v Pralhad Singh* 1972 MP LJ 473, the Madhya Pradesh High Court reviewed much of the case law on recovery for minors' contracts existing at the time and sought to explain why this approach was in accord with s 65. The decision is important because it expressly considered the bar in *Mohori Bibee* to be limited by its circumstances; that is, there the mortgagee had known of the incapacity of the mortgagor and sought to contract around it. The Court noted that

> [U]ltimately the basic principle of equity behind section 41, Specific Relief Act and section 65 of the Contract Act is the same, namely, a person who wants to get out of his obligation under an agreement or a contract, whether or not evidenced by an instrument, he may, if equitable considerations require, be compelled to disgorge the advantage gained by him. It is conceivable that the party seeking such restoration has by its own inequity forfeited the right to get it; but that would be another matter. As in all equitable matters, the Court will before granting relief consider whether the hands of the proposed recipient are clean.

Notably, the Court appears to have interpreted s 65's phrase 'discovered to be void' to only require the party seeking recovery to have discovered the contract's voidness after having conferred the advantage. The Court does not appear to have discussed how the phrase 'discover to be void' applies in a situation where the other party knew of the incapacity at the contract's inception.

[63] See eg *Monosseh Jacob Monosseh* (n 47). The Court noted that

> Therefore if one party seeks to enforce a contract which is void under s 12 of the Contract Act on account of the absence of capacity to contract in the other contracting party, it is not permissible to give equitable relief. However statutory relief can be given under ss 38 and 4 of the Specific Relief Act when rescission of a contract is asked for on this ground.

[64] The relevant part of the Specific Relief Act 1963, s 33 states that

> Where a defendant successfully resists any suit on the ground . . . that the agreement sought to be enforced against him in the suit is void by reason of his not having been competent to contract under section 11. . ., the court may, if the defendant has received any benefit under the agreement from the other party, require him to restore, so far as may be, such benefit to that party, to the extent to which he or his estate has benefited thereby.

provides no guidelines as to how judicial discretion is to be exercised in such cases. The text of section 33 permits recovery both by incapacitated parties who misrepresent their status and by those who proceed with knowledge of the other party's incapacity. Indian courts have, however, usually applied section 33 where 'there was equity in favour of the defendant'.[65] In practice, this has meant that recovery continues to be barred for those who knowingly contract with the incapacitated[66] so that the workings of section 33 of the Specific Relief Act 1963 in this respect are similar to those of section 65 of the Contract Act.

Relief for minors who misrepresent their age at the time of contracting has presented a greater challenge for Indian courts. The courts have differed on the extent to which the misrepresenting minor should be entitled to relief under section 41 of the 1887 Act. The Lahore High Court held that a misrepresenting minor who successfully resisted a suit on the ground of his minority was bound to restore both the property and the pecuniary benefit derived from the contract.[67] The Court took the view that this outcome was a negation of the contract, rather than its enforcement. The Allahabad High Court [68] and the Andhra Pradesh High Court[69] took a different view, requiring the misrepresenting minor to restore the specific property but not the pecuniary benefit since that would amount to enforcing the contract against the minor.[70] The Law Commission sided with the Lahore High Court, recommending the enactment of what would become section 33 of the Specific Relief Act 1963, requiring the restoration of all proprietary and pecuniary benefits received but requiring no compensation to be paid by the minor.[71]

The situation today therefore appears to be that the party who contracts with knowledge of the other's incapacity cannot recover any benefit conferred on the other, either under section 65 of the Contract Act or section 33 of the Specific Relief Act 1963. An incapacitated party who misrepresents or conceals that party's incapacity is required to return all proprietary and pecuniary benefit received under section 33, though no claim may lie against them under section 65.

[65] *Gurushiddswami v Parawa Dundaya Narendra* AIR 1920 Bom 269. There, the minor plaintiff had misrepresented herself as having attained majority, but the Bombay High Court found for her, noting that the defendant had made inquiries as to her status elsewhere and had proceeded with knowledge of the incapacity.

[66] ibid. See also *Maniyan Nadar v Harikumar* AIR 2015 Ker 183; and for the opposite result, where relief was granted to a buyer who had unknowingly contracted with a minor seller, *Thiru Arooran Sugars v State Bank of India* Mad HC (1990).

[67] *Khan Gul v Lakha Singh* AIR 1928 Lah 609, 617–18. The Madras High Court took a similar view in *TR Appasami Ayyangar v Narayanaswami Iyer* AIR 1930 Mad 945, as did the then Mysore High Court in *Dyaviah v Shivamma* AIR 1959 Mysore 188.

[68] *Ajudhia Prasad* (n 60).

[69] *Gokeda Latcharao v Vishwanadham Bhimayya* AIR 1956 AP 182; Law Commission of India, *The Specific Relief Act 1877* (Law Com Report No 9, 1958) 45–46.

[70] This would also mean that where the minor had converted a non-cash benefit conferred to cash, a tracing remedy would not be available because that would amount to 'enforcing a contract of loan': see *Gokeda Latcharao* (n 69).

[71] Law Commission of India, *The Specific Relief Act 1877* (n 69) 46.

2. Remedies in Cases Involving Incapacitation by Legal Disqualification

The case law on restitution of benefits conferred upon an incapacitated person has almost entirely developed in the context of contracts with minors. As a result, it is less clear whether, and how, restitution should be ordered where one party is subject to some other type of incapacity. This is particularly the case where one party is subject to a legal disqualification. Such contracts are void *ab initio* (and unlike minors' contracts, should be void *ab initio*), but could any recovery be permitted under either section 65 of the Contract Act or section 33 of the Specific Relief Act 1963 for such cases?

The case law on both provisions indicate that recovery is unlikely where the party seeking recovery contracted with knowledge of the other's incapacity or their own. In the case of contracts with minors and persons of unsound mind, such knowledge of the incapacity is a question of fact that must be proved in the ordinary course. But in cases where a party is subject to a legal disqualification, are parties presumed to have knowledge of the legal disqualification, as an extension of the presumption that contract parties know the law? For example, if an Indian judge, acting in ignorance of section 136 of the Transfer of Property Act 1872 proceeds to buy an actionable claim, it is unlikely that the judge could cite ignorance as a ground for recovery under either section 65 of the Contract Act or section 33 of the Specific Relief Act 1963. Could the errant judge seek recovery under section 72 of the Contract Act, which states that a person to whom money has been paid, or anything delivered, by mistake or under coercion, must repay or return it?

Section 21 of the Contract Act states that a contract is not voidable because it was caused by a mistake as to any law in force in India, while a mistake as to a law not in force in India has the same effect as a mistake of fact. The courts were split[72] on the question of whether section 72 of the Contract Act permitted recovery for amounts paid under a mistake of law, until first the Privy Council,[73] and then the Supreme Court of India,[74] confirmed that such monies were recoverable under section 72.[75] Yet, in permitting such recovery, the Supreme Court of India cited with approval the Privy Council's observation that not every sum paid under mistake is recoverable and that '[t]here may in a particular case be circumstances which disentitle a plaintiff by

[72] The Bombay and Madras High Courts took the view that no recovery under the Contract Act, s 72 was possible for amounts paid in mistake of law; see *Wolf and Sons v Dadiba Khimji and Co* AIR 1920 Bom 192; *AM Appavoo Chettiar v South Indian Railway Company* (1929) 56 MLJ 269, respectively. The Calcutta High Court ruled that amounts paid in mistake of law were recoverable under section 72 of the Contract Act. See *Jagdish Prosad Pannalal v Produce Exchange Corporation Ltd* AIR 1946 Cal 245.

[73] *Shiba Prasad Singh v Maharaja Srish Chandra Nandi* AIR 1949 PC 297.

[74] *Sales Tax Officer Banaras v Kanhaiya Lal Mukund Lal Saraf* AIR 1959 SC 135.

[75] Some Indian courts have also sought to draw a distinction between a 'pure mistake of law' contemplated under section 21, for which there is no recovery under section 72, and some category of mixed mistakes of fact and law, for which recovery may be possible. *AM Appavoo Chettiar* (n 72). This distinction, which seems unclear, did not affect the decision in *Appavoo Chettiar*, which held that the mistake in question was a 'pure mistake of law' and therefore subject to the Contract Act, s 21.

estoppel or otherwise'.[76] This observation is clearly significant for barring recovery by plaintiffs who misrepresent or conceal their legal disqualification but are plaintiffs who sign contractual clauses representing that they are under no legal disqualification similarly estopped, even if they did not actually know of their disqualification at the time of contracting?[77] The question is yet to be tested in litigation in the Indian courts, and it is certainly possible that a plaintiff who executes documents without due diligence as to their own status may find recovery barred under section 65 and section 72 of the Act, as well as under section 33 of the Specific Relief Act 1963.

Notably, the Supreme Court of India stated that courts should not use equitable principles to determine recovery because the text of section 72 is clear.[78] It is not clear, though, that equitable principles should never be considered in determining whether a legally disqualified person should be permitted to recover. First, in the same decision, the Supreme Court of India permitted the consideration of equitable factors such as waiver and estoppel. Second, the Supreme Court's decision permitting recovery for amounts paid under a mistake of law under section 72 did not specifically contemplate payments under a contract that was void *ab initio* as a result of a mistake of law. Where, for example, a legal disability is mandatorily imposed to further a particular policy promoting an important legislative goal (as with section 136 of the Transfer of Property Act 1872), it may be perverse to permit full recovery by persons who make payment with no knowledge of the disqualification. Permitting full recovery in such cases would effectively render such transactions risk-proof. Parties would receive their expected consideration if the contract was unchallenged, and even if the contract were declared void, they would recover all benefits conferred so that there would be no hazard to contracting in violation of the law.

One further wrinkle may be worth discussing in the context of incapacity caused by legal disqualification. Section 11 of the Act notes that a person lacks capacity if the person is 'disqualified from contracting by any law to which he is subject'. Where the disqualifying law is an Indian law, it is unclear what effect parties' ignorance of such laws would precisely have for recovery under sections 65 or 72 of the Contract Act or section 33 of the Specific Relief Act 1963. But what if one contracting party is a foreigner subject to a disqualification under a foreign law, and neither party actually knew of the disqualification? Section 21 of the Contract Act states that the parties' mistake regarding the foreigner's incapacity would amount to a mistake of fact, and, in the absence of misrepresentation or concealment of the incapacity, recovery under either of section 72 of the Contract Act or section 33 of the Specific Relief Act should be possible.

[76] *Kanhaiya Lal* (n 74), citing *Shiba Prasad Singh* (n 73). Elsewhere in *Kanhaiya Lal*, the Indian Supreme Court also recognised waiver and limitation as other grounds for barring recovery of an amount paid under mistake of law.

[77] The question is complicated by the fact that at least one High Court has held that ignorance of law or its deliberate disregard does not necessarily amount to a mistake of law; see *Anath Bandhu Deb v Dominion of India* AIR 1955 Cal 626. It is unclear, however, whether this proposition survives the Supreme Court's decision in *Kanhaiya Lal* (n 74); see *Modern Industries v State of Uttar Pradesh* (1973) 32 STC 555 All.

[78] *Kanhaiya Lal* (n 74), disapproving of an earlier observation of the Nagpur High Court in *Nagorao v Governor General-in-Council* AIR 1951 Ngp 372,374.

Much of the foregoing discussion on restitution for payments made under a contract with a person subject to a legal disqualification is only informed speculation. There appear to be no cases directly on the issue, and it would be dangerous to take a body of law developed specifically in the context of one particular kind of incapacity and apply it to a completely different type of incapacity.

3. Quasi-Contractual Remedies under the Contract Act

If section 65 of the Contract Act is unavailable to a plaintiff because no contract has formed, the plaintiff might seek recourse to one of the quasi-contractual remedies provided in Chapter V of the Contract Act. Unlike section 65, these provisions do not require a contract to have been in existence for a remedy to be available. Two provisions in particular—sections 68 and 72 of the Contract Act—may be relevant to benefits conferred upon the incapacitated.[79]

The first of these, section 68 of the Contract Act, states that a person who supplies an incapacitated person, or anyone the incapacitated person is bound to support 'with necessaries suited to his condition in life' is entitled to be reimbursed from the property of the incapacitated person. By its terms, the supplying of necessaries is likely to be something that is required to be done only for minors or persons of unsound mind so that it is unlikely that this provision applies to persons subject to a legal disqualification. The liability is not to pay an agreed price but only to reimburse,[80] and the liability attaches to the incapacitated person's estate rather than to that person personally.[81] Much of the litigation around the provision has revolved around the interpretation of the phrase 'necessaries suited to his condition in life', which the courts have rightly read to extend beyond necessities alone.[82]

Section 68 of the Contract Act provides a more secure basis for a claim against an incapacitated person's estate in that it does not require any contract. But this advantage may be negated by the plaintiff's need to prove that the money, goods, or services supplied were necessary for the minor's condition of life and that there was no other supply from other sources.

[79] A third provision on quasi-contracts, the Contract Act, s 70, states that a person who confers a non-gratuitous benefit on another is entitled to be compensated by that other. The courts have ruled that a minor is not liable to a suit under s 70 because if the minor cannot be sued on an express contract, the minor cannot be sued on an implied one. Courts have also been concerned that if s 70 covered such contracts, the Contract Act, s 68 would be rendered nugatory: *Re Ambica Textiles Ltd* AIR 1950 Cal 491; *Bapulal v Laxmi Bharat Trading Co* AIR 1966 Raj 14; *Shahbaz Khan v Bhangi Khan* AIR 1931 Lah 344; *Bankey Behari Prasad v Mahendra Prasad* AIR 1940 Pat 324.

[80] This also appears to bar a claim for interest: *Umrao Singh v Firm Banarsi Das-Dip Chand* AIR 1927 Lah 414; *Ramchandra v Hari* AIR 1936 Ngp 12, although this may sometimes be allowed on non-statutory grounds; see *RV Rajarathna Chettiar v Shari Shaick Mahboob Sahib* AIR 1940 Mad 106.

[81] See eg *Juggessur Sircar v Nilumbur Biswas* (1865) 3 WR 217; *Sadhu Laxmi Sundaramma v Sadhu Suryanarayana* AIR 1950 Mad 274; *Mahmood Ali v Chinki Shah* AIR 1930 All 128; *Sadasheo Balaji v Firm Hiralal Ramgopal* AIR 1938 Ngp 65, 68.

[82] See eg *Jagon Ram Marwari v Mahadeo Prosad Sahu* (1909) ILR 36 Cal 768, citing, among other decisions, *Peters v Fleming* (1840) 6 M & W 42.

The other relevant quasi-contractual provision, section 72 of the Contract Act, has been discussed in connection with persons who contract in ignorance of an applicable legal disability. The mistakes contemplated by section 72 typically appear to be unilateral,[83] and the text of the provision suggests it should permit recovery for a person who enters into an agreement in the mistaken belief that their counterparty is not incapacitated. Recovery under section 72 does not require any contract to have been formed and is not limited to necessities, unlike section 68—both of which make it suitable for plaintiffs who have conferred benefits in good faith.

V. Conclusion

Indian cases on recovery for contracts with the incapacitated do not appear to yield significant identifiable principles. One fairly consistent thread running through many of the cases after *Mohori Bibee* is that recovery usually depends on judicial perceptions of the competing equities. In particular, recovery has often turned on the question of one party's knowledge or misrepresentation of the situation, even where the statute does not necessarily restrict recovery along these lines, as, for example, section 33 of the Specific Relief Act 1963 does not. This common-sense approach to recovery usually results in restitution for parties who are not at fault (or parties whose conduct is less conspicuously capable of being faulted) and has generally lessened the impact of *Mohori Bibee* because it does not automatically disadvantage every individual who contracts with an incapacitated party. The principle (if it can be called that) is amorphous and has its limits, and a future case on recovery for a contract with the legally disqualified may highlight these. For now, however, this approach may have reduced the need to reverse *Mohori Bibee*.

The advent of online contracting, with its relative anonymity, could also have raised new issues of incapacity and misrepresentation before Indian courts. Curiously, however, the growth of e-commerce has not resulted in a rush of new cases on incapacity—perhaps because most online contracts are for relatively small sums, and customer redressal systems work reasonably efficiently for many online retailers. Whatever the reasons, the absence of an influx of new cases on incapacity and a lack of disgruntled litigants may have eased any real-world pressures *Mohori Bibee* created. Further, following the passage of the HMGA, and significant social changes over the past century, the unrepresented minor is rarely spotted in contemporary courtrooms. All of which suggests that the considerable accumulated doctrinal difficulties relating to contractual incapacity are unlike to be resolved in the near future.

[83] See eg *Kanhaiya Lal* (n 74); *Saseendrakumari v State Bank of Travancore* AIR 2011 Ker 58.

9

Coercion, Undue Influence, and Unconscionability

*Shivprasad Swaminathan and Veda Singh**

I. Isolating Central Issues

The Indian Contract Act 1872 (hereinafter 'the Contract Act') defines consent to be free when it is not caused by coercion, undue influence, fraud, misrepresentation, or mistake.[1] Coercion is defined in section 15 and undue influence in section 16 of the Contract Act. While the Act does not provide separately for unconscionability, the definition of undue influence in section 16, it will be argued, was deliberately designed to be capacious enough to incorporate a general principle of unconscionability—enough, in fact, to have subsumed the doctrine of undue influence within its ambit. This chapter explores the contours of the doctrines of coercion, undue influence, and unconscionability in Indian contract law.

Two prefatory comments about the arrangement of themes in this chapter may be in order here. First, since section 16 braided together the doctrines of unconscionability and undue influence (with the result that what would be classified as a case of unconscionability or inequality of bargaining power elsewhere in the common law world would be undue influence according to the definition in section 16), we are required to treat them conjointly here. Second, as the discussion here will reveal, there is a double dissonance between the design of sections 15 and 16 and the construction that courts have placed upon these provisions. On the one hand, courts have sought to pack into the definition of coercion in section 15 more than it can plausibly encompass within its scope, with the result that their attempts at accommodating, within the ambit of the provision, forms of illegitimate pressure like economic duress come across as tenuous and contrived. And on the other, they have unduly constricted

* This chapter is substantially based on 'Coercion, Undue Influence and Unconscionability' in Mindy Chen-Wishart, Stefan Vogenauer and Hiroo Sono (eds), *Studies in the Contract Laws of Asia IV: Invalidity* (OUP 2022). Many thanks are due to Hugh Beale, Tom Sebastian, Hiroo Sono, Ankur Sood, Ragini Surana, Stelios Tofaris, Niranjan Venkatesan, and Goh Yihan for their insightful comments on the earlier version of the chapter; and Samvit Ganesh, Angad Makkar, Manasa Ramakrishna, and Pulkit Goyal for their research assistance.

[1] Contract Act, s 14.

Shivprasad Swaminathan and Veda Singh, *Coercion, Undue Influence, and Unconscionability* In: *Foundations of Indian Contract Law*. Edited by: KV Krishnaprasad, Niranjan Venkatesan, Shivprasad Swaminathan, and Umakanth Varottil, Oxford University Press.
 DOI: 10.1093/9780191997211.003.0009

section 16 by refusing to invoke it in cases of unconscionability and inequality of bargaining power where its invocation was warranted, as they have erroneously projected the narrower notion of undue influence as understood in English law onto the provision. Consequently, they have neglected to use the width and potential versatility of section 16 to supplement attempts to overcome a rigid and ossified definition of coercion in section 15.

To bring out this double dissonance and the overlap between the provisions, we would do well to reverse the order in which the doctrines are enumerated in the Act and take up undue influence and unconscionability for discussion before coercion. A recent edition of the treatise by Sir Frederick Pollock and Sir Dinshah Mulla notes that 'provisions of ss. 15 and 16 as defined in the Contract Act are not flexible to deal with the new emerging principles, whether of inequality of bargaining power, economic duress or unconscionability'.[2] While section 15 will, indeed, be found 'not flexible' as charged, section 16, it will be argued, would be equal to the task if it were interpreted as envisioned by the drafters.

II. Undue Influence and Unconscionability

1. Section 16 Prior to the 1899 Amendment

Section 16, as it presently stands, owes its shape to a far-reaching amendment in 1899. Prior to this amendment, section 16 read:

> Undue influence is said to be employed in the following cases:
> (1) When a person in whom confidence is reposed by another, or who holds a real or apparent authority over that other, makes use of such confidence or authority for a purpose of obtaining an advantage over that other which but for such confidence or authority he could not have obtained;
> (2) When a person whose mind is enfeebled by old age, illness or mental or bodily distress is so treated as to make him consent to which but for such treatment he would have not consented although such treatment may not amount to coercion.

While the phraseology of section 16(1) mirrors that found in the Field Code,[3] elements of the definition can be found in *Smith v Kay*[4] and *Huguenin v Baseley*.[5] Section 16(2) appears to have slightly extended and codified one of the several categories of

[2] N Bhadbhade (ed), *Pollock and Mulla: Indian Contract Act 1872* (14th edn, Lexis Nexis Butterworths Wadhwa 2012) 355.
[3] *The Civil Code of the State of New York* (Weed Parsons & Co 1865) § 760(1) (hereinafter 'the Field Code').
[4] (1859) 11 ER 299.
[5] (1807) 33 ER 526.

unconscionable dealing that the 18th- and 19th-century English courts of equity had intervened in.[6] Section 16(2) gave the court the power to provide relief in cases distinct from either duress or undue influence[7] because the 'cornerstone' of unconscionability was the notion of 'special disadvantage', which is not encompassed by duress or undue influence.[8]

The cases of unconscionable dealing in which the English courts of equity gave relief were never subsumed under a general principle of unconscionability. And, by the turn of the century, the career of the doctrine was abruptly cut short due to a combination of factors.[9] Although there is little material to indicate reliably why the drafters omitted incorporating a principle of unconscionability in section 16 when the Act was drafted (between 1866 and 1872), one might hypothesize that this had something to do with its incompatibility with the Will Theory. The Will Theory was arguably the *Grundnorm* of the Contract Act.[10]

Also conspicuous by its absence from section 16, as it originally stood, were the categories of 'undue pressure'[11] and presumed undue influence.[12] For better or worse, Indian courts in the late 19th and early 20th centuries continued to be greatly influenced by English contract doctrine, even if it meant overlooking—as they often did—clear provisions of the Contract Act.[13] Accordingly, even though the definition of undue influence did not, as Pollock and Mulla noted, 'reflect the generality of the English doctrine',[14] it did not prevent courts in India from achieving much of what an English court could.[15]

[6] The Field Code (n 3) § 760(2) and (3) referred to 'weakness of mind' and 'distress', respectively. English courts of equity intervened in cases of illiteracy and ignorance, poverty, mental weakness of the claimant, or where one party used a sharp practice to induce another to enter into an unwise bargain, as in the case of 'catching bargains' with 'expectant heirs': KL Fletcher, 'Review of Unconscionable Transactions' (1973) 8 University of Queensland Law Journal 45, 56.

[7] SC Banerjee, *Law of Specific Relief in British India* (2nd edn, Cambray & Co 1917) 216 (Tagore Law Lectures 1905).

[8] A Chandler and J Devenny, 'Unconscionability and the Taxonomy of Undue Influence' (2007) Journal of Business Law 541, 543. The concept of 'special disadvantage', which is central to the doctrine of unconscionability, is more easily illustrated than defined. The paradigm cases of 'special disadvantage' are drunkenness, mental deficiency, and necessity (catching bargains): see n 6 above.

[9] A full account of these factors need not detain us. The primary reason is briefly explored later. After a long 'hibernation', the doctrine has made something of a return in England since the 1960s; D Capper, 'The Unconscionable Bargain in the Common Law World' (2010) 126 Law Quarterly Review 403.

[10] W Swain, *The Law of Contract 1670–1870* (CUP 2015) 276.

[11] Which is to say, the type of situation covered in *Williams v Bailey* (1866) LR 1 HL 200.

[12] Indian Evidence Act 1872, s 111, however, shifted the burden of proof in cases of transactions where there was 'active confidence' between parties: ML Sarin, 'Contract Unconscionability in India' (1972) 14 Loyola of Los Angeles International and Comparative Law Review 569, 576.

[13] RN Gooderson, 'English Contract Problems in Indian Code and Case Law' (1958) 16 Cambridge Law Journal 67.

[14] F Pollock and D Mulla, *Indian Contract Act* (2nd edn, Sweet & Maxwell 1909) 76.

[15] See eg *Mannu Singh v Umadat Pande* (1890) 12 All 523 (Allahabad HC): where a gift of all of his property was made by an old man to his spiritual adviser with a view to secure benefits in the afterlife, the Court raised a presumption of undue influence. And in *Pudishary Numbudry v Karampally Kunhunni Kurup* (1874) 8 Mad HC Rep 378 (Madras HC) following *Williams v Bailey* (n 11), the Court struck down an agreement induced by threat to prosecute—without citing any provision of the Act. As noted earlier, such undue pressure cases did not fall within the ambit of the original s 16.

Although section 16 of the Act, as it originally stood, did not empower the courts to relieve disadvantaged parties from hard or unconscionable bargains, the courts in India freely invoked this power in a good number of cases—again, taking their cue from English cases.[16] The predominant category of cases—though not limited to it—in which section 16 was invoked concerned usurious money-lending transactions involving excessive interest rates.[17] In *Kamini Sundari v Kali Prosunno*, the Privy Council set aside a transaction for being hard and unconscionable even though it was not covered by undue influence as defined by section 16.[18] The Privy Council further confirmed this power in two other Indian appeals in the 1890s, and Indian courts followed the lead.[19] Relief in these cases was not granted on the basis of undue influence under section 16 but rather 'on the grounds on which English courts of equity would have awarded relief', which is to say, on the ground of unconscionability.[20]

2. The 1899 Amendment to Section 16

As Pollock and Mulla point out, one of the primary aims of the 1899 amendment appears to have been to rest the doctrine of unconscionability on a firm statutory basis.[21] The motivation for legislative intervention was an acute problem of rural indebtedness and usurious money-lending in India in the second half of the 1890s and was shepherded by the ace draftsman Sir Mackenzie Chalmers, who was a law member in the Governor General in Council.[22] Although the mischief could, arguably, have also been tackled by a provision focused entirely on the specific problem of usury, Chalmers proposed recasting section 16 so as to rest it on a secure 'general principle' that empowered courts to intervene in cases where parties do not 'contract with each other on a footing of equality' and, consequently, the stronger imposes 'unfair terms on the other'.[23] The proposed provision, Chalmers added, would give courts a freer hand to 'go behind the terms of the contract and to see whether the transaction is fair and reasonable or not'.[24] To buttress this, Chalmers relied on the treatise by Stephen Leake, who had postulated a general principle uniting cases of unconscionable bargains and undue influence in the conventional sense.[25] Leake saw cases of 'catching bargains' with expectant heirs and reversioners,

[16] Indian courts being fused courts of equity and law acted on these principles even before the passing of the Act 'without any express letter of the law justifying them in doing so': Pollock and Mulla (n 14) 84.

[17] ibid 85. For an illustration see, *Chidambara Chetty v Renja Krishna Muthu* (1874) 12 BLR 509 (Madras HC), where the Court scaled down the interest rate to what was considered reasonable as an interest rate of 60 per cent was found to be unconscionable.

[18] (1885) ILR 12 Cal 225 (PC). Also see *Rajah Mokham Singh v Rajah Rup Singh* (1898) 20 IA, 137.

[19] *Kunwar Ram Lal v Nil Kanth* (1893) 20 IA 112 (PC) and *Rajah Mokham Singh v Rajah Roop Singh* (1893) LR 127 (PC); the Allahabad Court in *Lalli v Ram Prasad* (1886) 9 ILR All 74 (Allahabad HC) and *Madho Singh v Kashi Ram* (1887) ILR 9 All 228 (Allahabad HC) applied this doctrine following the Privy Council.

[20] *Kesavelu Naidu v Arithulai Ammal* (1913) ILR 36 Mad 533, 542 (Madras HC) (C Sankaran Nair J).

[21] Pollock and Mulla (n 14) 84.

[22] Incidentally, England was tackling a similar problem around the same time, leading to the enactment of the Moneylenders Act 1900.

[23] *The Gazette of India* Part VI (1899) 10–11.

[24] ibid.

[25] SM Leake, *A Digest of Principles of the Law of Contract* (3rd edn, Stevens & Sons 1892) 354–61.

usurious contracts, cases where advantage was obtained by a person in a fiduciary position, and cases of 'relations of special influence' where 'dominion may be exercised by one person over another' as manifestations of the same principle, which he named as undue influence.[26] Leake never formulated the general principle in so many words, but what appears to unite these cases is the proscription of 'oppressive bargain[s]'[27] or, to borrow Lord Hardwicke's words, 'weakness' or 'necessity on one side' and 'advantage taken of that weakness' on the other.[28] Having invoked Leake, Chalmers noted,

> I think . . . we are not embarking on an unknown sea. We are merely investing our courts with equitable powers which have long been possessed by English courts . . . I think too that this Bill may fairly be regarded as restoring to our Courts an ancient jurisdiction rather than as creating a wholly new one.[29]

The resultant section, although ostensibly still a provision on undue influence, incorporated a 'general principle' of unconscionability. It protected a party to an unequal transaction from being subject to an unfair bargain—which, along with Leake, Chalmers took to underlie all cases of undue influence and unconscionability. Interestingly, this was a marked shift from the original Contract Bill, as debated in April 1872. A plea made by the then Lieutenant Governor of Bengal, to 'mitigate the severity of the law in contracts of a hard and one-sided character'[30] was strongly opposed by many members of the legislative council, including James Fitzjames Stephen, who was instrumental in drafting of the Act.[31] With the 1899 amendment, Chalmers successfully brought in what Stephens had rejected as allowing for palm-tree justice and would 'shake up the whole system of law'.[32] The section, as amended in 1899, has come down to us in the following form:

> Undue Influence defined (1) A contract is said to be induced by 'undue influence' where the relations subsisting between the parties are such that one of the parties is in a position to dominate the will of the other and uses that position to obtain an unfair advantage over the other.
>
> (2) In particular and without prejudice to the generality of the foregoing principle, a person is deemed to be in a position to dominate the will of another—
> (a) where he holds a real or apparent authority over the other, or where he stands in a fiduciary relation to the other; or
> (b) where he makes a contract with a person whose mental capacity is temporarily or permanently affected by reason of age, illness, or mental or bodily distress.

26 ibid 360.
27 ibid 356 (quoting Stuart VC in *Barrett v Hartley* [1866] LR 2 Eq 409).
28 *Earl of Chesterfield v Sir Abraham Janssen* (1750) 1 Atk 301 (Court of Chancery) 352, 339.
29 *The Gazette of India* (n 23) 11.
30 IOR 55 Leg Proc 1871–72, 350.
31 See W Swain, Chapter 1 of this volume.
32 IOR 55 Leg Proc 1871–72, 360.

(3) Where a person who is in a position to dominate the will of another, enters into a contract with him, and the transaction appears, on the face of it or on the evidence adduced, to be unconscionable, the burden of proving that such contract was not induced by undue influence shall be upon the person in a position to dominate the will of the other.

Nothing in the sub-section shall affect the provisions of section 111 of the Indian Evidence Act, 1872 (1 of 1872).

The use of the phrase 'unfair advantage' in the provision bears out the drafters' desire to posit a general principle of unconscionability. The amendment also appended four illustrations to the provision.[33] The provision went well beyond undue influence in the conventional sense as restated in *Allcard v Skinner*.[34] For one thing, section 16(1) did not require any 'improper conduct', 'coercion form outside', or 'overreaching'[35] to constitute what is known as 'improper pressure';[36] nor did it restrict its application only to cases of relationships of confidence of the *Allcard v Skinner* variety. Rather, section 16(1) posited a general principle against obtaining an 'unfair advantage' by anyone who was 'in a position to dominate the will of the other'. No actual domination of will was required. For another, section 16(3) contemplated a presumption whose operation was nothing like the category of presumed undue influence in *Allcard v Skinner*. The presumption in *Allcard v Skinner* was to apply to a well-defined class of relationships that involved an element of trust and confidence, casting a special duty upon the donee.[37] The presumption in section 16(3) was not subject to this limitation and extended to any case where one party was in a position to dominate the will of the other and the transaction was apparently (substantively) unconscionable. In this, it followed Leake, who had, in fact, subsumed *Allcard v Skinner* within the last of his categories of undue influence, namely, 'relations of special influence'.[38] Both these differences are instantiated in Illustration (c)—added by the 1899 amendment:

A, being in debt to B, the money-lender of his village, contracts a fresh loan on terms which appear to be unconscionable. It lies on B to prove that the contract was not induced by undue influence.[39]

[33] Pollock and Mulla describe three of the four illustrations as 'elementary law' on undue influence: Pollock and Mulla (n 14) 75. However, Illustration (c) did something different, which is addressed later.

[34] *Allcard v Skinner* (1887) 36 Ch D 145 (COA).

[35] ibid 181 (Lindley LJ).

[36] *Royal Bank of Scotland v Etridge* [2002] 2 AC 773 (HL) 795 (Lord Nicholls of Birkenhead).

[37] *Allcard v Skinner* (n 34) 181 (Lindley LJ).

[38] ibid 360.

[39] Illustration (d) stated than a loan procured from a bank will not be presumed to be procured by undue influence.

The above facts alone would hardly constitute a case of undue influence in the sense familiar to English law. This would rather be in the territory of unconscionable dealing. For Chalmers, unconscionability was the *genus* of which undue influence, as was conventionally understood, was a *specie*. Accordingly, section 16(3) placed the onus on the dominant or powerful party in a far wider range of circumstances—Illustration (c) being a case in point—than those contemplated under *Allcard v Skinner*'s category of *presumed* undue influence.

Section 16(2), which is an abridged version of the original section 16, was an amalgam of undue influence in the conventional sense and one category of unconscionable dealing. Section 16(2) was somewhat superfluous, as it could be subsumed, without remainder, under the general principle set out in section 16(1). The amenders, however, chose to retain it by recasting it as an indicative list of *some* occasions in which undue influence might result—with the express cautionary note that the list was without prejudice to the 'generality' of the 'principle' in section 16(1).

3. Remedies for Undue Influence under Section 19A

Prior to the 1899 amendment, the remedy when a contract is vitiated by either coercion or undue influence, as contained in section 19, was to render it voidable at the option of the claimant. The 1899 amendment introduced a new provision—section 19A—that empowered courts to set aside the agreement 'either absolutely or, if the party who was entitled to avoid it has received any benefit thereunder, upon such terms and conditions as to the Court may seem just'. The aim of the amendment appears to have been to empower courts with the ability to provide relief that stopped short of rescinding the contract in its entirety. This would be particularly useful in the kind of case that had motivated the amenders to act—namely, the case of loans taken on usurious interest. Setting aside the contract in its totality would mean returning the borrowed amount under section 64. Section 19A allowed the borrower to retain the loan while the court scaled down interest to a reasonable sum, as Illustration (b) to the provision shows:

> A, a money-lender, advances Rs. 100 to B, an agriculturist, and, by undue influence, induces B to execute a bond for Rs. 200 with interest at 6 per cent. per month. The Court may set the bond aside, ordering B to repay the Rs. 100 with such interest as may seem just.

More generally, section 19A also made it possible for the courts to excise substantively unconscionable terms in appropriate cases. However, as we shall see, this section has largely remained a dead letter in practice.

4. The Fate of the General Principle of Unconscionability in Section 16

The rationalization of the doctrinally disparate heads of action scattered across the realms of duress, undue influence, and unconscionability under the rubric of 'inequality of bargaining power' attempted by Lord Denning MR in *Lloyds Bank Ltd v Bundy*,[40] three-quarters of a century later, has much in common with that attempted by Chalmers in 1899. From the core idea of parties dealing on an unequal footing (the procedural limb), where the stronger takes 'unfair advantage'[41] of the weaker to impose 'unfair'[42] terms on the other (the substantive limb), the contiguity between Chalmers' and Lord Denning's projects is hard to miss.[43] Both approaches had in common the ambition of not only having a normative sweep over unconscionable bargains across the board (which are produced by taking unfair advantage of another) but also subsumed, within them, the conventional category of undue influence. However, the best laid plans of draftsmen, even those of the eminence of Chalmers, often go awry—as did Lord Denning's, incidentally, on this occasion.[44] The general principle of unconscionability postulated by section 16, which purported to subsume conventional undue influence within its scope, came to be constricted by the pincers of *two* lines of judicial pronouncement.

i. The first pincer: Unfavourable attitude to unconscionability

The Privy Council came to take an unfavourable attitude towards unconscionability, mirroring the English courts' approach to the doctrine around the beginning of the 20th century.[45] The Privy Council's 1906 advice in *Dhanipal Das v Raja Maneshar Baksh Singh*[46] inaugurated the trend of constricting section 16. Lord Davey, speaking for the Board, observed,

> The Subordinate Judge . . . mistook the English law . . . an English Court of Equity could not give relief from a transaction or contract merely on the ground that it was a hard bargain.[47]

And then in *Rani Sundar Koer v Rai Sham Krishen*,[48] decided later in the same year, the Privy Council firmly shut the door on this jurisdiction. In deciding whether a loan was unconscionable, the Privy Council read section 16 as requiring the claimant to prove

[40] *Lloyds Bank Ltd v Bundy* [1975] QB 326.
[41] ibid 339 (Lord Denning MR).
[42] ibid.
[43] As Ewan McKendrick points out, Lord Denning MR's test required both substantive and procedural unfairness: E McKendrick, *Contract Law: Text, Cases and Materials* (6th edn, OUP 2014) 687.
[44] In *National Westminster Bank v Morgan* [1985] AC 686, the House of Lords expressed its reservations about the doctrine of 'inequality of bargaining power'.
[45] David Capper has pointed out that the jurisdiction was thought to give courts a vague power to do 'palm tree justice', which came to be seen as a threat to legal certainty: Capper (n 9) 417.
[46] (1906) 28 ILR 570 (PC), (1906) 8 BomLR 491.
[47] ibid 127.
[48] (1906) LR 32 IA 9 (PC).

undue influence in the conventional sense in order to get relief.[49] This interpretation frustrated the legislative plan of regulating usurious money-lending by incorporating a doctrine of unconscionability in section 16. In the circumstances, the legislature was constrained to enact the Usurious Loans Act 1918, which, like England's Money Lenders Act 1900, permitted courts to intervene in usurious money-lending transactions and expressly empowered them to provide relief against excessive interest.[50] This further took away the issue of unconscionability from the heartland of Indian contract law.[51] In *Raghunath Prasad v Sarju Prasad*,[52] even though a money-lending transaction was *prima facie* unconscionable, the Privy Council held that section 16 will not apply. There was no 'position to dominate will' under section 16(1), the Board held, as it was not a relationship in which undue influence could arise in the conventional sense. Apart from some stray decisions, the power to intervene in unconscionable transactions that the courts had assumed in India came to be a thing of the past.[53]

In 1958, the Law Commission of India, in its *13th Law Commission of India Report, Indian Contract Act 1872*, sided with the view that 'unless undue influence is proved, no relief can be given on the ground of unconscionableness of a contract' alone.[54] Subsequent Law Commission Reports in 1984[55] and 2006[56] have moved away from this position and recommended reforming Indian contract law so as to empower courts to give relief to disadvantaged parties in unconscionable transactions. None of the recommendations have resulted in amendments to the Contract Act.[57] However, the Consumer Protection Act 2019 empowers consumer courts to excise unfair terms in consumer contracts. Section 2(46) of this Act defines 'unfair' to include any unreasonable charge, obligation, or condition that puts a consumer to disadvantage. In *Central*

[49] These decisions were cited with approval in *Raja Balla Mal v Ahad Shah* (1919) 21 BomLR 558 (PC). Consequently, in many cases in which Indian courts hitherto gave relief, they no longer could do so: see eg *Haripada v Jagai Shao* [1934] AIR Cal 511 (Calcutta HC), where the Court did not interfere where interest at the rate of 75 per cent (patently unconscionable) was payable since no undue influence in the conventional sense was established.

[50] Bhadbhade (n 2) 387.

[51] AC Patra, *The Indian Contract Act, 1872* (Asia Law House 1966) 349.

[52] AIR 1924 PC 60 (PC).

[53] In a decision that strikes a discordant note, C Sankaran Nair J in *Kesavelu Naidu* (n 20) noted that the effect of the 1899 amendment was to allow courts to apply a general principle of unconscionability. However, this view has not found wide support and remains an aberration. See also *Diala Ram v Sarga* [1927] AIR Lahore 536 (Lahore HC), where a money-lending transaction at an exorbitant rate of interest was presumed to have been induced by undue influence by invocation of Illustration (c) to s 16. Given the Privy Council's decisions, it would seem that this case was wrongly decided.

[54] *13th Law Commission of India Report, Indian Contract Act 1872* (1958) 21 <https://cdnbbsr.s3waas.gov.in/s3ca0daec69b5adc880fb464895726dbdf/uploads/2022/08/2022080532.pdf> accessed 25 September 2023.

[55] *103rd Law Commission of India Report on Unfair Terms in Contract* (1984) <https://cdnbbsr.s3waas.gov.in/s3ca0daec69b5adc880fb464895726dbdf/uploads/2022/08/2022080820.pdf> accessed 25 September 2023. The Commission held that s 16 was 'not of much relevance' in grounding unfairness: ibid 5.

[56] *199th Law Commission of India Report on Unfair (Substantive and Procedural) Terms in Contract* (2006) <https://cdnbbsr.s3waas.gov.in/s3ca0daec69b5adc880fb464895726dbdf/uploads/2022/08/2022081093-2.pdf> accessed 25 September 2023. Placing reliance on Illustration (c) to s 16, the Law Commission notes that s 16(1) pertains to 'procedural' unfairness and unconscionability in s 16(3) to 'substantive' unfairness: ibid 18.

[57] Specific Relief Act 1963, s 20 allows the court the discretion to refuse specific performance:

> where the terms of the contract or the conduct of the parties at the time of entering into the contract or the other circumstances under which the contract was entered into are such that the contract, though not voidable, gives the plaintiff an unfair advantage over the defendant.

Inland Water Transport v Brojonath Ganguly, the Supreme Court of India sought to import the doctrine of 'inequality of bargaining power' into Indian contract law and assert a power to intervene in unconscionable transactions.[58] However, the authority of that proposition, as we will see later, has been held to be confined to a relatively narrow range of cases within contract law.

There is one class of unconscionable dealing in which Indian courts gave relief, even before the enactment of the Contract Act in 1872, and have continued to do so unencumbered by the fate of the general doctrine of unconscionability in Indian law: that of the *pardanashin* woman.[59] The courts have, however, been careful to keep this category strictly confined so as not to allow it to become a device to oil out of inconvenient contracts.[60]

ii. The second pincer: Reading 'position to dominate will' as exhausted by section 16(2)

The presumption in section 16(3), as argued earlier, was meant to apply to cases of undue influence as defined in section 16(1), which, as we have seen, incorporated a wide principle of unconscionability. Section 16(2), merely enumerated specific instances of undue influence. However, the courts have interpreted the provision narrowly so that the presumption is not invoked in the full spectrum of cases that ought to come within the sweep of the general principle under section 16(1). This constriction was locked in place by the Supreme Court's decision in *Subhas Prosad Das Mushib v Ganga Prosad Das Mushib*.[61] The donor, who was of advanced years, made a gift of properties in favour of his younger son's grandson (with whom he was residing) to the exclusion of his elder son (the plaintiff) and daughter. The Calcutta High Court had found the gift to be a 'complete departure from the course of normal inheritance' and the donee's father to be in a position to 'dominate the will' of the donor, which would invoke the presumption in section 16(3). Reversing the High Court's decision, the Supreme Court held that the donee's father was not in a position to dominate the will of the donor since the donor was not subject to senile decay or mental unsoundness, and the case did not otherwise fall within section 16(2). The premise of the Supreme Court's reasoning was that the 'position to dominate the will' contemplated by section 16(1) was exhausted by cases in section 16(2)—meaning that a presumption was only warranted if there was a position of trust and confidence assumed by the defendant or some special disability of the kind enumerated in section 16(2) in the claimant.[62] Mitter J went on to hold:

[58] *Central Inland Water Transport v Brojonath Ganguly* (1986) 3 SCC 156 (SC).
[59] *Moonshi Buzloor Raheem v Shumsoonnissa Begum* (1867) 11 Moor Ind App 551, 585 (PC); *Khurbuja Koer v Junbahadur Rai* [1963] AIR SC 1203 (SC).
[60] *Hodges v Delhi & London Bank* (1900) 23 ILR All 137 (PC).
[61] [1967] 1 SCR 331 (SC).
[62] ibid [9].

> Generally speaking the relation of solicitor and client, trustee and cestui que trust, spiritual adviser and devotee, medical attendant and patient, parent and child are those in which such a presumption arises.[63]

In *Afsar Sheikh v Soleman Bibi*,[64] the Supreme Court reiterated the assumptions in *Subhas Prosad*. An illiterate and simple villager aged ninety claimed to have been induced to execute a gift deed under false pretences by his relative, who also helped him cultivate his lands. Sarkaria J found no undue influence even if it could be established that the donor treated the donee like his son, relied on his advice, and was subject to his influence.[65] Since the case did not fall within section 16(2), no presumption could be made under section 16(3):

> The mere fact that he was illiterate and old, was no proof of such *mental incapacity*. None of the circumstances mentioned in sub-section (2) of s. 16, had been proved from which an inference could be drawn that the donee was in a position to dominate the will of the donor.[66]

This line of authority has unrealistically cranked up the threshold to create a presumption under section 16(3) to deny relief to claimants on the grounds of presumed undue influence in all but the most obvious of cases falling under section 16(2).[67] In this, it was following a five-judge bench of the Supreme Court of India in *Ladli Prashad Jaiswal v Karnal Distillery*. Now, *Ladli Prashad* also held that position to dominate will is not exhausted by instances under section 16(2) but can be provided by evidence.[68] However, the subsequent case law, starting with *Subhas Chandra Mushib*, seems to read position to dominate will in a more restricted sense. Reading 'position to dominate the will' in section 16(1) as being exhausted by section 16(2) is motivated by the assumption that 'the law in India as to undue influence as embodied in s.16 is based on the English Common Law'.[69] This, it is submitted, is not altogether an accurate comparison since

[63] ibid.

[64] (1976) 2 SCC 142 (SC).

[65] ibid 150–51.

[66] ibid 150 (emphasis added). Another illustration of this is *Reshmi v Ghungaria* [1952] AIR HP 20 (Himachal Pradesh HC). The Court found that the defendant was not in a position to dominate the will of the claimant since the case did not fall within one of the circumstances enumerated in s 16(2).

[67] *Lakshmi Ammal v T Bhatta* [1970] AIR SC 1367 (SC) (Weakness of mental ability); *Sethani v Bhana* [1993] AIR SC 956 (SC) (claimant was a blind and illiterate woman); *Chinamma v Devanga Sangha* [1973] AIR Kant 338 (Karnataka HC) (claimant suffered from cancer and was in mental and bodily distress). As the recent edition of Pollock and Mulla puts it, summing up the law on s 16(3), 'the mere existence of fiduciary relationship raises the presumption of undue influence': Bhadbhade (n 2) 341; *Rajamani Ammal v Bhoorasami Padayachi* [1974] AIR Mad 36 (Madras HC), where a brother who was in a quasi-parental position to his sister got a release deed executed by her in respect of properties she had inherited from her deceased parents; *Sandersons and Morgans Solicitors v Mohanlal* [1955] AIR Cal 319 (Calcutta HC) (lawyer and client relationship); *Gouri Shanker v Fakir Mohan* AIR 1989 Ori 201 (Orissa HC) (unfavourable deed executed in favour of a lawyer without fully appreciating its terms); *Ramu Mahabir v Ghurhoo Samu* [2006] AIR All 273 (Allahabad HC), where an old man sold property to his nephew for inadequate consideration in circumstances where the Court found that there was physical or mental infirmity of which advantage was taken, the presumption was raised.

[68] AIR 1963 SC 1279, [25] (JC Shah J).

[69] *Subhas Prosad Das Mushib* (n 61) [9] (Mitter J).

this reading of section 16 makes undue influence in India much narrower than the English doctrine.

The extant English doctrine of undue influence provides relief in two kinds of cases. Class 1, also known as actual undue influence, covers cases of 'overt acts of improper pressure'.[70] Class 2, also known as presumed undue influence, covers cases of relationships where 'one of them is disposed to agree a course of action proposed by the other'.[71] Class 2 typically includes relationships of 'trust and confidence', of which the fiduciary type is a sub-set, and the presumption of undue influence is invoked where the transaction 'is not readily explicable' by conventional motives.[72] Indian courts do not give relief in 'Class 1'-type cases under section 16—this is a direct fallout from holding that 'position to dominate will' is exhausted by section 16(2). This result goes against what Chalmers envisaged.

Relief in 'Class 2'-type cases is limited to cases where the relationship is of the fiduciary type. Consider, for instance, *Shrimati Motiram Sakharam v Sudhakar Bhatkar*,[73] wherein an illiterate widow made a gift of her house to her tenant, whom she treated as her son and who was also an important officeholder in the local village government (*panchayat*), in circumstances where it was obvious that she was amenable to persuasion by him. The Court still did not find presumed undue influence under section 16. Indian courts have read 'position to dominate will' in section 16(1) as being exhausted by section 16(2), meaning that it requires some kind of a fiduciary relationship or mental incapacity caused due to illness or mental or bodily distress.

Adhering to the precedents scrupulously means rendering presumed undue influence incredibly difficult to find in Indian law. On the few occasions that Indian courts have found presumed undue influence by travelling outside section 16(2), they have done so by disregarding the precedents completely, which means that the authority of these breakaway decisions is feeble.[74]

iii. Unconscionability regained and lost again: *Brojonath Ganguly*

The Supreme Court of India sought to introduce a general principle of unconscionability in *Brojonath Ganguly*.[75] The Court did not do this, however, by seeking to resurrect Chalmers's project and, instead, held that section 16 is too narrow to ground a doctrine of unconscionability, situating the doctrine under 'public policy' in section 23 of the Act instead.[76] The terms of employment of the Central Inland Water Transport Corporation, which was a state-owned entity, allowed it to terminate the employment

[70] *Royal Bank of Scotland* (n 36) 795 (Lord Nicholls).
[71] ibid.
[72] ibid 798.
[73] [1998] AIR Bom 122 (Bombay HC).
[74] *Dharman v Marimuthu* [1996] 2 CTC 279, [17] (Madras HC); *Vinayakappa v Dulichand Murarka* [1986] AIR Bom 193 (Bombay HC) places reliance on the American Uniform Commercial Code; *Vinayakappa* was followed by the Bombay High Court in *Carl Estate Private Limited v Jagdish Counte* 2005 (4) Bom CR 630. See also *Ramaswami Gounder v Elaiya Pillai* [1972] AIR Mad 336 (Madras HC), where an illiterate man made a gift and the Court invoked presumption, albeit without reference to the Act or any precedent.
[75] *Brojonath Ganguly* (n 58).
[76] The Contract Act, s 23 renders an agreement unenforceable inter alia if it is 'opposed to public policy'.

of an employee by giving a three-month notice and payment of fifteen days' basic pay along with dearness allowance for every completed year of service. The Supreme Court struck down the term for unconscionability.

Madon J found, in Article 14 of the Indian Constitution, the principle that the courts will 'strike down an unfair and unreasonable contract or clause in a contract, entered into between parties who are not equal in bargaining power'.[77] *Brojonath Ganguly*, therefore, was, at heart, a public law decision that proscribed specifically a State instrumentality from exploiting its inequality in bargaining power and imposing unconscionable terms on the weaker party.[78] Madon J located the fulcrum of the issue as being 'whether an unconscionable term in contract of employment entered into with a corporation which is "the State" within the meaning of the expression in Article 12 is void as being violative of Article 14'.[79] Madon J further specifically observed that limitations on government corporations are not the same as those on private ones.[80] In this case, therefore, the issue of positing a general contractual principle against imposing unconscionable terms by using inequality of bargaining power did not arise.

Madon J found that the principle of inequality of bargaining power could not fit 'within the four corners of the definition of "undue influence" given in section 16(1)'.[81] Madon J hung the doctrine on the peg of 'public policy' under section 23 of the Act instead: a provision which rendered contracts that were 'against public policy' to be unenforceable.[82] However, 'public policy'—as the 103rd Law Commission report noted—is a tenuous ground to base contractual unconscionability upon.[83] Even if one were to grant *arguendo* the plausibility of public policy (s 23) as a peg on which to hang inequality of bargaining power, another problem appears. One of the consequences of pegging inequality of bargaining power on section 23 is that the offending contract would be void in its entirety. Excising just the unconscionable part and enforcing the unoffending rest—which could be achieved under section 19A—is not an option permitted by section 24 of the Act.

To get around this hurdle, Madon J invoked the notion of severance—to excise just the offending part, leaving the rest of the bargain intact—by citing an English case,

[77] *Brojonath Ganguly* (n 58) 216; Constitution of India 1950, art 12 makes fundamental rights available against the State. One of the fundamental rights guaranteed by art 14 to all persons is 'equality before the law' and 'equal protection of the laws'. This has been held by judicial interpretation to incorporate a principle against arbitrary action by governmental agencies and instrumentalities of the State. The employer in this case was a 'State' instrumentality, and hence fundamental rights were available against it. A principle as open-ended and abstract as 'arbitrariness' has made it possible for courts to read a whole host of moral values into art 14, the present case being an illustration of this.

[78] *Brojonath Ganguly* (n 58) 222–24.

[79] ibid 202.

[80] ibid 185.

[81] ibid 217.

[82] ibid 212.

[83] *103rd Law Commission of India Report* (n 55) 5. Although Madon J does not rely on it, there is a line of cases which have held that champertous agreements stipulating for an extortionate or unconscionable share in the proceeds of the litigation are void for being violative of 'public policy' under s 23: see eg *Valluri Ramanamma v Marina Viranna* (1931) 33 Bom LR 960 (PC). The basis of these decisions, however, is champerty, which is a recognized head of public policy rather than contractual unfairness. Indian cases merely posit a higher threshold for refusing to enforce champertous agreements.

Pickering v Ilfracombe Ry Co.[84] This sidestep is hard to sustain.[85] As Whitley Stokes pointed out, section 24 is a departure from the English law on severance;[86] and as Pollock and Mulla warned, 'reference to English cases where the rule has been recognized would be of no practical use for Indian purposes'.[87] All the same, *Brojonath* has since been invoked by Indian High Courts to support the idea of severance.[88]

Subsequent decisions of the Supreme Court of India have read *Brojonath Ganguly* as being inapplicable to contracts that do not involve the 'State'. In *Binny Ltd v Sadasivam*, where an employee of a private company whose services were terminated sought to have a clause in the employment contract that resembled the one in *Brojonath Ganguly* set aside for unconscionability, the Supreme Court declined to do so, holding that *Brojonath Ganguly* had no applicability to 'private bodies'.[89] Recently, in *Pioneer Urban Land and Infrastructure v Raghavan*, the Supreme Court invoked *Brojonath Ganguly* in a consumer dispute.[90] The Supreme Court sought to strike down a one-sided term in an agreement for the sale of an apartment. The Supreme Court seems to have fallen back on *Brojonath Ganguly* since the Consumer Protection Act 2019—which enabled unfair terms to be excised—was not yet enacted at the time this decision was handed down.

All said and done, a general doctrine of unconscionability of the kind envisaged by Chalmers—and written into the design of section 16—still remains unrecognized in Indian contract law. Although the English law on unconscionability has not quite turned out as Lord Denning had envisioned in *Lloyds Bank v Bundy*, it does recognize a pared down version of a general doctrine of unconscionability, which kicks in whenever one party 'imposes objectionable terms in a morally reprehensible manner' on the other.[91]

III. Coercion

1. Definition and Its Travails

The scope of the doctrine of duress in English law 'has been shifting over the years'.[92] Early on, duress in English law was limited to threats to person of the kind that would

[84] (1868) LR 3 CP 235, 250; *Brojonath Ganguly* (n 58) 206.

[85] For a discussion, see S Swaminathan, 'Contractual Unfairness: Another Way of Skinning the Cat' (2019) 3 Indian Law Review 299, 304 ('s 24 does not prevent the enforcement of a distinct agreement supported by a distinct consideration, but failing this, the entirety of the agreement will be void').

[86] W Stokes, *Anglo-Indian Codes* (1888) vol 1, 561.

[87] Pollock and Mulla (n 14) 145.

[88] *Ganganagar Sugar Mills v Madanlal* [2000] SCC OnLine Raj 411 (Rajasthan HC); *Director General, All India Radio v Casual Labour Employees Association, Radio Kashmir* 2019 (160) FLR 374 (Jammu and Kashmir HC); *Syed Sharji Hussain v IDBI Bank Ltd* 2016 (3) RLW 2235 (Raj) (Rajasthan HC).

[89] [2005] 6 SCC 657, 672. This was reiterated in *SK Jain v State of Haryana* (2009) 4 SCC 357; Pasayat J held that 'concept of unequal bargaining power has no application in case of commercial contracts': ibid 360.

[90] [2019] 5 SCC 725.

[91] *Boustany v Pigott* (1995) 69 P & CR 298 (PC) (Lord Templeman). Consumers contracts, however, are policed by a more robust notion of unconscionableness. The Consumer Rights Act 2015 (UK) protects consumers from unfair contractual terms. An unfair term is defined as one that is contrary to 'good faith' or causes 'significant imbalance' between parties.

[92] N Enonchong, *Duress, Undue Influence and Unconscionable Dealing* (1st edn, Sweet & Maxwell 2006) 7.

impair free agency in a mind of ordinary firmness;[93] duress of goods and economic duress came to be recognized later.[94] Duress is now defined in capacious terms as consent obtained by 'illegitimate pressure'.[95] The wider the concept of duress has become in English law, the more it has come to overlap with undue influence.[96] There is arguably even a case for complete assimilation of the category into undue influence.[97] The Contract Act in section 15 defined coercion in terms wider than English law's duress stood in the mid-19th century:

> 'Coercion' is the committing, or threatening to commit, any act forbidden by the Indian Penal Code (45 of 1860) or the unlawful detaining, or threatening to detain, any property, to the prejudice of any person whatever, with the intention of causing any person to enter into an agreement.

What also contributed to its width was the prescription that (a) the actions threatened could be to the prejudice of any person whatsoever and (b) the threat may also be issued by anyone not party to the contract. The width of this definition is demonstrated in *Chikham Ammiraju v Chikkam Sheshamma*,[98] wherein a husband threatened to take his own life if his wife and son did not sign a release deed, the effect of which would be to transfer some properties to the husband's brother. When the wife and son afterwards sought to have the deed rescinded, the two questions before the court were (a) whether suicide is an act forbidden by the Indian Penal Code, although it is, strictly speaking, not punishable under it, and if (a) was answered in the affirmative, (b) whether this was an act that was 'to the prejudice of any person whatever' as contemplated in section 15. A two-judge bench of the Madras High Court was divided on question (b) despite agreeing on question (a).[99] Sadasiva Ayyar J—with whom Moore J disagreed—was of the opinion that prejudice to the husband's life would suffice to constitute coercion as long as 'it was intended by the person using the threat to bring about the agreement thereby', and it did bring it about.[100] Ayyar J went on to point out just how wide the scope of the provision was in this regard:

> [Mr Patanjali Sastri, counsel for the defendant] put the following question in support of his contention: 'Suppose A threatens to blow up the Taj Mahal unless B gives C a pronote for Rs. 10,000 and suppose B is a man of such fine artistic feelings that to save the noble structure, he gives the pronote, is the note voidable for coercion?' I see no

[93] *Skeate v Beale* [1841] 113 ER 688 (threat to deprive of goods was held not to be duress).
[94] *Maskell v Horner* [1915] 3 KB 106. *Occidental Worldwide Investment Corporation v Skibs A/S Avanti* ('*The Siboen and The Sibotre*') [1976] 1 Lloyd's Rep 293 (QB); *North Ocean Shipping Co Ltd v Hyundai Construction Co Ltd* [1979] QB 705; *Pao On v Lau Yiu Long* [1980] AC 614 (PC).
[95] *Universe Tankships of Monrovia v International Transport Workers Federation* ('*The Universe Sentinel*') [1983] 1 AC 366 (HL).
[96] Enonchong (n 92) 36.
[97] ibid.
[98] [1916] 3 LW 490 (Madras HC).
[99] See also *Purabi Bannerjee v Basudeb Mukherjee* AIR 1969 Cal 293.
[100] *Chikham Ammiraju* (n 98) 491–92.

difficulty in answering the question in the affirmative, provided . . . the threat (which was to do an act of mischief or vandalism prohibited by the Penal Code to the prejudice of Government) was intended to bring about the execution of the pronote and did have that effect.[101]

'Detention' of property in section 15 has been read widely. A payment made by a father to prevent attachment of cattle belonging to him and his son, which was ordered upon his son's criminal conviction and subsequent inability to pay the fine, was held to amount to a threat of 'detention' of property within the meaning of the definition of coercion in section 15.[102] The refusal by an agent to hand over account books unless the agent was released from some debts has been held to amount to coercion.[103] The Andhra Pradesh High Court in *Superintending Engineer, Irrigation Department v Progressive Engineering* sought to widen 'detention of property' even further by seeking to include harm to economic and commercial interests within it.[104] In this case, refusal by a government department to release the payment of a contractor unless he gave up his claim for extra rates was held to amount to 'coercion' under the category of detention of property. Some of these cases appear to be an attempt to force-fit the category of economic duress within the confines of section 15. This reading is not without serious conceptual difficulties, as we shall see below in section III.2 on economic duress.

Although section 15 was wider than duress in English law as it stood at the time of drafting, the phraseology of the provision linking it to offences in the Indian Penal Code meant that the provision was liable to ossification—rendering it unable to accommodate forms of unwarranted pressure that called out for interference from the courts. The English common law, which is not committed to such rules with a canonical form of words, has been able to adapt to circumstances and innovate a lot better, with the result that duress in English law—which is defined in terms of 'illegitimate pressure'—is now much wider than coercion in Indian law. This rigidity was the principal limitation of section 15. An early decision of the Madras High Court, *Ranganayakamma v Alwar Setti*, shows the Court grapple with this inherent limitation in the face of what was obviously illegitimate pressure due to the rigid phraseology in section 15.[105] In this case, the brother and other relatives of the deceased threatened to obstruct his mortal remains from cremation unless his widow, who was a minor, consented to an adoption that would disinherit her of a large share in the husband's property. The Court found the consent to be vitiated by coercion (and undue influence), albeit without stating which section of the Indian Penal Code forbids obstruction so as to make it

[101] ibid 492 (parenthesis in original); On intra-court appeal a three-judge bench affirmed Sadasiva Ayyar J's view: (1918) 41 ILR Mad 33 (Madras HC) (Oldfield J dissented). The *13th Law Commission of India Report* (n 54) 21 recommended widening s 15 to include all penal laws, not just the Indian Penal Code.

[102] *Bansraj v Secy of State* 1939 AWR 247 (Allahabad HC). The Allahabad High Court relied on *Dulichand v Ram Kishan Singh* (1881) 7 Cal 648 and *Ganga Prasad Sinha v Brindaban Chandra* AIR 1935 Cal 176 (Calcutta HC).

[103] *Muthia Chetti v Muthu Karuppan* [1927] AIR Mad 852 (Madras HC).

[104] (1997) 4 Andh LD 489 DP (Andhra Pradesh HC). Followed in *Krishna Bhagya Jala Nigam v Harishchandra Reddy* 2005 (2) Kar LJ 409 (Karnataka HC).

[105] *Ranganayakamma v Alwar Setti* (1889) 13 ILR Mad 214 (Madras HC).

'coercion'.[106] Pollock and Mulla were critical of this decision, as the facts did not constitute coercion as understood by section 15.[107] In this instance, there was undeniably hard and overwhelming pressure, which did not straightforwardly amount to coercion within the terms of section 15. Therefore, the Court presumably additionally invoked section 16 as a basis for its decision. It must be noted that this decision was handed down at a time—even though it predated the 1899 amendment—when section 16 was interpreted liberally (as seen in section II above). Later, as section 16 came to be constricted further, the latitude for accommodating hard cases spilling over from section 15 that did not strictly fall within the four corners of the definition of coercion has drastically reduced.

The narrowness of section 15 is particularly evident in 'pressure' cases. Causing someone to enter into an agreement with threats of prosecution has long been held not to amount to coercion under section 15 unless the charge is a false one.[108] This is because threatening prosecution does not, in itself, amount to an offence under the Indian Penal Code.[109] And the problem with the case of threats of prosecution is equally applicable to all other 'pressure cases'. For instance, a threat to launch a strike by workers to induce the management to arrive at concessions or favourable terms has been held not to amount to coercion.[110] Section 15, as it stands, cannot address them, yet courts have resorted to it to provide relief in some such pressure cases. Consider, for instance, *Kishan Lal v New Delhi Municipal Corporation*.[111] During the Constitutional Emergency in India (1975–77), a business owner running a restaurant on premises under lease from the government was asked by the authorities to surrender possession of the premises or face arrest under the Maintenance of Internal Security Act 1971—an oppressive and controversial law giving sweeping powers of preventive detention (repealed in 1977). The Delhi High Court set aside the surrender as vitiated by coercion in terms of section 15, without naming the section of the Indian Penal Code involved. This is a 'pressure case' that cannot be straightforwardly covered by the definition of coercion in section 15. Oddly, what has remained overlooked is that not only was section 16, as envisaged by Chalmers, broad enough to subsume such cases, but also the amenders, in fact, specifically envisaged such 'pressure' cases to be covered by it by making it the subject of Illustration (a) to section 19A.

[106] ibid 224.

[107] Pollock and Mulla (n 14) 73–74.

[108] *Askari Mirza v Bibi Jai Kishori* (1912) 16 IC 334 (Allahabad HC); *Rameshwar Marwari v Upendranath Das Sarkar* AIR 1926 Cal 455 (Calcutta HC), where it was held that refusal to withdraw an already launched criminal case, unless a bond for the amount due is executed, would not amount to coercion.

[109] *London and Lancashire Insurance Co Ltd v Binoy Krishna Mitra* [1945] AIR Cal 218, [68] (Calcutta HC). As a corollary, threatening to do something that is 'legal' can never amount to coercion. However, any money paid under a threat of prosecution of any nature can be recovered by virtue of s 72, which provides for restitution of any money paid under 'coercion' although an agreement entered into in like circumstances would not amount to coercion under s 15. Coercion in s 72 has been held to be wider than that in s 15: *Kanhaya Lal v National Bank* (1913) Cal 598 (PC).

[110] *Workmen of Appin Tea Estate v Presiding Office, Industrial Officer, Assam* [1966] AIR Gau 115 (Gauhati HC).

[111] (2001) DLT 67 (Delhi HC). The Delhi High Court relied on the Privy Council decision in *Barton v Armstrong* (1975) 2 All ER 465. Also see *Kishanlal v Ashok Kumar* FA No 169/1996, judgment dated 28 February 2013 (Madhya Pradesh HC), where it was held that the signature on a document procured under fear of unlawful detention by police amounted to coercion.

> A's son has forged B's name to a promissory note. B under threat of prosecuting A's son, obtains a bond from A for the amount of the forged note. If B sues on this bond, the Court may set the bond aside.

In English law, this would amount to a Class 1 undue influence case, namely, one of *undue pressure*. Chalmers seems to have based the illustration on *Williams v Bailey*. As noted earlier, the *Williams v Bailey*-type pressure case did not fall within the original section 16. The broad principle of unfairness envisaged by Chalmers was meant to subsume these Class 1 pressure cases under amended section 16. Given the construction that the authorities have put upon section 16 (that position to dominate will is exhausted by situations in section 16(2), an Indian court guided by precedent will presently find it difficult to reach the result arrived at in this illustration.[112] The extant reading of section 16 virtually rules out 'Class 1' undue influence cases (pressure cases) at English law from coming under the sweep of the provision.

The Andhra Pradesh High Court has, however, invoked this illustration (and *Williams v Bailey*) to hold that consent to a compromise decree induced by threat to initiate contempt of court proceedings would amount to undue influence.[113] It does not, however, discuss any Indian precedent or try to justify how 'Class 1' undue influence cases at English law fit within the scheme of section 16. For this reason, the authority of this decision is somewhat doubtful.[114] The only way pressure cases can be taken to constitute undue influence under section 16 is if 'position to dominate will' is understood in broad terms as incorporating a principle of unfairness, subsuming the principle of undue pressure—as Chalmers intended section 16 to operate.

2. Economic Duress

A problem similar to that found with 'pressure cases' can also be seen in cases of economic duress. Ever since the Bombay High Court recognized the doctrine of economic duress in *Dai-ichi Karkaria v Oil and Natural Gas Corporation*[115] by reading it into section 15, it has steadily become a part of Indian law.[116] In *Dai-ichi*, the claimant, who supplied materials to Oil and Natural Gas Corporation of India, was required by the latter to execute a bank guarantee to cover a levy of customs duty that constituted a variation in terms of the agreement between the parties. The defendant induced the

[112] See *London and Lancashire Insurance Co Ltd* (n 109) [69] (Pal J) ('Undue influence usually arises in contracts made between relatives or persons in a fiduciary position').

[113] *C Balakrishnaian v A Kanniah* 2007 (2) ALT477 (Andhra Pradesh HC).

[114] Another decision that supports this (ie a finding of undue influence in these circumstances by relying on *Williams v Bailey* (n 11)) is *Ram Kumar Das v Nanda Kumar Shaha* AIR 1924 Cal 248 (Calcutta HC). However, this decision dates back to before when s 16 began to be read constrictively. A recent decision of the Madras High Court held—albeit without any discussion of the provisions—that a second agreement signed in the presence of police officers repaying advance sale consideration received under a valid contract, amounted to exerting pressure on the party and therefore resulted in coercion and undue influence: *S Duraivelu v N Thangamani* AS No 25/2017 decided on 29 April 2022 (Madras HC).

[115] [1992] AIR Bom 309 (Bombay HC). As it happens, this decision by a single judge was stayed by a larger bench of the court in appeal in *ONGC v Dai-ichi Karkaria* (1994) 2 Mah LJ 1084. However, since it is the single judge's decision that has made its way into academic commentary as widely cited as the *fons et origo* of economic duress in Indian contract law, it merits detailed analysis.

[116] See IC Saxena, 'Commercial Law' in *Indian Legal System* (Universal Law Publishing 2006) 506–57.

claimant to execute the bank guarantee by threatening to pay at a rate lower than the contract price, which would have meant certain financial ruin for the claimant. The Bombay High Court found for the claimant and, in doing so, recognized the principle of economic duress. Dhanuka J held:

> I am in complete agreement with the principles of law to be applied in cases involving economic duress. It is not possible to accept the submission . . . that the principles of law enunciated in English, American and Australian judgments have no relevance in Indian legal system . . . The, above-referred principles are also relevant for interpretation and elucidation of law of coercion contained in Section 15 of Indian Contract Act, 1872.[117]

Dhanuka J then also went on to hold that section 15 was broad enough to bring 'within its sweep the concept of "Economic Duress"'.[118] The doctrine of economic duress has since been pressed into service by the Bombay High Court,[119] the Andhra Pradesh High Court,[120] and the Delhi High Court.[121] The doctrine is now so well ensconced that even the Supreme Court of India has invoked it, albeit without justifying its basis or locating it in the scheme of the Contract Act.[122] These decisions have proceeded on the basis that economic duress is to be easily found in section 15; there is considerable difficulty in such an approach. This difficulty is palpable in the very fount of the doctrine, namely, Dhanuka J's reasoning in *Dai-ichi*. One law report has Dhanuka J point out that '[t]he underlined portion of the section brings within its sweep the concept of "Economic Duress"' but omits to underline the portion of the section he had in mind.[123] Another law report, by contrast, has Dhanuka J point out that '[t]he portion [here shown in italics] brings within its sweep the concept'.[124] The latter two-thirds of section 15 is shown to be italicized. It matters little, however, how much of the section is underlined or italicized because, whichever bits of the provision one looks at, by itself it is incapable of encompassing economic duress. It cannot accommodate economic duress unless it contingently coincides with a threat to commit an offence or detention of property. For instance, the facts in *The Universe Sentinel*,[125] where

[117] *Dai-ichi* (n 115) 336.
[118] ibid 337.
[119] *National Insurance Co Ltd v Opera Clothing* [2015] Indlaw MUM 913 (Bombay HC); *Bajranglal Anilkumar Jaju v The Vyasya Bank Ltd* Suit No 824/1980 decided on 12 March 2015 (Bombay HC); *Balaji Pressure Vessels Ltd v Bharat Petroleum Corporation Ltd* Arb Pet 729/2012 decided on 15 November 2014 (Bombay HC) (do not cite *Dai-chi*).
[120] *Superintending Engineer* (n 104).
[121] The Delhi High Court formulated the principle by basing it on English law: *Unikol Bottlers Ltd v M/s Dhillon Kool Drinks* AIR 1995 Delhi 25 (Delhi HC); *AEC Enterprises v Peacock Chemicals* (1998) 94 Comp Cas 912 (Delhi HC); *Double Dot Finance Ltd v Goyal MG Gases Ltd* ILR (2005) 1 Del 161, which was affirmed in *Goyal MG Gases Ltd v Double Dot Finance Ltd* FAO (OS) 210/2005 decided on 18 May 2009 (Delhi HC); *Sara International Limited v Rizhao Steel Holding Group Company Ltd* (2013) DLT 262 (Delhi HC). Also see *Essar Steel v Union of India* (2006) 1 GLR 436 (Gujarat HC) (without specifically naming the doctrine or referring to *Dai-ichi*).
[122] *Associated Construction v Pawanhans Helicopters Ltd* (2008) 16 SCC 128 (SC); *National Insurance Company Ltd v Boghara Polyfab Pvt Ltd* 2009 1 SCC 267 (SC); *Oriental Insurance Co Ltd v Dicitex Furnishing Ltd* 2019 SCC OnLine 1458 (SC).
[123] *Dai-ichi* (n 115) 336.
[124] (1991) 93 BLR 183, 210 (original in parenthesis).
[125] *The Universe Sentinel* (n 95).

the trade union blocked the claimant's ship—refusing to tug it—would arguably, and purely contingently, constitute a threat to 'detain' property, thereby bringing the case under section 15. And no doctrine of 'economic duress' need be invoked here. Barring such contingent congruencies, section 15 does not lend itself to be invoked in cases of economic duress. It is rather undue influence under section 16 that is—on a proper construction—the appropriate provision for such cases, as it is for other 'pressure cases' discussed earlier. One decision of the Delhi High Court, *Puri Construction v Larsen & Toubro*, makes a marked departure and situates economic duress under section 16, albeit reaching that result without basing it on the genealogy of the provision discussed here.[126] While this is the correct reading of the section, the decision remains somewhat of an anomaly in so far as it hangs economic duress on the peg of section 16. The Supreme Court approved it as good law in relation to another point of law[127] but has not considered this finding on economic duress.

Perilous though its foundations might be, economic duress is now an important fixture in Indian contract law—with some cases pegging it on section 15 and others going straight to English law for support.[128] One can find a line of Supreme Court decisions involving discharge of obligations to the opposite party by a subsequent agreement, which invoke the doctrine without reference to section 15 and through an entirely different line of reasoning in cases.[129] In *Parmar Construction*, for instance, the Court seems to rest the notion of economic or financial duress on something resembling the notion of inequality of bargaining power (between the small contractors and the state-run Indian Railways), albeit without naming the doctrine.[130]

The contours of the doctrine of 'economic duress' in India are, therefore, still amorphous. Having borrowed the doctrine from English law, Indian courts are likely to follow the lead of English decisions in defining its boundaries. English courts have been slow to extend the doctrine of 'economic duress' to cases of refusal to contract except on certain terms (as opposed to threatening to commit breach of contract).[131] Consequently, it is likely that Indian courts will be inclined to take a similar position.[132]

[126] *Puri Construction v Larsen & Toubro* 1 FAO(OS) 21/2009 decided on 30 April 2015 (Delhi HC).

[127] *NHAI v Hakeem* (2021) 9 SCC 1.

[128] See *Sara International* (n 121), which followed the Privy Council's decision in *Pao On* (n 94).

[129] *Union of India v Parmar Construction Co* (2019) 15 SCC 682; *Union of India v Master Construction Co* (2011) 12 SCC 349; *New India Assurance Co Ltd v Genus Power Infrastructure Ltd* (2015) 2 SCC 424, in addition to *Boghara Polyfab* (n 122) and *Dicitex* (n 122).

[130] *Parmar Construction* (n 129) [34], [36]. The SCC Law Report in fact includes a headnote on 'unconscionable bargain', despite there being no such mention in the text of the judgment.

[131] *CTN Cash and Carry Ltd v Gallagher Ltd* [1994] 4 All ER 714 (CA).

[132] An example of this is *M/s Palbro International v The Federal Bank Ltd* [2005] SCC OnLine Bom 407 (Bombay HC). Refusal to extend fresh credit facilities except on the settlement of some other dues, held not to amount to economic duress, but merely 'commercial pressure'. The Court did not, however, refer to *CTN Cash* (n 131). However, the line of cases like *Parmar Construction* (n 129) seem to be operating without any such limitations.

10

Fraud, Misrepresentation, and Mistake

*KV Krishnaprasad**

I. Introduction

This chapter examines the provisions of the Indian Contract Act 1872 that govern fraud, misrepresentation, and mistake. These provisions are remarkable in a number of respects. The rules governing mistake were significantly ahead of English courts and commentators.[1] The fraud and misrepresentation provisions are notable for their notoriety. Sir Frederick Pollock described them as being 'rather worse, if anything, than the average badness of the whole'.[2]

Despite their obvious significance, these aspects of the Contract Act have not been the subject of detailed study. It was sixty-five years ago that the Law Commission of India last reviewed these sections.[3] They are, therefore, in need of careful reconsideration. This chapter attempts to do that.

The chapter proceeds in four sections. Section II considers the historical background. Fraud and misrepresentation are examined in Section III. Section IV considers the Indian law on mistake. Section V offers some concluding observations.

II. Drafting History

The drafting history of the Contract Act is examined by Warren Swain in Chapter 1 of this volume. For the present purposes, three points merit emphasis.

First, the drafting process commenced with the constitution of the Third Indian Law Commission on 2 December 1861. The Third Law Commission produced its second report in July 1866, which contained the first draft of the Contract Act (the '1866 Draft').[4]

* I am grateful to Shubham Jain and Ritwik Bhattacharya for their research assistance. This chapter is substantially based on KV Krishnaprasad, 'Fraud, Misrepresentation, and Mistake in Indian Contract Law' in M Chen-Wishart and others (eds), *Invalidity* (OUP 2022).

[1] S Tofaris, 'A Historical Study of the Indian Contract Act' (PhD thesis, University of Cambridge 2011) 146.

[2] F Pollock and DF Mulla, *The Indian Contract Act: With a Commentary, Critical and Explanatory* (1st edn, Sweet & Maxwell 1905) v.

[3] Law Commission of India, *Report on Indian Contract Act, 1872* (Law Com Report No 13, 1958).

[4] Third Indian Law Commission, *Second Report on the Substantive Law of India* (31 July 1866) 6–48.

KV Krishnaprasad, *Fraud, Misrepresentation, and Mistake* In: *Foundations of Indian Contract Law.* Edited by: KV Krishnaprasad, Niranjan Venkatesan, Shivprasad Swaminathan, and Umakanth Varottil, Oxford University Press. © Oxford University Press 2024.
DOI: 10.1093/9780191997211.003.0010

Second, the Act evolved into its final form through a drafting process that lasted more than a decade. The Act passed through many hands during that period. Among others, Sir Henry Maine and Sir James Fitzjames Stephen (both of whom were law members of the Government of India) and William Macpherson (Secretary to the Third Indian Law Commission) shaped the Act in significant ways. As Pollock puts it, the Contract Act was 'not only the work of different hands, but work done from quite different points of view'.[5] As explained below, many internal incongruities of the fraud, misrepresentation, and mistake provisions of the Contract Act are attributable to the lack of continuity in its drafting process, both temporally and in respect of its draftsmen.

Third, it is often said that the Contract Act is a codification of English law.[6] That is substantially true. However, as Swain explains in Chapter 1 of this volume, the Act was also influenced by non-English sources. For the purposes of this chapter, there are two significant sources of non-common law influence: Pothier's 'Will Theory' and the Draft of a Civil Code for New York prepared by David Dudley Field (the 'Field Code'). As the following sections of this chapter will show, Pothier's Will Theory and the Field Code had a profound influence on the fraud, misrepresentation, and mistake provisions of the Contract Act. Regrettably, however, neither of these influences has featured prominently in the judicial and academic analyses of these provisions.

III. Fraud and Misrepresentation

Section 17 (Fraud) and section 18 (Misrepresentation) are both concerned with the implications of pre-contractual misrepresentation on contractual validity. Section 17 provides that

> "Fraud" means and includes any of the following acts committed by a party to a contract, or with his connivance, or by his agent, with intent to deceive another party thereto of his agent, or to induce him to enter into the contract:—
> (1) the suggestion, as a fact, of that which is not true, by one who does not believe it to be true;
> (2) the active concealment of a fact by one having knowledge or belief of the fact;
> (3) a promise made without any intention of performing it;
> (4) any other act fitted to deceive;
> (5) any such act or omission as the law specially declares to be fraudulent.

Section 18 provides that

[5] Pollock and Mulla (n 2) iv–v.
[6] J Minattur, 'The Indian Contract Act: Its Wanderlust and Warmer Climes' [1972] Journal of the Indian Law Institute 107, 109; B Acharyya, *Codification in British India* (SK Banerji 1914) 66.

'Misrepresentation' means and includes—

(1) the positive assertion, in a manner not warranted by the information of the person making it, of that which is not true, though he believes it to be true;
(2) any breach of duty which, without an intent to deceive, gains an advantage to the person committing it, or any one claiming under him; by misleading another to his prejudice, or to the prejudice of any one claiming under him;
(3) causing, however innocently, a party to an agreement, to make a mistake as to the substance of the thing which is the subject of the agreement.

When examined through the common law lens, section 17 concerns fraudulent misrepresentations whereas section 18 applies to negligent and innocent misrepresentations. Due to their considerable overlap, fraud and misrepresentation are examined together in this section under the four heads: (1) The Legislative Scheme (2) Representation (3) Causation and (4) Remedies.

1. The Legislative Scheme

In my view, the legislative scheme of the fraud and misrepresentation provisions in the Contract Act is obscured by a drafting flaw. I will identify the drafting error before examining the legislative scheme.

i. The drafting error

The drafting flaw is apparent from the incompatibility between section 19, on the one hand, and sections 10 and 14 on the other. Consider an example:

> *Example 1*: *P* sold a car to *X*. *P* did so relying on *X*'s misrepresentation about *X*'s creditworthiness. Having obtained possession of the car, *X* sold it on to *D*. *D* purchased the car in good faith, at the market price and unaware of *X*'s misrepresentation. *P* wishes to recover the car from *D*.

Whether *P* has a claim against *D* depends on whether *D* received good title to the car. That, in turn, depends on whether *X*'s misrepresentation rendered the contract between *P* and *X* void or voidable.[7]

For the present purposes, let us assume that, as against *X*, *P* can satisfy the requirements of 'misrepresentation' under section 18 or 'fraud' under section 17. What consequence does *X*'s fraud/misrepresentation have for the *P*–*X* contract? Remarkably, the Contract Act does not offer a clear answer. On the one hand, section 19 suggests that the *P*–*X* contract is voidable. It provides that

[7] See Sale of Goods Act 1930 (India), s 29.

> When consent to an agreement is caused by coercion, fraud or misrepresentation, the agreement is a contract voidable at the option of the party whose consent was so caused.

Based on section 19, Indian Courts have held that the *P–X* contract is voidable.[8] However, one could argue that the *P–X* contract is void. That argument runs as follows. Section 14 provides that:

> Consent is said to be free when it is not caused by—
> ...
> (3) fraud, as defined in section 17, or
> (4) misrepresentation, as defined in section 18, or
> ...

Thus, if *P* can satisfy the requirements of misrepresentation or fraud then, pursuant to section 14, *P* did not 'freely consent' to the contract. According to section 10, 'agreements' are 'contracts' only if they are made by the 'free consent' of the parties. Reading sections 10 and 14 together, the *P–X* contract is only an 'agreement', not a 'contract'. The distinction between 'agreements' and 'contracts' is drawn in section 2: agreements enforceable by law are contracts;[9] agreements not enforceable by law are void.[10] On this analysis, the *P–X* contract is void. Thus, whereas section 19 provides that contracts affected by fraud or misrepresentation are voidable, sections 10 and 14 do not preclude the argument that they are void on account of the parties' lack of free consent.[11]

This inconsistency arises from a drafting error. The source of the error lies in the fact that sections 10 and 14 on the one hand and section 19 on the other are based on different legislative frameworks. Section 19 has its genesis in clause 6 of the 1866 Draft. Section 14, by contrast, is based on § 548 of the Field Code. Unfortunately, both provisions came to be retained in the Contract Act. The problem is compounded by the phrase '*free* consent' in section 10. This phrase suggests that fraud and misrepresentation render a contract void by virtue of section 10, not merely voidable under section 19.

In my view, the drafting error outlined above requires legislative rectification. In particular,

[8] *Haryana Power Purchase Centre v Sasan Power Ltd* (2023) SCC Online SC 577, [93]; *Texco Marketing Pvt Ltd v Tata AIG General Insurance Co Ltd* (2023) 1 SCC 428, [25]–[26]; *Central National Bank v United Industrial Bank* AIR 1954 SC 181, [9]; *Hiraben Chaudhari v RC Raval* (1993) 1 GLR 66, [20] (Gujarat High Court).

[9] The Contract Act, s 2(h).

[10] The Contract Act, s 2(g).

[11] In *Janakiammal v Kumarasamy* (2021) 9 SCC 114, [42]–[44] and *Avitel Post Studioz Limited v HSBC PI Holdings* (2021) 4 SCC 713, [16]–[17], the Supreme Court of India recognised the relevance of ss 10 and 14 in determining whether a contract vitiated by fraud/misrepresentation is void or voidable. However, with respect, in both cases the Court glossed over the difficulty posed by the incompatibility of these provisions with s 19.

(1) With the exception of the second paragraph of section 14,[12] which concerns causation, the remainder of section 14 is rendered redundant by section 19. Therefore, section 14, save for its second paragraph, ought to be deleted. The second paragraph of section 14 should be moved to section 19; it fits better alongside the causal rule set out in that provision.[13]
(2) The word 'free' in the phrase 'free consent' in section 10 should be deleted. This will help avoid the incompatibility between sections 10 and 14 on the one hand and section 19 on the other.

ii. The two-stage approach

Once the drafting error is rectified, the scheme of the fraud and misrepresentation provisions in the Contract Act becomes clear. The Act proceeds in two stages.

The first stage, which consists of sections 10 and 13, concerns consent. These provisions apply where, as a consequence of fraud or misrepresentation, the parties did not 'agree upon the same thing in the same sense'.[14] Consider an example:

> *Example 2*: *D* induced *P*, an illiterate person, to sign a document. *P* signed the document believing *D*'s fraudulent misrepresentation that it was a gift deed; *P* believed that it was a gift of Blackacre from *D* to *P*. In fact, it was a sale deed purporting to record *D*'s sale of Blackacre to *P* for consideration.

Indian courts have held that the sale deed between *P* and *D* is void, not voidable.[15] In the case law, this has been justified by reference to the common law doctrine of *non est factum*.[16]

The best statutory explanation for this result is based on sections 10 and 13. Section 10 requires that parties must have 'consented' in order for there to be a contract. Section 13 defines consent as agreement 'upon the same thing in the same sense'. In Example 2, *P* and *D* did not agree upon the same thing in the same sense. Thus, as per section 13, *P* did not 'consent' to the sale deed. According to section 10, therefore, the sale deed is only an 'agreement', not a 'contract'. It is consequently void.[17]

In many cases, despite one party's misrepresentation or fraud, parties will have consented to the agreement. Consider Example 1, for instance. In that example, *P*'s complaint was not that they did not agree to buy the car. Rather, it was that they were

[12] It reads,

> Consent is said to be so caused when it would not have been given but for the existence of such coercion, undue influence, fraud, misrepresentation or mistake.

[13] See the Contract Act 1872, s 19 (Explanation), which reads,

> A fraud or misrepresentation which did not cause the consent to a contract of the party on whom such fraud was practised, or to whom such misrepresentation was made, does not render a contract voidable.

[14] ibid s 13.

[15] *Ningawwa v Byrappa* AIR 1968 SC 956, [5]; *Dularia Devi v Janardan Singh* AIR 1990 SC 1173, [7]; *Brindaban Adhikary v Dhruba Roy* AIR 1929 Cal 606, [3]–[4]; *Sanni Bibi v Siddik Husain* [1919] 23 CWN 93, [3] (Calcutta High Court).

[16] *Bismillah v Janeshwar Prasad* AIR 1990 SC 540, [6]; *KM Madhavakrishnan v SR Sami* (1980) 2 MLJ 398, [14] (Madras High Court).

[17] See the Contract Act 1872, s 2(g).

misinformed about one of the buyer's attributes. Claims of this nature are governed by sections 17 and 18. These provisions constitute the second stage of the legislative scheme.

As stated above, the first stage is entirely consent-based. Consent plays a crucial role in the second stage too. But a wider range of factors come into play at the second stage. Many of these are unrelated to the plaintiff's consent. Consider two examples:

Example 3A: *X* fraudulently misrepresented to *P* that *D* was an authorised retailer of Apple computers. In fact, this was untrue. Relying on *X*'s misrepresentation, *P* entered into a contract with *D*. *D* was unaware of, and played no part in, *X*'s misrepresentation. *P* wishes to avoid the contract.

Example 3B: *D* negligently misrepresented to *P* that *D* was an authorised retailer of Apple computers. In fact, this was untrue. Relying on *D*'s misrepresentation, *P* entered into a contract with *D*. Had *P* carried out basic enquiries, *P* would have realised that *D*'s representation was false. *P* wishes to avoid the contract.

P is not entitled to avoid the contract in either case. In Example 3A, this is because the definition of 'fraud' under section 17 of the Contract Act only covers 'acts committed by a party to a contract, or with his connivance, or by his agent'. Thus, a fraudulent misrepresentation by *X*, a non-party, falls outside the purview of section 17. *P* cannot rescind the contract in Example 3B either. This is because *P* had 'means of discovering the truth with ordinary diligence'. According to the Exception to section 19, this precludes *P* from avoiding the contract.

Neither of these examples is explicable solely by reference to *P*'s consent. In Example 3A, the identity of the representor is irrelevant to *P*'s consent. Similarly, in Example 3B, the analysis that *P* was at fault for failing to make enquiries is also unrelated to *P*'s consent.

In summary, the fraud and misrepresentation provisions in the Contract Act proceed in two stages: a consent-based first stage and a more pluralistic second stage. The second stage takes into account a range of non-consent based factors, including the plaintiff's fault and the defendant's wrongdoing.[18] The drafting flaw outlined in section I.i, quite apart from obscuring the contractual consequences of fraud and misrepresentation, conflates these two distinct stages. This is yet another reason why it requires legislative rectification.[19]

2. Representation

In this and the following two sections, I examine the substantive elements of the fraud and misrepresentation provisions. This section will consider three kinds of representations: (i) statements, (ii) silence, and (iii) conduct.

[18] For the argument that the common law follows a similar 'two-stage defeasibility' approach, see HLA Hart, 'The Ascription of Responsibility and Rights' (1949) 49 Proceedings of the Aristotelian Society 171, 174–78; M Chen-Wishart, 'The Nature of Vitiating Factors in Contract Law' in G Klass, G Letsas, and P Saprai (eds), *Philosophical Foundations of Contract Law* (OUP 2014).

[19] I am grateful to Yihan Goh for encouraging me to clarify this point.

i. Statements

The Contract Act offers limited guidance on the kind of statements that fall within the purview of sections 17 and 18. On this issue, Indian courts have generally followed English law.

As a general rule, only statements of fact constitute fraud or misrepresentation.[20] For these purposes, statements of fact are distinguished from statements of opinion and statements of future intention.[21] However, statements of opinion may sometimes involve implied factual assertions,[22] especially when the facts are not known to both parties.[23] Consider an example:

> *Example 4*: *D*, a retired navy officer, owns a house in the countryside. *P*, an engineer, wishes to purchase it and convert it into a sheep farm. During the negotiations, *D* said that 'surely, the land will be good for 2,000 sheep'. After the purchase, *P* realises that the land will only sustain up to 500 sheep and thus will not be viable for *P*'s purposes.

D's statement is an expression of opinion. However, it may involve an implied representation that *D* is aware of facts that justify that opinion. Whether *D*'s statement has this effect depends on whether the facts were known to both *P* and *D*. For instance, assume that *P* had personally inspected the property. Then *P* cannot rely on *D*'s statement as an implied assertion of facts. On the other hand, if the property was unknown to *P*, *P* may rely on *D*'s assertion as an implied representation that *D* was aware of facts that justified their opinion.[24]

ii. Silence

A number of Indian cases have assumed that silence constitutes fraud or misrepresentation only when there is a duty to speak. Thus, in *Vibha Mehta v Hotel Marina*, the Delhi High Court observed that

> [M]ere silence as to fact likely to affect the willingness of a person to enter into a contract is not fraud unless the circumstances of the case are such that regard being had to them, it is the duty of the person, keeping silent, to speak . . . Silence is fraud only when there is an obligation to speak up.[25]

With respect, this is an over-simplification. As explained below, the legislative position on this issue consists of a general rule qualified by four exceptions.[26]

[20] *Bhagwani Bai v Life Insurance Corporation* AIR 1984 MP 126, [11]; *Orient Underwater Engineers v Cochin Port Trust* 2017 (1) KHC 833, [8].

[21] Y Vardhan and C Narayan (eds), *Pollock and Mulla: The Indian Contract & Specific Relief Acts* (15th edn, LexisNexis 2017) 399.

[22] The same is true of statements of future intention. For an example, see the Contract Act, s 17(3).

[23] *Subramanian Chetti v Official Assignee of Madras* AIR 1931 Mad 603a, [6].

[24] It has been suggested that the best statutory explanation for this reasoning is based on s 17(4): A Briggs and A Burrows, *The Law of Contract in Myanmar* (Oxford Faculty of Law 2017) 105 <www.law.ox.ac.uk/sites/files/oxlaw/briggsburrowsbook_-_thelawofcontractinmyanmar.pdf> accessed 5 August 2023.

[25] *Vibha Mehta v Hotel Marina* 2014 (142) DRJ 528 (Delhi High Court) [32]. See also *Orient Underwater* Engineers (n 20) [7] (Ninan J).

[26] For the purposes of this section, fraud and misrepresentation are considered separately.

(a) Silence as fraud

The general rule is that silence does not constitute fraud. This is so even if the defendant was aware that the plaintiff was proceeding under a misapprehension about the facts.[27] This is clear from the first part of the Explanation to section 17: '[m]ere silence as to facts likely to affect the willingness of a person to enter into a contract is not fraud'. This view is reinforced by Illustration (a) to section 17, which reads,

> A sells, by auction, to B, a horse which A knows to be unsound. A says nothing to B about the horse's unsoundness. This is not fraud in A.

Now consider an example:

> *Example 5*: *D* sells *D*'s country estate to *P*, who tells *D* that *P* wishes to use it as a quiet weekend escape from a demanding job in the city. *P* pays the purchase price. Before *P* moves in, *P* learns that a pig farm for 400 pigs is about to be built within a distance of a hundred metres from the house and that *D* had been aware of the imminent establishment of the farm.

P cannot avoid the contract. *P*'s misapprehension was not caused by *D*. Therefore, *D* is not under an obligation to correct it. The contract between *P* and *D* is not vitiated by fraud.

However, this general rule is qualified by four exceptions. These are instances when *D*'s silence may amount to fraud. The exceptions apply when

(1) 'Silence is, in itself, equivalent to speech' (Explanation to section 17);
(2) 'It is the duty of the person keeping silence to speak' (Explanation to section 17);
(3) one person intentionally induces another to enter into a contract through 'the active concealment of a fact' that they had knowledge or belief of (section 17(2)); and
(4) law specifically declares silence to be fraudulent (section 17(5)).

I examine each of these exceptions below.

First, silence may constitute fraud when 'silence is, in itself, equivalent to speech'.[28] There are at least three circumstances when silence is considered equivalent to speech. The first among these is 'half-truths'. In these cases, the representor states certain facts but omits to state some others. The effect of what is left unsaid is to render the positive representation misleading. Here is an example:

> *Example 6*: *D* offers *D*'s car for sale to *P*. *D* tells *P* that the car was purchased new only a week ago. But *D* does not disclose that the car was badly damaged in an accident almost immediately after it was purchased. Relying on *D*'s representation, *P* enters into a contract to purchase the car.[29]

[27] *Sarabjit Singh v Indu Sabharwal* 211 (2014) DLT 171 (Delhi High Court). See also Briggs and Burrows (n 24) 106.

[28] The Contract Act, s 17 (Explanation).

[29] Based on Briggs and Burrows (n 24) 105.

D's silence about the accident is 'equivalent to speech'. It may constitute fraud. There is extensive support for this analysis in the case law. Consider, for example, the decision of the Madras High Court in *Subramanian Chetti v Official Assignee of Madras*.[30] The plaintiff executed a deed of transfer assigning a decree to the defendant. The plaintiff did so because he was told by the defendant's agent that the decrees were 'unrealizable' and 'not worth even 20 per cent of their face value'.[31] The defendant's agent did not mention, however, that the decree was secured. The defendant was not under an obligation to speak. Therefore, this case was *not* covered by exception (2). Nevertheless, Curgenven J said,[32]

> [I]t seems impossible to hold that what passed at the interview between [the plaintiff] and [the defendant's agent] amounted to no more than "mere silence" about the existence of the security.

A second category of case where silence is equivalent to speech arises when a change of circumstances renders an initial representation untrue. In this context, the representor's failure to correct an initial statement may constitute fraud. This scenario is examined in greater detail below.[33]

Illustration (c) to section 17 offers a third instance when silence is considered equivalent to speech. It reads,

> B says to A—"If you do not deny it, I shall assume that the horse is sound." A says nothing. Here, A's silence is equivalent to speech.

Now consider the second exception: silence may constitute fraud when there is a duty to speak.[34] This rule is exemplified by Illustration (b) to section 17:

> [*A* sells, by auction, to *B*, a horse which *A* knows to be unsound. *A* says nothing to *B* about the horse's unsoundness.] B is A's daughter and has just come of age. Here, the relation between the parties would make it A's duty to tell B if the horse is unsound.

Indian courts have applied the 'the duty-to-speak' exception to a wide range of cases, including those relating to insurance contracts,[35] familial relationships,[36] and fiduciary obligations.[37]

[30] *Subramanian Chetti* (n 23).
[31] Ibid, [1].
[32] Ibid, [5]. See also *Budha Singh v Lakshmi Chand* AIR 1929 Lah 880, [4]; *Jogendra Goswami v Chandra Mazumdar* AIR 1914 Cal 661, [5].
[33] See section III.2.ii.(b) below.
[34] The Contract Act, s 17 (Explanation).
[35] *Sea Lark Fisheries v United India Insurance* (2008) 4 SCC 131; *Krishna Puri v Life Insurance Corporation* AIR 1975 Del 19.
[36] *Kishan Lal v Musammat Kashmiro* (1916) 31 MLJ 362 (Allahabad High Court) [22].
[37] *Muthia Chettiar v Shanmugham Chettiar* AIR 1969 SC 552, [4].

The third exception, by contrast, rarely features in the case law. It applies when one person intentionally induces another to enter into a contract through 'the active concealment of a fact' of which the inducer had knowledge or belief.[38] This may amount to fraud within the meaning of section 17(2).[39] The class of case to which this exception is meant to apply is clarified by Illustrations (d) and (e) of section 19:[40]

(d) B, having discovered a vein of ore on the estate of A, adopts means to conceal, and does conceal, the existence of the ore from A. Through A's ignorance B is enabled to buy the estate at an under-value. The contract is voidable at the option of A.
(e) A is entitled to succeed to an estate at the death of B. B dies. C, having received intelligence of B's death, prevents the intelligence reaching A, and thus induces A to sell to B A's interest in the estate. The sale is voidable at the option of A.

As these illustrations, and indeed the language of section 17(2), indicate this exception only applies if the defendant took active steps to conceal information from the plaintiff.

The fourth exception is provided in section 17(5). It applies to 'any such act or omission as the law specially declares to be fraudulent'. Consider the following example:

Example 7: *P* enters into a contract to purchase Blackacre from *D*. *D* had previously sold Blackacre to *X*. Consequently, *D* no longer has title to Blackacre. *D* does not disclose this to *P*.

D was under a statutory obligation to disclose to *P* that *D* no longer had title to Blackacre. *D*'s failure to do so is declared 'fraudulent' by statute.[41] Accordingly, pursuant to section 17(5), *D*'s silence may constitute fraud.[42]

(b) Silence as misrepresentation

As a general rule, non-fraudulent failure to disclose information does not render a contract voidable. This is clear from the phrase 'positive assertion' in section 18(1).

However, there is at least one circumstance in which negligent non-disclosure may constitute misrepresentation. This is provided in section 18(2), which reads,

Misrepresentation means and includes—
(2) any breach of duty which, without an intent to deceive, gains an advantage to the person committing it, or any one claiming under him; by misleading another to his prejudice, or to the prejudice of any one claiming under him;

[38] The Contract Act, s 17(2). See Vardhan and Narayan (n 21) 401; W Macpherson, *Outlines of the Law of Contracts as Administered in the Courts of British India* (2nd edn, RC Lepage & Co 1864) 8.
[39] It is likely that the genesis of s 17(2) lies in Macpherson's commentary: see Macpherson (n 38) 8.
[40] See also Illustrations (c), (d) and (e) to 1866 Draft, cl 5.
[41] Transfer of Property Act 1882 (India), s 55.
[42] See *Akhtar Begam v Hazari Lal* AIR 1927 All 693 and the explanation of this decision in Vardhan and Narayan (n 21) 403.

Section 18(2) applies if the representor negligently failed to disclose facts despite being under a duty to do so. Unlike the 'duty-to-speak' exception in section 17, however, section 18(2) has two additional requirements: the representor must have gained an advantage, and the representee must have been misled to the representee's prejudice.

Outside this limited exception, non-fraudulent silence does not render a contract voidable under the Act. This statutory position has the potential to lead to odd consequences. Consider the following example:

> *Example 8*: *D* offers *D*'s car for sale to *P*. *D* tells *P* that the car was purchased new only a week ago. After the representation is made, but before the contract is concluded, the car meets with an accident and is badly damaged. *D* intends to inform *P* about the accident, but negligently fails to do so. *P* enters into a contract with *D* on the assumption that the car is in good condition.

D was not under a duty to speak. Therefore, section 18 suggests that *D*'s silence does not constitute misrepresentation. It follows that *P* cannot avoid the contract. That is an odd result.

The leading practitioners' commentary in India attempts to avoid it by applying section 18(2) to cases such as Example 8. It is said that:

> [Section 18(2)] would also cover the position where a true statement is made, but it becomes false to the knowledge of the maker before it has been acted upon . . . This non-disclosure would appear to be a breach of duty within cl 2.[43]

In support of the proposition that *D* was under a 'duty' to disclose the change of circumstances to *P*, the commentary relies on English cases such as *With v O'Flanagan*[44] and *Davies v Provincial Insurance Company*.[45] The courts in these cases did use the language of 'a duty to communicate the change of circumstances'.[46] It is clear, though, that they were not referring to a primary legal duty the breach of which carries remedial consequences. At common law, only consequence of a party's failure to comply with the 'duty' to disclose a change of circumstance is to render the contract voidable. Whether the representor's negligent failure to disclose a change of circumstance has the effect of rendering a contract voidable is the very question that Example 8 raises. To read the common law cases which suggest that the representor's failure to disclose a change of circumstance has the effect of rendering a contract voidable along with section 18(2) to argue that there was a breach of 'duty' in Example 8 is therefore circular reasoning.

If the result in Example 8 is thought to be unsatisfactory (in my view it is), the solution lies in legislative clarification. This may be achieved by adding an Explanation to section 18, which states that non-fraudulent silence may constitute misrepresentation when such 'silence is equivalent to speech'.

43 Vardhan and Narayan (n 21) 424–25.
44 *With v O'Flanagan* [1936] Ch 575.
45 *Davies v Provincial Insurance Company* (1878) 8 Ch D 469.
46 *With* (n 44) 583; *Davies* (n 45) 474 and 475.

iii. Conduct

In addition to statements and silence, representations may also be made through conduct.

The circumstances in which conduct may amount to fraud are relatively clear. A suggestion through conduct 'as a fact, that which is not true'[47] may amount to fraud.[48] In addition, there are three specific instances when conduct may constitute fraud. 'Active concealment' of a fact within the meaning of section 17(2) is one example.[49] Section 17(5), which concerns 'any such act or omission as the law specially declares to be fraudulent', is another.[50] A third example may be found in section 17(4). It applies to 'any other act fitted to deceive'. Save for some passing references to section 17(4),[51] Indian courts have not yet had to determine the scope of this ambiguously worded provision.[52] As Briggs and Burrows say, section 17(4) may have been intended as a 'sweeping up provision'.[53]

As to the circumstances in which conduct may constitute non-fraudulent misrepresentation, the position in India is less clear. At first blush, the phrase 'positive assertion' in section 18(1) may appear to exclude conduct from its purview. This, however, would be a surprising conclusion. The preferable approach is to treat conduct as falling within the purview of section 18 when it has the effect of making a representation as to a fact.

3. Causation

To render a contract voidable, in addition to establishing the elements of sections 17 or 18, the plaintiff's consent must also have been 'caused' by fraud or misrepresentation. This requirement is reflected in the Explanation to section 19, which provides that[54]

> A fraud or misrepresentation which did not cause the consent to a contract of the party on whom such fraud was practised, or to whom such misrepresentation was made, does not render a contract voidable.

This section will consider two causal issues: (i) the standard by which causation is assessed; and (ii) the relevance of the common law test of materiality.

[47] The Contract Act, s 17(1).
[48] *Ayyasamy v Paramasivam* (2016) 10 SCC 386, [10]; *Ramesh Kumar v Furu Ram* (2011) 8 SCC 613, [12].
[49] Considered in section III.2.ii.(a) above.
[50] Considered in ibid.
[51] *Rajesh Choudhury v United India Insurance* 2005 (2) GLT 149 (Gauhati High Court); *Sarabjit Singh* (n 27); *Chartered Bank of India v Imperial Bank of India* (1933) ILR 60 Cal 262.
[52] See *Karnaphuli Paper Mills v Amanullah* 23 DLR (1971) 150 (Delhi High Court).
[53] Briggs and Burrows (n 24) 105.
[54] See also Illustration (b) to s 19.

i. The causal standard

By what standard must the causative relevance of fraud or misrepresentation be assessed? Indian courts have not adopted a consistent stance on this issue. In some cases, it has been suggested that 'the representee must in fact, have been induced to enter into the contract by the misrepresentation in question'.[55] In some other cases, it has been said that the misrepresentation must 'have materially induced the contract'.[56] With respect, neither formulation is helpful. There is also some judicial support for a higher causative standard. For instance, the Kerala High Court has held that 'fraud or misrepresentation would render the contract voidable only if the said act was *the* reason, *the* cause, for the grant of consent by the party'.[57]

Despite the ambiguity in the case law, the applicable causal standard is clear from the second paragraph of section 14. It provides that

> Consent is said to be so caused when it would not have been given but for the existence of such coercion, undue influence, fraud, misrepresentation or mistake.

Thus, the 'but for' standard of causation applies to both fraud and misrepresentation. In this respect, the Contract Act departs from the common law position. At common law, causation is assessed using the 'a reason' standard for fraudulent misrepresentation (ie it will suffice if the misrepresentation was one of the reasons why the representee entered into the contract),[58] whereas for negligent and innocent misrepresentation, it is tested using the 'but for' standard.[59]

ii. Materiality

In English law, in addition to causation, a representee who wishes to avoid a contract on the basis of misrepresentation (other than fraudulent misrepresentation) must also establish 'materiality'. Materiality requires the representee to establish that their representation would have affected the judgement of a reasonable person in deciding to enter into the contract.[60] If the representee can establish materiality, then the burden is on the representor to prove that their representation did not induce the contract.[61]

Unlike the position at common law, section 18 does not require 'materiality'. Nevertheless, Indian courts have applied this test.[62] For instance, in *Bhagwani Bai v Life Insurance Corporation*, the Madhya Pradesh High Court said,

[55] *RC Thakkar v Gujarat Housing Board* AIR 1973 Guj 34, [65].
[56] *GM Birla and Co v Johurmull Premsukh* AIR 1920 Cal 908, [3] (emphasis added). See also *Mithoolal Nayak v Life Insurance Corporation* AIR 1962 SC 814, [11].
[57] *Orient Underwater Engineers* (n 20) [9] (emphasis added).
[58] *Barton v Amstrong* [1976] AC 104, 106–107.
[59] *Raiffeisen Zentralbank v Royal Bank of Scotland* [2010] EWHC 1392 (Comm) [171] (Clarke J).
[60] E Peel, *Treitel on the Law of Contract* (15th edn, Sweet & Maxwell 2020) [9-023].
[61] ibid 373–74.
[62] Vardhan and Narayan (n 21) 399.

> It may be said that a misrepresentation will not be effective to ground the avoidance of a contract unless it was material in the sense that a reasonable man would have been influenced by it in deciding whether to enter into the contract.[63]

In cases where materiality can be established, Indian courts have also drawn the inference that the representation induced the representee's decision to enter into the contract. Consider, for example, the decision of the Madras High Court in *Raghava Mannadiar v Sivasankara Menon*.[64] In that case, Iyer J said,

> If it is proved that the defendant with a view to induce the plaintiff to enter into a contract made a statement to the plaintiff of such a nature as would be likely to induce a person to enter into a contract, and it is proved that the plaintiff did enter into the contract, it is a fair inference of fact that he was induced to do so by the statement.[65]

With respect, it is difficult to justify the application of 'materiality' as a mandatory pre-condition for misrepresentation claims in India. Section 18 does not require it. Moreover, even English courts[66] and commentators[67] have expressed doubts as to whether materiality should be a mandatory requirement. However, materiality may legitimately play a more limited role in the causation analysis under section 19. If the representation is one that would have induced a reasonable person to enter into a contract, it may be likely that the representee was so induced. In the absence of contrary evidence this may be, as Iyer J put it, 'a fair inference of fact'.[68]

4. Remedies

There are three main remedial consequences that flow from fraud or misrepresentation: rescission, restitution, and damages.[69] These remedial issues are examined by Mihir Naniwadekar (Chapter 13 of this volume), Katy Barnett (Chapter 16 of this volume), and Steven Elliott KC and Divya Behl (Chapter 19 of this volume). This chapter will confine itself to highlighting a particularly difficult aspect of damages following rescission that arises from the second paragraph of section 19. The second paragraph of section 19 provides that

> A party to a contract whose consent was caused by fraud or misrepresentation, may, if he thinks fit, insist that the contract shall be performed, and that he shall be

[63] *Bhagwani Bai* (n 20) [11].
[64] *Raghava Mannadiar v Sivasankara Menon* 1921 MWN 340 (Madras High Court).
[65] ibid [1].
[66] *Primus Telecommunications v MCI WorldCom* [2004] EWCA Civ 957, [31] (Mance LJ).
[67] H Beale, *Chitty on Contracts* (34th edn, Sweet & Maxwell 2021) [9-049].
[68] *Raghava Mannadiar* (n 64) [1].
[69] As to their remedial consequences, the Act does not distinguish between fraud and misrepresentation. They are both dealt with in s 19.

put in the position in which he would have been if the representations made had been true.

Indian cases have relied on this provision for two propositions:

(1) It has been suggested that, following rescission, the representee is entitled to damages that would put them in the position that they would have been in had the representation been true.[70]
(2) More radically, the Delhi High Court has held that the effect of the second paragraph is to exclude claims for tortious damages following rescission for fraud or misrepresentation.[71]

In my view, the second paragraph of section 19 requires legislative reconsideration. Its effect is to treat all false representations as enforceable promises whether or not they are contractual terms.[72] This is particularly difficult to justify as the second paragraph applies to fraudulent, negligent, and innocent misrepresentations. Its application to innocent misrepresentation leads to especially absurd consequences. If read as the source of a positive claim for damages, the second paragraph has the effect of holding a no-fault representor liable for damages. To make matters worse, these damages are assessed by reference to the contractual expectation measure, they are not damages to compensate the representee for loss that they would not have suffered if the misrepresentation had not been made. This is indefensible.

The drafting history of the second paragraph of section 19 offers two insights.

First, it may be that this provision was intended merely to operate as a bar on rescission (in cases where the representor is willing and able to put the representee in the position that they would have been in if the representation had been true), rather than as a basis for claiming damages. This is how the corresponding provision in the 1866 Draft was worded. That provision read:

> A person who, either knowingly or ignorantly, makes a false representation whereby he induces another to enter into a contract with him, is bound to place the other in the same position as if the representation had been true, and in default of his doing so the contract is voidable at the option of the person who has been misled.[73]

[70] *Prithuram Kalita v Mayaram Sarma* AIR 1925 Cal 555, [4]; *Sorabshah Pestonji v Secretary of State* AIR 1928 Bom 17, [6]. On some occasions, Indian courts have held (disregarding the second para of s 19) that damages for misrepresentation are intended to put the plaintiff in the 'same position as if the contract had never come into existence'; in other words, 'the same financial position as they would have been, if no false misrepresentation had been made': see *Chhanga Lal v MCD* AIR 2008 Del 146, [21].

[71] *Gaurav Monga v Premier Inn India* 237 (2017) DLT 67 (Delhi High Court).

[72] Briggs and Burrows (n 24) 118. A similar concern may arise in relation to s 75 of the Act, which provides that 'A person who rightfully rescinds a contract is entitled to compensation for any damage which he has sustained through the non-fulfilment of the contract.' At first blush, this section may appear to contemplate a claim for contractual damages following rescission for fraud or misrepresentation. However, the better view is that s 75 is inapplicable to such cases: see eg *Mirza Javed Murtaza v UP Financial Corporation* AIR 1983 All 234, [13]. As the Supreme Court of India has clarified in *Trojan & Co Ltd v Nagappa Chettiar* AIR 1953 SC 235, [15], the measure of damages in such cases is the tortious one.

[73] Clause 6 of the 1866 Draft.

Much like the second paragraph of section 19, this provision also applies to fraudulent, negligent, and innocent misrepresentations. It also requires the representor to 'place the [representee] in the same position as if the representation had been true'. The critical difference is in the concluding words. They make clear that the only consequence of the representor failing to put the representee in the position that they would have been in if the representation had been true is that the representee may rescind the contract. Regrettably, these words appear to have been omitted from section 19.

The view that the second paragraph must be interpreted restrictively also derives support from the 13th Indian Law Commission's *Report on the Indian Contract Act, 1872*.[74] The following passage from the Law Commission's review of this provision is instructive:[75]

> A sells a house to B and by some blunder of A's agent, the annual value is represented as being Rs. 2,000 when it is in truth only Rs 1,000. According to the letter of the present paragraph, so say the learned authors, we may insist on completing the contract and on having the difference between actual and the stated value paid to him by A and A's successor-in-title for all time. Obviously, such could not be the intention of the Legislature.

A second possibility is that the second paragraph of section 19 means what it says: the representor is liable for damages that put the representee in the position that they would have been in if the misrepresentation had been true. This analysis is supported by Macpherson's commentary on contract law in British India.[76] The relevant passage is as follows:

> If a man by his acts or words represents his property as alienable, he will not be permitted afterwards to dispute on his own behalf its capability of being alienated. Where a jaghiredar raised money upon mortgage of his jaghire, it was held that he was not at liberty afterwards to dispute the validity of the alienation, and generally, <u>if a person induces another to enter into a contract, upon incorrect representation of facts, he is bound to make good the representation</u>.[77]

The underlined words appear to reflect the nineteenth-century equitable doctrine of 'making representations good'.[78] It states that if a deliberate representation is made by one person to another with the intention that it be relied upon, the representor may be held to the statement and compelled to make good the representation.[79] At common

[74] Law Commission of India (n 3).
[75] ibid 22.
[76] As mentioned in section II above, Macpherson was Secretary to the Third Indian Law Commission, which produced the 1866 Draft.
[77] Macpherson (n 38) 7–8 (emphasis added).
[78] I am grateful to Shivprasad Swaminathan for drawing my attention to this doctrine and to the fact that it is also reflected in cls 60, 61, and 62 of the 1866 Draft, none of which were retained in the Contract Act.
[79] F Dawson, 'Making Representations Good' (1982) 1 Canterbury Law Review 329, 330.

law, this doctrine had become 'defunct'[80] and 'had to vanish'[81] in the latter half of the nineteenth century.

In either case, in my view, the second paragraph of section 19 ought to be removed from the Contract Act. Alternatively, it should be reformulated such that it operates as a bar on rescission in cases where the representor is willing and able to put the representee in the position that they would have been in if the representation had been true. In its current form, the provision is difficult to justify.

IV. Mistake

When, if ever, can self-induced mistakes invalidate a contract? In answering that question, this section considers three categories of mistakes: common mistakes (where both parties make the same mistake), mutual mistakes (where the parties mistake each other and are therefore at cross-purposes) and unilateral mistakes (where only one party is mistaken).[82]

The remainder of this section will proceed in four parts. Sub-section (1) will highlight a conflict underlying the mistake provisions of the Act. Sub-sections (2)–(4) will then examine common mistakes, unilateral mistakes, and mistakes of law respectively. Mutual mistakes will be considered alongside unilateral mistakes.

1. Pothier, Mistake and Objectivity

As Swain explains in Chapter 1 of this volume, Pothier's Will Theory had a profound impact on nineteenth-century contract law, both in England and in India. In broad terms, Will Theory's influence had two consequences for English law: the recognition of consent as the basis of contractual liability and the evolution of mistake as a vitiating factor.[83]

In one important respect, Pothier's Will Theory sat uneasily with the pre-existing contract rules. This incompatibility arose as a consequence of the doctrine of objectivity.[84] By the late eighteenth century, the doctrine of objectivity had become firmly

[80] B McFarlane, 'Proprietary Estoppel: Undermining the Law of Succession?' in B Häcker and C Mitchell (eds), *Current Issues in Succession Law* (Hart 2016) 81–82.

[81] JD Davies, 'Promises in Equity' [2000] Singapore Journal of Legal Studies 162, 164. See also G Spencer Bower, *The Law of Actionable Misrepresentation* (Butterworth & Co 1911) 192 (describing the doctrine as 'the unhappy monster' created by 'the equitable Frankensteins'); P Sales, 'Proprietary Estoppel: Great Expectation and Detrimental Reliance' (Modern Studies in Property Law Conference, 29 March 2022) [41]–[43] <www.supremecourt.uk/docs/Proprietary%20Estoppel%20-%20Oxford%20Property%20Conference%20-%20Lord%20Sales.pdf> accessed 6 August 2023 (analysing the doctrine as a precursor to the concept of proprietary estoppel).

[82] The terminology is based on GC Cheshire, 'Mistake as Affecting Contractual Consent' (1944) 60 Law Quarterly Review 175, 175.

[83] See Chapter 1 of this volume.

[84] Doctrine of objectivity is the idea that the validity and construction of a contract are approached from the perspective of a reasonable person in the position of the parties to the contract rather than on the basis of the parties' subjective intentions.

entrenched in the common law.[85] Yet, as Ibbetson explains, 'the objective theory obviously sat ill with [Pothier's] theory that contractual liability stemmed from the meeting of the minds of the parties'.[86] During the course of the nineteenth century, English courts and commentators resorted to an estoppel-style reasoning to explain away this conflict.[87] The following passage from Parke B's judgment in *Freeman v Cooke*[88] is a classic example of this:

> [I]f whatever a man's real intention may be, he so conducts himself that a reasonable man would take the representation to be true . . . the party making the representation would be . . . precluded from contesting its truth.

The common law also had to reconcile the doctrine of mistake, a progeny of the Will Theory, with the rule of objectivity. This was done by adopting a severely truncated version of Pothier's notion of 'error'.[89] For Pothier, 'error' included a wide range of defects, including defects in subjective consent, such as unilateral mistakes.[90] By contrast, at common law, a unilateral mistake could only invalidate a contract if it had the effect of defeating the parties' objective agreement.[91]

The conflict between Will Theory and objectivity is reflected in the provisions of the Contract Act. For example, section 10 provides that 'consent' is a pre-requisite for a valid contract. Section 13 defines 'consent' as agreement 'upon the same thing in the same sense'. At first blush, cases of unilateral mistake fall squarely within this definition. Consider the following illustration:

> *Example 9*: *P*, the Deputy Head of a primary school, orders a new server for the school from a retailer (*D*). She enters the request for '5.0 petabyte' (PB) storage capacity in the order form. When the retailer makes delivery of the server with 5.0 PB capacity, she realises that she had not been aware of the correct meaning of the term 'petabyte'. In fact, 5 terabyte storage (TB) capacity would have sufficed.

Applying section 13, one may think that *P* and *D* did not 'agree upon the same thing in the same sense'.[92] Despite what she wrote on the order form, *P* only meant to purchase a 5.0 TB server. A 5.0 PB server and a 5.0 TB server are not the 'same thing'. Yet, section 22 provides that the contract is not invalid for this reason. It reads,

> A contract is not voidable merely because it was caused by one of the parties to it being under a mistake as to a matter of fact.

[85] See W Paley, *The Principles of Moral and Political Philosophy* (Faulder 1785) 107.
[86] D Ibbetson, *A Historical Introduction to the Law of Obligations* (OUP 2001) 221–22.
[87] For examples of this, see C MacMillan, *Mistakes in Contract Law* (Hart 2010) 113ff.
[88] *Freeman v Cooke* (1848) 2 Ex 654, 656–657. See also *Smith v Hughes* (1870–71) LR 6 QB 597, 607.
[89] Ibbetson (n 86) 225–26; MacMillan (n 87) 98.
[90] MacMillan (n 87) 102.
[91] In modern English contract law, this is captured by the requirement that a unilateral mistake must be 'operative': see *Treitel on the Law of Contract* (n 60) [8-051]–[8-057].
[92] As shown below, this is not the correct interpretation of s 13.

The apparent conflict between sections 10 and 13 on the one hand and section 22 on the other reflects the uneasy relationship between the Will Theory and the doctrine of objectivity. Sections 10 and 13 are a legislative restatement of the Will Theory.[93] The exclusion of unilateral mistakes by section 22 is, by contrast, a product of common law's objective approach.

The case law in India has resolved this conflict by firmly prioritising the doctrine of objectivity. Indian courts have achieved this outcome in two different ways. First, 'consent' in section 13 has been interpreted as an objective notion.[94] For the purposes of section 13, therefore, what matters is whether, judged from the perspective of a reasonable observer, the parties appeared to agree upon the same thing in the same sense.

Second, courts in India have held that sections 20–22, the specific provisions that relate to the doctrine of mistake, are conditioned by the overarching rule of objectivity. To illustrate this point, consider section 22. It provides that contracts are not invalidated by unilateral mistakes. Nevertheless if, as the result of a unilateral mistake, the parties did not objectively agree upon the same thing in the same sense, then there is no contract according to section 13.[95] Thus, and as explained in more detail below, the central enquiry in many cases of unilateral mistake and mutual mistake is whether the parties' mistake had the effect of precluding their objective agreement.[96]

2. Common Mistake

This section considers cases where, at the time of concluding the contract, both contracting parties were proceeding under the same mistake. These cases are governed by section 20, which provides that:

> Agreement void where both parties are under mistake as to matter of fact.—Where both the parties to an agreement are under a mistake as to a matter of fact essential to the agreement, the agreement is void.

As the first edition of Pollock and Mulla points out, the kind of cases to which this provision was intended to apply is not immediately apparent from its wording.[97] Rather unhelpfully, section 20 does not state that the parties must have been acting under the same mistake.[98] However, that requirement is clear from the illustrations. For instance, Illustration (b) reads,

[93] W Swain, 'Contract Codification and the English: Some Observations from the Indian Contract Act 1872' in J Devernney and M Kennedy (eds), *The Transformation of European Private Law* (CUP 2013) 183.
[94] *ITC Ltd v George Fernandes* (1989) 2 SCC 1, [21].
[95] This point is examined in greater detail at sub-section (3) below.
[96] For a similar analysis of the doctrine of mistake at common law, see J Smith, 'Contracts—Mistake, Frustration and Implied Terms' (1994) 110 Law Quarterly Review 400.
[97] Pollock and Mulla (n 2) 135.
[98] Briggs and Burrows (n 24) 57.

> A agrees to buy from B a certain horse. It turns out that the horse was dead at the time of bargain, though neither party was aware of the fact. The agreement is void.

Strictly, based on the criteria set out in section 13, the agreement between *A* and *B* is valid. They did agree upon the same thing in the same sense.[99] However, the defect in their contract arises from the fact that both parties were proceeding on the mistaken assumption that the horse was alive. Their agreement was premised on a condition that was never effective. That is why the contract between *A* and *B* is void.[100]

Against the backdrop of those preliminary remarks, I will consider two specific aspects of the treatment of common mistakes under the Contract Act.

First, for the purposes of section 20, the parties' mistake must relate to an existing fact. Thus, cases where contractual performance is rendered impossible by an event subsequent to the conclusion of a contract fall outside the purview of section 20. As West J said in *Babshetti v Venkatramana*,

> A mistake as to existing facts may make a contract void, when an erroneous expectation which events entirely falsify, has no influence at all.[101]

When contractual performance is rendered impossible by subsequent events, the parties may be discharged from performance by the second paragraph of section 56, the Indian variant of the doctrine of frustration.[102]

Second, section 20 requires the court to determine whether the parties' mistake was as to 'a matter of fact essential to the agreement'. This is a fact-specific enquiry. However, two general propositions may be derived from the Indian authorities on this topic:

i. If, unknown to the parties, performance of the contract was impossible from the very beginning, the contract will be void under section 20

There are three categories of cases that illustrate this proposition. The first concerns cases where the subject matter of the agreement was non-existent at the time of conclusion of the contract. Illustration (b) to section 20 exemplifies this category. So does the decision of the Calcutta High Court in *Ananda Das v Kali Bepari*.[103] In that case, the parties had entered into a compromise agreement to settle their claims. In doing so, they proceeded on the mistaken assumption that there was pending litigation between them. In fact, the proceedings had ended in judgment. Therefore, the compromise agreement was held to be void.[104]

A second example relates to cases where, at the time of conclusion of the contract, contractual performance was unlawful. The Madras High Court decision in

[99] This is why common mistakes are conceptually different from mutual and unilateral mistakes.

[100] Cheshire (n 82) 175–76.

[101] *Babshetti v Venkatramana* ILR 1879 (3) Bom 154, 158. See also *UP Government v Lala Gupta* AIR 1960 All 420, [10].

[102] Frustration is examined in N Bhadbhade, Chapter 14 of this volume.

[103] *Ananda Das v Kali Bepari* AIR 1919 Cal 330.

[104] ibid [2].

Lakshmanprasad v Achutan Nair[105] is an example. In that case, the defendant had purchased a motor car from the plaintiff for 9,350 Rupees. The price was more than what was permissible under the Madras Motor Cars Control Order 1947. Therefore, the Court held that the contract was vitiated by common mistake.[106]

A third example consists of cases where, although performance of the contract is strictly possible, the contractual purpose could not be achieved. This is illustrated by the decision of the Bombay High Court in *Purshottam Talreja v Coover Bharucha*. In that case, Deshmukh J said,

> [P]erusal of the agreement shows that the land was agreed to be purchased by the Plaintiffs for the purpose of raising construction on the land . . . Therefore, the purpose for which the land is permitted to be used was of vital importance.[107]

On this basis, the Court concluded that the purpose for which the land could be used was a 'fact essential to the agreement'. Since that purpose could not have been achieved at the time when the agreement was concluded, the contract was held to be void.

ii. The parties' erroneous opinion regarding the value of the subject matter will not render a contract void; however, a common mistake as to one of its essential qualities will

The distinction between the first[108] and second sentences of proposition (ii) is not easy to draw. The case law suggests that the court will be guided by the contractual purpose in distinguishing between 'erroneous opinions as to value' and 'essential qualities' of the subject matter.

An example of the former may be found in the early decision of the Travancore-Cochin High Court in *TV Kochuvareed v Mariappa Gounder*.[109] In that case, in the context of a lease agreement, the parties were mistaken as to whether the lessee had the right to be compensated for improvements to the property. The Court treated this as a mistake regarding one of the lessee's rights. It was, thus, held to be incidental to the contractual purpose. Therefore, the parties' mistake was categorised as 'an erroneous opinion as to the real value of the subject-matter of the agreement'.[110]

The decision in *TV Kochuvareed* may be contrasted with the Allahabad High Court's decision in *Walker v Meaney*.[111] There, the dispute arose in the context of an agreement for the sale of land. The parties believed that the plot was more than five *bighas*. In fact, it was less. At first blush, this may seem like a mistake regarding the value of the property. However, the applicable municipal by-laws did not permit land less than five

105 *Lakshmanprasad v Achutan Nair* AIR 1955 Mad 662.
106 ibid [3].
107 *Purshottam Talreja v Coover Bharucha* (2008) 2 MahLJ 173 (Bombay High Court) [8].
108 See the Contract Act, s 20 (Explanation).
109 *TV Kochuvareed v Mariappa Gounder* AIR 1954 TC 10 (Travancore-Cochin High Court).
110 ibid [44].
111 *Walker v Meaney* AIR 1947 All 332.

bighas to be built upon. For this reason, the area of the land was held to be part of the contractual purpose. Malik J said,

> This would be a case of a mutual mistake as to a matter of fact essential to the agreement inasmuch as if the area was less than five bighas, the Plaintiff would not be entitled to build on the land.[112]

The centrality of the contractual purpose in assessing whether the mistake relates to an essential quality of the subject matter becomes even more apparent when the decision in *Walker* is compared with the Calcutta High Court's judgment in *Banerjee v Goswami*.[113] In that case too, the parties were mistaken about the area of the land. They had both proceeded on the incorrect basis that the land measured more than 100 *bighas*. Unlike in *Walker*, however, the area of the land was found not to be relevant to the contractual purpose. Page J said,

> I approach the issue whether there was a mutual mistake as to the fact essential to the agreement. I am not satisfied that the exact area of 100 bighas more or less was essential for the colliery purposes for which the agreement was arrived at.[114]

On this basis, the contract was found to be valid.

3. Unilateral Mistake

> *Example 10A*: *P* owns a painting that *P* believes is worth Rs 20,000. *P* enters into a contract with *D* to sell the painting for Rs 30,000. Subsequently, *P* realises that the painting is a Picasso worth Rs 20 million. *P* wishes to avoid the contract.

Despite *P*'s unilateral mistake, *P* is bound by the contract. That is the effect of section 22:

> A contract is not voidable merely because it was caused by one of the parties to it being under a mistake as to a matter of fact.

The rule set out in section 22 is based on the doctrine of objectivity. In Example 10A, the parties' objective agreement was to buy and sell a particular painting for Rs 30,000. That agreement was independent of *P*'s subjective belief as to the value of that painting. Consequently, the falsification of *P*'s belief does not invalidate the agreement.

The principle is illustrated by the Bombay High Court's decision in *Allarakha v The Bombay and Persia Steam Company*.[115] The plaintiff chartered a steamer to sail from

[112] ibid [5]. See also *Nursing Kothari v Chuttoo Misser* (1923) ILR 50 Cal 615.
[113] *Banerjee v Goswami* AIR 1929 Cal 547.
[114] ibid [4].
[115] *Allarakha v The Bombay and Persia Steam Company* ILR (1892) 16 Bom 561.

Jeddah to Bombay. The ship was meant to convey pilgrims returning to India after *Haj*. The charter-party was due to commence on 10 August 1892. The plaintiff proposed this date on the assumption that it fell fifteen days after *Haj*. In fact, this was not the case. Nevertheless, the Court found that there was a valid charter for 10 August 1892. Farran J said,

> I am inclined to think that [the plaintiff] intended to charter the vessel for [the fifteenth day of Haj], but what he really did was to charter it for the 10th of August, believing that date to correspond with the fifteenth day after the Haj.[116]

In other words, despite the plaintiff's unilateral error, the parties had reached objective agreement.

Notwithstanding what was said above, section 22 does not mean that unilateral mistakes may never invalidate a contract. It only provides that a contract is not void 'merely because' of a unilateral mistake. This general principle is subject to three exceptions. The exceptions are cases where a unilateral mistake has the effect of defeating the parties' objective agreement.

The first exception applies when one party is aware of the other's mistake as to the terms of the contract. Consider the following example:

> *Example 10B*: *D* owns a painting that *D* believes is worth £20,000. *D* enters into a contract with *P* to sell the painting for that price. *P* mistakenly believes that the sale price under the contract is $20,000. *D* was aware of *P*'s mistake when the contract was concluded. Subsequently, *P* realises the mistake and wishes to avoid the contract.

Here, the contract is invalid. Section 22 is inapplicable. This is because, having been aware of *P*'s unilateral mistake as to the terms, *D* cannot hold *P* to the objective agreement. As Sharma J said in the Delhi High Court judgment in *NCT of Delhi v Bhushan Kumar*,

> Contracts are rarely rescinded on the ground of unilateral mistake unless the other side is aware of the said mistake and had actual knowledge of the said mistake.[117]

The second exception applies when the unilateral mistake relates to the subject matter of the agreement and it was caused, even if innocently, by the other party. As a matter of principle this rule follows, *a fortiori*, from the first exception. The Act deals with this category of cases by equating 'induced mistakes' with misrepresentations. It does so in section 18(3), which provides that:

[116] ibid 566.

[117] *NCT of Delhi v Bhushan Kumar* (2008) 151 DLT 158 (Delhi High Court). See also *William Binns v Avery Ltd* AIR 1934 Cal 778. Indian courts have not always clearly distinguished between mistakes as to terms and mistakes as to facts: see eg *Punnen v United India Insurance Co Ltd* (2022) 3 SCC 655, [21]–[22]. Nevertheless, the better view is that a contract is void on the basis that the mistake was known to the other party only when the mistake was as to terms: see *Smith* (n 88). I am grateful to Professor Hugh Beale for drawing this point to my attention.

'Misrepresentation' means and includes—

...

(3) causing, however innocently, a party to an agreement, to make a mistake as to the substance of the thing which is the subject of the agreement.

The third exception applies when the effect of a unilateral mistake is to defeat one of the requirements of contract formation. A unilateral mistake as to the identity of the other party is an example of this. Consider the following illustration:

Example 11: *D*, who bears a striking resemblance to a well-known pop star, walks into *P*'s jewellery store and selects a diamond ring. *D* says to *P*, 'I've forgotten my credit card, but I assure you that I can pay.' *P* is overawed and says, 'Yes, of course!' *P* allows *D* to take the ring.

Here, the question is whether, objectively, *P* concluded a contract with *D* rather than the pop star. In some cases, as a result of *P*'s unilateral mistake, and when judged objectively, there may be no valid contract between *P* and *D*.[118] Whether that conclusion can be reached will depend on fact-specific issues, including the nature of the pre-contractual communications between the parties.[119]

Mutual mistakes (ie cases where the parties mistake each other and are, therefore, at cross-purposes) are also explicable on this basis. Consider this example:

Example 10C: *P* owns two paintings: one is a Picasso worth Rs 20 million and the other, the work of a less-known painter valued at Rs 20,000. *P* offers to sell the latter painting to *D* for Rs 30,000. *D* accepts the offer, under the impression that *P* was offering the Picasso.

Here, whether the parties' mutual mistake had the effect of invalidating the contract depends on whether the parties reached objective agreement. As the Allahabad High Court held in *UP Government v Lala Gupta*,

> In a case of mutual mistake the contracting parties misunderstand each other and there is no real correspondence of offer and acceptance. The parties are really not consensus ad idem and there is in fact no agreement at all. In this case also the contract is void.[120]

Notably, the mere fact that the parties were at cross purposes does not necessarily mean that they did not reach objective agreement. In Example 10C, for instance, the court will need to determine whether a reasonable person would have understood *P*'s offer as one to sell the Picasso. Equally, could *D*'s acceptance be construed, objectively, as relating to the painting worth Rs 20,000? If so, there may be a valid contract despite the mutual mistake.[121]

118 *AY Reily v Rajkumri* AIR 1922 Cal 493, [8]. See also N Bhadbhade, *Contract Law in India* (Kluwer International 2010) 125.

119 Cf *Nanotech (P) Ltd v Assam State Electricity Board* (2009) 5 GauLR 370 (Gauhati High Court) [122]–[124], relying on s 20 to suggest that a mistake as to identity always renders a contract void. This analysis is incorrect because, as explained above, s 20 applies to common mistakes, not unilateral mistakes.

120 *Lala Gupta* (n 101) [9]. See also *Ramanujulu Naidu v Gajaraja Ammal* AIR 1950 Mad 146, [6].

121 See Cheshire (n 82) 179.

4. Mistakes of Law

The Contract Act distinguishes between mistakes of fact and mistakes of law. While the former may render a contract void, the latter does not. Section 21 provides that:

> A contract is not voidable because it was caused by a mistake as to any law in force in India; but a mistake as to a law not in force in India has the same effect as a mistake of fact.

Viewed against the historical context in which the Act was drafted,[122] this provision is unsurprising. The nineteenth century was the high point of the mistake-of-law bar at common law.[123] Soon thereafter, the tide turned against this rule. Ultimately, it was abolished by the House of Lords in 1998.[124]

In my view, the exclusionary rule in section 21 requires legislative reconsideration. The reasons why the mistake-of-law bar was abolished in England support that view. In summary, the reasons were three-fold. First, the supposed rationale for the mistake-of-law bar—the maxim *ignorantia juris non excusat*—does not, in fact, justify it. This maxim only means that ignorance of law does not excuse a person from performing their obligations.[125] It does not follow that mistakes of law are always legally irrelevant.

Second, the distinction between mistakes of law and mistakes of fact leads to capricious results. For example, this distinction had led English courts to conclude that an insurer who pays the insured forgetting that the premium had not been paid had made a mistake of fact (and therefore could recover the payment),[126] whereas an insurer who pays out forgetting that the facts in the insurer's knowledge would have enabled them to repudiate liability had made a mistake of law (and therefore could not recover the payment).[127]

Third, from the perspective of the parties' consent, it is difficult to justify the distinction between mistakes of fact and mistakes of law. Both impact the parties' consent in the same way.[128]

In addition to these, there is yet another reason why section 21 requires reconsideration: the Indian courts' interpretation of section 72 of the Contract Act. Section 72 provides that '[a] person to whom money has been paid, or anything delivered, by mistake or under coercion, must repay or return it'. In the context of this provision, the Indian Supreme Court has repeatedly rejected the distinction between mistakes of

[122] Section 21 is based on cl 8 of the 1866 Draft.
[123] See *Bilbie v Lumley* (1802) 2 East 469; *Brisbane v Dacres* (1813) 5 Taunton 143.
[124] *Kleinwort Benson Ltd v Lincoln City Council* [1999] 2 AC 349 (HL).
[125] W Evans, 'An Essay on the Action of Money Had and Received' in W Evans (ed), *Essays: On the Action for Money Had and Received, on the Law of Insurances, and on the Law of Bills of Exchange and Promissory Notes* (Merritt & Wright 1802).
[126] *Kelly v Solari* (1841) 9 M&W 54, 55.
[127] *Brisbane* (n 123).
[128] Even Birks, who did not favour abolishing the mistake of law bar in England, admitted this: see P Birks, *An Introduction to the Law of Restitution* (Clarendon Press 1985) 164.

law and fact.[129] Thus, section 21 is inconsistent with the modern Indian approach to section 72.

In the light of the abolition of the corresponding rule in England, the near unanimous extrajudicial criticism of this rule,[130] its abrogation in much of the rest of the common law world,[131] and its inconsistency with the Indian courts' approach to section 72, in my view, section 21 must be removed from the Contract Act.

V. Conclusion

The study of the Indian law on fraud, misrepresentation, and mistake in this chapter has revealed three underlying themes.

The first relates to the complex relationship between the Contract Act and English common law. On some occasions, common law has functioned as an interpretive aid. On some others, it has filled in the interstices. More radically still, at least in some instances, English contract law has supplanted the statutory scheme. As a consequence, the provisions of the Contract Act can only be analysed against the backdrop of common law principles.

The second theme relates to the sources. Where is the substantive content of the Contract Act derived from? A number of its provisions codify English contract law. However, as this chapter tried to show, there were significant non-English law influences too. The interplay between the civilian influences and pre-existing contract law doctrines was a problem that the common law courts of the nineteenth century had to grapple with. It is not a problem that present-day Indian courts can avoid either.

The final theme is legislative reform. As this chapter attempted to demonstrate, in a number of respects, the Act is in need of revision. Part of the problem arises from antiquity: in many respects, the Act represents nineteenth-century English contract law. Another difficulty is internal incompatibility. This is attributable to the discontinuities in the Contract Act's drafting process and the incongruity of the sources that it tries to piece together. Sixty years after they were last reviewed by the Indian Law Commission, a careful reconsideration of the fraud, misrepresentation, and mistake provisions in the Act is now long overdue.

[129] *Mafatlal Industries v Union of India* (1997) 5 SCC 536, [28]; *State of Kerala v Aluminium Industries* (1965) 16 STC 689.

[130] Summarised in Law Commission of England and Wales, *Restitution of Payments Made under a Mistake of Law* (Law Com CP No 120, 1991) [2.24]–[2.26].

[131] Summarised in *Kleinwort Benson* (n 124) 372–74 (Lord Goff).

11
Illegality

*Thomas Sebastian and Aman Ahluwalia**

I. Introduction

The rule against enforceability of illegal agreements reflects the reluctance of the private law of contract to facilitate conduct that is prohibited by other laws or otherwise disfavoured as a matter of policy or morality.[1] The illegality defence is an anomaly of sorts as it allows a party to extricate from an agreement made with full capacity and free consent. It is, however, a necessary anomaly, as the law as a whole would be internally inconsistent if binding contracts could be used to undermine its various other regulatory objectives. For example, allowing gangs of smugglers to enter into enforceable contracts with each other would be self-defeating because it would facilitate the evasion of customs duties. Likewise, enforcing agreements between co-conspirators to defraud a third party would undermine the regulatory objective of preventing fraud. Nevertheless, it is important to recognise that while the illegality defence can serve to promote regulatory objectives, it can also lead to injustice. It has the potential to lead to enrichment of a party who is complicit in the illegality and can impose financial losses that are far in excess of the fines imposed or compensation provided for under the specific legal regime that would have been infringed by the illegal conduct.

These complexities have led two common law jurisdictions, New Zealand (in 1970) and England (far more recently, following the UK Supreme Court ruling in *Patel v Mirza* in 2016) to conclude that the appropriate solution is to confer discretion on courts to determine how the private law of contract should respond to illegality (or other disfavoured conduct) in any individual case. The Indian Contract Act 1872 (hereinafter 'the Contract Act'), however, leaves limited, if any, room for discretion as it lays down clear rules regarding the effect of illegality (or other disfavoured conduct).

In this chapter, we describe those rules in the following sequence: first, we outline the relevant statutory framework; second, we describe the degree of connection that

* We thank KV Krishnaprasad, Niranjan Venkatesan, and the participants in the Conference on 150 years of the Indian Contract Act 1872 for their extremely helpful comments on this chapter. The responsibility for any remaining errors rests entirely with us. We also thank Deanna Barmakian and Michelle Pearse, Reference Librarians at Harvard Law School, for their assistance with research relevant to the drafting history of section 23.

[1] For a more detailed account of the policies that underlie the illegality rule, see English Law Commission, *Illegal Transactions: The Effect of Illegality on Contracts and Trusts* (Consultation Paper No 154, 1999) [6.1]–[6.12]; S Green and A Bogg (eds), *Illegality after Patel v Mirza* (Hart 2018).

Thomas Sebastian and Aman Ahluwalia, *Illegality* In: *Foundations of Indian Contract Law.* Edited by: KV Krishnaprasad, Niranjan Venkatesan, Shivprasad Swaminathan, and Umakanth Varottil, Oxford University Press. © Oxford University Press 2024.
DOI: 10.1093/9780191997211.003.0011

the law requires between illegal conduct and a contract before it will intervene to make the contract unenforceable; third, we describe the various categories of illegal and disfavoured conduct which result in non-enforcement; and fourth, we deal with the consequences of illegality, including mitigating rules allowing for proprietary transfers, severability, and restitution.

II. The Statutory Framework

The key provision in the Contract Act is section 23.[2]

Under that section, if an agreement's 'object or consideration' is unlawful, it will be void. Section 23 sets out five instances in which an 'object or consideration' will be treated as unlawful. These are (a) where it is forbidden by law, (b) where it would defeat the provisions of any law, (c) where it is fraudulent, (d) where it involves injury to another's person or property, and (e) where the court considers it to be immoral or opposed to public policy. In addition to the general rule set out in section 23, four further provisions—sections 26, 27, 28, and 30—define particular types of agreements that are declared unenforceable on account of their content. Furthermore, illegality is addressed in sections 24, 57, 58 (dealing broadly with severability or non-severability of the illegal parts of a contract), section 56 (dealing with frustration where performance becomes illegal on account of a change in the law *after* formation of a contract), and section 65 (dealing with restitutionary relief).

These provisions of the Contract Act have to be considered alongside section 27(1)(b) of the Specific Relief Act 1963, [3] section 6(h) of the Transfer of Property Act 1882, and sections 4 and 84 of the Trusts Act 1882. Section 27(1)(b) of the Specific Relief Act 1963 allows for a court to make a declaration rescinding a contract if the contract 'is unlawful for causes not apparent on its face and the defendant is more to blame than the plaintiff'.[4] Sections 6(h) of the Transfer of Property Act 1882 and section 4 of the Trusts

[2] Section 23 reads,

> 23. What considerations and objects are lawful, and what not.—
> The consideration or object of an agreement is lawful, unless—
> it is forbidden by law; or
> is of such a nature that, if permitted, it would defeat the provisions of any law; or
> is fraudulent; or
> involves or implies injury to the person or property of another; or
> the Court regards it as immoral, or opposed to public policy.
> In each of these cases, the consideration or object of an agreement is said to be unlawful.
> Every agreement of which the object or consideration is unlawful, is void.

[3] Formerly the Specific Relief Act 1877, s 35(b).

[4] There is very little case law on the interpretation of this provision, and it does not neatly cohere with the Contract Act, s 23. If the Specific Relief Act, 1963, s 27 and the Contract Act, s 23 refer to the same kinds of illegality, it is not apparent why the rescission of an unlawful contract should be dependent on a finding that one party is less blameworthy than the other (given that the contract is, in any event, unenforceable by operation of the Contract Act, s 23). If the Specific Relief Act, 1963, s 27 and the Contract Act, s 23 do not refer to the same kinds of illegality, then s 27 must cover agreements with a lawful object and for lawful consideration, which are nevertheless unlawful on other grounds, but it is unclear what those grounds might be.

Act 1882 are similar to section 23 of the Contract Act and provide, respectively, that no transfer of property can be made for an 'unlawful object or consideration' and that no trust can be made to effect an unlawful purpose. Section 84 of the Trusts Act 1882 deals with transfers of property for an illegal purpose and provides for the transferee to hold property on trust for the benefit of the transferor in certain circumstances.

In addition to these statutory provisions, the courts have also relied on common law rules reflected in two Latin maxims, *ex turpi causa non oritur actio* ('From a dishonourable cause an action does not arise') and *in pari delicto potior est condition defendentis* ('If both parties are in the wrong, the position of the defendant is stronger'). As far as matters of contract are concerned, the reliance on these maxims seems unnecessary and only serves to complicate matters, given that the issue of how illegality affects contractual obligations is directly addressed in the Contract Act. However, the practice of relying on the maxims is now well entrenched.[5] Although courts refer to these maxims, it is difficult to identify decided cases where reliance on these maxims has led to substantive results regarding contractual enforcement, which could not otherwise have been arrived at, more directly, under the provisions of the Contract Act and/or the Specific Relief Act.

Contractual invalidity may also be addressed, expressly or impliedly, in substantive statutes which declare that particular kinds of contracts or contractual terms are void. To give two examples, an agreement for the giving or taking of dowry is made void by section 5 of the Dowry Prohibition Act 1961, and restrictive terms in patent licensing agreements are made void by section 140(1) of the Patents Act 1970. Often, where there is such an express provision in substantive statutes other than the Contract Act, there will be little need to consider the Contract Act in order to arrive at conclusions regarding enforceability.[6]

In other cases, complex questions of statutory interpretation will arise, and the courts will have to determine whether the scheme of the individual statute is meant to displace the more general provisions of the Contract Act. *BOI Finance Ltd v Custodian*[7] is one example. In *BOI*, the Supreme Court held that contracts entered into in contravention of requirements set out in a binding circular issued by the Reserve Bank of India (RBI) under the Banking Regulation Act 1949 remained enforceable, because the circular in question was not disclosed to the borrowing public. On this basis, it concluded that the RBI circular was not intended to affect contractual rights.[8] That may answer the plea of illegality based solely on the Banking Regulation Act 1949. But it does not fully resolve a plea of illegality based on the more general provisions of the Contract Act. As discussed further below, under section 23 of the Contract Act, a contract to do something that is penalised under an enactment (here, the Banking

[5] See eg *Kedar Nath Motani v Prahlad Rai* AIR 1960 SC 213; *Immani Appa Rao v Gollapalli Ramalingam* AIR 1962 SC 370; *Sita Ram v Radhabai* AIR 1968 SC 534; *Narayanamma v Govindappa* (2019) 19 SCC 42 (these cases can be understood as cases about the law of property as opposed to cases about the law of contract).

[6] There may, nevertheless, be a need to consider provisions of the Contract Act to deal with remedial consequences.

[7] (1997) 10 SCC 488.

[8] ibid [30], [33], [34].

Regulation Act 1949) is void. Accordingly, some further analysis was required before the Supreme Court could safely conclude that the contract was valid notwithstanding section 23. A similar concern arises in cases where defendants argue that contractual terms contravene the Foreign Exchange Management Act 1999 (FEMA). Courts (and arbitral tribunals) have dismissed FEMA defences on the basis that, in sharp contrast to its predecessor Foreign Exchange Regulation Act 1973 (FERA), FEMA does not contain a specific provision invalidating non-compliant contracts.[9] They appear to overlook the fact that it is entirely possible for FEMA to proscribe certain conduct, and for section 23 of the Contract Act to render unenforceable a contract to carry out such proscribed conduct. The dismissal of FEMA defences may not be justified in the absence of a specific statutory provision saving contracts that contravene FEMA requirements.

Finally, we note that the drafting history of section 23 has played little, if any, role in how that provision has been interpreted. The general approach of the Indian courts has been to take the provision as it stands and to refer to English precedents where relevant (and occasionally, even where irrelevant). The provision on illegality[10] in the original Draft Bill of the Indian Law Commissioners was referred to as 'somewhat clumsy'[11] in the *Report of the Select Committee*[12] comprising Mr Fitzjames Stephen and others. The provision substituted for it by the Select Committee is section 23 in its present form. While the text of the original draft clause changed considerably, most of the illustrations survived, with minor adaptations.[13]

III. Nexus between Illegality and the Agreement: 'Object or Consideration'

Not every illegality/immorality connected with an agreement will result in unenforceability. For section 23 to apply, either the 'object' or the 'consideration' of

[9] See eg *SRM Exploration v N&S* (2012) 129 DRJ 113; *Vijay Karia v Prysmian* (2020) 11 SCC 1. It is noteworthy that the RBI does not appear to accept this argument: see *Docomo v Tata* (2017) SCC Online Del 8078, [27], [31].

[10] The Draft Bill accompanying the Third Indian Law Commission, *Second Report on the Substantive Law of India* (31 July 1866) had a clause that required a contract to have a lawful object and a good consideration. It was further specified that a good consideration had to be lawful. Thus, lawful object and lawful consideration were necessary ingredients of a valid contract, even in the early draft prepared by the Indian Law Commissioners. As to what constituted a lawful object and lawful consideration, cl 10 only specified that they should 'not (be) contrary to law or to morality'. It did not specifically enumerate what constituted unlawful object and consideration, and nor did it expressly state (although it implied) that an unlawful agreement would be void. The Draft of the Indian Law Commissioners underwent some changes at the hands of the Council of the Governor General, and the Draft Indian Contract Bill was then referred to a Select Committee in December 1867. In the Bill, as referred to the Select Committee, illegality was dealt with in cl 13.

[11] Legislative Department, *Gazette of India (Extraordinary)* 28 March 1872. Quite apart from effecting major changes in s 23, the Select Committee also 'recommended distinct provisions to be made for the effect of an unlawful object or consideration, the absence of consideration, contracts in restraint of marriage or trade, and contracts in restraint of legal proceedings; contracts the meaning of which cannot be ascertained, and contracts by way of wager'.

[12] The Indian Contract Bill underwent significant revisions at the hands of the Select Committee, and Mr Fitzjames Stephen presented the *Report of the Select Committee* to the Council of the Governor General, in March 1872.

[13] Illustrations (a)–(i) of the present s 23 of the Contract Act are, in substance, similar to the illustrations appended to the original Draft clause.

the agreement has to be unlawful. Accordingly, the term 'object or consideration of an agreement' in section 23 is crucial because it determines when an illegality will be sufficiently connected to an agreement to result in its non-enforcement.[14]

The term 'object . . . of an agreement' has been interpreted as the purpose or design behind an agreement.[15] Parties to an otherwise legitimate agreement will find that it is unenforceable if their purpose or design was to facilitate illegality. For instance, an ordinary agreement to loan money will be rendered unenforceable if both parties intended that the funds be used to finance an illegal child marriage.[16] Even though the child marriage forms no part of the performance provided for under the loan agreement, the fact that the ordinary loan agreement was intended to further a broader unlawful enterprise (ie the child marriage) suffices for section 23 to apply. Likewise, where the intent of the parties was that an agent should purchase goods that would then be exported in breach of binding regulations, the ordinary agency contract regulating their relationship became unenforceable.[17]

For an unlawful/immoral purpose to be treated as the 'object' of an agreement *both* parties to the agreement must share it. In *Pragilal v Ratanlal*, one party (the borrower) desired funds for gambling activities, but the other party (the lender) did not know about or seek to facilitate that immoral purpose. Section 23 could not be invoked to invalidate the loan agreement.[18] Likewise, if one party to a sale agreement seeks to defraud that party's creditors and the other party does not know about or share this objective, section 23 cannot be invoked.[19]

The term 'consideration of an agreement' may appear to be incongruous because consideration is given for a promise, not for an agreement. However, the use of this language has not led to any difficulty in practice.[20] What needs to be assessed is (a) the promised performance (ie each and every term of the contract) or (b) any other conduct that constitutes consideration within the meaning of section 2(d) of the Contract Act (ie past conduct if the consideration is 'past consideration' or the condition for a unilateral promise if the agreement is unilateral). It is clear that if the promised

[14] An interesting example comes from the 2G cases where contracts between the Government of India and telecom companies were invalidated by the Supreme Court because of public law illegalities in the process of allocation antecedent to those contracts. In a subsequent proceeding regarding restitution, the Telecom Disputes Settlement and Appellate Tribunal (TDSAT) ruled that the Contract Act, s 23 was not attracted because the presence of antecedent public law illegalities did not imply that either the 'consideration' or the 'object' of the licence contracts was unlawful: see *Loop Telecom v Union of India* (2015) SCC Online TDSAT 99.

[15] See *Gurmukh Singh v Amar Singh* (1991) 3 SCC 79. Note that object appears to be used in a different sense in the Contract Act, s 24.

[16] *Chandra Sreenivasa Rao v Korrapati Raja* AIR 1952 Mad 579. Doubts have been expressed in subsequent cases about whether the act of entering into a child marriage is actually illegal. That does not affect the point made here: assuming entering into a child marriage is illegal, a contract to provide funds for a such a marriage would be unenforceable.

[17] *Appana Radha v VKM Kodandarama Chetti* AIR 1960 AP 190.

[18] *Pragilal v Ratan Lal* AIR 1931 All 458.

[19] Illustration taken from *Nathusa v Munir Khan* AIR 1943 Nag 129. See also *Shahabuddin Sahib v Tota Venkatachalam* AIR 1938 Mad 911; *Duggirala Sadasiva Vittal v Bolla Rattalu* AIR 1956 AP 145; *Gulabchand Gambjirmal v Kudilal Govindram* AIR 1959 MP 151.

[20] *13th Law Commission of India Report, Indian Contract Act 1872* (1958) 23 <https://cdnbbsr.s3waas.gov.in/s3ca0daec69b5adc880fb464895726dbdf/uploads/2022/08/2022080532.pdf> accessed 9 May 2023.

performance or any other conduct constituting 'consideration' is illegal (or otherwise disfavoured), then the agreement will be void.

A particularly difficult issue arises when an agreement does not require illegal performance but one of the parties chooses to perform the agreement in an illegal manner. Can it be said that the guilty party loses its contractual rights because of its conduct? Does the law go even further and invalidate the contract itself, thus depriving both parties of the ability to enforce the contract?

On the latter question, existing authorities tend to support the view that a post-formation decision by one party to perform illegally will not invalidate the contract as a whole. In *Sree Ramakrishna Mining Company v CIT*, an income tax case, the Mysore High Court concluded that post-formation illegality in how a partnership business was conducted could not affect the validity of the partnership agreement itself (which was lawful at the time of its formation). [21] The Mysore High Court cited the English case of *Marles v Phillip Trant & Sons*[22] in favour of the proposition that 'a contract which is not illegal when made, does not become illegal by reason of illegality in performance'. The Kerala High Court reached a similar conclusion in *Janardhanan v Sreedharan* when it observed that 'the question of illegality of a partnership must be distinguished from illegality of any acts done in the course of its business by the firm or some or all of its members'.[23] However, critically, in both of these cases it was the position of the innocent party that had to be considered. Neither of these cases involved a claim by a guilty party against an innocent counterparty.

The courts have not addressed the issue of whether the guilty party (ie the party that chooses to perform illegally) can retain its contractual rights against the innocent party. In this regard, it is worth noting that English law apparently allows for a result whereby a guilty party is deprived of contractual rights, while the innocent party retains its contractual rights.[24] The position in India, however, remains open.

The text of section 23 militates against a result where the guilty party loses its contractual rights if an otherwise legal contract is performed illegally.[25] Section 23 is not really directed at the contractual rights of individual parties. It is concerned with the enforceability of the 'agreement' more generally: it says '[e]very agreement of which the object or consideration is unlawful is void'. Therefore, within the textual framework of section 23, an agreement is either void or it is not, and it is difficult to fit within that text a result where the contract is enforceable by one party but not by the other. Moreover, it is difficult to say that the post-formation decision by the guilty party to perform illegally implies that the 'consideration' or the 'object' of an agreement, which was initially legal,

[21] ILR 1966 Mys 1045.
[22] (1954) 1 QB 29. This case involved the position of the innocent party.
[23] AIR 1985 Ker 199.
[24] See RA Buckley, *Illegality and Public Policy* (4th edn, Sweet & Maxwell 2017) [3.13].
[25] Another solution, proposed by Banerji, is for the innocent party to have recourse to the Specific Relief Act, s 27(1)(a). However, no explanation is given by Banerji as to how illegal performance by one party makes a contract voidable under the Contract Act. SC Banerji, *The Law of Specific Relief in British India* (2nd edn, R Cambray & Co 1917) 465 ('If one of the parties is ignorant of such design and purpose, it is voidable at his option, if executory, and, upon becoming aware of the same, he may repudiate it. Such a case may be treated as one under clause (a), section [27], Specific Relief Act, for the plaintiff is innocent'.)

has changed so as to subsequently become illegal because of the guilty party's unilateral decision to perform illegally.[26] 'Consideration' is something that needs to exist at the time of formation of a contract: it cannot change after formation. Likewise, the 'object' of the agreement is the joint purpose of the parties and, therefore, cannot be altered by means of a unilateral decision of the guilty party. For these reasons, the text of section 23 does not provide fertile ground for the view that one party's choice to perform illegally will result in that party losing its ability to enforce its contractual rights. [27] Quite apart from the textual hurdles, there are also policy considerations that weigh against depriving a guilty party of its contractual rights for having elected to perform illegally. For example, in the case of trivial violations in the course of performance (for instance, speeding in a contract for the transport of goods) or for an illegality that is not central to the guilty party's performance of the contract (for instance, income tax evasion by a building contractor in a construction contract), preventing a guilty party from exercising its contractual rights can lead to disproportionate sanctions and injustice, especially because the contract itself does not materially encourage illegal conduct in these situations. Moreover, introducing such a rule can delay and complicate the resolution of contractual disputes more generally, as it may encourage defendants to frequently (and frivolously) invoke such defences to wriggle out of difficult contracts.

On the other hand, there are potentially sound arguments that may be advanced in favour of depriving a guilty party of its contractual rights—principally, that it would disincentivise illegal conduct, as parties would elect to perform legally so as to retain their contractual rights. It would also allow an innocent party to extricate itself from a contract when it discovers that its counterparty is performing illegally. Otherwise, the innocent party would have to tolerate illegal performance and the prospect of guilt by association.

On balance, our view is that section 23 can be usefully supplemented by a common law rule[28] that guilty parties will lose their contractual rights if they have intentionally

[26] For a statement that illegality must exist at the time of inception of a contract, see *Govind Subrao v FS Pacheco* (1902) 4 Bom LR 948.

[27] Against this textual reading of s 23 is the pragmatic argument by Pollock and Mulla that 'consideration' can be understood as both the legally required consideration described in s 2(d) (which is established at formation) and any actual performance given in exchange for a promise (which can only be determined after formation). As noted, in our view, this reading is difficult to reconcile with the text of s 2(d) (and Pollock and Mulla themselves appear to acknowledge this). See F Pollock and DF Mulla, *The Indian Contract Act* (2nd edn, Thacker & Co and NM Tripathi & Co 1908) 114–15:

> in discussing the subsequent duties of the parties as to performance the word 'consideration' is sometimes applied, in a loose and extended sense, to those cases where the duty of performance on the one party is, according to the original intent of the agreement, conditional on previous or simultaneous performance on the other. In this inaccurate but not so uncommon sense it may be said that, when a promisor who might have performed his promise lawfully performs it unlawfully the consideration for the reciprocal promise becomes unlawful; and the language of the Act may have been designed to cover such cases . . . Practically it is convenient to treat these cases under the head of unlawful agreement, as the broad principles and the results are the same.

[28] We note that one may object that the statutory scheme on illegality should not be modified by way of common law rules. This is a difficult point but, in our view, s 23 is better understood as a provision that is silent about unilateral decisions to perform illegally (as opposed to a provision that treats such conduct as irrelevant to enforceability). The Contract Act is not a complete code, and while it is, no doubt, true that where it deals with a certain subject it would be exhaustive on the point and oust common law principles, there is room for supplementary rules on points where the Contract Act is silent.

committed a serious illegality that is central (and not collateral or peripheral) to their contractual performance.[29] This supplementary rule would have the salutary effect of deterring serious wrongdoing and would give innocent counterparties the option of exit when faced with such serious wrongdoing.[30]

There are two further points to be made about the 'object or consideration' test in section 23.

First, the Supreme Court has held that the mere possibility that the object or consideration of a contract will give rise to illegality or other disfavoured conduct will not be enough to invalidate a contract. It must be inevitable or certain that the object or consideration will give rise to illegality or other disfavoured conduct.[31] This is a perfectly sensible rule, which ensures that contracts are not invalidated more often than necessary.

Second, the courts have sometimes sought to distinguish between the object and consideration of an agreement and the motives of the parties.[32] It is not always apparent how this distinction is to be drawn or whether it leads to satisfactory conclusions about the applicability of section 23. Starting with the distinction between object and motive: as noted above, it is clear that the motive of one party, which is not shared by the other party, cannot be described as the object of an agreement. However, where a motive is shared, as opposed to unilateral, it is not excluded that such a (shared) motive could be understood as the object of an agreement. To this extent, motive can be relevant to the analysis under section 23. As for the distinction between motive and consideration, it is plain that these two concepts are distinct, and an unlawful motive will not imply that the consideration under an agreement is unlawful. However, courts have sometimes (wrongly) used this distinction to remove inconvenient features of an agreement from the scope of the analysis under section 23. In *Union Carbide v Union of India*, the Supreme Court was faced with a contention that part of the consideration for a promise to pay a settlement sum was the withdrawal of criminal proceedings. The Court concluded that the withdrawal of criminal proceedings was the motive for entering into the agreement (to pay the settlement sum) but could not be described as part of the consideration. The basis for this specific conclusion is difficult to follow, given that the agreement contained a term requiring withdrawal of criminal proceedings. This clearly implies that withdrawal was part of the consideration for the reciprocal promises contained in the settlement agreement.[33]

[29] See, in this regard, the English case of *ParkingEye Limited v Somerfield Stores Limited* [2012] EWCA Civ 1338, [75] (Toulson LJ).

[30] Absent such a rule, the innocent party would only be able to exit the contract if the parties included a term specifying that illegal performance will give rise to a right to terminate the contract.

[31] *Neminath v Kocheri* AIR 1966 Mys 154; *Kocheri v Neminath* AIR 1968 SC 1358; *Lachoo Mal v Shri Radhey Shyam* AIR 1971 SC 2213.

[32] See eg *In re Dehra Dun Mussoorie Electric Tram-way Company Limited (In Liquidation)* AIR 1930 All 357; *Ouseph Poulo v Catholic Union Bank* AIR 1965 SC 166; *Union Carbide v Union of India* (1991) 4 SCC 584. See also *Singh* (n 15).

[33] *Union Carbide* (n 32). For an earlier illustration of relying on the alleged irrelevance of motive to permit enforcement (despite evidence of an illegal object, albeit one that had been consummated), see *Kashinath v Bapurao* AIR 1940 Nag 305.

IV. Categories of Illegality

1. Object/Consideration is 'Forbidden by Law'

The first subclause of section 23 applies where performance of a contract involves conduct that is 'forbidden by law'. The relevant conduct will either be the promised performance (the 'consideration') or the conduct involved in some broader scheme (the 'object'), which is facilitated by performance of the contract.

In most cases, the law prohibiting the relevant conduct is to be found in a statute. It is obvious that conduct that is made punishable by a criminal statute, such as the Indian Penal Code, will be treated as conduct that is 'forbidden by law'. It will also suffice if a statute provides that the relevant conduct gives rise to civil penalties.[34] However, if a statute does not penalise and prohibit particular conduct but merely provides for other legal consequences, that will be insufficient. In *Gherulal Parakh v Mahadeodas Maiya*, the Supreme Court held that a partnership contract that had the object of facilitating wagers was valid because the conduct of entering into wagers was not prohibited or penalised under the relevant statutory provision (in that case, the relevant statutory provision was section 30 of the Contract Act, which only operates to deprive wagering contracts of binding effect).[35]

The law prohibiting the relevant conduct may also be found in uncodified rules.[36] Thus, conduct might be considered 'forbidden by law' if it contravenes uncodified personal law.[37] By way of contrast, conduct that is in breach of contract is not conduct that is 'forbidden by law'. The provisions of private contracts are distinct from the general law.[38] Similarly, conduct that runs contrary to statements of governmental policy will not be treated as prohibited conduct: policies or non-binding executive instructions/notifications are not the same thing as binding laws or binding provisions of delegated legislation.[39]

In certain cases, a statute may go further than prohibiting certain conduct, and it may specifically and expressly prohibit or render illegal or invalid the making of certain contracts.[40] Such specifically declared illegal contracts would naturally be void. But this

[34] *Mannanlal Khetan v Kedar Nathan Khetan* (1977) 2 SCC 424. See also *Asha John Divianathan v Vikram Malhotra* (2021) 19 SCC 629.

[35] AIR 1959 SC 781.

[36] See ibid [9] (citing the following statement from Pollock and Mulla (n 27): 'An act or undertaking is equally forbidden by law whether it violates a prohibitory enactment of the legislature or a principle of unwritten law').

[37] *Mahmud Ali v Mt Ghulam Fatima* AIR 1935 Lah 902.

[38] *Ram Chander v Jagan Nath* AIR 1957 HP 70. See also *Govind Subrao* (n 26). If an agreement requires the commission of a breach of contract, it may well be that the agreement is unenforceable on the separate basis that it involves an agreement to commit a tort, more specifically, an agreement to commit an 'economic tort'. If *A* and *B* enter into an agreement for *B* to breach its contract with *C*, this can amount to the economic tort of inducing a breach of contract (provided certain further requirements relating to intent are met). Accordingly, the existence of a breach of contract (the breach of *B*'s contract with *C*) may become relevant under s 23. We note that the Indian law on economic torts remains underdeveloped.

[39] *Union of India v Col LSN Murthy* (2012) 1 SCC 718. Paragraph 17 of this case appears to be overbroad in assuming that only statutory provisions can be relevant under s 23. See to this effect *GT Girish v Y Subba Raju* (2022) 12 SCC 321. Furthermore, as noted earlier, uncodified rules of law can also be relevant under s 23.

[40] Such as eg the Securities Contracts (Regulation) Act 1956, s 16.

is not strictly required, as under section 23, it is sufficient if the conduct required by way of performance is prohibited by a statute. One need not identify a specific statutory provision that goes so far as to expressly prohibit the making of particular contracts. This important point was highlighted by the Malaysian Federal Court when it observed as follows:

> To decide if [section 23, second paragraph] makes a contract illegal and unenforceable in connection with a statute, and this bears repeating, one must find out first if the statute prohibits or forbids the act which the parties have contracted to do by the contract in question, and not whether the statute prohibits the contract or the making of the contract in question by the parties. The difference is real, though very subtle. In my view, the failure to bear in mind this fine distinction has given rise to some difficulties.[41]

2. Object/Consideration 'Defeat(s) the Provisions of Any Law'

Section 23 also applies where a contract, if performed, would 'defeat' the provisions of any law. This is a wide provision, which implies that a contract can be invalidated if its performance would result in the circumvention of a law. To this extent, this sub-clause goes beyond the English law position, which requires the commission of a legal wrong.[42] Two illustrative cases are discussed below.

In *Fateh Singh v Sanwal Singh*, *A* stood surety for *B*'s good behaviour before a magistrate. Unknown to the magistrate, *B* deposited money with *A* on the understanding that the money would be returned if the surety was not invoked. The surety was not invoked (because *B* behaved appropriately), but *A* refused to return the deposit. In subsequent proceedings by *B* for the return of the deposit, *A*'s defence was that the agreement between them was unlawful: it defeated the object of the law relating to the grant of surety. There was no suggestion that the conduct of making a deposit was expressly prohibited by the law relating to the grant of surety. Nevertheless, the Court concluded that the transaction defeated the object of that law. The effect of the agreement is that the surety becomes 'responsible only in name'. That was sufficient to render the agreement unenforceable.[43]

In *Sundara Gownder v Balachandran*, *A* was ineligible to bid for toddy shops under the Abkari Shops (Disposal in Auction) Rules. *B* successfully bid for certain toddy shops in auction. *A* then agreed with *B* that *B* would transfer those toddy shops to *A*. There was no suggestion that the transfer itself would violate Abkari Shops (Disposal in Auction) Rules. Nevertheless, the Kerala High Court refused to enforce the contract on the basis that its object was to defeat those rules.[44]

41 *Sababumi (Sandakan) Sdn Bhd v Datuk Yap Pak Leong* [1998] 3 MLJ 151, 176 (per Peh Swee Chin FCJ).
42 See H Beale (ed), *Chitty on Contract*, vol 1 (33rd edn, Sweet & Maxwell 2018) [16-043].
43 (1875) ILR 1 All 751. As to whether a restitutionary claim would have succeeded, in our view a statutory restitutionary claim under the Contract Act, s 65 would not have succeeded.
44 AIR 1990 Ker 324.

Finally, Pollock and Mulla's observation that the words 'defeat the provisions of any law' must be 'taken as limited to defeating the intention which the Legislature has expressed, or which is necessarily implied from the express terms of an Act' and that 'it is not defeating the provisions of a law to take advantage of the lack of any provision for some particular case . . . [as] the Court cannot assume that the omission was not intended' is worth endorsing.[45] In practice, however, it is naturally more difficult to ascertain when a contract is defeating legislative intention, as opposed to when it is simply in violation of an express prohibition. The Supreme Court's ruling in *MG Brothers Lorry Service v Prasad Textiles*[46] is illustrative of the difficulties that can arise when attempting to ascertain legislative intention. In that case, a contractual provision that shortened the period for bringing a claim against a carrier to thirty days was struck down on the basis that it would defeat the legislation establishing a limitation period of six months. The Court, citing the preamble to the legislation, held that the statutory intent was not only to limit the liability of carriers but also to declare their liability for negligent or criminal acts. According to the Court, the contractual limitation clause was designed to avoid liability by effectively emasculating the statutory remedy and, therefore, defeated the provisions of section 10 of the Carriers Act. However, in circumstances where the legislature refrained from imposing any minimum limitation period, it is arguable that the contractual limitation clause was not, in fact, defeating any legislative intention. While the result in this particular case may be defensible, it illustrates how contestable assumptions about legislative intent can have far-reaching effects and underlines the importance of restricting the operation of section 23 to situations where legislative intent can be inferred without doubt.

3. Object/Consideration Involves 'Injury' or is 'Fraudulent'

It is convenient to consider the third and fourth subclauses of section 23 together as they both relate to agreements that adversely affect a third party. The scope of these subclauses is quite clear: if the contemplated performance involves harm to a third party, either in the form of fraud or in the form of other tortious or criminal conduct causing injury to them, the contract will not be enforceable.

A fraudulent contract within the meaning of the third subclause is one that involves the deceit of a third party. An example comes from *Manikka Mooppanar v Peria Muniyandi Pandithan*.[47] In that case, which concerned the sale of certain lands, the seller's agent arrived at an agreement with a prospective purchaser to settle the sale profitably for that purchaser even if there were other better offers. The agent was promised a commission by the purchaser, which was not disclosed to the seller. The sale was completed, but the purchaser reneged on the commission, contending that the

[45] Pollock and Mulla (n 27) 116.
[46] AIR 1984 SC 15.
[47] AIR 1936 Mad 541.

contract was unenforceable. Here, the agent was deceiving a third party—the seller (his principal). Section 23 applied, and the agent was unable to recover the undisclosed commission from the purchaser.

Injury in the fourth subclause should be wrongful injury; that is, it should arise from a tort or crime.[48] Accordingly, a contract to establish a competing business will not infringe this subclause because economic competition is perfectly lawful.

In certain cases, the third party being defrauded could also be the government. There is some case law which suggests that if defrauding the revenue is only an incidental purpose of the parties, the third subclause will not apply. In *Anand v Oswal Trading*, the Delhi High Court treated a contract for sale of goods that envisaged payment in 'black money' as enforceable on two grounds, one of which was that defrauding the revenue was only an 'incidental purpose' of the parties, their primary purpose being 'to do business'.[49] It is not clear to what extent the parties shared the objective of defrauding the revenue. If they did not, then the decision may be defensible. However, if there was such joint intention, the Delhi High Court's conclusion appears difficult to defend. The distinction between substantial design and incidental purpose is overbroad—in every case where a third party is defrauded, it would be open to the parties to say that their primary objective was 'to do business'.[50]

4. Object/Consideration is Contrary to 'Public Policy' or 'Morality'

The fifth subclause of section 23 applies if an agreement contemplates conduct that is contrary to judicially recognised notions of 'public policy' and 'morality'. Both notions are to be interpreted restrictively. In *Gherulal Parakh v Mahadeodas Maiya*,[51] the Supreme Court observed that notions of conduct that are contrary to public policy have been 'crystallised under different heads'. The Court held that although it is theoretically open to the courts to create new heads of public policy, this should only be done exceptionally where there is a clear and incontestable case of harm to the public. In the same case, the Supreme Court clarified that immorality in section 23 is likewise confined to 'principles recognised and settled by Courts' and should have a restricted meaning. The Court held that immorality, in this context, meant only 'sexual immorality'. It gave as illustrations agreements that facilitate prostitution, divorce, and cohabitation outside marriage.

As to the heads of conduct that have been judicially recognised as contrary to public policy, there are four broad headings: (i) conduct that undermines the administration of justice, (ii) conduct that undermines public administration, (iii) conduct that

[48] *Jai Ram v Kanha Ram Hans Raj* AIR 1963 HP 3.

[49] AIR 1976 Del 24, [38]. The other ground was that rejecting the claim would result in a windfall for the defendant, who was equally guilty. This could be said of every case in which the illegality defence is raised.

[50] For a more conventional case finding that a contract designed to defraud the revenue could not be enforced, see *Kanhayyalal Madhavlal Khandelwal v Roshan Eruch Mehta* (2015) SCC Online Bom 4845.

[51] *Gherulal Parakh* (n 35).

undermines the institution of marriage and family life (although this category overlaps considerably with the category of immorality), and (iv) the rule in *Brojo Nath*.[52] We discuss each of these headings below. We also discuss two potential further categories, namely, (v) conduct that breaches foreign law and (vi) 'constitutional' public policy.

i. Administration of justice

An agreement providing for the withdrawal of a criminal complaint in respect of a non-compoundable offence is contrary to public policy.[53] There is a public interest in ensuring that those guilty of serious non-compoundable criminal offences are tried and punished. Agreements to withdraw complaints create impediments to the prosecution of such offences. Likewise, agreements that compromise the integrity of the legal process (for instance, agreements to reward a witness for giving false testimony) are contrary to public policy.[54] Agreements to fund litigation are not *per se* contrary to public policy.[55] The rigid rules of the torts of champerty and maintenance were not recognised in India, and it has long been accepted that litigation funding arrangements are enforceable, provided they have 'fair terms' and the funder is not acting out of malice.[56] However, agreements by advocates to fund litigation, or to take a share of the proceeds of litigation, are contrary to their professional obligations and are highly likely to be contrary to public policy.[57]

ii. Public administration

Agreements to bribe government officials in order to obtain contracts from the government or posts in the government are contrary to public policy. These agreements will also usually involve conduct that is contrary to law (the Prevention of Corruption Act and/or the Indian Penal Code (IPC)). As a consequence, it will not be necessary for a defendant to invoke public policy in order to resist enforcement of such an agreement.

Agreements with private persons to influence the government to grant posts[58] are also contrary to the public policy. They compromise the public interest in ensuring that administrative posts are allocated purely on merit.[59] In *Rattan Chand v Jung*, the Supreme Court held that an agreement with a private person to use that person's influence with government officials to achieve certain outcomes regarding the allocation of an estate was also barred by public policy. The Court held that the agreement promoted

[52] *Central Inland Water Transport Corpn v Brojo Nath Ganguly* (1986) 3 SCC 156.

[53] *V Narasimharaju v V Gurumurthy Raju* AIR 1963 SC 107.

[54] *Ko Pa Tu v Azimulla* AIR 1940 Rang 73. See also *Adiraja Shetty v Villal Bhutta* AIR 1914 Mad 366(1), finding that a payment to a witness to give true evidence is also contrary to public policy. No detailed reasoning is provided for this ruling, and it is arguably *obiter* because the case was also decided on the basis of an absence of consideration.

[55] *Ram Swarup v Court of Wards* AIR 1940 PC 19. See also *In Re Mr G* 1955 1 SCR 490 and the more tentative observation in *Bar Council v AK Balaji* (2018) 5 SCC 379, [38].

[56] See *Ram Coomar Coondoo v Chunder Canto Mookerjee* (1876–77) 4 IA 23. See also S Naravane, Chapter 7 of this volume.

[57] See *Kathu Jairam Gujar v Vishwanath Ganesh Javadeker* AIR 1925 Bom 470; *B Sunitha v State of Telangana* (2018) 1 SCC 638. Compare *Bar Council* (n 55) [35], [38].

[58] Contract Act, Illustration (f) to s 23. See also *Virender Singh v Laxmi Narain* ILR (2006) II Delhi 1183.

[59] See *Kolaparti v Kolaparti* AIR 1964 AP 465.

'a pernicious practice of procuring decisions by influencing authorities when they should abide by the law'.[60] This ruling suggests that agreements to provide lobbying services are unenforceable purely because lobbying efforts have the potential to affect governmental decision-making. However, absent specific evidence of corruption or suppression of material facts (such as the fact that the lobbyist has been paid by a party with an interest in a particular administrative outcome), it is not apparent that lobbying activity necessarily compromises the public interest.[61]

iii. Marriage and family life

There are a number of cases where agreements relating to marriage and family life have not been enforced on the basis that they are contrary to public policy or involve immorality. However, there is very little clarity in this area of the law. The authorities are often contradictory, outdated, and dependent on the personal laws of the parties involved in the litigation. It is therefore difficult to describe the legal position with any degree of certainty.

Promises to marry are not enforceable in English law.[62] By way of contrast, Indian law has not (to date) adopted the position that promises to marry are unenforceable. Mutual promises of marriage by the groom or bride, or their parents that do not involve any exchange of money or property are likely to be enforceable. The Bombay High Court case of *Tulshiram v Roopchand* is an example of a case where a prospective groom was forced to pay damages for breach of a promise to marry the daughter of the plaintiff.[63] However, agreements to marry, or ensure a marriage, in exchange for money or property (ie dowry), are invalid under section 5 of the Dowry Prohibition Act. Indeed, even prior to the Dowry Prohibition Act, agreements creating financial incentives in connection with decisions about marriage were questioned in cases decided under section 23.[64] While these cases are now mainly of historical interest given the wide definition of dowry in section 2 of the Dowry Prohibition Act, the principles they lay down could have some contemporary relevance to contracts underlying commercial marriage brokerages, which may arguably be unenforceable (both under section 23 and under the Dowry Prohibition Act).

Agreements to marry where one, or both, parties are already married have been held to be contrary to public policy on the basis that they encourage divorce.[65] There are

[60] (1991) 3 SCC 67.

[61] Compare *Shri Saran Lal v Kesho Prasad Singh* AIR 1917 Pat 92. The Supreme Court also failed to address the statutory restitutionary claim advanced by the plaintiff in *Rattan Chand*. Compare in this regard *Amresh Chandra Pandey v Firm Kalyan Mal Dharam Narain Saraf* AIR 1972 All 130 (granting restitution, albeit without explicit consideration of the statutory position).

[62] See Law Reform (Miscellaneous Provisions) Act 1970, s 1.

[63] AIR 2006 Bom 183.

[64] The Madras High Court held, in *Devarayan Chetty v VKM Muthuram Chetty* AIR 1914 Mad 551, that all agreements providing for payments to parents in connection with marriage were contrary to public policy. By way of contrast, other High Courts have held that a public policy concern only arises in cases where the effect of the payment was to encourage marriage to an ineligible bride or groom; see *Dharnidhar v Kanhji* AIR 1949 Pat 250. There is also case law dealing with agreements to reward third parties (who are not relatives). In these cases, there is no concern that the third party will misuse a position of familial trust or authority in connection with a marriage decision. Nevertheless, the Madras and Bombay High Courts have held that such agreements are contrary to public policy: see eg *Pitamber v Jagjivan* (1889) ILR 13 Bom 131.

[65] See the comments in *Skipp v Kelly* AIR 1926 PC 27. See also *Kamla Bai v Arjan Singh* AIR 1991 MP 275.

contradictory authorities on whether an agreement to loan money to facilitate a divorce is also contrary to public policy.[66] Likewise, agreements for future separation of a married couple have been held to be contrary to public policy (unless they are part of an agreement aimed at reconciliation),[67] although agreements for immediate separation are valid.[68] Underlying these decisions is a discernible emphasis on preserving the marital bond, and it is questionable to what extent this is in keeping with contemporary legislative views about the permissibility of divorce. Along similar lines, agreements providing for cohabitation outside marriage have been treated as contrary to morality in a number of High Court cases.[69] However, agreements involving a reward for past cohabitation but no promise of future cohabitation have been upheld by certain High Courts.[70] It is difficult to defend the distinction made in these cases between past and future cohabitation. More importantly, it is not apparent that moral concerns about discouraging relationships outside marriage are fully in keeping with contemporary norms. In this regard, it is significant that the Protection of Women from Domestic Violence Act 2005 provides rights of maintenance and residence to women in informal relationships. In our view, the relevance of earlier precedents falls away in light of changing norms reflected in more recent legislative enactments.

There are differing views on whether agreements to relinquish statutory rights of maintenance are contrary to public policy. In *Muniammal v Raja*,[71] the Madras High Court observed that an agreement relinquishing the statutory right to maintenance would be enforceable. More recent cases have disagreed with that conclusion and have treated agreements relinquishing statutory rights to maintenance as contrary to public policy.[72] In any event, regardless of the contractual position, it will usually be open to a court to depart from a bilateral agreement when exercising its discretion in giving effect to statutory rights and obligations.[73] This holds true for statutory rights to maintenance but also other statutory rights such as rights to custody/guardianship and rights to remain in the matrimonial residence. While agreements can be reached on all of these matters, they are unlikely to bind a court adjudicating statutory rights, as the statute would be given overriding effect over the contract. The issue, here, is less to do with the unenforceability of the agreement and more to do with the extent of freedom of the parties to waive or opt out of beneficial statutory provisions.

[66] Compare *Narayan v Laxman* AIR 1925 Nag 111 (payment to facilitate divorce may be alright if personal law of the parties permits divorce) to *Thunki v Bajirao* AIR 1956 Nag 160 (payment to facilitate divorce is contrary to public policy).

[67] *Gogineni Subbayya v Gogineni Govinamma* AIR 1945 Mad 36.

[68] *Sandhya Chatterjee v Sahil Chandra Chatterjee* AIR 1980 Cal 244 (see, however, the contrary Madras High Court precedents cited in the judgment). This distinction is made on the basis that agreements for immediate separation do not encourage separation but merely formalise a decision that has already been made.

[69] *Sabava v Yamanappa* AIR 1933 Bom 209; *Istak v Ranchod Zipru* AIR 1947 Bom 198; *Manicka v Muniammal* AIR 1968 Mad 392. In *Dwarampudi v Kunuku* AIR 1968 SC 253, the Supreme Court avoided a ruling on this matter.

[70] *LB Godfrey v Mt Parbati* AIR 1938 Pat 502; *Subhashchandra v Narbadabai* AIR 1982 MP 236; *Payare Mohan v Narayani* AIR 1982 Raj 43.

[71] AIR 1978 Mad 103.

[72] *P Archanda v Varda Siva Rama Krishna* AIR 2008 AP 216; *Kamble v Kamble* (2018) SCC Online Bom 7039.

[73] See *Usha Devi v Mahinder* 2009 SCC Online P&H 6179; *Mohinder Singh v Ravneet Kaur* AIR 2007 P&H 49.

Finally, agreements regarding reallocations of assets upon divorce or separation ought to be valid, regardless of whether they are pre-nuptial or post-nuptial agreements. This is because there is no overarching statutory regime in India providing for an equitable division of assets upon divorce.[74] While such a legislative void might legitimately invite criticism, in the absence of such a statutory regime, pre-nuptial and post-nuptial agreements regarding assets cannot be said to be contrary to any broader policy of ensuring equitable division.

iv. The rule in *Brojo Nath*

In the case of *Central Inland Water Transport Corporation v Brojo Nath Ganguly*, a two-judge bench of the Supreme Court developed a novel and potentially boundless head of public policy: 'unfair and unreasonable' terms that 'shock the conscience of the court' will be treated as contrary to public policy provided the agreement is 'between parties who are not equal in bargaining power'.[75] In *Brojo Nath*, the two-judge bench concluded that terms in a service contract[76] permitting a state corporation to dismiss employees at will and without a hearing (with three months' notice or three months' pay) were unconscionable and therefore contrary to public policy, given that there was, apparently, a 'gross disparity' between the state corporation and its employees.[77]

This ruling confers a wide power on the courts to test contractual terms for reasonableness. It is difficult to reconcile with the three-judge bench decision in *Gherulal Parakh*,[78] which concluded that new heads of public policy should only be created where there is a clear and incontestable case of harm to the public. The Court does not explain how terms that allow for dismissal at will necessarily result in harm to the public. Insecure labour arrangements are commonplace in the private sector and cannot be characterised as necessarily harmful to the public interest. And if they are harmful to the public interest, it is not apparent why they should be condemned only when they result from a disparity in bargaining power. The Court relied heavily on the requirements of non-arbitrariness and non-discrimination set out in Article 14 of the Constitution, and the relevant service rules were concurrently struck down as being violative of Article 14.[79] There was little need, therefore, to expand the notion of public policy in section 23 of the Contract Act and declare the (struck-down) rule additionally void under section 23. In subsequent cases, the Supreme Court has clarified that the reasonableness test developed in *Brojo Nath* does not apply in the context of

[74] See F Agnes, *Family Law: Marriage, Divorce and Matrimonial Litigation*, vol 2 (OUP 2012) 224–26. Note that jointly held property acquired at the time of marriage under the Hindu Marriage Act can be the subject of a court order for equitable division: Hindu Marriage Act 1955, s 27.

[75] *Brojo Nath* (n 52) [89], [93].

[76] The relevant rules were held to be a part of the contract of employment.

[77] *Brojo Nath* (n 52) [100].

[78] *Gherulal Parakh* (n 35).

[79] The service rules, in that case, were held to be a part of the contract of employment. An issue arises on whether contract terms can be 'struck down' or declared void in exercise of writ jurisdiction. However, regardless of how that question is answered, the same practical result can be achieved by granting an order that the state corporation refrain from imposing or enforcing clauses that offend art 14.

commercial transactions.[80] As a consequence, commercial contracts between private parties ought not to be affected[81] and—in our view—the rule in *Brojo Nath* should be redundant. As noted above, similar outcomes can be achieved by invoking Article 14 of the Constitution and the public law duty on state entities to impose, and/or enforce, only just, fair, and reasonable contractual terms on their counterparties.[82]

v. Foreign illegality

An interesting question arises in relation to contracts where the contemplated performance involves a breach of foreign (as opposed to Indian) law. Would such a contract be void in terms of section 23 of the Contract Act? The rule in English law is that if performance is illegal in the place where a contract is required to be performed, the contract will not be enforceable (even if performance is legal under English law).[83] That rule has been rationalised as a choice-of-law rule and as part of the law of contract dealing with frustration, but it can also be understood as an aspect of comity.[84] This issue has not directly arisen before the Indian courts, but there are indications that similar principles based on comity would weigh with Indian courts in denying the enforcement of a contract that necessarily entailed the violation of the law of a foreign country.[85] The statutory basis for doing so would be that the contract is against 'public policy' within the meaning of section 23, more specifically that it contravenes a public policy of facilitating the ability of foreign states to ensure compliance, with their own laws, on their own territory.

vi. Constitutional policy

Academic discussion by Gautam Bhatia[86] of the judgment in *Zoroastrian Cooperative Housing Society v District Registrar*[87] has brought to the fore the argument that a further category of public policy should be developed to prevent contracts from undermining constitutional values such as non-discrimination. In *Zoroastrian Cooperative*, the Supreme Court upheld contractual restrictions on rentals to non-Parsis. In that

[80] *SK Jain v State of Haryana* (2009) 4 SCC 357, [8]; *Icomm Tele Ltd v Punjab State Water Supply* (2019) 4 SCC 401, [11], [13]. See also *DTC v DTC Mazdoor Congress* (1991) Supp 1 SCC 600, [286] and the English decision of *Deepak v ICI* [1998] 2 LR 139.

[81] For a recent case, which arguably failed to respect this limitation, see *Pioneer Urban Land v Govindan Raghavan* (2019) 5 SCC 725.

[82] There exists precedent for the application of art 14 in situations when a state entity acts in the purely contractual realm. See eg *United India Insurance v Manubhai Dharamsinhbhai Gajera* (2008) 10 SCC 404 and *LIC v CERC* (1995) 5 SCC 482. While this position is by no means uncontested, and there exists case law both ways, addressing the problem through art 14 prevents the distortion of the more general law of contract (which also applies to contracts between private parties). We do not mean to suggest that the result in *Brojo Nath* is correct as a matter of constitutional law. Compare *Joshi Technologies v Union of India* (2015) 7 SCC 728 (expressing some scepticism about the use of constitutional law to impose broad controls on state contracts).

[83] See *Ralli Bros v Compania Naviera Sota y Aznar* [1920] 2 KB 287.

[84] See W Day, 'Contracts, Illegality and Comity: *Ralli Bros* Revisited' (2020) 79 Cambridge Law Journal 64.

[85] See *Taprogge v IAEC* AIR 1988 Bom 157 (endorsing the rule in *Ralli Bros* (n 83) as a matter of private international law rather than the law of contract). *PASL Wind Solutions v GE Power* (2021) 7 SCC 1 discusses the rule in *Ralli Bros* as an aspect of English law but does not discuss the import of that rule in Indian law.

[86] G Bhatia, *The Transformative Constitution: A Radical Biography in Nine Acts* (Harper Collins India 2019) 121–28.

[87] (2005) 5 SCC 632.

case, it was argued that contractual restraints that give effect to discrimination on the basis of religion are contrary to public policy as reflected in constitutional provisions guaranteeing equality. The Court rejected the argument on the basis that this should be a matter for the legislature and that public policy is to be assessed only by reference to a particular enabling legislation (the relevant cooperative act) rather than more general principles. This approach fails to recognise that the Court can develop new heads of public policy provided there is a clear case of harm to the public. As the Court has recently observed in another case, 'freedom of contract needs to be balanced with clear and undeniable harm to the public, even if the facts of a particular case do not fall within the crystallized principles enumerated in well-defined "heads" of public policy.'[88]

This raises the question of whether there is a compelling public interest in ensuring that private parties conduct their affairs in a manner that is consistent with constitutional values. For example, is it open to a private restaurant to enter into a contract with a supplier, stipulating that the supplier shall not employ any person of a certain religion? Would such a contract be valid and enforceable?

One powerful counter-argument to Bhatia, and indeed the example above, was put forward by Niranjan Venkatesan in discussions on this chapter in the working conference. The argument, simply put, is that the matter depends entirely on the constitutional question of the extent to which such dealings between private parties are subjected to constitutional scrutiny in the same manner as state action is. If such actions are subject to such constitutional scrutiny, then the 'object' and/or 'consideration' of the agreement is forbidden by law (in this case, the Constitution), and the contract is rendered void under section 23. But if the Constitution does not apply to (nor proscribe) such contracts, the matter ends there. If the Constitution itself does not apply to such private contracts, the 'constitutional policy' is to leave private arrangements alone and, accordingly, the Constitution cannot be invoked to invalidate the terms of a private contract (via the backdoor of section 23).[89]

In our view, there is a genuine difficulty in invoking the Constitution to justify an extension of certain values into the private sphere if, by its own terms, the Constitution limits relevant obligations to the public sphere. Nevertheless, the Supreme Court's evolving jurisprudence on 'constitutional morality'[90] does leave room open for even private contracts to be subjected to a certain core set of constitutional values. And, as Bhatia points out, the South African courts appear to have made such an extension even in respect of constitutional provisions that lack horizontal effect; that is, the provisions do not directly apply to private parties.[91] Section 23, as interpreted by the Supreme Court, allows new heads of public policy to be added and, having already, in practice,

[88] *PASL Wind Solutions* (n 85) [89].

[89] We note that even if a constitutional policy test were applied, the outcome in *Zoroastrian* itself (n 87) is arguably defensible on the ground that there is a competing constitutional interest in preserving minority culture. However, as addressed below, it remains an open question whether the frontiers of public policy should be extended so as to invalidate contracts that run contrary to core constitutional principles.

[90] See, for instance, the observations in *Navtej Johar v Union of India* (2018) 10 SCC 1.

[91] Bhatia (n 86) 120.

loosened requirements for accepting new heads of public policy, the Supreme Court is not necessarily bound to accept the proposition that the content of section 23 cannot be informed by core constitutional values solely because those values are denied horizontal effect in the Constitution itself.[92] Accordingly, our view is that the courts *can* seek inspiration from core constitutional values that it identifies in developing new heads of public policy. However, it must be able to present specific additional reasoning for concluding that constitutional requirements that are lacking in horizontal effect should, nevertheless, be extended to the private sphere (so as to invalidate contracts).

V. Consequences of Illegality

An illegal agreement is void and cannot be enforced. Nevertheless, there exist various principles that operate to mitigate the harshness of that rule. First, in certain circumstances, the courts can sever the unlawful portion of an agreement from the lawful portion and enforce the remainder of the agreement. Second, a transfer of property that has taken place pursuant to an illegal agreement may not be reversed, as the court may refuse to come to the aid of a party to the illegality. Third, restitutionary remedies under section 65 of the Contract Act may be available. We briefly discuss each of these below.

1. Severance

Often, in practice, the taint of illegality may not attach to the entirety of the agreement, and it then becomes necessary to ascertain whether some part of the agreement can be severed such that it remains enforceable as a contract. Sections 24, 57, and 58 are the relevant statutory provisions on severance.

If any part of the 'consideration' is unlawful, the text of section 24 might appear to suggest that the entire agreement is void. Fortunately, it has not been interpreted in this manner, and courts have clearly limited its application to cases where the terms are not severable. It is only when the terms are indivisible, and incapable of severance, that the agreement as a whole would be void. Thus, if *A* agrees to pay *B* Rs 100 to bring and deliver to *A* rice and smuggled opium, the agreement would be void in its entirety. Implicit in this illustration is the fact that it would be impossible to apportion the Rs

[92] Certain fundamental rights, in any event, apply to non-state entities, and in those cases, an agreement to carry out activities that are constitutionally forbidden would be hit by s 23 and be void. Similarly, in other matters, where there is no express application to private bodies, horizontal effect may be the result of judicial innovation in constitutional law (for instance, treating the judiciary as state, in which case judicial enforcement of certain contracts would offend Part III of the Constitution), contract law (by developing the concept of public policy), or both. While theoretically possible, it is unclear whether such developments are desirable. The expansive fundamental rights jurisprudence in public law presents a genuine risk that the incursion of public law standards into the private law of contract may become unwieldy and overbroad. The desirability of such an incursion is therefore very directly correlated with the ability of courts to restrict such horizontal application to only well-delineated core constitutional values, which give rise to narrow and specified new heads of public policy where the case for intervention in private transactions is compelling.

100 so as to ascertain which part of it related to the rice and which part to the smuggled opium. The test is whether there is a *distinct* consideration that is wholly lawful for the promise called into question.[93] If the consideration is capable of being severed, the entire agreement would not be rendered void by the operation of section 24. *Muhammad Khalilur Rahman Khan v Mohammad Muzammilullah Khan*[94] is an early illustration where the Court looked past the text of section 24 and held that it was inapplicable in cases where severance was possible. By way of a composite deed, a borrower had taken a loan of a certain amount and undertaken to repay it personally on demand. The same deed also created a mortgage that, at the time, the borrower was incompetent to make. The Allahabad High Court held that there was a distinct personal covenant to pay that was separate from the creation of a security by way of mortgage. Effectively, by the same deed, the debtor had entered into 'two agreements'—he took a loan which he undertook to repay, and he (wrongly) mortgaged his property. It ruled that there was no reason why 'the creditor should not be entitled to enforce his remedy under the first part of the agreement when that part is distinct and separate from the second part which is not legal'.

In summary, section 24 has not been interpreted in a manner that is at substantial variance from the English common law.[95] It is now well accepted that a court can sever the unlawful portion of an agreement from the lawful portion of an agreement.[96] The agreement must allow for a clean textual excision of the unlawful part, and rewriting, or rearrangement, of the remainder is not possible. Moreover, severance should not alter the fundamental nature of the agreement—the remaining lawful portion should be such that the parties would have agreed to perform in those terms had they known the unlawful part would not be enforced.[97]

Two further provisions need to be considered: sections 57 and 58 of the Contract Act. These provisions provide for severance in particular cases (but they could just as easily be accommodated under the general principle that has been read into section 24).

Section 57 of the Contract Act provides for severance where there are two distinct sets of reciprocal promises—one of which is to do things that are legal and the other, under specified contingencies, to do certain additional things that are illegal. The first agreement is valid and the second void. Thus, if *A* and *B* agree that *A* shall sell *B* a house for Rs 1,000, and further agree that if *B* uses that house to smuggle opium, *B* shall pay *A* Rs 5,000 for it, those are distinct reciprocal promises within the meaning of

[93] See *Bhagabai v Narayan Gopal* ILR (1907) 31 552, where the Bombay High Court, citing *Pickering v Ilfracombe Railway Co* (2) 1868 LR 3 CP 250, held that it was well settled that where several distinct promises were made for one and the same lawful consideration, and one or more of them be such as the law would not enforce, that will not, of itself, prevent the rest from being enforceable.

[94] AIR 1933 All 468.

[95] See *VRM Ramaswamy Chettyar v CTNM Nachiappa Chettyar* AIR 1940 Rang 45.

[96] *Dharamchand v Jhamsa* AIR 1931 Nag 6; *Asaram v Ludheshwar* AIR 1938 Nag 335 (Bose J).

[97] *Shin Satellite v Jain Studios* (2006) 2 SCC 628, [27]. The Court noted that the position in India was not different from that in England. In this regard, reference may be made to the recent decision of the UK Supreme Court in *Egon Zehnder v Tillman* [2019] UKSC 32, where the law on severance is clarified and an earlier precedent overruled. However, much of the discussion is in the specific context of policy considerations that are relevant to restrictive covenants in employment contracts.

section 57—the agreement to sell the house is a contract, but the further agreement on *B* paying a certain amount if *B* uses the house to smuggle opium is a void agreement. In a securities contract comprising a ready leg and a forward leg, the Supreme Court applied section 57 to hold that the ready leg was severable (and valid), whereas the forward leg was void.[98]

Section 58 offers another instance of severance, where there are alternative promises, one branch being legal and the other illegal. This lends itself very easily to severance. By its very nature, since the promises are in the alternative, the entirety of the consideration is capable of supporting either promise. And if one branch of the alternative promises is legal, the consideration shall support that branch, thereby creating a valid contract. Thus, if *A* agrees to pay *B* Rs 100 to bring *A either* rice or smuggled opium, those would be alternative promises within the meaning of section 58, and it would be a valid contract to deliver rice but void in respect of the smuggled opium. In *Mahadeo Prasad Singh* v *Mathura Chaudhari*,[99] one party held itself out as being the reversioners to the estate of a Hindu widow. Although there were nearer reversioners, they were of an advanced age, and the party expected to succeed to the estate. It agreed that within a stipulated period after the inheritance takes place, it would execute a sale deed in favour of the counterparty. It further agreed that if, for any reason, the inheritance did not fructify or it could not execute the sale deed, it would sell some part of its own estate to the counterparty. The first promise, to sell the (expected) inheritance, fell foul of section 6 of the Transfer of Property Act, the sale of a chance of succession being void. However, the alternative promise—to sell a part of its own estate—was perfectly valid and therefore enforceable.

2. Passing of Property

The leading English law authority for the proposition that title can pass under an illegal contract is a Privy Council case: *Singh* v *Ali*.[100] The proposition laid down in *Singh* v *Ali* is, however, in some tension with section 6(h) of the Transfer of Property Act, which specifies that no transfer of property can be made for an unlawful object or consideration. Under section 6(h), it is clear that an illegal agreement cannot be enforced to *effect* a transfer of property (which has not yet occurred).[101] But what is to happen when a transfer has already occurred pursuant to the illegal agreement, especially when the transferee has taken possession? Is such a transfer to be regarded as void under section 6(h); is it to be left untouched; or is there a discretionary middle ground? Any answer entails an assessment of the extent to which the principle in *Singh* v *Ali* is consistent

[98] *BOI Finance Limited* (n 7).
[99] AIR 1931 All 589 (2).
[100] [1960] AC 167.
[101] In *Narayanamma* (n 5), the Supreme Court declined to enforce an agreement entered into in violation of law.

with section 23 of the Contract Act, section 6(h) of the Transfer of Property Act, and various principles and maxims that have been endorsed by the Indian courts.

In *Deivanayaga Padayachi v Muthu Reddi*,[102] the Court allowed title to pass under an illegal agreement and refused to assist the guilty transferor. In that case, the defendant had settled some land on his concubine for her maintenance. She later executed a usufructuary mortgage in favour of two other persons, who brought a suit for possession when the defendant attempted to obstruct their possession. The defendant resisted the suit, inter alia, on the ground that the deed of settlement having been executed for an immoral purpose, the plaintiffs acquired no title in the land. The Court rejected that contention, holding instead that it was well settled that when a transaction had been entered into for an unlawful or immoral purpose, and the purpose had been achieved, the Court would not interfere at the instance of a guilty transferor to relieve the transferor of the legal effects of the transaction. It specifically considered and rejected the argument predicated on section 6(h) of the Transfer of Property Act, holding that the section did not modify the long-standing English rule laid down in *Ayerst* v *Jenkins*[103] and followed consistently by the Indian courts. The Court held that the section is meant to ensure that it 'will not enforce a transfer which would have the effect of carrying out its unlawful object'; that is, it is only meant to prevent a guilty transferee from approaching a court to effect a transfer of property that has not yet occurred.

However, the Bombay High Court disagreed with the view put forward in *Deivanayaga Padayachi*. It did so on the ground that, in India, transfers for an immoral consideration are expressly prohibited under section 6(h) of the Transfer of Property Act.[104] Citing a Madras High Court judgment, the Court concluded that transactions in exchange for immoral cohabitation could be impeached by a guilty transferor (and the transferor's successors).

Various conflicting decisions were again considered in the judgment of the Calcutta High Court in *Pranballav Saha v Tulsi Bala Dashi*.[105] Here again, the Court allowed for impeachment of a transaction by a guilty transferor (or rather her legal representatives). The Court held that if a person lets out his/her house for the purpose of prostitution, the apparent lessee is not a lessee at all, and the lessor has, in fact, not parted with the leasehold interest in the estate. The transfer was unlawful or immoral, and therefore, the effect of section 6(h)(2) of the Transfer of Property Act was that there was no successful transfer of property to the transferee. It held that, on the facts of that case, the plaintiff could utilise the procedures of the Court and the property would 'remain where it was, namely with the owner . . . (who) cannot divest himself of ownership by disregarding the law'.

The above cases pre-date *Singh v Ali*. *Surasaibalini Debi v Majumdar* is an early decision where *Singh* v *Ali* was considered, and endorsed in principle, by one judge of the Supreme Court.[106] In that case, the plaintiff was seeking to assert title on the basis

[102] ILR 1921 44 Mad 329.
[103] (1873) LR 16 Eq 275.
[104] See *Istak Kamu Musalman v Ranchhod Zipru Bhate* (1946) 48 Bom LR 775.
[105] AIR 1958 Cal 713.
[106] AIR 1965 SC 1364.

of an agreement which, it was alleged, involved an attempt to defraud the revenue. Ultimately, the Supreme Court found for the plaintiff on the basis that there was no illegality in the underlying agreement (Shah J and Gajendragadkar CJ). Ayyangar J, concurring, found for the plaintiff on the basis that his claim was not based on the illegal agreement but could be made out otherwise[107] and, in this context, endorsed the ruling in *Singh v Ali*.

In *BOI Finance Limited v Custodian*,[108] the Supreme Court once again endorsed the rule set out in *Singh v Ali*. It did so over the objections of the respondents, who argued that

> decisions of the courts in England should not be applied in India where the validity of the contract has to be judged according to the statutory law applicable in this country ... under the Indian Contract Act the entire contract was void. The original contract could not be legally entered into and the title in securities did not, in law, pass to the appellants.[109]

However, the precedential value of *BOI Finance* on this point is open to question. No doubt, it is a conscious adoption of the *Singh* v *Ali* principle by the Supreme Court, but on the facts of the case, it is apparent that title did not, in fact, pass pursuant to an illegal agreement but pursuant to a perfectly legal one. The Supreme Court held that the agreement could be severed into a lawful part and an unlawful one. The ready leg of the contract was the lawful part and was perfectly valid. Title passed under this valid legal agreement, and the question of title having passed under an illegal agreement did not, therefore, arise in that case.[110]

In view of the above, the position under Indian law is difficult to discern. The early decisions of the High Courts, prior to *Singh* v *Ali*, though conflicting with each other, made a clear attempt to deal with section 6(h) of the Transfer of Property Act and the interest in denying relief to a transferor who was party to a tainted transaction. The subsequent acceptance of *Singh* v *Ali* has complicated matters. The Supreme Court case law endorsing *Singh v Ali* is arguably *obiter* and does not, in our view, satisfactorily address the implications of section 6(h) of the Transfer of Property Act.[111] Accordingly, it

[107] On the somewhat doubtful basis of a failure to redeliver when demanded, which was said to be contrary to a specific understanding reached between the parties.

[108] *BOI Finance* (n 7) [62]. In that case, title had passed at the time of the execution of the ready leg of the contract, which was held to be distinct and severable from the forward leg of the contract, which was void.

[109] ibid [55].

[110] A distinction that was noticed by the Bombay High Court in *Shirish Finance and Investments Ltd* v *M Sreenivasulu Reddy* (2002) 1 Bom CR 419, where reliance on *BOI Finance* was found to be misplaced. The case concerned shares acquired in violation of the Securities and Exchange Board of India (SEBI) Regulations. A subsequent case, *Canbank Financial Services Ltd v Custodian* (2004) 8 SCC 355, which appears to endorse the principle in *BOI Finance* (n 7), is again of questionable precedential value on this point. In that case, there is a clear finding that the arrangement by which certain securities were transferred may have been unethical but was not illegal. Thus, it does not raise the issue of whether property passes pursuant to an illegal agreement.

[111] In particular, the Court's attempt to distinguish the validity of a transfer from the validity of the agreement preceding it, at [62], does not appear to be correct. The Court reasons that if title in moveable property passes upon payment for delivery, then the payment is the consideration, and the validity of the preceding agreement is of no relevance. This does not account for the fact that s 6(h) invalidates transfers made for an unlawful object. And therefore, even if a transfer is made for consideration and title passes, that does not foreclose the applicability of s

would be unwise to view *BOI Finance* (read with *Singh v Ali*) as establishing a binding rule that, in all cases where title has apparently passed and possession has changed hands pursuant to an illegal agreement, the estate must lie where it falls. Nor is it clear that section 6(h) of the Transfer of Property Act forecloses the argument that title can pass notwithstanding the presence of an illegal agreement. The frequent application of more open-textured common law principles[112] by High Courts (and the Supreme Court in certain contexts) implies that a degree of discretion resides with courts, and there are statutory provisions that engraft and recognise such discretion, such as section 31 of the Specific Relief Act. In summary, the case law as it stands does not, in our view, divest the courts of the ability to exercise discretion when deciding who retains property in any given case.[113]

3. Restitution

Even if an illegal agreement cannot be enforced, the parties may nevertheless be able to seek restitution of sums paid pursuant to the illegal agreement.

Section 65 allows for restitution '[w]hen an agreement is discovered to be void' or 'when a contract becomes void'. The latter condition, a contract 'becom[ing] void', will not be met in cases of initial illegality under section 23 of the Contract Act. The issue is whether the former condition may be met (ie whether an agreement that is illegal from its inception) can be characterised as one that is 'discovered to be void'. The original view of Pollock and Mulla was that section 65 could not apply 'to agreements which are void ab initio on the ground of the object or consideration being unlawful within the meaning of s.23 of the Act'.[114] However, this view did not find favour with the courts. In *Asaram v Ludheshwar*, Bose J and Digby J observed that section 65 could apply to agreements that were void for illegality under section 23.[115] In *Budhulal v Deccan Banking Company*, the Hyderabad High Court concluded that section 65 could be invoked in cases where the parties were initially of the mistaken view that they had entered into a valid agreement but later discover their error.[116] In *Gupta v Murli Prasad*[117] and *Kuju Collieries v Jharkhand Mines Ltd*,[118] the Supreme Court endorsed this interpretation.

6(h). Even as a matter of policy, the mere fact that a transfer has taken place cannot be a reason to treat it as valid when there is a statutory provision to the contrary.

[112] *Ex turpi causa, in pari delicto* and, possibly, the principle in *Bowmakers Case* [1945] KB 65 and *Tinsley v Milligan* [1994] 1 AC 340 (to the effect that a plaintiff who does not rely on an illegal agreement can obtain the assistance of a court).

[113] See *Kamarbai Ahmed v Badrinarayan Narayandas Agarwal* AIR 1977 Bom 228. See also the academic discussion in V Ramaseshan, 'Some Aspects of the Indian Law Relating to Illegal Contracts and Recovery by Possession' (1961) 7 Journal of the Indian Law Institute 206.

[114] Pollock and Mulla (n 27) 279.

[115] *Asaram* (n 96). Digby J took the view that this provision amended English law relating to illegality, with the result that 'the rule "the loss will remain where it lies" no longer applied'.

[116] AIR 1955 Hyd 55.

[117] (1974) 2 SCC 266.

[118] (1974) 2 SCC 533.

As a consequence, parties can claim restitution of sums paid under illegal agreements pursuant to section 65 provided that they had no knowledge of illegality at the time of their conclusion. The absence of knowledge could be because the parties were mistaken about relevant facts or because they were mistaken about the applicable law.

In the recent case of *Loop Telecom v Union of India*,[119] a two-judge bench of the Supreme Court has relied on a more open-ended requirement that the party claiming restitution under section 65 cannot be *in pari delicto*. The two-judge bench observed that 'if the party claiming restitution was equally or more responsible for the illegality (in comparison to the defendant) there shall be no cause for restitution. This has to be determined on the facts of each case.'[120] Applying this novel test, the Supreme Court denied relief because Loop Telecom was 'complicit in obtaining benefits'[121] under a specific government policy. The reasoning of the Court appears to be at variance with the test laid down in *Gupta v Murli Prasad* and *Kuju Collieries*, which focuses on the ignorance of the party seeking restitution as opposed to relative responsibility for illegality.

The question of whether restitutionary relief can be sought under common law and outside the boundaries of section 65 of the Contract Act is one that has not been definitively resolved. In the old case of *Gulabchand Paramchand v Fulbai Harichand*, the Bombay High Court gave restitutionary relief for sums paid pursuant to an illegal marriage brokerage agreement under the common law.[122]

VI. Conclusion

In conclusion, the Indian law of illegality strikes a defensible balance between promoting regulatory objectives and minimising injustice to individual contracting parties. It is notable that despite a statutory framework that potentially allows for considerable interference with contracts to promote the regulatory demands of the state (as well as judicial dictates about what public policy and morality require), the Indian courts have sought to narrow the impact on contracts by a variety of means, including seeking to limit the heads of public policy, allowing for severance and restitution, and retaining some discretion to allow for title to pass between parties to an illegal contract.

Indian law is largely aligned with English law (as that law stood prior to the UK Supreme Court's revolutionary judgment in *Patel v Mirza*), and it is plain, from the frequency of English case citations if nothing else, that English law has exerted a strong gravitational pull. Two notable divergences from English law (pre-*Patel v Mirza*) are the ability to invalidate a contract on the basis that the contract 'defeats' a particular law (which does not feature in English law) and the lack of clarity on whether a choice to perform illegally invalidates the contractual rights of the guilty party making that

[119] (2022) 6 SCC 762.
[120] ibid [52].
[121] ibid [54].
[122] 1909 SCC Online Bom 70. There is, however, a reference to s 84 of the Trusts Act in the judgment, so it is not entirely clear whether restitution was granted under that provision or the common law.

choice (which does feature in English law, but the position remains unclear under Indian law). There is scope for further development of the law by the courts, especially in the area of restitutionary remedies.

It is undeniable that the decision of the UK Supreme Court in *Patel v Mirza* effected a seismic shift in the English law on illegality. Whatever the merits of the more flexible approach in *Patel v Mirza* may be, they are not easily reconcilable with the text of section 23 of the Contract Act, and, absent legislative change, the development of Indian law must continue to be within existing statutory contours. We note that, in some areas, the need to balance regulatory considerations with the private interests of the parties has been implicitly recognised by Indian courts, for example, in cases about the passing of property under illegal agreements. In other areas, working within the constraints of section 23, Indian courts have, by and large, applied that provision in a satisfactory manner. A root-and-branch displacement of the Indian law on illegality in favour of the discretionary regime in *Patel v Mirza*, therefore, appears to be unnecessary.

12

Restraint of Trade in India

Reason (Un)restrained?

*Zhong Xing Tan and Umakanth Varottil**

I. Introduction

Across the common law world, the restraint-of-trade doctrine seeks to mediate between two competing policies: freedom of contract, on the one hand, and the protection of a person's fundamental liberty to earn a living, on the other.[1] It is said,

> The common law strikes the balance between these two policy imperatives by holding a restrictive covenant to be void unless certain conditions are satisfied. The threshold condition is that the restrictive covenant protects a legitimate interest of the employer. If it does, the restrictive covenant will be enforceable if in addition: (a) it is reasonable in the interests of the parties; and (b) it is reasonable in the public interest.[2]

The rise of a 'rule of reason', or a 'reasonableness' analysis, is a dominant motif in the development of the restraint-of-trade doctrine. In a recent UK Supreme Court decision on the topic, *Tillman v Egon Zehnder Ltd*,[3] Lord Wilson traced this theme through an abbreviated historical tour of the case law.[4] As early as 1711, *Mitchell v Reynolds*[5] recognized that a baker's bond not to trade as a baker elsewhere in Holborn for a period of five years, given as a term of the baker's assignment to a purchaser for the lease of a bakery in the said locality for that period, was reasonable and enforceable. Hence, 'the concept of reasonableness [was] authoritatively grafted on to the doctrine by way of

* We are grateful to Ragini Surana for excellent research assistance. Errors or omissions remain ours.

[1] *Herbert Morris, Limited v Saxelby* [1916] 1 A C 688, 699, 701 (Lord Atkinson).

[2] *Lek Gwee Noi v Humming Flowers & Gifts Pte Ltd* [2014] SGHC 64, [2014] 3 SLR 27, [34]. See also *Man Financial (S) Pte Ltd (formerly known as E D & F Man International (S) Pte Ltd) v Wong Bark Chuan David* [2008] 1 SLR(R) 663, [70]; *Smile Inc Dental Surgeons Pte Ltd v Lui Andrew Stewart* [2012] 4 SLR 308, [19].

[3] [2019] UKSC 32. For a more recent enunciation of the restraint-of-trade doctrine in the United Kingdom, see *Peninsula Securities Ltd v Dunnes Stores (Bangor) Ltd* [2020] UKSC 36.

[4] *Tillman* (n 3) [22]–[29].

[5] (1711) 1 P Wms 181.

Zhong Xing Tan and Umakanth Varottil, *Restraint of Trade in India* In: *Foundations of Indian Contract Law.* Edited by: KV Krishnaprasad, Niranjan Venkatesan, Shivprasad Swaminathan, and Umakanth Varottil, Oxford University Press. © Oxford University Press 2024.
DOI: 10.1093/9780191997211.003.0012

modification of it'.[6] In the seminal decision of *Nordenfelt v The Maxim Nordenfelt Guns and Ammunition Co Ltd*,[7] a manufacturer's covenant with the purchaser of his business not to engage in the production of guns and ammunition anywhere in the world over a twenty-five-year period was held reasonable and enforceable. Lord Macnaghten's dictum eschewed rigidity in favour of flexibility, thereby relaxing the rule.[8]

The Indian incarnation of the doctrine, however, has achieved notoriety in appearing to repudiate an express appeal to reason as a general approach in dealing with restrictive covenants. The rule governing agreements in restraint of trade is found under section 27 of the Indian Contract Act 1872 (hereinafter 'the Contract Act'):

> **27. Agreement in restraint of trade, void.**—Every agreement by which any one is restrained from exercising a lawful profession, trade or business of any kind, is to that extent void.[9]

There appears to be almost universal consensus amongst commentators on the strictness of the rule under section 27. Professors Briggs and Burrows, in their commentary on the similarly worded provision under Myanmar contract law, observe that

> [o]ne might have expected the law to provide that an unreasonable restraint of trade is void, but the position is more extreme: it does not matter how reasonable the restraint was ... [t]he fact that it was in restraint of trade is sufficient to render it void, no matter how rational it might otherwise have appeared to be.[10]

An early edition of the leading treatise of Pollock and Mulla[11] explains the somewhat uninspired history of the provision. It was suggested that, in the legislature's zeal to protect trade, it 'may have wished to make the smallest number of exceptions to the rule'[12] and adopted section 833 of Field's draft of the New York Code of 1862.[13] This attempted to narrow the common law just as it was embracing an approach looking to reasonableness with reference to the interest of the parties and public, moreover doing so without proper reflection on the competing policy considerations.[14] In restating the contemporary state of jurisprudence, it appears that not much has changed. The current edition of *Pollock and Mulla* comments that '[t]he Indian law is rigid, in that it invalidates all restraints, whether general or partial'.[15]

[6] *Tillman* (n 3) [25].
[7] [1894] AC 535.
[8] ibid 564.
[9] Certain exceptions accompany s 27, which we discuss in section III.1 below.
[10] Myanmar contract law adopts the Contract Act; see A Briggs and A Burrows, *The Law of Contract in Myanmar* (OUP 2017) 73–76.
[11] F Pollock and D Mulla, *The Indian Contract Act, with a Commentary, Critical and Explanatory* (2nd edn, Sweet & Maxwell 1909) 164.
[12] *Oakes & Co v Jackson* (1876) 1 Mad 134, 145.
[13] This approach was justified on the ground that 'contracts in restraint of trade have been allowed by modern decisions to a very dangerous extent'. See Pollock and Mulla (n 11) 164.
[14] ibid.
[15] N Bhadbhade, *Pollock and Mulla: The Indian Contract Act, 1872* (14th edn, Lexis Nexis Butterworth Wadhwa 2013) 627.

In this chapter, we explore what appears, on the surface, to be a curious case of Indian exceptionalism.[16] Contrary to the dominant narrative, which presumes that a reasonableness analysis is, for the large part, impeded by the language of section 27 and hence absent from the case law, we explain how Indian courts have, nevertheless, adopted a variety of techniques to reach 'reasonable' results in restraint of trade cases.

From our survey of close to 150 years of key classic and contemporary cases, we identify such techniques[17] and demonstrate that they allow Indian courts to incorporate some measure of sensitivity to the legitimate interests of parties in stipulating restraints, while protecting the autonomy of those subject to the relevant restrictive covenants. We touch more briefly on a number of outstanding themes and topics,[18] including whether there is a need to reform the current approach, as well as a select number of boundary issues between the restraint doctrine and cognate areas of law, such as the developing law on severance, and the interfaces with competition law, economic torts, and constitutional law. We conclude[19] that reasonableness does not, in fact, appear to be completely constrained by the jurisprudence developed under section 27, though there certainly remains room for the doctrine to develop in a more coherent, consistent, and transparent way.

II. Section 27 of the Contract Act: Indian Exceptionalism?

It is true that many cases have affirmed a strict approach eschewing a reasonableness analysis. In *Madhub Chunder v Rajcoomar Doss*,[20] one of the earliest leading decisions on the interpretation of section 27, an agreement to stop business in a particular locality for consideration was held void. The Court was keen to emphasize that section 27 extended to both absolute and partial restraints, stating that it 'was intended to prevent not merely a total restraint from carrying on trade or business, but a partial one' and further that '[w]e have nothing to do with the policy of such a law. All we have to do is to take the words of the Contract Act, and put upon them the meaning which they appear plainly to bear.'[21] The current editors of *Pollock and Mulla* take this to mean: 'Neither the test of reasonableness, nor the restraint being partial apply to a case governed by s. 27 of the Contract Act, unless they fall within the exception to that section.'[22]

In *Oakes & Company v Jackson*,[23] a restriction against the defendants setting up business within 800 miles of Madras contained in a five-year service agreement was held void, the Court reasoning that the only exceptions were partnership and sale of

[16] See section II below.
[17] We list and discuss these techniques in section III below.
[18] See section IV below.
[19] See section V below.
[20] (1874) 14 BLR 76.
[21] ibid [7]. The inclusion of both partial and absolute restraints in the ambit of s 27 was said to derive support from the fact that if the legislature intended to limit it to absolute restraints, it would have used the term 'absolutely', as it did in the Contract Act, s 28, which makes agreements in restraint of legal proceedings void.
[22] Bhadbhade (n 15) 627.
[23] *Oakes* (n 12).

goodwill cases, which did not apply. Again, in *The Brahmaputra Tea Co Ltd v Scarth*,[24] a post-service five-year non-competition covenant in respect of the cultivation, manufacture, or sale of tea was held void, 'although the restriction only extended to a distance of forty miles from any of the Company's gardens', given that section 27 applied to partial restrictions as well. Similarly, in *Shaikh Kalu v Ram Saran Bhagat*,[25] an exclusive supply agreement between the defendant and twenty-nine comb manufacturers (including the petitioner) lasting during the lifetime of the latter was held void. The Court endorsed the authority of the narrow rule adopted from the draft New York Code, which it noted had been applied in Indian law, despite it exhibiting a 'startling dissimilarity' to the modern English approach.[26] In *Har Bilas v Mahadeo Prasad*,[27] an exclusive supply agreement for the defendant to sell silica sand to the plaintiff and not to four other factories was held void as a restraint of trade, regardless of how great or small the restriction was.[28]

The emphasis on the strict approach[29] appears not only to persist in the modern era but also to receive recognition by the Supreme Court of India. In the important decision of the Supreme Court in *Superintendence Company of India v Krishan Murgai*,[30] Sen J's oft-cited concurring judgment emphasized that '[n]either the test of reasonableness nor the principle of . . . the restraint being partial . . . are applicable to a case governed by Section 27 . . . unless it falls within Exception 1'.[31] Sen J further explained that amending section 27 to include a reasonableness analysis, as suggested by the Law Commission in its *Thirteenth Report*,[32] was ultimately a matter for Parliament.[33] Similarly, in *Gujarat Bottling Co Ltd v Coca Cola Company*,[34] the Supreme Court proceeded on the basis that 'an enquiry into reasonableness of the restraint is not envisaged by Section 27'.[35] In *Ambiance India Pvt Ltd v Shri Naveen Jain*,[36] post-employment restraints in the form of a two-year non-competition and a three-year non-disclosure restrictive covenant were held unenforceable, with the Delhi High Court emphasizing that 'all contracts in restraint of trade are void and hit by section 27'.[37]

At the same time, a closer inspection of this narrative reveals that Indian exceptionalism is not necessarily watertight. As one commentator astutely observes,[38] the

[24] (1885) 11 ILR Cal 545.
[25] [1908] 13 CWN 388.
[26] ibid [7].
[27] AIR 1931 All 539.
[28] ibid [6].
[29] Other older cases emphasizing the strict approach include *Nur Ali Dubash v Abdul Ali* 1892 ILR 19 Cal 765; *G Hurry Krishna Pillai v M Authilachmy Ammal* AIR 1916 LB 51; *Parasullah v Chandra Kent* AIR 1918 Cal 546; *Mohamed v Ona Mohamed Ebrahim* AIR 1922 UB 9.
[30] [1981] 2 SCC 246. See also *Raj Chopra v Narender Anand* 1991 (21) DRJ 53, [16].
[31] *Superintendence Company* (n 30) [51]. Tulzapurkar J's majority decision, however, expressly avoided the question of whether s 27 involves a reasonableness analysis: ibid [7].
[32] *13th Law Commission of India Report, Indian Contract Act 1872* (1958) <2022080532.pdf (s3waas.gov.in)> accessed 19 June 2023.
[33] *Superintendence Company* (n 30) [50].
[34] AIR 1995 SC 2372.
[35] ibid [24].
[36] 122 (2005) DLT 421.
[37] ibid [6].
[38] S Naravane, 'The Place of Reasonableness in the Restraint of Trade: Just How Much Does India Depart from the Common Law?' (2010) 5 NALSAR Student Law Review 105.

apparent rigour of section 27 was directed at the distinction between absolute and partial restraints, viz, attempts to validate restraints by introducing some limitation to a particular place or time. This, in itself, does not directly speak to the question of reasonableness, despite Sen J's apparent conflation of the two issues, viz, the absolute/partial nature of the restraint and the question of reasonableness. It could, of course, be that one interprets the underlying policy concern of promoting trade to extend section 27's ambit to partial restraints *and* preclude validation based on reasonableness. However, it is just as likely that section 27's expansion to partial restraints is *complemented* by a less blunt tool of assessing restraints by reference to reasonableness. This was the position taken after *Nordenfelt*,[39] where the 'consideration [is] whether [the covenant] exceeds what is necessary for the protection of the covenantee, [and hence] the distinction between general and particular restraints ceases to be a distinction in point of law'.[40]

Moreover, it appears that courts do not entirely neglect reasonableness even in cases affirming the (apparent) strict rule. In *Oakes*, for instance, Kindersley J observed that if the validity of the contract depended on the law of England, 'the limit of 800 miles was unreasonable, as being much in excess of that which the protection of the plaintiffs' interests required'.[41] In *The Brahmaputra Tea Co Ltd*, we see indications that courts use as a proxy for reasonableness a distinction between restraints during the term of the contract as opposed to restraints after: the former can be understood as essential to the fulfilment and protection of the interests of the employer.[42] In *Shaikh Kalu*,[43] the Court also considered reasonableness to buttress its conclusion: the exclusive dealing agreement was seen as obviously larger than necessary for protection and undoubtedly oppressive and unreasonable, given that it was simply an attempt to suppress competition by contracting with manufacturers for their entire product so as to monopolize the market.

Likewise, in *Har Bilas*,[44] the Court appeared to entertain some consideration of whether the plaintiff had a legitimate interest in the restraint, holding that the prohibition was not necessary to ensure supply of sand to the plaintiff before supplying to other factories. There was no evidence that the defendant could not have supplied to the plaintiff as well as other factories simultaneously. Again, in *Ambiance India*,[45] while there was no express reference to a reasonableness analysis, such considerations appear to have arisen. In respect of the non-disclosure covenant, the Court found that the plaintiff had not meaningfully identified relevant trade secrets or technical know-how and, in respect of the non-competition covenant, the two-year restraint was seen as 'an arm twisting tactic adopted by an employer against a young man who was looking for a job'.[46] Hence, it appears that Indian courts, while applying the strict approach and

[39] *Nordenfelt* (n 7).
[40] ibid 548.
[41] *Oakes* (n 12) 145. The reference to English law was raised as an alternative.
[42] *The Brahmaputra Tea Co Ltd* (n 24) 550. We discuss this trend in detail in section III.3 below.
[43] *Shaikh Kalu* (n 25).
[44] *Har Bilas* (n 27).
[45] *Ambiance India* (n 36).
[46] ibid [7]–[8].

avoiding the language of reasonableness, do, at times, incorporate such considerations into their analysis. With this background, we turn to specific manifestations of the application of 'reason' in Indian courts' analysis of restraint-of-trade clauses.

III. Techniques for Reaching 'Reasonable' Results in Restraint-of-Trade Cases

1. Statutory Exceptions

In escaping the confines of the strict approach, Indian courts have recourse to a number of techniques to reach decisions based on 'reasonableness'. The first and perhaps most clear-cut method is to have reference to express statutory exceptions. The sale of goodwill exception under section 27 of the Contract Act is framed as follows:

> Exception 1.—Saving of agreement not to carry on business of which good-will is sold.—One who sells the good-will of a business may agree with the buyer to refrain from carrying on a similar business, within specified local limits, so long as the buyer, or any person deriving title to the good-will from him, carries on a like business therein, provided that such limits appear to the Court reasonable, regard being had to the nature of the business.[47]

The above exception expressly introduces a reasonableness analysis and allows the restraint to operate insofar as the goodwill is not extinguished and where the restraint is within specified local limits.[48] In *Chandra Kanta Das v Parasullah Mullick*,[49] the respondent purchased from the appellant the goodwill of his trade in plying ferry boats and proprietary interests in several river landing places, in consideration of which the latter undertook to close the business of plying the particular ferry boats. This amounted to a sale of real goodwill and fell within exception 1 to section 27. The respondent had a legitimate interest in the restraint, which presumably was necessary and not excessive in this regard. Recent cases, too, have applied the reasonableness analysis in exception 1. In *Affle Holdings Pte Ltd v Saurabh Singh*,[50] the Delhi High Court upheld a thirty-six-month non-compete clause requiring the respondents not to engage in business or commercial activity competitively affecting the business of the petitioner, contained in an addendum to a share purchase agreement by which they sold their entire controlling interest and goodwill of a business. The Court viewed this as reasonable in time and space and falling within the ambit of exception 1.[51]

[47] Certain other exceptions originally in the Contract Act were subsequently relocated to the Indian Partnership Act 1932 upon its enactment, in the form of ss 11, 36, 54, and 55.
[48] Bhadbhade (n 15) 646.
[49] (1922) 24 BomLR 602.
[50] MANU/DE/0152/2015.
[51] ibid [10].

Of course, there are, at times, issues arising as to the scope of exception 1. In *Arvinder Singh v Lal Pathlabs Pvt Ltd*,[52] two doctors sold their medical diagnostic centre to the respondent and agreed to various non-compete and non-solicitation covenants that were to last five years thereafter, though they later took up employment with another company within that time period. Noting the wording of exception 1 (validating an agreement 'to refrain from carrying on a similar business'), the Delhi High Court distinguished 'business' (economic activities connected with production and purchase of goods and services), 'trade' (a subset of business involving buying and selling of goods), and 'profession' (economic activities requiring special knowledge and skill).[53] It held that while the doctors could not run a business venture such as a diagnostic centre, they could carry on their professions as pathologists and radiologists and that any wider prohibition on the latter would be contrary to section 27.[54] Perhaps a simpler way of putting the point would be to acknowledge that business, trade, and profession often overlap.[55] Hence, exception 1 would apply to govern the activities of the doctors by a reasonableness standard, but any restraint would be potentially unreasonable the greater the dissimilarity between the post-sale type of business engaged in (eg as an employed doctor) and the business sold (running a diagnostic centre).[56]

2. Applying a Reasonableness Analysis Despite Statutory Language

A somewhat more uncommon approach involves decisions that do not appear to focus very much on the strict rule with limited statutory exceptions and that instead apply a common law standard of reasonableness akin to that found in English law.

In *VD Deshpande v Arvind Mills Ltd*,[57] the Court upheld non-competition and confidentiality covenants imposed on a weaving master in a three-year fixed-term service agreement and, in doing so, observed that '[t]he question whether a particular covenant in a particular agreement was unreasonably wide has to be decided by the nature of the agreement, the qualifications of the employee and the service he has to render'.[58] The Court referred to English decisions in determining the reasonableness of the restraint and found that the restraint on taking up service in the whole of India was not unreasonable, given that the cloth manufactured by the respondents was sold all over India and textile mills were likewise geographically dispersed.[59]

[52] 2015 (149) DRJ 88.
[53] ibid [43]–[63].
[54] ibid [69]–[71].
[55] A single judge, whose judgment was appealed against in ibid, adopted this line: ibid [15], [25].
[56] Although the exceptions to restraint of trade under the Indian Partnership Act are outside the scope of this chapter, an examination of post-dissolution restraints in partnership situations pursuant to s 54 of the legislation indicates that courts are free to directly invoke a reasonableness standard, which they have done with some regularity. See eg *Premji Damodar v Firm LV Govindji* AIR 1943 Sind 197; *Krishanrao Chawathe v Shankar Sahadeo Mungekar* [1954] ILR Bom 1409; *Deva Sharma v Laxmi Narain Gaddodia* AIR 1956 P&H 49; *Hukmi Chand v Jaipur Ice & Oil Mills Co* AIR 1980 Raj 155.
[57] (1946) 48 BomLR 90.
[58] ibid [5].
[59] ibid [14].

In *Shree Gopal Paper Mills Ltd v Surendra K Ganeshdas Malhotra*,[60] the Court applied a test of reasonableness to evaluate a fixed-term agreement to work exclusively for the plaintiff for seventeen years. The Court cited Lord Macnaghten's test[61] that the restraint should be in the interests of the parties and the public.[62] It then found that the restraint was too wide, unreasonable, and not for the protection of any proprietary interest of the plaintiff.[63]

Likewise, in *Jet Airways (I) Ltd v Mr Jan Peter Ravi Karnik*,[64] while the Court referred to section 27 of the Contract Act, it immediately followed this by asserting that '[w]hether or not the contract is in restraint of trade would depend upon whether the contract was unreasonable, unfair or unconscionable'. It noted that while a general restraint would be void, partial restraints would have to be reasonable in the interests of the parties and the public to be valid.[65] Applying this test, it held that a pilot's seven-year exclusive employment covenant was 'unconscionable, one sided, unreasonable and not for the protection of any proprietary interest of the plaintiff', especially given the fact that the pilots had, in fact, financed their own training, and the sole purpose of the covenant was to prevent them from leaving for a competitor airline.[66]

An alternative plausible interpretation of these cases is that they turn on a distinction between restraints within the term of the employment, as opposed to after the period of the contract, and that the courts' omission to emphasize the strict rule arises from the fact that restraints of the former kind do not engage section 27 at all.[67] We turn to the case law emphasizing this distinction below.

3. Distinction between Restraints Operating during and after the Term of a Contract

In interpreting section 27, courts have clarified that negative covenants operating during the period of a contract (such as of employment) are generally not regarded as a restraint of trade, unless the contract is unconscionable, excessively harsh, unreasonable, or one-sided, while a non-competition restraint operating after termination is, in all likelihood, void.[68] It must be emphasized that this somewhat formalistic-sounding distinction, though not evident from the plain text of the statute, itself rests on a conception of reasonableness: section 27, on the face of it, would have the potential to catch an agreement to serve exclusively for a week, a day, or even an hour.[69] Hence, to

[60] AIR 1962 Cal 61.
[61] *Nordenfelt* (n 7).
[62] *Shree Gopal Papermills Ltd* (n 60) [27].
[63] ibid [28].
[64] 2000 (4) BomCR 487.
[65] ibid [15].
[66] ibid [17]–[19].
[67] *VD Deshpande* (n 57) [4].
[68] *Niranjan Shankar Golikari v Century Spinning and Manufacturing* [1967] AIR SC 1098, distinguishing *Shree Gopal Paper Mills Ltd* (n 60).
[69] *VD Deshpande* (n 57) [4].

ascertain the gravamen of the section, one needs to apply some notion of reasonableness in identifying what types of restraints are meant to be caught.[70]

In doing so, one might adopt a fairly intuitive distinction: there is more likely to be a legitimate interest in restraining trade during the period of the contract to ensure adequate commitment to the venture and facilitate trade compared with a post-termination non-competition restraint that appears to be for no legitimate purpose except to secure freedom from competition.[71] In this sense, the 'during/after' distinction serves as a roughproxy for reasonable restraints, as we will see from the extensive case law on this point. Moreover, it will also emerge that courts do not solely use this distinction to decide cases but, at times, start with it and thereafter invoke further considerations of reasonableness in crafting a fair and equitable result on the validity of a restrictive covenant.

In *Charlesworth v Macdonald*,[72] the defendant agreed to be an assistant of a medical practitioner in Zanzibar for a period of three years, and the contract contained a negative covenant construed by the court to mean that the defendant would not practise on his own account in Zanzibar during the period of the contract. In an oft-cited dictum, Farran CJ commented that 'a man who agrees to exercise his calling for a particular wage and for a certain period agrees to exercise his calling, and such an agreement does not restrain him from doing so'.[73] In *Lalbhai Dalpatbhai & Co v Chittaranjan Chandulal Pandya*,[74] a non-compete obligation during a three-year fixed-term contract was upheld applying the rule in *Charlesworth*, the Court observing that '[i]t is now well settled that restrictions that are to operate only while the employer [*sic*] is contractually bound to serve his employer are never regarded as in restraint of trade'.[75]

This principle was endorsed and more fully explicated in the *locus classicus* decision of *Niranjan Shankar Golikari v Century Spinning and Manufacturing*,[76] concerning a positive obligation of exclusive devotion and a negative non-competition covenant in a five-year fixed-term employment agreement, which was valid and not caught by section 27. The Supreme Court emphasized the above distinction in the following passage:

> [C]onsiderations against restrictive covenants are different in cases where the restriction is to apply during the period after the termination of the contract than those in cases where it is to operate during the period of the contract. Negative covenants operative during the period of the contract of employment when the employee is bound to serve his employer exclusively are generally not regarded as restraint of trade and therefore do not fall under section 27 of the Contract Act. A negative covenant that the employee would not engage himself in a trade or business or would not get himself employed by any other master for whom he would perform similar or substantially

[70] See also Naravane (n 38) 113–15.
[71] *Taprogge Gesellschaft MBH v IAEC India Ltd* AIR 1988 Bom 157.
[72] (1899) ILR 23 Bom 103.
[73] ibid 112.
[74] (1966) GLR 493.
[75] ibid [2].
[76] *Golikari* (n 68).

> similar duties is not therefore a restraint of trade unless the contract as aforesaid is unconscionable or excessively harsh or unreasonable or one sided.[77]

Applying the rule in *Golikari*,[78] the Court in *Karam Chand Thapar & Bros v HH Jethanandani*[79] held that section 27 did not catch an eleven-year fixed-term exclusive employment agreement on the basis that the restraint operated during the period of employment. It also appeared to invoke further considerations of reasonableness to distinguish a twenty-year contract (coupled with an employer's arbitrary power of termination), which was considered unreasonable and unenforceable in *Shree Gopal Paper Mills*.[80]

In *Taprogge Gesellschaft MBH v IAEC India Ltd*,[81] the Bombay High Court invalidated a post-contractual restraint and emphasized that

> The distinction between the restraints imposed by a Contract, operative during the subsistence of the contract and those operative after the lifetime of the contract is of a fundamental character . . . For instance the restraints which operate during the term of the contract have to fulfil one kind of purpose viz. furthering the contract. On the other hand, the restraints operative after the termination of the contract strive to secure freedom from competition from a person who no longer works within the contract.[82]

These principles found a place in another leading case in the modern era, *Gujarat Bottling Co Ltd v Coca Cola Company*,[83] where a non-competition covenant in a franchise agreement for the duration of the agreement and its notice period were not hit by section 27. The Supreme Court emphasized that the franchise model often incorporates exclusive dealing conditions facilitating the distribution of goods and that, apart from cases where the contract is wholly one-sided, the restraint doctrine would not normally be attracted where the covenant operates during the period of the contract as opposed to after.[84] In that sense, the principle that evolved in *Golikari*[85] in an employment situation was extended to other contractual arrangements as well. More recent restatements of the principle include *Percept D'Mark (India) Pvt Ltd v Zaheer Khan*[86] and *Wipro Ltd v Beckman Coulter International SA*,[87] where the latter Court observed that, in construing restraint clauses, 'the courts take a stricter view in employer-employee

[77] ibid [20]. See also *High Polymer Labs Pvt Ltd v RK Mutreja* ILR (Delhi Series) 1983 vol 1 213, [16] to similar effect.
[78] *Golikari* (n 68).
[79] 1972 76 CWN 338.
[80] *Shree Gopal Papermills Ltd* (n 60).
[81] *Taprogge Gesellschaft MBH* (n 71).
[82] ibid [10].
[83] *Gujarat Bottling Company* (n 34).
[84] ibid [33]–[36].
[85] *Golikari* (n 68).
[86] AIR 2006 SC 3426.
[87] 131 (2006) DLT 681.

contracts than in other contracts', with the 'reason being that in the latter kind of contracts, the parties are expected to have dealt with each other on more or less an equal footing, whereas in employer–employee contracts, the norm is that the employer has an advantage over the employee'.[88]

In the past three decades, courts have regularly applied this set of considerations.[89] As we have argued, the 'during/after' distinction suggests something akin to a presumption of reasonableness for restraints operating within the contractual period and, conversely, a presumption of unreasonableness for restraints operating beyond the contractual period (and hence targeted by section 27). It is true that in a number of cases, this distinction has been applied without any *further* consideration of reasonableness, which has had the consequence of making the law operate somewhat bluntly. So it is said that 'the applicability of Section 27 . . . cannot be withered by the test of reasonableness or the partial applicability of the restraint',[90] and there are cases like *VFS Global Services* that expressly resist resort to a test of reasonableness even for a short (three-month) post-contractual restraint,[91] which appears rather harsh.

At the same time, we would hazard that courts do use the 'during/after' distinction as a starting point for a fuller reasonableness analysis. As we have established, a restraint operating during the contractual period is only *prima facie* valid—there is a proviso for unreasonable, harsh, or one-sided fixed-term contracts.[92] Hence, a reasonableness inquiry is necessary to determine whether the proviso applies, or alternatively confirms validity in questionable cases. In *Dr S Gobu v State of Tamil Nadu*,[93] a six-year medical bond was not hit by section 27, the Court emphasizing that the bond was reasonably necessary to protect the respondent's interests and that the doctor had not suffered from unequal bargaining power and had obtained the benefits of medical training with financial support.[94] In cases involving post-contractual restraints, while there is almost an irrebuttable presumption of voidness, the courts also sometimes gesture towards the unreasonableness of the restraint, such as in *Iec School of Art & Fashion*, where the Court commented on the unlimited period and the width of the restraint extending to the whole of Chandigarh.[95] To take an example, in *Tapas Kanti Mandal v Cosmo Films Ltd*,[96] while holding that a three-year post-employment non-competition restraint was void, the Court further emphasized the length of the restraint as well as the fact that

[88] ibid [47].

[89] For a representative sampling of the case law, see *M/s Interlink Services Pvt Ltd v Shri SP Bangera Sole Prop* 65 (1997) DLT 228; *Iec School of Art & Fashion v Mr Gursharan Goyal* 72 (1998) DLT 833; *Weiler International Electronics Private Ltd v Punita Velu Somasundaram* (2003)(3) ALLMR 577; *VFS Global Services Private Limited v Suprit Roy* 2008(2) BomCR 446; *M/S Paramount Coaching Centre Pvt Ltd v Rakesh Ranjan Jha* LNIND 2017 Del 3077; *SVF Entertainment Pvt Ltd v Mr Anupriyo Sengupta* LNIND 2018 Cal 1851; *Avantika Elcon Private Limited v Miraenan Tech Co Ltd* LNIND 2018 Del 3425; *Navigatothers Logistics Ltd v Kashif Qureshi* LNIND 2018 Del 4110.

[90] *Avantika Elcon* (n 89) [22] citing *Percept D'Mark* (n 86).

[91] *VFS Global Services* (n 89) [10].

[92] *Golikari* (n 68) [20].

[93] 2010 Mad 2532.

[94] ibid [17], [29].

[95] *Iec School of Art & Fashion* (n 89) [20].

[96] LNIND 2018 Aug 260. A useful up-to-date list of the case law emphasizing the 'during/after' distinction is set out in ibid [43], where the Court also noted, 'Most of the decisions have been given with reference to section 27 of the Contract Act and enforceability of restrictive covenant post service period has been held in the negative.'

there was no consideration given for it, in contrast with an earlier decision in which a three-month garden leave clause supported by remuneration was upheld.[97]

In *KD Campus Pvt Ltd v Metis Eduventures P Ltd India*,[98] the plaintiff-employer sought to enforce a restraint against the defendant-tutors from competing with their coaching institute for the agreed term of their employment, which was repudiated through premature termination by the latter. Interestingly, while the plaintiff contended that it should be entitled to an injunction given that it was only seeking restraint against the defendants for the contractual period of employment and not any period beyond, the Court took the view that the plaintiff's acceptance of the defendants' repudiation and its own treatment of the contract as terminated (albeit illegally), in likewise ceasing to perform its side of the bargain (including the payment of emoluments to the defendants), meant that 'the present case would fall in the genre of employer seeking to enforce the negative covenant after the termination of service and which is not permissible in law'.[99] Because the contract of employment was seen as coming to an end, any negative covenant sought to be enforced would be considered after the period of service. The Court further noted that the plaintiff had shown no proprietary right that may be infringed by the defendants in joining employment elsewhere or continuing the activity of tutoring. Hence, the restraint was simply anti-competitive, driving the defendants to idleness and a state of penury, and ultimately unenforceable.

This decision is another example of courts applying a more fine-grained analysis. Perhaps the Court was rather quick in departing from case law that had validated restraints operating during the period of certain fixed-term contracts. It could be argued that the law does, at times, fetter an innocent employer's election to affirm a repudiated contract by requiring it to come to an end, in order that a personal services contract is not specifically enforced against the liberty of an employee and a less burdensome remedy of damages in award instead. But this is a different matter from holding that (now that employment has presumably ended) a separate and expressly provided period of non-competition has also come to an end. Nonetheless, it is clear that the Court sought to characterize the restraint as operating 'after' in order to question its validity under section 27. Moreover, it buttressed its conclusion through the language of a reasonableness analysis, taking into account the lack of proprietary interest on the employer's end and countervailing public interests in autonomy on the side of employee-tutors.

Consequently, it cannot be said that by making a distinction between those restraints operating during and beyond the contractual period, Indian courts have abdicated all considerations of reasonableness. They have, in fact, used this distinction to police the boundary between reasonable and unreasonable restraints, while leaving room for a closer, context-specific enquiry in some cases.

[97] *M/s Kuoni Travel (I) Pvt Ltd v Ashish Kishore* 2007 6 All MR 808.
[98] (2018) 248 DLT 453.
[99] ibid [15].

4. Distinction between Non-competition and Other Forms of Restrictive Covenants

It is clear that courts treat non-compete obligations quite differently from covenants relating to confidentiality or non-solicitation of customers and employees and are more open to enforcing a non-competition covenant where it is necessary to protect trade secrets, confidential information, and business connections.[100] To the extent that these types of covenants or interests are hived off from the core of the section 27 prohibition, Indian courts are essentially allowing for the validation, where appropriate, of well-recognized 'legitimate interests' in the common law. As Stephen Smith explains, '[t]he classic examples of legitimate interest—trade secrets, customer connections, goodwill—are all properly described as investments necessary for the positive endeavour (the job, developing a business).'[101]

Of course, the identification of such proprietary information undergirding a restrictive covenant is often a difficult question of law and/or fact. As observed in *Star India Pvt Ltd v Laxmiraj Seetharaman Nayak*, '[a]cquisition of excellence is a very long process in the career of every one. No one else can have proprietary rights or interest in such acquisition of excellence.'[102] The status of an employee, the nature of his/her work, the fact that an employer impresses upon an employee the confidentiality of information and that the restricted information might be isolated from other information that an employee is free to use are all relevant factors in determining whether or not information can be classified as highly confidential.[103]

As we will see, Indian courts often take into account the above guidelines implicitly in determining whether there is a relevant legitimate interest to protect and whether the covenant is reasonably necessary for the protection of such an interest. In doing so, they appear to be proceeding on an enquiry not unlike the reasonableness approach undertaken in other common law jurisdictions.

In *Mundipharma AG v Wockhardt Ltd*,[104] a three-year post-termination covenant in a pharmaceutical licence restricting the respondent from making preparations using the petitioner's product and its derivatives was hit by section 27 (being a post-termination restraint). However, the Court also held that, assuming it is valid, it would be unreasonable to enforce the clause, given that the formulations that had gone into the preparations were public knowledge; viz, there was no legitimate interest in confidentiality. In another oft-cited case, *Sandhya Organic Chemicals P Ltd v United Phosphorous Ltd*,[105] the plaintiff sought, unsuccessfully, to injunct the defendant from

[100] Bhadbhade (n 15) 642. For other overviews of how confidential information is protected not only by contract but also by intellectual property law, tort law, and equity, see A Kumar and A Mishra, 'Protecting Trade Secrets in India' (2015) 18 Journal of World Intellectual Property 335; V Pai and R Seetharaman, 'Legal Protection of Trade Secrets' (2004) 1 SCC J-22.

[101] SA Smith, 'Reconstructing Restraint of Trade' (1995) 15 Oxford Journal of Legal Studies 565, 574–76.

[102] 2003(3) BomCR 563, [14].

[103] Bhadbhade (n 15) 643.

[104] (1991) ILR 1 Delhi 606.

[105] AIR 1997 Guj 177.

producing aluminium and zinc phosphide using their process on the basis of a confidentiality clause that extended post-employment. The Court held that there was no proper evidence of the defendant divulging any secrets and that the defendant could not be restrained 'for all times to come from using his knowledge and experience which he gained during the course of his employment', especially given that the defendant was a qualified chemical engineer whose experience constituted his own assets.[106] Again, in *Ambiance India*,[107] the Court emphasized,

> In a business house, the employees discharging their duties come across many matters, but all these matters are not trade secrets . . . If the defendant on account of his employment . . . has learnt some business acumen or ways of dealing with the customers or clients, the same do not constitute trade secrets or confidential informations [*sic*], the divulgence of which should be prohibited.[108]

More recent decisions have also applied the above principles, showing similar circumspection in identifying where information should be impressed with an obligation of confidence, especially where this would appear to limit the defendant's freedom of occupation. In *American Express Bank Ltd v Priya Puri*,[109] the Court refused an interim injunction against the defendant in relation to using or disclosing information and trade secrets and soliciting the plaintiff-bank's customers. It observed that '[c]reating a data base of the clients/customers and then claiming confidentiality about it, will not permit such bank to create a monopoly about such customers that even such customers cannot be approached',[110] and that '[r]ights of an employee to seek and search for better employment are not to be curbed by an injunction even on the ground that she has confidential data' (an allegation that was not established).[111] Likewise, in the more recent decision of *Manipal Business Solutions Private Limited v Aurigain Consultants Private Limited*,[112] the Court held that the defendant ex-employees of the plaintiff could not be injuncted against operating a competing business in breach of a non-disclosure agreement, referring to the fact that the plaintiff had failed to prove that the defendant had used any proprietary information belonging to it and that client–customer lists would not necessarily qualify as confidential information or trade secrets.

Of course, each case is quite context-specific in identifying legitimate interests that can support a covenant and take it out of the purview of section 27. In *Wipro Ltd*,[113] a non-solicitation-of-employees clause in a distributorship agreement that would extend to two years post-termination was upheld. The Court commented that the

[106] ibid [16].
[107] *Ambiance India* (n 36).
[108] ibid [7].
[109] 2006 (11) FLR 1061.
[110] ibid [34].
[111] ibid [47]. See also *Financial Software and Systems v Mudassir Naik* LNIND 2013 MAD 1008; *MS Stellar Information Technology Private Ltd v Mr Rakesh Kumar* LNIND 2016 Del 4084; *EV Motothers India Private Limited v Anurag Agarwal* LNIND 2017 Del 5539.
[112] 2022 SCC OnLine Del 2480.
[113] *Wipro Ltd* (n 87).

non-solicitation provision was not a bar on the employees of the petitioner but operated as between the petitioner and the respondent and 'has to be viewed more liberally than a restriction in an employer–employee contract', hence not amounting to a restraint of trade, business, or profession within the meaning of section 27. In *Embee Software Private Limited v Samir Kumar Shaw*,[114] the Court held that the respondents could not be prevented from carrying on the business of reselling software after leaving the employment of the plaintiff. But it prohibited the respondents from dealing in programmes, files, and data using the plaintiff's source code and disallowed them from soliciting the clients of the plaintiff. Hence, it is possible that, in some cases, courts do recognize trade connections and perhaps the maintenance of a stable and well-trained workforce as a type of legitimate interest, separate from trade secrets and confidential information.[115]

Accordingly, in deciding whether or not there exists some form of a proprietary legitimate interest, and in determining whether the confidentiality, non-solicitation, or non-compete covenant is necessary to protect such an interest and take it out of the ambit of section 27, Indian courts do appear to be working through the same range of factors animating a reasonableness inquiry.

5. No Restraint from 'Exercising a Lawful Profession, Trade or Business'

Another technique to escape the confines of section 27 involves courts interpreting the section so as not to include restraints that do not implicate a 'profession, trade or business', or restraints in the course or in the manner of trade, or where the restraint might be said to be ancillary to trade, which itself is not prohibited.

The types of covenants covered in this category tend to be horizontal or vertical agreements such as market-sharing, price-regulating, exclusive dealing, or land use-covenants that typically do not involve employment relationships and where the focus does not necessarily appear to be on the protection of legitimate interests in customers, clients, or proprietary information. To be clear, this carve-out does not technically revive an exception for 'partial' restraints that was discarded early on in *Madhub Chunder*;[116] rather, the idea appears to be that the restraint is reasonable or acceptable as facilitative of trade generally, arguably coupled with the fact that the particular restraint itself is not especially onerous.[117]

To give a few illustrations: in *Carlisles, Nephews & Co v Ricknauth Bucktearmull*,[118] a buyer's stipulation in a contract prohibiting sales of 'animal-bordered dhooties' to others for a particular period was not caught by section 27. The Court suggested that 'it

[114] AIR 2012 Cal 141.
[115] Such a view has been endorsed in other jurisdictions, such as the Singapore Court of Appeal in *Man Financial (S) Pte Ltd* (n 2) [93], [136], referring also to *Herbert Morris* (n 1). See also *MS Eli Research India Pvt Ltd v Mr Deepak Gupta* LNIND 2017 Del 1693, [14] (binding the defendant to a non-poaching undertaking).
[116] *Madhub Chunder* (n 20).
[117] Bhadbhade (n 15) 625.
[118] (1882) ILR 8 Cal 809.

was never intended to prohibit such a stipulation as that with which we are now dealing in contracts for the sale of goods'.[119] Likewise, in *Prem Sook v Dhurum Chand*,[120] an agreement to sell goods at one price if sent to Cuttack and another price if sent for sale in Madras was not 'a contract in restraint of trade whatsoever'. This is because the sellers 'had a right to refuse to sell to the defendants at all this small parcel of goods, and they had a right to fix the price at which they were willing to sell them'.[121] In similar vein, a fixed-rate agreement is said not to prevent sales but only to require the observance of certain terms within an agreement to trade.[122] Again, in *Mackenzie v Striramiah*,[123] an exclusive supply agreement to sell all salt manufactured during a certain period at a fixed price escaped the scrutiny of section 27. The Court held that 'a reasonable construction must be put upon the section' and that it did not aim at 'contracts by which in the exercise of [a person's] profession, trade or business, he enters . . . which are really necessary for the carrying on of his business';[124] in other words, restrictive covenants that are deemed to be facilitative of trade more widely.[125]

In such situations, one can argue that a reasonableness analysis is implicitly being undertaken, as courts interpret the legislative purpose as excluding from the ambit of section 27 such categories of restraints that do not prohibit a profession, trade, or business per se but regulate some aspect of it (say, price, supply, scope of business, and so on) as a precondition for entry into the principal transaction (such as a franchise or distributorship agreement or a commercial lease), and is thus considered on the whole as being supportive of trade.

Consistent with this rationale, however, courts do not universally validate all such horizontal or vertical agreements where these are not, in fact, beneficial for trade. For instance, in *Carew v North Bengal Sugar Mills*,[126] a zoning agreement to divide territories within which parties would obtain raw materials was hit by section 27. The Court distinguished inter alia *Carlisles*,[127] *Prem Sook*,[128] and *Mackenzie*,[129] by highlighting that the very essence of the contract was that one should not carry out business within a particular area and also that the length of the restraint was for all time to come.[130] In this sense, it is clear that some form of reasonableness analysis is being undertaken, having reference to the time and geographic scope of the restraint. Onerous or unreasonable restraints of this sort that are, on balance, injurious of trade are still deemed void.[131]

[119] ibid [18].
[120] (1890) ILR 17 Cal 320.
[121] ibid 322.
[122] *Kuber Nath v Mahali Ram* (1912) ILR 34 All 587.
[123] (1890) ILR 13 Mad 472.
[124] ibid [5].
[125] See also *Pothi Ram v Islam Fatima* (1915) 37 ILR All 212; *Vidya Wati v Hans Raj* (1993) DLT 625.
[126] (1951) 2 ILR Cal 386.
[127] *Carlisles* (n 118).
[128] *Prem Sook* (n 120).
[129] *Mackenzie* (n 123).
[130] *Carrew* (n 126) [388]–[389].
[131] It is also worth observing here that what courts appear to be doing in some of these early cases is a primitive form of competition regulation dealt with through the blunt tool of s 27. The division of labour between restraint of trade and the competition regulation regime is an issue we touch upon in section IV.2.ii of this chapter.

6. Reading Down Scope of Ambiguous Restraints

Where there exists some interpretive ambiguity in the scope of a restrictive covenant (or how it relates to other covenants), some Indian courts have seized upon this as an opportunity to read down an otherwise offensive clause or otherwise reinterpret the contract to avoid the compass of section 27. Through this, 'reasonable' results may obtain without courts being overtly interventionist or appearing to introduce novel legal principles. Courts simply construe the parties' intentions in a particular contract in a manner that reduces the reach of what may initially appear to be an unreasonable restraint. Accordingly, this technique is quite context-specific.

For instance, in the leading decision of *Superintendence Company*,[132] a two-year post-service non-competition covenant that operated 'after you leave the company' was held by the majority to refer only to a case where the employee had voluntarily left the services of the employer and not to a situation where the latter had terminated the employee's services. 'Leave' having been given a restricted meaning, the covenant was simply not triggered as applying to restrain the employee in such circumstances. Sen J's minority judgment endorsed a similar rule of construction on this point, arguing that the policy of section 27 leans in favour of an employee's autonomy and hence supports this form of *contra proferentem* reasoning: 'even if the word "leave" . . . is susceptible of another construction as being operative on termination however accomplished . . . [I] would, having regard to the provisions of Section 27 . . . try to preserve the covenant . . . by giving it a restrictive meaning, as implying volition i.e. where the employee resigns or voluntarily leaves the services'.[133]

Likewise, in *Bhavesh J Bhatt v Cyrus N Baxter*,[134] an agreement between the proprietor of coaching classes and one of his teachers contained a negative covenant that the latter would not serve in 'any other coaching classes conducted by any other person or institution' during the subsistence of the six-year contract. This was interpreted as prohibiting employment elsewhere in other coaching classes but not coaching classes conducted by the teacher himself or in partnership with someone else. Hence, the restraint was read down and the question of validity under section 27 avoided. In a very similar context, a clause stating that the 'teacher shall not indulge in teaching in any other Institute as long as associated with this Institute, or start his own Institute' as part of a five-year agreement in *Paramount Coaching Centre Pvt Ltd v Gopal Krishan @ Gopal Verma*[135] was read as inapplicable once the defendant started his own institute and effectively ceased association with the plaintiff.[136] Hence, the clause was read very narrowly to mean only that the teacher could not work in multiple positions during the

[132] *Superintendence Company* (n 30).
[133] ibid [63].
[134] (1990) Vol XCII The Bombay Law Reporter 474.
[135] 2017 Del 5649.
[136] ibid [19].

term of the contract, but that he could teach in a competing business if he chose to leave anytime during the fixed term.

It is clear that some of these constructions adopted are sensible, while others are more strained. The limited reading given to 'leave' in *Superintendence Company*[137] is quite plausible. Yet, in *Bhavesh J Bhatt*,[138] the purpose of the non-competition covenant would conceivably extend to situations where the teacher had set up an institution by himself or in partnership with another, and, in *Paramount Coaching*,[139] the possibility that the non-competition provision was meant to last during the whole term of the fixed contract cannot be gainsaid.

Relatedly, some courts read a questionable clause in a manner that escapes the scrutiny of section 27 in so far as the clause in question is not tainted by a separate restrictive covenant, although these clauses may initially appear to come together as part of a 'package deal' in a horizontal arrangement. In *Haribhai Maneklal v Sharafali Isabji*,[140] the plaintiff was held to be entitled to recover under an agreement to charge a uniform rate for ginning cotton where parts of the sums earned would be carried to a common fund and divided. The part of the agreement sought to be enforced was the agreement to divide the profits, which was founded upon the mutual agreement of profit-sharing and not price-fixing.[141] Similarly, in *SB Fraser v Bombay Ice Manufacturing Company*,[142] an agreement included a resale price maintenance clause and arrangements to establish a scale of manufacture and sale as well as a contribution to a common fund. Again, in so far as the obligation to contribute to the fund was concerned, this was a valid covenant.[143]

7. Reintroducing Reasonableness Analysis at Remedial Stage

A final technique we have identified is where courts incorporate reasonableness considerations at the remedial stage, such as when deciding whether, and on what terms, to grant injunctive relief or uphold a liquidated damages clause. This enables courts to adhere, in theory, to the idea that section 27 apparently operates in a fairly formalistic manner of determining either validity or voidness where the section bites, while in fact making room for reasonableness at a subsequent level of analysis, in order to achieve an ultimately fair and equitable result.

[137] *Superintendence Company* (n 30).
[138] *Bhavesh J Bhatt* (n 134).
[139] *Paramount Coaching* (n 135).
[140] (1897) 22 ILR Bom 861.
[141] ibid 867, 873–74.
[142] (1904) 29 ILR Bom 107.
[143] ibid 119. The idea appears similar to that found in the contractual illegality doctrine in common law, where an illegality that is 'remote' from the contract is less likely to render it void or unenforceable. See eg *21st Century Logistical Solution v Madysen* [2004] 2 Lloyd's Rep 92, [2004] EWHC 231. In such situations, parts of a contract that are not directly affected by illegality are construed as valid and enforceable. This technique has clear resonances with the severance doctrine, which we discuss briefly in section IV.2.i of this chapter.

In the *locus classicus* of *Golikari*,[144] the non-competition covenant during the five-year contract was upheld, yet the Court was willing to tailor the remedy, noting that 'there is nothing to prevent the court from granting a limited injunction to the extent that is necessary to protect the employer's interests where the negative stipulation is not void'.[145] A recent example of this type of reasoning is found in *Ozone Spa Private Limited v Pure Fitness and Others*,[146] where the Court upheld a non-competition covenant in a franchise agreement but awarded an interim injunction limited by a particular geographic scope. The result of this 'should be fair, just and reasonable as the absolute restriction on the basis of negative covenant . . . would be too harsh upon the defendants and would be even greater than the licensed area'.[147] In *Electrosteel Castings Ltd v Saw Pipes Ltd*,[148] the Court emphasized some measure of weighing and balancing at the remedial juncture when considering a restraint operating during a fixed-term contract. It noted, '[i]t is because the Court has to deal with propriety of passing an order of injunction during the unexpired term of the agreed period of employment, that questions and consideration of reasonableness and fairness come in.'[149]

In some cases, reasonableness will point against granting an injunction at all, despite the covenant being valid. For instance, in *Lalbhai Dalpatbhai*,[150] while the non-competition obligation was considered valid as within a three-year fixed term, the Court referred to section 12 of the Specific Relief Act 1963 and held that in exercising its discretion to award specific performance, it was necessary to consider the 'reasonableness of the matter and examine whether the grant of the injunction would impose a reasonable restriction or an unreasonable restriction on the right of the employee to follow the occupation of his choice'.[151] Applying the reasonableness standard, it declined to award an interim injunction, given that there was no material showing how the enforcement of the restraint would be 'necessary for the protection of the legitimate interests of the plaintiffs'.[152]

Other examples in this vein include *Karam Chand Thapar*,[153] which upheld the non-competition covenant within a eleven-year contract but attenuated the harshness of the result considerably by holding that a breach of the obligation entitled the employer not to an injunction but merely to terminate the employee's service without notice as per the terms of the employment agreement.[154] Likewise, in *Modern Food Industries India Ltd v Shri Krishna Bottlers Pvt Ltd*,[155] an injunction was not granted for breach of an obligation in a franchise agreement not to sell similar products, the Court observing that it would generally not be reasonable to award an injunction where damages would

[144] *Golikari* (n 68).
[145] ibid [21].
[146] 222 (2015) DLT 372.
[147] ibid [53].
[148] (2005) (1) CHN 612.
[149] ibid [48].
[150] *Lalbhai Dalpatbhai* (n 74).
[151] ibid [13].
[152] ibid [14].
[153] *Karam Chand Thapar* (n 79).
[154] ibid [8]–[10].
[155] AIR 1984 Del 119.

work efficaciously.[156] In *Nazir Maricar v Marshalls Sons and Co (India) Limited*,[157] an engineer breached a five-year bond with his employer, which was agreed in consideration for overseas training. The Court held that the exclusive employment clause, operating during the term of the agreement, was not in restraint of trade and was hence valid, but the Court watered down the claim for liquidated damages. Consequently, we see there is substantial room for courts to introduce considerations of reasonableness and proportionality in awarding remedies, notwithstanding the apparently formalistic language of section 27.

In all, our analysis in this section demonstrates that despite the historical evolution of section 27 and its often strict interpretation, courts have not altogether abandoned the concept of reasonableness. To the contrary, they have embraced it expressly or by necessary implication, usually relying upon one or more of the techniques outlined herein.

IV. The Future of the Restraint-of-Trade Doctrine in India

1. Suggested Trajectories

Our analysis has implications for the way in which the restraint-of-trade doctrine might develop in future years. The principal question in this regard is whether section 27 should be reformed in line with the model of reasonableness presently applied in the United Kingdom and other common law jurisdictions. Suggestions for reform of the section are by no means novel. The Law Commission, in its *13th Report*, observed that

> today, trade in India does not lag far behind that in England or the United States and there is no reason why a more liberal attitude should not be adopted by acknowledging such restraints as are reasonable not only as between the parties to the agreement but also as regards the general public. We recommend that section 27 be suitably amended to permit such reasonable restraint.[158]

Various commentators have echoed similar suggestions. Subrahmanyan, writing in 1968, noted: 'The 'reasonableness' rule could be adopted ... which would give adequate powers in the armoury of the judiciary to give necessary relief according to the circumstances of each case.'[159] Clerk suggested

[156] ibid [21].
[157] 2005(2) CTC 478. Compare also *Independent News Service Pvt Limited v Sucherita Kukreti* (2019) 257 DLT 426 (invalidating a negative covenant against competition in a broadcaster's employment contract pursuant to s 27, as well as holding that no injunction should be awarded given the interests of the defendant in pursuing her profession and the public interest in the dissemination of news and recognizing that any losses of the plaintiff-employer could be measured in monetary terms).
[158] Law Commission of India (n 32) at 27.
[159] VS Subrahmanyan, 'Restraint on Trade' (The Indian Law Institute, Discussion Meet on Contract Law In India, Nainital May 1968) 9–10.

> that Parliament take up the question of amendment of section 27 of the Contract Act either to bring it more in line with the common law in UK, or better still, to provide for rights and remedies which are more suitable in the context of policies of the present day Government in India.[160]

More recently, Govindjee and Bhat call for a reform of Indian law to 'necessitate a Court's enquiry into the reasonableness of such clauses and not imply holding them to be invalid *per se*—despite the wording of s 27 of the Contract Act'.[161]

Given our analysis of the myriad ways in which Indian courts have *already* introduced considerations of reasonableness, we might put these calls for reform in wider perspective. As Naravane has pointed out, 'it appears that an amendment is not the only means to make the Indian position on restraint of trade commercially appropriate, and . . . the law as it stands, also permits and mandates a "reasonableness" inquiry'.[162] The various judicial carve-outs from the scope of section 27 have somewhat mitigated its harshness and allowed Indian courts to balance, often through proxies and rules of thumb, notions of legitimate interests and the need to protect free trade. In that sense, we would be hard-pressed to conclude that Indian courts have got the majority of decisions on restraint of trade wrong. On the contrary, it is likely that the techniques we have identified above have allowed Indian courts to reach decisions not radically dissimilar from English cases in many circumstances, notwithstanding how section 27 is worded.

Nonetheless, there remain certain advantages in moving more openly towards a reasonableness standard with the components of an identifiable legitimate interest and the necessity of the provision being reasonable in the interests of the parties and the public. First, it goes without saying that a transparent approach to reasonableness accords more completely with the ideal of the rule of law. To take one well-known theoretical explication of this ideal, Fuller's internal morality of law,[163] it might be said that reform would promote the desiderata of adequate publicity, comprehensibility, non-contradiction, constancy over time, and congruence between announced rules and actual administration. While one might, on closer examination (as we have done here), conclude that the law already includes some degree of reasonableness analysis, from an expressive point of view, the *prima facie* strict default position that is constantly reiterated by leading courts and commentators sends the wrong signal: that reason is to be excluded when considering a restraint of trade.

Second, following from the above to a more practical implication, this disjunction is inimical to commercial certainty. Lawyers and businesspersons must know where they stand. By disconnecting the 'paper' rules from the 'real' rules, parties are in a difficult

[160] R Clerk, 'Law of Restrictive/Negative Covenants in Contract of Employment and Their Specific Performance: Case for Legislative Reform' (1996) 38 Journal of the Indian Law Institute 83, 89.

[161] A Govindjee and S Bhat, 'Restrictive Covenants in Employment Contracts: A Comparison between the Legal Positions in India and South Africa' (2008) 20 National Law School of India Review 46, 61.

[162] Naravane (n 38) 119.

[163] L Fuller, *The Morality of Law* (Yale University Press 1964).

position up front when drafting restraints that may or may not have a chance of being validated, and this would tend to increase subsequent litigation costs *ex post* as parties attempt to enforce or escape potentially unenforceable clauses.

Third, a reasonableness analysis is, to some extent, inescapable. The formalist approach to contract adjudication, which tends to emphasize the transaction costs of judicial intervention,[164] is attractive in theory but almost impossible to institute as a one-size-fits-all model for all contracting regimes. Courts will invariably be pointed to the equities of each case and, in the area of illegality and public policy, the extent to which a particular clause contravenes such values. In the same way that courts have moved towards a proportionality balancing approach in looking at the issue of illegality more generally,[165] it is natural that courts are drawn towards a reasonableness analysis in the closely related topic of restraints of trade. The enforceability of a one-month non-compete provision differs from a twenty-year clause; just as the enforceability of a contract for murder would be different from a contract involving a minor regulatory infraction. To the extent this is true, it is better to be up front about it and develop a case law jurisprudence that can give guidance to parties on specific issues, such as what sort of scope of activities, time, and geographic restrictions courts conventionally find to be valid, rather than stick to the half-baked myth that Indian courts avoid reasonableness altogether.

2. Boundary Issues and Interfaces

Indian courts have often been called upon to decide the nature, scope, and validity of restraints clauses not merely under section 27 but also in conjunction with associated legal fields such as the severance doctrine, competition law, tort law, and constitutional law. While it will be remiss on our part if we omit this increasingly important interface, our discussion on this point is necessarily compressed.

i. Severance doctrine

One boundary issue that warrants further exploration in the future is the relationship between the doctrine of severance and the approaches that Indian courts have taken to validating otherwise unenforceable clauses.[166] Interestingly, there do appear to be circumstances under which some form of severance is implicitly adopted in restraint-of-trade cases. An uncontroversial example might be the situation where a contract may have a restraint during the term of an employment contract, which extends beyond the contract; the post-contractual restraint is caught by section 27 and 'to that extent void'. This could be understood as section 27 creating a type of 'blue pencil test'[167] specifically for post-employment restraints.

[164] See eg A Schwartz and RE Scott, 'Contract Theory and the Limits of Contract Law' (2003) 113 Yale LJ 541; A Schwartz and RE Scott, 'Contract Interpretation Redux' (2010) 119 Yale LJ 926.

[165] See *Patel v Mirza* [2016] UKSC 42, [101].

[166] For a recent enunciation of the approaches to severance developed in common law, see *Tillman* (n 3).

[167] Under this test, severance may be permitted if 'the unenforceable provision is capable of being removed without the necessity of adding to or modifying the wording of what remains': *Tillman* (n 3) [85].

While courts have not always appeared to make explicit reference to one or more versions of the severance tests developed in common law, where there is, in fact, an interpretive technique used that amounts to rewriting an otherwise offensive clause, it is arguable that Indian courts are using something akin to notional severance[168] without overtly endorsing the doctrine. For instance, in reading down a non-compete to cover only situations where one takes up similar employment elsewhere but not situations where one starts another business,[169] the court might effect notional severance under the guise of interpreting an ambiguous clause. Identifying extant functional equivalents to notional severance, for example, may underscore the fact that Indian courts are more activist than they appear at first glance and help to direct attention towards crafting a consistent approach to delimiting the appropriate scope of judicial intervention across restraint of trade cases.

ii. Competition law

Some decisions brought under the ambit of section 27 at times raise wider systemic concerns as to the limits of fair competition, which, in any developed system of law, will involve a division of labour between the private law of contract and the regulatory law of competition, with its specialized procedures, practices, and jurisprudence aimed at dealing with polycentric, rather than primarily bilateral, considerations.[170] In India, section 3 of the Competition Act 2002 invalidates anti-competitive agreements to the extent that they have an appreciable adverse effect on competition (AAEC) within India.

For instance, horizontal agreements (akin to situations arising in restraint-of-trade cases) may necessitate a complex enquiry into the structure of the market to consider whether they result in AAEC.[171] In the case of vertical restraints, likewise, the anticompetitive effects must be weighed against any pro-competitive effects, taking into account the width of the market and the ultimate impact on consumer welfare.[172] For our purposes, the straightforward assertion is that section 27 is too blunt an instrument to deal with such horizontal or vertical agreements, particularly because it does not purport to raise the sort of considerations that the Competition Act 2002 does. This means that judges either ignore such considerations, which must be relevant where competition concerns are involved, or covertly smuggle some of them into the analysis in an impressionistic way, such as when they refer loosely to concerns of monopolization or the unfair exercise of market power in contract cases.[173] Either scenario is not ideal.

[168] Under this more flexible doctrine, courts effectively modify or replace an offensive clause with a more reasonable construction. See *Transport v New Solutions* (2001) 200 DLR (4th) 560; *Uber Technologies Inc v Heller* 2020 SCC 16.

[169] *Bhavesh J Bhatt* (n 134).

[170] See Smith (n 101) 576.

[171] See further A Roy, *Competition Law in India: A Practical Guide* (Kluwer Law International 2016) ch 2.

[172] ibid.

[173] For some key rulings involving an overlap between contractual and competition law considerations, see *Sanjeev Mittal v M/s Tirupati Infraprojects Pvt Ltd* LNIND 2014 Del 764; *Orchid-Hospira* Combination Registration No C-2012/09/79 (Competition Commission of India, 21 December 2012).

iii. Economic torts

A further interface worth mentioning is that of the operation of section 27 and economic torts of inducing breach of contract, the unlawful means tort, and (lawful and unlawful means) conspiracy, in so far as the latter also serve as a means of regulating unfair competition in commerce.[174] The law in these areas is exceedingly intricate, and to trace the twists and turns in its evolution is beyond the scope of this chapter.[175]

The interaction between economic torts and issues of section 27 is very much context-specific and depends on the positions of the parties, usually involving two or more competitor firms and often employees or customers of one firm. At times, the direction of argument may overlap, while in other situations, it is important to keep these issues distinct. For instance, in *Bhola Nath-Shankar Das v Lachmi Narain*,[176] the Court found that where a claim of organized conspiracy was founded upon tort, section 27 of the Contract Act does not apply. Hence, to be clear, section 27 invalidates only restrictive covenants in bilateral contractual settings; where there is a conspiracy among firms or persons to target a rival's business through interfering with the rival's employees or customers, this would fall more naturally within the domain of the economic torts. Section 27 on its own accord does not generate tortious liability and is not meant to be used to regulate all forms of unfair competition in private law.

However, it appears that section 27 has the potential to become relevant in more narrowly defined situations where a restrictive covenant is present in a contractual relationship as between the plaintiff and defendant. In *Modicare Limited v Gautam Bali*,[177] the plaintiff sought an injunction to restrain the defendant ex-employees from enticing the customers and consultants in the plaintiff's marketing network, inter alia on the basis of the tort of unlawful interference with business or enticement to commit a breach of contract. In the course of rejecting this claim, the Delhi High Court noted that any non-compete restriction in the defendants' employment agreements would be void and unenforceable owing to section 27, and hence it would be incongruous 'to enable the same plaintiff to the same relief under the law of tort'.[178]

To be clear, while the reasoning in *Modicare* is not illogical, there is no inexorable logic dictating that an invalid restrictive covenant invariably negates all potential tortious liability. It is trite that a claim for inducing breach of contract requires that there be a breach of contract.[179] Hence, where a restrictive covenant between an employer *A* and employee *B* is hit by section 27, rival *C* (who may or may not be an ex-employee of *A*) cannot be liable for inducing any breach of the *A*–*B* contract. Here, section 27 may be relevant. However, as between rivals *X* and *Y* (an ex-employee of *X* with a restrictive covenant), the fact that the restrictive covenant in *Y*'s employment contract is

[174] H Carty, 'The Modern Functions of the Economic Torts' (2015) 74 Cambridge Law Journal 261.
[175] Note the present position in the UK in *OBG v Allan* [2007] UKHL 21, [2008] 1 AC 1 leading from *Lumley v Gye* (1853) 2 E & B 216, (1853) 118 ER 749.
[176] AIR 1931 All 83.
[177] 2019 SCC OnLine Del 10511.
[178] ibid [29]–[30]. The Delhi High Court reached a similar conclusion in *INOX Leisure Limited v PVR Limited*, CS (OS) No 196/2018 (Delhi High Court, 18 May 2020).
[179] WE Peel and J Goudkamp (eds), *Winfield and Jolowicz on Tort* (19th edn, Sweet & Maxwell 2014) [19-009].

hit by section 27 does not mean that the default protection offered by the law of economic torts is completely out of the window as well. The situation would simply be equivalent to that of rivals who never had prior contractual relations—if *Y* fulfilled the elements of inducing a breach of contract,[180] there is no reason why such claims are precluded. Accordingly, the relationship between economic torts and section 27 must be scrutinized on a case-by-case basis.

iv. Constitutional law

One final boundary issue concerns cases where parties have invoked public law norms, most markedly constitutional norms, to buttress arguments that a restraint is valid or void, as the case may be. In *Mumbai Mazdoor Sabha v SA Patil*,[181] the clause in question, which required that the employer obtain the consent of a union before retrenching, terminating, or discharging any workman, was held to be hit by section 27 as imposing a restraint on the employer more than reasonably necessary to protect the interests of the workmen.[182] Interestingly, the Bombay High Court alluded to Article 19(1)(g) of the Constitution conferring fundamental rights on the citizen to carry on business, profession, or vocation, subject to Article 19(6) providing for reasonable restrictions imposed in the public interest. This was a case where the employers were subject to an unreasonable restrictive condition, which was struck down as a matter of contractual public policy as well as constitutional warrant.

A useful comparison may be made with the decision of *Association of Medical Super Specialty Aspirants and Residents v Union of India*.[183] In this case, medical students were required to execute indemnity bonds to serve the state government for various periods of time after the successful completion of their postgraduate medical and super-specialty courses, which they challenged as being in restraint of trade. The Supreme Court rejected this argument.[184] For our purposes, the Supreme Court also rejected the contention that Article 19(1)(g) was violated, given that the students had, without protest, agreed to the bonds.[185]

It is worth pointing out that this form of reasoning in the above cases has some affinity with the burgeoning case law on the 'horizontal effect' of constitutional law in

[180] See *Lumley* (n 175).
[181] 1993(3) BomCR 265.
[182] ibid [26].
[183] LNIND 2019 SC 651.
[184] ibid [39].
[185] ibid [20]. This decision has spawned related litigation in various High Courts of India, with these courts consistently dismissing a variety of challenges to the enforceability of such service bonds on contractual, constitutional, and other grounds. See *Ranjan Sinha v State of Bihar* AIR 2020 Pat 117 (High Court of Patna dismissing petition for study leave from performing mandatory service and observing that the compulsory bond did not violate the Contract Act, s 27 or the Constitution, art 19(1)(g)); *Chandar Shekhar v State of Himachal Pradesh* 2021 SCC OnLine HP 8067 (High Court of Himachal Pradesh at Shimla upholding the conditions of the compulsory bonds executed by the petitioners and refusing to order a reduction of compulsory service to two years on the grounds that the Supreme Court in the *Association of Medical Super Specialty Aspirants* (n 183) decision had not given any direction to the state governments to amend the bond period but only directed it to consider a two-year period); as well as *Sunil Chillalshetti v State of Chhattisgarh* 2020 SCC OnLine Chh 1402; *State of Tamil Nadu v PS Sairam* (2020) 7 Mad LJ 513 (High Court of Chhattisgarh at Bilaspur and High Court of Madras decisions, holding that the Supreme Court's judgment regarding the enforceability of service bonds extended to students occupying All India quota seats as well as state seats, since these educational facilities were on a par with each other).

private law settings.[186] To be fair, in both *Mumbai Mazdoor Sabha*[187] and *Association of Medical Super Specialty Aspirants*,[188] the constitutional arguments appear to run *alongside* the section 27 arguments. Hence, it is not entirely clear whether these cases genuinely embrace horizontal-effect reasoning, which usually suggests some *integration* of such public–private considerations. A fuller resolution of this issue, however, is beyond the scope of our chapter, given that it would require a closer comparative interrogation into the receptivity of Indian courts to invoking public norms in private disputes.[189]

V. Conclusion: Reason (Un)restrained?

Our analysis of 150 years of Indian case law has suggested that a complete resistance to reason, as seen at first glance from the strict wording of section 27 of the Contract Act, is something of a myth. It is true that the strict approach has been endorsed by the Indian judiciary in the letter of the law. Yet, its spirit reveals an unfolding narrative of the rise of reason, no doubt in fits and starts, and often through the circuitous techniques that we have identified, preserving the outward appearance of an aberration within the common law world that has, for the most part, embraced the less formalistic reasonableness tests inaugurated in the *Nordenfelt* decision.

Nonetheless, as we have demonstrated, these techniques allow Indian courts to introduce some degree of balancing between the legitimate commercial interests of parties and the autonomy interests of those subject to restraints. At the same time, the resultant state of affairs is something of a tangled (rather than seamless) web, woven through decades of case law. We have suggested that there remains impetus for reform in the direction of a more express endorsement of the reasonableness approach in pursuit of the values of consistency, coherence, and the rule of law. While not purporting to articulate the precise boundary lines of the restraint doctrine, we have also indicated that there exist potentially productive and disruptive interfaces between the doctrine and evolving areas, including the rules on severance, competition regulation, the economic torts, and constitutional law. The restraint doctrine, as we have seen, is nothing if not dynamic, and we hope our analysis has provided a map for the development of the law as we look to its next horizon.

[186] For an overview by a leading commentator, see H Collins, 'Private Law, Fundamental Rights, and the Rule of Law' (2018) 121(1) West Virginia Law Review 1.

[187] *Mumbai Mazdoor Sabha* (n 181).

[188] *Association of Medical Super Specialty Aspirants* (n 183).

[189] See eg S Balganesh, 'The Constitutionalisation of Indian Private Law' in S Choudhry, M Khosla, and PB Mehta (eds), *The Oxford Handbook of the Indian Constitution* (OUP 2016); C Chandrachud, Chapter 23 of this volume.

13

Performance, Breach, and Termination

*Mihir Naniwadekar**

I. Introduction

The Contract Act regulates the performance of contracts in some detail and devotes nearly thirty sections to the topic.[1] This chapter examines how these provisions have been applied since 1872. It would appear that there remains immense scope for Courts—even after 150 years of the Act—to provide surer foundations for the law governing performance of contracts. This chapter begins by considering issues relating to *who* is to perform the contract (section II). Section III then considers issues relating to *how* the performance of the contract is to happen, and section IV covers when *non-performance* can be justified. Section V considers the question of when a breach can result in the *termination* of the contract. Before proceeding, it will also be helpful to note what this chapter does not cover. Frustration can be considered to be a factor justifying non-performance: however, frustration is not covered in this chapter. Questions relating to the consequences of breach other than termination are not dealt with in this chapter. These aspects have been dealt with in separate chapters in this book.[2]

II. Who Should Perform the Contract?

1. Personal Performance

If a famous artist agrees to sketch my portrait for me in return for a handsome remuneration, the artist must do so himself: it will not be sufficient if he gives me a sketch drawn by his novice student.[3] On the other hand, if I agree to provide a photocopy of parts of a book that I own to my neighbour, the neighbour should not really complain if I ask my son to take the book to a nearby stationer, get an appropriate copy made, and deliver

* The author thanks Dr KV Krishnaprasad and the participants at the conference where this chapter was initially presented for their comments and suggestions.

[1] The Contract Act, ch IV is titled 'Of the Performance of Contracts' and covers ss 37–67.

[2] See N Bhadbhade, Chapter 14 of this volume.

[3] See the Contract Act, s 40, Illustration (b).

Mihir Naniwadekar, *Performance, Breach, and Termination* In: *Foundations of Indian Contract Law.* Edited by: KV Krishnaprasad, Niranjan Venkatesan, Shivprasad Swaminathan, and Umakanth Varottil, Oxford University Press. © Oxford University Press 2024.
DOI: 10.1093/9780191997211.003.0013

that to the neighbour.[4] The difference between these two cases is that in the first case, it is plain that the intention of the parties was that the performance should be done personally by the promisor, using his personal skills and qualities;[5] in the second case, parties would be more concerned with getting the performance done rather than with who is to do the necessary acts.

This general rule is found in section 40 of the Contract Act. In the language of section 40, the test is: does it appear 'from the nature of the case' that the intention of the parties is that the contract must be performed personally by the promisor?

Simple though this may seem in principle, difficulties may arise in practical application. Consider my agreement with the artist. I, of course, want my sketch to be drawn by the artist personally: but does this mean that everything from sharpening the pencil onwards must be done by the artist? What extent of assistance by the novice student would be acceptable? As an early commentary on the Act noted, '[i]n ascertaining what is contemplated by the parties, usage as well as express terms must be regarded'.[6] If the general practice in the relevant art is that their novice students may assist so long as the artist retains overall supervision, then that will suffice.[7]

2. Death of a Party: Representatives and Heirs

It may so happen that a party is no longer alive when the time for performance arrives. Section 37 addresses this situation, when it provides, 'Promises bind the representatives of the promisors in case of the death of such promisors before performance, unless a contrary intention appears from the contract.' The language used here ('unless a contrary intention appears from the contract') is different from that of section 40 ('if it appears from the nature of the case'). However, the underlying principle is the same: if a promise is intended (that intention to be objectively ascertained) to be personally performed, it cannot be delegated; nor can performance then be insisted from the legal heirs or representatives after the death of the promisor.

The common law position at the time the Contract Act was enacted was summarised by Willes J in 1869 in the following terms:[8]

> Generally speaking, contracts bind the executor or administrator, though not named. Where, however, personal considerations are of the foundation of the contract, as in

[4] See ibid s 40, Illustration (a). Ordinarily, promises of delivery of goods and payment do not involve any 'personal' element: see *Tod v Lakhmidas* (1892) ILR 16 Bom 441. This principle has been applied to immovable properties also, and it has been held that, ordinarily, contracts for the purchase of immovable property cannot be considered 'personal': see *Joshi v Shimpi* (1925) 27 Bom LR 1261.

[5] The proviso to the Specific Relief Act 1963, s 15 contains some bars to specific performance in cases of contracts 'where the learning, skill, solvency or any personal quality . . . is a material ingredient'. It would seem that is the same principle at play.

[6] F Pollock and D Mulla, *The Indian Contract Act, with a Commentary, Critical and Explanatory* (2nd edn, Sweet & Maxwell 1909) 225 (emphasis added).

[7] See S Naravane, Chapter 7 of this volume.

[8] *Farrow v Wilson* (1868–69) 4 CP 744, 745.

cases of principal and agent and master and servant, the death of either party puts an end to the relation.

Section 37 did not intend to depart from this rule. Thus, an agreement for repurchase of immovable property was held to be binding on the heirs.[9] On the other hand, a contract for managing the property as a 'dewan' was held to be personal in nature and terminable on the death of one of the parties.[10] The Court expressly took notice of the fact that '[t]he relationship between the Dewan and the proprietor of an impartible estate is of a somewhat intimate and personal nature though much of the work of the Dewan is connected with the administration of the estate' and was also influenced by the fact that the evidence demonstrated previous knowledge on the part of both parties regarding the personal merits of the 'dewan'. It is respectfully submitted that while the decision appears to be correct, the latter consideration, on its own, may not be determinative: one may *know* of the personal skills of another; yet, the contract may not necessarily be one *based* only on those personal qualities.

Of course, legal representatives or heirs cannot be bound personally in the sense that damages from breach cannot be recovered from their personal assets. Rather, it is the estate of the deceased party that will be liable. Consider a case where *A* agrees to sell goods to *B*, and *A* dies prior to the completion of the sale. In such a case, the contract will not cease to exist and will have to be performed by the legal heirs of *A*: but damages for breach (if any) will be recovered not from the heirs personally but from the estate of *A*.[11]

3. Abatement of Suits

Under Indian civil procedure rules, 'the death of a plaintiff or defendant shall not cause the suit to abate if the right to sue survives'.[12] Does the right to sue for breach of contract survive the death of the wronged party? Section 306 of the Indian Succession Act 1925—the Indian version of *actio personalis moritur cum persona*—reads,

> All demands whatsoever and all rights to prosecute or defend any action or special proceeding existing in favour of or against a person at the time of his decease, survive

[9] *Khatoon v Haq* (1997) 7 SCC 452.

[10] *Patnaik v Harichandan* AIR 1954 Ori 241.

[11] This was effectively conceded in *Vasudeo v Govind* AIR 1945 Bom 21, but it seems that the concession was entirely correct. Pollock and Mulla quote, in this context, the following extract from PJ Fitzgerald, *Salmond on Jurisprudence* (12th edn, Sweet & Maxwell 1966) 443–44:

> Just as many of a man's rights survive him, so also do many of his liabilities; and these inheritable obligations pass to his representative, and must be satisfied by him. Being, however, merely the representative of another, he is not liable in propria persona, and his responsibility is limited by the amount of property which he has acquired from the deceased.

See F Pollock and D Mulla, *The Indian Contract Act, with a Commentary, Critical and Explanatory* (Padia ed, 13th edn, Sweet & Maxwell 2006) 966. See also A Briggs and A Burrows, *The Law of Contract in Myanmar* (OUP 2016) 152.

[12] Code of Civil Procedure 1908, Order XXII, Rule 1.

> to and against his executors or administrators; except causes of action for defamation, assault, as defined in the Indian Penal Code, 1860 (45 of 1860) or other personal injuries not causing the death of the party.

Though the section expressly speaks of 'executors or administrators', the principle equally applies to all legal representatives after the death of the concerned party.[13] At one point of time, there was some ambiguity as to the scope of 'defamation, assault . . . or other personal injuries not causing the death'. The Calcutta High Court held that this means that, in addition to defamation and assault, only actions for bodily injuries not causing death would abate.[14] But a Full Bench of the Madras High Court held that the phrase means that, in addition to defamation and assault, all wrongs (and not just bodily injuries) to the person that do not necessarily cause damage to the *estate* of the person wronged would be barred.[15] The latter view has now been endorsed by the Supreme Court on multiple occasions.[16] However, as we will see shortly, breach of contract cannot be considered as falling within the scope of the phrase.

A statement of the present position of Indian law is found in the judgment of the Supreme Court in *Veerappa v Sequeira*.[17] In that case, the Supreme Court held—in considering a case involving alleged negligent professional services—that if a pleaded cause of action is solely in tort, the suit will abate on the death of the injured party; however, if the pleaded cause of action is contractual in nature, the suit can continue:

> We leave the matter open for the trial court to decide whether the suit is founded entirely on torts or on contract or partly on torts and partly on contract and deal with the matter according to law. If the entire suit claim is founded on torts the suit would undoubtedly abate. If the action is founded partly on torts and partly on contract then such part of the claim as relates to torts would stand abated and the other part would survive. If the suit claim is founded entirely on contract then the suit has to proceed to trial in its entirety and be adjudicated upon.[18]

It may be argued that whether an action is in contract or in tort is not always determinative. In *Patel v Chowgule*,[19] *Veerappa* was relied on to argue that a suit for a declaration that a will executed by the plaintiff was void would abate on the death of the plaintiff. The Bombay High Court held that 'the test whether the cause of action and the right to sue survives cannot be made solely depending on the classification of the action as a tort or a contract'.[20]

[13] *Ezhuthasan v Nair* AIR 1986 SC 411.
[14] *Sen v Corporation of Calcutta* ILR 31 Cal 993. The same view was taken by the High Court of Rangoon in *Cassim v Bibi* AIR 1936 Rang 17.
[15] *Dorabji v Nurse* AIR 1921 Mad 1.
[16] *Ezhuthasan* (n 13); *Veerappa v Sequeira* (1988) 1 SCC 556.
[17] *Veerappa* (n 16).
[18] ibid [15].
[19] *Patel v Chowgule* (2008) 2 Bom CR 567.
[20] ibid [16].

Patel was an unusual case. Ordinarily, a plaintiff who seeks to cancel his/her own will can simply duly execute a fresh will to be the last will and testament. The complication arose because the original suit was instituted by the plaintiff, who suffered from mental infirmity and was already acting through the next friend (his wife) at the inception of the suit itself. The plaintiff (through the next friend) sought cancellation of the will in favour of the daughter. That plaintiff died, and the wife sought to substitute herself. The daughter relied on *Veerappa* and argued that (a) a will is not a contract and (b) the suit was therefore not based on contract but based on tort and, consequently, must abate. The Court rejected this contention. The Court's decision does not—indeed, cannot—detract from *Veerappa*. In any case, it is not clear whether analysing the cause of action as a 'tort' is helpful: the better analysis is that the suit was one that engaged the equitable jurisdiction of the Court.

A complete analysis of when the right to sue can survive in cases of torts or equitable wrongs would carry us too far away from the subject of this chapter,[21] but the trend is to limit the application of the *actio personalis* rule.[22] The point, however, remains that—following *Veerappa*—it seems very difficult to imagine a case where a suit based on a breach of contract would abate on the death of a party.[23]

4. Effect of Accepting Performance from Third Party

Section 41 of the Contract Act states,

> When a promisee accepts performance of the promise from a third person, he cannot afterwards enforce it against the promisor.

It is not necessary that performance from a third person should be authorised or ratified by the promisor: the acceptance of the performance by the promisee is sufficient. At the time the Contract Act was enacted, one view in English law[24] was that where a payment was made to a creditor by a third person without the authority of the debtor, the creditor and the third person could rescind the transaction before the debtor's ratification. In such a case, the performance would remain outstanding. Section 41 makes the position clear that, in Indian law, there is no need for any ratification. Performance is complete—and the contract would consequently be discharged by performance—the moment the creditor accepts the payment.

[21] A large body of law has developed on when cases involving the declaration of status/office abate. See, for instance, *Qutubuddin v Saifuddin* (2017) 3 Bom CR 322.

[22] See *Manjhi v Management of Sangramgarh Colliery* (1994) 1 SCC 292.

[23] The principle of *Veerappa* (n 16) applies in determining whether a vested cause of action to sue for breach of contract continues to survive the death of one of the parties; and not in determining whether the obligations under a contract itself continue or not. The latter question is determined by looking at the principles emerging from the earlier discussion around the Contract Act, ss 37 and 40.

[24] *Walter v James* (1871) LR 6 Ex 124.

This section may be attracted in some situations, even when the third person does not make the full payment but the creditor accepts a lesser payment from the third party towards discharge of the full liability: section 41 will apply together with section 63 in such cases. This was illustrated by the Supreme Court in *Godha v Khan*.[25] The Prince of Berar purchased some jewellery from a jeweller in the late 1930s but did not make payment. Interest accrued on the outstanding amounts. The debt was acknowledged from time to time. After Indian independence, a committee was set up by the Military Governor of Hyderabad, and the committee recommended payment of Rs 20,00,000 in full and final satisfaction of the outstanding debt (which, by that time, was around Rs 27,00,000). The Comptroller General refused to make the payment when the jeweller insisted that he retained the right to claim the balance amounts. Sometime thereafter, the jeweller accepted the amount of Rs 20,00,000 from the Comptroller General of the Military Governor and issued a receipt to the effect, which recorded that the jeweller had 'received payment in full'. In 1950, the jeweller commenced proceedings for the balance amount from the Prince. The trial judge took the view that the jeweller was entitled to proceed against the Prince, on the reasoning that the acknowledgment of 'received payment in full' meant that the payment due from the Military Governor was received in full but that the balance payment could be recovered from the Prince. The Supreme Court noted that section 63 of the Contract Act entitles a promisee to dispense with the whole or any part of the performance, and that had been done. Further, having accepted the payment from the Military Governor, section 41 applied as well.

Of course, if section 63 is not attracted (for instance, if the promisee does not dispense with the full performance but expressly reserves his/her rights for the balance payment[26]), then the third person will have to make the full payment in order for the debtor to be discharged.[27] For section 41 to be invoked in such cases, it is not enough if the contract is performed in part by a third person.[28]

It is clear from the language of section 41 that where the creditor has accepted performance from a third person, then the creditor cannot enforce performance again from the debtor. But does the third person have a claim against the debtor? In a few specific situations, statutory provisions expressly provide for subrogation.[29] But one High Court has suggested that '"subrogation" means substitution. A substitution is always

[25] *Godha v Khan* AIR 1963 SC 250.

[26] Indeed, it has been held that unless there is an unequivocal dispensation at the time of accepting a part-payment, the mere acceptance of a part-amount does not result in a waiver to the claim for the balance: See *Bharat Coking Coal v Annapurna Construction* (2003) 8 SCC 154. Ultimately, it would seem that this is a question to be ascertained on the facts of each individual case; and the continued acceptance of substandard performance without demur may result in an inference that there is a dispensation from performance of the optimal standard: *Bhagwati Oxygen v Hindustan Copper* (2005) 6 SCC 462. Dispensation does not require express language but can also be through conduct, so long as the conduct is unequivocal: See *Kanchan Udyog v United Spirits* (2017) 8 SCC 237.

[27] A mere promise will not suffice: what s 41 contemplates is actual performance by a third person and not simply the promise to perform: *Lal v Singh* AIR 1916 PC 68; *Citibank v Standard Chartered Bank* AIR 2003 SC 4630.

[28] *Hebbar v Bhandari* AIR 1966 Kar 84.

[29] See, for instance, the Transfer of Property Act 1882, s 92 (which applies to subrogation in the case of mortgages), the Contract Act, s 140 (which deals with subrogation in the case of sureties), or the Marine Insurance Act 1963, s 79.

permissible under section 41 of the Contract Act.'[30] This suggests that subrogation is possible in every situation where section 41 is attracted. It is respectfully suggested that the issue merits deeper consideration.

If the third party is to have a claim against the debtor, what (leaving aside any specific statutory provisions) is the basis of such a claim? If the creditor cannot recover from the debtor, then on what basis can rules of subrogation apply such that the third person can, nonetheless, maintain a claim against the debtor? In the context of insurance contracts, the Supreme Court has held that subrogation is inherent in the contract of insurance.[31] In an insurance contract, though, the position is slightly different. If *C* and *D* enter into a contract, and *C* insures herself against losses caused by *D*'s non-performance, the insurer is not really 'performing' the contract between *C* and *D*.[32] Accordingly, section 41 does not apply in such situations. Hence, there is no difficulty with the principle of subrogation being applied in such a case. *C*'s rights are not extinguished by section 41 here; and as *C*'s right to obtain performance is retained, the insurer can (as a matter of the law of insurance) step into the shoes of *C*.

On the other hand, in a situation where section 41 applies, *C*'s right to insist on performance will not exist. Thus, there is nothing left for the third person to 'step into'.[33] How would subrogation then work? It has been suggested that the answer (in English law) may lie in viewing the situation through an unjust enrichment lens.[34] But this result—if transposed into the Indian context in every situation where section 41 applies—may sometimes produce unfair results. In particular, a potentially unfair result could arise in cases where the subrogation would have occurred without the debtor having ratified—or indeed, known about—the payment made by the third party to the creditor.[35] It is submitted that the answer would, indeed, turn on unjust enrichment; but one cannot assume the existence of the cause of action in unjust enrichment merely because section 41 applies. In particular, the question of whether there is an unjust factor must be squarely addressed in each case. The provisions of section 41 may result

[30] *Bhamini v Kerala State Road Transport* MACA 637 of 2003 decided on 18 December 2008 (Kerala High Court).

[31] *Economic Transport Organisation v Charan Spinning* (2010) 4 SCC 114. See also *Union of India v Sri Sarada Mills* AIR 1973 SC 281.

[32] Cf *Textiles & Yarn v Indian National Steamship* AIR 1964 SC 362, holding that if *C* has received payment from an insurance company, *C*'s claim against *D* is barred by virtue of s 41. However, the Supreme Court has held that a payment made to a consignor by an insurer on account of the loss of the consignor's goods by the railways does not operate to discharge the obligation of the railways, and s 41 is not attracted in such cases (though *C* may be accountable to the insurer for the moneys received from *D*): *Sri Sarada Mills* (n 31). See also *Union of India v Orissa Textile Mills* AIR 1979 Ori 165.

[33] Professor Mitchell describes such situations as 'reviving subrogation'—simple subrogation is the remedy where the creditor's rights subsist notwithstanding the third person's payment; and reviving subrogation is the remedy when the creditor's rights have been extinguished. See C Mitchell, 'Subrogation: Persistent Misunderstandings' in A Burrows and A Rodger (eds), *Mapping the Law* (OUP 2006) 105.

[34] See *Banque Financière de la Cite v Parc (Battersea)* [1999] 1 AC 221. See also A Burrows, 'Absence of Basis' in Burrows and Rodger (n 33) 33, 43–44.

[35] If unjust enrichment is the cause of action, the limitation would start from the date of enrichment. Presumably, the debtor is enriched at the time the third person makes the payment to the creditor. It is probably fair that the limitation period will run afresh from then, if the debtor has ratified—or is at least aware—of the payment. But it is not clear whether the same can be said in situations when the debtor has no such knowledge whatsoever. In particular, there would be a possibility of the limitation period being continually extended irrespective of the debtor's actions or knowledge.

in an enrichment in every case where the section is attracted, but whether there is an unjust factor must be separately analysed.

5. Joint Liabilities and Joint Rights

The cases of joint promisors and joint promisees are dealt with in sections 42–45 of the Contract Act. This series of sections was intended to diverge from English common law.[36]

So far as joint rights are concerned, the position is stated in section 45: joint rights can be enforced jointly and, in the event of the death of one of the promisees, by the surviving promisees jointly with the legal representatives of the deceased promisee. So far as joint liabilities are concerned, section 42 provides that joint promises must be fulfilled by 'all [joint promisors], during their joint lives, and, after the death of any of them, his representative jointly with the survivor or survivors, and, after the death of the last survivor, the representatives of all jointly'. This rule can be displaced if a contrary intention appears from the contract. Under section 43, the promisee can claim performance from any one or more joint promisors (and the concerned promisor can claim contribution from the other promisors). The liability of the joint promisors is thus joint and several.[37] Section 44 provides that a release of one joint promisor by the promisee does not discharge the other joint promisors; nor does the release free the released promisor from responsibilities (of contribution) to the other joint promisors.

If a decree is obtained against one of many joint promisors and such decree remains unsatisfied, will a second claim against another joint promisor be maintainable? There was some divergence of views in the High Courts on this aspect,[38] but it seems that the view that the second suit is not barred has now been accepted by most High Courts.[39]

[36] See *Khimji v Haridas* (1882) ILR 6 Bom 700, 710 (speaking of the 'series of sections materially altering the rules of English common law as to the devolution of the benefit of and liability on joint contracts'); Pollock and Mulla, *The Indian Contract Act* (2nd edn) (n 6) 225–26.

[37] *Das v Chaudhari* AIR 1927 Pat 426.

[38] See *Mullick v Monshee* (1878) ILR 3 Cal 353 and *Chand v Cherty* (1916) ILR 39 Mad 548, where the Calcutta and Madras High Courts, respectively, held that the second suit would be barred; and *Askari v Singh* (1900) ILR 22 All 307, where the Allahabad High Court held that there is no bar to the second suit. The Calcutta High Court subsequently held that the rule in *Mullick* would not apply to bar a second suit when the first suit was before a foreign court rather than a domestic court: *Mukhopadhyay v Cooch Behar Loan Office* AIR 1941 Cal 64. The Allahabad view has since been followed by other High Courts, including the Calcutta and Madras High Courts themselves in the cases cited in n 39 below.

[39] Following the principle of *Askari v Singh* (n 38); *In re Vallibhai Adamji* (1933) 35 Bom LR 881; *Solomon v Martin & Co* 163 Ind Cas 331 (Cal); *Chettiar v Chettiar* AIR 1970 Mad 337; *Punjab Co-operative Bank v Official Liquidator* (1984) 55 Comp Cas 1 (P&H). Of course, these decisions do not mean that double recovery would be permissible. The Law Commission of India accepted the correctness of *Askari* in its *13th Law Commission of India Report, Indian Contract Act 1872* (1958) [70] <https://cdnbbsr.s3waas.gov.in/s3ca0daec69b5adc880fb46 4895726dbdf/uploads/2022/08/2022080532.pdf> accessed 24 August 2023.

III. How Should Performance Happen?

1. Exact Performance

The starting point is that the promisor must perform exactly what he or she has undertaken to perform. However, courts have, from time to time, accepted that trivial defects in performance could be excused on an application of the principle of *de minimis non curat lex*.[40] *De minimis does not* mean that there is no breach whatsoever. As the Canadian Supreme Court has noted, 'a finding of de minimis means that no fundamental breach permitting rescission has been committed, not that there has been no breach giving rise to an action in damages'.[41] Ultimately, the issue may simply turn on construction. As a matter of interpretation of the contract, is substantial performance sufficient?[42] If, on interpreting the contract, the obligation is such that substantial compliance suffices (or a small margin of error is permissible), then there is no breach at all: the obligation, indeed, has been 'exactly' performed. On the other hand, if, on interpretation, there is no room to deviate from exact performance, then substantial performance will not suffice: there will be a breach. But the consequences of that breach may only be that there is a right to merely nominal damages.

In substance, how performance should happen is essentially a matter of interpreting the substantive content of the contract.[43] Nonetheless, the Act provides for a somewhat detailed set of default rules in this regard,[44] to which we can now briefly turn.

2. Time and Place for Performance

If the place for performance is not fixed,[45] then it is for the promisor to apply to the promisee to appoint a reasonable place for performance and to complete performance at the appointed place.[46] And where no time for performance is specified, performance must be within a 'reasonable time'.[47] The Supreme Court has held that this principle is

[40] *Kumar v Koya & Sons* AIR 1990 Ker 20.

[41] *Sail Labrador v Navimar* [1999] 1 SCR 265 (Supreme Court of Canada). Questions of termination are discussed in section V below.

[42] See *Nadgouda v Reddy* AIR 1969 SC 447, which hints at treating the question as one of interpretation. Similarly, the 'rule' that *de minimis non curat lex* does not apply to commercial credit transactions may be explained on the basis that the nature of such transactions does not leave any scope for implying that the exact performance can be derogated from. See *Arosan Enterprises v Union of India* (1993) 51 DLT 280.

[43] In this regard, see G Yihan, Chapter 3 of this volume.

[44] In the case of sale of goods, even more detailed rules are found in the Sale of Goods Act 1930. The relevant provisions pertaining to sale of goods were initially enacted in the Contract Act, ss 76–123 until the separate specific enactment of 'an Act to define and amend the law relating to the sale of goods', that is, the Sale of Goods Act 1930.

[45] This section applies when performance is to be made without application by the promisee: it does not apply to 'on-demand' obligations: *Chettiyar v Gopalachari* (1908) 31 Mad 223.

[46] The Contract Act, s 49.

[47] ibid s 46: 'the engagement must be performed within a reasonable time'. 'Engagement', here, refers to the promise: it appears that the nomenclature of 'engagement' was carried forward from an earlier draft of the Act. In the case of reciprocal promises, where the order of performance is not fixed by contract, the order of performance is determined by the nature of the transaction: the Contract Act, s 52.

a term implied by law[48] and that determination must be made 'having regard to those circumstances of which the actor . . . knows or ought to know'.[49] The Act expressly notes that the question of what is reasonable time is a question of fact.[50] This means that there will usually be no second appeal possible on the issue of what is reasonable time; and that an arbitrator's finding in this regard would generally not be interfered with by the courts.[51]

When the date of performance is fixed by contract, it must be performed 'during the usual business hours' at the place of performance.[52] Thus, if goods are to be delivered at a warehouse on a certain date but are brought to the warehouse after the usual business hours, the contract cannot be said to have been performed.[53] Consequences of not performing on time turn on whether time is of the essence of the contract or not.[54] This aspect is discussed in section V below.

3. Appropriation of Payments and Exchange Rates

Questions of how a payment is to be appropriated towards multiple debts are governed by sections 59–61 of the Contract Act. These sections apply only if there are distinct debts: principal and interest on the same debt do not form distinct debts.[55] If there are, indeed, multiple debts, then, in the first place, the intimation of the debtor (either express or by implication from the circumstances) would prevail.[56] If there is no such express or implied implication from the debtor, then it is for the creditor to decide to which debt to apply the payment. If there are two debts, the recovery of one of which is time-barred on account of limitation, it will be open to the creditor to apply the payment to that time-barred debt.[57]

There is a conflict of views on whether it is possible for a creditor to appropriate a payment partly to all outstanding debts such that there is a part-payment of each outstanding debt (resulting in limitation periods getting extended for all debts).[58] On one

[48] *Hungerford Investment Trust v Mundhra* (1972) 3 SCC 684.

[49] *Municipal Corp of Delhi v Kumar* (1987) 4 SCC 497.

[50] Contract Act, s 46 (Explanation). An early commentary noted that 'it is difficult to understand why decisions should be reported on the question of what is reasonable time': Pollock and Mulla, *The Indian Contract Act* (2nd edn) (n 6) 236. See also the Contract Act, s 48 (Explanation): the question of 'what is a proper time and place' is a question of fact.

[51] See *Trustees of the Port of Madras v Engineering Constructions Corp* (1995) 5 SCC 531.

[52] The Contract Act, s 47.

[53] The illustration to s 47 appears to suggest that even if the warehouse is actually open, it is still a breach if the goods are delivered after the usual business hours. The illustration perhaps slightly modifies the conclusion reached in an earlier English decision, *Startup v Macdonald* (1843) 6 Man & G 593. In respect of payment obligations, modern methods of money transfer render these types of issues obsolete in most situations.

[54] Contract Act, s 55.

[55] *Industrial Credit & Development Syndicate v Patel* AIR 1999 SC 1036; *Singh v Union of India* (2006) 8 SCC 457; *Kerala State Electricity Board v Kalathil* (2018) 4 SCC 793. In so far as appropriation between principal and interest is concerned, the presumption in law is that the payment must first be appropriated to the interest: *In re Gopiram Govindram* (1936) 4 ITR 157 (Cal); *Meghraj v Bayabai* [1970] 1 SCR 523. The presumption can be displaced by agreement between the parties.

[56] Contract Act, s 59.

[57] ibid s 60 expressly makes this clear. The underlying principle seems to be that limitation precludes the remedy but does not extinguish the right: *BK Educational Services v Gupta* (2019) 11 SCC 633.

[58] See Pollock and Mulla, *The Indian Contract Act* (13th edn) (n 11) 1220.

view, the creditor cannot extend limitation in respect of all outstanding debts: what section 60 entitles the creditor to do is to apply 'the payment to any lawful debt . . . whether its recovery is or is not barred (due to limitation)'. In support of this view, the language does not speak of multiple debts at all. However, it is submitted that the contrary view is better.[59] First, section 60 applies only if the debtor fails to have made his/her choice clear under section 59. If the debtor fails to do so, there is no injustice in giving greater scope to the creditor to do as he or she pleases to place him- or herself in the most advantageous position.[60] Second, there is no difficulty posed by the use of the singular 'the payment' and 'debt': legal provisions are often interpreted such that the singular includes the plural.[61] Third, there is no basis to suggest that the payment cannot be split up: indeed, if neither the debtor nor the creditor makes any choice, the default position in section 61 is that the payment is to be applied chronologically, but 'if the debts are of equal standing, the payment shall be applied in discharge of each proportionately'. Thus, there cannot be said to be any conceptual hurdle in appropriating one payment to multiple debts.

Complexities may also arise when sums are expressed in foreign currency. Suppose a contract is entered into on 1 January 2020, which involves a payment of US$ 100 on 1 January 2022, then is the exchange rate applicable that of 2020 or of 2022? Additionally, if there is a delayed payment, then is the relevant date to be taken as the date on which the payment is due or the one on which the payment actually takes place? And what if there is no payment, and the claimant is driven to the courts: is the appropriate date then the date of commencement of action, the date of the decree, the date when execution is awarded, or the date when the decreed amount is actually realised? It would appear that the choice between the date of contract and the date of payment is simply a matter of interpretation: is the obligation one to pay US$ 100 on the fixed date, or is the obligation to pay the value of what is today US$ 100 on the fixed date? When the obligation is fixed in terms of amounts and dates specifically, it would appear that the obligation would generally be the former one. In that case, the appropriate date of conversion would be the date on which the payment is due. In relation to the choice between the various dates possible in the case of breaches, the Supreme Court has held that the appropriate date of conversion would be the date of the decree.[62]

It will be apparent from what was said above that most issues relating to how performance should happen may be resolved by interpreting the agreed terms of the

[59] This contrary view in favour of the creditor was preferred in *Nath v Narain* AIR 1961 Raj 154.

[60] *Shah v Chand* AIR 1940 PC 63 (on the point that if the election is with the creditor, there can be no rigid rule, but the matter must depend entirely on the volition of the creditor).

[61] General Clauses Act 1897, s 13(2). The General Clauses Act should apply even in the interpretation of pre-1897 legislations because it was purely a consolidating enactment and not intended to effect any change in the prior law. In particular, s 13 applies to 'all' central enactments and not just to those enacted after 1897.

[62] *Forasol v Oil & Natural Gas Commission* AIR 1984 SC 241. The answer reached by the House of Lords on these issues in *Miliangos v George Frank Ltd* (1975) 3 All ER 801 was rejected as being unsuited for Indian conditions: the date on which execution is permitted by the executing court would not be workable in India due to the fact that, in the Indian procedural scheme, execution can only issue for a sum that has been expressed in Indian currency, and the executing court cannot fix the sum at the time of execution. A subsequent decision of the Supreme Court has expressly rejected a request that the principle in *Forasol* be reconsidered: *Renusagar Power v General Electric* AIR 1994 SC 860.

contract. Against that backdrop, we can now turn to when a contract need *not* be performed and what happens if a contract is not performed.

IV. Justifications for Non-performance

Other than the case of frustration or the case where a contract is rescinded *ab initio* (typically due to defective consent at the inception of the contract), non-performance may be justified in several other situations as well. We will consider a few of these situations in this section. Situations where a contract need not be performed because it can be validly terminated are considered in section V below.

1. Novation and Alteration

It stands to reason that if parties have agreed to do something, they should also be able to agree that that thing need not be done or that a different thing be done instead. Section 62 of the Contract Act provides that the original contract need not be performed if the parties agree[63] to substitute a new contract for an existing contract or to rescind or alter it. There must be a meeting of minds, and all elements of a new contract must be satisfied; save that putting an end to mutual obligations under the old contract may, in itself, amount to consideration for the new agreement.[64] Novation may occur by the introduction of new parties altogether (with the consent of all existing parties) or by the agreement of new terms between the same parties such that the new terms amount to a wholesale substitution of the earlier agreement.[65] The novated agreement, then, is an independent agreement between the parties. However, there is no novation—but merely an alteration of the existing contract—if the parties agree to vary some of the terms but without substituting or replacing the entire contract.[66] The difference may often have practical consequences. Thus, if a contract contains an exclusive jurisdiction clause, the efficacy of that clause may well depend on whether the subsequent agreement between the parties is a novation or merely an alteration.[67] Whether there is, indeed, a novation or not depends on the intention of the parties (ascertained objectively).

[63] A new agreement for variation may not be necessary if a contract gives a specific power of unilateral variation to one of the parties. In *Build India v Union of India* (2002) 5 SCC 433, it was held that, in principle, such a unilateral variation clause would be effective. But it would seem that this must usually be an express clause in the original contract. It is difficult to think of cases where a power of unilateral variation may arise as an implied term of the contract.

[64] See *Gouri Dutt Ganesh Lall Firm v Madho Prasad* AIR 1943 PC 147.

[65] Unless, of course, a contract gives a specific power of unilateral variation to one of the parties. It was held, in *Build India* (n 63), that, in principle, such a unilateral variation clause would be effective.

[66] The mere description by the parties as 'variation' or 'novation' is not determinative of the matter: *Andheri Bridge View Co-op Housing Society v Deo* AIR 1991 Bom 129.

[67] See *Young Achievers v IMS Learning Resources* (2013) 10 SCC 535.

Contracts sometimes have a 'no oral variation' clause: the efficacy of such clauses has been called into question in various jurisdictions. One argument is that even if there is a 'no oral variation' clause, why can parties not alter that clause itself orally and then alter the rest of the contract?[68] This view has been rejected at the highest level in England and Wales in *Rock Advertising*,[69] where the UK Supreme Court confirmed the effectiveness of 'no oral variation' clauses. *Rock Advertising* was cited before the Bombay High Court in a challenge to an arbitral award holding that a 'no oral variation' clause was ineffective. Having considered *Rock Advertising*, the Court held:

> It is one thing to say that 'no oral modification' clause, such as what we are concerned with in the present case, is by itself enforceable and should be ordinarily honoured, but quite another to say that *the parties having not only made a variation in a manner different from the one agreed to, but having acted in pursuance of such variation, the party objecting to such variation later would be precluded by its conduct from relying on a 'no oral modification' clause* included in the original contract. There is no contradiction between the two propositions; both may well hold good.[70]

The Bombay High Court did not really have to go into much detail on this issue. On the facts before the High Court, the supplier was supplying goods to the purchaser at an agreed rate. The arbitrator found that there was an oral variation of the rate and also found that, in pursuance of that variation, there were some payments at the varied rate made by the purchaser. In those circumstances, it was no longer open to rely on the 'no oral variation' clause. The Court was hearing a challenge to an arbitral award and only had to satisfy itself that there was no patent illegality on the face of the award. In the circumstances of the case, the conclusion of the High Court that the award of the arbitrator required no interference is unsurprising.

One alternative way to understand the result is that a 'no oral variation' clause is effective, but a party may choose to 'waive' or dispense with its right to enforce that clause. On that view, a waiver may be established not simply by parties orally agreeing to waive the 'no oral variation' clause but, equally, by acting in furtherance of the oral variation. Had there been no payment at the varied rate whatsoever, it would perhaps have been open to the purchaser to contend that the variation was ineffective.

[68] *Beatty v Guggenheim Exploration* (1919) 225 NY 380.

[69] *Rock Advertising v MWB Business Exchange Centres* [2018] UKSC 24, [2019] AC 119.

[70] *John Distilleries v Brihan Maharashtra Sugar Syndicate* 2019 SCC OnLine Bom 67, [6] (emphasis added). Questions of how deviations from a 'no oral variation' can be proved—particularly in view of the parol evidence rule in the Indian Evidence Act—appear not to have been considered in any Indian court. See G Yihan, Chapter 3 of this volume for a discussion on how principles of the Evidence Act have a bearing on interpretation of contracts generally.

2. Dispensation or Remission of Performance

Section 63 of the Contract Act reads,

> Every promisee may dispense with or may remit, wholly or in part, the performance of the promise made to him, or may extend the time for performance, or may accept instead of it any satisfaction which he thinks fit.

This section marks a break with English law;[71] and the principle of *Foakes v Beer* is not applicable in India.[72] The Privy Council has confirmed that unilateral remission or dispensation is sufficient to discharge performance of the balance promise, and there does not need to be any consideration or agreement between the parties in this regard.[73] It is also clear that dispensations under this section—unlike the case of novation—do not result in a new agreement between the parties.[74]

There has been some confusion about whether this section applies to unilateral extensions of time for performance.[75] The language of the section clearly contemplates extensions of time and does not prescribe any different requirement in that regard. But extensions of time have, nonetheless, troubled the courts.

In *Patel v Lalbhai Trikumlal Mills*,[76] the Supreme Court considered a situation where the appellant had placed an order with the respondent for the purchase of certain goods. The goods were agreed to be delivered in the months of September and October 1942. In August 1942, however, workers at the respondent's unit went on strike in support of the then raging Quit India movement. The respondent wrote to the appellant that time for delivery should be automatically understood as being extended by the period during which the operations had ceased. Normal working resumed in November 1942. The appellant demanded delivery in December 1942 and January 1943, but the respondent refused to deliver. A suit for damages was filed in January 1946. Whether the suit was within limitation or not turned on whether there was an extension of the time for performance (such that the breach did not occur in October 1942 but occurred only in December or later). The appellant relied on section 63 in support of its contention that time had been extended. Here, the 'extension' of time was not a unilateral dispensation or remission by the *promisee*. The relevant promise was the promise to deliver goods: the promisor was the respondent and the promisee was the appellant. It was the promisor that had sought to extend time: the promisee was only latching on to this to strategically overcome objections that the suit was barred by limitation.

[71] This has been the understanding from the very inception of the Act; see W Stokes, *Anglo-Indian Codes* (Clarendon Press 1888) 582.

[72] *Foakes v Beer* [1881–85] All ER Rep 106.

[73] *Firm Chunna Mal v Firm Mool Chand* AIR 1928 PC 99. This has also been confirmed by the Supreme Court: *Chatterjee v Rani* (1969) 3 SCC 445; *Gopal v State of Punjab* (1973) 1 SCC 204.

[74] Thus, if time to perform a contract is extended, it may attract s 63: but the underlying agreement itself is not superseded by any fresh agreement: a dispute resolution clause in the original agreement will therefore continue to be applicable. If an entirely new bargain is struck between the parties, that would, however, amount to novation and be governed by the principles under section 62. See *Bhairadan v Hoare Miller & Co* (1914) 41 Cal 35. See also *Citibank v Standard Chartered Bank* (n 27) (distinction between ss 62 and 63).

[75] Also see the discussion on s 55 in section V below.

[76] *Patel v Lalbhai Trikumlal Mills* AIR 1958 SC 512.

Section 63 ought not to apply in such a case at all: section 63 in terms applies when the promisee dispenses performance; and it is not a license for the promisee to unilaterally extend time in its own favour without expressly agreeing to the promisor's request for extension. In order to show that there was an extension of time in this case, therefore, it was essential to show that there was, indeed, an agreement between the parties resulting in an extension. Surely, the promisee cannot sit on the promisor's request for extension (and leave it open to argue that it had never agreed to such a request) and yet, when the time to sue comes, say that time has been extended and the 'breach' therefore happened later than the due date under the contract.

On the facts, the Supreme Court held that the 'agreement' between the parties was vague and therefore unenforceable.[77] The Supreme Court, it is respectfully submitted, reached the correct result that there was no extension; but some potential for confusion crept into the law when the Court held, in its reasons,

> The true legal position in regard to the extension of time for the performance of a contract is quite clear under section 63 of the Indian Contract Act. Every promisee, as the section provides, may extend time for the performance of the contract. The *question as to how extension of time may be agreed upon* by the parties has been the subject-matter of some argument at the Bar in the present appeal. *There can be no doubt, we think, that both the buyer and the seller must agree to extend time for the delivery of goods. It would not be open to the promise by his unilateral act to extend the time for performance of his own accord for his own benefit*... Forbearance on, the part of the buyer to make a demand for the delivery of goods on the due date as fixed in the original contract may conceivably be relevant on the question of the intention of the buyer to accept the seller's proposal to extend time. It would be difficult to lay down any hard and fast rule about the requirements of proof of such an agreement. It would naturally be a question of fact in each case to be determined in the light of evidence adduced by the parties.[78]

This reasoning is similar to what was said by the Bombay High Court in an earlier case:

> Under section 63 of the Indian Contract Act, the promisee may make certain concessions to the promisor which are advantageous to the promisor, and one of them is that he may extend the time for such performance. But it is clear again that *such an extension of time cannot be a unilateral extension on the part of the promisee. It is only at the request of the promisor that the promisee may agree to extend the time of performance and thereby bring about an agreement for extension of time.* Therefore it is only as a result of the operation of section 63 of the Indian Contract Act that the time for the performance of the contract can be extended and that time can only be extended by an agreement arrived at between the promisor and the promisee.[79]

[77] The agreement was held to be void under the Contract Act, s 29.
[78] *Patel v Lalhai Trikumlal Mills* (n 76) [8] (emphasis added).
[79] *Mangturam v Tanumal* (1945) 47 Bom LR 719, [16] (Chagla J) (emphasis added).

This reasoning does not sit easily with the proposition that section 63 requires neither consideration nor agreement. In a subsequent decision,[80] the Supreme Court has held that it is always open to the promisee to extend time for the promisor's performance unilaterally when the extension is for the benefit of the promisor. This result follows from the plain language of the section.

But does this mean that purchasers can effectively wriggle out of the law of limitation at any time by claiming to be 'extending' time for performance for the sellers' benefit? Surely, the position cannot be that limitation periods extend indefinitely in this way. The answer is perhaps that in so far as section 63 speaks of extending the time for performance, it is implicit that the section applies only so far as it benefits the promisor. The thrust of the Supreme Court's reasoning in *Patel* must therefore be seen in the following statement: 'It would not be open to the promisee by his unilateral act to extend the time for performance of his own accord *for his own benefit*' (emphasis added). If the purpose behind granting the extension is to obtain a benefit for oneself,[81] then the extension cannot be termed as being within the scope of section 63. Thus, an 'extension' granted to the seller by the purchaser, but with a view to claiming heavier damages (on the footing of changed market rates on the 'new' date of performance) is no real 'extension' within the meaning of section 63: in the event of a breach of this extended date, the purchaser will be able to claim damages based only on the original date of performance.[82]

Another limitation was read in to section 63 by the Supreme Court in *Sasan Power*: waiver of rights under section 63 would not be given effect if the waiver affects public interest.[83] In that case, a waiver of certain terms of a power purchase agreement was considered as not being effective, on the basis that the waiver would result in an adverse effect on electricity tariffs, and consequently not be in the public interest: 'if there is any element of public interest involved, the court steps in to thwart any waiver which may be contrary to such public interest'.[84]

With great respect, it is submitted that this 'public interest' exception—especially one framed in the broad terms used by the Court—may need reconsideration. The Court relied on three prior decisions to hold that a 'public interest' exception exists; but those decisions turn on the question of whether rights granted under a statute can be waived or not. In *Lachoo v Shyam*,[85] the Court considered an agreement between a tenant and a landlord, where the landlord had agreed to waive some rights granted to the landlord under a statutory provision. The landlord sought to avoid the waiver on the ground that the waiver was contrary to the statutory rights of the landlord. The Court rejected the argument of the landlord and, in doing so, stated that there is no

[80] *Kailash Nath Associates v Delhi Development Authority* (2015) 4 SCC 136.

[81] The fact that an extension is sought for by the promisor and acceded to would perhaps indicate that the purpose of granting the extension was, indeed, to benefit the promisor and not the promisee; see *Bramanand v Muthugopal* (2005) 12 SCC 764.

[82] *Sundareswaran v Sri Krishna Refineries* AIR 1977 Mad 109. See also the Contract Act, s 55.

[83] *All India Power Engineer Federation v Sasan Power* (2017) 1 SCC 487.

[84] ibid [25].

[85] *Lachoo v Shyam* (1971) 1 SCC 619.

bar on waiving benefits of agreements or rules of law made to protect private interests. In *Indira v Nandkishore*,[86] the Court stated that it may be difficult to set up estoppel as a defence in a case where the general welfare of society was in question. On the facts, estoppel was held to be a valid defence against a right of pre-emption under a local enactment. There was no discussion on 'public interest' in the context of waiver of contractual rights at all. And finally, in *Krishna v Purna Theatre*,[87] the question was whether the rights of workmen under section 25F of the Industrial Disputes Act could be waived. On the facts, it was held that no such waiver was possible because the plea as to waiver was not taken at first instance: such a plea could not be raised for the first time in appeal. The decision of the Court does not rest on any 'public interest' exception. In any case, section 25F requires certain measures to be taken before retrenchment of workmen, including notice to the workmen, compensation, and notice to the relevant government. This requirement has been consistently held to be mandatory. Thus, an agreement to waive this requirement would be hit simply by the illegality/public policy bars without raising any independent 'public interest' exception to the waiver of contractual rights.

To put matters at the lowest, none of the three decisions involved the 'public interest' exception being applied to negate a waiver of contractual rights. It is difficult to see what role such an exception can have in private contracts.[88] A case can perhaps be made for a narrower exception. Let us assume that there is a contract between a company and a franchisee, which contains a non-compete clause in favour of the franchisor but grants an exclusive franchise over a certain geographical area to the franchisee. An outright non-compete clause may be invalid under section 27 of the Act; but a non-compete clause limited to the term of the franchise may be valid.[89] In such circumstances, it may be possible to contend that a waiver on the part of the franchisee of his/her right to the franchise may be ineffective: the waiver may result in the agreement effectively being transformed into one hit by section 27 of the Act. Thus, where the contract would (after waiver of one party's rights) result in invalidity under another clause (section 27 or perhaps section 23), then it may potentially be a justification for a court holding such a waiver to be non-effective. But the justification is perhaps that such contracts contain cross-bargains that are not really severable from one another.

An independent 'public interest' exception may be prone to creating uncertainty and does not appear to promote coherence in this area of law. It is respectfully submitted that this aspect of the matter may need to be revisited by the Supreme Court.

86 *Indira v Nandkishore* (1990) 4 SCC 668.

87 *Krishna v Purna Theatre* (2004) 8 SCC 229.

88 This is not to say that the decision in *Sasan Power* (n 83) itself was wrong: it was also held on facts that there was no clear waiver. Further, a power purchase agreement is a specific type of contract governed by a specific statutory regime: the Court was not hearing a pure contractual dispute. This, with respect, is an additional reason why its discussion of s 63 may need to be revisited.

89 The point of this example presently is only to indicate the possible contours of an exception to s 63. A detailed analysis of the law on restraint of trade can be found in T Zhong Xing and U Varottil, Chapter 12 of this volume.

3. Refusal to Accept Performance; or Neglect/Refusal to Afford Reasonable Facilities for Performance

Section 67 of the Contract Act specifies that if a promisee neglects or refuses to afford the promisor reasonable facilities for performance, then the promisor's non-performance caused by such neglect or refusal is excused. So too, where a promisor offers to perform but the promisee refuses to accept the offer of performance, the promisor is no longer responsible for the non-performance. This is made clear by section 38. For the principle of section 38 to apply, the offer of performance must be (a) unconditional; (b) made at a proper time and place and under circumstances where the promisee has a reasonable opportunity of ascertaining that the promisor is able and willing to perform; and (c) in cases where the offer is of performance by delivery, the promisee must have a reasonable opportunity of inspecting the thing to be delivered.

Having looked at some instances where non-performance is excused, we can now turn to the question of what happens in the absence of such excuse.

V. Termination for Breach

A leading (English law) textbook defines a breach of contract as follows:

> a breach of contract is committed when a party without lawful excuse fails or refuses to perform what is due from him under the contract, or performs defectively or incapacitates himself from performing.[90]

Thus, when there is no performance (or a refusal to perform), and there is no valid reason for this failure, a contract is breached. Breach of the primary contractual obligation will generally give rise to a secondary obligation in damages. But, in some situations, a breach by one party will also entitle the innocent party to put an end to the contract.

1. Termination vis-à-vis Rescission

English common law today clearly recognises the 'distinction between contracts terminated de futuro for breach and those rescinded ab initio for initial invalidating cause'.[91] This chapter is concerned essentially with termination for breach.[92] The enunciation of the distinction, however, is a relatively recent development in the common

[90] E Peel (ed), *Treitel on the Law of Contract* (14th edn, Sweet & Maxwell 2015) [17-049].
[91] D O'Sullivan, S Elliott, and R Zakrezewski, *The Law of Rescission* (2nd edn, OUP 2014) [3.30].
[92] Rescission is considered in S Elliott KC and D Behl, Chapter 19 of this volume.

law: the law can be taken as being settled only in the early 1980s.[93] Given this, it is not really surprising that the Contract Act does not clearly distinguish between the two concepts.

Indeed, one could be forgiven for thinking that the Act uses different words to mean the same thing and the same words to mean different things. Thus, section 39 says that when a party to a contract has refused to perform (or disabled him- or herself from performing) the promise, the promisee 'may put an end to the contract'. Under Illustration (a), if a singer enters into a contract with a theatre manager to perform at the theatre for two nights every week and on the sixth night absents herself, then the manager is at liberty to put an end to the contract. Section 55 notes that if time is of the essence of the contract and the promisor fails to perform on time, then the contract 'becomes voidable' at the option of the promisee. Section 64 notes that a person 'rescinding' a voidable contract must restore benefits received under the contract to the other party. Section 65 notes that when a contract 'is discovered to be void . . . or becomes void', any person who has received any advantage under such agreement is bound to restore it, or to make compensation for it, to the person from whom he or she has received it. Illustration (c) to this section is similar to the illustration about the singer and the manager but clarifies that the theatre manager must pay the singer for the five nights which she had sung. Section 75 then provides that a person who 'rightfully rescinds' a contract is entitled to compensation for damage sustained through the non-fulfilment. The illustration carries the singer–theatre example further and notes that the theatre is entitled to claim compensation from the singer.

The confusion arising from the language was highlighted by the *Privy Council* in *Muralidhar Chatterjee*.[94] Chatterjee was a distributor of films. He entered into a contract with the International Film Company (IFC), under which he was to maintain, at his own cost, IFC's office in Calcutta. IFC agreed to deliver to him the prints for new cinematographic films and to pay royalties to the producer of the films. Chatterjee was to pay IFC certain amounts for each film, and the print was to be delivered within a few weeks of the payment. There was also a formula in the contract for sharing of the revenues from the film screenings between Chatterjee and IFC. Chatterjee paid IFC Rs 4,000 on account for two films. However, claiming that IFC was delaying delivery, Chatterjee sought to put an end to the contract. He claimed that he was entitled to both the refund of Rs 4,000 together with recoupment of expenses incurred and lost profits of Rs 3,000. IFC denied that it had committed any breach and instead averred that Chatterjee had breached the contract, for which breach it reserved its rights to sue in damages. At trial, it was found that IFC had not committed any breach. However, the trial judge passed a decree for Rs 4,000 on the basis that Chatterjee had a valid claim to the Rs 4,000 under section 64 of the Act. The Appeal Court reversed this decree, holding that section 64 had no application to cases of rescission under section

[93] O'Sullivan, Elliott, and Zakrezewski (n 91) [1.08], referring to academic literature in the 1970s and noting that the law was 'definitively restated' in *Johnson v Agnew* [1980] AC 367.

[94] *Chatterjee v International Film Co* AIR 1943 PC 34, (1943) 56 LW 283.

39. Chatterjee carried the matter to the Privy Council. He no longer contended that IFC was in breach, but his appeal was confined to the recovery of Rs 4,000 decreed to him at first instance. It was contended on behalf of Chatterjee before the Judicial Committee that he was entitled to the Rs 4,000 both under section 64 and also 'on general principles of law': assuming Chatterjee was in breach, IFC would be entitled to compensation for breach but allowing it to retain the Rs 4,000 would amount to unjust enrichment. In counsel's words, '[i]t is not the policy of the law to enrich a party to a contract, but merely to compensate him if he has suffered any damages'. IFC contended that the Rs 4,000 had, indeed, been paid to them: but IFC had used that to procure the positives of two films and had rendered an account of the expenses to Chatterjee. As the amounts had already been used in furtherance of the contract, there could be no liability to refund. The Judicial Committee accepted that the language of the statute gave rise to problems of construction, but it held:

> no view which can be taken upon these matters can provide an escape from the conclusion that a liability to make restitution attaches to the party putting an end to a contract under s 39 . . .
>
> . . . From these sections it must be conceded that, as language is used in this Act, the right to treat a contract as voidable and to rescind it may be accompanied by a right to recover damages for the wrongful act which grounds the right of rescission. The ordinary notion of an English lawyer that the right to recover damages must be based upon a valid and subsisting contract, and that a plaintiff could not declare upon a contract as being void, cannot be taken as a guide to the use of the words "void" and "voidable" in the Indian Statute . . .
>
> . . . Their Lordships are not concerned to make the Act agree in its results with the English law . . . the fact that a party to a contract is in default affords good reason why he should pay damages, but further exaction is not justified by his default. Where a payment has been made under a contract which has—for whatever reason—become void, the duty of restitution would seem to emerge. A cross claim for damages stands upon an independent footing, though it arises out of the same contract and can be set off.[95]

The appeal was accordingly allowed, but it was directed that IFC would be entitled to raise its claims in damages by way of set-off against the Rs 4,000.

Stepping back to the language of the sections, it is possible to analyse the position in a manner compatible with the distinction between termination for breach and rescission *ab initio*. Thus, if one looks at the illustrations to sections 39, 65, and 75, it is clear that the singer has committed a breach and repudiated the contract. The theatre manager can accept the breach and put the contract to an end. The singer is, nonetheless, entitled to be paid for the first five days at the contractual rate. And the theatre owner is entitled to claim compensation for breach. The difficulty is that section 65 is not restricted

[95] ibid 287–88.

only to such situations: it also applies to contracts that are *ab initio* void. One solution could be this: section 65 says, 'when an agreement is discovered to be void, or when a contract becomes void', then the person receiving an advantage is bound to 'restore it, or make compensation for it'. One could conceivably suggest that when an agreement is 'discovered to be void' (ie is avoided *ab initio*), then the benefit must be restored as a matter of restitution. On the other hand, when a contract 'becomes void' in the sense that it is terminated, future non-performance is at an end, but past performance is not wiped away, and hence, compensation must be paid for that earlier performance.

The distinction between termination for breach and rescission *ab initio* has been accepted in Malaysia,[96] where the relevant Act[97] is similar to the Indian Act. It has been held there at the highest level:

> the decision in Muralidhar Chatterjee v. International Film Co Ltd. is readily explainable on the basis of the doctrine of restitution. There the plaintiff had paid moneys to the defendants but had received nothing in return. It would be an unjust enrichment to have permitted the defendants to keep the money when they had put an end to the contract. However, the defendants had a valid counterclaim for damages for breach of contract against the plaintiff. And they would, in recovering those damages, be obliged to give the plaintiff credit for the monies he had already paid. The true principle is this. A contract breaker must pay damages to the innocent party. However, if he has made any payment under the contract (not being a true deposit for the purchase of movable or immovable property) the contract breaker is entitled to have that payment set off against the damages he has to pay. However, he cannot seek to recover any benefit he may have conferred upon the innocent party where he is himself guilty of a breach of contract. Were it otherwise, a contract breaker will be in a position to take advantage of his own wrong. This is against principle and the policy of the law. In my judgment Muralidhar Chatterjee v. International Film Co Ltd. does not decide any opposite principle.[98]

In this chapter, the terminology of 'termination' is used to refer to the act of 'putting an end' to the contract for breach.[99]

[96] The following statement in *Johnson v Agnew* (n 93) has been expressly adopted in that country in this context in *Abdul Razak v Shah Alam Properties* (1999) 2 MLJ 500 (Gopal Sri Ram JCA):

> In the case of an accepted repudiatory breach the contract has come into existence but has been put an end to or discharged. Whatever contrary indications may be disinterred from old authorities, it is now quite clear, under the general law of contract, that acceptance of a repudiatory breach does not bring about 'rescission ab initio'.

[97] Contract Act 1950 (Malaysia). The Malaysian Act, s 40 corresponds to the Indian Act, s 39. The Malaysian Act, s 66 corresponds to the Indian Act, s 65. The Malaysian Act, s 76 corresponds to the Indian Act, s 75. The singer–theatre illustration is found in all these sections.

[98] *Berjaya Times Squares v M Concept* 2009 SCC OnLine MYFC 82, [33] (Malaysian Federal Court) (Gopal Sri Ram FCJ). The learned judge appears to have considered that Indian decisions after *Chatterjee v International Film Co* (n 94) do not detract from this proposition: in particular, he refers to *Chettiar v Mooppannar* AIR 1953 Mad 380 and *Shree Hanuman Cotton Mills v Tata Air Craft* (1969) 3 SCC 522.

[99] In *Damodar Valley Corporation v Kar* (1974) 1 SCC 141, the Supreme Court has held (holding that an arbitration clause can be relied on even after the agreement has been terminated for breach):

> in certain circumstances, it may be that there has been a termination of the contract unilaterally and as a consequence the parties may agree to rescind the contract. In such a situation the rescission would

2. Breaches Giving Rise to a Right to Terminate

In the case of anticipatory breaches,[100] there is no compulsion that the innocent party must terminate the contract: the innocent party may choose to keep the contract alive and sue for the agreed sum (or for specific performance) when performance becomes due.[101] It is, of course, not each and every breach that gives rise to a right to the innocent party to terminate the contract. A repudiation of a contract by a party is a 'serious matter, not to be lightly found or inferred'.[102] In the language of section 39, there must be a 'refusal to perform . . . or [disabling oneself] from performing . . . promise in its entirety'.

The point that not all breaches entitle the aggrieved party to terminate is plain from other provisions as well. Section 55 grants the right to terminate, in case of delay, only if time is of the essence. Section 12 of the Sale of Goods Act 1930 adopts the terminology of 'condition' and 'warranty': a condition is a stipulation 'essential to the main purpose of the contract' and a warranty is a stipulation 'collateral to the main purpose of the contract'. Breach of a condition expressly gives rise to treat the contract as repudiated, while breach of a warranty expressly does not.[103] Thus, it is clear that not all breaches give rise to the right to terminate the contract.

The position on whether Indian law recognises the tripartite division of terms (into conditions, warranties, and innominate/intermediate terms) is not clear. The Sale of Goods Act divides terms into 'conditions' and 'warranties' based on whether the term is essential or collateral to the main purpose of the contract; but those provisions do not mean that there can be no scope for the tripartite approach being adopted in general law. The law laid down in *Hong Kong Fir Shipping*[104] was accepted as applicable in India by the Delhi High Court.[105] However, the result in that case did not depend on this issue. Further, the Delhi High Court's summary of the principles in that case is not entirely illuminating. For instance, the Court appears, at one place, to suggest that in assessing the validity of termination, relevant considerations include, among others, 'whether the party seeking termination of the contract for any breach, can be

put an end to the performance of the contract in future, but it may remain alive for claiming damages either for previous breaches or for the breach which constituted the termination.

[100] See *Nandi v Acharjya* AIR 1924 Cal 185, applying *Hochster v de la Tour* 95 RR 747.

[101] If this course of action is chosen, then the innocent party will have to be at least ready and willing to perform its future obligations: see *Wadhwa v Chakroberty* (1989) 1 SCC 76. The principles governing the award of an agreed sum/suits for price, the relevance of the principle of *White & Carter v McGregor* (1962) AC 413 in Indian law, and any limitations on the right of the innocent party to keep the contract alive, are discussed in N Venkatesan, Chapter 18 of this volume.

[102] *Parulekar v Sakal Papers* (2005) 11 SCC 73.

[103] Sale of Goods Act 1930, ss 12(2) and 12(3). The nomenclature of 'condition' or 'warranty' is, in itself, not conclusive of the matter: ibid s 12(4).

[104] *Hong Kong Fir Shipping v Kawasaki Kisen Kaisha* [1961] EWCA Civ 7, [1962] 2 QB 26.

[105] *Unikol Bottlers v Dhillon Kool Drinks* AIR 1995 Del 25. The Court did not expressly cite *Hong Kong Fir* (n 104), but it suggested that the tripartite division of terms between conditions, warranties, and innominate terms is part of Indian law.

compensated with damages for that breach'. If this consideration is meant to suggest that 'adequacy of damages' is a bar to *termination*, that is plainly incorrect.

A leading commentary on the Contract Act of Myanmar—which has the same text as the Indian Act—suggests that the tripartite division of terms is not part of Myanmar law but that reform in this regard is perhaps desirable.[106] In India, the Supreme Court appears to have accepted the principle that 'one way of looking at the matter would be to ask whether the party in breach has by its breach produced a situation fundamentally different from anything which the parties as reasonable men have contemplated when the contract was made'.[107] The language of 'by its breach . . . produced a situation' can be read as meaning that what matters is not the breach on its own but the effect produced as a result.[108]

It is respectfully submitted that there is scope for Indian law to be developed on the lines noted by Lord Diplock in *Hong Kong Fir Shipping*. Lord Diplock said, in that case,

> Once it is appreciated that it is the event and not the fact that the event is a result of a breach of contract which relieves the party not in default of further performance of his obligations two consequences follow. (1) The test whether the event relied upon has this consequence is the same whether the event is the result of the other party's breach of contract or not . . . (2) The question whether an event which is the result of the other party's breach of contract has this consequence cannot be answered by treating all contractual undertakings as falling into one of two separate categories: 'conditions' the breach of which gives rise to an event which relieves the party not in default of further performance of his obligations, and 'warranties' the breach of which does not give rise to such an event . . . here are, however, many contractual undertakings of a more complex character which cannot be categorised as being 'conditions' or 'warranties' . . . Of such undertakings all that can be predicated is that some breaches will and others will not give rise to an event which will deprive the party not in default of substantially the whole benefit which it was intended that he should obtain from the contract.[109]

In a recent decision, the Supreme Court had occasion to clarify the relevant principles further.[110] An insurance policy contained a term that the insured should not give a lift to any other person in the insured vehicle. This term was breached. The insurer sought to terminate the policy due to this breach. The Supreme Court refused to accept this, holding, 'the violation . . . should be . . . a fundamental breach . . . the insurance company . . . must show that the breach of the policy is so fundamental in nature that it brings the contract to an end'.[111] With respect, while the result is, indeed, justified,

[106] Briggs and Burrows (n 11) 175–76.
[107] *HPA International v Daswani* (2004) 6 SCC 537; *MSEDCL v Datar Switchgear* (2018) 3 SCC 133, citing *Suisse Atlantique Société d'Armament SA v NV Rotterdamsche Kolen Centrale* [1967] 1 AC 361.
[108] *Hong Kong Fir* (n 104).
[109] ibid.
[110] *Singh v National Insurance* (2018) 2 SCC 108.
[111] ibid [5].

the reasoning somewhat begs the question: it does not clarify what type of breach is regarded as being 'so fundamental'. It is hoped that the Supreme Court clarifies that 'fundamental breach' is to be understood in Indian law in a manner similar to that in English law:

> Where the event resulting from the failure by one party to perform a primary obligation has the effect of depriving the other party of substantially the whole benefit which it was the intention of the parties that he should obtain from the contract, the party not in default may elect to put an end to all primary obligations of both parties remaining unperformed. (If the expression 'fundamental breach' is to be retained, it should, in the interests of clarity, be confined to this . . .).[112]

3. Delay: 'Time of the Essence'

Finally, section 55 of the Contract Act provides further guidance for breaches on account of delayed performance in cases of contracts where the time to perform is specified. The right to terminate arises if it was intended that time is of the essence of the contract. If it was not so intended, then there is a right to claim compensation but no right to terminate. The question turns on whether time is of the essence or not. The Supreme Court has clarified the relevant principles for ascertaining when time is of the essence in *Hind Construction Contractors v State of Maharashtra*.[113] The test for determining the essence of the contract is a question of intention to be gathered from the terms of the contract. Mere description by the parties that time is of the essence is not conclusive (though an emphatic declaration must be entitled to some weight, of course). The presence of clauses such as those providing for extension of time—or clauses prescribing specific 'penalties' on a daily or weekly basis for delays—would suggest that time was not considered to be of the essence. The normal presumption is that time is not of the essence in contracts for the sale of immovable property:[114] however, there have been calls for reconsidering this presumption.[115]

Where a contract is one where time is not of the essence, it is possible for a party in case of delay by the other party to give notice requiring the other party to perform within reasonable time. In such a case, time will then be considered to be of the essence.[116] This principle is not the same as a unilateral variation to the contract. Rather, this principle appears to be recognising that, even if time is not of the essence, that is not an excuse to allow one party to delay performance beyond all reasonable limits. If performance is not forthcoming, principles analogous to those contained in section 39

[112] *Photo Production v Securicor* [1980] AC 827.

[113] *Hind Construction Contractors v State of Maharashtra* (1979) 2 SCC 70. See also *McDermott International v Burn Standard* (2006) 11 SCC 181.

[114] *Chaturvedi v Shastri* (1977) 2 SCC 539. See also *Rani v Rani* (1993) 1 SCC 519.

[115] Particularly in the context of urban land, where India has seen enormous price variations in short time periods: see *Vidyanadan v Vairavan* (1997) 3 SCC 1.

[116] See *Pillai v Nadar* AIR 1967 SC 868, applying *Stickney v Keeble* [1915] AC 386.

may justify termination by the innocent party: the mechanism of giving notice to make time of the essence may simply be the mechanism to achieve this result.

VI. Conclusion

It is true that the Contract Act—in Part IV—has codified the law governing performance and termination to a large extent. However, a survey of how the Act has been applied in the 150 years of its existence may call into question whether codification itself can be a panacea to all problems. Writing in 1909 in the preface to the second edition of Pollock and Mulla, Sir Frederick Pollock commented,

> This is not the season to complain of the Government of India for not having leisure to undertake a thorough revision of the Contract Act. One can only repeat that it has remained unrevised longer than any codifying Act ought, and hope that the Legislative Department will not lose sight of the matter.[117]

There have, of course, been sporadic efforts at reform; but it is perhaps time to acknowledge that the learnings of one-and-a-half centuries need not all be rejected. Of course, in several places, the drafting leaves ambiguities of interpretation that provide room for courts to step in. In other places, there is scope for the principles underlying various provisions to be explained further. The continued role and value of courts in rationalising and ordering the foundational principles on a principled basis cannot be underestimated, even after 150 years.

[117] Pollock and Mulla, *The Indian Contract Act* (2nd edn) (n 6) iii.

14

Frustration

Nilima Bhadbhade

I. Introduction

The law relating to frustration of contracts discharges a promisor when subsequent events or circumstances beyond the promisor's control make its performance impossible or substantially frustrate the principal purpose of the contract.[1] Frustration ends the contract prospectively and relieves a party from that party's contractual obligations.

This doctrine of frustration (the 'doctrine') reconciles the rule of absolute contracts with the need for making exceptions to meet the demands of justice.[2] The Indian Contract Act 1872 (hereinafter 'the Contract Act') uses the term 'impossibility' and not 'frustration', but the two terms are often used interchangeably in legal materials.[3] In the Contract Act, the effect of supervening events on contracts is stated in two parts: contingent contracts (ss 31–36) and subsequent impossibility and unlawfulness (s 56).

II. Theories of the Doctrine of Frustration

In the English law, the doctrine developed as a departure from the strict rule of absolute liability stated in *Paradine v Jane*.[4] It was formally recognised in *Taylor v Caldwell*,[5] where a theatre let out for a performance was destroyed. The Court implied a condition of the continued existence of the theatre and held that the parties were released. This was a case of literal or physical impossibility. Later, cases of frustration arising from delay in fulfilling charterparties were decided as 'frustration of adventures'.[6] This reasoning was adopted in *Krell v Henry*,[7] where rooms were let out to a tenant for watching a coronation procession. The tenant was discharged from paying rent when the coronation was cancelled. Although performance was possible, the state of things that formed the basis on which the contract was made had been lost.

[1] B Garner (ed), *Black's Law Dictionary* (9th edn, West Group 2009).
[2] *Hirji Mulji v Cheong Yue Steamship Co Ltd* [1926] UKPC 12.
[3] *Satyabrata Ghose v Mugneeram Bangur and Co* AIR 1954 SC 44 (Mukherjea J): the question is whether a contract 'stood dissolved by frustration or in other words became impossible of performance'.
[4] *Paradine v Jane* 82 ER 897 (KB).
[5] *Taylor v Caldwell* 122 ER 309 (KB).
[6] *Jackson v Union Marine Insurance Co Ltd* (1874–75) LR 10 CP 125.
[7] *Krell v Henry* [1903] 2 KB 740.

Nilima Bhadbhade, *Frustration* In: *Foundations of Indian Contract Law*. Edited by: KV Krishnaprasad, Niranjan Venkatesan, Shivprasad Swaminathan, and Umakanth Varottil, Oxford University Press.
DOI: 10.1093/9780191997211.003.0014

By the 1940s, English courts began to recognise that discharge by frustration occurred not by the will of parties but because courts exercised a positive function releasing a party from further performance in order to reach a just and reasonable result.[8] The test, based on 'disappearance of the foundation of the contract', asked the question: are the events or circumstances of such a nature as to cause the foundation of the contract to disappear?[9] The 'radical change in the obligation' test[10] was formulated later, where subsequent circumstances would render performance a thing radically different from that which was undertaken by the contract: '[i]t was not this that I promised to do'. This test is generally accepted and applied in English law.[11]

These theories provided juristic bases that allowed the doctrine to evolve across cases involving different circumstances. These theories not only justified the doctrine but also provided a formula for deciding its operation.[12]

Indian courts have discussed these theories.[13] For example, early Indian judgments decided under the Contract Act adopted the implied term theory.[14] Later judgments adverted to the development of the doctrine in the English law as applicable to particular contracts like charterparties, sale of goods, leases, etc.

In *Satyabrata Ghose,*[15] the Supreme Court preferred the foundation of contract theory over the implied term theory, and observed that relief can be given where

> the whole purpose or basis of a contract was frustrated by the intrusion or occurrence of an unexpected event or change of circumstances. . . . When such event . . . is so fundamental as to be regarded by law as striking to the root of the contract as a whole,

Later, in *Naihati Jute Mills Ltd,*[16] Shelat J said,

> The Court can grant relief . . . when it finds that the whole purpose or the basis of the contract was frustrated by the intrusion or occurrence of an unexpected event or change of circumstances which was not contemplated by the parties at the date of the contract. There would . . . be no question of finding out an implied term . . . because the parties did not think about the matter at all nor could possibly have any intention regarding it.

In *VL Narasu v PSV Iyer,*[17] with facts similar to *Taylor v Caldwell,*[18] the Madras High Court held that the continued existence of the cinema-house was the fundamental basis on which the agreement rested.

[8] *Joseph Constantine Steamship Line Ltd v Imperial Shipping Corporation Ltd* [1942]AC 154 (HL).
[9] *FA Tamplin Steamship Co Ltd v Anglo-Mexican Petroleum Products Co Ltd* [1916] 2 AC 397 (HL).
[10] *Davis Contractors Ltd v Fareham Urban District Council* [1956] AC 696 (HL).
[11] J Beatson, A Burrows, and J Cartwright (eds), *Anson's Law of Contract* (29th edn, OUP 2010) 487.
[12] E Peel (ed), *Treitel on the Law of Contract* (15th edn, Sweet and Maxwell 2020) [19.123] (hereinafter *Treitel on the Law of Contract*).
[13] *Satyabrata Ghose* (n 3).
[14] See eg *Goculdas Madhavji v Narsu Yenkuji* (1889) ILR 13 Bom 630.
[15] *Satyabrata Ghose* (n 3).
[16] *Naihati Jute Mills Ltd v Khyaliram Jagannath* AIR 1968 SC 522.
[17] *VL Narasu v PSV Iyer* AIR 1953 Mad 300.
[18] *Taylor* (n 5).

Theories of 'disappearance of foundation' or 'basis of contract'[19] and terms like 'totally upset the basis of the bargain and commercial object'[20] and 'fundamental' or 'radical change of circumstances'[21] are also referred to in Indian cases.

III. Frustration under the Contract Act

Nine years after *Taylor v Caldwell*,[22] the Contract Act adopted the doctrine in two parts: contingent contracts in sections 31 and 32 and subsequent impossibility and unlawfulness in paragraphs 2 and 3 of section 56.

The Bill for enacting the Indian Contract Act 1867 proposed in the *Second Report of Her Majesty's Commissioners*[23] placed subsequent impossibility and unlawfulness in the chapter titled 'Conditional Contracts', as an exception to the rule of absolute liability.[24] Section 31 in the draft excused a promisor only if the promisor had not taken the risk upon him- or herself.

In the Contract Act as enacted, these provisions appeared as substantive provisions in section 56 in Chapter IV that deals with performance of contracts. It was observed,

> nothing resembling this section [56] has been found in the materials known to have been used by the framers of the act. It varies the Common Law to a large extent, and moreover, the Act lays down positive rules of law on questions which English and American Courts have more and more tended . . . to regard as matters of construction depending on true intention of parties.[25]

Thus, the language of section 56 was unqualified, and the distinctions observed in English Law about different types of conditions frustrating transactions were not necessary in India.[26] This, it was stated, gained simplicity at 'the expense of considerable departure from the principles of English law'.[27]

[19] *Ram Kumar Agarwala v PC Roy & Co Ltd* AIR 1952 Cal 397; *Parmeshawari Das Mehra and Son v Firm Ram Chand Om Prakash* AIR 1952 Pun 34; *State of Rajasthan v Madanswarup* AIR 1960 Raj 138.

[20] *Satyabrata Ghose* (n 3).

[21] *Industrial Finance Corporation of India Ltd v The Cannanore Spinning and Weaving Mills Ltd* AIR 2002 SC 1841; *Easun Engg Co Ltd v Fertiliser & Chemicals Travancore Ltd* AIR 1991 Mad 158; *Energy Watchdog v Central Electricity Regulatory Commission* (2017) 14 SCC 80.

[22] *Taylor* (n 5).

[23] *Second Report of Her Majesty's Commissioners* appointed to prepare a body of substantive law for India published by the Order of the House of Commons, 1868.

[24] S 31:

> Liability of person failing to do an act which he has engaged to do: A person who fails to do an act, which he has engaged by contract to do shall make compensation to the person in whose favour the act was to be done.
>
> *Exceptions:* A man incurs no liability through the non-performance of an act which he has engaged by contract to do, where, since the date of the contract, the performance of the act has rendered unlawful, or has been made impossible by some event, of which he did not expressly, or by implication, take upon himself the risk.

[25] F Pollock and DF Mulla, *The Indian Contract Act: With a Commentary, Critical and Explanatory* (2nd edn, Sweet & Maxwell 1909) 253.

[26] ibid 254; see also *Kesarichand v Governor General in Council* (1949) ILR Nag 718; *Satyabrata Ghose* (n 3).

[27] F Pollock, *Principles of Contract: At Law and in Equity* (2nd edn, Stevens and Sons 1878) 379.

In the Contract Act, contingent contracts were placed separately in Chapter III, and were 'the original work of the 'Indian' Legislative Department'.[28] Sections 31–36 of the Contract Act cover all promises conditional upon happening of future events, including acts of persons.

Sections 32 and 56 of the Contract Act incorporated the doctrine of frustration as a special case of impossibility that discharged a contract by physical and legal impossibility after its formation.[29] Hence, Indian courts primarily look at the law as stated in these two sections.[30]

The doctrine in Indian law is of impossibility. It 'is really a positive rule enacted in section 56'[31] and does not leave the matter to be determined by the intention of the parties,[32] providing better justice and greater certainty than has been achieved in the English decisions.[33]

IV. Absolute Obligation

To a large extent, the rule of absolute obligation applies in India.[34] Thus, a mere change of circumstances affecting performance does not excuse a party from performing that party's promise.[35]

In *Alopi Parshad and Sons Ltd v Union of India*,[36] goods were supplied to the government on agreed rates. Following the Second World War, the price of the goods rose, and the supplier demanded revised rates. Shah J stated this famous dictum:

> The [Contract Act] does not enable a party to a contract to ignore the express covenants thereof, . . . on some vague plea of equity.

and further,

> There is no general liberty reserved to the courts to absolve a party from liability to perform . . ., merely because on account of an uncontemplated turn of events, the performance of the contract may become onerous. . . . [T]here is . . . no general rule to which recourse may be had . . ., relying upon which a party may ignore the express covenants on account of an uncontemplated turn of events since the date of the contract.

[28] Pollock and Mulla (n 25) 196.
[29] W Stokes, *Anglo-Indian Codes* (Clarendon Press 1888) 507; *Kesarichand* (n 26); *Satyabrata Ghose* (n 3).
[30] *Ganga Saran v Firm Ram Charan Ram Gopal* AIR 1952 SC 9.
[31] *Naihati Jute Mills Ltd* (n 16).
[32] *Satyabrata Ghose* (n 3); G Rankin, *Background to Indian Law* (CUP 1946) 109 ('Section 56 deals with impossibility of performance not by making assumptions as to the intention of the parties in the particular case but by positive rules').
[33] Rankin (n 32) 108–109.
[34] *Bombay and Persia Steam Navigation Company Ltd v Rubattino Company Limited* (1889) 14 Bom 147.
[35] The Contract Act, s 37 states, 'The parties to a contract must either perform, or offer to perform, their respective promises, unless such performance is dispensed with or excused under the provisions of this Act, or of any other law.'
[36] *Alopi Parshad and Sons Ltd v Union of India* AIR 1960 SC 588 (Shah J).

Later, in the *Naihati* case,[37] a buyer of Pakistani jute was denied permission to import jute required by subsequent regulations. He defended the seller's claim for compensation, alleging frustration because of an unforeseen change in government policy. Rejecting this defence, Shelat J observed,

> A contract is not frustrated merely because the circumstances in which it was made are altered. The Courts have no general power to absolve a party from the performance of his part of the contract merely because its performance has become onerous on account of an unforeseen turn of events.

In *Noor Mohammad v Sonu Mistri*,[38] a hirer of lights and decorations for a marriage procession could not return them because they were destroyed in riots. While decreeing the suit against him, the Patna High Court has observed,

> The general rule is that when a party has not qualified his obligation, he is liable to make compensation in damages 'for non-performance, although the performance has been rendered impracticable by some unforeseen cause over which he had not control.'

Following this general rule, the doctrine will not to be lightly invoked 'to relieve contracting parties of the normal consequences of imprudent commercial bargains'.[39]

The scope of the doctrine is very narrow. Treitel[40] outlines some reasons: (a) a party should not have an easy escape from his/her bargain, (b) it is difficult to draw a line between cases of frustration and cases where liability under the contract is strict, (c) commercial parties are very likely to make express provision for dealing with 'obstacles to performance', (d) whether the court holds that the contract is discharged, or refuses to do so, one party will always suffer loss, and the court is not in a position to modify their contract to allocate or adjust losses.

V. Allocation of Risks

A party is not excused if the law puts risk on such party. Thus, there is no excuse if parties have taken calculated risks of various future events and contingencies in express terms or as demanded by their transaction.

Risk may also fall upon one party by law. In a contract for sale of goods, risk *prima facie* passes with property, unless otherwise agreed.[41] Property passes to the buyer when it is intended to pass.[42] Property and risk pass to the buyer of specific goods in

[37] *Naihati Jute Mills Ltd* (n 16).
[38] *Noor Mohammad v Sonu Mistri* AIR 1941 Pat 429.
[39] *Pioneer Shipping Ltd v BTP Tioxide Ltd (The Nema)* [1982] AC 724 (HL) (Roskill J).
[40] *Treitel on the Law of Contract* (n 12) [19-006].
[41] Sale of Goods Act 1930, s 26.
[42] ibid s 19.

a deliverable state at the time the contract is made.[43] Other provisions indicate when property will pass if the agreed goods are unascertained, or not in a deliverable state, or sold on sale-or-return basis, or where right of disposal is reserved.[44] A bailee is not liable for damage to or loss of goods bailed because of causes beyond the bailee's control.[45] A buyer of immovable property must bear the loss arising from destruction, injury, or decrease in value of the property.[46] However, where a leased property is destroyed, the lessee can end it.[47] The lessee is bound to repair the leased property to keep it in its original condition;[48] the lessee will not be liable if the property is damaged by any natural cause or by fire not caused by the lessee's negligence.

It may appear, or be implied or construed from the terms of the contract or the nature of the transaction, that the promisor undertook the risk of the event that prevented the promisor's performance.[49] Thus, a seller bears the risk that the seller's source of supply may fail. The seller is expected to arrange alternative supplies. A toll contractor having the right to collect tolls on a bridge undertakes the risk that traffic might be suspended due to government orders or events such as floods.[50] A fixed-rate or fixed-price contract puts the risk of price increase on the seller or contractor, because price fluctuations are taken into account while quoting the price.[51] Neither rise nor fall in prices[52] affect performance, even if the prices are later modified by law;[53] the contract merely becomes burdensome. A party quoting non-escalable tariffs, takes the risk of unexpected rise in prices.[54] The risk of disease exists in every crowded emigrant ship, and the shipper cannot be excused from operating the voyage for this reason.[55] In all these cases, one party has knowingly taken the risk of such circumstances that make performance difficult or expensive.

VI. Contingent Contracts

Contracting parties may agree that the contract shall become void when a particular event occurs.[56] Chapter III of the Contract Act refers to such conditional contracts as

[43] ibid s 20.
[44] ibid ss 21–25.
[45] Contract Act, s 151 ('Unless it be shown that the bailee has not taken as much care of the goods as a man of ordinary prudence would take of his own goods under similar circumstances').
[46] Transfer of Property Act 1882, s 108(5)(c).
[47] ibid s 108(e).
[48] ibid s 108(m): subject to reasonable wear and tear and irresistible force.
[49] *Marshall and Co v Naginchand Fulchand* AIR 1917 Bom 182 (a sale of goods on cost, insurance, and freight (CIF) terms).
[50] *President of the District Board South Kanara v G Santhappa Naik* AIR 1925 Mad 907; *Panakkattan Sankaran v District Board of Malabar* AIR 1934 Mad 85.
[51] *South East Asia Marin Engineering and Constructions Ltd (Seamec Ltd) v Oil India Limited* AIROnline 2020 SC 552; *Energy Watchdog* (n 21); but see *Easun Engg Co Ltd* (n 21) (400 per cent increase in price excused the promisor because the difference in price struck at the foundation or basis of the contract and affected a radical change in obligations).
[52] *Kunjukrishnan v State of Kerala* AIR 1983 Ker 73.
[53] *Dominion of India v Raja Bahadur Bhikhraj Jaipuria* AIR 1957 Pat 586.
[54] *Energy Watchdog* (n 21).
[55] *Bombay and Persia Steam Navigation Company* (n 34).
[56] Stokes (n 29) 502.

'contingent contracts' where performance is dependent on the happening of an event that may be specified or may be known to the parties. Such condition can also be implied into their contract.[57] Parties are discharged by the terms in their contract. It is stated,

> In cases . . . where the Court gathers as a matter of construction that the contract itself contained impliedly or expressly a term, according to which it would stand discharged on the happening of certain circumstances the dissolution of the contract would take place under the terms of the contract itself and such cases would be outside the purview of section 56 altogether. Although in English law these cases are treated as cases of frustration, in India they would be dealt with under section 32 of the Contract Act.[58]

A contingent contract is a contract to do or not to do something, if some event, collateral to such contract, does or does not happen.[59] Such event must be collateral to the contract, that is, neither a performance directly promised as part of the contract nor the whole of the consideration for the promise.[60] The event must be contingent and future and beyond the control of parties.[61]

A contingent term may be implied in a contract from its other terms[62] or from its type.[63] A court may also refuse to imply a term.[64]

Whether the contract is contingent or absolute is a matter of construction. In *Harnandrai Fulchand v Pragdas Budhsen*,[65] an agreement to sell a specified quantity of dhotis provided 'to be taken delivery of as and when the same may be received from the [specified] mills'. The mills did not supply. The Court held that the words did not mean 'if and when' supplies were received, especially because a time was named for delivery. The seller was not excused. In *Ganga Saran v Firm Ram Charan Ram Gopal*,[66] the seller agreed to deliver cloth manufactured by Victoria Cotton Mills to the buyer 'as they are prepared' by the mills and would be delivered to the buyer 'as soon as soon as the goods are supplied to the sellers'. The mills did not supply. It was held that delivery

[57] Nevertheless, courts have applied s 56 in such cases: *Punj Sons Pvt Ltd v Union of India* AIR 1986 Del 158 (supply of goods after processing using metal available only with permission); *Ramani Ammal v Susilammal* AIR 1991 Mad 163 (sale of property after eviction of tenants); *Air Construction Consultants Private Limited v Reena Das* AIR 2015 Cal 9 (development of property after eviction of tenants).

[58] *Satyabrata Ghose* (n 3).

[59] Contract Act, s 31.

[60] *Maung Kywe v Maung San Tin* AIR 1923 Rang 26 (a surety bond to assure attendance of an accused, else to pay the amount of bond, is not a contingent contract).

[61] *Balwant Singh v Rajaram* AIR 1975 Raj 73.

[62] *Kirpal Das Jivraj Mal v Manager, Encumbered Estates* AIR 1936 Sindh 26 (sale of undivided share in land shall happen only if the seller got the share after partition); *Govindbhai Gordhanbhai Patel v Gulam Abbas Mulla Allibhai* AIR 1977 SC 1019 (sale of property in possession of lessee shall happen only if the lessee surrendered the lease).

[63] *Firm Bachhraj Amolakchand v Firm Nand Lal Sitaram* AIR 1966 MP 145 (essence of a *bilticut* contract that railway wagons will be available).

[64] *Samuel Fitz and Co Ltd v Standard Cotton and Silk Weaving Co* AIR 1945 Mad 291; *Bombay and Persia Steam Navigation Company* (n 34).

[65] *Harnandrai Fulchand v Pragdas Budhsen* AIR 1923 PC 54; see also *F Ranchoddas v Nathmal Hirachand & Co* AIR 1949 Bom 356.

[66] *Ganga Saran* (n 30).

was not contingent on the supply by the mills, and the words merely described the goods and stated the process of delivery.

Contingent contracts to do or nor to do anything if an uncertain future event happens cannot be enforced by law unless and until that event has happened. If the event becomes impossible, such contracts become void.[67] Such an event must become finally impossible.[68] Thus, where performance is subject to a permission, the contract becomes void only if permission is refused.[69] Contingent contracts to do or not to do anything if an uncertain future event does not happen can be enforced when the happening of that event becomes impossible and not before.[70] The party alleging that performance is contingent must prove it.[71]

Such event can also be a way in which a person will act at an unspecified time,[72] for example, where performance depends upon any permission, permit, consent, sanction, or approval of any authority or another person. If performance requires permission and the contract does state which party must obtain the permission, a term may be implied that one party shall do all things necessary to obtain it.[73] Specific performance can also be ordered that application for such permission shall be made.[74]

The party whose obligation it is to obtain permission must make best efforts to obtain it[75] from the appropriate authority,[76] and prove it.[77] In a suit by the bridegroom for enforcing a contract to marry made by a father of the bride, the father sought an excuse because his daughter refused to get married for the next four years. Rejecting this defence, the Bombay Court in 1896 observed[78] that the act 'is neither impossible in itself, nor impracticable in the ordinary sense of the term'. It was the duty of the father to use the utmost persuasive powers as a parent: '[H]e, like this Court, must also regard the matter from the strictly legal point of view.'

The scope of sections 32 and section 56 is different, yet 'it is sometimes a matter of doubt whether a contract falls under section 32 or section 56'.[79] *Force majeure* clauses[80] are enforced under the general principles that parties are bound by their contracts[81] but are also resolved under the provisions of sections 32 and 33.[82]

[67] Contract Act, s 32

[68] *Govindbhai Gordhanbhai Patel* (n 62); *Dinanath v Premchand* AIR 1957 MB 186.

[69] *National Agricultural Cooperative Marketing Federation of India v Alimenta SA* AIROnline 2020 SC 522 (export permission).

[70] Contract Act, s 33.

[71] *Dinanath* (n 68).

[72] Contract Act, s 34.

[73] *Motilal v Nanhelal* AIR 1930 PC 287; *Nathulal v Phoolchand* AIR 1970 SC 546; *GA Galia Kotwala and Co Ltd v KRL Narasimhan* AIR 1954 Mad 119.

[74] *Chandnee Vidyawati Madden v Dr CL Katyal* AIR 1964 SC 978; *Nirmala Anand v Advent Corporation Pvt Ltd* AIR 2002 SC 2290.

[75] *Motilal* (n 73); *Raghuvir Singh Bhatty v Ram Chandra Waman Subhedar* AIR 2002 All 13; *DR Mehta v Tin Plate Dealers Association Ltd* AIR 1965 Mad 400; *TV Kochuvareed v P Mariappa Gounder* AIR 1954 TC 10.

[76] *Govindbhai Gordhanbhai Patel* (n 62).

[77] *Bansilal Fomra v Thadava Co-op Agricultural and Industrial Society Ltd* (1976) 1 Mad LJ 39.

[78] *Purshotamdas Tribhovandas v Purshotamdas Mangaldas Tribhovandas* (1896) 21 ILR Bom 23.

[79] *Kirpal Das Jivraj Mal* (n 62).

[80] See notes following 176 below for discussion about *force majeure* clauses.

[81] *National Agricultural Cooperative Marketing Federation of India* (n 69).

[82] As observed in *Satyabrata Ghose* (n 3).

VII. Impossibility

Section 56 of the Contract Act, appearing in Chapter IV about performance of contracts,[83] has three paragraphs about impossibility:

> *56. Agreement to do impossible act.* An agreement to do an act impossible in itself is void.
>
> *Contract to do act afterwards becoming impossible or unlawful*: A contract to do an act which, after the contract is made, becomes impossible, or, by reason of some event which the promisor could not prevent, unlawful, becomes void when the act becomes impossible or unlawful.
>
> *Compensation for loss through non-performance of act known to be impossible or unlawful*: Where one person has promised to do something which that person knew, or, with reasonable diligence, might have known, and which the promisee did not know, to be impossible or unlawful, such promisor must make compensation to such promisee for any loss which such promisee sustains through the non-performance of the promise.

1. Paragraph 1 of Section 56

This deals with physical impossibility or legal impossibility apparent on the face of the promise.[84] It closely resembles section 20 of the Contract Act, which deals with mutual mistakes.[85] This difference was considered in *Sheikh Brothers Ltd v Ochsner*,[86] where a question arose whether the contract to cut trees from an estate that, as the parties later realised, could not produce the minimum trees required for performance of the contract, was void under section 20 or section 56 of the Contract Act. If it was void under section 56, compensation could be ordered under the third paragraph because the licensor with reasonable diligence would have known that it was impossible to produce the minimum quantities. It was held that the agreement was vitiated by mistake of both parties and was not a contract. The Court observed that section 56 applied where there was 'apart from any question of performance, an enforceable agreement'.

[83] It has been suggested that it should have been placed with void agreements: Stokes (n 29) 580.

[84] Illustration (a) to s 56 provides: 'A agrees with B to discover treasure by magic. The agreement is void.'

[85] The Contract Act, s 20 provides: 'Where both the parties to an agreement are under a mistake as to a matter of fact essential to the agreement, the agreement is void.' See also *Joseph Constantine Steamship Line Ltd* (n 8) 186. For an analysis of the two doctrines, see S Swaminathan, 'Frustration and Force Majeure: A Guide for the Perplexed' (*IndiaCorpLaw*, 12 May 2020) <https://indiacorplaw.in/2020/05/frustration-and-force-majeure-a-guide-for-the-perplexed-part-i.html> accessed 1 August 2020.

[86] *Sheikh Brothers Ltd v Ochsner* [1957] AC 136 (a case from Kenya decided by the Privy Council applying the Contract Act).

2. Paragraph 2 of Section 56

The second paragraph covers the effect of subsequent impossibility and unlawfulness, that is, illegality.[87] It states that if

(i) an event occurs after the contract is made, and
(ii) the event makes the act (i.e. the promise) impossible or unlawful
(iii) the contract becomes void when the act becomes impossible or unlawful, and
(iv) in case of subsequent unlawfulness, the event should be one that the promisor could not prevent.

Illustration (d) to section 56 states an example: 'A contracts to take in cargo for B at a foreign port. A's Government afterwards declares war against the country in which the port is situated. The contract becomes void when war is declared.'

This paragraph uses the word 'impossible' and not 'frustration', but its application is not restricted to 'impossibility'. Thus,

> The word 'impossible' has not been used in the sense of physical or literal impossibility. The performance of an act may not be literally impossible but it may be impracticable and useless from the point of view of the object and purpose which the parties had in view; and if an untoward event or change of circumstances totally upsets the very foundation upon which the parties rested their bargain, it can very well be said that the promisor finds it impossible to do the act which he promised to do.[88]

Cases in which courts have held that the promise had, or had not, become impossible are discussed later.

3. Paragraph 3 of Section 56

The third paragraph provides that the non-performing party becomes liable to pay compensation where that party knew or would have known about the impossibility or unlawfulness, whether initial or subsequent.[89] Hence, a plaintiff seeking compensation is likely to make a claim under section 56 rather than section 20 (mistake) or 32 and 34 (contingent contracts).[90]

[87] Since the Contract Act uses the term 'unlawful', it is preferred to the term 'illegal' in this chapter.
[88] *Satyabrata Ghose* (n 3).
[89] Illustration (c) to s 56 states, 'A contracts to marry B, being already married to C, and being forbidden by the law to which he is subject to practise polygamy, A must make compensation to B for the loss caused to her by the non-performance of his promise.'
[90] *Kirpal Das Jivraj Mal* (n 62); *Sheikh Brothers* (n 86).

The liability to compensate arises when

(i) the act agreed is impossible or unlawful,
(ii) the promisor knew, or would have known with reasonable diligence, that the act was unlawful or impossible,
(iii) the promisee did not know, and
(iv) in case of unlawfulness, the promisor could not have prevented the event which rendered the act unlawful.[91]

VIII. Subsequent Impossibility

Discharge by subsequent impossibility operates when

(i) there is a valid and subsisting contract between the parties,
(ii) some part of the contract is yet to be performed; and
(iii) after the contract is made, it becomes impossible to perform.[92]

The party that alleges subsequent impossibility must plead and prove it,[93] and all its components, and that the event prevented that party from performing it.[94]

1. Event Must Be Unforeseen

If parties knew, or could have known, contemplated, or foreseen, the future event or the circumstances that might affect their contract, they cannot be excused from performance,[95] either because they understood or took the risks or because that they could have made an express provision for it but chose not to.[96] In this context, foreseeability informs an analysis of the allocation of risks.

Parties' knowledge or contemplation can be ascertained from the terms of the contract. In the *Naihati Jute Mills* case,[97] the Supreme Court refused to excuse a purchaser

[91] *Firm of Hussainbhoy Karimji v Haridas* AIR 1928 Sind 21 (in this case, the Court held that both parties were aware of the circumstances and contracted on the basis that ships would be available but also made efforts. Hence the act was impossible); see also *Sheikh Brothers* (n 86).
[92] *Industrial Finance Corporation of India Ltd* (n 21).
[93] *Harishchandra Dwarkadas Cloth Market, Indore v Firm Murlidhar Chironjilal* AIR 1962 SC 366; *Dinanath* (n 68); *Sri Amuruvi Perumal Devasthanam v KR Sabapathi Pillai* AIR 1962 Mad 132; *Parmeshawari Das Mehra* (n 19).
[94] *Manasseh Film Co v Gemini Picture Circuit* AIR 1944 Mad 239.
[95] *Satyabrata Ghose* (n 3) (war restrictions); *Sannadhi Gundayya v Illoori Subbayya* AIR 1927 Mad 89 (requirement of priority certificates for transport during war times); *Afshar MM Tacki v Dharamsey Tricamdas* AIR 1947 Bom 98; *Gwalior Rayon Silk Mfg Co Ltd v Shri Andavar & Co* AIR 1991 Ker 134; *Gujarat Housing Board v Vipul Corporation* AIR 2004 Guj 319.
[96] *Davis Contractors* (n 10) (Lord Radcliffe); *Bombay and Persia Steam Navigation Company* (n 34).
[97] *Naihati Jute Mills Ltd* (n 16).

who could not obtain an import licence, because the contract indicated that parties were aware about import restrictions.

It can also be ascertained from surrounding circumstances. Thus, parties who contracted after declaration of war cannot claim discharge for inability to perform due to circumstances arising from the war.[98] A seller who contracted while the seller's supplier's mill was shut due to labour strike is not excused.[99]

2. Event Must be Beyond the Control of Parties

Such subsequent event must be beyond the control of parties. The event must not merely make performance impossible for the promisor, but it must be impossible in itself.[100] The party seeking the excuse is expected to take steps to avoid the situation or event,[101] to attempt to avoid the happening of the event,[102] or to have performed before the event happened.[103] It must have explored alternative modes of performance,[104] even if expensive,[105] unless the contract requires strict compliance.[106]

3. Factors Relevant to Deciding Impossibility

Many factors are relevant in determining whether performance has 'become impossible'.

In *Satyabrata*,[107] a developer agreed to develop and sell plots out of a large tract of land and complete the sale within a specified time after the development was completed. No time was specified for completing development. The land was requisitioned by the government for use by troops for the war. The developer asked the purchaser of a plot either to take the land as it was or accept refund of price; and if the purchaser did not exercise any choice, the agreement would stand cancelled and the earnest money forfeited. The purchaser sued for a declaration that the purchaser's contract subsisted. The developer pleaded that the requisition made performance impossible.[108] While deciding against the developer, the Court considered that a very small amount was

[98] *Satyabrata Ghose* (n 3).
[99] *Firm Rampratap Mahadeo Prasad v Sasansa Sugar Works* AIR 1964 Pat 250.
[100] *Ezekiel Abraham Gubray v Ramjusray Golabray* AIR 1921 Cal 305; *Firm of Hussainbhoy Karimji* (n 91).
[101] *MMTC of India Ltd v Interore Fertichem Resources SA* AIR 2012 Del 123.
[102] *Firm of Hussainbhoy Karimji* (n 91) (ships were not available to load Java Sugar for Karachi port); *Kirpal Das Jivraj Mal* (n 62) (other owners having share in land did not partition it); *Ram Kumar Agarwala* (n 19) availiability of railway wagon).
[103] *Karl Ettlinger v Chagandas & Co* AIR 1915 Bom 232.
[104] *Shree Kishen v Gambhirmal* AIR 1955 Hyd 233.
[105] *Gurdit Singh v Secretary of State* AIR 1931 Lah 347.
[106] *Edmund Bendit v Edgar Raphael Prudhomme* AIR 1925 Mad 626.
[107] *Satyabrata Ghose* (n 3).
[108] The conduct of the developer immediately after the requisition showed readiness of some obligations, but the only issue before the Supreme Court was about discharge by impossibility.

paid at the time of the agreement, the balance price was payable over a long period of time, the nature of requisition was temporary, and other factors, thus:

> having regard to the nature and terms of the contracts, the actual existence of war conditions at the time when it was entered into, the extent of the work involved in the development scheme and last though not the least the total absence of any definite period of time agreed to by the parties within which the work was to be completed, it cannot be said the requisition order vitally affected the contract or made its performance impossible.[109]

Such a 'multi-factorial' approach later enunciated in the *Sea-Angel* case,[110] was adopted and approved again by the Supreme Court:[111]

> the application of the doctrine of frustration requires a multi-factorial approach. Among the factors which have to be considered are the terms of the contract itself, its matrix or context, the parties' knowledge, expectations, assumptions and contemplations, in particular as to risk, as at the time of the contract, at any rate so far as these can be ascribed mutually and objectively, and then the nature of the supervening event, and the parties' reasonable and objectively ascertainable calculations as to the possibilities of future performance in the new circumstances.

IX. Situations of Impossibility

Circumstances discharging a contract for subsequent impossibility can be grouped under these heads:

1. Destruction of Subject Matter or of Something Essential to Performance

Performance of a contract becomes impossible when a specific thing that is the subject matter of the contract, or essential to the performance, is destroyed. In *VL Narasu v PSV Iyer*,[112] the owner of a cinema-hall who exhibited films of a producer, was excused when a wall of his cinema-hall fell down due to rain, and the local authority ordered its demolition. In *Piarey Lal v Hori Lal*,[113] the seller of land was discharged when he was allotted another land in place of the agreed land under a subsequent law. In the early case of *Inder Pershad Singh v Campbell*,[114] a seller of indigo was excused under his

[109] *Satyabrata Ghose* (n 3) (Mukherjea J).
[110] *Edwinton Commercial Corporation v Tsavliris Russ (Worldwide Salvage & Towage) Ltd* [2007] EWCA Civ 547.
[111] *Energy Watchdog* (n 21).
[112] *VL Narasu* (n 17).
[113] *Piarey Lal v Hori Lal* AIR 1977 SC 1226.
[114] *Inder Pershad Singh v Campbell* (1881) 7 Cal 474.

contract of cultivating and selling indigo that he grew on the land as sub-lessee, when his lessor (the main lessee) was evicted for non-payment of rent.

2. Non-availability

Performance of a contract is excused for non-availability of supplies, or something essential to performance (eg transport) only if the particular source is considered important and essential by the parties; for example, they intend that the source, and no other, should be used.[115] The court can consider whether the seller's attempt to deliver from supplies from other sources would amount to breach of the contract.[116]

A contract for supply of goods will be frustrated if the ship, or other mode of transport carrying the goods, is requisitioned[117] or transport is not available.[118] Thus, a contract to deliver Java sugar to Karachi was discharged when the ship was requisitioned, and no ships left from Java for Karachi during the period of the contract.[119]

A temporary interruption from the source of supply will end the contract only if the interruption is likely to continue close to or beyond the period of the contract. Often the answer depends on whether performance in full is possible after the termporary non-availability ceases and whether such performance will be the same or there will be a 'radical change in the obligation'.

3. Death or Incapacity of Parties

The Contract Act provides for cases where the promisor dies.[120] 'Personal' contracts[121] end with the promisor's death, because they involve the exercise of individual skill or taste of the promisor or are based on the confidence between parties. In other cases, the legal representatives may perform the promise themselves or appoint a competent person to perform it.[122] Whether the contract is personal or not depends on the construction of the contract.[123]

The Contract Act has no general provision about subsequent incapacity of parties.[124] However, subsequent disablement of any party, viz. subsequent physical or

[115] *Energy Watchdog* (n 21).
[116] *Firm Rampratap Mahadeo Prasad* (n 99).
[117] *Firm of Hussainbhoy Karimji* (n 91); *Noorbux Mohmoodbux Musalmal v Kalyandas Jugaldas Gujrathi Mode* AIR 1945 Nag 192.
[118] *Ram Kumar Agarwala* (n 19).
[119] *Firm of Hussainbhoy Karimji* (n 91).
[120] Contract Act, s 37: promises bind legal representatives of the promisors in case the promisor dies before performance, unless a contrary intention appears from the contract.
[121] ibid s 40 indicates that the promise is personal where 'it appears from the nature of the case that it was the intention of the parties to any contract that any promise contained in it should be performed by the promisor himself' and gives an illustration about a painter.
[122] ibid.
[123] *Jagannath Patnaik v Sri Pitamber Bhupati Harichandran Mohapatra* AIR 1954 Ori 241.
[124] Except the Contract Act, s 201: other than unsoundness of mind of a principal or agent.

mental illness, or imprisonment, can invite the doctrine of impossibility, as suggested by Illustration (e) to section 56.[125]

If disability is imposed by a subsequent law, it is a case of subsequent unlawfulness, viz. the promisor becoming an alien enemy,[126] or prohibition disabling the promisor from rendering the particular kind of performance[127] or nature of relationship.[128]

4. Delay

Delay is a commercial risk that the parties undertake. Where the subsequent event causes temporary delay, the proportion that the period of event has to the contract term is important.[129] Delay will not discharge if it has not affected the main purpose of the contract.[130] In *Satyabrata*, the Supreme Court held that an order requisitioning land would not excuse the land developer because there was no 'delay so great and of such a character that it would totally upset the basis of the bargain and commercial object which the parties had in view'.[131]

A subsequent event of temporary effect can discharge the promisor for performances during that period, as suggested by Illustration (e) to section 56 where a promisor is discharged from performance during the period of illness in a long term contract.

5. Impracticality

Performance is impractical, as contrasted with 'impossible', where the promisor is able to perform but the performance will involve difficulty, expense, or unreasonable loss[132] or would impose a burden on one party quite different from the one contemplated when the contract was made. It also refers to commercial impossibility. In English law, mere impracticality is not an excuse.[133]

In 1887, Whitley Stokes suggested,[134] with reference to section 56, that impracticality should excuse the promisor: 'a thing is said to be impossible *if it be practically out of the question because it can only be accomplished at an unreasonable cost*'.

In *Satyabrata*, the Court[135] observes that performance becomes impossible where it is 'impracticable and useless from the point of view of the object and purpose which the

[125] ibid illustration (e) to s 56: *A* contracts to act at a theatre for six months in consideration of a sum paid in advance by *B*. On several occasions, *A* is too ill to act. The contract to act on those occasions becomes void.
[126] *Textile Mfg Co Ltd v Salomon Brothers* (1916) 40 Bom 570.
[127] *Sri Madana Gopalswamy Temple v Saride Manikyam* AIR 1957 AP 643 (a law abolishing devdasi practices).
[128] *Jagannath Patnaik* (n 123) (relationship of confidence between a dewan, that is, the manager of estate and a nobleman employer).
[129] *Panakkattan Sankaran* (n 50).
[130] *CT Xavier v PV Joseph* AIR 1995 Ker 140 (construction for purposes of lease of godowns).
[131] *Satyabrata Ghose* (n 3).
[132] *Treitel on the Law of Contract* (n 12) [19-033].
[133] ibid [19-033]; *British Movietonews Ltd v London and District Cinemas* [1952] AC 166 (HL); *Davis Contractors* (n 10).
[134] *Stokes* (n 29) 495.
[135] *Satyabrata Ghose* (n 3).

parties had in view'. In *Delhi Development Authority v Kenneth Builders and Developers Ltd*,[136] a developer undertook a large development project for construction of flats for a development authority and was responsible to obtain all permissions required for the development from various authorities. Some of these permissions were refused. The developer sought to cancel the tender process and claim return of money that had been paid. Pending these legal proceedings, a judgment of a High Court in another proceeding involving another piece of land indicated that lands that were morphologically a ridge required permission of a ridge authority and could not be developed without such permission. This judgment affected the land under development. The Supreme Court, having regard also to many other impediments in the development work, applied section 56 of the Contract Act, that 'circumstances made it impracticable for [the developer] to construct' and ordered refund of amount.

X. Subsequent Unlawfulness

A contract to do an act which, after the contract is made, becomes unlawful by reason of some event, which the promisor could not prevent, becomes void when the act becomes unlawful.[137] This occurs when the precise obligation[138] that the promisor promises is prohibited, restricted, or made punishable by a law passed after the contract was made, including by orders of courts[139] or government authorities.[140]

Performance has been excused where it was affected by export or import[141] restrictions, or by laws prohibiting transfers,[142] or the activity involving the performance,[143] or transport.[144] Restrictions on prices by law do not excuse performance.[145]

A promisor is not excused if the promisor could have prevented unlawfulness. Where the subsequent law allows performance with permissions, the promisor is not excused if the promisor has not sought permissions.[146] It is excused if it has sought permission, but it is refused.[147]

[136] *Delhi Development Authority v Kenneth Builders and Developers Ltd* AIR 2016 SC 3026.
[137] See the Contract Act, s 56(2).
[138] *Markfed Vanaspati & Allied Industries v Union of India* (2007) 7 SCC 679: supply of rapeseed oil was not prohibited, but its use in manufacture was.
[139] *In Re: HEH The Nizam's Jewellery Trust, Shanti Vijay & Co* AIR 1980 SC 17; *Delhi Development Authority* (n 136).
[140] *Raj Kumar Gupta v Des Raj* AIR 1995 HP 107; *National Agricultural Cooperative Marketing Federation of India* (n 69); most import and export restrictions are issued by authorities by notification.
[141] *Boothalinga Agencies v VTC Poriaswami Nadar* AIR 1969 SC 110; *Boggiano & Co v Arab Steamers Co Ltd* AIR 1916 Bom 265.
[142] *K Narendra v Riviera Apartments (P)Ltd* AIR 1999 SC 2309 (law imposing ceiling on holdings of urban land prohibited transfers); *Rozan Mian v Tahera Begum* AIR 2007 SC 2883 (law prohibition on transfer of particular tenancy rights); *Raj Kumar Gupta* (n 140) (town planning law).
[143] *Syed Khursed Ali v State of Orissa* AIR 2007 Ori 56 (law prohibiting cowslaughter ended the contract for supply of meat as animal feed to zoos); *Sri Madana Gopalswamy Temple* (n 127) (law prohibiting dancing by devadasis in temples).
[144] *Shree Kishen* (n 104); *Seth Mohan Lal v Grain Chambers Ltd* AIR 1968 SC 772; *Har Prasad Chaubey v Union of India* AIR 1973 SC 2380.
[145] *Seth Mohan Lal* (n 144).
[146] *RK Motishaw & Co v Mercantile Bank of India* (1916) 41 Bom 566; *Sahas Karan v Nath Mal* AIR 1951 Ajmer 65.
[147] *VR Lakshmanan Chettiar v SK Kamrajendara Kadir Velluswami Pandian* AIR 1955 Mad 606.

Subsequent unlawfulness must be reckoned with reference to the date specified for performance; that is, it should affect performance on the day or during the time in which the promise has to be performed.[148]

Where performance becomes impossible because of wartime requisitions or restrictions of import, export, or price, the contract ends forthwith, even if one party has indicated waiver by extending time for performance.[149] Similarly, a contract ends, and does not merely remain suspended, if it involves trading with an alien enemy[150] or the ship carrying goods is captured and condemned as prize.[151]

Indian courts will not enforce a promise affected by subsequent foreign law if the promise must be performed in the foreign country where it is rendered unlawful.[152]

XI. Leases and Transfers of Property

The doctrine does not apply to completed transfers, viz. leases or sales.[153] A lease is a transfer of property under the Transfer of Property Act 1882. The Supreme Court has held, '[t]here is a clear distinction between a completed conveyance and an executory contract, and events which discharge a contract do not invalidate a concluded transfer'.[154] The doctrine does apply to agreements to lease,[155] contracts for sale of land, and agreements for reconveyance.[156]

In *Raja Dhruv Dev Chand v Raja Harmohinder Singh*,[157] a leased land fell into the territory of Pakistan after Partition. The lessee sued to claim refund of rent for failure of consideration because 'the lease had become impossible of performance as a result of communal riots in the District . . . and the inability of non-Muslims to continue to reside in that area'. The agreement did not provide that rent was payable only if the lessee could personally attend or supervise agricultural operations. The Supreme Court held, after referring to earlier cases taking the same view,[158] that the doctrine of impossibility did not apply to leases, them being completed transfers. This settled the law relating to frsutration of leases.

If the lease, in express terms, casts an absolute obligation, a lessee is not excused from paying rent, nor is the lessee entitled to surrender the lease.[159] Sections 55 and

[148] *Mugneeram Bangur and Co (P) Ltd v Gurbacharan Singh* AIR 1965 SC 1523.

[149] *Textile Mfg Co Ltd* (n 126).

[150] *AF Ferguson & Co v Lalit Mohan Ghosh* AIR 1954 Pat 596. See also *Textile Mfg Co Ltd* (n 126); *Manasseh Film Co* (n 94).

[151] *Gouri Shankar Agarwalla v HP Moitra* AIR 1921 Cal 509.

[152] *Rabindra N Maitra v Life Insurance Corporation of India* AIR 1964 Cal 141; *Energy Watchdog* (n 21).

[153] *Raja Dhruv Dev Chand v Raja Harmohinder Singh* AIR 1968 SC 1024; *Rajendra Nath Sarma v Ramdhin Rajbhor* AIR 1971 Assam 160.

[154] *Raja Dhruv Dev Chand* (n 153) (Shah J).

[155] *Sushila Devi v Hari Singh* AIR 1971 SC 1756.

[156] *Ahmad Khan v Shahanshah Jehan Begum* AIR 1973 All 529.

[157] *Raja Dhruv Dev Chand* (n 153) overruling *Gurdarshan Singh v Bishan Singh* AIR 1963 Punj 49 (FB).

[158] *Abdul Hashem v Balahari Mondal* AIR 1952 Cal 380; *Tarabai Jivanlal v Padamchand* AIR 1950 Bom 89; *Alanduraiappar Koil Chithakkadu v TSA Hamid* AIR l963 Mad 94.

[159] *Surpat Singh v Sheo Prasad Gupta* AIR 1945 Pat 300; *Merla Suramma v Kakileti Sitaramaswamy* AIR 1957 AP 71; *Sri Mahalingaswami Devasthanam v AT Sambanda Mudaliar* AIR 1962 Mad 122; *Velur Devasthanam v S Sundaram Nainar* (1959) 1 Mad LJ 24.

108 of the Transfer of Property Act 1882, which provide for destruction and damage to property that has been agreed to be sold or has been leased, are subject to contrary agreement. The doctrine has limited application without express provisions in the contract.[160] The real question arises as to whether there can be a discharge outside these provisions.

Under section 108(e) of the Transfer of Property Act,[161] a lease does not end even if the leased property or its material part is destroyed or rendered substantially and permanently unfit for the purpose for which it was let by fire, tempest or flood, or violence of an army or of a mob, or other irresistible force. The lessee can terminate it. This is an exhaustive provision.[162]

Firstly, the possibility of termination arises only if the property or its material part is (a) destroyed or (b) is rendered substantially and permanently unfit, that is, has undergone positive actual destruction or injury by some violent force.[163] In *Dhuramsey Soonderdas v Ahmedbhai Habeebbhoy*,[164] it was held applying section 108(e), and despite the English law at that time, that the lessee of a godown with a lease of twelve months could effectively terminate the lease after the godown was destroyed by fire, even though it was possible to repair it within three months.

A lease cannot be terminated under section 108(e) if the property has become unprofitable or unfit for cultivation.[165] A lessee is not excused from paying rent, nor does a lease end if the lessee's enjoyment is affected by an event such that the lessee cannot enter the property or use it.[166] Hence, temporary non-use of premises due to the lockdown during the COVID-19 pandemic does not entitle a lessee to avoid or to seek remission in the payment of rent.[167]

Secondly, the lessee can terminate only if the property is so affected by events of fire, tempest or flood, or violence of an army or of a mob, or other irresistible force.

Lastly, such event does not end the lease. The lessee only, and not the lessor,[168] has the option to terminate it. If the lessee terminates, the lessee can claim remission or return of the rent for the unexpired term of the lease under section 65 of the Contract Act.[169] If the lessee does not terminate, the lease continues, and the lessee must continue to pay rent despite destruction of property.[170]

160 *Ramanand v Girish Soni* CM App 10848/2020 (Delhi High Court, 21 May 2020).

161 The Transfer of Property Act, s 108(e) provides:

Rights and Liabilities of Lessor and Lessee—

In the absence of a contract or local usage to the contrary, the lessor and the lessee of immovable property, as against one another, respectively, possess the rights and are subject to the liabilities mentioned in the rules next following . . .

(e) if by fire, tempest or flood, or violence of an army or of a mob, or other irresistible force, any material part of the property be wholly destroyed or rendered substantially and permanently unfit for the purposes for which it was let, the lease shall, at the option of the lessee, be void.

162 *Mahadeo Prosad Shaw v Calcutta Dyeing & Cleaning Co* AIR 1961 Cal 70.

163 *Ghulam Mahomed v Sahebsingh* AIR 1914 Sind 75.

164 *Dhuramsey Soonderas v Ahmedbhai Habeebbhoy* (1898) 23 Bom 15.

165 *Ghulam Mahomed* (n 163) (failure of water supply).

166 *Raja Dhruv Dev Chand* (n 153); *Hari Laxman Joshi v Secretary of State* AIR 1928 Bom 61.

167 *Ramanand* (n 160).

168 *Shyam Kumari v Ejaz Ahmad Ansari* AIR 1977 All 376.

169 *Dhuramsey Soonderdas* (n 164) (Contrary to English Law); *Shrawan v Sheoratan* AIR 1935 Nag 208.

170 *Kundal Lal v Shamshad Ahmad* AIR 1966 All 225.

XII. No Frustration

A promisor is not excused by a subsequent event if the contract provides for the event or if the act has become impossible because of the promisor's own conduct. Subsequent frustrating events do not generally end arbitration clauses or certain contracts.

1. Contractual Provisions

Parties can impose absolute obligations in their contract. They can also make provisions for subsequent events in *force majeure* clauses. In doing so, they allocate risks between themselves.

i Absolute obligation

A party may promise to perform irrespective of any subsequent event, in which case that party is not excused if the event happens. Such a provision excludes the operation of the doctrine:[171]

> [I]f the parties do contemplate the possibility of an intervening circumstance which might affect the performance of the contract, but expressly stipulate that the contract would stand despite such circumstances, there can be no case of frustration because the basis of the contract being to demand performance despite the happening of a particular event, it cannot disappear when that event happens.[172]

Whether the obligation is absolute, depends on the construction of its terms.[173] A clause in a performance bond in an employment contract provided that a treasurer of a post office shall be liable for losses and 'he shall be solely responsible for all and any loss or damages forever ... otherwise than by the act of God or the King's enemies'. This showed that parties had frustrating events in mind and that the parties deliberately intended to limit frustrating events to two, even though the contract indicated that losses for other reasons were likely to occur. Hence, the treasurer was not excused where articles were lost because of riots.[174]

ii. *Force majeure* clauses

Parties can provide *force majeure* clauses in their contracts to deal with supervening events. The term '*force majeure*' is wider in import than 'vis major', and such clauses also cover events such as strikes, breakdown of machinery, non-availability of supplies

[171] *Kesarichand* (n 26).
[172] *Satyabrata Ghose* (n 3).
[173] *Naihati Jute Mills Ltd* (n 16). It has been held that in a fixed-rate contract, parties undertake the risk of price fluctuations; see *Seamec Ltd* (n 51); *Energy Watchdog* (n 21).
[174] *Kesarichand* (n 26).

or transport, etc that are not natural events. Such provisions save promisors from the consequences of events over which they do not have control.[175]

A *force majeure* clause may provide for (a) a list of events, which list may be exhaustive, general, or a list of related events followed by words of general import; (b) the procedure that parties must follow if any listed event occurs; (c) the effect of the happening of the event, that is, whether it will discharge one or both parties, or suspend performance, or will give to one or both parties the right to terminate,[176] or to seek extension of time, or change prices or rates. A contract 'subject to the "usual force majeure clause" can also be enforced because its true meaning [can] be ascertained in evidence from surrounding circumstances'.[177]

The event affecting performance must fall within the scope of such clause.[178] This is a matter of interpretation. The party relying on such provision must also show that the event was beyond that party's control:[179] 'It is absolutely necessary to go further and establish by satisfactory evidence that the circumstance or occurrence which is called force majeure was the real cause, which . . . prevented the performance of the contract.'[180] Thus, where listed 'unprecedented' events exempted liability, it was for the party seeking exemption to lead evidence that the rain and floods that affected performance were unprecedented.[181]

A *force majeure* clause must be strictly complied with. Where the seller had the option to extend time for delivery or to cancel, the seller could not insist on another mode of delivery.[182]

A *force majeure* clause is 'construed in each case with a close attention to the words which precede or follow it, and with due regard to the nature and general terms of the contract. The effect of the clause may vary with each instrument.'[183] It is narrowly construed. A clause in a development agreement that the project land was available on an 'as is where is' basis was applied to the physical characteristics and condition of the land. It did not cover the legal compliances required for development and, hence, did not excuse the developer from because permissions to construct were refused.[184] In *Energy Watchdog v Central Electricity Regulatory Commission*,[185] electricity-generating companies sought discharge from the performance of their power purchase agreement under a 'change-in-law' clause, because prices of Indonesian coal rose considerably following a change in Indonesian law. This price was the basis of its bid calculations. The Supreme Court held that the 'change in law' was restricted to Indian law.

175 *Dhanrajmal Gobindram v Shamji Kalidas and Co* AIR 1961 SC 1285.
176 *Firm Bachhraj Amolakchand* (n 63).
177 *Dhanrajamal Gobindram* (n 175).
178 *Naihati Jute Mills Ltd* (n 16).
179 *MMTC of India* (n 101).
180 *Edmund Bendit* (n 106) (Srinivasa Aiyangar J).
181 *State of UP v Allied Constructions* AIR 2004 SC 586.
182 *Firm Bachhraj Amolakchand* (n 63).
183 *Lebeaupin v Crispin* [1920] 2 KB 71 (*Justice* McCardie), quoted with approval in *Edmund Bendit* (n 106).
184 *Delhi Development Authority* (n 136).
185 *Energy Watchdog* (n 21).

Where the clause states a list of events followed by general words like 'and other events of a like nature', the general words will be construed *ejusdem generis*. Thus, the words 'other unforeseen circumstances which might prevent goods from reaching the port of embarkation' covered inability to obtain tonnage so as to discharge and relieve the seller under a CIF contract.[186] But in *Serajuddin v State of Orissa*,[187] the lessee of a mine sought excuse under a *force majeure* clause from completing setting up a manufacturing unit on the ground that the government did not supply electric power, land, etc. The *force majeure* clause listed 'act of God, War, Insurrection, Riot, Civil Commotion, Strike, Earthquake. Tide, Storm, Tidal Wave, Flood, Lightning, Explosion, Fire and any other happening which the lessee could not reasonably prevent or control'. The Court held that non-availability of land and electric power was not covered by the clause.

There seems to be a trend of applying the doctrine to situations falling outside *force majeure* clauses. In *Easun Engg Co Ltd v Fertiliser v & Chemicals Travancore Ltd*,[188] a supplier in a firm-price contract claimed revision in rates arising from a 400 per cent rise in prices of transformer oil following war conditions in the Middle East. The contract provided that the supplier shall not be considered in default of performance if it was prevented or delayed by war, etc 'or any other cause which is beyond the control of the parties'. The arbitral tribunal held that the 400 per cent price rise was a *force majeure* condition being caused by conditions of war. Relying upon the dictum in *Alopi Pershad v Union of India*,[189] the Madras High Court observed that the abnormal increase due to the unexpected war condition was a 'fundamentally different situation' that 'unexpectedly emerged' but upheld the award 'not because the Court in its discretion thinks it just and reasonable to qualify the terms of the contract, but because on its true construction it does not apply in that situation'. The Supreme Court has also hinted that a *force majeure* clause in a contract does not exhaust the possibility of unforeseen events occurring outside natural or non-natural events.[190]

2. Self-Induced Frustration

Following English law, Indian law recognises that a promisor who is at fault cannot take the benefit of the doctrine. A promisor is not discharged if the frustrating event is caused by the promisor's own conduct or the conduct of those for whom the promisor is responsible, or if the promisor has committed breach,[191] or if the promisor did not prevent the event having the means and opportunity to prevent it[192] and was expected to prevent it. In *Inder Pershad Singh v Campbell*,[193] the sub-lessee of a piece of land

[186] *Edmund Bendit* (n 106).
[187] *Serajuddin v State of Orissa* AIR 1969 Ori 152.
[188] *Easun Engg Co Ltd* (n 21).
[189] *Alopi Pershad* (n 36).
[190] *Energy Watchdog* (n 21).
[191] *GA Galia Kotwala* (n 73); *Ganga Singh v Santosh Kumar* AIR 1963 All 201.
[192] *MMTC of India Ltd* (n 101); *Gujarat Housing Board* (n 95).
[193] *Inder Pershad Singh* (n 114).

claimed discharge from a contract to cultivate and supply indigo grown on the land because of the eviction of the lessee for non-payment of rent. It was argued that the sub-lessee could have paid off the arrears of rent. The Court observed that he could not be expected to do so and that there was no material to show that he could.

Mere negligence is not enough to deprive the promisor of the discharge. In *VL Narasu v PSV Iyer*,[194] a question arose whether the owner of a cinema-hall was negligent in not taking proper steps to ensure that it was fit enough for performances. The Madras High Court allowed the defence of frustration, observing

> that the appellant was negligent in not taking proper steps for ensuring that the theatre was in a fit condition for performing the contract, that is not . . . sufficient to deprive him of the benefit of the plea of frustration. In neglecting to effect the repairs to the theatre he was not actuated by any intention to break the contract . . . or injure the plaintiff. His conduct had no relation to the suit contract and he did 'nothing against the faith of the contract which would amount to repudiation and would justify rescission'. There was no act or election on the part of the appellant made 'in order to get out of the engagement'.

The burden of proving that frustration is self-induced is on the party alleging it.[195]

3. Particular Agreements

An arbitration clause survives even if the contract containing it is discharged by impossibility, because the arbitral tribunal must decide whether contract has ended by impossibility.[196] However, a party cannot be forced to arbitrate where that party is unable to attend the proceeding due to travel restrictions, except at high cost or great risk to life.[197]

An unforeseen event discharging a primary contract may not affect a secondary independent contract. A guarantee, being an absolute contract giving an unqualified undertaking, will not be discharged even if the primary contract were affected by impossibility.[198] Payment under letters of credit could not be injuncted on the ground of frustration because of circumstances arising from the COVID-19 pandemic, because they formed an independent transaction; the *force majeure* clause in the primary contract did not apply to the bank, and the lockdown was a temporary event and did not excuse the buyer from paying the seller.[199]

[194] *VL Narasu* (n 17).
[195] *MD, Army Welfare Housing Organisation v Sumangal Services Pvt Ltd* AIR 2004 SC 1344.
[196] *Naihati Jute Mills Ltd* (n 16); *Union of India v Kishori Lal Gupta & Bros* AIR 1959 SC 1362; *Khardah Co Ltd v Raymon & Co (India) Pvt Ltd* AIR 1962 SC 1810.
[197] *Rama Nand Vijay Parkash v Gokal Chand Gian Chand* AIR 1951 Simla 189 (but see *Parmeshawari Das Mehra* (n 19): parties did not show that personal presence at Karachi, the seat of arbitration, was required).
[198] *Industrial Finance Corporation of India Ltd* (n 21); *Suresh Narain Sinha v Akhauri Balbhadra Prasad* AIR 1957 Pat 256.
[199] *Standard Retail Pvt Ltd v GS Global Corp* Comm Arb Petn (L) No 404 of 2020 (Delhi) (29 May 2020).

The doctrine does not apply to statutory contracts.[200] Parties' obligations under such contracts are strict. In *Alluri Narayana Murthy Raju v Dist Collector*,[201] the lessee having a right to quarry sand under a statutory contract was prevented from taking away sand by villagers in the area. In *Mary v State of Kerala*,[202] the licensee of a liquor-vending licence could not start her shop because people in the area resisted physically. In both cases, it was held that the contractors had no right to recover amounts they paid for obtaining rights.

XIII. Effect of Frustration

Frustration ends the contract forthwith. In Indian law, the party that has obtained an advantage under the agreement must return it or compensate.

1. Automatic Discharge

In cases of initial impossibility, the agreement is void, though the parties might discover the impossibility later.

A valid contract 'becomes void'[203] (a) where it is contingent on happening of an event, and the event becomes impossible under section 32, and (b) in case of subsequent impossibility or unlawfulness under paragraph 2 of section 56. Like the English law, subsequent impossibility discharges all parties from future performance[204] when the event happens.[205] The discharge is automatic and does not depend on the choice or election of either party.[206]

2. Compensation

If the contract is discharged by impossibility or unlawfulness, and the promisor knew, or with reasonable diligence might have known, and to be impossible or unlawful, the promisor is liable to compensate the promisee.[207]

[200] These are contracts governed by statutory provisions that stipulate their terms. The relationship between parties is governed by the applicable statute. Examples include electricity supply, liquor licences, etc.
[201] *Alluri Narayana Murthy Raju v District Collector* AIR 2008 AP 264.
[202] *Mary v State of Kerala* AIR 2014 SC 1.
[203] Contract Act, s 2(j): a contract that ceases to be enforceable by law becomes void when it ceases to be enforceable.
[204] *Satyabrata Ghose* (n 3).
[205] Illustration (d) to s 56 states, 'A contracts to take in cargo for B at a foreign port. A's Government afterwards declares war against the country in which the port is situated. The contract becomes void when war is declared.'
[206] *Satyabrata Ghose* (n 3); *Boothalinga Agencies* (n 141).
[207] See n 89 above.

3. *Force Majeure* Clauses

Where the court discharges a promisor under the terms of a *force majeure* clause, relief will be granted according to the terms of that clause.

4. Return of Advantage or Compensation

Section 65 applies where the agreement is 'discovered to be void', as under paragraph 1 of section 56, or 'becomes void', as under section 34 or under paragraph 2 of section 56. Section 65[208] provides a restitutionary obligation to (a) return the advantage under the agreement, or (b) restore the advantage, or (c) make compensation for it to the person from whom it was received.

Section 65 allows recovery of payments made before the discharge,[209] viz. return of deposits or advances.[210] Section 65 applies also to leases. Where the leased property is destroyed, and the lessee terminates the lease,[211] the lessee is entitled to refund of proportionate rent.[212]

The term 'advantage' is relative and must be understood in context. It is not mere 'profit' or 'clear profit'. It does not matter what the party receiving money has done with it.[213] The claim for return of amount is subject to adjustment for the expenses incurred by the other party.

In *Boggiano & Co v Arab Steamers Co Ltd*,[214] a shipper procured freight on the carrier's ship. Government orders prohibited import of those goods, the ship did not leave harbour, and was unloaded. The shipper claimed return of freight, the amount that the shipper had deposited for covering expenses and losses incurred by the ship. The carrier was ordered to return the freight amount but was entitled to retain expenses for unloading of cargo and demurrage at the rate the carrier accounted for, since the shipper failed to prove that the carrier could have obtained cheaper rates for work.

In *Govindram Seksaria v Edward Radbone*,[215] after the greater part of the purchased machinery had arrived from Germany and half the purchase price was paid, war was

[208] The Contract Act, s 65 provides,
Obligation of person who has received advantage under void agreement, or contract that becomes void—When an agreement is discovered to be void, or when a contract becomes void, any person who has received any advantage under such agreement or contract is bound to restore it, or to make compensation for it to the person from whom he received it.

[209] *Gandha Korliah v Janoo Hassan* AIR 1926 Mad 175, unlike the English law at the time; following *Boggiano* (n 141); *Bahadur v Mohammad Din* AIR 1934 Lah 979; *CVRM Ramaswami Chettiar v AKRMCT Chidambaram Chettiar* AIR 1954 Mad 1040; *Orissa State Electricity Board v Indian Metals & Ferro Alloys Ltd* AIR 1991 Ori 59.

[210] *Textile Mfg Co Ltd* (n 126).

[211] Under the Transfer of Property Act 1882, s 108(e).

[212] *Dhuramsey Soonderdas* (n 164).

[213] *Muradlidhar Chatterjee v International Film Co Ltd* AIR 1943 PC 34.

[214] *Boggiano* (n 141).

[215] *Govindram Seksaria v Edward Radbone* AIR 1948 PC 56, followed in *State of Rajasthan v Associated Stone Industries (Kotah) Ltd* AIR 1985 SC 466.

declared. The seller (custodian) sued the purchaser for value of machinery. He would have recovered it if he could show that the value of the delivered machine part was more than the amount paid by the purchaser. For this purpose, the value of the machinery would be its value after the contract became void. The Court took into account the fact that the balance of the machinery could not be supplied, and the services of the seller's qualified personnel would not be available. The Court also considered whether the purchasers could procure the remaining machinery from other sources and at what price and within how much time.

In *Dhuramsey Soonderdas v Ahmedbhai Habeebbhoy*,[216] the Bombay High Court calculated return of amount on a frustrated lease on the basis of rent proportionate to the period during which the property destroyed was not available. The Court was willing to take into account the fact that rent would differ during different seasons of the year but did not do so for lack of evidence.

Compensation will be ordered only if the court cannot order return or restoration.[217]

5. Events after Discharge

Events occurring after the frustrating event will not be taken into account, because that would mean making a new contract for the parties. Where the ship captured during war arrived at the destination two years after the date fixed under the contract, the capture ended the contract, and the seller was not bound to deliver the goods to the buyer,[218] nor was the buyer bound to purchase.[219] Where the damaged cinema-theatre was reconstructed after two years, the promisee could not seek to exhibit his films in the new theatre.[220] Where, in consolidation proceedings of lands under a law, the piece of land agreed to be sold was substituted by another, the agreement could not be specifically enforced. [221] Once a contract became unlawful, it could not be revived once the prohibition imposed by law was removed.[222]

XIV. Conclusion

The Indian law of frustration or subsequent impossibility, contained in section 56 of the Contract Act, does not depend on intention of parties. While seeking to remain detached from the English law, it has drawn upon principles of English law, like the 'foundation or basis of contract' test, the 'radical change of foundation' test and the

[216] *Dhuramsey Soonderdas* (n 164).
[217] *Fakira Mal v Nabbu* AIR 1915 Lah 310.
[218] *Gouri Sankar Agarwalla* (n 151); *Banghy Abdul Razack Sahib v Khandi Rao* AIR 1918 Mad 515; *Soorthingjee Sakalchand v Mahomed Nasruddin* AIR 1918 Mad 1124.
[219] *Madhoram Hurdeo Dass v GC Sett* AIR 1918 Cal 830.
[220] *VL Narasu* (n 17).
[221] *Piarey Lal* (n 113).
[222] *K Narendra* (n 142) (Repeal of the Urban Land Ceiling Act 1976 will not revive the contract).

'multifactorial' approach, to name a few. Its strength lies in maintaining that contractual obligations are generally absolute, but recognising situations of frustration where necessary to achieve just results. Contractual provisions dealing with subsequent events have primacy. The doctrine of subsequent impossibility remains within narrow limits, as default or residuary principle.

The COVID-19 pandemic and the lockdown orders following it raised new issues and challenges for the application of this doctrine. Difficult situations faced by parties will be too diverse to be brought under one principle, if one were to attempt to create one for the pandemic. A liberal approach favouring discharge from obligations will encourage uncertainty, and allow parties to indulge in sharp practices. The current law can sufficiently cover the new situation. Orders given in interim matters have followed the set rule. Strict application of the doctrine can drive parties to negotiated settlements for mutual benefit.

15
The Duty of Good Faith

*Manasi Kumar and Poorna Mysoor**

I. Introduction

The mention of a positive obligation of good faith in contract law is bound to attract animated discussion, especially within English law. Although Lord Mansfield expressed strong support for the duty of good faith in contract law in the eighteenth century,[1] English common law was not swayed by this in the subsequent years. The explanation, to a great extent, seems to lie with the history of English common law as it developed through the Industrial Revolution and flexed its imperial muscles forging its identity as a mercantilist power. The ideological objection is that a positive duty of good faith is an illiberal interference with the freedom of contract, with the pragmatic concern being that a general principle of law imposing such a duty would be 'of uncertain ambit and distinctly dubious pedigree'.[2] While this debate rages on in English law, jurisdictions that owe their origin to the English common law of contract have gone on to successfully introduce a duty of good faith as a persuasive guideline or into their case law.[3] This suggests that at least some of the fears of introducing good faith into English contract law may be overstated.

Barring specific references in relation to certain special contracts,[4] the Contract Act does not impose a general duty of good faith. At the same time, there is also no express mandate against such an obligation. Whatever the intention of imperial Britain in enacting the Contract Act in its original form, and whatever the reasons for the current scepticism in the United Kingdom towards a duty of good faith, there is no reason to assume that no duty of good faith can be read into the interpretation of the Contract Act itself or into Indian common law. Therefore, the starting point for the Indian courts

* The authors wish to thank Afrrin Advani for her research assistance.

[1] *Carter v Boehm* (1766) 3 Burr 1905, 1910.

[2] E McKendrick, 'Good Faith: A Matter of Principle?' in ADM Forte (ed), *Good Faith in Contract and Property Law* (Bloomsbury 2000) 48.

[3] See eg Restatement (Second) of Contracts, s 205 in the United States; *Paciocco v Australia and New Zealand Banking Group Ltd* [2015] FCAFC 50, [287] in Australia; and *Bhasin v Hyrnew* [2014] 3 SCR 495, [33] in Canada.

[4] For example, the Indian Contract Act 1872, s 166 provides that a bailee returning goods in good faith to the bailor is not liable to the actual owner of goods, and s 178 protects a good-faith pawnee when there is a pledge made by a mercantile agent.

Manasi Kumar and Poorna Mysoor, *The Duty of Good Faith* In: *Foundations of Indian Contract Law*. Edited by: KV Krishnaprasad, Niranjan Venkatesan, Shivprasad Swaminathan, and Umakanth Varottil, Oxford University Press. © Oxford University Press 2024.
DOI: 10.1093/9780191997211.003.0015

need not be an objection to the very principle of imposing a duty of good faith, even as English common law is itself coming under pressure to recognise this duty. Certain very senior members of the judiciary in the United Kingdom have indicated strong support for imposing a duty of good faith, writing within and outside their judicial capacity.[5] Chen-Wishart and Dixon, among other scholars, make a powerful case as to why a legal system must consider imposing a duty of good faith, the most persuasive being that it enhances the autonomy of the institution of contract and upholds its integrity.[6] As such, the Indian courts will be well served being open to it. This chapter examines the contexts in which the issue has arisen in Indian contract law, and whether the courts acknowledge it using the language of good faith or not.

Given that a major criticism of a general obligation of good faith is its scope, this chapter begins by examining, in section II, what is generally understood by good faith and fair dealing within the scholarly literature. Having laid this foundation, we provide a quick survey in section III of the provisions of the Contract Act and ancillary legislation to demonstrate that these already owe their existence to an underlying notion of good faith. We then move on to investigate, in section IV, the Indian case law. The difficulty is with courts not acknowledging expressly that their conclusion is attributable to a reasoning rooted in good faith. Therefore, we examine those decisions that are explicable only because of an underlying duty of good faith. We focus on instances where Indian courts have modified seemingly clear contractual obligations in order to prevent certain kinds of conduct that could be classified as bad faith. The case law in this section is divided into three broad categories: first, provisions granting unfettered discretion to one party by the express terms of a contract and the courts agreeing or resisting the placing of certain fetters on the discretion; second, the provisions in contracts that exclude liability for breach of contract and the different mechanisms that the courts have adopted to avoid parties to the contract being left with no remedies; and third, contracts governed by other legislation where a general duty of good faith does exist. We bring the analysis together in our conclusion in section V and examine the future of the duty of good faith in Indian contract law.

II. What Is the Duty of Good Faith?

One of the biggest challenges in this debate is to define good faith. Its amorphous nature does no favours in converting sceptics into believers. But, one can take a stab at providing different approaches to its conceptualisation. A good starting point is the law in the United States, where there is a greater acceptance of the duty of good faith, given its

[5] M Arden, *Common Law and Modern Society: Keeping Pace with Change* (OUP 2015) 57; J Steyn, 'Contract Law: Fulfilling the Reasonable Expectations of Honest Men' (1997) 113 Law Quarterly Review 433; Leggatt J's (now Lord Leggatt) landmark judgment in *Yam Seng Pte v International Trade Corporation Ltd* [2013] EWHC 111 (QB).

[6] M Chen-Wishart and V Dixon, 'Good Faith in English Contract Law: A Humble "3x4" Approach' in PB Miller and J Oberdiek (eds), *Oxford Studies in Private Law Theory: Volume 1* (OUP 2020) 196–97.

express mention in the Uniform Commercial Code[7] and the Restatement (Second) of Contracts ('US Restatement').[8] Although not binding, these documents have a strong persuasive influence. The essential ingredients of the duty of good faith include honesty in fact in the conduct or transaction concerned, requiring the observance of reasonable standards of fair dealing in trade.[9] It emphasises the agreed common purpose of the contract and consistency with the reasonable expectations of the counterparty.[10] In effect, good faith excludes conduct characterised as involving 'bad faith' or conduct that violates 'community standards of decency, fairness or reasonableness'.[11] Scholars support the usefulness of this excluder analysis.[12] These principles have been adopted and applied in different contexts in the United States case law.

In the United Kingdom, despite resistance to a general duty of good faith, scholarly literature has identified aspects that inform the duty of good faith. Scholars in general use terms such as honesty and fair dealing to describe the duty of good faith, and it is difficult to understand the remit of these words without a context in which to view them. Steyn brings greater clarity to these expressions by asserting that there is both a subjective and an objective element to the duty of good faith. The subjective element simply requires parties to act honestly,[13] believing themselves to be doing so. While a subjective state of mind does lead to individualised justice, it is not the concern of English law for the obvious pitfalls that it presents. Therefore, this subjective requirement is paired with an objective standard that requires the observance of reasonable commercial standards of fair dealing in the conclusion and performance of the relevant transaction,[14] which can be calibrated and imposed externally. For Steyn, this is captured within 'the reasonable expectation of honest men'.[15] Similarly, Arden explains that a contracting party should not only believe reasonably that their conduct is honest, but also that such conduct should be regarded to be 'fair and reasonable by right-thinking people engaged in the same business'.[16]

One of the most authoritative works is by Chen-Wishart and Dixon, who have developed a framework for understanding the content of the duty of good faith. They regard good faith at its core as an attitude of respect for (a) the counterparty's legitimate interests, manifesting as a duty of honesty and fair dealing, and (b) for the contract itself, manifesting in fidelity to contractual purpose.[17] One may see areas of overlap

[7] Article 2 of the Uniform Commercial Code (UCC) references good faith in several contexts, including the rights of a 'good faith purchaser'. See generally, UCC, art 2, pt 4. It also, however, imposes an obligation upon the parties to conduct themselves in a manner that comports with good faith where the contractual terms permit one party to set the particulars of performance: UCC § 2-311(1); see also, §§ 2-305 (open price term must be fixed in good faith) and 2-306(1) (outputs and requirements to be measured in good faith).

[8] Restatement (Second) of Contracts, § 205 (imposing a duty of good faith and fair dealing upon every contract).

[9] See UCC (n 7) § 1-201(19), read with § 2-103(1)(b).

[10] US Restatement (n 8), § 205, comment (a).

[11] ibid.

[12] See eg R Summers, 'The General Duty of Good Faith—Its Recognition and Conceptualization' (1981–82) 67 Cornell Law Review 810.

[13] Steyn (n 5) 438.

[14] ibid.

[15] ibid 439.

[16] Arden (n 5) 49.

[17] Chen-Wishart and Dixon (n 6) 188, 204–205.

between (a) and (b). However, this approach is attractive for being simple, yet pithy, in its essence as a workable framework. This chapter draws on this framework broadly to inform the analysis of good faith in the Indian context.

The duty of good faith as an attitude of respect can inform every stage of the life of a contract. However, the US Restatement and the UCC impose the obligation specifically on the performance and enforcement of the contract.[18] Since parties perform and enforce contracts according to its terms, if the terms do not say so (which, in most cases, they will not), then a duty to perform and enforce the contract in good faith will have to be implied. Implying a term is the mechanism adopted by the UK courts, with *Yam Seng* leading the way.[19] Leggatt J (as he then was) likens a contract to other human communications, all of which must be considered against a background of unstated shared understandings, values, norms of behaviour, and expectations of honesty, which inform their meaning.[20]

There is much debate as to whether a duty of good faith is a term implied-in-fact or a term implied-by-law.[21] A term that is implied-in-fact is a bespoke term that is reflective of the parties' unexpressed joint intentions in the specific transaction,[22] whereas a term implied-by-law is one that is imposed upon a particular type of contract as a default rule for all contracts of that type as a matter of policy.[23] While a term implied to fulfil the duty of good faith must be specific to the context of the particular contract, and therefore a bespoke term, the implication is also a reflection of a general policy of contract law.[24] Therefore, instead of focusing the debate on whether the implication is in-fact or by-law, it would better serve the discussion to focus on whether the implication brings about a real change in the outcome of the case, in the face of the parties' express written terms.

While this debate informs the common law courts developing the contexts in which the duty of good faith can be implied, civilian jurisdictions such as France, Italy, and Germany expressly incorporate the duty of good faith into their civil codes. In this context, it would be worthwhile to examine the Contract Act to see whether a duty of good faith can be found. This leads us to a brief overview in section III below.

III. Duty of Good Faith underlying Statutory Provisions in Indian Law

Speaking of English law, McKendrick gives several examples of how the English contract law already embodies the duty of good faith.[25] In English law, these will have

[18] US Restatement (n 8), § 205 and UCC, § 1-203.
[19] *Yam Seng Pte* (n 5).
[20] ibid [133]–[135].
[21] See generally H Collins, 'Implied Terms: The Foundation in Good Faith and Fair Dealing' (2014) 67 Current Legal Problems 297.
[22] E Peel (ed), *Treitel: The Law of Contract* (13th edn, Sweet & Maxwell 2012) [6-032] (hereinafter *Treitel on the Law of Contract*).
[23] ibid [6-043].
[24] Summers (n 12) (noting that the US Restatement § 205 demonstrates a commitment to 'justice according to law').
[25] McKendrick (n 2) 42–44.

developed as precedents of common law over time, whereas the Contract Act has codified these rules. The Contract Act is punctuated with examples that are premised on a duty of good faith. An obvious example of respect for a counterparty's legitimate interests includes provisions imposing negative duties against misrepresentation, duress, and undue influence.[26] While positive duties of disclosure are imposed only on specific types of contracts outside the purview of the Contract Act,[27] a party's silence is tantamount to fraud when he or she has a duty to speak and fails to do so, rendering the contract voidable, unless the fraudulent concealment or misrepresentation could have been discovered through 'ordinary diligence'.[28] Respect for contractual purpose is evident from the provision rendering a contract void if both parties were 'under a mistake as to a matter of fact essential to the agreement', though a unilateral mistake of fact would not render the contract voidable unless it related to the subject matter of the agreement and was caused by the other party's assertions.[29] Additionally, if performance has been rendered impossible or unlawful after the contract has already been entered into, the contract becomes void.[30]

Fair dealing as an ingredient of good faith requires an element of reasonableness. Thus, for example, where the contract fails to provide a time for performance, the promisor must perform within a 'reasonable time',[31] a promisee must provide the promisor 'reasonable facilities for the performance of his promise',[32] and an indemnified party can only recover costs and settlement payments from the indemnifier if they acted prudently.[33]

The Contract Act singles out certain contractual relations for specific treatment where respect for the legitimate interests of the counterparty might be at risk. Thus, contracts of bailment, pledge, and agency subject the parties to heightened duties.[34] Bailors have a duty to disclose material faults in the bailed goods, failing which they are liable for all damage the bailee suffers due to the faults.[35] Further, bailees, who are in possession of the other party's property, are required to act reasonably at all times.[36] Specifically, the Contract Act requires a bailee 'to take as much care of the goods bailed to him as a man of ordinary prudence would, under similar circumstances, take of his own goods of the same bulk, quantity and value as the goods bailed'.[37] In an agency relationship, a principal must indemnify their agent for loss occasioned by acts done in good faith.[38]

[26] Contract Act, ss 14–20. Substantive unfairness is addressed outside the Contract Act and only in relation to consumer contracts under the Consumer Protection Act 2019, which explicitly prohibits any 'unfair contract', defined under s 2(46) as a contract 'having such terms which cause significant change in the rights of such consumer'.

[27] For example, the Transfer of Property Act 1882 imposes specific duties of disclosure on the seller and the buyer, lessor and lessee under ss 55(1)(a), 55(5)(a), and 108(a), (k).

[28] Contract Act, explanation under s 17(2) read with s 19 exception.

[29] ibid s 18(3), read with ss 20 and 22.

[30] ibid s 56.

[31] ibid s 46.

[32] ibid s 67.

[33] ibid s 125.

[34] See generally, G Pearson, Chapter 21 in this volume.

[35] Contract Act, s 150.

[36] ibid ss 154, 156–57.

[37] ibid s 151.

[38] ibid s 223.

Thus, the Contract Act has detailed provisions that govern contract formation, leaving fewer provisions governing the performance or the enforcement of the contract. This is, in part, because parties are free to decide what the subject matter of the performance is, how it is to be performed, and how the contract is to be enforced if it is not performed as agreed—specifically what liberties the parties provide themselves in termination and limitations of liability. If, in the exercise of this freedom, one party conducts themselves in an egregiously self-interested manner, the courts will have to decide whether and how such a term must be given effect. And where the court chooses to limit a party's contractual freedom to minimise (perhaps even eliminate) their risk, it can be fairly understood to be doing so in order to protect the counterparty's reasonable expectations. According to us, such an outcome would be no less than an imposition of a duty of good faith, whether or not the courts actually refer to such a duty. This leads us to the discussion in section IV, reviewing the approach of the Indian courts in this regard.

IV. Duty of Good Faith in Indian Case Law

It is entirely plausible for the contracting parties to grant unfettered discretion to one of the parties in relation to the performance or the enforcement of the contract or both, but without providing for the manner of the exercise of this discretion. It is in these cases that a duty being implied to mandate the exercise of the discretion in a manner respectful of counterparty's legitimate interests, while maintaining fidelity to the contractual purpose, makes a big difference to the outcome of the case. However, as will be evident from the discussion below, in a vast majority of cases, the courts do not use the language of good faith. It follows also that courts do not speak of how the duty of good faith is implied—whether they imply terms in-fact or by-law.

More than the performance of the contract, enforcement has been the most litigious. There are, first, clauses that grant unfettered powers to a party to terminate the contract without cause, and, second, those that permit a party to exclude or limit their liability for damages for breach. The duty of good faith may manifest itself as a term implied into such contracts restricting the discretionary power such that its exercise does not disrespect the counterparty's reasonable expectations. Since, in most cases, the terms implied are bespoke, Indian courts appear to favour the implied-in-fact approach to the duty of good faith.

A third category of cases is where the courts adopt the language of implying a duty of good faith due to the very nature of the contractual relationship, be it employer–employee, debtor–creditor, or insurer–insured. Here, the duty of good faith is being implied into a contract of a particular type as a default rule to achieve a policy goal (such as addressing inequality of bargaining power). Therefore, the courts seem to favour the implied-by-law approach to duty of good faith in these cases. This section deals with each of these categories of contract in turn.

1. Contractual Discretion on Termination

A rough line may be drawn between matters that were decided by the courts on merits and those that were decided by the courts in exercise of their jurisdiction to review arbitral awards. This is because the Arbitration and Conciliation Act 1996 ('ACA') was amended in 2015 to require the arbitral tribunal to '*take into account* the terms of the contract,[39] instead of deciding 'in accordance with the terms of the contract'.[40] This change was brought about due to the recommendations of the Law Commission of India, which wanted to ensure that 'any contravention of a term of the contract by the tribunal should not *ipso jure* result in rendering the award becoming capable of being set aside'.[41] Therefore, courts now only intervene if they find that the tribunal's interpretation of the parties' contract 'is not a possible one',[42] as opposed to if they believe that the tribunal's interpretation is not the correct one. It is worthwhile to examine whether the courts adopt different approaches in these contexts.

i. Judgments on the merits

This discussion may start with the judgment of the Bombay High Court in *Chunilal Dayabhai & Co v The Ahmedabad Fine Spinning and Weaving Co Ltd*,[43] a pre-independence decision where the plaintiff ordered certain manufactured goods from the defendant. The contract provided not only that the defendant could terminate the contract for no cause but also that the plaintiffs could only treat the contract as cancelled and not seek damages. The Court held that the defendant was required to give reasons for termination and that the defendant could not himself bring about a state of affairs that would avoid the contract, denying the plaintiffs their damages.[44] This can be seen as the Court toning down a seemingly absolute termination clause by implying a modification to insert the need to give reasons for termination, although the Court did not frame it as an implied term.[45] One can see that the Court in *Chunilal* insisted on respect for not only the reasonable expectation of the counterparty but also the contractual purpose that had been endangered by the self-interested exercise of one party's powers of termination.[46]

[39] Arbitration and Conciliation (Amendment) Act 2015, s 14 (emphasis added).

[40] Arbitration and Conciliation Act 1996 (India), s 28(3).

[41] *246th Law Commission of India Report, Amendments to the Arbitration and Conciliation Act 1996* (2014) 22, 53 <https://cdnbbsr.s3waas.gov.in/s3ca0daec69b5adc880fb464895726dbdf/uploads/2022/08/2022081615.pdf> accessed 8 April 2023 (expressly stating that the aim was to 'overrule the effect of *ONGC Ltd v Saw Pipes*'); see *Oil and Natural Gas Corp Ltd v Saw Pipes* (2003) 5 SCC 705, 736.

[42] *HRD Corp v GAIL India* (2018) 12 SCC 471, 493; *Ssangyong Engineering & Construction Co Ltd v National Highways Authority of India* (2019) 15 SCC 131, [29].

[43] (1921) 46 ILR 806 (Bombay High Court).

[44] ibid 810, following an English court decision in *New Zealand Shipping Company v Societe des Ateliers* [1919] AC 1.

[45] This decision was followed in *Chotalal Lallubhai v Champsey Umersey & Sons* (1922) 24 BOMLR 877.

[46] In the United Kingdom, see *Abu Dhabi National Tanker Co v Product Star Shipping Ltd (The Product Star) (No 2)* [1993] 1 Lloyd's Rep 397, 404 (stating that 'not only must the discretion be exercised honestly and in good faith, but, having regard to the provisions of the contract by which it is conferred, it must not be exercised arbitrarily, capriciously or unreasonably'). See also M Bridge, 'The Exercise of Contractual Discretion' (2019) 135 Law Quarterly Review 227.

The courts in independent India started on a different note. In *Maddala Thathiah v Union of India*,[47] the Madras High Court refused to enforce a unilateral termination clause as a rule of law. The approach adopted by the Court was markedly different. Here, the plaintiff had successfully bid with the government to supply jaggery. After granting the tender, the government placed an order for the entire quantity and asked for delivery in four instalments. After delivery of the first instalment, the government, unilaterally, and without assigning a reason, cancelled the contract, citing a clause in the tender document that permitted it to do so.[48] The plaintiff brought a claim against the government, claiming he had already invested a substantial sum of money to fulfil the remaining instalments and that he was ready and willing to perform.

If *Chunilal* were to be applied, the Court should have held that the government could not cancel the contract without providing proper and sufficient reasons. The Court expressly did not wish to go down this route.[49] Instead, the Court held that an unfettered contractual discretion to unilaterally terminate the contract would be unenforceable for want of mutuality, that is, that it served to give one party an arbitrary option to declare its main covenants unenforceable at any time.[50] According to the Madras High Court, therefore, a unilateral termination clause that subjected the main contractual promises to the promisor's own whims was void, and no clever drafting could remedy such infirmity. On merits, the Madras High Court found that the tender document did not require the government to place orders but that once it did, the termination clause could not be invoked.[51] This construction of the contract resolved the issue at hand, since the government had, in fact, placed an order, and it was the sole basis upon which the Supreme Court of India affirmed the judgment on appeal.[52]

The Court in *Maddala Thathiah* did not require the clause in the contract granting discretion to be modified by an implied term to require its exercise in good faith. Instead, the Court held the very clause to be unenforceable. In effect, the Court ruled that a term of this nature should not find a place in the contract, pointing to something having gone awry in the negotiation of the contract. One of the most plausible explanations is that the lack of mutuality gnaws at the fair dealing aspect of good faith while negotiating the contractual terms. Although this focuses on a different stage in the life of a contract, it is arguable that it is still informed by the duty of good faith.

At the turn of the twenty-first century, the Supreme Court of India attempted to embrace the approach of the High Court in *Maddala Thathiah* and declare such unilateral termination clauses generally unenforceable for 'interfering with the integrity of the contract'.[53] However, the subsequent year, a larger bench of the Supreme Court in

[47] 69 LW 835 (1956) (Madras High Court).
[48] The clause provided: 'This Administration reserves the right to cancel the contract at any stage during the tenure of the contract without calling upon the outstandings on the unexpired portion of the contract': ibid 836.
[49] ibid 839–40.
[50] ibid 838, 840 (oddly the Court read *Chotalal Lallubhai* (n 45) as a precedent for such a proposition even though that argument was rejected in that case).
[51] *Maddala Thathiah* (n 47) 837.
[52] *Union of India v Maddala Thathiah* AIR 1966 SC 1724, [12], [20].
[53] *National Fertilizers v Puran Chand Nangia* (2000) 8 SCC 343, 351.

Maharani Shantidevi v Savjibhai Haribhai Patel overruled that judgment, declaring it to have misconstrued the precedent.[54] Here, the Supreme Court held that a contractual clause giving absolute discretion to a party to unilaterally terminate the contract is a valid clause, stating categorically that any clause giving absolute power to one party to cancel the contract does not amount to interfering with the integrity of the contract. It went on to support a unilateral termination clause on the grounds of freedom of contract.[55] Such a broad, and stern, statement in favour of freedom of contract appears to sound the death knell for the *Maddala Thathiah* approach in India, although it does not negate the possibility of the implication of terms as seen in *Chunilal*, as the discussion below suggests.[56]

A court is likely to uphold a contractual term that grants both parties the right to terminate at will. In *Central Bank of India (CBI) v Hartford Fire Insurance*,[57] the Supreme Court was faced with insurance policies that provided both the insured and the insurance company with the ability to terminate 'at any time' the insurance contract with notice to each other.[58] The three-judge bench refused to imply a term that the insurance policy can be cancelled only for 'reasonable cause', holding that it must give effect to the plain language of the contract.[59] The Court also seemed persuaded by the fact that this was a common clause in insurance policies that extended the same discretion also to the insured.[60]

A year later, in *General Assurance Society Ltd v Chandumull Jain*,[61] a five-judge bench of the Supreme Court held unanimously that a mutual termination right is perfectly legal in insurance contracts, as is the wide discretion to do so without assigning reasons.[62] The Court conceived this outcome as one that was rooted in the parties' freedom to contract as they desire, without the court intervening, no matter how reasonable the court deems such intervention.[63] Although *General Assurance* purported to do no more than apply the plain language of the contractual language, and follow *CBI*, it made one rather significant amendment. The Court carved out an exception within the insurance contract—the insurer cannot cancel the policy if the loss has already occurred 'or has become so imminent that it must inevitably take place'.[64] Finding no evidence to establish that loss had become imminent at the time of cancellation, the

[54] (2001) 5 SCC 101, 127–28.
[55] ibid 130.
[56] Such court judgments, along the lines of *Maddala Thathiah* (n 47), still occasionally surface. See eg *The State of Bihar v PK Jain* AIR 1981 Pat 280 (Patna High Court) 288–89 (holding that where any unfettered discretion is provided to the commercial party, including a clause that gave one party the sole discretion to increase or decrease its orders depending upon their own necessity for bricks, such a unilateral clause is 'arbitrary' and void as a 'point of law').
[57] AIR 1965 SC 1288.
[58] The contract language at issue was 'This Insurance may be terminated at any time at the request of the Insured [...]. This Insurance may also at any time be terminated at the option of the Company, on notice to that effect being given to the insured, [...]': ibid.
[59] ibid [6]–[8].
[60] ibid [12].
[61] AIR 1966 SC 1644.
[62] ibid [17]–[18].
[63] ibid [19].
[64] ibid [20].

Supreme Court held that the insurer was entitled to cancel the policy, as it did without assigning reasons.[65] This exception means that the insurer is restrained from cancelling their insurance policy even in the face of plain contractual language permitting unlimited discretion if the cancellation is a purely opportunistic attempt to evade an imminent contractual liability. Therefore, the *General Assurance* Court would imply a term that prohibits a party to enforce the termination clause in bad faith. To this extent, it can be argued that this decision took away the sharpness of the decision in *CBI*.

In summary, the line of cases on discretion to terminate a contract indicates that if both parties have the same rights of termination, *CBI* confirms that a court does not interfere with the reasonable expectation of the counterparty, as the counterparty has exactly the same rights of termination. *General Assurance* demonstrates that it is possible, even when there are equal rights of termination, that the clause is exercised in a manner that disrespects the counterparty's legitimate interests. The Supreme Court has rightly given effect to the good faith obligation here, although it does not state this in so many words. Since *General Assurance* leaves open the possibility of a court modifying an express clause on termination even in a bilateral termination clause, in an appropriate case, it might be possible to argue that *General Assurance* also applies to unilateral termination clauses. Although *Maharani Shantidevi* regards a unilateral termination clause to be valid in law, since it did not eliminate the possibility of implying a term, it may be possible to tone down a unilateral termination clause to confine its exercise to proper purpose, along the lines of *Chunilal*. It would be worthwhile to examine whether the courts adopted this line of reasoning in their exercise of review jurisdiction, which brings us to section IV.1.ii below.

ii. Judgments reviewing arbitral awards

Due to the ever-increasing use of commercial arbitration to resolve disputes, there has been plenty of litigation surrounding termination clauses when courts have been asked to review arbitral awards. In this context, the change in the ACA to the threshold of review appears to have emboldened some High Courts to declare a unilateral termination clause as unjustifiable in some cases.

In *Eastern Coalfields v Rungta Projects*, the contract between the parties gave the petitioner the discretion to terminate the contract for, among others, 'administrative reasons'.[66] The contract also provided that if such a termination occurs, then the respondent would only receive payment for such work as it had 'satisfactorily completed as decided by the [petitioner] Company and the [respondent] contractor shall have no further claim on this account'.[67] The petitioner terminated the contract by notice alleging 'administrative reasons', and the respondent brought a claim for, among other things, mobilisation costs in preparation of performance, idle charges, and demobilisation costs upon termination. While the arbitrator held the termination to be a valid

[65] ibid [21]–[22].
[66] 2018 SCC Online Cal 6555.
[67] ibid [9].

exercise of contractual discretion, they also permitted recovery of such costs.[68] The petitioner challenged the award on the grounds that the contract limited its liability to paying for work that was completed.

The Calcutta High Court confirmed the arbitrator's assessment of damages as 'what is right and justifiable'.[69] However, in its reasoning the Court observed that terminating the contract by merely citing 'administrative reasons' was 'arbitrary and wreaks of high-handedness', especially since the petitioner terminated the contract after three months.[70] Again, although the Court did not use the language of good faith, it is clear that the manner of exercise of contractual discretion was in utter disregard of the legitimate interests of the counterparty. Since the contractual term explicitly did not allow the damages that were awarded, it is arguable that the Court implied a term that required the demonstration of justifiable grounds for termination, along similar lines as *Chunilal*.

The Kerala High Court held similarly, and clearly attributed this to the implication of a duty of good faith. In *Kerala Minerals and Metals Ltd v Doshion Ltd*,[71] the contract gave the petitioner, a public-sector company, the right to unilaterally terminate the contract 'at any time' by giving three months' notice, and limited the respondent's remedies in such an instance to a proportionate value of the contract based upon the amount of work completed. It also explicitly provided that the petitioner was not liable to pay consequential damages.[72] The petitioner decided some time later that the project was no longer feasible and actively lobbied the Government of Kerala to decommission the project, which the government did.[73] The petitioner also sent a notice terminating the contract, but, before the notice period expired, it prevented the respondent's workers from accessing the work site.[74]

When the matter went to arbitration at the respondent's behest, the arbitrator determined the petitioner's termination to be unjustifiable, despite the contractual discretion, and awarded damages for loss of profits.[75] The petitioner appealed against this award, but the Kerala High Court held that under the new standard of review in section 28(3) of the ACA, it did not find the decision to be illegal. Indeed, the Court agreed with the respondent's argument that, due to the change in the standard of review, arbitrators were authorised to depart from the contractual language.[76] The Court stated that it agreed with the arbitrator's reasoning because '[i]n every contract, there is an implied covenant of good faith and fair dealing', which the petitioner had clearly violated.[77] This is the only case the authors have been able to find where the modification

[68] ibid [5].
[69] ibid [18].
[70] ibid [21].
[71] 2020 SCC Online Ker 9357.
[72] ibid [3].
[73] ibid [6].
[74] ibid [19].
[75] ibid [7], [8].
[76] ibid [15] (respondent's counsel argued, 'Arbitrators can, in fit cases, depart from or ignore a term of the contract in order to do justice to a party').
[77] ibid [21].

of contractual discretion was attributed to an implied duty of good faith. It makes transparent what the courts have been doing in many cases without attributing their approach to an implied duty of good faith.

Not all High Courts agree with the above decisions, however. The Delhi High Court has vacated arbitral awards that have ignored a unilateral termination clause. In *Pipavav Energy Pvt Ltd v Madhavi Procon Pvt Ltd*,[78] where the arbitrator awarded loss of profit as damages for wrongful termination, in the face of a unilateral termination clause, the Delhi High Court held the award to be arbitrary and capricious and vacated it. The Court read the unilateral termination clause, which permitted the petitioner to terminate the contract 'at any time' and 'for any reason', as a valid term that was properly invoked by the petitioner.[79] The Court specifically read the *Maharani Shantidevi* judgment to hold that there was no legal justification for inserting a requirement that a unilateral termination clause be 'exercised for a good and reasonable cause' in the face of express language to the contrary.[80] Essentially, the Court held that infusing reasonableness into an express provision is not a permissible interpretation of the clause. This, it is submitted, is an incorrect reading of *Maharani Shantidevi* because, as argued above,[81] that case did not eliminate the possibility of implying terms but merely held that such clauses were not bad at law. Additional reasons exist in *General Assurance*, which acknowledges the possibility of an express provision on termination to be toned down to avoid its exercise in bad faith. Unfortunately, the Delhi High Court has also reiterated this decision in a subsequent matter.[82]

It is, however, worth noting that where the state is a contracting party, it is not permitted to invoke such unilateral termination clauses without justification due to the constitutional restrictions placed upon it.[83] This is an exception based in public law and seems to have drawn quite some inspiration from the unconscionability jurisprudence,[84] which has itself been limited to contracts with the state or state instrumentalities.[85] It is possible to also argue that this is a limited instance of a term implied-by-law, as this is a term (that termination of a contract be for justifiable reasons) implied into all contracts of a particular type, being contracts made with the state.[86]

[78] *Pipavav Energy Pvt Ltd v Madhavi Procon Pvt Ltd* 2018 SCC Online Del 13100.

[79] ibid [14].

[80] ibid [15] ff.

[81] See text accompanying nn 54–56.

[82] *Altus Group India Pvt Ltd v Darrameks Hotels & Developers Pvt Ltd* 2018 SCC Online Del 8263 (judgment by the same judge as in *Pipavav Energy*, n 78), *affirmed* by a larger bench of the Delhi High Court in MANU/DE/2073/2018, [11].

[83] *Indian Oil Corp Ltd (IOCL) v Nilofer Siddiqui* (2015) 16 SCC 125 (a standard form contract that gave a state instrumentality unfettered discretion to terminate a distributorship agreement without any justification was declared unconscionable and read down in light of the Constitution of India 1950, art 14). See also *Golden Trust Financial Services v Union of India* 2016 SCC Online Cal 1546 (Calcutta High Court) (in part, distinguishing the Supreme Court decisions in *CBI* (n 57) and *General Assurance* (n 61)as cases involving two private parties). See generally C Chandrachud, Chapter 23 of this volume.

[84] See *Central Inland Water Transport Corp Ltd (CIWT) v Brojo Nath Ganguly* (1986) 3 SCC 156.

[85] See S Swaminathan and V Singh, Chapter 9 of this volume.

[86] There was one notable exception to this constraint upon the state. Where the state provided a grant of property, it was deemed unconstrained by any other statutory or legal provision as a result of the Government Grants Act 1895. Therefore, an unfettered unilateral termination clause was deemed valid and enforceable: *Hajee SVM Mohamed Jamaludeen v Govt of Tamil Nadu* (1997) 3 SCC 466. The Act has, however, been repealed as of 2018: Act 4 of 2018 dated 8 January 2018.

The question before us now is whether the courts have come up with a different jurisprudence while exercising their review jurisdiction over arbitral awards. In *Maharani Shantidevi*, the Court leaving open the possibility of implying a term to tone down the exercise of a termination clause in an appropriate case has resulted in high courts reading this as a negation of such a possibility. While we have the Kerala High Court decision that explicitly recognises implying a duty of good faith, there are others that threaten to negate any such argument. Although *General Assurance* is a high authority that does acknowledge modification of an express term to accommodate concerns of the counterparty, it does not recognise this, in so many words, as an implied term and does not attribute it to the duty of good faith. Until the Supreme Court hands down a decision clearly acknowledging the existence of a duty of good faith to tone down termination clauses, parties should be able to rely on *General Assurance*.

Further, it is worth noting that the Calcutta and Kerala High Courts have affirmed arbitral awards that ignored the express limitations and exclusions of liability contained in the contracts. And the courts have done so in a manner that demonstrated agreement with the outcome. The fact that the courts' agreement was provided merely by way of dicta makes this a more interesting development in commercial jurisprudence. As will be demonstrated in section IV.1.iii below, limitations and exclusions of liability is another fraught area of law in India, perhaps more so than contractual discretion, where the Supreme Court is struggling to develop a coherent legal principle by which to curtail parties' worst impulses. As we explore the flawed approaches below, it is worth remembering that with the change in the threshold of review of arbitral awards, a court is free to view the award as being based on 'a possible' interpretation of the terms of the contract, regardless of whether it is 'the correct' interpretation of the contract. In this vein, it is possible that a court, which might not have implied a duty of good faith if it had the opportunity of considering the matter on its own, might find nothing objectionable about an arbitrator doing so.

iii. Exclusions of liability

Contracting parties frequently tailor the remedies available to them to reallocate risk amongst themselves. Within this context, although it may be considered rational for a party to put all the risk of loss upon the other party, the law does not always permit this. A classic example is the limitation placed upon sums stipulated in the contract under section 74 of the Contract Act—penalties are not permitted.[87] Another example arises when parties limit or exclude their liability for breach, negligence, or any wrongdoing. This may be considered an aspect of good faith because respect for the counterparty's legitimate interests means that the counterparty cannot be assumed to have accepted all the risks that arise from such limitation or exclusion of liability[88] and be deprived of an effective remedy.

[87] For an excellent explanation of the social considerations that shaped the language of the Contract Act, s 74 in its current form, see TT Arvind, Chapter 17 of this volume, section III.

[88] Chen-Wishart and Dixon (n 6) 217; *Treitel on the Law of Contract* (n 22) [7-018] (making no comment about good faith, but noting that English courts find it improbable that commercial parties agreed to a complete exclusion).

In England, before the enactment of the Unfair Contract Terms Act 1977 (UCTA), onerous exclusions of liability were sought to be excised through the use of the doctrine of fundamental breach.[89] The substance of the doctrine was that where there was a fundamental breach, the breaching party could not, as a rule of law, avoid liability through the use of an exemption clause.[90] However, this approach was discarded shortly after the enactment of the UCTA in *Photo Production Ltd v Securicor Transport Ltd*,[91] where the House of Lords held that any decision regarding the fate of exclusion clauses must rest entirely upon the construction of the contract. By so holding, the House of Lords clarified its previous judgment in *Suisse Atlantique Société d'Armement Maritime SA v NV Rotterdamsche Kolen Centrale*,[92] where certain parts of the judgment seemed to suggest that a doctrine of fundamental breach still existed.

Indian courts do not appear to have followed the English courts' approach to exclusion clauses at the time that such jurisprudence was in its heyday in England.[93] Instead, their preferred approach seems to be to construe narrowly the relevant statutory provision and not permit parties to contract out of these provisions. This practice began pre-independence in *Shekh Mahamad Ravuther v The British India Steam Navigation Co Ltd*,[94] where the defendant bailee had completely excluded itself from liability in negligence. Sections 151 and 152 of the Contract Act require a bailee to take due care of the goods bailed as an ordinary person would. The Court held that the defendant was subject to this standard of care, which could not be excluded. The Court came to this conclusion despite there being no express statutory mandate prohibiting parties from excluding duty of care provisions under the Contract Act. The logic behind this might be that the ability to sue for negligence (breach of duty of care) is so fundamental that a contractual provision cannot exclude it. If the language of implied terms is to be used, the implied duty of good faith helps read down the exclusion clause to bring the contract in compliance with a statutory provision.

Post-independence, however, the Indian Law Commission observed that such reasoning was not favoured by the various high courts and that the 'majority view' is to permit a bailee to exclude their liability for negligence. The Law Commission concluded that this was the correct approach and recommended inclusion of express statutory language making the standard of care subject to contract.[95] Nevertheless, courts continue to disallow contracting out of statutory provisions.

[89] J Beatson, A Burrows, and J Cartwright, *Anson's Law of Contract* (30th edn, OUP 2016) 199.

[90] ibid; M Furmston, *Cheshire, Fifoot & Furmston's Law of Contract* (17th edn, OUP 2017) 238.

[91] [1980] AC 827.

[92] [1967] 1 AC 361.

[93] See generally V Ramaseshan, 'Fundamental Obligation and the Indian Law of Contract' (1968) 10 Journal of the Indian Law Institute 301 (exploring the possibilities of having a doctrine of fundamental breach apply to contracts dealing with sale of goods, bailment, and insurance).

[94] [1908] ILR 32 Mad 95 (Madras High Court).

[95] *13th Law Commission of India Report, Indian Contract Act 1872* (1958) 59–60 <https://cdnbbsr.s3waas.gov.in/s3ca0daec69b5adc880fb464895726dbdf/uploads/2022/08/2022080532.pdf> accessed 26 October 2023 (citing various Madras and Bombay High Court judgments for support of the majority view). Although in a more recent case, the Supreme Court has held that hotels cannot contract out of their statutory liability for negligence in safeguarding the vehicles of hotel guests who use the hotel valet parking service, the Court was insistent that its holding was limited solely to the specific context at hand and that it was not commenting upon 'other kinds of contracts': *Taj Mahal Hotel v United India Insurance Co Ltd* (2020) 2 SCC 224, 255.

An illustration of it can be seen in *General Manager Northern Railways v Sarvesh Chopra*,[96] where time was of the essence of the contract. Section 55 of the Contract Act provides that when time is of the essence of the contract, as per the parties' intention, failure to meet the contractually stipulated timelines renders the contract voidable at the option of the promisee. The section goes on to provide that if the promisee elects to stay with the contract, then they cannot claim compensation unless they affirmatively reserve the right to do so. A long line of cases had upheld exclusion-of-liability clauses that disentitle a contractor from recovering damages for delays caused if an extension of time had been granted.[97] However, the *General Manager Northern Railways* bench held that where time is of the essence and the contractor has elected not to stay with the contract due to the delays, by virtue of section 55, their claim for damages is not prevented by any contrary contractual language. The logic seems to be that where the counterparty does not have the benefit of continuing with the contract, they must at least have a remedy, which arguably is reflective of respect for the legitimate interests of the counterparty.

Another example of the application of section 55 read with section 73 of the Contract Act can be seen in *Simplex Concrete Piles (India) Ltd v Union of India*.[98] As stated above, while section 55 addresses a contract where time is of the essence, section 73 of the Contract Act provides that a non-breaching party is entitled to damages. Neither section provides that it is 'subject to contract', much like the sections pertaining to the standard of care for bailment. And yet, a single judge of Delhi High Court held that all exclusionary clauses are against public policy for violating the statutory provisions of sections 55 and 73 of the Contract Act. No judgment by the Supreme Court of India has gone so far as to support such an indictment of the exclusionary clause as an unfair term as a matter of law. In more recent times, the Delhi High Court itself seems to be distancing itself from the *Simplex Concrete* judgment,[99] although, once again, arbitrators appear to be drawn to this reasoning, and courts do not interfere with those awards.[100] Again, the logic appears to be to not eliminate all remedy for the counterparty.

[96] (2002) 4 SCC 45.

[97] Several Supreme Court judgments set aside arbitral awards that awarded compensation to contractors in the face of such an exclusion of liability clause. See eg *ONGC v Wig Brothers Builders and Engineers Pvt Ltd* (2010) 13 SCC 377; *Ramalinga Reddy v Superintending Engineer* (1999) 9 SCC 610. See also S Bindal and RV Prabhat, 'Limitation of Liability Clause: Position in India' (2019) 4 Supreme Court Cases Journal 25 (summarising various conflicting judgments and arguing that the *General Manager Northern Railways* judgment (n 96) is the proper approach). See also G Pachnanda, 'Effect of Limitation of Liability and Exclusion of Liability Clauses in the Event of Fundamental breach of Contract' (2020) 5 Supreme Court Cases Journal 1, 2.

[98] (2010) 115 DRJ 616 (Delhi High Court).

[99] *C & C Constructions Ltd v Ircon International Ltd* 2021 SCC Online Del 3148 (Delhi High Court) (noting but not acceding to the argument that an exclusionary clause was contrary to the Contract Act, s 23 and refraining from interfering with the arbitral award that enforced such a clause); *KSS–KSSIIPL Consortium v GAIL India Ltd* 2019 SCC Online Del 10388 (Delhi High Court) (surprisingly reading *Simplex Concrete* (n 98) to provide a public interest exception; that is, where there is a public interest at stake, then ss 55 and 73 can be amended by way of contractual stipulation).

[100] See *Delhi Metro Rail Corp Ltd v J Kumar Crtg JV* 2022 SCC Online Del 1210 (where the arbitral panel refused to enforce the exclusionary clause in light of *Simplex Concrete* (n 98), the Court refused to interfere with the arbitral award); *Ircon International Ltd v GPT-Rahee JV* 2022 SCC Online Del 839 (Delhi High Court) (same).

The core tension here is that such a strict reading of the statutory framework is evidently strained as it fails to explain why certain contractual limitations that are subject to the same statutory provisions are permissible. For example, a clause that limits the recoverable damages is permissible,[101] although this also goes against damages having to be available under section 73 of the Contract Act. Even the previously discussed clauses that provide for unilateral termination could be deemed impermissible under section 39 of the Contract Act. Section 39 of the Contract Act only permits an innocent party to elect to terminate the contract where the promisor has refused to perform the promise 'in its entirety'. A unilateral termination for any reason could be argued to contradict this provision, as it does not provide that it is subject to an agreement to the contrary. Therefore, statutory interpretation seems to be too blunt a tool for the task at hand, yielding a contradictory patchwork of decisions.

More recently, the Kerala High Court has alluded specifically to the duty of good faith in *DLF Home Developers Ltd v Martin George*.[102] In this case, the contract provided for limiting the liability of the defendant developer to return the sums paid and for interest payments under certain circumstances (such as *force majeure*). The Court upheld the interpretation by the arbitrator in refusing to limit the liability. In support of this, the Court held that 'in every contract, there is an implied covenant of good faith and fair dealing' and that each party must act in such a manner 'as not to destroy the right of the other party to receive the benefit of the contract'.[103] It is significant to note that the courts are applying their mind to the obligation of good faith and without using the logic of previous decisions in avoiding certain exclusionary clauses.[104] However, once again, the Court in *DLF Home Developers* made the remarks about good faith merely by way of dicta because, even if there was a duty of good faith, the circumstances that triggered limiting the liability had not arisen.

Without a readily apparent solution to exclusionary clauses being found in the Contract Act, and the ill ease with explicitly recognising a duty of good faith, it is perhaps not surprising that, in recent times, the doctrine of fundamental breach appears to be getting fresh wind in India.[105] Especially noteworthy in this regard is the judgment by the Supreme Court affirming an arbitral award providing damages in the face of an exclusionary clause, characterising as a 'proposition of law' that if the innocent party is justified in terminating the agreement for fundamental breach, then it is entitled to the full measure of damages, irrespective of contractual terms.[106] The Supreme Court went on to cite one of the controversial passages in the House of Lords' *Suisse Atlantique* judgment, without making any reference to the *Photo Production* clarification.[107] On

[101] *Bharathi Knittings v DHL Worldwide* (1996) 4 SCC 704.
[102] 2021 SCC Online Ker 2867, [40].
[103] ibid.
[104] Here, one may recall *Eastern Coalfields* (n 66) and *Kerala Minerals and Metals* (n 71) discussed in section IV.1.ii as well; see text accompanying nn 66–77.
[105] See generally S Khanderia, 'The Ambivalent Notion of "Fundamental Breach" in Indian Law of Contract: Towards a New Paradigm' (2022) 43 Liverpool Law Review 391.
[106] *Maharashtra State Electricity Distribution Co (MSED) v Datar Switchgear* (2018) 3 SCC 133, 176.
[107] ibid. The Supreme Court drew specific attention to the following quote from the *Suisse Atlantique* case (n 92): 'I do not think that there is generally much difficulty where the innocent party has elected to treat the breach as a repudiation, bring the contract to an end and sue for damages. Then the whole contract has ceased to exist,

this point, the Supreme Court's reasoning has largely escaped notice, although some have noted and criticised the Court's reliance upon *Suisse Atlantique* in a manner that could be understood to support an independent doctrine of fundamental breach, separate from an inquiry into the parties' intention.[108] However, adopting the *doctrine* of fundamental breach may pose the risk of being overbroad for the task for which it is employed, suffocating commercially negotiated risk re-allocations.[109]

It is interesting, however, that within the context of exclusions of liability, unlike with contractual discretion, in the face of bad faith action, the Supreme Court seems receptive to a rule of law that prevails over any contract language, no matter how unambiguous. What is apparent is the Court's desire to intervene in cases where an innocent party is left essentially without a remedy, in the face of express terms. In *MSED*, for example, the state entity was unresponsive to requests from the supplier to provide a complete list of sites where the work needed to be done, and the arbitrator had made extensive findings that the contractor was ready and willing to perform but the state entity remained uncooperative.[110] In the face of such bad faith conduct, it is only natural for a court to want to provide the innocent party with an adequate remedy.

In summary, although there is a discernible impulse to modify the contractual language as to exclusion of liability to bring it in line with the duty of good faith, there is no acknowledgment that this is what courts are doing. While courts have been sufficiently consistent in this line of cases in their effort to limit or eliminate the impact of conduct in bad faith, greater certainty may only be achieved by legislative intervention.[111]

iv. Specific categories of contracts

Indian contract law also encompasses case law on specific types of contracts where the duty of good faith is explicitly acknowledged and implied. In these cases, courts recognise that there is something inherent in these types of contracts that makes the duty of good faith acquire a heightened importance. As such, the duty of good faith is implied-by-law into these contracts as a default rule to set right information asymmetry or inequality of bargaining power. Although the courts recognize the language of the duty of good faith, they do not identify it as implied-by-law.

In *Mardia Chemicals v Union of India*,[112] the Court was faced with interpreting the Securitisation and Reconstruction of Financial Assets and Enforcement of Security

including the exclusion clause': *MSED* (n 106) 176 (citing [1967] 1 AC 361, 398 (Lord Reid)) (emphasis supplied by the *MSED* Court).

[108] Khanderia (n 105); Pachnanda (n 97).

[109] This is not to say that the seriousness of the breach may not be a relevant consideration for the court to ascertain whether the parties intended the exemption clause should apply in such a situation: *Treitel on the Law of Contract* (n 22) [7-026].

[110] *MSED* (n 106) 168–69.

[111] Two different Law Commission of India reports have recommended curtailing exclusionary clauses by inserting a requirement of reasonableness: *103rd Law Commission of India Report, Unfair Terms in Contracts* (1984) <https://cdnbbsr.s3waas.gov.in/s3ca0daec69b5adc880fb464895726dbdf/uploads/2022/08/2022080820.pdf> accessed 17 April 2023; *199th Law Commission of India Report, Unfair (Procedural and Substantive) Terms in Contracts* (2006) <https://cdnbbsr.s3waas.gov.in/s3ca0daec69b5adc880fb464895726dbdf/uploads/2022/08/2022081093-2.pdf> accessed 17 April 2023.

[112] *Mardia Chemicals v Union of India* (2004) 4 SCC 311.

Interest Act 2002 (SARFAESI Act). The Act had been instituted to help creditors recover on non-performing assets without a court's intervention by, in part, permitting them to foreclose upon secured interests. However, the absence of a judicial procedure whereby creditors' actions could be subject to review before they foreclosed led to an action challenging the constitutionality of the statute as arbitrary.[113] The Supreme Court held that the SARFAESI Act was constitutional[114] but imposed upon the creditors a duty to meaningfully consider a debtor's objections to foreclosure and to communicate the reasons for rejecting those objections.[115] The Court went further to create a common law principle of lender's liability in the face of perceived inaction by Parliament. Specifically, the Court observed,

> it cannot be denied that the financial institutions namely, the *lenders owe a duty to act fairly and in good faith*. There has to be a *fair dealing* between the parties and the financial companies/institutions are not free to ignore performance on their part of the obligation as a party to the contract (...) *Possessing more drastic powers calls for exercise of higher degree of good faith and fair play.*[116]

In addition to the Court's eagerness to recognise a duty of good faith, this decision hints at the Court's willingness to view any such duty on a spectrum, paying attention to the nature of the commercial relationship. This judgment, however, has not received any attention for this approach of implying a duty of this nature into this type of transactions.

There is also, of course, a recognition by Indian courts that insurance agreements are contracts that are *uberrima fides*, of utmost good faith. This notion seems to be expanding, however, to also incorporate actions by the insurer.[117] In a recent case, the Supreme Court held that the duty of utmost good faith required sufficient disclosures by the insured and the insurer.[118] In the case at hand, the insurer had sent a policy renewal document but not affirmatively drawn the insureds' attention to the change in coverage amounts. This was deemed to be a breach of the duty of good faith, and the insureds were held to be entitled to the full coverage under the previous policy's terms.[119] In so holding, the Supreme Court held that this was a deficiency in service under the Consumer Protection Act 1986, overruling the decisions by the State and National Consumer Disputes Redressal Commissions, which had held the insureds to

[113] ibid 331–33.

[114] Except s 17(2) of the Act, which required an aggrieved debtor to deposit 75 per cent of the demand amount with the Debt Recovery Tribunal before it could have its grievance adjudicated before the tribunal: ibid 350–54.

[115] ibid 362.

[116] ibid 358 (emphasis supplied).

[117] At least at the time of the *General Assurance* judgment, the Supreme Court understood the *uberrima fides* narrowly to require disclosures by the insured: *General Assurance* (n 61) [11]:

> In other respects there is no difference between a contract of insurance and any other contract except that in a contract of insurance there is a requirement of *uberrima fides* i.e. good faith on the part of the assured and the contract is likely to be construed *contra proferentem* that is against the company in case of ambiguity or doubt.

[118] *Jacob Punnen v United India Insurance Co Ltd* (2022) 3 SCC 655, 671–73.

[119] ibid 680.

the terms of renewed policy, imposing upon them the duty to read.[120] The Supreme Court's reasoning was clearly based upon concerns regarding the use of standard-form contracts in the insurance industry and a person's need for health insurance coverage, especially as they get older.[121]

The Delhi High Court recognised an implied duty of good faith in contracts between private companies and the government for the provision of telecom services by requiring the private companies to submit to an audit by the Central Auditor General.[122] The Court did so because the contract was for 'mutual gain', 'similar to a joint venture', and the government had 'reposed trust and confidence' in the licensee.[123] However, on appeal, the Supreme Court affirmed the judgment only upon the constitutional grounds.[124]

Finally, courts also evince concern with an employer's actions in an employment contract. In this area, the doctrine of unconscionability, introduced in India through the Supreme Court judgment of *Brojo Nath Ganguly*,[125] is normally called upon to declare unenforceable clauses that provide the employer unlimited discretion. *Brojo Nath Ganguly* was itself an employment agreement that gave the employer wide discretion to unilaterally terminate the agreement even for permanent employees. However, in at least one recent case, the Supreme Court has called upon the unconscionability doctrine as a substitute for a duty of good faith.

In *Assistant General Manager v Radhey Shyam Pandey*,[126] the State Bank of India (SBI) Central Board of Directors approved a voluntary retirement scheme that lowered the retirement age from twenty years to fifteen years and circulated the details of the decision to the employees. The circular informed employees that those who had hit the new retirement age as of 31 December 2000 would be eligible to apply for the new scheme.[127] According to the SBI, however, the scheme was notified to be subject to the SBI Pension Fund Rules and those rules retained the retirement age as twenty years and were never amended.[128] Therefore, only those who retired after putting in twenty years of service were entitled to pension, and the SBI refused to pay all other employees who availed of the lower retirement age. The employees sued the SBI to avail of the pension benefits under the voluntary retirement scheme.

The Court in *Radhey Shyam Pandey* relied extensively on *Brojo Nath Ganguly* regarding unconscionability and found the SBI's defence that it retained discretion to amend the rules and was, thus, entitled not to amend the rules, 'unconscionable'.[129] The Court concluded that the SBI could not invalidate a decision that was otherwise valid because of an 'exclusive superior power to amend or not to amend the rule and

[120] ibid 664.
[121] ibid 673ff.
[122] *Association of Unified Telecom Service Providers of India v Union of India* 2014 SCC Online Del 82.
[123] ibid [29]–[30].
[124] *Association of Unified Telecom Service Providers of India v Union of India* (2014) 6 SCC 110.
[125] *CIWT* (n 84).
[126] (2020) 6 SCC 438.
[127] ibid 449.
[128] ibid 452.
[129] ibid 477.

act unfairly and make the entire contract unreasonable based on misrepresentation'.[130] There appears to be some judicial sleight of hand, however, as the Court's decision here was not that the Pension Fund Rules, or the discretion to amend them, were unconscionable terms that were against public policy and therefore unenforceable; rather, their invocation by the SBI within these circumstances was unconscionable. In other words, the Court restrained the SBI's freedom to engage in opportunistic and exploitative conduct by requiring it to act in good faith vis-à-vis its employees.

One can observe, therefore, that while certain types of clauses invite the courts' heightened scrutiny, Indian courts are also alert to different kinds of commercial relationships invoking specific considerations where a duty of good faith would be appropriate. This could be an encouraging sign that an implied duty of good faith as a rule of construction may have a more promising future within India.

V. Conclusion

Although the question of the existence of a general duty of good faith in English contract law continues to be controversial, one need not maintain a similar scepticism in relation to Indian contract law. Good faith is as much about the attitude of the contracting parties as it is of the legal system that has a vision to see it and of institutions that recognise and give effect to it. The Indian legal system should, therefore, forge its own path reflective of its value system and business realities. If the duty of good faith can be understood as a duty that requires contracting parties to have regard for the justifiable expectations of the other such that they interact with each other honestly and fairly and maintain fidelity to the contractual purpose, then there is plenty of evidence that Indian contract law is concerned with such a principle. While the legislative provisions address good faith at all other stages of the contract, case law addresses performance and enforcement of contracts where the contractual freedom and, therefore, the likelihood of utter disregard for the legitimate interests of the counterparty are most evident.

Like many jurisdictions, Indian courts have also recognised explicitly the duty of good faith in the performance and enforcement of certain types of contracts such as those between employer and employee, creditor and debtor, insurer and insured, and so on. In more generic circumstances, where courts are not necessarily dealing with a specific type of contract, whether a general duty of good faith can be implied is a more controversial question.

While the inherent vagueness of such a general duty might cause some concern about the desirability of its incorporation into Indian contract law, in its absence, Indian courts will continue to struggle with some of the challenges presented by modern commercial practices—challenges to which the courts are not impervious. Thus, for example, in relation to exclusion clauses, one cannot lose sight of the courts' efforts to

[130] ibid 494 (emphasis supplied).

protect a party from the counterparty's conduct in bad faith, whether by reading down the exclusion clauses or by the doctrine of fundamental breach. Although legislative intervention may be considered desirable in certain instances, it is arguably also important for Indian courts to develop a coherent framework to restrain the varied excesses indulged in by stronger commercial parties in different scenarios. An implied contractual duty of good faith holds promise in being able to provide such a framework due to the emphasis it places upon the legitimate expectations of the parties and fidelity to the larger contractual purpose.

In this context, *General Assurance* is an underappreciated Supreme Court authority, which has the potential to be the basis for implying a general duty of good faith not only to govern contractual discretion for termination of contracts but also for the manner of performance of contract. This Supreme Court authority should not be lost sight of in the midst of contradictory High Court authorities, at least until another Supreme Court authority clearly affirms the existence of a duty of good faith applicable to contractual discretion along the lines of the decision in *Kerala Minerals and Metals*. Indeed, the time may be right for a robust and critical engagement in this area, with jurists paying closer attention to what Indian courts actually do and not just what they say they do. It may be that the twenty-first century will see the development of a uniquely Indian conception of good faith in contracts.

16

Damages

*Katy Barnett**

I. Introduction and the History behind the Remedial Structure of the Indian Contract Act 1872

This chapter seeks to outline the principles governing the availability, quantum of, and limitations upon damages for breach of contract in the Indian Contract Act 1872 (hereinafter 'the Contract Act'). At the beginning of the 19th century in Britain, contract damages were not a subject of great interest in textbooks, and little attention was paid to them until *Hadley v Baxendale* was decided in 1854.[1] As Richard Danzig has noted, Britain underwent a 'Great Boom' from 1842 to 1874, and the underdeveloped common law of contract had to shift to catch up, with *Hadley v Baxendale* being an important part of that shift.[2]

On the other hand, as Niranjan has noted, the rule in *Hadley v Baxendale* was initially regarded as controversial,[3] and in 1873, the US editors of the American edition of *Smith's Leading Cases* described it as 'a merely arbitrary rule, laid down in our courts for the first time'.[4] From this point of view, the decision to codify *Hadley v Baxendale* in section 73 of the Contract Act only eighteen years after it was handed down may seem surprising. Here, I suggest that the following factors contributed to its inclusion. First, in Chapter 1 in this volume, Professor Swain has considered how the Indian codification project was influenced by the work of the French jurist, Robert-Joseph Pothier, and his Will Theory of Contract,[5] as well as by David Dudley Field's Draft New York Civil Code of 1862.[6] It is also reasonably clear, as Niranjan has also noted,[7] that the rule in

* I am grateful to KV Krishnaprasad and V Niranjan for their detailed comments on a draft of this chapter. Thanks also to the helpful suggestions and comments from participants in the conference on 150 Years of the Contract Act held remotely on 15 August 2020, 22 August 2020, and 12 September 2020.

[1] *Hadley v Baxendale* (1854) 9 Ex 341, 156 ER 145.

[2] R Danzig, '*Hadley v Baxendale*: A Study in the Industrialization of the Law' (1975) 4 Journal of Legal Studies 249.

[3] N Venkatesan, 'The Contract Remoteness Rule: Exclusion, Not Assumption of Responsibility' in A Dyson, J Goudkamp, and F Wilmot-Smith (eds), *Defences in Contract* (Hart 2017) 187, 198.

[4] JI Clark Hare, H Bonney Wallace, and JW Wallace, *Smith's Leading Cases*, vol 2 (7th edn, T and JW Johnson & Company 1873) 492. This quote has previously been attributed to the 5th English edition, an error that seems to have originated in Danzig (n 2) fn 20.

[5] W Swain, Chapter 1 of this volume. The text is R-J Pothier, *A Treatise on the Law of Obligations or Contracts* (W Evans (tr), Strahan 1806).

[6] *Draft of a Civil Code for the State of New York prepared by the Commissioners of the Code* (Albany, Weed and Parsons 1856).

[7] N Venkatesan, 'The Contract Remoteness Rule' (n 3) 187, 198.

Katy Barnett, *Damages* In: *Foundations of Indian Contract Law.* Edited by: KV Krishnaprasad, Niranjan Venkatesan, Shivprasad Swaminathan, and Umakanth Varottil, Oxford University Press. © Oxford University Press 2024.
DOI: 10.1093/9780191997211.003.0016

Hadley v Baxendale was derived from the writings of American legal scholar Theodore Sedgwick, who was, in turn, explicitly inspired by Pothier's works.[8] Moreover, in the 1862 Draft New York Code, *Hadley v Baxendale* had been explicitly codified in § 1496.[9]

In other words, the rule in *Hadley v Baxendale* was consistent with the general approach to, and the normative underpinnings of, the codification project (precisely because the rule drew on Pothier and Will Theory), and there was precedent for codifying the rule as had occurred in 1862 Draft New York Code (although, as Professor Swain has noted, the influence of the New York Code cannot be overstated).[10] Consequently, despite the fact that it had not yet become fully settled law in its home jurisdiction, the rule in *Hadley v Baxendale* represented a good 'fit' for the general approach of the Contract Act in 1872. It may, indeed, be that the codification of the rule in India influenced the later acceptance of the rule in *Hadley v Baxendale* in England and Wales.

II. The Provision: Section 73 of the Contract Act

Section 73 of the Contract Act is a short and simple attempt to codify the common law principles regarding damages for breach for contract:

> 73. Compensation of loss or damage caused by breach of contract
>
> When a contract has been broken, the party who suffers by such breach is entitled to receive, from the party who has broken the contract, compensation for any loss or damage caused to him thereby, which naturally arose in the usual course of things from such breach, or which the parties knew, when they made the contract, to be likely to result from the breach of it.
>
> Such compensation is not to be given for any remote and indirect loss of damage sustained by reason of the breach.
>
> Compensation for failure to discharge obligation resembling those created by contract: When an obligation resembling those created by contract has been incurred and has not been discharged, any person injured by the failure to discharge it is entitled to receive the same compensation from the party in default, as if such person had contracted to discharge it and had broken his contract.

[8] T Sedgwick, *A Treatise on the Measure of Damages* (JS Voorhies 1847) 64–67 (this is the 1st edition, which was cited in *Hadley* (n 1)).

[9] *Draft of a Civil Code* (n 6) 568, § 1840 stated:

> For the breach of an obligation arising from contract, the measure of damages, except where otherwise expressly provided by this Code, is the amount which will compensate the party aggrieved for all the detriment proximately caused thereby which the party in fault had notice, at the time of entering into the contract, or at any time before the breach, and while it was in his power to perform the contract upon his part, would be likely to result from such breach, or which, in the ordinary course of things, would be likely to result therefrom.

[10] W Swain, Chapter 1 in this volume at section VI. He notes that it had rather more influence on the Specific Relief Act 1877.

> *Explanation*: In estimating the loss or damage arising from a breach of contract, the means which existed of remedying the inconvenience caused by non-performance of the contract must be taken into account.

The section is said to be declaratory of the common law position with regard to contract damages as it stood in England in 1872,[11] although it is worth heeding the warning of MV Swaroop that the wording of the Act makes 'certain beguiling departures' from the common law that are not always heeded by the courts.[12] Underneath the section are eighteen illustrations ((a)–(r)) explaining how contract damages are to be calculated in various circumstances.

These illustrations will be mentioned where relevant to factual scenarios or limitations upon damages discussed in this chapter. Unfortunately, the illustrations to this section are not in logical order (they jump from goods to services, back to goods, and so forth), which makes them harder to rationalise than might otherwise be the case. Part of my aim in this chapter is to rationalise them, a work I hope will be useful to Indian contract law practitioners and scholars.

As always with statutory provisions, the first port of call is the wording of the statute itself, but as is often the case with statutory provisions governing damages,[13] the section is broad-textured, and thus case law from India and other common law jurisdictions provides guidance in the principles to be applied.

It follows that, as a starting point, there must a breach of the contract, leaving aside, for present purposes, the third paragraph of section 73 of the Contract Act dealing with compensation for contract-like obligations. If there is a breach, the 'party who suffers by such breach' is entitled to receive 'compensation for loss or damage' from the breaching party, as a matter of course. The illustrations form part of the statute and are usually read as explaining the words of the section to which they are appended;[14] thus, they can be useful in ascertaining how the broad-textured 'loss or damage' is to be interpreted and how the limitations operate. However, the section does not exhaustively outline how such loss or damage is to be measured.

III. Assessment of Compensation: Measuring 'Loss or Damage'

1. Protection of the Plaintiff's Expectation Interest

When the words 'loss or damage' are used in private law statutes, there are two main ways in which we can think of compensating for loss that compete for

[11] *AKAS Jamal v Molla Dawood Sons & Co* [1916] 1 AC 175 (Privy Council (Burma)).
[12] MV Swaroop, 'Performance Interest and Money Awards in India' in M Chen-Wishart, A Loke, and B Ong (eds), *Studies in the Contract Laws of Asia I: Remedies for Breach of Contract* (OUP 2016) 84, 85.
[13] See eg Competition and Consumer Act 2010 (Cth), sch 2 ('Australian Consumer Law') s 236.
[14] *Mohomed Syedol Ariffin v Yeoh Ooi Gark* 1916 PC 242; *Mumma Masjid v Kodimanaindra Deviah* AIR 1962 SC 847; *Muralidhar Chatterjee v International Film Co* AIR 1943 PC 34, 38. See Swaroop (n 12) 86.

acceptance: expectation loss and reliance loss.[15] Of course, in a contractual setting, the presumption is that expectation loss is the default measure. Hence, the common law rule is that famously noted by Parke B in *Robinson v Harman*:

> The rule of the common law is, that where the party sustains a loss by reason of a breach of contract, he is, so far as money can do it, to be placed in the same situation, with respect to damages, as if the contract had been performed.[16]

Unsurprisingly, the term 'expectation loss' is not used in the Contract Act, as it came into currency after the statute was enacted, as a result of Fuller and Perdue's seminal article on the topic.[17] In any case, it would not be advisable to confine damages for breach of contract simply to expectation loss, as it has been recognised that, in some circumstances, reliance losses (or damages for wasted expenditure) may be appropriate for breach of contract where expectation damages are unable to be calculated, upon the presumption that the plaintiff would at least have broken even if the contract had been performed. Moreover, in other circumstances, 'loss or damage' may possibly be restitutionary in nature where the plaintiff's loss reflects the defendant's gain, although the presence of restitutionary liability in contract remains controversial. At any rate, it seems clear that the section cannot encompass purely gain-based relief for breach of contract, because that looks only to the defendant's gain, not to the plaintiff's loss or damage, and thus that question is put on one side in this chapter.[18]

This section of the chapter focuses on how the expectation loss is calculated in the Indian context and turns to questions of reliance losses and restitutionary liability later. The Indian Supreme Court has confirmed, in *Murlidhar Chiranjilal v Harishchandra Dwarkadas*, that the primary measure for breach of contract is expectation loss, subject to the limiting principles of mitigation:

> The first is that he who has proved a breach of a bargain to supply what he has contracted to get, is to be placed so far as money can do it in as good a situation as if the contract has been performed; but this principle is qualified by a second which imposes on a plaintiff the duty of taking all reasonable steps to mitigate the loss consequent on the breach, and debars him from claiming any part of the damage which is due to his neglect to take such steps.[19]

[15] *Gates v City Mutual Life Assurance Society Ltd* (1986) 160 CLR 1, 11 (Mason, Wilson and Dawson JJ).
[16] *Robinson v Harman* (1848) 1 Ex 850 at 855; (1848) 154 ER 363 at 365.
[17] L Fuller and W Perdue, 'The Reliance Interest in Contract Damages: 1' (1936) 46 Yale Law Journal 52, 53.
[18] RY Vardhan and C Narayan, *Pollock & Mulla: The Indian Contract & Specific Relief Acts*, vol 2 (16th edn, LexisNexis 2019) [s 73.10.7]; cf in England and Wales *Attorney General v Blake* [2001] 1 AC 268 (*Blake*), but cf again *Morris-Garner v One Step (Support) Ltd* [2018] UKSC 20, [2019] AC 649, which seems to back away from *Blake* without totally overruling it. See also *Prudential Assurance Co Ltd v Revenue and Customs Commissioners* [2018] UKSC 39, [2018] AC 929, [47].
[19] *Murlidhar Chiranjilal v Harishchandra Dwarkadas* (1962) 1 SCR 653, 657 (Wanchoo J).

This is in accordance with the illustrations supplied to the section, which show that clearly, the default measure of damages is intended to be expectation loss.

2. Measure of Expectation Loss in Particular Contexts

Adam Kramer argues that, when courts calculate expectation damages for breach of contract, they contrast the hypothetical breach position (the actual gains and harms that occurred, subject to certain assumptions about how the non-breaching party should respond) and the non-breach position (the hypothetical gains and harms that would have occurred but for the breach).[20] The object of the damages award is to compensate for the difference. This analysis—like the illustrations to the Contract Act—focuses our attention upon the necessity of considering the hypothetical non-breach position. Courts must look to the objective the non-breaching party had hoped to achieve if the contract had been performed.[21] The non-breaching party's objective in entering the contract provides a useful (but not necessarily determinative) indication of what measure will be appropriate. When a contract is for financial advantage, the non-breaching party is *more likely* to be able to find a substitute on the market. This is, in fact, the position in the Contract Act: the non-breaching party is deemed to obtain a substitute performance. By contrast, where the non-breaching party has some subjective, difficult-to-quantify interest in performance, a market substitute is less likely to be available, and different measures, such as cost-of-cure or damages reflecting reliance losses or non-pecuniary losses, may be appropriate.

i. Damages for Breach of Contract for Sale of Goods

There are multiple ways in which a contract for sale of goods may be breached. Where a seller breaches a contract for sale of goods, this may be because of a failure to deliver, delay, or provision of defective goods. When a buyer breaches a contract for sale of goods, this is generally because they refuse to accept goods as agreed. Fascinatingly, Indian contract law was codified before Sale of Goods legislation had been enacted in Britain or any Commonwealth dominions, but the illustrations confirm that primary measure is 'difference in value', which has a deemed mitigation built into it. Sale of Goods was originally part of the Contract Act but was hived off into the Sale of Goods Act 1930, and the Indian experience was used to inform the later British legislation.

The general principle in relation to goods is that expressed in *Murlidhar Chiranjilal v Harishchandra Dwarkadas*:

> Where goods are available in the market, it is the difference between the market price on the date of the breach and the contract price which is the measure of damages.[22]

[20] A Kramer, *The Law of Contract Damages* (3rd edn, Hart 2022) 15–16, 345.
[21] D Friedmann, 'Economic Aspects of Damages and Specific Performance Compared' in D Saidov and R Cunnington (eds), *Contract Damages: Domestic and International Perspectives* (Hart 2008) 65, 68–71.
[22] *Murlidhar Chiranjilal* (n 19).

In fact, most of the illustrations to section 73 of the Contract Act deal with the measure for sales of goods in various contexts, namely, (a), (c), (d), (h), (j), (k), (m), (o), (p), and (q). Some of these illustrations are primarily designed to illustrate the limitations upon awards of damages, so will be discussed in that context.

(a) Non-delivery by seller

Section 57 of the Sale of Goods Act 1930 confirms that if a seller refuses to deliver goods to a buyer, the buyer is entitled to sue for damages for non-delivery. The general principle for a total failure to deliver a good is outlined in Illustration (a), which states that if a seller fails to deliver a good, the buyer is entitled to compensation according to the difference in value between the price the buyer was going to pay the seller and what it would have cost the buyer to buy a similar quantity of goods at the date when they should have been delivered.[23] This is an entirely orthodox illustration of the 'difference-in-value' measure used for sale of goods across the common law world.[24] In Kramer's terms, there is a comparison between the non-breach situation (what the buyer would have paid the seller) and the presumed breach situation (that the buyer obtained replacement goods from someone else). Note that it does not matter whether the buyer *actually* obtains 50 *maunds* of saltpetre of like quality from another supplier: he or she is deemed to have purchased replacement goods and mitigated accordingly in the difference-in-value measure. Thus, mitigation is effectively built into the difference-in-value measure because it is deemed that a buyer will go out and buy a replacement good. In this sense, perhaps this substitutive analysis may have some application in Indian law, because the 'deemed purchase' masks the reality of what the real losses are and awards a substitute for the right.

Illustration (j) quite properly provides (applying *Hadley v Baxendale*, as will be discussed later) that if a seller of goods knows that the goods are needed for a follow-on sale and fails to deliver, the seller will be liable for the loss of profits from the follow-on sale, which makes it clear that loss of profits from the follow-on sale will be recoverable if the contract was in the contemplation of the parties.

Conversely, Illustration (k) outlines an example where a seller fails to deliver goods, and the buyer has made a follow-on contract of which the seller did not know. The buyer is forced to purchase goods at a higher price than the buyer would have done otherwise and also loses profits from the follow-on contract. Illustration (k) confirms that the measure of damages is the difference in value between the price the buyer would have paid the seller and the price they actually had to pay for replacement goods but that the buyer is *not* entitled to the loss of profits of the follow-on contract because it was not known to the seller. Similarly, Illustration (o) provides that if there is a failure to deliver on a particular date, and the seller does not know of a profitable follow-on

[23] *Muthaya Manigaran v Lakku Reddiar* AIR 1914 Mad 573 (HC); *Gopal Das Agarwala v L Hari Kishan Das* AIR 1936 All 514 (HC); *Maharajsingh Swaisingh v Narayasingh Devisingh* AIR 1951 MB 103 (HC); *Dominion of India v All India Reporter Ltd* AIR 1952 Nag 32 (HC); *Divakaruni Samasiva Ras & Bros v Kurnala Ventkatarao Tobacco Seed Oil Firm Ltd* AIR 1955 AP 148 (HC).

[24] K Barnett, *Damages for Breach of Contract* (2nd edn, Sweet & Maxwell 2022) [2-009].

sale concluded *after* the original contract is entered into, then the proper measure of difference in value is the difference in value between the contract price and the market value as at the date of delivery, and the follow-on sale is not relevant. Illustration (o) is consistent with the well-known cases of *Rodocanachi Sons & Co v Milburn Bros*[25] and *Williams Brothers v Ed T Agius Ltd*,[26] both of which post-date the enactment of the Contract Act, which hold that the resale price (whether higher or lower) is generally irrelevant to calculating market value if it is not within the contemplation of the parties. In *Rodocanachi Sons* , Lord Esher MR famously said that in circumstances of non-delivery by the seller or non-acceptance by the buyer, 'the value is to be taken independently of any circumstances peculiar to the plaintiff'.[27]

The issue of follow-on profits from a failure to deliver was considered in *Karsandas H Thacker v Saran English Co Ltd*.[28] The buyer sought to purchase 200 tons of scrap iron from the seller and subsequently made a follow-on contract to sell the scrap iron to a third party. As a result of the seller's failure to deliver, the buyer breached its contract with the third party and was forced to pay the third party difference-in-value damages. The buyer then sought damages from the seller based on the difference in value between the price he would have paid the seller and the price he would have obtained from the third party. Following Illustration (k), the Court said that because the seller had not known of the follow-on contract, the buyer was not entitled to damages calculated on this basis and that damages should simply be calculated based on the difference in value between what the buyer had promised to pay and the market value at that time, which was nil.

(b) Failure to take delivery by buyer

Section 55 of the Sale of Goods Act 1930 holds that if a buyer refuses to take delivery of goods, the seller may sue for the price of the goods, which is confirmed by Illustration (c) to section 73 of the Contract Act. Illustration (c) outlines a failure on the part of a buyer to accept goods and states that if a seller refuses to deliver to a buyer, the buyer is entitled to the difference in value between the price the buyer could obtain from that seller and the price at which the buyer could sell the rice on the market at the time of the repudiation. This is, of course, simply the obverse of Illustration (a), a failure to deliver by the seller. Illustration (d), involving the sale of a ship, expresses the same basic principles to Illustration (c), albeit in a slightly different factual situation. Multiple cases confirm that, if a buyer refuses to take delivery of part of a shipment of goods, then the seller is entitled to damages reflecting the difference in value of that portion, calculated in a similar way.[29] If the buyer refuses to take delivery of a chattel and there is not an

[25] *Rodocanachi Sons & Co v Milburn Bros* (1886) 18 QBD 67.
[26] *Williams Brothers v Ed T Agius Ltd* [1914] AC 510.
[27] *Rodocanachi Sons and Co* (n 25) 77.
[28] *Karsandas H Thacker v Saran English Co Ltd* AIR 1965 SC 1981.
[29] *AKA Jamal v Molla Dawood Sons & Co* AIR 1915 PC 148; *PSNS Ambalavana Chettiar & Co Ltd v Express Newspapers Ltd* AIR 1968 SC 741; *Narsinggirji Mfg Co v Budansaheb Abdulsaheb Kaji* AIR 1924 Bom 390 (HC); *Ramalingam Chettiyar v Gokuldas Madavji & Co* AIR 1926 Mad 1021 (HC); *Seth Roda Ladha Chhatri v Abdul Gafoor* AIR 1943 Ngp 2010 (HC); *H Sham Sunder & Sons v Ram Chand Spinning and Weaving Mills* AIR 1957 P&H 90 (HC); *Union of India v S Kesar Singh* AIR 1978 J&K 102 (HC).

available market, the difference in value will reflect the date when the seller could sell the property to another buyer.[30]

Illustration (h) clarifies that, using iron as an example, if the seller of goods has agreed to sell at a higher price than the market price and the buyer repudiates, damages are the difference in value between the contract price and the sum the seller can obtain from another buyer at the same time. In this sense, damages could be seen as compensating for loss of profit, as Mason CJ and Dawson J noted in the seminal Australian case of *Commonwealth v Amann Aviation Pty Ltd* later.[31]

ii. Delay by seller

Illustration (e) deals with delay in a falling market and delivery of goods (the scenario in question is a carrier service, and the good is jute, but the principles would apply to a seller who delayed in delivery too). The carrier must compensate for the amount the recipient would have received if the jute had arrived on time and the market price at the time it in fact arrived.

However, it is worth noting that the same measurement would be applied if the seller of goods was the one who delayed in delivery. Again, we have a situation where there is a comparison between the non-breach situation (jute arriving on time and being sold for a higher price) and actual breach situation (jute arriving late and a lesser price being obtained because of the falling market). In *R Nataranjan Ramalingom Chettiar v Parasuram Parumal & Co*,[32] the sellers delayed in sending bags in a falling market, and the bags were necessary for the buyers to sell sugar in a falling, fluctuating market. The Court averaged the prices at which sugar could be sold over the period when the bags were not delivered, rather than taking the lowest price as an indication.

Unlike non-delivery, failure to accept and defective goods, in delay cases, courts consider the price that the buyer in fact received in on-sales. *Wertheim v Chicoutimi Pulp Co*,[33] a Privy Council case that post-dates the Contract Act, has been generally accepted in common law countries such as England, Australia, and Canada. In that case, the fact that the buyer managed to sell delayed goods at a higher price than the market price was considered. The prevailing view in the current edition of *Pollock and Mulla* seems to be that Indian law must take this into account[34] and follow suit, but it is submitted that there is no reason for it to do so, particularly since the terms of section 73 of the Contract Act do not, on the face of it, justify a different treatment for delay.

Scrutton LJ was highly critical of the decision in *Wertheim* in *Slater v Hoyle & Smith*, saying, 'I should myself have thought the principles applying to these two cases were the same as those applying to non-delivery, and that the Privy Council judgment [in *Wertheim*] was erroneous as departing from those principles.'[35] There is nothing in the

[30] *Sampatraj v Pokar* AIR 1955 Raj 70 (HC).
[31] *Commonwealth of Australia v Amann Aviation Pty Ltd* (1991) 174 CLR 64, 81 (Mason CJ and Dawson J).
[32] *R Nataranjan Ramalingom Chettiar v Parasuram Parumal & Co* AIR 1963 Ker 13 (HC).
[33] *Wertheim v Chicoutimi Pulp Co* [1911] AC 301.
[34] Vardhan and Narayan (n 18) [s 73.23.1.5].
[35] *Slater v Hoyle & Smith* [1920] 2 KB 11, 24.

terms of the section or the illustrations to section 73 of the Contract Act to prevent Indian courts from rejecting *Wertheim*, and such an approach would have the advantage that it was more consistent and principled.

Indeed, McGregor has suggested that English law should reject *Wertheim* and that the *prima facie* position should be to ignore follow-on sales (regardless of whether the breach was non-delivery, non-acceptance, delay, or defect), but the seller should be able to adduce facts to the contrary *if* the seller can show that the buyer has not bought substitute goods and is not subject to a damages claim.[36] This would render the outcomes in *Williams Brothers* and *Rodocanachi* incorrect. The terms and illustrations of section 73 of the Contract Act may not make such an approach possible in an Indian context: liability rests upon whether the follow-on sale was in the natural course of things or whether the parties knew, when they made the contract, of the existence of the follow-on sale (see eg Illustration (o) discussed above).

(a) Supply of defective goods by seller

The question of defective goods always gives rise to difficulties involving follow-on sales and whether they should or should not be considered in determining the difference in value. Illustration (m) provides that if a seller warrants that merchandise is of a particular quality, and the buyer, in reliance on this warranty, then on-sells it to another with a similar warranty, the buyer will be liable to the third party, but the original seller will be liable to reimburse the buyer for that sum.

Illustration (m) can be compared with the later English case of *Bence Graphics International Ltd v Fasson UK Ltd*.[37] In that case, the buyer received vinyl film from the seller, from which it made labels for shipping containers. The vinyl film turned out to be defective and peeled off the containers, but the English Court of Appeal did not award the difference in value between the defective film and the value the film would have had it complied with the warranty. It awarded the buyer the cost of having to reimburse the third parties (in the event, only one party, in fact, sued). In fact, *Bence Graphics* is broadly consistent with Illustration (m) (subject to the requirement under section 73 of the Contract Act to show that the loss was in the contemplation of the parties), although it could be argued that the buyer should also recover any consequential losses incurred from dealing with the defective film or loss of goodwill.[38]

Bence Graphics is often criticised as being inconsistent with *Slater & Co v Hoyle & Smith Ltd*,[39] an earlier case (which, nonetheless, post-dates the Contract Act) also involving defective goods. In that case, the seller delivered defective goods that were worth less than what the buyer had contracted for, but the buyer managed to on-sell the defective goods at the price at which non-defective goods could have been sold. The English Court of Appeal awarded the buyer the difference in value between

[36] J Edelman, J Varuhas, and S Colton (eds), *McGregor on Damages* (20th edn, Sweet & Maxwell 2018) [9-183].
[37] *Bence Graphics International Ltd v Fasson UK Ltd* [1998] QB 87.
[38] K Barnett, 'Substitutive Damages and Mitigation in Contract Law' (2016) 26 Singapore Academy of Law Journal 795, 817.
[39] *Slater* (n 35).

non-defective goods and the market value of defective goods without considering that this particular buyer had managed to sell the goods at a different value, saying that it was not relevant to take into account resale value. In fact, Indian law takes a similar approach (as Illustrations (k) and (o) to the Contract Act show) and, as Dyson and Kramer have argued, *Slater v Hoyle* can be distinguished from *Bence Graphics* in any case.[40] In *Slater v Hoyle*, the defect was patent and known to the parties at the time of the sale, and the Court expected the buyer to go onto the market and ameliorate its losses. The fact that it was very skilled in mitigating its loss was held to be irrelevant. In *Bence Graphics*, the defect was latent, and the buyer was unaware of it when it on-sold the products to third parties. There was no way (in the absence of any knowledge of the defect) that it could have mitigated its losses on the market, and thus, in accordance with Illustration (m), it was appropriate to award damages reflecting what the buyer had to pay third parties in damages.

Consequently, both *Slater v Hoyle* and *Bence Graphics* can be rationalised as consistent with the Contract Act and its illustrations. In fact, Illustration (m) proves prescient as to the *Bence Graphics* problem, although it surely requires the loss in question to be in the contemplation of the parties, having regard to the first paragraph of section 73 of the Contract Act.

iii. Failure to convey land as promised

A vendor of land may breach a contract for sale of land in several ways: by conveying the land later than promised, by not conveying the land at all, or by providing defective title. Interestingly, none of the illustrations to section 73 of the Contract Act discuss the conveyance of land.

The traditional English common law rule is that the general measure for land is the same as goods, subject to the rule in *Bain v Fothergill*,[41] which provides that an innocent vendor's liability for providing defective title is limited to compensating the purchaser for expenses incurred in inspecting the title. However, this rule does not apply in India.[42] In *Ranchhod Bhawan v Manmohandas Ramji*,[43] a case involving a wilful default on the part of the vendor in completing the title, Macleod J held that the rule in *Bain v Fothergill* did not apply, first because of the wilful nature of the vendor's default, but even so, second, the rule should not apply because it had not existed when the Contract Act was enacted, and there was no reference to it in the wording of the Act. As Farran CJ in *Nagardas v Ahmedkhan* noted, 'The legislature has not prescribed a different measure of damages in the case of contracts dealing with land from that laid down in the case of contracts dealing with commodities.'[44] This has later been confirmed in the 1992 case, *Jagdish Singh v Nathu Singh*.[45] However, it has sometimes been

[40] A Dyson and A Kramer, 'There Is No "Breach Date Rule": Mitigation, Difference in Value and Date of Assessment' (2014) 130 Law Quarterly Review 259, 273–75.

[41] *Bain v Fothergill* (1874-75) LR 7 HL 158.

[42] Vardhan and Narayan (n 18) [s 73.23.7.1].

[43] *Ranchhod Bhawan v Manmohandas Ramji* (1907) 9 BOMLR 1087.

[44] *Nagardas v Ahmedkhan* (1895) ILR 21 Bom 175, 185.

[45] *Jagdish Singh v Nathu Singh* AIR 1992 SC 1604, (1992) 1 SCC 647. See Vardhan and Narayan (n 18) [s 73.23.7.1].

held that difference in value damages will not always been awarded if the vendor is not guilty of fraud and a lesser award made.[46] It is suggested that any cases that hold this should be regarded as incorrect in light of *Jagdish Singh*.

Although the principles for sale of interests in land are generally the same as those that apply to sale of goods (a comparison of the hypothetical position the non-breaching party would have been in if the contract had been performed with the position the non-breaching party is in, taking into account reasonable mitigation), the market for interests in land is less liquid than that for goods. For this reason, a purchaser may be entitled to an order of specific relief in relation to a contract for sale of land,[47] but if this is not possible or sought after, he or she may also be entitled to return of the deposit and damages calculated according to difference in value measure. In *Ghaziabad Development Authority v Union of India*, the Supreme Court held:

> A vendor who breaks the contract by failing to convey the land to the purchaser is liable to damages for the purchaser's loss of bargain by paying the market value of the property at the fixed time for completion less the contract price. The purchaser may claim the loss of profit he intended to make from any particular use if the vendor had actual or imputed knowledge thereof. For delay in performance the normal nature of damages is the value of the use of the land for the period of delay, *viz.*, usually its rental value. In our opinion, compensation for mental agony cannot be awarded.[48]

There is also authority to suggest there is a little flexibility regarding the calculation of difference in value, as sometimes the difference is taken between the agreed price, and the value either at the date when proceedings were started[49] or at the date of judgment.[50]

If a purchaser wrongfully refuses to complete a contract of sale, the current edition of *Pollock and Mulla* says that the vendor can obtain the difference in value between the initial contract price and the eventual price at which the property is sold, as long as it is sold within a reasonable time.[51] A question has arisen in other jurisdictions, such as England and Australia, as to whether the proper date for ascertaining damages can be adjusted to take into account lack of liquidity in the property market in circumstances where the purchaser repudiates the contract. Thus, generally, damages will be calculated as at date of breach,[52] but if the vendor makes a reasonable effort to resell the property and cannot do so until a much later date, the purchaser may have to pay the difference in value between the original price and the later sale price, notwithstanding that there may have been a falling market.[53] It is unclear how Indian courts would deal

[46] See eg *Dhanrajgirji Narsinggirji v Tata Sons Ltd* AIR 1924 Bom 743 (HC).
[47] Specific Relief Act 1963 (Ind), s 10.
[48] *Ghaziabad Development Authority v Union of India* AIR 2000 SC 2003, 2006.
[49] *Polavarapu Venkataswami v Nalluri Venkayya* AIR 1953 Mad 529 (HC).
[50] Vardhan and Narayan (n 18) [s 72.23.7.2].
[51] ibid.
[52] *Ng v Filmlock Pty Ltd* [2014] NSWCA 389, (2014) 88 NSWLR 146; *C&P Syndicate Pty Ltd v Reddy* [2013] NSWSC 643, (2013) 16 BPR 31, 771.
[53] *Hooper v Oates* [2013] EWCA Civ 91, (2014) Ch 287; *Lords v Von Thomann (No 2)* [2014] WASC 320, (2014) 47 WAR 473 (Supreme Court of Western Australia).

with this problem, but it is suggested that it would be similar to English and Australian courts, particularly given that section 73 of the Contract Act explicitly clarifies that when measuring the loss or damage, 'the means which existed of remedying the inconvenience caused by the non-performance of the contract must be taken into account'.

iv. Failure to build or repair property as promised

Damages representing 'cost-of-cure' for a failure to build or repair property are *prima facie* available as 'loss or damage' arising from the breach. Illustration (f) deals with repair of property and discusses an example where a builder contracts to repair a house in a certain manner for payment in advance. The builder repairs the house, but not according to the contract, and the example confirms that the home owner is entitled to recover 'the cost of making the repairs conform to the contract'. Swaroop notes that this illustration (unlike many others in the section) is not based on a particular case but was simply added as an illustration of the application of the principle of damages for breach of contract.[54]

Illustration (l) outlines a situation where a builder contracts to erect and finish a building by 1 January and knows that this completion date is necessary so that the owner may lease it out to a third party at a given date. The house is so badly built that it must be reconstructed, and the owner has to compensate the third party for breaching the lease. Illustration (l) states that the builder must compensate the owner for the cost of rebuilding the house, for the rent lost from the third party, and for the compensation paid to the third party.

It is thus clear under the statute that Indian contract law presupposes a 'cost-of-cure' measure for defective repairs or buildings, as well as consequential losses flowing from that (as long as the possibility of such consequential losses is known to the repairer or builder). In this way, Indian law reflects the law from other Commonwealth countries such as England and Wales and Australia, both of which contemplate a 'cost-of-cure' measure.[55]

However, as Swaroop has noted, unlike England and Wales and Australia, the illustrations do not include a 'reasonableness' qualification (namely, that the repair be necessary and reasonable in the circumstances). Nonetheless, in a situation where the defective performance is substantially similar to the contracted-for performance, rectification costs may not be awarded, as in the US case of *Jacob & Youngs v Kent*,[56] where the homeowner contracted for his house to be built with a certain specified brand of pipe made by Reading. In fact, half of the piping was not 'Reading' pipe but 'Cohoes'

[54] Swaroop (n 12) 88. Nonetheless, some early English cases establish the general principle: see eg *Thornton v Place* (1832) 1 Mood & R 218; 174 ER 74, in which it was held that if a tradesman did not conform to the specification, he was only entitled to the agreed sum for the work minus the amount it would take to redo the work according to the specification.

[55] Australia: *Bellgrove v Eldridge* (1954) 90 CLR 613; *Tabcorp Holdings Ltd v Bowen Investments Pty Ltd* [2009] HCA 8, (2009) 236 CLR 272; cf, however, *Stone v Chappel* [2017] SASCFC 72, (2017) 128 SASR 165. England and Wales: *Radford v De Froberville* [1977] 1 WLR 1262; *Dean v Ainley* [1987] 1 WLR 1729; *Ruxley Electronics and Construction Ltd v Forsyth* [1996] AC 344 (HL).

[56] *Jacob & Youngs v Kent* 129 NE 889 (CA NY).

pipe; a different brand, which was otherwise the same in quality, appearance, market value, and cost as Reading pipe, but the owner refused to pay for the house. In order to replace the piping, the builder would have needed to tear down the completed house and rebuild it, at a massive expense. A majority of the New York Court of Appeals held that the measure of damages was not 'cost-of-cure' but a 'difference in value' between the house built entirely using Reading pipe and the house built with using some Cohoes pipe (ie nominal or nil) because it was unreasonable to expect the builder to tear it down. Swaroop argues that this case shows a shortcoming of the illustrations regarding building repair and that it would have been preferable to have a reasonableness qualification. Moreover, there is a conflict between the unqualified nature of Illustration (f) and the requirement in the main section that damages can only be for 'loss or damage', which has in fact occurred, and thus Illustration (f) should be read as ancillary only.[57]

It may not matter that Illustration (f) does not contain a reasonableness qualification because the Explanation to section 73 of the Contract Act allows courts to consider the 'means which existed of remedying the inconvenience caused by the non-performance', which might allow an Indian court to read in a reasonableness requirement into section 73 of the Contract Act, particularly in these cost-of-cure cases. Nonetheless, it would be preferable to have an express qualification in Illustration (f) for the avoidance of doubt.

Indian courts have applied the 'cost-of-cure' measure, as in *Nikhera v Chitnavis*,[58] where a building was so badly built as to be unusable, where it was clearly reasonable to require cost-of-cure.

v. Failure to provide services as promised

The illustrations to section 73 of the Contract Act deal primarily with carrier contracts, which were, as *Hadley v Baxendale* illustrates, a primary concern at this time in contract law. We have already discussed (in the context of goods) Illustration (e), which dealt with a carrier contract to transport jute, and which held that in a falling market, the seller of the jute was to be awarded the difference in value between the price the seller could have obtained had it been awarded on time and the market price at the time it arrived.

Illustration (b) deals with a situation where a seller hires a ship to take his cargo, but the ship does not go. The seller finds another ship on terms as advantageous as the first, and hires it but is put to trouble and expense in doing so and is entitled to damages reflecting that trouble and expense. In his commentary on the *Anglo-Indian Codes*, Whitley Stokes notes, in a footnote, that this example reflects an obligation to mitigate and cites *Hochster v De La Tour*,[59] saying that if an agent or servant is wrongfully discharged, he or she is obliged to try to obtain fresh employment, and the wages he or she did obtain (or should have obtained) will be deducted from the damages.[60]

[57] Swaroop (n 12) 86–88.
[58] *Nikhera v Chitnavis* AIR 1941 Nag 111 (HC).
[59] *Hochster v De La Tour* 118 ER 922 (QB).
[60] W Stokes, *The Anglo-Indian Codes* (OUP 1887) 589 fn 1.

Illustration (g) also deals with a contract to hire a ship for a year, but the cost of freight rises, and thus the ship owner breaches to obtain a more favourable contract from someone else. Illustration (g) provides that the ship owner must pay the difference in value between the contract price and the price for which the non-breaching party could hire a similar ship for a year as at the same date.

Many of the other illustrations regarding services raise issues of remoteness and mitigation and what liability carriers should be aware of, and will be discussed in section IV.2.i. Carriers are, by their very nature, generally less likely to have an awareness of the ramifications of a failure to deliver or late delivery on the seller.[61] Thus, more detailed consideration of these matters is deferred to that discussion.

vi. Failure to pay money

Illustration (n) to the Contract Act covers the failure to pay a debt in a timely fashion, meaning that the creditor cannot pay his her own debts and is 'totally ruined'. Rather than being an 'illustration' as billed, it seems to provide a rule.

Illustration (n) confirms that the debtor is not liable to pay the creditor anything except the principal sum together with interest to the day of payment. This confirms the principle that, ordinarily, such a loss is too remote and not within the contemplation of the parties. The situation may be different where the consequential loss was in the contemplation of the parties.[62]

In *Bengal Nagpur Railway Co Ltd v Ruttanji Ramji*,[63] it was held that Illustration (n) did not confer upon a creditor a right to interest upon a debt where the creditor was not otherwise entitled to it under the law. Section 73 has been held to be merely declaratory of the common law as to damages,[64] and thus consequential losses arising from the delay in payment of money will not be recoverable where they would not be recoverable under common law.

3. Compensation of Reliance Loss

As noted earlier, section 73 of the Contract Act does not specify how 'loss or damage' is to be measured, and it is possible that in some circumstances, a reliance measure (or 'wasted expenditure'[65]) measure might be applied, as has occurred in other common law countries, particularly in Australia and England.[66] It has been confirmed by the

[61] Vardhan and Narayan (n 18) [s 73.23.6.1].

[62] ibid [s 73.23.4].

[63] *Bengal Nagpur Railway Co Ltd v Ruttanji Ramji* AIR 1938 PC 67, 70.

[64] ibid, citing *AKAS Jamal* (n 11) followed in *District Local Board Nawabshah v Bulchand Chandiram* AIR 1942 Sind 165 and *S Kotrabasappa v Indian Bank* AIR 1987 Kant 236 (HC).

[65] 'Wasted expenditure' has been suggested as the preferable term by MB Kelly, 'The Phantom Reliance Interest in Contract Damages' [1992] Wisconsin Law Review 1755; D McLauchlan, 'Reliance Damages for Breach of Contract' [2007] New Zealand Law Review 417.

[66] See *McRae v Commonwealth Disposals Commission* [1951] HCA 79, (1951) 84 CLR 377; *Anglia Television v Reed* [1972] QB 60; *CCC Films (London) Ltd v Impact Quadrant Films Ltd* (1985) 1 QB 16; *Amann Aviation* (n 31); *Omak Maritime Ltd v Mamola Challenger Shipping Ltd* [2010] EWHC 2026 (Comm), [2011] Lloyd's Rep 47; *Cessnock City Council v 123 259 932 Pty Ltd* [2024] HCA 17.

Indian Supreme Court that a party cannot apply for expectation loss and reliance loss simultaneously.[67]

It is suggested that in these cases, courts address four issues:

(1) whether reliance damages are appropriate in the circumstances;
(2) whether the expenditure was incurred in performance of the contract;
(3) whether the expenditure was reasonable;
(4) whether the plaintiff would have recouped the expenditure had the contract been performed.[68]

In regard to the first issue, whether reliance damages are appropriate in the circumstances, there is a divergence between Australian and English law. Some English cases appear to suggest that the plaintiff may elect to obtain reliance damages,[69] whereas the High Court of Australia has repeatedly said, in the two most detailed judicial considerations of this issue, that reliance damages are in the discretion of the court, and only appropriate in a narrow range of circumstances, as a proxy for expectation loss where it is impossible or very difficult to measure that loss.[70] The Australian approach has been followed in the most recent English case.[71] The situations in which reliance damages appear to be appropriate are where the defendant has rendered the expectation interest impossible or very difficult to calculate through its own actions[72] or where the plaintiff incurred expenses in excess of the profit expected from the contract breached in the expectation that further contracts would be entered into.[73]

Regarding the second issue, it is not necessary for the moneys spent to be stipulated in the contract, as long as the money is spent in reliance upon the contract. However, expenditure that would have been incurred anyway (such as capital expenditure) will not be recoverable.[74] The burden of proof is on the plaintiff is to establish it.

Regarding the third issue, it is clear from the majority judgments in *Amann Aviation* and *Cessnock* that the expenditure must be reasonable and that, again, the burden of proof is on the plaintiff to establish the reasonableness.[75]

Regarding the fourth issue, it seems from *Amann Aviation* and *Cessnock* that the burden of proof is on the *defendant* to prove that the plaintiff would *not* have recouped the expenditure had the contract been performed. In *Amann Aviation*, the plaintiff entered into a contract for aerial surveillance with the Australian government and

67 *Kanchan Udyog Ltd v United Spirits Ltd* (2017) 8 SCC 237.

68 See K Barnett and S Harder, *Remedies in Australian Private Law* (2nd edn, CUP 2018) [5.63]; Barnett, *Damages for Breach of Contract* (n 24) [3-004].

69 *Anglia Television* (n 66); *CCC Films (London) Ltd* (n 66).

70 *McRae* (n 66) 414; *Amann Aviation* (n 31) 86, 105–107, 126–27, 142–43, 155–56, 166; *Cessnock* (n 66) [119], but cf [9]. Cf also *Soteria Insurance Ltd v IBM United Kingdom Ltd* [2022] EWCA Civ 440, [2022] 2 All ER (Comm) 1082.

71 *Omak Maritime* (n 66).

72 See eg *McRae* (n 66); *Anglia Television* (n 66); *Cessnock* (n 66) [50]–[51], [127], [134], [139] but cf [4], [13]–[14], [34]–[35], [226]–[229].

73 *Amann Aviation* (n 31).

74 *McRae* (n 66); *Cessnock* (n 66).

75 *Amann Aviation* (n 31); *Cessnock* (n 66) [55], [61], [67], [120], [139], [164], [191], [236] but cf [3]–[4].

expended more than the profit made from the initial contract in preparing surveillance airplanes on the expectation that the option to renew in the contract would be exercised. The plaintiff had breached the contract;, however, the government wrongfully terminated it. There were two possible contingencies: the government might have renewed the initial contract (favouring the plaintiff) or it might have lawfully terminated the contract (disfavouring the contract). Six of the seven judges of the High Court took the possibility of renewal into account, arguing that it was in the contemplation of the parties that the plaintiff was expecting renewal. Four of the seven judges did not take the possibility of lawful termination into account, and accordingly, damages were not discounted by the possibility of lawful termination.[76] It is worth observing that if a favourable contingency is taken into account, it seems fair to take into account a unfavourable contingency,[77] and the author has expressed the view that Deane J's minority judgment on this is preferable.[78]

It is suggested that if a suitable case involving wasted expenditure comes up before Indian courts, the terms of section 73 of the Contract Act would allow such 'loss or damage' to the compensated. It is also suggested that guidance could be taken from the English and Australian case law on this, particularly the Australian cases, as they contain the most detailed consideration of the matter.

4. 'Restitutionary Damages'

As noted earlier, although English courts have moved to award accounts of profits for breach of contract in exceptional circumstances, there seems no possibility of awarding relief based on disgorgement of gain under section 73 of the Contract Act because of the necessity to show 'loss or damage'.[79] The point of awarding an account of profits for breach of contract is that the plaintiff has not suffered any easily identifiable loss or damage, but the defendant has gained by breach.

However, there remains a possibility that section 73 of the Contract Act could encompass 'restitutionary damages' for breach of contract in situations where the defendant's gain mirrors the plaintiff's loss, with the latter providing the requisite 'loss or damage' for the purposes of the section.

Typically, these issues arise where there is no easily quantifiable expectation loss in the ordinary sense, but an award is made for breach of contract on the basis that the plaintiff should be awarded a reasonable fee reflecting the sum that they could have demanded if the defendant had sought consent to breach. In *Morris-Garner v One-Step (Support) Ltd*, Lord Reed called these damages for breach of contract 'negotiating damages'.[80]

[76] ibid 97–98 (Mason CJ and Dawson J), 115 (Brennan J), 158 (Gaudron J).
[77] ibid 131–32 (Deane J), 145 (Toohey J), 176–77 (McHugh J).
[78] Barnett and Harder (n 68) [2.116].
[79] There may, however, be a separate common law right to claim disgorgement damages on the basis that the Contract Act is not an exhaustive code.
[80] *Morris-Garner* (n 18) [48] (Lord Reed).

The position of 'restitutionary damages' in the common law world is radically unclear. While there is considerable academic support, and some support in case law, for the notion that reasonable fee awards are restitutionary, the precise way in which such damages operate is contested. The most recent case law on the topic from the UK Supreme Court, *Morris-Garner*, suggests negotiating damages are an exceptional species of compensatory damages, related to 'user damages' for proprietary torts and to damages awarded in lieu of specific relief pursuant to *Lord Cairns' Act*.[81] *Wrotham Park* is said to reflect the fact that 'the refusal of an injunction had the effect of depriving the claimant of an asset which had an economic value'.[82]

A similar but subtly different approach has been suggested by the Singaporean Court of Appeal in *Turf Club Auto Emporium Pte Ltd v Yeo Boong Hua*.[83] The main differences between *Turf Club* compared to *Morris-Garner* are as follows. First, no importance is placed on whether such damages are called 'negotiating damages' or '*Wrotham Park*' damages.[84] Second, the Singapore Court of Appeal does not confine compensatory awards to economically valuable assets because it considers that the meaning of 'asset' is unclear.[85] Third, and finally, the Singapore Court of Appeal does not distinguish between 'reasonable fee' damages awarded in the absence of *Lord Cairns' Act* and those available pursuant to *Lord Cairns' Act*.[86]

On this point, it is worth noting that the Indian version of *Lord Cairns' Act* is quite different to those in most other common law jurisdictions, including the United Kingdom and Singapore,[87] and the author of this chapter has argued the specificity of the pre-2018 Indian provisions means that there is limited room for judicial creativity, and they would not allow for any form of 'restitutionary damages'.[88] This is even more the case since section 21(1) of the Specific Relief Act 1963 was amended in 2018 to remove the possibility of damages being awarded 'in substitution of' performance (without section 40 being correspondingly amended to provide that damages 'in substitution of' an injunction are unavailable).[89]

It is also worth noting that the 2018 amendments created a new remedy of 'substituted performance' in section 20 of the Specific Relief Act 1963, providing that where a promisee engages a third party to provide performance, it can recover costs from the breaching promisor. However, as Niranjan has noted in Chapter 18 of this volume,[90]

[81] ibid [30], [79], [81] (Lord Reed, with whom Lady Hale and Lord Wilson agreed, and Lord Carnwath in a separate judgment rejecting Lord Sumption's analysis) [113]–[114] (Lord Sumption).
[82] ibid [63] (Lord Reed).
[83] *Turf Club Auto Emporium Pte Ltd v Yeo Boong Hua* [2018] SGCA 44 [179], [191], [271].
[84] ibid [270].
[85] ibid [278]–[281].
[86] ibid [284]–[286].
[87] England: Senior Courts Act 1981 (UK), s 50. Singapore: Supreme Court of Judicature Act 1908 (Cap 322), 2013 Reprint, s 16A; cf India: Specific Relief Act 1963, ss 21 and 40. Of course, Pakistan and Malaysia have similar provisions to India: Malaysia: Specific Relief Act 1950, s 18; Pakistan: Specific Relief Act 1877, s 19. However, other common law countries such as Singapore but also Australia, Canada, Hong Kong, and New Zealand, borrowed from the earlier or later English versions of the Act.
[88] K Barnett, 'Lord Cairns' Act and Statutory Interpretation: Give the Court an Inch, They'll Take a Mile' in P Vines and M Scott Donald (eds), *Statutory Interpretation in Private Law* (Federation Press 2019) 207.
[89] N Venkatesan, Chapter 18 of this volume, section IV.
[90] ibid.

the draftsmanship of the provision is not ideal, and it is not clear why the amendment is necessary at all, as the way in which contract damages operate in general always allow for promisees to recover from breaching promisors when they have had to mitigate by getting a third party to complete the performance.

In any case, if the Indian courts take the approach of the UK Supreme Court or the Singaporean Court of Appeal, 'negotiating damages' or a reasonable fee for breach of contract are simply an exceptional form of compensatory damages,[91] awarded when the usual kinds of expectation losses are unavailable, and there would be no problem with making such an award pursuant to section 73 of the Contract Act. As noted earlier in section II, the focus of section 73 of the Contract Act seems to be on factual loss (and the concomitant limiting factors upon liability), but there seems to be no reason on the face of the section why 'loss or damage' cannot also encompass a substitutionary award of this nature in exceptional circumstances.

As for when such awards are to be made, these cases often arise where there is a breach of negative covenant and no factual loss has been suffered, but the plaintiff could have been awarded specific relief if they had been aware of the breach or if they had not delayed in seeking such relief. Unfortunately, the way in which the quantum of the reasonable fee is to be calculated is still very unclear, and in Australia, for this reason, courts have tended to shy away from making such awards.

5. Non-pecuniary Loss

Despite the fact that there is nothing in the terms of section 73 of the Contract Act itself to suggest that loss or damage should be confined to pecuniary loss, and that even under an understanding of loss that takes a factual loss approach, damages for non-pecuniary factual losses should be recoverable, MV Swaroop has noted that Indian courts have been slow to award non-pecuniary amounts for breach of contract.[92] He hypothesises that part of the reason for this is because the illustrations focus so heavily on pecuniary loss, and only Illustration (b), with its reference to 'trouble and expense' caused by a failure to provide a chartered ship, seems to contemplate the award of damages for non-pecuniary losses. He also notes that the more usual way to seek damages for mental trauma and inconvenience are thus more often brought under the Consumer Protection Act 1986.

The Indian Supreme Court has indicated, in *Ghaziabad Development Authority*, that there is no room for damages for breach of contract causing injury to feelings, mental distress, anguish, annoyance, loss of reputation, or social discredit caused by breach of contract except if the purpose of the contract is to provide peace of mind or freedom from distress.[93] However, Swaroop argues that the court relies on the English textbook,

[91] For a detailed discussion of how the damages now work in English law see Barnett, *Damages for Breach of Contract* (n 24) ch 4.
[92] Swaroop (n 12) 91.
[93] *Ghaziabad Development Authority* (n 48).

Chitty on Contract, to hold this, without paying attention to the wording of the statute, which is drawn more widely.[94] He notes that courts have sometimes awarded damages for distress in Indian contract cases,[95] including breach of a contract of marriage (an action that still persists in India).[96]

IV. Attribution of Responsibility

The provision makes it clear that there must be a causal link between the breach and the loss or damage, and that the loss or damage must not be too remote, and that the means taken by the plaintiff to remedy the inconvenience caused by the non-performance of the contract will be taken into account.

1. Causation

The provision infers a causal link by saying that the loss or damage must be caused 'thereby', as a result of the breaching party's actions. In *Kanchan Udyog Ltd v United Spirits Ltd*, the Indian Supreme Court said that it must be shown that the breach was a cause, or the dominant cause, of the loss or damages suffered.[97] As the current edition of *Pollock and Mulla* outlines, the usual test for causation is the 'but for' test, namely, 'but for' the defendant's breach would the plaintiff have suffered the injuries?[98] Famously, the 'but for' test does not resolve the issue of multiple causes or new intervening causes.

The Indian Supreme Court's reference to 'cause' or 'dominant cause' underlines the fact that in all common law jurisdictions there has been a question as to how the test of causation in private law works, namely, whether a 'break in the chain of causation' caused by a new intervening act is really a question of causation or whether it is, in fact, a question more related to scope of liability, as suggested by Jane Stapleton.[99] It seems that, presently, Indian law ascertains what the 'cause' or 'effective or dominant cause'

[94] Swaroop (n 12) 93. The Court in *Ghaziabad Development Authority* (n 48) cited a passage from AG Guest (ed), *Chitty on Contracts*, vol 1 (27th edn, Sweet & Maxwell 1994) [26.041]. Australia has, in fact, had a case involving damages for distress for contravention of statutory consumer guarantees (*Moore v Scenic Tours Pty Ltd* [2020] HCA 17), in which the author and two other participants in this volume have argued that the High Court also unduly read down statute by reference to common law principles, without paying enough attention to the wording of the statute: E Bant, K Barnett, and J Paterson, '"Plain Sailing?': Damages for Distress under the ACL and the Performance Interest in Contract' (2020) 36 Journal of Contract Law 272.

[95] *Raj Kishore Sahay v Binod Kumar* AIR 1989 Pat 111 (HC); *Prema Korgaokar v Mustak Ahmed* AIR 1987 Guj 106 (HC); *N Sukumaran Nair v P Narayanan* (1996) 2 MLJ 184 (HC).

[96] Vardhan and Narayan (n 18) [s 73.23.12]. Note that the personal law of the parties to the marriage may affect outcomes.

[97] *Kanchan Udyog* (n 67) [11].

[98] The example often given is *Barnett v Chelsea and Kensington Hospital Management Committee* [1969] 1 QB 428 (where the defendant hospital was negligent, but the deceased patient would still have died from arsenic poisoning even if the defendant hospital had not been negligent).

[99] J Stapleton, 'Legal Cause: Cause-in-Fact and the Scope of Liability for Consequences' (2001) 54 Vanderbilt Law Review 941.

is and then treats a new intervening act as a break in the chain of causation. Australian contract law treats the matter similarly, looking at whether, as a matter of 'common sense', the breach caused the loss or whether a new intervening act was the dominant or effective cause of the loss.[100]

In terms of what events break the chain of causation, Indian courts have taken a similar approach to other jurisdictions: new intervening acts may be an abnormal act of nature extraneous to the parties, the voluntary intervening action of a third party, or even the action of the plaintiff him- or herself.[101]

2. Remoteness of Damage

i. Codification of the *Hadley v Baxendale* test

As Indian courts have noted,[102] section 73 of the Contract Act displays a clear intention to codify a paraphrased version of Baron Alderson's two-limbed test from *Hadley v Baxendale*,[103] because the only loss or damage that is compensable is that 'which naturally arose in the usual course of things from such breach, or which the parties knew, when they made the contract, to be likely to result from the breach of it'. It is further reiterated in the second paragraph to section 73 of the Contract Act, 'Such compensation is not to be given for any remote and indirect loss of damage sustained by reason of the breach.'

Illustration (i) is clearly a variation upon the facts of *Hadley v Baxendale*:

> A delivers to B, a common carrier, a machine, to be conveyed without delay, to A's mill, informing B that this mill is stopped for want of machine. B unreasonably delays the delivery of the machine, and A, in consequence, loses a profitable contract with the Government. A is entitled to receive from B, by way of compensation, the average amount of profit which would have been made by the working of the mill during the time that delivery of it was delayed, but not the loss sustained through the loss of the Government contract.

In fact, the illustration also anticipates the result of *Victoria Laundry (Windsor) Ltd v Newman Industries Ltd*,[104] where the non-breaching party was compensated for expected loss of profit but not for unusually lucrative follow-on contracts.

Illustration (p) is also a variation upon *Hadley v Baxendale*, involving a delay in delivery of manufacturing materials rather than a common carrier:

[100] See *Alexander v Cambridge Credit Corporation Pty Ltd* (1987) 9 NSWLR 310.

[101] Vardhan and Narayan (n 18) [ss 73.17.1.2], [73.18], and [73.18.1].

[102] *Shantilal Mutha & Co (Firm) Cotton Merchants, Jalna v Chirala Co-op Spinning Mills Ltd* (1986) 2 APLJ 291, (1986) 2 Andh LT 379.

[103] *Hadley* (n 1).

[104] *Victoria Laundry (Windsor) Ltd v Newman Industries Ltd* (1949) 2 KB 528.

A contracts to sell and deliver 500 bales of cotton to B on a fixed day. A knows nothing of B's mode of conducting his business. A breaks the promise, and B, having no cotton, is obliged to close his mill. A is not responsible to B for the loss caused to B by closing of the mill.

Many of the other illustrations also raise issues of remoteness, including (j), (k), (l), (m), (o), (q), and (r), because they all raise questions of whether the breaching party knew of more unusual kinds of loss (in which case, they will be liable) or did not know (in which case, they will not be liable).

ii. The 'usual course of things'

Pannalal Jankidas v Mohanlal indicates that, notwithstanding the illustrations, it remains difficult to ascertain whether an event is in the 'usual course of things'.[105] The facts are unusual. The plaintiffs were agents for the defendants and obtained certain goods on behalf of the defendants, which they stored in a warehouse while awaiting a government permit to allow them to send the goods. The agents were contractually obliged to obtain fire insurance, but they did not. Section 212 of the Contract Act provides that an agent is obliged to make compensation in relation to the 'direct consequences' of his own negligence and not for loss that is indirect or remote. A massive explosion caused the goods to be destroyed. The government passed an ordinance which provided, among other things, that the government would compensate owners for the entire value of insured goods, and 50 per cent of the value of uninsured goods destroyed in the explosion. Ordinary fire insurance would not have covered an explosion of this kind.

The principal was paid 50 per cent of the value of the goods by the government and then sought to recover the other 50 per cent of the value from the agents for failing to insure the goods, arguing that but for the agents' failure, they would have received 100 per cent of the compensation from the government. The agent argued that although it had breached its contract, even if it had taken out fire insurance, in the usual course of things, the principal would not have received any compensation, and the fact that the government later passed a law allowing for compensation dependent upon the existence of insurance was not in the contemplation of the parties.

The Supreme Court was divided on whether this was a direct consequence (which is generally thought to be relevant to 'the usual course of things' for the purposes of section 73 of the Contract Act). The majority (Kania CJ and Das J) held that it was a 'natural consequence', holding that the liability was incurred by reason of the breach of duty, and the agents made themselves liable to pay damages thereby, such damages being measured according to the loss suffered by the respondents on account of the goods not being insured. Pantanjali Sastri J dissented and held that the government's action was not in the usual course of things and could not have been contemplated by the parties at the time of entering into the contract.

[105] *Pannalal Jankidas v Mohanlal* AIR 1951 SC 144, (1950) SCR 979.

Swaroop argues that the dissenting opinion of Sastri J is the better opinion[106] and that the statements of Lord Hoffmann in *South Australia Asset Management Corporation v York Montague Ltd*[107] show why this is so. Lord Hoffmann, in *SAAMCO*, gives the example of a mountain climber who seeks medical advice before undertaking a dangerous climb because he or she is concerned about whether his or her knee is fit for climbing. The doctor gives a negligent inspection of the knee and says it is fine (when, in fact, the knee is not). The climber undertakes the climb and injures him- or herself in an entirely different (but reasonably foreseeable) way. Lord Hoffmann says that it could be argued that the doctor 'caused' the loss in the sense that, 'but for' the negligent advice about the knee, the climber would not have gone on the climb and injured him- or herself, but the doctor should not be liable for this. At [22], Lord Hoffmann says,

> it makes the doctor responsible for consequences which, though in general terms foreseeable, do not appear to have a sufficient causal connection with the subject matter of the duty. The doctor was asked for information on only one of the considerations which might affect the safety of the mountaineer on the expedition. There seems no reason of policy which requires that the negligence of the doctor should require the transfer to him of all the foreseeable risks of the expedition.

Hence, this is beyond the scope of the doctor's liability. The approach, Swaroop says, is not to look at what occurred and then look back to see whether the loss was direct or indirect. The approach should be to look at what was in the contemplation of the parties at the time of the contract and measure the loss accordingly.[108]

With respect, it is suggested that Swaroop's suggestions have merit. In fact, his approach is reinforced by the language of section 73 of the Contract Act itself: the section expressly mentions that the breaching party may be liable for loss or damage 'which the parties knew, when they made the contract, to be likely to result from the breach of it'.

The other case that raises similar issues and is often raised in this context is *Firm Kishanlal Shrilal Patna v Union of India*.[109] In that case, the government railway administration delayed a shipment of goods, and in the meantime, a price control order was issued by the government, which reduced the price that the owner of the goods could get for the goods. The High Court held that this loss was too remote, as government price control orders could not have been contemplated at the time. This approach is in accordance with principle in other countries.[110]

iii. The significance of the defendant's knowledge of the plaintiff's circumstances

Although the section says 'which the *parties* knew', the relevant knowledge is clearly that of the breaching party or defendant.

106 Swaroop (n 12) 95–96.
107 *South Australia Asset Management Corporation v York Montague Ltd* [1997] AC 191 (*SAAMCO*).
108 Swaroop (n 12) 96.
109 *Firm Kishanlal Shrilal Patna v Union of India* AIR 1960 MP 289 (HC).
110 See *Alexander* (n 100).

Swaroop has argued that, although section 73 of the Contract Act displays an intention to codify *Hadley v Baxendale*, there is, in fact, a subtle difference between section 73 of the Contract Act and *Hadley v Baxendale*.[111] Section 73 of the Contract Act indicates that for liability to be imposed under the second limb, the parties must know the consequence (actual knowledge), whereas *Hadley v Baxendale* itself says that liability will be imposed under the second limb where knowledge 'may reasonably be supposed to have been in the contemplation of both parties, at the time they made the contract, as the probable result of the breach of it'[112] ('supposed' indicates that constructive knowledge is sufficient). Swaroop also notes that Indian courts have consistently applied section 73 of the Contract Act as if it was identical to *Hadley v Baxendale* without noting the difference in language and have sometimes allowed constructive knowledge for the second limb accordingly.[113] Indeed, in *Hussain v Chartered Bank*,[114] the judge appears to suggest that Indian Courts are limited strictly by how *Hadley v Baxendale* was understood in 1872.

Of course, section 73 of the Contract Act was enacted well before *Victoria Laundry*,[115] in which Asquith LJ held the following, regarding *Hadley v Baxendale*:

> For this purpose, knowledge 'possessed' is of two kinds; one imputed, the other actual. Everyone, as a reasonable person, is taken to know the 'ordinary course of things' and consequently what loss is liable to result from a breach of contract in that ordinary course. This is the subject matter of the 'first rule' in *Hadley v. Baxendale*. But to this knowledge, which a contract-breaker is assumed to possess whether he actually possesses it or not, there may have to be added in a particular case knowledge which he actually possesses, of special circumstances outside 'the ordinary course of things,' of such a kind that a breach in those special circumstances would be liable to cause more loss. Such a case attracts the operation of the 'second rule' so as to make additional loss also recoverable.[116]

In any case, *Victoria Laundry* means that the common law has subsequently ended up in the same place as section 73 of the Contract Act (imputed knowledge for the first limb of *Hadley v Baxendale*, actual knowledge for the second limb of *Hadley v Baxendale*), thus any inconsistency between section 73 of the Contract Act and *Hadley v Baxendale* may have been ironed out by *Victoria Laundry*. It is suggested that the wording of section 73 of the Contract Act should be applied, rather than applying *Hadley v Baxendale* in the way it was understood in 1872, as suggested in *Hussain v Chartered Bank*.[117]

111 Swaroop (n 12) 96–97.
112 *Hadley* (n 1) 151.
113 Swaroop (n 12) 97 gives the examples of *Sind Biscuits Manufacturing Co v Delight Engineering Works* 1984 AWC (Supp) 211 (HC) and *Union of India v Central Gulf Steamship Corporation* (1978) 83 CWN 75.
114 *N Mohamed Hussain Sahib v Chartered Bank* AIR 1965 Mad 266, [65].
115 *Victoria Laundry (Windsor) Ltd* (n 104).
116 ibid 539.
117 *N Mohamed Hussain Sahib* (n 114) [65].

iv. Assumption of responsibility and *The Achilleas* in Indian law

Some scholars suggest that where contract damages are concerned, courts exclude liability for events for which the defendant did not voluntarily assume the risk.[118] This argument is contentious, and others have argued that remoteness rules in contract are better seen as 'gap-filling' rules.[119]

In *Transfield Shipping Inc v Mercator Shipping*,[120] Lord Hoffmann of the House of Lords famously adopted the 'assumption-of-responsibility' line of argument, and suggested that the *Hadley v Baxendale* two-limbed test could be reduced to one single test: looking at the intentions of the parties in an objective manner, did the defendant assume responsibility for the risk? In that case, while the loss in question was a 'first-limb' loss in *Hadley v Baxendale* terms,[121] Lord Hoffmann (with whom Lord Hope and Lord Walker agreed) held that, in the context of industry practice in that industry (the shipping industry), the breaching party could not have assumed responsibility for the loss of a follow-on charter caused by the late return of a ship. Lord Rodger and Lady Hale (with whom Lord Walker also agreed) applied *Hadley v Baxendale* and held that while the kind of loss was foreseeable, the precise extent of it was not foreseeable. (With respect, it seems that this conclusion cannot be correct, as it has long been held that it is unnecessary to foresee the extent of a loss, as long as the kind of loss is foreseeable.)

Of course, the corollary of the proposition that parties will not be liable for unusual losses for which they did not assume responsibility is that if a party *did* assume responsibility for unusual losses, they will be liable for them.[122]

In the United Kingdom, the 'assumption-of-responsibility' test now seems to operate primarily as a 'gloss' on both limbs of *Hadley v Baxendale*, rather than as a new test. This may be important to how it is received in Indian law, because if assumption of responsibility has always been an aspect of *Hadley v Baxendale* prior to *The*

[118] J Cartwright, 'Remoteness of Damage in Contract and Tort: A Reconsideration' (1996) 55 Cambridge Law Journal 488, 489; D Harris, D Campbell, and R Halson, *Remedies in Contract and Tort* (2nd edn, CUP 2005) 88–97; H Collins, *The Law of Contract* (4th edn, LexisNexis 2003) 413; D Campbell and H Collins, 'Discovering the Implicit Dimensions of Contracts' in D Campbell, H Collins, and J Wightman (eds), *Implicit Dimensions of Contract: Discrete, Relational and Network Contracts* (Hart 2003) 25, 45; A Kramer, 'An Agreement-Centred Approach to Remoteness and Contract Damages' in N Cohen and E McKendrick (eds), *Comparative Remedies for Breach of Contract* (Hart 2005) 249; A Tettenborn, 'Hadley v Baxendale Foreseeability: A Principle beyond Its Sell-By Date?' (2007) 23 Journal of Contract Law 120.

[119] A Robertson, 'The Basis of the Remoteness Rule in Contract' (2008) 28 Legal Studies 172; M Stiggelbout, 'Contractual Remoteness, "Scope of Duty" and Intention' [2012] Lloyd's Maritime and Commercial Law Quarterly 97; KW Lawson, 'The Remoteness Rules in Contract: Holmes, Hoffmann, and Ships that Pass in the Night' (2012) 23 Kings Law Journal 1; A Robertson, 'The Limits of Interpretation in the Law of Contract' (2016) 47 Victoria University of Wellington Law Review 191, 200–207.

[120] *Transfield Shipping Inc v Mercator Shipping* [2009] 1 AC 61, [2008] UKHL 48 ('*The Achilleas*'). This was one of a series of cases where Lord Hoffmann advanced a series of interlinked principles regarding limitations on liability and interpretation of contracts, including *SAAMCO* (n 107) and *Attorney General of Belize v Belize Telecom Limited* [2009] UKPC 10.

[121] Initially, it was suggested in Harris, Campbell, and Halson (n 118) that it should apply particularly to unusual *second-limb* losses.

[122] *Siemens Building Technologies FE Ltd v Supershield Ltd* [2010] EWCA Civ 7.

Achilleas, then it can be more readily accommodated by section 73 of the Contract Act. The 'assumption-of-responsibility' test has been rejected by the Singaporean Court of Appeal, which has opted to stay with a traditional *Hadley v Baxendale* formulation, on the basis that this test can already accommodate concerns about assumption of responsibility.[123] However, *The Achilleas* is mentioned by the Supreme Court of India with apparent approval in *Kanchan Udyog Ltd v United Spirits Ltd.* The Court notes the English decision of *Wellesley Partners LLP v Withers LLP*[124] (a case of concurrent liability in tort and contract) and goes on to say,

> *Wellesley Partners LLP* . . . itself carves out an exception to the principle that a contract breaker is liable for damage resulting from his breach, if at the time of making the contract, a reasonable person in his shoes would have had damage of that kind in mind as not unlikely to result from a breach. After noticing *The Achilleas* ... it was observed:
>
> 69 . . . *The Achilleas* shows that there may be cases, where based on the individual circumstances surrounding the making of the contract, this assumed expectation is not well founded.[125]

It seems, therefore, that the Indian Supreme Court is not averse, in principle, to adopting an *Achilleas*-style 'assumption-of-responsibility' test. The question is then whether the terms of section 73 of the Contract Act allows them to do so. Swaroop argues that paragraph 2 of section 73 of the Contract Act would allow Indian courts to adopt a position that is consistent with Lord Hoffmann's analysis in *The Achilleas*, as it requires the court not to give compensation for 'any remote and indirect loss of damage sustained by reason of the breach'. He argues, first, that the 'assumption-of-responsibility' test is older than *The Achilleas*; second, that paragraph 2 calls for a consideration of whether a party has, in fact, assumed responsibility for a risk; and third, that Illustration (i) to the section (noted above) further lends credence to this interpretation.[126]

There are cases that might support an assumption-of-responsibility approach, although not in those terms explicitly. The analysis proceeds rather on an argument that the losses are not natural and proximate.[127]

In *Monindra Lall Sen v Union of India*,[128] the plaintiff, a lawyer, purchased some rail tickets for himself and his family from Patna to Calcutta. When he arrived at the train, he discovered that the seats had been mistakenly double-booked, and the station could

[123] *MFM Restaurants Pte Ltd v Fish & Co Restaurants Pte Ltd* [2010] SGCA 36, [2011] 1 SLR 150, [112]; *Out of the Box Pte Ltd v Wanin Industries Pte Ltd* [2013] SGCA 15, [2013] 2 SLR 363, [24]–[47].

[124] *Wellesley Partners LLP v Withers LLP* [2015] EWCA Civ 1146.

[125] *Kanchan Udyog* (n 67) [26].

[126] Swaroop (n 12) 98–100.

[127] I am indebted to Niranjan Venkatesan for drawing my attention to these cases: *Monindra Lall Sen v Union of India* AIR 1960 Pat 411 (HC) and *State of Kerala v Bhaskaran* AIR 1985 Ker 49 (HC). I am also indebted to Mihir Naniwadekar for useful discussions on *Monindra Lall Sen*.

[128] *Monindra Lall Sen* (n 127).

not find alternative transport for him. As a result, he missed an appointment with a client in Calcutta and suffered damage as a consequence. The plaintiff could not recover damages as the loss was too remote: it was not natural and proximate. However, the Court also said that the railway company

> would also be entitled to damages if the Railway Administration knew at the time of the reservation of the seats that the plaintiff had an engagement in Calcutta at 9-00 hours on 29-9-1954, and that he had booked the tickets and reserved the seats in order to go there to fulfil the engagement.

The difficulty with this is that it does not fit with the policy of the rule in *Hadley v Baxendale.* Baron Alderson states explicitly that if you know you are being exposed to a higher risk, you can require a higher fee to reflect the greater risk.[129] It is doubtful whether a railway company would be able to demand a higher fee from a passenger in any case (presumably ticket prices are fixed), which means that perhaps it should not be liable for this loss, particularly if it is providing some kind of public service.

In fact, *Monindra Lall Sen* is a classic example of the 'taxi driver' problem averted to by Campbell, Harris, and Halson, which led them to develop the notion of 'assumption of responsibility': where a carrier is liable for a consequential loss stemming from a failure to transport a person on time, it is suggested that the carrier has not assumed responsibility for it.[130] It is precisely the kind of case where we might wish to say that the railway company should not be held to assume responsibility for this loss.

Ultimately, paragraph 2 represents the best option a court would have for Indian courts to interpret section 73 of the Contract Act in such a way as to take into account assumption-of-responsibility concerns, and thus it may not be necessary to adopt *The Achilleas* expressly, particularly given that several other common law countries have either rejected it (as is the case with Singapore, mentioned above in section IV.2.iv), or shown no particular appetite to adopt it.[131] This may be particularly the case if one takes the approach in *Hussain v Chartered Bank* that section 73 of the Contract Act must be understood by reference to how *Hadley v Baxendale* was understood in 1872.[132] On the other hand, it could be argued that the 'assumption-of-responsibility' test is slightly easier (although still not necessarily straightforward) to apply than the test of whether the loss is 'natural' and 'proximate'.

3. Mitigation

The Explanation to section 73 of the Contract Act states, 'In estimating the loss or damage arising from a breach of contract, the means which existed of remedying the

[129] *Hadley* (n 1) 251.
[130] Harris, Campbell, and Halson (n 118) 88–97.
[131] Australia has shown no particular appetite to adopt the test: see Barnett and Harder (n 68) [5.102]–[5.104].
[132] *N Mohamed Hussain Sahib* (n 114).

inconvenience caused by the non-performance of the contract must be taken into account.' This is, as others have noted, an unusual 'explanation': it does not clarify a matter already mentioned in the section but seems to add an additional element.[133] Whitley Stokes says, in his commentary, that the Explanation was put in to ensure that the means taken of 'obviating or lessening the damage' was taken into account but does not explain why it was done in this way, as an explanation rather than as part of the section.[134] It is clearly accepted by Indian courts, however, that this Explanation and the illustrations to section 73 of the Contract Act requires a court to consider mitigation, and that mitigation is an important limitation upon the calculation of contract damages. As noted earlier, the Indian Supreme Court in *Murlidhar Chiranjilal* has confirmed that contract damages are subject to a 'duty' upon the plaintiff 'of taking all reasonable steps to mitigate the loss consequent on the breach, and debars him from claiming any part of the damage which is due to his neglect to take such steps'.[135] Although the Court uses the term 'duty', as is well known, there is not, in fact, a duty upon the plaintiff to do anything at all.[136] It is simply that the plaintiff will be deemed to have behaved as if he or she had mitigated, even if he or she has not. As Dyson and Kramer have argued, it requires contract damages to be assessed as if the plaintiff had acted reasonably, even if he or she did not.[137] Consequently, in Kramer's terms, the Court, in fact, compares the *hypothetical* non-breach position (the gains and harms that should have occurred if the plaintiff had acted reasonably) and the breach position (the gains and harms that occurred as a result of the breach).[138]

McGregor on Damages has said that the doctrine of mitigation has three aspects. First, the plaintiff must take all reasonable steps to mitigate his or her loss, and he or she cannot recover for reasonably avoidable loss (the 'avoidable loss' rule). Second, if the plaintiff does take reasonable steps to mitigate and suffers greater loss, the defendant will still be liable. Third, if the plaintiff takes reasonable steps to mitigate the loss and reduces the loss, this should be considered (the 'avoided loss' rule).[139]

To an extent, these rules overlap. The first rule involves 'avoidable loss', the second rule involves the consequences of incurring more loss through attempting to avoid avoidable loss, and the third rule involves 'avoided loss'. 'Avoided loss' is not simply the result of carrying out a 'duty' to avoid loss: a plaintiff's benefit will be considered only when he or she has gone further than he or she needed and avoided *more* loss than required by law.[140] These rules have been criticised as unnecessarily complex, on

[133] Swaroop (n 12) 100.
[134] Stokes (n 60) 588.
[135] *Murlidhar Chiranjilal* (n 19) 657 (Wanchoo J).
[136] Swaroop (n 12) 101–102; cf, however, the unfortunate case of *Nannapaneni Narasingayudu v Nannapaneni Ankineedu* AIR 1962 AP 192 (HC), noted in Swaroop (n 12) 101–102, where the Court seems to have found that a plaintiff had a 'duty' to mitigate his losses by appealing a legal decision, even though he was not aware of the law or any changes to the law.
[137] Dyson and Kramer (n 40) 259. Recently judicially affirmed in *Sharp Corp Ltd v Viterra BV* [2024] UKSC 14, [85].
[138] Kramer, *The Law of Contract Damages* (n 20) ch 15, especially the helpful diagram at 345.
[139] Edelman, Varuhas, and Colton (n 36) [9-004]–[9.006].
[140] ibid [9-108].

the basis that the second rule and the third rule are simply qualifications that establish when mitigatory principles do not apply.[141]

i. Avoidable losses

The doctrine of mitigation most often operates in contract law as a separate standalone doctrine to limit the availability of damages, but the concept of avoidable loss is also built into the difference in value measure used in so many of the illustrations, as Kramer's analysis makes clear. Take, for example, the simple example in Illustration (a):

> A contracts to sell and deliver 50 maunds of saltpetre to B, at a certain price to be paid on delivery. A breaks his promise. B is entitled to receive from A, by way of compensation, the sum, if any, by which the contract price falls short of the price for which B might have obtained 50 maunds of saltpetre of like quality at the time when the saltpetre ought to have been delivered.

The Court is required to compare the difference in value between the breach position (failure to deliver the 50 maunds of saltpetre) and a hypothetical breach position (where the buyer obtains 50 maunds of saltpetre of like quality at the time when the saltpetre ought to been delivered). In other words, this measure deems the buyer to behave reasonably and to mitigate by obtaining a substitute performance from another supplier at the time of breach.

Mitigation also features in Illustration (b) (where the non-breaching charterer is deemed to have hired an alternative ship), Illustration (c) (where the non-breaching seller is deemed to have tried to sell the 50 maunds of rice to an alternative buyer), Illustration (d) (where the non-breaching seller is deemed to have tried to sell the ship to an alternative buyer), Illustration (g) (where the non-breaching charterer is assumed to have hired out a similar ship), Illustration (k) (which assumes the non-breaching party purchases alternative machinery), Illustration (q) (which seems to assume that the non-breaching party should have obtained cloth from another supplier) and Illustration (r) (which assumes the non-breaching party hires another vessel after the breaching shipowner delays in a journey).

Illustration (q) raises complex issues of remoteness and mitigation that deserve greater consideration: it is suggested that it does not give enough detail to be helpful. The illustration contemplates a situation where a seller contracts to deliver cloth on a certain date to a buyer, who intends to manufacture the cloth into caps for which there is only demand in that season. The cloth is delivered late. The illustration specifies that the seller is liable to pay the difference in value between the contract price of the cloth and the market price at time of delivery but is not liable to pay the profits the buyer

[141] Kramer, *The Law of Contract Damages* (n 20) 339; *Thai Airways International Public Co Ltd v KI Holdings Co Ltd* [2015] EWHC 1250, [33] (Leggatt LJ).

expected to make from selling the caps, nor the expenses to which the buyer was put in preparing for manufacture. Presumably, one of the reasons why the seller may not be liable to pay for the loss of the cloth is because the buyer failed to mitigate and attempt to obtain cloth from other sources; at the least, there is no mention of him doing so. Another reason why the seller may not be liable is because the seller may not be aware of the special circumstances of the buyer, which raises *Hadley v Baxendale* issues of knowledge.

This raises another question: what is the relationship between causation, remoteness, and mitigation? English courts have tended to describe mitigation in causal terms,[142] and Dyson and Kramer have made similar arguments.[143] However, as Dyson and Kramer acknowledge, it is also necessary to take into account questions of legal causation (or scope of liability).[144] Conversely, Australian courts have disavowed the causal approach to mitigation and have tended to see it as a question of remoteness, as indicated by the dissenting judgment of Brennan J in the High Court of Australia in *Burns v MAN Automotive Pty Ltd*:

> A party who, when he gives a warranty, has such knowledge that he can foresee that the loss which will result from a breach of the warranty, will continue until the other party acts to stop the loss, can foresee that the loss will continue until it is reasonable to expect that the injured party will act to stop it. Foreseeability extends until it would be unreasonable for the injured party to fail to act to mitigate his loss, and the onus of proving such a failure is on the party in breach.[145]

Wayne Courtney has argued that notions of causation do play into the assessment of avoidable loss, particularly in regard to intervening causes of breach, and that this relates to the extent to which the plaintiff is able to rely on the contract or must rely on his or her own actions.[146] He argues that 'but for' causation has no place in mitigation, and nor do new intervening acts, but that causation can be relevant if one takes into account the reasonableness of the plaintiff's reliance on the defendant's promise to

[142] In W Courtney, 'Contract Damages and the Promisee's Role in Its Own Loss' (2019) 42 Melbourne University Law Review 406, 410–11, Courtney traces the development of English causal-based approaches to mitigation back to *Koch Marine Inc v D'Amica Societa di Navigazione; The Elena D'Amico* [1980] 1 Lloyd's Rep 75, 88 (Goff LJ) but also cites *Kaines (UK) Ltd v Osterreichische Warrenhandelsgesellschaft Austrowaren GmbH* [1993] 2 Lloyd's Rep 1, 10 (Bingham LJ); *Standard Chartered Bank v Pakistan National Shipping Corp [No 3]* [1999] 1 Lloyd's Rep 747, 758 and on appeal, [2001] 1 All ER (Comm) 822, 837, [41] (Potter LJ; Henry LJ and Wall J agreeing); *Bunge SA v Nidera BV* [2015] 3 All ER 1082, 1106–107, [81] (Lord Toulson; Lord Neuberger, Lord Mance and Lord Clarke agreeing); *Thai Airways International Public Co Ltd* (n 141) [33]; *Nuclear Decommissioning Authority v EnergySolutions EU Ltd* [2017] 1 WLR 1373, 1392, [32]; *Hughes-Holland v BPE Solicitors* [2017] UKSC 21, [2017] 2 WLR 1029, 1039, [20].

[143] See particularly Dyson and Kramer (n 40) 259.

[144] ibid 263. As many scholars observe, factual causation alone cannot adequately explain the rule; see MG Bridge, 'Mitigation of Damages in Contract and the Meaning of Avoidable Loss' (1989) 105 Law Quarterly Review 398, 401–402, Edelman, Varuhas, and Colton (n 36) [9-019] and SM Waddams, *The Law of Damages* (5th edn, Canada Law Book Co 2012) [15.70].

[145] *Burns v MAN Automotive Pty Ltd* [1986] HCA 81, (1986) 161 CLR 658, 673 (Brennan J).

[146] Courtney (n 142) 426–34.

perform. In other words, once it becomes unreasonable for the plaintiff to rely upon an expectation that the defendant will perform his or her obligations, the defendant's actions no longer cause the loss. This is a helpful analysis.

It is the view of the author of this chapter that causation, remoteness (in the broader sense of scope of liability), and mitigation are intertwined to a degree.[147] Thus, a defendant will no longer be liable for loss once it becomes reasonable for the plaintiff to mitigate that loss. Alternatively, it can be argued that the plaintiff has caused his or her own loss by failing to help him- or herself once it becomes evident that he or she cannot rely on the contract any longer and must rely on his or her own actions. Or it can be argued that the loss has become too remote because it is not foreseeable that a reasonable plaintiff would fail to mitigate, and as a matter of policy, we wish to curtail the scope of liability of a defendant and ensure plaintiffs who are best placed to heal a breach act to help themselves.

ii. Further losses from attempts to mitigate

It was noted above that *McGregor on Damages* stated that it was a corollary of the avoidable loss rule that if a plaintiff incurs more loss in a reasonable attempt to avoid loss, the plaintiff can recover that loss. In fact, Illustration (b) confirms that this is the case for the Contract Act, as the non-breaching charterer is deemed to have hired an alternative ship to transport his cargo 'upon terms as advantageous as those upon which he had chartered the ship' but is entitled to receive compensation for the additional 'trouble and expense' incurred in hiring the alternative ship. There are good policy reasons for this: the law seeks to provide incentives to plaintiffs to help themselves.[148]

This rule has been confirmed in Indian case law. In *RJ Mohammad Jacub Sahib v Indian Bank Ltd*,[149] the Madras High Court approved the statement of Lord Macmillan in *Banco de Portugal v Waterlow* that as long as a plaintiff has acted reasonably, it is not for the defendant to say that there was a less costly course of action to be taken.[150] On the other hand, *Burn and Co Ltd v Thakur Sahib Shree Lakhdirjee* confirmed that if the plaintiff has acted *unreasonably* in attempting to mitigate his or her losses, the court will not compensate him or her.[151]

iii. Avoided losses

Avoided loss does not cover situations where the plaintiff has simply avoided a loss by obtaining a substitute performance of the same quality: it only covers circumstances where the plaintiff has gone further and avoided more loss than was reasonable in the

[147] See Barnett, 'Substitutive Damages' (n 38); K Barnett, 'Mitigation and Remoteness in Contract: Policy and Principle' (2019) 36 Journal of Contract Law 5.
[148] Barnett, 'Substitutive Damages' (n 38) 808.
[149] *RJ Mohammad Jacub Sahib v Indian Bank Ltd* AIR 1975 Mad 220 (HC).
[150] *Banco de Portugal v Waterlow* (1932) AC 452.
[151] *Burn and Co Ltd v Thakur Sahib Shree Lakhdirjee* AIR 1924 Cal 427 (HC).

circumstances.[152] It is simply an arithmetical *quid pro quo*: if the plaintiff is worse off or better off as a result of the breach, it will be considered. If the plaintiff is left in an identical situation, the court is satisfied that a reasonable substitute performance has been obtained, and compensates the plaintiff for that.[153]

Regarding avoided loss, the defendant is entitled to benefit from any mitigating steps taken by the plaintiff, even if it would have been reasonable for the plaintiff not to have taken those steps.[154] Thus, in *British Westinghouse Electric & Manufacturing Co Ltd v Underground Electric Railways Co of London Ltd*, the defendant supplied substandard turbine engines to the plaintiffs. Despite efforts on the part of the defendant to fix the turbines, they never performed according to the contractual specifications. The plaintiffs purchased new turbines from a different manufacturer, which were vastly superior and more efficient. They claimed the cost of installing the new turbines, but the Court found that the new turbines were so vastly superior that the savings effectively compensated for the losses caused by the defective turbines. This subsequent transaction (buying the new turbines) was to be considered because it arose out of the consequences of the breach and occurred in the ordinary course of business.[155]

Conversely in other circumstances, subsequent transactions will not be considered, as the famous case of *AKAS Jamal v Moolla Dawood & Sons* shows.[156] In that case, the plaintiff had contracted to sell certain shares to the defendant on a particular date, but the defendant refused to accept them. The plaintiff retained the shares and sold them at a later date to someone else when the market price was higher. The plaintiff then sought the difference in value between the contract price and the market price as at the date of breach. The defendant attempted to argue that the later transaction should be considered, but the Privy Council said that the subsequent transaction could not be taken into account in this case, and the only question was what the means of rectifying the breach was as at the date of breach.

This raises questions of the date of breach rule. As will be evident from several of the examples, and the discussion of goods transactions, the illustrations to section 73 of the Contract Act seem to contemplate that generally, the rule for measuring damages is that it is measured as at date of breach (see Illustrations (a), (b), (d), (e), (g), (h), (o)) and subsequent transactions are generally not relevant. Thus, Illustration (o) states,

[152] This is why the avoided loss rule did not apply in *Clark v Macourt* (2013) CLR 253 1, [2013] HCA 56, [18]–[22] (Hayne J) [142]–[143] (Keane J): the doctor obtained sperm straws that were identical in quality to the (ultimately defective) sperm straws promised under the contract for the purposes of conducting an in vitro fertilisation medical practice.

[153] Barnett, 'Substitutive Damages' (n 38) 810–11.

[154] *British Westinghouse Electric & Manufacturing Co Ltd v Underground Electric Railways Co of London Ltd* [1912] AC 673, 688–90 (Viscount Haldane LC).

[155] In *Thai Airways International Public Co* (n 141) [45] (Leggatt LJ) argued that *British Westinghouse* (n 154) was not a case of avoided loss and simply demonstrated that, as long as the plaintiff's course of action was reasonable, the measure of damages is the loss the plaintiff has actually suffered, taking into account both losses and benefits from the breach of contract.

[156] *AKAS Jamal* (n 11).

> A contracts to deliver 50 maunds of saltpetre to B on the first of January, at a certain price, B afterwards, before the first of January, contracts to sell saltpetre to C at a price higher than the market price on the first of January. A breaks his promise. In estimating the compensation payable by A to B, the market price of the first of January, and not the print which would have arisen to B from the sale to C is to be taken into account.

The general date-of-breach rule reflects the principle that, particularly in a liquid market, the court presumes that the plaintiff mitigates on the date of breach. This is really a principle of convenience. However, the date-of-breach rule is only a general rule of thumb, and if mitigation is impossible to achieve for some reason, the court will generally not expect the plaintiff to mitigate and may use a later date to assess damages. As Dyson and Kramer have noted, if a plaintiff is legally or practically 'locked out' from accessing the market, or financially 'locked in' such that he or she cannot limit losses, he or she may generally recover such losses until mitigation becomes reasonable or possible.[157]

V. Liability for Obligations Resembling Contract

The third paragraph of section 73 of the Contract Act states,

> Compensation for failure to discharge obligation resembling those created by contract: When an obligation resembling those created by contract has been incurred and has not been discharged, any person injured by the failure to discharge it is entitled to receive the same compensation from the party in default, as if such person had contracted to discharge it and had broken his contract.

This paragraph can be dealt with briefly. It has been held, in *Great Eastern Shipping Co Ltd v Union of India*,[158] that 'an obligation resembling those by contract' is effectively a restitutionary obligation (which, back at the time when section 73 of the Contract Act was enacted, would have been thought to be an obligation in 'quasi-contract'). It is thus also related to section 70 of the Contract Act, which provides for liability for unjust enrichment in certain circumstances, including mistake. Thus, in *Great Eastern Shipping Co Ltd v Union of India*, the Court said,

> In assessing the compensation payable under Section 70 and (sic) third paragraph of Section 73 of the Act, the Court shall take into account what the parties contemplated to be a reasonable compensation at the time when the works were done or the goods

[157] Dyson and Kramer (n 40) 276–81. For extensive discussion of how this works practically, see Barnett, 'Mitigation and Remoteness' (n 147) 9–17.

[158] *Great Eastern Shipping Co Ltd v Union of India* AIR 1971 Cal 150, 155 (HC).

> were delivered. So far as compensation for goods are concerned, the court will always take into consideration the market rate of those goods prevailing on the date on which they were delivered. In the case of works done the Court will similarly consider the remuneration that would have been charged by other persons on the date on which the plaintiff has rendered the said services to the defendant.[159]

In this sense, Indian courts face the same questions as courts in other common law countries that are called upon to provide a fair value for restitutionary remedies.

[159] ibid.

17
Stipulated Sums and Limitation Clauses

*TT Arvind**

I. Introduction

The law governing stipulated sum clauses and limitation clauses in India has long been complex. In part, this is because these clauses bring into direct conflict two principles, both of which are fundamental to contract law: the principle of freedom of contract and the principle that the law provides full compensation for breach. But it also reflects the fact that these clauses are used in a very wide range of transaction types, ranging from employment contracts to complex, cross-border commercial transactions. Although the judiciary has shown a clear understanding that the law must have the flexibility to deal differently with different types of transactions, the doctrinal tests they use are not well suited to considering contextual factors specific to a particular type of transaction. The result, as this chapter shows, is a law that is characterised by a lack of clarity, is over-interventionist, and contains a surprisingly large number of different tests for deciding when these clauses are enforceable. These tests draw not only on the statutory provisions themselves but also on broader ideas of unconscionability, inequality of bargaining power, and public policy.

Against this background, this chapter seeks, first, to discuss the different approaches that the courts have taken to stipulated sums and limitation clauses (collectively referred to in this chapter as 'remedial clauses'). Second, it seeks to identify and analyse the problems from which each of the approaches that the courts currently take to remedial clauses suffer. Third, it draws on previously unexamined documents in the India Office Records on the history of the 1899 amendment to the Indian Contract Act to argue that its legislative history gives us the basis for restating the law on remedial clauses in a way that resolves the complexity in the current law and also provides a clearer guide to the types of circumstances in which it is appropriate for the judiciary to intervene in contracts. The starting point is the relationship between contract law and the social context in which it operates; and, in particular, the social purpose that the courts' powers to intervene in remedial clauses can, and should, serve. The question of whether or not contract law should seek to discharge broader social functions is a heavily contested topic in academic writing about contracts. In the Indian context,

* I am grateful to participants in the symposium and to the editors of this volume for their comments on an earlier draft of this chapter. All archival material cited in this chapter is held in the India Office Records at the British Library, London.

TT Arvind, *Stipulated Sums and Limitation Clauses* In: *Foundations of Indian Contract Law*. Edited by: KV Krishnaprasad, Niranjan Venkatesan, Shivprasad Swaminathan, and Umakanth Varottil, Oxford University Press. © Oxford University Press 2024.
DOI: 10.1093/9780191997211.003.0017

however, the question must be taken to have been settled in favour of such a social role: as this chapter shows, the Indian Contract Act 1872 (hereinafter 'the Contract Act') assumes that contract law should be applied in a way that is sensitive to its social context, and it seeks to ensure that courts have the legal tools needed to intervene when necessary while also protecting *bona fide* commercial transactions from judicial intervention. Put together, these points have a strong resonance with the type of factors that underpin judicial intervention in remedial clauses today, and they provide a basis for framing a more structured and systematic approach to stipulated sums and limitation clauses.

II. Stipulated Sums and Limitation Clauses: The Current State of the Law

1. Stipulated Sums

The law on stipulated sums is contained in four leading Supreme Court cases: *Fateh Chand v Balkishan Das*,[1] *Maula Bux v Union of India*,[2] *Kailash Nath Associates v Delhi Development Authority*,[3] and *ONGC Ltd v Saw Pipes Ltd*.[4] These cases have consistently held that Indian law does not distinguish between liquidated damages and penalty clauses but adopts a single rule that applies to both types of clause. Nevertheless, the way in which they express that single rule relies heavily on the traditional common law approach of only giving effect to a stipulated sum if it is a 'genuine pre-estimate'.

The reliance of Indian courts on the 'genuine pre-estimate' test is somewhat surprising, because nothing in the Contract Act suggests that a 'genuine pre-estimate' should be treated differently from other contractually stipulated sums. Section 74 of the Contract Act gives courts a wide discretion to disregard any contractually stipulated sum and, instead, award reasonable compensation of any amount up to the stipulated sum, regardless of whether the stipulation would have been treated as a liquidated damages clause or a penalty at common law and regardless of whether the plaintiff is actually able to prove loss. Why, then, have the courts adopted a test based on the classical form of the rule against penalties? The answer is that section 74 does not answer a particularly challenging question with which courts around the common law world have struggled, namely, whether there are circumstances in which it is reasonable to award the sum stipulated in the contract, simply *because* it is stipulated in the contract and not because an assessment of the loss caused by the breach shows the sum to be a reasonable one. The leading cases on section 74 have all involved precisely this question,[5] and their approach to stipulated sums can be boiled down to three principles:

[1] AIR 1963 SC 1405.
[2] AIR 1970 SC 1955.
[3] (2015) 4 SCC 136, [43].
[4] (2003) 5 SCC 705, [64]–[65], [68].
[5] See the cases cited at nn 1–4.

(1) Regardless of whether or not a sum has been stipulated in the contract, compensation will only be awarded if loss or damage has, in fact, been suffered. Although section 74 gives the court the power to award reasonable compensation even where loss or damage has not been proved, the courts have taken this to simply mean that the *quantum* of loss or damage need not be proved. The *fact* of loss or damage, in contrast, must be proved. The law will not give one party a windfall if there has been no loss.
(2) The starting point in determining what is 'reasonable' is that the court will award a sum of compensation calculated in accordance with general principles of Indian contract law. That ordinary measure of compensation is the measure of what is 'reasonable' under section 74.
(3) If, however, the quantum of damage or loss is difficult or impossible to prove, *and* if the court, after due scrutiny, finds that the sum named in the contract is a 'genuine pre-estimate of damages fixed by both parties', the court will award the full sum named in the contract. Both conditions must be satisfied.

This approach has not, however, provided a satisfactory answer to the question of when the courts should give effect to a contractually stipulated sum. Because it draws on the *Dunlop*[6] principles that governed English law until the recent shift of direction in *Cavendish Square*[7] is striking, it suffers from precisely the same difficulties as the *Dunlop* approach in determining when something is a 'genuine pre-estimate'.

Two recent cases illustrate these difficulties. The first relates to a common practice in which companies include in their trainees' employment contracts provisions requiring their trainees to pay a substantial sum of money to the company to compensate the company for training expenses in the event that the trainee does not pass probation.[8] The second case related to a settlement agreement arising out of an allegation of forgery, which provided for the payment of a very large sum of money—US $3.5 million—in the event of a breach of the agreement.[9] Both, arguably, involved situations where the quantum of damage or loss was impossible to prove. On what basis, then, could a court decide whether the sum named in the contract was a 'genuine pre-estimate' of damages?

Case law from High Courts suggests that they have taken two routes around this difficulty. A few High Courts, and in particular the High Court of Bombay, have added a gloss to the third of the principles outlined above, stressing that the party seeking the award of the named sum must prove that the quantum of damage or loss is difficult or impossible to prove, that the court must find to its satisfaction that the named sum was a genuine pre-estimate, and that the court retains a discretion to determine whether to award the named sum, which it must exercise with reference to the injury or loss

[6] *Dunlop Pneumatic Tyre Co Ltd v New Garage and Motor Co Ltd* [1915] AC 79 (HL).
[7] *Cavendish Square Holding BV v Talal El Makdessi* [2015] UKSC 67.
[8] *Sandhya Nayak v Larsen and Toubro Infotech*, Arbitration Petition 761 of 2015 (Bombay High Court, 5 February 2019).
[9] *Jackie Shroff v Ratnam Sudesh Iyer* (2020) 3 AIR Bom R 161.

actually caused by the breach. Both cases discussed above were decided on the basis of this approach, with the court in both cases holding that the plaintiff had failed to discharge this burden of proof.

The difficulty with this approach, however, is that it relies on evidentiary difficulties to achieve what is clearly intended to be a substantive position, which is hardly satisfactory. Equally, it arguably sets the bar so high as to make it virtually impossible to clear—and, in doing so, makes no distinction between commercial contracts negotiated with the benefit of full legal advice and contracts marked by a high degree of asymmetry. An approach that treats the reasonableness of a sum stipulated in a contract between two evenly matched commercial concerns, or between two high net-worth individuals, as being, in principle, no different from a sum stipulated in contract between a company and a trainee is not easy to justify.

A second route around this difficulty, taken in a small number of cases, involves deciding the case without any reference to section 74, relying instead on the doctrine of unconscionability in Indian law—a move also seen in other common law jurisdictions such as Canada.[10] The Contract Act does not expressly enact a doctrine of unconscionability. Nevertheless, such a doctrine was read into the Contract Act in 1986 by the Supreme Court in *Central Indian Water Transport Corp v Brojo Nath Ganguly*,[11] which held that a contract that was unconscionable would violate public policy and, hence, be void under section 23 of the Contract Act, which deals with contracts against public policy. What is unconscionable is somewhat expansively defined:[12] it depends on the unfairness or unreasonableness of the clause, whether the term shocks the conscience of the court, the extent of inequality in bargaining power, differences in the economic strength, lack of meaningful choice, and so on; but the courts have been at pains to stress that commercial transactions marked by an equality of bargaining power are unlikely to be unconscionable. The High Courts of Madhya Pradesh[13] and Gujarat[14] have used the notion of unconscionability, rather than the powers conferred by section 74, in cases involving agreements signed by medical students that committed them to spend a certain period of time as a resident in a named hospital and required them to pay a substantial sum of money if they failed to do so.

The attractions of unconscionability are easy to see. Unlike the current approach to section 74, it does permit a substantial degree of context-sensitivity, and it enables the courts to consider the extent to which the approach taken in relation to commercial contracts produced by symmetric or equal bargaining should be the same as

[10] See eg *Liu v Coal Harbour Properties Partnership* [2006] BCCA 385, (2006) 273 DLR (4th) 508, [24]; *Birch v Union of Taxation Employees* [2008] ONCA 809, (2008) 305 DLR (4th) 64.

[11] AIR 1986 SC 1571.

[12] The Law Commission of India, in its 199th report (2006), recommended putting the doctrine on a statutory footing, but no government has taken up this recommendation, although private members' bills to do so are periodically introduced in Parliament (and one is currently pending). Please refer to S Swaminathan and V Singh, Chapter 9 of this volume.

[13] *Anshul Jain v Medical Education Department,* Writ Petition 7982 of 2019 (Madhya Pradesh High Court, 13 May 2020).

[14] *Shitanshushekhar Manoharlal Sharma v State of Gujarat,* Special Civil Application 18840 of 2014 (Gujarat High Court, 12 April 2019).

that taken in other contexts. Yet, it is not clear whether unconscionability applies to bodies other than public bodies that are part of the state as defined in Article 12 of the Constitution: although the concept has been applied to wholly private bodies, dicta suggest that it should be confined to public bodies. Equally, the fact that unconscionability as applied in these cases is rooted in public policy rather than the specific provisions of section 74 also raises questions in relation to the appropriateness of applying it to an area such as stipulated sums, which are the subject of a specific statutory provision.

2. Limitation Clauses

The position in relation to limitation clauses can be discussed more briefly. The Contract Act does not directly provide for any rules in relation to limitation clauses, either to permit or to restrict them. Nevertheless, Indian courts have developed a range of techniques to deal with these clauses, which have been influenced by the common law approach developed in cases like *Spurling v Bradshaw*[15] in relation to the extent of notice that must be given for a limitation clause to be incorporated, as well as by the approach to construction developed in the *Suisse Atlantique* line of cases.[16] Whilst these individually pose fewer problems than the law in relation to stipulated sums, the question of their relationship to each other remains unresolved.

The first approach asks whether the limitation clause has been validly incorporated into the contract if the incorporation is by notice rather than through a signed document. The Contract Act itself does not deal directly with incorporation, but the Indian courts have consistently applied a body of rules derived from English law and substantially identical with it. Notice of the clause must be given prior to the time of contract, with the result that clauses contained in post-contractual documents, such as receipts or consignment notes, do not form part of the contract and have no legal effect.[17] The courts also consider the nature of the document containing the term and the extent of notice that was given. A notice contained on the reverse of a laundry receipt, for example, will not be binding if the owner of the laundry did not draw the customer's attention to the clause,[18] and the rule also applies to other types of documents such as tickets.[19]

A second approach to limitation clauses is derived from the *Suisse Atlantique*[20] rule in English law. Under this approach, courts read down exclusion clauses that conflict with the main purpose of the contract. The aim, as the Supreme Court described it in *Skandia Insurance v Kokilaben Chandravadan*,[21] is to ensure that the exclusion clause

[15] [1956] 1 WLR 461 (CA).
[16] *Suisse Atlantique Société d'Armament SA v NV Rotterdamsche Kolen Centrale* [1967] 1 AC 361 (HL).
[17] *Road Transport Corporation v Kirloskar Brothers* AIR 1981 Bom 299; *Road Transport Organisation of India v Barunai Powerloom Weavers' Cooperative Society Ltd* (1997) 2 OLR 106.
[18] *RS Deboo v Dr MV Hindlekar* AIR 1995 Bom 68.
[19] *Special Secretary to the Government of Rajasthan v Vedakantara Venkataramanna* AIR 1984 AP 5.
[20] *Suisse Atlantique Société d'Armament SA* (n 16).
[21] AIR 1987 SC 1184.

'does not cross swords' with the contract's main purpose. The court will, accordingly, try to 'harmonize the two instead of allowing the exclusion clause to snipe successfully at the main purpose'. As in English law, this is a rule of interpretation rather than a substantive rule, and effect will be given to a clearly worded clause no matter how onerous the result. A number of cases have arisen, for example, out of a standard term in public-sector construction contracts, under which public bodies are not liable to compensate contractors for any losses arising out of construction delays caused by the public body if the contractor has been given an extension of time for completing the project. The courts have generally tended to give full effect to these clauses.[22] Where statutory policies are also at play, as in motor insurance contracts, courts will go further in reading down exclusion clauses to make them conform to the statute.[23] As in English law, the courts also draw on the *contra proferentam* rule to read down limitation clauses.[24]

A third technique uses the doctrine of unconscionability set out in *Brojo Nath Ganguly*,[25] discussed above, to hold exclusion clauses void under section 23. Much as with stipulated sums, the application of unconscionability to exclusion clauses is influenced by context. In insurance cases, for example, the courts have read in a duty on insurance companies, based on the duty of utmost good faith, to explain all exclusions to the assured and have held exclusion clauses void where this has not been done.[26] A far more interesting field of application of unconscionability has been in housebuilding contracts. Developers of residential housing appear to not infrequently introduce a standard term in their contracts which is written in the form of a liquidated damages clause, but in reality operates to cap the liability of the developer at a very low amount in the event of delay. Clauses of this type have come up before the consumer courts on several occasions, and their response in every instance has been to use the doctrine of unconscionability to hold the clause void for unconscionability.[27]

A final, and somewhat startling, approach was taken by the High Court of Delhi in a 2010 decision, *Simplex Concrete Piles v Union of India*.[28] The High Court in this case held that section 73 created a legal right to compensation for breach which, as a matter of public policy, cannot be waived:

> It therefore is a matter of public policy that the sanctity of the contracts and the bindingness thereof should be given precedence over the entitlement to breach the same by virtue of contractual clauses with no remedy to the aggrieved party.

[22] See eg *Ramnath International Construction Ltd v Union of India* AIR 2007 SC 509; *ONGC v Wig Brothers* (2010) 13 SCC 377.
[23] *BV Nagaraju v Oriental Insurance Co* (1996) 5 SCC 71.
[24] *Iffco Tokio General Insurance Co v Permanent Lok Adalat (Public Utility Service), Gurgaon* 2011 SCC OnLine P&H 11047.
[25] *Central Indian Water Transport Corp* (n 11).
[26] *Modern Insulators v Oriental Insurance Co Ltd* 2002 (2) SCC 734; *Iffco Tokio General Insurance Co* (n 24).
[27] See eg *Smita Uban v Pioneer Urban Land* 2020 SCC OnLine NCDRC 1094.
[28] 2010 SCC OnLine Del 821.

Any clause that sought to exclude liability would, therefore, be void for 'being against public interest and public policy'.

This approach has thus far exerted a rather limited influence over subsequent cases, and it is to be hoped that it stays that way. The approach resembles the doctrine of substantive fundamental breach with which English courts experimented in the 1970s and is likely to suffer from problems similar to those which that doctrine created.[29] There is little in the language of section 73 or in its history to suggest that the Contract Act was intended to prohibit exclusion clauses. Given that nineteenth-century English law already had statutes limiting exclusion clauses in specific circumstances,[30] it is likely that if the Contract Act had been intended to create a general policy against exclusion clauses, it would have done so expressly.

III. Towards a Diagnosis: Rediscovering the Social Function of Contract Law

Drawing on case law from elsewhere in the common law world is an obvious way to deal with difficult questions, and it is unsurprising that the Indian courts have done so. Nevertheless, case law and scholarly writing from other jurisdictions should be approached with some caution when dealing with remedial clauses in Indian law. The Contract Act makes a number of deliberate departures from common law rules, including in relation to remedial clauses. Crucially, and as this section discusses in more detail, these departures were made not only in the interest of simplifying the law but also based on a clear view as to the role of contract law in responding to social concerns.

There are several reasons why it is worth engaging with these aspects of Indian law at this point in time. The growing move across the common law world away from the 'genuine pre-estimate' test makes it likely that Indian law, too, will shift away from that test in due course. Rather than simply following the path taken by English law, it is worth investigating why the Contract Act sought to depart from English law in the nineteenth century and examining whether those factors have any relevance to the path Indian law should take in the present day. As this section argues, both these questions should be answered in the affirmative. A closer examination of the historical origins of the discretion conferred by section 74, and the purposes that underlay it, suggests a very different path that Indian law can and should take, which will resolve not only the problems with the current state of Indian law itself but also problems from which the common law elsewhere continues to suffer.

This section begins by discussing the ways in which the Contract Act departed from the common law rules on stipulated sums (section III.1). It then draws on the legislative

[29] See *Photo Production Ltd v Securicor Transport Ltd* [1980] AC 827 (HL), which abolished the doctrine in English law, for a discussion of its background and the difficulties to which it gave rise.

[30] For an overview, see J Paterson and E Bant, 'Contract and the Challenge of Consumer Protection Legislation' in TT Arvind and Jenny Steele (eds), *Contract Law and the Legislature: Autonomy, Expectations, and the Making of Legal Doctrine* (Hart 2020).

history to show that these departures were animated by an underlying view that saw contract law as having a central role in responding to social problems (section III.2) and concludes by arguing that this social role remains relevant in the present day (section III.3).

1. Section 74 and the Nineteenth-Century Common Law

The Contract Act made several changes to English contract law as it stood in the nineteenth century.[31] Section 74 was one of these changes. As prior work has discussed, the section sought to avoid the technicalities of the distinction between penalty clauses and liquidated damages in English law.[32] Instead, it set out a single rule applicable to all clauses providing for a named sum to be payable on breach, regardless of whether they would have been considered liquidated damages clauses or penalty clauses in English law. In effect, it abolished the distinction between liquidated damages and penalties and the distinction between relief against forfeiture and against penalties.[33] In addition, it departed from English law by giving the courts a broad discretion to award any sum they consider reasonable in place of the stipulated sum. This departure is of greater importance than the first, and it therefore merits some explanation.

Nineteenth-century treatises demonstrate that English lawyers saw the rule against penalties as being grounded in a legal principle that contracting parties were, in general, entitled to no more than compensation for the loss that could be proven to have been suffered in consequence of the breach. Liquidated damages formed a narrow exception to that rule. Contemporary treatises suggest that this exception was seen as a pragmatic concession to evidentiary problems. Both Addison and Chitty linked liquidated damages to contractual covenants whose nature was such as to make the precise amount of damages occasioned by their breach uncertain.[34] Liquidated damages, on this view, were enforceable because it was likely that the damages incurred by breach would be more than merely nominal but, nevertheless, be 'of an uncertain character', making it desirable to permit the parties to 'by their contract, assess and fix them beforehand'.[35] Treatises on equity tended to draw on a slightly broader range of factors, but they also agreed that a clause would be enforceable as a liquidated damages clause if it covered contractual stipulations 'the damages from the breach of which cannot be measured', or where 'there is no adequate means of ascertaining the precise damage that may result to the plaintiff from the breach of contract'.[36] In such a case, parties were

[31] For an overview, see W Swain, *The Law of Contract: 1670—1870* (CUP 2015) 262—70.

[32] S Swaminathan, 'De-Inventing the Wheel: Liquidated Damages, Penalties and the Indian Contract Act 1872' (2018) 6 Chinese Journal of Comparative Law 103.

[33] Australian law has recently made a similar shift; see *Andrews v ANZ Bank* [2012] HCA 30.

[34] J Chitty, *A Practical Treatise on the Law of Contracts Not Under Seal* (T Chitty ed, 3rd edn, S Sweet 1841) 866. The rule continued to be described in similar terms into the twentieth century.

[35] CG Addison, *A Treatise on the Law of Contracts and Rights and Liabilities Ex Contractu* (W Benning 1847) 176.

[36] EHT Snell, *The Principles of Equity* (1st edn, Stevens and Haynes 1868) 273.

permitted 'to fix a given amount of compensation in order to avoid the difficulty'.[37] Liquidated damages clauses, in other words, were only enforceable because they were a pragmatic way of dealing with the fact that it would be hard to ascertain how much loss certain types of breaches had caused.[38]

The Contract Act took a very different route to resolving this evidentiary problem by eliminating the need to reflect the actual loss in determining how much compensation to award. Instead, section 74 gives the court discretion to award any sum, not exceeding the sum named in the contract, which it considers to be 'reasonable' compensation. In other words, unlike the position at English law or section 73 of the Contract Act on the award of damages generally, both of which require courts to award exact compensation for the loss, Indian courts have a broad power to award any compensation they consider reasonable, including in situations where no loss is proved to have been caused by the breach.[39] This departure is of considerable significance because it obviates the need to have a special rule applicable to situations where damages are difficult to quantify and, thus, to treat 'genuine pre-estimates' any differently from other stipulated sums. The question in every case, instead, ought to be the reasonableness of the sum stipulated. It is open to a court under section 74 to refuse to enforce a clause which provides for the payment of an amount that is unreasonable, even if damages are difficult to measure. Equally, it also leaves open the possibility of enforcing a clause providing for the payment of a penalty as long as it is reasonable. Most significantly, it creates a new possibility—unknown to nineteenth-century common law or to modern English law—of awarding a third sum, which is neither the sum stipulated in the contract nor the precise amount of the actual loss but rather a sum that is reasonable, given the nature of the harm suffered by the plaintiff as a result of the breach.

The importance of this possibility will be discussed in greater detail in section IV, but it is evident that it makes the importation of the 'genuine pre-estimate' test problematic, and it suggests that there is a need to reconsider whether the current reading of section 74 is the correct one. As section III.2 discusses, this is reinforced by the legislative history of section 74, which shows that the discretionary power conferred by that section was intended to give the courts the ability to respond to the social problems posed by asymmetric or imbalanced social and economic relations.

2. Balancing Legal, Social, and Commercial Considerations

The initial draft of the Contract Act suggested abolishing the rule against penalties in its entirety and replacing with it a rule making the stipulated sum always payable.[40] Clause

[37] ibid 274.

[38] Other matters that would later become central—such as the question of whether or not the clause was *in terrorem*—do not play an important role in nineteenth-century English treatises.

[39] The reference to cases where no loss is proved to have been caused by the breach is likely to have been intended to refer to situations of debt. A creditor seeking to recover a debt can recover the amount of the debt and stipulated interest without having to prove anything beyond the fact of breach.

[40] India Office, *Papers Showing the Present Position of the Question of a Contract Law for India* (HC-239, 1867–68) 5–6.

50 of the draft bill annexed to the Commissioners' Second Report on the Substantive Law of India provided that 'when a contract has been broken, if a sum is named in the contract itself as the amount to be paid in case of such breach, the amount so named shall be paid accordingly'.[41] The illustrations to the draft clause, too, unambiguously repudiated the rule against penalties. The paradigmatic example of a penalty clause in late-nineteenth-century England was a bond requiring the borrower to pay double the original sum in the event of default.[42] Illustration (a) to clause 50 used precisely this scenario but inverted the outcome: a contract that immediately doubled the debt if the borrower failed to repay it on the due day would be fully enforceable.[43]

Strong objections were raised to this proposal by judges of first instance in different provinces, who argued that it would cause considerable practical difficulty and have adverse social consequences. Judges responding to the proposals argued that social conditions in India made it necessary to legally protect individuals against the consequences of 'over-reaching contracts', not least by restraining the power of money lenders over borrowers.[44] These arguments about the social consequences of the Commissioners' proposal to abolish the jurisdiction to relieve against stipulated sums ultimately convinced the Legislative Council to choose a different course.

These social problems were not trivial, and the history of the 1899 amendment to section 74, which put the section in its current form, gives a clear picture of what they were and what purpose the discretion conferred by section 74 was intended to serve. The original version of section 74, enacted in 1872, could be circumvented by requiring a party to provide a penal bond that would be forfeited in the event of breach. Because this was not a stipulated sum, several courts had held that it did not fall within section 74. In 1899, the statute was amended to expand the court's power beyond clauses stipulating a sum to also cover 'any other stipulation by way of penalty'.

The immediate reason for the amendment was the problem of agricultural debt. The colonial government had repealed the Usury Laws in 1855, making any contractually stipulated interest rate enforceable.[45] Procedural and remedial laws compounded the problem. The Code of Civil Procedure 1859, which applied outside the presidency towns, gave creditors an unrestricted power to imprison debtors for unpaid debts[46] and permitted all property to be attached and sold in satisfaction of the debt with no reservation for necessities.[47] The consequences were troubling and were described by the Deccan Riots Commission as, in effect, enabling creditors to 'compel his debtor to work for him as a slave'.[48] In 1879, the government sought to deal with the problem through a special enactment, the Deccan Agriculturalists' Relief Act 1879, but the

41 ibid 16.

42 EHT Snell, *The Principles of Equity* (A Brown ed, 4th edn, Stevens and Haynes 1878) 332.

43 India Office (n 40) 16.

44 See especially IOR/L/PJ/5/15, Comment from Canoba; ibid, Comment from Deputy Commissioner of Delhi.

45 Usury Laws Repeal Act 1855, s 2.

46 Code of Civil Procedure 1859, s 201.

47 ibid s 205.

48 Deccan Riots Commission, *Report of the Commission Appointed to Inquire into the Causes of the Riots in 1875* (C (2nd series) 2071, 1878) 40.

regime it created failed to address this problem. A Government Commission appointed to enquire into the problem suggested amending the Usury Laws Repeal Act 1855 to give courts a wide discretion to reduce unconscionable interest rates[49] and amending the Contract Act to clarify how undue influence applied to agreements to pay interest.[50] The 1899 amendments to sections 16 and 19 of the Contract Act gave effect to the latter recommendation. The government was, however, unwilling to create a special power in relation to interest and, instead, chose to amend section 74, expanding the courts' powers over stipulated sums to cover a wider range of penal stipulations.

Administrative and judicial officials welcomed the proposed amendment's 'highly advantageous' character in dealing with pressing social issues and particularly 'the removal of inequalities so common in India where the poor man is generally at the mercy of the rich man from whom he has borrowed money'.[51] The expansion of the powers under section 74 was thought to be 'just and necessary for the equitable decision of many cases which come before judicial officers'[52] and for dealing with cleverly worded contractual stipulations.[53] It was imperative for the courts to be able to 'protect the agriculturist from the unfair dealings and rapacity of the money-lender', and the revision to section 74 would introduce a much-needed reform enabling them to do that.[54]

As this demonstrates, section 74 was intended to serve a *social* function. The fact that oppressive agricultural lending was a social problem that required a remedy was a significant factor in the amendment of section 74, and the power it gave courts was seen as a tool to respond to that problem. The problem had arisen from the introduction into India of common law rules without adequate consideration being given to their social consequences. It was, therefore, only logical to resolve that problem by giving courts the power to be more socially responsive in applying the law.

This social function, however, was not unlimited. The historical record shows that the drafters of the amendment were also anxious about protecting freely agreed commercial transactions. The statement of objects and reasons accompanying the Bill said so explicitly, and in his speech introducing the Bill to the Legislative Council, Sir John Woodburn, the Bill's initial sponsor, explained that the primary reason for choosing to amend the substantive law of contract, rather than the law regarding interest, was to avoid the risk that courts would 'interfere largely with legitimate trade'. High rates of interest could be 'perfectly legitimate' in some circumstances, and they should be enforced as long as the parties 'enter upon an engagement in equal terms'. This, it was felt, could be achieved by giving the courts more discretion:

[49] ibid [77].
[50] ibid [41].
[51] IOR/L/PJ/6/483, File 1213, Comment from the Chief Commissioner of Coorg.
[52] IOR/L/PJ/6/488, File 1748, Comment from the Commissioner of Ajmere-Merwara.
[53] IOR/L/PJ/6/483, File 1213, Comment from Coorg District Judge.
[54] IOR/L/PJ/6/488, File 1748, Comment from Pritchard.

> in the direction of varying the terms of a contract which they believed to be inequitable, so that they may not be required . . . to give a creditor judgment for sums which they actually consider to be unconscionable.[55]

When the Bill returned to the Council after consideration by a Select Committee, Mackenzie Chalmers, who had taken over responsibility for the Bill following John Woodburn's appointment as Lieutenant Governor of Bengal, stressed that the Committee had gone to some lengths to show that the Bill was not 'intended in any way to apply to, or to affect, *bona fide* business transactions'[56] or to 'interfere with freedom of contract where the parties to a contract are really free and contract with each other on a footing of equality'.[57] Respondents to the consultation on the draft Bill, including judges, similarly worried that the change would 'lower the standard of commercial morality by relaxing the bonds of contract and encouraging litigation to avoid bargains which ought to be carried out'.[58] It was not the law's role to assist individuals 'who deal recklessly when they are in a proper state of mind and have grown in worldly experience'.[59] Members of the legislative council, too, expressed worries about the sweeping nature of the Bill[60] and feared it might be 'applied by ill-informed courts to classes of contracts it was never intended to apply to'.[61]

Two concerns underpinned this. The first was the risk of encouraging speculative litigation and undermining the security of commercial transactions.[62] As one respondent put it, any alteration to the general law of contract ran the risk of 'offering new opportunities for doubtful litigation to an already over litigious people', causing 'gross injustice' to ordinary merchants and adding 'to the terrors with which litigation tends to paralyse all dealings' in India.[63] The second was that judges in smaller towns and districts in the provinces were less experienced than the judges of the presidencies and would be more easily swayed to favour borrowers.[64]

The final form of the amendment reflected these concerns. It sought to protect genuine commercial transactions by circumscribing the 'general lines' on which courts should proceed without leaving them (as Chalmers put it) 'free to wander at will over all English and American jurisprudence'.[65] The point was to legislate not against moneylenders but against unconscionable bargains,[66] and the introduction of the terminology

[55] Governor General's Council Proceedings of 21 March 1898, *Gazette of India Part VI* (Calcutta, 26 March 1898) 294.
[56] Governor General's Council Proceedings of 17 February 1899, *Gazette of India Part VI* (Calcutta, 18 February 1899) 28.
[57] Governor General's Council Proceedings of 20 January 1899, *Gazette of India Part VI* (Calcutta, 21 January 1899) 10.
[58] IOR/L/PJ/6/497, File 2310, Comment from HF Aston (District Judge, Satara).
[59] IOR/L/PJ/6/496, File 2269, Petition from the Panchayat of Ghotki, Sind.
[60] Proceedings of 17 February 1899 (n 56) 37 (Ananda Charlu).
[61] ibid 37 (Evans).
[62] ibid 28 (Maharaja of Darbhanga).
[63] IOR/L/PJ/6/450, File 1205, Letter No 1505-96 from the Secretary, Bengal Chambers of Commerce to the Officiating Secretary to the Government of Bengal, 6 November 1896.
[64] Proceedings of 17 February 1899 (n 56) 29 (Smeaton).
[65] ibid 39 (Chalmers).
[66] ibid 40 (Chalmers).

of 'penalty' as well as the specific examples discussed in the illustrations were intended to highlight the fact that the discretion conferred by the section was not a general discretion to relieve against financial hardship or to intervene merely because a bond contained hard stipulations. Several judges, in commenting on the draft amendment, had pointed to the hardship that acceleration clauses (which provided that the whole debt immediately fell due if a single instalment was missed) caused borrowers.[67] The contrast between Illustrations (f) and (g) to the final section were a specific response to this: a mere acceleration clause was enforceable, but an acceleration clause that also doubled the amount payable was not. This balance between enabling intervention to deal with social harms, while also upholding commercial freedom in bona fide transactions, was fundamental to the scheme of the amendment, which sought to ensure that the courts exercised their discretion in a manner that did not interfere with commercial transactions where parties were on an equal footing in terms of bargaining power.

3. Implications for the Present Day

Understanding the purpose underlying section 74 is not just of historical interest. It also matters to how we understand the law in relation to remedial clauses today. The Contract Act, like many other laws around the world, was transplanted from the jurisdiction in which it originated to a new social and cultural context.[68] Legal transplants almost inevitably involve a significant degree of adaptation and alteration.[69] The history of section 74 sheds light on precisely such an adaptation. Yet, as the discussion in this section has shown, the courts' reliance on the 'genuine pre-estimate' test has led section 74 to fall well short of the outcomes its drafters envisaged. It has led the courts to interfere in fully negotiated transactions between parties of equal bargaining power, in sharp contrast to the intention that underlay section 74. At the same time, it has provided an inadequate basis for the courts to intervene in transactions where intervention is arguably required and compels judges to either use a legal fiction to set a very high evidentiary bar or to resort to a completely different doctrine such as public policy.

These issues remain because the general law of contract law continues to have a broad field of application in India. Cases that would elsewhere be decided on the basis of a special statutory regime fall to be decided under the ordinary principles of contract law in India, and a significant proportion of the case law on stipulated sums or limitation clauses arises out of such contracts. Employment contracts, for example, are subject to an extensive system of statutory regulation in England but, in India, are largely governed by the ordinary law of contract. The same applies to a considerable

[67] See eg IOR/L/PJ/6/488, File 1748, Comment from Khandekar (Judicial Assistant Commissioner, Ajmere-Merwara); IOR/L/PJ/6/497, File 2310, Comment from James (Commissioner, Sind).

[68] A Watson, *Legal Transplants: An Approach to Comparative Law* (2nd edn, University of Georgia Press 1993).

[69] TT Arvind, 'The "Transplant Effect" in Harmonization' (2010) 59 International and Comparative Law Quarterly 65.

proportion of consumer contracts. Although consumer courts in India operate a special regime for product liability[70] and have a higher degree of remedial flexibility than the ordinary civil courts, when it comes to any issue beyond liability for defective products (and, possibly, defective services),[71] they operate under the general law of contract. India also incorporates a somewhat distinctive approach to defining a consumer: a self-employed individual is considered a consumer even in relation to contracts entered into for the purpose of their business.[72] A contract between the self-employed owner of a clothing store and a transport company is, as a result, treated as a consumer contract in Indian law.[73] Equally, the wall of separation between public law and private law set up in English cases like *Re Racal*[74] and *O'Reilly v Mackman*[75] has no counterpart in Indian law, and it is far from uncommon to see arguments and decisions in cases involving public-sector contracting juxtaposing principles of contract law with principles of administrative law or constitutional law.[76]

The consequence is that Indian contract law operates in a very different context from English law. The steady retreat of general contract law in England from a significant number of areas of interaction means that the courts can refocus principles on the needs of commercial transactions.[77] That option is not tenable in the Indian context, where the transactional context, and the nature of the social and economic relations to which a transaction relates, matter in a way they do not elsewhere. Whatever the desirability in purely normative terms of the positions in relation to freedom of contract that have been taken elsewhere in the common law world,[78] in the Indian context, emphasis has to be placed on the purposes that the statutory discretion created by section 74 was intended to serve.

The complexities of the case law arise from the complexity of the contractual landscape in India—and, in particular, the very wide range of contexts and transaction types in which remedial clauses are used as well as the very different situations they present in relation to the parties' relative bargaining power. This makes the bright-line approaches and binary categories that dominate this area of law elsewhere less suited to India. As section IV discusses, re-grounding the law in an approach that assigns appropriate weight to social context and the social function of contract law has the potential

[70] The Consumer Protection Act 2019, ss 82–87.

[71] The Consumer Protiection Act, s 2(34) defines 'product liability' to include deficient services, and 'product seller' is similarly defined to include a service provider by s 2(37), but the wording of ss 82–87 is not particularly well suited to services and suggests that the draftsmen had physical products in mind.

[72] ibid, s 2(7)(ii)(a).

[73] See eg *Tridev Express Cargo v Ipsita Shah*, Revision Petition 27 of 2020 (National Consumer Disputes Redressal Commission, 25 February 2020).

[74] [1981] AC 374 (HL).

[75] [1983] 2 AC 237 (HL).

[76] See eg *Anshul Jain* (n 13).

[77] Although, as Lord Burrows JSC has recently pointed out, the growing separation between general contract law and specific bodies of law in relation to areas such as employment contracts is not necessarily a positive development; see A Burrows, 'Preservation, Removal and Freezing of the Common Law by Statute' in Arvind and Steele (n 30).

[78] See eg S Worthington, 'Common Law Values: The Role of Party Autonomy in Private Law' in A Robertson and M Tilbury (eds), *The Common Law of Obligations: Divergence and Unity* (Hart 2016).

to resolve the issues that make the current approach to section 74 unsatisfactory, as well as the problems Indian courts have faced in relation to limitation clauses.

IV. Rethinking the Law

What, then, can we learn from the history that is of relevance to the present day? The most important lesson is that it is both feasible and appropriate for the judiciary to move the law onto a different path that is more in keeping with the original purpose that section 74 was intended to serve. A discretionary power is, at its heart, a legal tool; and a central task for the courts in dealing with powers conferred by a long-lived statute is maintaining and improving the tools it provides to adapt them to the changing context.[79] This task can be easily achieved if courts have close regard to the operational context of the discretionary power[80] and to the social function it was intended to serve within the framework of the statute that created it. If section 74's actual effect has been materially different from the effect it was intended to have, the answer is a change of direction to bring the law closer to the manner in which it was intended to function. Legal theorists have paid considerable attention to this task, and their work provides us with a ready methodology for going about it.[81]

What direction, then, should the law take? This chapter argues that four basic insights must lie at the heart of any approach to remedial clauses in Indian law. The first is that the Contract Act is, by design, concerned not only with markets but also with society. The history discussed above demonstrates that in structure, purpose, and intent, section 74 resembles neither an English statute nor a civilian code as much as it resembles the US Uniform Commercial Code—a law that was explicitly drafted to permit a more socially and contextually aware form of judging.[82] The fact that contracts were used in a wide variety of transactions, some of which reflected social asymmetries, was widely understood, as was the fact that the law needed to adopt a position that would let the courts be responsive to the legal needs created by asymmetric transactions, while also adopting a more hands-off stance when it came to more balanced market transactions.

Second, the law must also be cognisant of the fact that any approach to penalty clauses will be applied by not only the courts themselves but also other actors. To some extent, this is already recognised in practice. The superior courts have expressly sought to temper the propensity of the consumer courts to err in a more pro-consumer direction; and the case law of the Bombay High Court on section 74 is characterised by a sense of exasperation with the propensity of arbitrators to routinely award stipulated

[79] See K Llewellyn, 'The Normative, the Legal and the Law-Jobs: The Problem of Juristic Method' (1940) 8 Yale Law Journal 1355, 1392.

[80] TT Arvind and J Steele, 'History, Context and the Problem of Juristic Method: The Chancery Amendment Act 1858 and the Law of Contract' in Arvind and Steele (n 30).

[81] For an overview, see TT Arvind, 'Vilhelm Lundstedt and the Social Function of Legislation' (2013) 1 Theory and Practice of Legislation 33.

[82] For a fuller discussion, see W Twining, *Karl Llewellyn and the Realist Movement* (2nd edn, CUP 2012).

sums without entering into the broader enquiry on reasonableness that the Contract Act requires.[83] Making the law's social purpose fully effective in such an environment will require the courts to give greater weight to law's hortatory function, seeking to induce those who draft remedial clauses to do so in a manner that adheres both to the letter and the spirit of the law, rather than devoting their energies to circumventing the law through clever drafting.[84] To do so, it must provide an avenue that permits parties to stipulate sums in their contract if they have legitimate commercial reasons to do so.

Third, the law must be sensitive to the fact that, in some contexts, stipulated sums can, and do, serve legitimate commercial purposes. An awareness of these purposes led English law to move away from the old penalties-liquidated damages distinction in *Cavendish Square*[85] and, as the history discussed above has shown, it guided section 74 well over a century before it entered English law. The literature on contracting gives several examples,[86] and Indian law should be more open to giving them weight when they occur in fully negotiated transactions entered into between parties of approximately equal standing and where they serve a mutual purpose or provide mutual benefit. In keeping with the hortatory function, the law should encourage parties to be transparent in drafting contracts by expressly setting out the specific (and not generic) mutual purpose the clause serves, the basis on which the stipulated sum was calculated, and the specific (and not generic) reason why it is reasonable under the circumstances. Consider, for example, demurrage clauses, which have posed considerable problems under section 74.[87] On its face, there are good reasons to permit a party to seek to set a higher price for having to remain in possession of the other party's goods for a period beyond what was contractually agreed; and there is an obvious mutual benefit to both parties in continuing to have the goods attended to and not abandoned. The approach suggested here would place the focus on the question of whether the price is reasonable, while giving the parties the ability to set out in the contract the basis for the stipulated sum. Other clauses—for example, the payment of compensation for early termination of an agency—will be approached similarly.

Fourth, and finally, the law must be expressly cognisant of, and responsive to, the fact that the cases that come before the courts continue to reflect a broad variety of transactions, ranging from employment contracts to contracts for maritime salvage. This requires the courts to go beyond the distinction between consumer and commercial transactions that is often made in English law.[88] As the 1899 amendment recognised, and as the agricultural loans that were prompted it instantiate, transactions that are

[83] See eg *Sandhya Nayak* (n 8).

[84] The nature and importance of the hortatory function of law is discussed more fully in the work of Professor Atiyah; see PS Atiyah, 'From Principles to Pragmatism: Changes in the Function of the Judicial Process and the Law' (1980) 65 Iowa Law Review 1249.

[85] *Cavendish Square Holding BV* (n 7) [32], and in particular the reference to the 'legitimate interest' that a penalty may be designed to protect.

[86] See eg S Rowan, 'For the Recognition of Remedial Terms agreed *Inter Partes*' (2010) 126 Law Quarterly Review 448; CJ Goetz and RE Scott, 'Liquidated Damages, Penalties, and the Just Compensation Principle' (1977) 77 Columbia Law Review 554; IR Macneil, 'Power of Contract and Agreed Remedies' (1962) 47 Cornell Law Quarterly 495.

[87] *Ultratech Cement Ltd v Sunfield Resources Pvt Ltd* 2016 SCC OnLine Bom 10023.

[88] JN Adams and R Brownsword, 'The Ideologies of Contract' (1987) 7 Legal Studies 205.

commercial may, nevertheless, be characterised by an imbalance between the parties, just as non-commercial transactions may be perfectly balanced.[89] Jenny Steele and I have recently argued that English contract law embeds not just two but four distinct approaches to contract law, which respond as much to structural asymmetries—that is to say, to market structures and propensities in a particular field—as they do to transactional asymmetries.[90] The concerns that underlay section 74 require distinguishing between, for example, a contract engaging a trainee (which is unlikely to ever be entered into between parties dealing on an equal footing) and a contract between two evenly matched commercial parties seeking to settle a long-running dispute (which will, save in exceptional circumstances, involve parties dealing on an equal footing)—something existing approaches struggle to achieve.[91] Equally, section 74 permits the courts to combine this with the remedial flexibility permitted by the section in that the courts faced with an asymmetric transaction can award compensation on a discounted scale, depending on the extent of inequality and its impact on the final form of the contract: unlike the position in English law, Indian courts are not restricted to the binary option of either allowing the stipulation or disallowing it entirely.

The approach can be summarised in the form of four propositions, which are offered here by way of a restatement of the law:

(1) The purpose of an enquiry under section 74 is to identify a reasonable sum to be awarded by way of compensation for breach. Depending on the circumstances, this may be the sum named in the contract, the actual loss suffered by the innocent party, or a different sum, which is lower than the named sum.

(2) The sum named in the contract will be treated as reasonable compensation only if all the following conditions are satisfied. If any of them are not satisfied, the named sum will be treated as exceeding the amount of compensation that is reasonable and a lesser sum will be awarded:

   (i) the transaction is a *bona fide* commercial transaction between parties with comparable bargaining power;

   (ii) the named sum serves a legitimate commercial purpose, which is expressly set out in the contract or is otherwise identifiable from the contract and is proportionate to the importance of that purpose to the party to whom the named sum is payable on breach;

   (iii) where the clause is framed in terms of a formula rather than a specific amount, the application of that formula does not produce effects that would have been outside the parties' reasonable contemplation at the time of contracting; and

   (iv) although the breach must affect the interests of the innocent party for the named sum to be payable, it need not cause economic loss: the courts

[89] See eg the discussion of the market for agricultural loans in South India in Proceedings of 17 February 1899 (n 56) 42–46 (Rees).

[90] TT Arvind and J Steele, 'Remapping Contract Law: Four Perceptions of Markets' in Arvind and Steele (n 30).

[91] See the discussion in section II.1 above.

should recognise that in a *bona fide* commercial transaction, the loss of a contractual right can itself be the loss that the clause was intended to remedy.

(3) If the sum named in the contract is not reasonable compensation because one of the above conditions has not been met, the court will award the actual loss suffered by the innocent party if it can be quantified in accordance with the usual principles of contract law.

(4) Where the circumstances of an individual case make it impossible to specify the actual loss suffered in that particular case (eg in relation to delayed completion in construction contracts), the court will estimate reasonable compensation with reference to the types of loss that a breach of that type has a propensity to produce. This may be assessed from broader sectoral evidence or from evidence of market conditions. Where such evidence is unavailable, a court may use the named sum as a starting point and reduce it to take account of the impact of any inequality between the parties on the contract, or to make it more proportionate to the purpose it was intended to serve, or otherwise to make it more reasonable. This process of adjustment of the named sum is of particular importance in cases where the relationship between the parties is asymmetric, either due to transactional factors or due to social or structural factors.

Whilst the approach outlined above does depart from the 'genuine pre-estimate' test, it is submitted that it nevertheless comes far closer to embodying the spirit of the intent behind section 74 and will also do a much better job than the current approach of balancing the socially directed objective and policy behind section 74 with the commercial concern of non-interference in freely negotiated commercial transactions.

Whilst the discussion in this section has focused on stipulated sums, it is equally applicable to limitation clauses. Limitation clauses serve a commercial purpose but also create potential issues much like stipulated sums. The gradual moves by Indian courts to extend unconscionability to limitation clauses arguably reflect their recognition of this similarity, but it nevertheless runs the risk of disturbing a mutually agreed and commercially reasonable allocation of risk. Given this, the approach suggested above can also guide the manner in which unconscionability is applied to exclusion clauses, including—critically—by stressing the importance of the principle that the courts should not disturb a *bona fide* allocation of risk in a freely negotiated commercial transaction and should, accordingly, give effect to exclusion clauses in all such contracts.

V. Conclusion

This chapter has argued that the approach of the courts to section 74 of the Contract Act requires reconsideration. The general move in the common law world away from the 'genuine pre-estimate' approach provides an opportune moment to do so. As this chapter has also argued, the language of section 74, and the less-differentiated character of contract litigation in India, make it inappropriate to simply follow the approaches taken in other common law jurisdictions. A distinctively Indian approach is needed.

This chapter has argued that the historical background to section 74 indicates what the broad contours of such an approach could be. Any approach should take account of the different contexts in which stipulated sums are used, the social function of contract law in relation to those contexts (in particular in relation to systemic asymmetry), and the broader need to strike a balance with the imperative of non-interference in *bona fide* commercial transactions. These principles are important, and they matter not just to the question of the approach to stipulated sums but also, more broadly, for understanding the approach that the Contract Act takes to the question of the relationship between law, contract, and broader social concerns. The 150th anniversary of the Contract Act is an appropriate time to engage more closely with them.

18

The Action for the Agreed Sum and Specific Performance in Indian Law

Niranjan Venkatesan[*]

I. Introduction

A chapter I wrote on this subject in 2013 concluded with the observation that 'it is difficult to predict what the future holds for the primacy of damages in Indian law'.[1] That is no longer the case. In 2018, Parliament chose to abolish the rule, which had stood since 1877, that a contract may be specifically enforced only if damages would not be an adequate remedy for its breach. That this amendment has fundamentally altered the shape of the Indian law of remedies is beyond doubt. Whether it has done so for the better is not.

Section II of this chapter considers the action for the agreed sum in India. The distinctive feature of this area of the law is the adoption by the Indian courts of the civilian doctrine of the 'fiction of fulfilment', according to which a claimant who is wrongfully prevented from performing its contractual obligations is deemed to have performed them. The consequence of (erroneously) adopting this doctrine is that the action for the agreed sum in India is considerably wider than the drafters intended it to be.

Section III considers the law relating to specific performance as it stood prior to 2018. The framework for specific performance was established by the enactment of the Specific Relief Act in 1877 (hereinafter 'the 1877 Act'). Despite Sir Henry Maine's proposal to the contrary, that Act retained the rule that specific performance may be granted only if damages would not be an adequate remedy. The 1877 Act was eventually replaced by the Specific Relief Act 1963 (hereinafter 'the 1963 Act'). The 1963 Act made a number of important changes to the law but did not disturb the adequacy rule. That rule stood until 2018, when, as noted above, Parliament amended the 1963 Act to provide that specific performance shall be available as of right, subject only to certain grounds for refusing it, of which the adequacy of damages is not one.

* This chapter is based substantially on my paper titled 'Specific and Agreed Remedies in Indian Law: A Code of English Law?' in M Chen-Wishart, A Loke, and B Ong (eds), *Studies in the Contract Laws of Asia I: Remedies for Breach of Contract* (OUP 2016).

[1] See note above.

Niranjan Venkatesan, *The Action for the Agreed Sum and Specific Performance in Indian Law* In: *Foundations of Indian Contract Law.*
Edited by: KV Krishnaprasad, Niranjan Venkatesan, Shivprasad Swaminathan, and Umakanth Varottil, Oxford University Press.
 DOI: 10.1093/9780191997211.003.0018

Section IV considers the 2018 amendment which, it is fair to say, does not represent the draftsman's finest hour. Indeed, as explained below, it appears to have introduced a number of oddities or anomalies, which Parliament probably did not foresee but are the effect of the words it used.

II. The Action for the Agreed Sum in Indian Law

An action for an agreed sum is a claim in debt. For this reason, it is (at any rate, in English law) subject neither to the restrictions on the availability of specific performance nor to the rules governing the assessment of damages.[2] It is therefore not necessary to prove, for example, that damages are an inadequate remedy or that loss was caused by the non-payment of the agreed sum. How does Indian law characterise such a claim? The answer to this question is not beyond doubt. Its importance is not merely taxonomical, significant though that is: if a claim for an agreed sum is treated as a claim for specific performance, it would be governed by the 1963 Act (as amended in 2018) and accordingly be subject to the restrictions there set out. If it is treated as a claim in debt, it would not be.

1. The Characterisation of a Claim for an Agreed Sum

The better view, although there is little modern authority for it, is that Indian law, like English law, treats a claim for an agreed sum as a claim in debt. Three points may be made in support of this proposition.

First, an early line of authority concerning the sale of judgment debts suggests that Indian law treats a claim for an agreed sum as a claim in debt. In *Vithaldas Vishram*,[3] the claimant sold a judgment debt in his favour to the defendant. The claimant's judgment debtor was subsequently declared insolvent. The defendant refused to complete the transaction. He was sued for the price. Counsel for the claimant sought to distinguish a Privy Council authority[4] on the ground that the (unsuccessful) claim in that case was for 'specific performance of a contract . . . and the whole basis was therefore different from that in the present suit, which is a suit *not for specific performance but for price*'.[5] Blackwell J accepted this contention, observing that the claimant sued for the 'price of goods alleged to have been bargained and sold', not specific performance.[6] In a similar case in the Madras High Court, Krishnan J said that 'the plaintiff is entitled to the price arranged under the contract and need not sue for damages'.[7] Krishnan J did

[2] HG Beale, *Chitty on Contracts* (33rd edn, Sweet & Maxwell 2019) [26-009].
[3] *Vithaldas Vishram v Jagjivan Gordhandas* (1939) 41 Bom LR 33.
[4] *JN Basu v Peyer Deye Debi* (1915-16) 43 IA 108, 112.
[5] *Vithaldas Vishram* (n 3) 37 (emphasis added).
[6] ibid 42.
[7] *KS Krishna Iyer v Nynadikkam Pillai* (1920) 20 LW 329 (Madras HC) 330 (emphasis added).

observe that 'recovery of the price is in the nature of a specific performance of the contract', but this, it is suggested, does not mean that the restrictions on specific performance are applicable to an action for the agreed sum. This view of the case is consistent with Krishnan J's conclusion that 'the payment of the price is the proper remedy that should be allowed . . . in such a contract as this',[8] without considering whether compensation in money is an adequate remedy, as he would have had to do had he taken the view that a claim for the price is in fact a claim for specific performance.

Second, there are a number of cases,[9] apart from those concerning judgment debts discussed above, in which a claim for the agreed sum has succeeded without reference to the rules on damages or specific performance. Many of these concern a claim by an unpaid seller for the sale price. Such claims are now governed by section 55(1) of the Sale of Goods Act 1930, which is based on (and virtually identical to) section 49(1) of the old English Act of 1893.[10] As is well known, that provision, in general,[11] allows an unpaid seller to sue for the price only if title has passed or the price is payable on a 'day certain' irrespective of delivery and passing of title. Although the predecessor to the 1930 Act[12] did not contain an equivalent provision, the Indian courts had held consistently that an unpaid seller may sue for the price at common law if title had passed, irrespective of the rules governing damages and specific performance.[13]

Third, Indian procedural law classifies an action for the price as debt, not damages. This is apparent from Order 37, rule 2(b)(ii) of the Code of Civil Procedure 1908, which allows a claimant to institute a 'summary suit'[14] if he or she seeks to recover 'a debt or a liquidated demand in money payable by the defendant . . . on a written contract or on an enactment'. In holding that an action for the agreed sum under an oral contract is not maintainable under this rule, the courts appear to have proceeded on the basis that such an action constitutes a claim in debt.[15]

It follows from the foregoing that an action for the agreed sum, in Indian and English law alike, is not subject to any of the restrictions on specific performance or damages. The real controversy, again in English and Indian law alike, is whether this remedy is available to the claimant notwithstanding a repudiation by the defendant. Indian law

[8] ibid 330.

[9] In addition to those cited in the text, see *Sales Tax Officer, Pilibhit v Budh Prakash Jai Prakash* [1955] 1 SCR 243, [6] (Venkatarama Aiyar J) (*obiter*) and *ML Devender Singh v Syed Khaja* (1973) 2 SCC 515, 521 (Beg J).

[10] Sale of Goods Act 1893. The corresponding provision in the 1979 Act is also s 49. The only difference is that the Indian Act uses the word 'sue' in place of the words 'maintain an action' that appear in the English Act.

[11] The scope of the exceptions remains controversial, but the general rule is not in doubt: see *The Res Cogitans* [2016] AC 1034, [57]–[58] (Lord Mance).

[12] Contract Act, Chapter 7.

[13] See eg *Shoshi Mohun Pal Chowdhury v Nobo Kristo Poddar* [1879] ILR 56 Cal 801, [6]; *Mohammad Abdul Subbhan v Ghulam Hussain Ahmed Ali & Co* AIR 1935 Nag 66, [4] (cf *PR and Co v Bhagwandas Chaturbhuj* (1908) 10 Bom LR 1113). See also *Kedarnath & Sons v India United Mills Ltd* [1956] 58 Bom LR 907, 911 and CO Remfry, *Commercial Law in British India* (Butterworth & Co (India) Ltd 1912) 299.

[14] The advantage to a claimant of instituting a summary suit under this rule is that the defendant is not entitled to defend the suit without leave: see Code of Civil Procedure (CPC) Order 37, r 3(5).

[15] See eg *West Bengal Decorating Co v Damodar Das Daga* AIR 1982 Cal 386, [13]; *Simba FRP Pvt Ltd v Department of Tourism, Lucknow* (1995) 34 DRJ 273, 275; *Penguin Books Ltd v Book Sales Co* (2002) 64 DRJ 279, 282; *Lohmann Rauscher Gmbh v Medipshere Marketing* [2005] 80 DRJ 9, 14.

gives a very different answer to this question. As section II..2 demonstrates, this may be by accident rather than design.

2. *White and Carter v McGregor* in Indian Law

The law in India as to the effect of a repudiatory breach and the doctrine of anticipatory breach is not different in any material respect from the English law on the subject.[16] The well-known aphorism of Asquith LJ that an unaccepted repudiation is a 'thing writ in water'[17] has been cited with approval on many occasions[18] and is reflected in section 39 of the Contract Act.[19].The question has therefore arisen: is it open in Indian law to the innocent party to reject a repudiation by the other party and sue for the price? The leading case on this point in English law, *White and Carter (Councils) Ltd v McGregor*,[20] is familiar. The defender, a garage proprietor in Clydebank, entered into a three-year contract for the display of advertisements on litter receptacles maintained by the pursuer in Clydebank. When the defender discovered that his sales manager had made this contract, allegedly without authorisation, he purported to repudiate the contract on the same day. The pursuer rejected the repudiation, displayed the advertisements, and sued for the price under an acceleration clause. By a bare majority, the House of Lords held that it was entitled to do so. This was because there is, subject to two exceptions that appear in Lord Reid's speech,[21] no '*general equitable jurisdiction*' to compel the innocent party to accept the repudiation and sue for damages. The two exceptions are that the claimant cannot sue for the price if he or she requires the cooperation of the defendant to perform the obligation for which the price is payable[22] or if he or she has no 'legitimate financial or other interest'[23] that cannot adequately be compensated by an award of damages. These exceptions, which are controversial in Indian law, are considered below; but it suffices, for present purposes, to observe that Lord Reid did not anywhere suggest the innocent party may sue for the price even if he or she does not (or is unable to) perform his or her own obligation: that the claimant is allowed to keep the

[16] See eg *Mansuk Das v Rangayya Chetti* [1862] 1 MHCR 162 (Madras HC); *Bilasiram Thakurdas v Ezekiel Abraham Gubbay* [1916] ILR 43 Cal 305; *Manindra Chandra Mandy v Aswini Kumar Acharyya* [1921] ILR 48 Cal 427, [3]–[5].

[17] *Howard v Pickford Tool Co Ltd* [1951] 1 KB 417, 421.

[18] See eg *Rockweld Electrodes v KC Vijayan* (1979) 92 LW 332 (Madras HC) [12]; *Cochin Port SCS Association v Harrisons and Crosfields Ltd* (1982) 2 KLT 141 (Kerala HC) [8]; *Kerala State Electricity Board v G Gopinathan* [1990] 3 ILR 749, 767; *Potluri Babu Rao v Sistla Neelagriva Sastry* (1994) 3 ALT 669, [30].

[19] A provision that has, however, given rise to difficult questions: *Muralidhar Chatterjee v International Film Co* (1942-43) 70 IA 35. See for discussion M Naniwadekar, Chapter 13 of this volume.

[20] *White and Carter (Councils) Ltd v McGregor* [1962] AC 413. *White and Carter* was a Scottish case, but it was accepted in argument (at 417) that English law is not different, and it has been subsequently applied in English cases.

[21] Lord Hodson, with whom Lord Tucker agreed, did not expressly adopt these two exceptions, although his Lordship comes close to endorsing the cooperation exception, observing (445) that the innocent party may choose to accept or reject the repudiation 'where the assistance of the court is not required'. In any event, Lord Reid's exceptions have been subsequently treated as part of the *ratio* of *White and Carter*, ibid.

[22] *White and Carter* (n 20) 428–29.

[23] ibid 431.

contract alive does not absolve him or her of the obligation to render the promised performance by which the price is earned.

The general rule in *White and Carter* has been endorsed by the Indian courts, including by the Indian Supreme Court in 1968.[24] However, since most of these cases were concerned with a claim for damages, neither the rule nor the exceptions to it had to be examined closely.

The first point to make about the cooperation exception is that the very existence of this exception shows that the mere fact that the defendant wrongfully prevented the claimant from performing its obligation does not dispense with the need for the claimant to perform in order to sue for the price.[25] If it did, cooperation would not be an exception to the claimant's right to sue for the price: it would be irrelevant, since the claimant would be 'deemed' to have performed and thus be entitled to the price. Indian law, however, has virtually excised the cooperation exception by adopting the civilian doctrine sometimes known as the 'fiction of fulfilment',[26] namely, the proposition that the wrongful prevention of performance is deemed to constitute, or is equivalent to, performance. Since the interaction of the fiction of fulfilment and the action for the agreed sum is the main controversy in this area of Indian law today, it requires careful consideration. It derives from the well-known Scottish case, *Mackay v Dick*,[27] which the Indian courts have, with respect, both misunderstood and erroneously assumed to be reflected in section 53 of the Contract Act.

i. The principle in *Mackay v Dick*

In *Mackay v Dick*, the defender agreed to purchase a digging machine capable of filling 350 cubic yards of clay per day into waggons. The payment of the agreed price of £1,115 was conditional upon the outcome of a test to be made of the machine at the defender's cutting to establish whether the machine, indeed, had this capacity. By the defender's default, the test was not performed. The House of Lords held that the pursuer was nonetheless entitled to the agreed price. The headnote to the case undoubtedly contains the doctrine of constructive or deemed performance.[28] The question is whether it is accurate. That depends on three passages in the case: two in the speech of Lord Blackburn and one in the speech of Lord Watson. The first passage does not furnish any support for deemed performance: all it says is that if a contract can be performed effectively only if both parties are to do something, a term may be implied that each agrees to do all that is necessary on its part for that thing to be done.[29] As explained

[24] *State of Kerala v Cochin Chemical Refineries Ltd* (1968) 3 SCR 556, [10]. See also *Zainab Begum v Khursheed Begum* AIR 1963 AP 370, [24]; *Aiyaswami Nadar v Subbaih Setty* (1965) KLJ 766 (Kerala HC) 767A-D.

[25] As Salmon LJ has pointed out, '[t]he fact that the contract breaker has prevented you from earning it by breach cannot entitle you to claim it as due under the contract. All you are entitled to is damages': *Decro-Wall International SA v Practitioners in Marketing Ltd* [1971] 1 WLR 361, 370E–F.

[26] R Stevens, 'Justified Enrichment' (2005) 5 Oxford University Commonwealth Law Journal 141, 144–45.

[27] *Mackay v Dick* (1881) 6 App Cas 251.

[28]

> If, in the case of a contract of sale and delivery, which makes acceptance of the thing sold and payment of the price conditional on a certain thing done by the seller, and the buyer prevents the possibility of the seller fulfilling the condition, the contract is to be *taken as satisfied* [emphasis added].

[29] *Mackay* (n 28) 263 (Lord Blackburn).

below, the second passage in Lord Blackburn's speech (at 264) does not support the proposition either. The third, which appears in Lord Watson's speech, reads as follows:

> [The pursuers] have been thwarted in their attempt to fulfil that condition by the neglect or refusal of the [defender] to furnish the means of applying the stipulated test; and their failure being due to his fault, I am of opinion that, as in a question with him, they *must be taken to have fulfilled the condition*.[30]

This does appear to endorse the proposition that a party wrongfully prevented by the other party from rendering the performance in exchange for which the sum is payable may, nevertheless, sue for the sum. This is, in fact, not the position in relation to contracts of sale, because there is a rule at common law and under the 1893 and 1979 Acts that the seller's right to sue for the price is conditional on the passing of title or the existence of special terms in the contract.[31] As McCardie J explained in *Colley*,[32] the true explanation of *Mackay v Dick* is that title *had* passed to the buyer: the stipulation as to the test was a 'resolutive condition',[33] namely, a condition that (unlike a 'suspensive condition') did not prevent the passing of title but permitted the buyer to call upon the seller to remove the machine should it be fulfilled.

But sale of goods apart, does *Mackay v Dick* decide that a condition wrongfully prevented from being performed should be taken to have been performed? There are two possible views of this aspect of the case. The first is that the House adopted the fiction of fulfilment. On this view,[34] the seller's obligation to provide a machine that satisfied the test was, in that case, deemed to have been performed, and the headnote to *Mackay v Dick* is accurate except, ironically, in the case of sale of goods. This has the support of Professor Treitel, who considers that *Mackay v Dick* did adopt the doctrine of fiction of fulfilment but that it was wrong to do so.[35] The second—and it is suggested the better[36]—view is that *Mackay v Dick* deals with the implication of terms, not with the fulfilment or non-fulfilment of terms. On this view, the seller succeeded because the price became payable once the title to the digging machine passed to the buyer; and the resolutive condition (allowing the buyer to return the machine and refuse payment should the machine fail the test) was not fulfilled because that condition, as a matter of construction or implication, was applicable only if the buyer provided adequate

[30] ibid 270 (Lord Watson) (emphasis added).

[31] Before the 1893 Act was passed (on which the 1930 Act in India is founded), an action for the price would lie only on the *indebitatus* counts of 'goods sold and delivered' (where title had passed) or 'goods bargained and sold' (where title had passed and delivery was not a condition precedent): the Act of 1893 did not change this, and *Mackay* (n 28) did not create any fiction that title had passed or, where necessary, delivery had been made: *Colley v Overseas Exporters (1919) Ltd* [1921] 3 KB 302, 309–11.

[32] *Colley* (n 32).

[33] ibid 308. Professor Treitel explains that the distinction between suspensive and resolutive conditions in the civil law generally corresponds to that between conditions precedent and subsequent in the common law: see GH Treitel, *Remedies for Breach of Contract: A Comparative Account* (Clarendon Press 1988) 262.

[34] See eg *Société General (London Branch) v Geys* [2013] 1 AC 523, [131] (Lord Sumption dissenting but not on this point).

[35] Treitel, *Remedies for Breach of Contract* (n 34) 268, 269.

[36] It must be acknowledged, however, that Lord Watson's speech favours the first view; nor did Lord Blackburn say in terms that the implied term required the buyer to perform *before* the seller.

facilities for the machine to be tested, which he failed to do. In other words, the House of Lords did not hold that the test was deemed to have been satisfied, but rather that the obligation to satisfy the test only arose if the buyer provided adequate facilities. If this is right, *Mackay v Dick* did not adopt the fiction of fulfilment but decided only that there may be an implied term which renders inoperative an obligation that would otherwise have to be performed in order for the creditor to earn the price.[37]

ii. The analysis of *Mackay v Dick* in the Indian Courts

In 1954, an Indian judge of great distinction approved *Colley* and came to the conclusion that Indian law does not permit an action for the price unless title has passed or the buyer has agreed to pay the price irrespective of delivery or the passing of title.[38] One might think that this, as a judgment of the Supreme Court, would have disposed of the controversy. However, it was a tax case, and the question of whether goods can be deemed to have been delivered, by fiction, was not before the Court. Nor was there any occasion to consider the effect of *Mackay v Dick* on contracts other than for the sale of goods. When these questions did arise, the Indian courts chose to adopt the principle in *Mackay v Dick*, without, it must respectfully be said, a complete analysis of what that case really decides.[39] Three of these cases have proven to be influential, one decided by the Andhra Pradesh High Court and two by the Kerala High Court.

In the Andhra case, *Nagayya v Bappama*,[40] the claimant entered into a settlement agreement under which she was to (a) receive, absolutely, certain immovable property and (b) take the defendant's son in adoption. She expressed herself to be ready and willing to adopt the defendant's son, but the defendant refused to consent. The question was whether she was, nevertheless, entitled to the property. The Court held that she was, relying almost entirely on *Mackay v Dick*, which it took to decide that 'if a promisor is prevented by the promisee from fulfilling her part of the contract, she should be deemed to have performed it'.[41] The Court rejected the contention that the rule in *Mackay v Dick* (if there is one) is confined to sale of goods, holding that 'the Indian Law on the subject is identical with the English Law that prevention by one party is *constructively tantamount to fulfilment* by the other'.[42] It relied on section 53 of the Contract Act for this proposition.

The Court's construction of section 53 is wrong in principle. The prevention by *D* of *C*'s performance of the contract gives rise to two different questions. The first is whether the contract remains in existence if *C* is prevented from performing. The second is

[37] Even if *Mackay* (n 28) did (contrary to the view preferred here) adopt the fiction of fulfilment, it is clear from recent authority that this principle no longer forms part of English law: see eg *Thompson v ASDA-MFI Group plc* [1998] Ch 241, 266; *Little v Courage* [1995] CLC 164, 170; *Cream Holdings Ltd v Davenport* [2011] EWCA Civ 1287, [2012] 1 BCLC 365, [33]; *Yam Seng Pte Ltd v International Trade Corporation Ltd* [2013] EWHC 111, [2013] 1 All ER (Comm) 1321, [139]; Stevens (n 26) 145.

[38] *Budh Prakash Jai Prakash* (n 9) [6] (Venkatarama Aiyar J).

[39] *Mackay* (n 28) has been cited with approval by the Indian courts on a number of occasions: see eg (in addition to the text above) *Nilakanta Roy Chowdhury v Lalit Mohan Banerjee* [1915] 19 CWN 933 (Calcutta HC); *Alagu Pillai v Veluchami* AIR 1923 Mad 576, [2]; *Valli Ammal v Arunachala Moopanar* AIR 1938 Mad 385, [12].

[40] *Makineni Nagayya v Makineni Bapamma* AIR 1958 AP 504.

[41] ibid [9] (emphasis added).

[42] ibid [13] (emphasis added).

whether, if the contract remains in existence, *C* is entitled to sue for the agreed sum payable under that contract. The error in the Court's analysis is to conflate these two questions. The first is a question of law. The answer section 53 gives to it is that *C* may, even if he or she is wrongfully prevented from performing, keep the contract alive. The second is a question of fact as to which section 53 has nothing to say: it turns on what *C* was required to do under the contract in order to earn the price and whether *C* did this. This is apparent from the language of section 53, which is that the contract becomes 'voidable' at the option of the party prevented from performing. This means that the contract becomes 'an agreement which is enforceable by law at the option of one of the parties' only,[43] namely *C*, since he or she is entitled either to terminate[44] the contract or to enforce it; but to suggest that the ability to enforce a contract means that the contract is deemed to have been performed is a *non sequitur*. The word 'enforced' means no more than that *C* may pursue the remedies available to him or her; it cannot tell us what those remedies are. It follows that if *C* has not rendered the promised performance before the repudiation and requires *D*'s cooperation to do so, section 53 allows him or her to do no more than sue for specific performance or damages. Curiously, the Court in *Nagayya* recognised that the remedy of specific performance was available to *C* but had no 'hesitation in holding that . . . she should be deemed to have fulfilled her promise and thus become entitled to enforce the obligation resting on the defendants'.[45]

In the second case, *Millars Machinery*,[46] *D* agreed to buy a hot mix plant, 90 per cent of the price payable on delivery, and 10 per cent payable after the plant had been commissioned. *D* paid 90 per cent but refused to incur the expenses necessary for the plant to be commissioned and refused to pay the balance. There was a finding that title to the plant had passed to *D*. The Kerala High Court—in what appears to be the only reported Indian case to have done so—recognised the cooperation exception: 'in certain cases where the contract cannot be fulfilled without co-operation of the party in default and if the party in default repudiates the contract, the other party may be forced to accept the repudiation and sue for damages'.[47] Oddly, it then proceeded to apply the fiction of fulfilment, observing that *C* could '*take the contract as satisfied*' since *D* had wrongfully prevented performance. Like the Andhra Pradesh High Court in *Nagayya*, the Kerala High Court also thought, erroneously, that section 53 of the Contract Act adopts the fiction of fulfilment.

In the third case,[48] a contractor who was hired to construct a branch canal was allowed to sue for the price although he had not completed the work, because the defendant had failed to provide land free of obstruction to enable him to do so.

What is perhaps striking about these cases is that their use of the fiction of fulfilment is inconsistent with the advice of the Judicial Committee in *Florrie Edridge v Rustomji*

[43] Contract Act, s 2(f).

[44] I use the word 'terminate' because it is familiar to common lawyers, but the Contract Act uses the word 'rescind' to describe this concept.

[45] *Makinenni Nagayya* (n 41) [15] (emphasis added).

[46] *Secretary of Department of Irrigation v M/s Millars Machinery* (1985) KLJ 734 (Kerala HC).

[47] ibid 743E, 744A.

[48] *State of Kerala v Kurian Paul* (1991) 2 KLJ 349 (Kerala HC).

Sethna.[49] In that case, Mr Smith agreed to pay Mr Sethna £5,000 if the latter wrote certain letters to the receiver of Mr Smith's company and paid certain costs. Mr Sethna expressed himself to be ready and willing to do this but had not, in fact, done so when Mr Smith allegedly repudiated the contract. Mr Sethna sued for the agreed sum. Lord Wright, giving the advice of the Board, explained why the claim failed, in a classic passage:

> The respondent might have accepted that as a final repudiation and thus treated the contract as determined and brought a claim for damages under s. 53. He did not do so. But a wrongful repudiation by one party cannot, except by the election of the other party so to treat it, put an end to an obligation; if the other party still insists on performance of the contract the repudiation is what is called '*brutum fulmen*,' that is the parties are left with their rights and liabilities as before. *A wrongful repudiation of a contract by one party does not of itself absolve the other party if he sues on the contract from establishing his right to recover by proving performance by him of conditions precedent*.[50]

It is impossible to reconcile this passage, which is the correct analysis, with the subsequent Indian cases that adopt the fiction of fulfilment. It is suggested that those cases should not be followed. It may be open, in the light of Lord Wright's observations, for the courts at any level so to hold, but the area is ripe for review by the Indian Supreme Court. Until then, it would appear that the action for the agreed sum in Indian law is significantly wider in scope than in English law.

III. Specific Performance

The equitable counterpart to the common law's action for an agreed sum is traditionally a claim for specific performance, which is the subject matter of this section of the chapter. It begins with an overview of the history of the law of specific performance in India. It then considers the principal features of the 1963 Act as they stood prior to the 2018 amendment. Section IV deals briefly with the 2018 amendment.

1. The History of the Law of Specific Relief in India

It has been said that India is the first country in which an attempt was made to codify the English law of contract.[51] This process began with the constitution of the Third Indian Law Commission in 1861. The twists and turns thereafter, culminating in the

[49] *Florrie Edridge v Rustomji Sethna* (1933) 38 LW 972 (PC).
[50] ibid 977 (Lord Wright) (emphasis added). Lord Wright observed that Rangnekar J was wrong in the court below to have relied on the fact that Mr Smith had 'prevented' performance: 'in such a case the claim must have been not in debt, but for damages in accordance with s 53 of the Contract Act'. See also *Gajjala Nagisetti v Maddi Venkatasubbayya* (1935) 41 LW 440, 441.
[51] D Ibbetson, *A Historical Introduction to the Law of Obligations* (OUP 2001) 227.

enactment of the Contract Act in 1872, have been analysed elsewhere in this collection.[52] The basic framework of Indian private law—and large parts of its substantive content—were, at the time of codification, and in many respects continue to be, identical to the common law; indeed, some provisions of current Indian legislation exactly reproduce the words used by English judges in well-known cases.[53] But some rules of the common law were thought to owe their origin principally to the division of jurisdiction in England or were otherwise unsuitable for codification in India.[54] The attempt to codify gave the drafters an opportunity to modify them. As a result, there are also important differences not only in particular rules of the common law in India but also in the characterisation of certain causes of action.

Three examples illustrate the point. First, the fiction created by the forms of action that unjust enrichment is quasi-contractual was first discarded in India.[55] This development was heralded some years before the enactment of the Contract Act by a judgment of a Full Bench of the Calcutta High Court, which recognised that a quasi-contract is not a contract at all.[56] The question in that case was whether a certain subordinate court had jurisdiction, which depended on whether a claim by a co-sharer of an estate for contribution could be characterised as a claim for 'money due on an (implied) contract'. Sir Barnes Peacock CJ, referring to the work of Pothier and to Roman law, said that the conception that these claims are founded on an 'implied contract' was a 'fiction adopted by the common law . . . for the purpose of obtaining jurisdiction in cases which would otherwise have been cognisable only by the courts of equity' and that it had no place in a country with neither the forms of action nor divided jurisdiction. Second, the Indian legislature abolished the rule in *Pinnel's Case*[57] that a debt cannot be satisfied by the payment of a lesser sum by enacting that a promisee may accept, as full satisfaction of the original promise, such performance as he thinks fit, either from the promisor or a third party.[58] Third, the common law rules governing contracts in restraint of trade were ignored, the legislature instead following Field's New York Civil Code. Sir Frederick Pollock's comment that the Code was 'the evil genius of this Act' is probably borne out by the difficult litigation generated by this unsatisfactory provision.[59]

The story of the codification of specific relief is closely related to that of contract, although it probably first made its appearance in an Indian code when the Civil

[52] W Swain, Chapter 1 of this volume. See also W Stokes, *The Anglo-Indian Codes* I (Clarendon Press 1887) x–xxviii; G Rankin, *Background to Indian Law* (CUP 1946) 22–46; W Macpherson, *Outlines of the Law of Contracts as Administered in the Courts of British India* (2nd edn, RC Lepage & Co 1864). Ibbetson observes that Macpherson followed Colebrooke's *Treatise on Obligations and Contracts* (1818), which was based upon Roman, not English, law: see Ibbetson (n 52) 227 and Rankin (n 53) 89.

[53] For eg, ss 69 and 70 of the Contract Act, around which the law of unjust enrichment in India is organised, largely reproduce the words used in *Lampleigh v Brathwait* 80 ER 255; and s 73 those of Alderson B in *Hadley v Baxendale* (1854) 9 Ex 341, 354.

[54] Examples of both types of provision are briefly considered below.

[55] Ibbetson (n 52) 284.

[56] *Rambux Chittangeo v Modhosoodun Pal Chowdhry* (1867) 7 WR 377, 380, 383–84.

[57] *Pinnell's Case* (1602) 5 Co Rep 117a.

[58] The Contract Act, ss 41 and 63. See also Rankin (n 53) 103.

[59] Contract Act, s 27; F Pollock and D Mulla, *The Indian Contract Act: With A Commentary, Critical and Explanatory* (2nd edn, Sweet & Maxwell 1909) 164. See further, T Zhong Xing and U Varottil, Chapter 12 of this volume.

Procedure Code was enacted in 1859. Section 192 of this Code provided that 'a court . . . may with the consent of the plaintiff decree the specific performance of the contract within a time to be fixed by the court . . . if it appear that the defendant is able to perform the contract'. Broughton notes that the courts had held that, under this provision (as, indeed, its plain language indicates), damages were subordinate to performance.[60]

By this time, the subject of specific relief had become politically sensitive.[61] On the one hand, owners of plantations, especially indigo plantations in Bengal, were aggrieved by the tendency of workers to desert after receiving payment. An award of damages would be readily available but was of no use to them since it could not, in practice, be enforced against the (usually impecunious) worker.[62] The owners therefore pressed for the intervention of the criminal law, which led to proposals in the early 1860s to make 'fraudulent breaches' of agricultural contracts punishable by imprisonment. That proposal was contentious and ultimately unsuccessful, partly because there was a widely held view that the owners had abused the system and made unjustifiably harsh demands of the workers.[63] Sir Henry Maine, who seems to have shared that view, did not think that imprisonment was the answer, but did think that the remedy of specific performance was.[64] This, he said, was because

> there is no country in which damages afford practically so imperfect a redress for breach of contract as they do in India, and none in which the prospect of having to pay damages operates so slightly to compel the performance of agreements.

Thus, Maine, says Sir George Rankin,

> was not minded to let a particular difficulty about indigo in a part of Bengal dictate a limited rule for the general law. His standpoint was that in a code worked by a simple procedure it was not necessary to exhibit the timidity of the Chancery any more than

[60] LPD Broughton, *The Code of Civil Procedure, Act VIII of 1859, and the Acts Amending It* (2nd edn, Wyman Bros 1867) 164. There were, however, procedural difficulties in the application of this provision, which, as a consequence, was not widely used: see S Tofaris, 'A Historical Study of the Indian Contract Act' (PhD thesis, University of Cambridge, 2011) 115–16.

[61] For a more detailed account, see Rankin (n 53) 77–80; Tofaris (n 61) 109–20.

[62] Rankin (n 53) 77.

[63] This led to a memorable exchange between Sir George Campbell, the Lieutenant Governor of Bengal, and Sir James Stephen, the Law Member. Sir George proposed the insertion of this illustration to the provision in the Contract Act dealing with 'undue influence':

> A, a rich and powerful zamindar, induces B, C and D, poor and ignorant ryots holding under him, to engage to grow certain produce and deliver it to him, for a term of 20 years in consideration of an inadequate price for which no independent ryot would have so engaged. A employs undue influence over B, C and D.

Sir James Stephen rhetorically asked why this illustration should not also be inserted:

> C, a rich and powerful Lieutenant-Governor of remarkable force of character, induces S, a member of Council of feeble intellect, to sell him a horse for a totally inadequate price. C employs undue influence.

Needless to say, neither illustration was inserted: see Rankin (n 53) 77, 78. On Sir James Stephen's contribution to codification in India (and his 'epigrammatic wit', of which, no doubt, Sir George Campbell was a victim in this episode), see JD Heydon, 'The Origins of the Indian Evidence Act' (2010) 10 Oxford University Commonwealth Law Journal 1.

[64] 'The Indian Contract Law', Bill Submitted to the Governor General (Simla, 9 July 1867), Statement of Objects and Reasons.

> to exercise the full freedom of the French law which had ordered Dumas to write a novel, or of the Civil Procedure Code of 1859 under which it would seem possible to order A to marry B.[65]

Accordingly, Maine drafted a bill to amend section 192 of the 1859 Code, but this never saw the light of day.[66]

The next attempt to amend the law of specific relief was made in the Contract Bill drafted by the Third Law Commission in 1866. Clauses 51–59 of the Bill dealt with specific performance and would, if enacted, have required the repeal of section 192.[67] They were opposed by Maine, mainly on two grounds.[68] The first was that the appropriate home for provisions relating to specific performance was a code of procedure, not a code of substantive contract law. The second was that these clauses 'are, in truth, directed against indigo planting'.[69] Although there was some resistance, the Governor General, Sir John Lawrence, ultimately consented to their omission, and they did not form part of the Contract Act when it came to be enacted in 1872.[70]

What is of interest is that when specific relief was finally codified in India in 1877, the code entirely inverted the premise of section 192 of the 1859 Code: damages, and not specific relief, became the rule, and the rules governing when specific relief can be given came closely to resemble English law. It is difficult to pinpoint exactly when this shift occurred, but it seems that the impetus came from a bill drawn by Whitley Stokes in or around 1875. As Stokes has himself said,[71] his Bill largely codified the work of Sir Edward Fry, although, to the trenchant disapproval of Sir Frederick Pollock,[72] he used the Field Code as his model for some of the less important parts. The Bill was revised by Sir Arthur (later Lord) Hobhouse,[73] who added illustrations to each provision, which (nearly without exception) codify cases decided in the English courts. This Bill was referred to a Select Committee of the Legislative Council in December 1875 and enacted in 1877.[74] It was in force until the current legislation, the Specific Relief Act, 1963, replaced it.

[65] Rankin (n 53) 79 (emphasis added).

[66] Largely because the Secretary of State and Governor General took the view that the indigo planters would be able to use the remedy to coerce the workers: Tofaris (n 60) 116–17.

[67] See generally Editor, 'The Code of Civil Procedure in India' (1907) 8 Journal of the Society of Comparative Legislation 235.

[68] This is partly why that Bill was not enacted until 1872, after cls 51–59 had been omitted.

[69] See further Tofaris (n 61) 118–19.

[70] ibid 119.

[71] Stokes (n 53) 939.

[72] Sir Frederick Pollock, commenting on the use of the New York Code in the Contract Bill, said,

> the framers of the Indian Codes . . . were tempted to borrow a section here and a section there from the draft Civil Code of New York which the sounder lawyers of that State have been happily successful so far in averting from its citizens. This code is in our opinion, and we believe in that of most competent lawyers who have examined it, about the worst piece of codification ever produced.

See Pollock and Mulla (n 59) vii.

[73] Sir Henry Maine was the Law Member of the Governor General in Council from November 1862 to September 1869, when Sir Arthur Hobhouse was appointed. It thus happened that the task of moving the Specific Relief Bill fell to Sir Arthur: see Rankin (n 53) 73, 74.

[74] See further ibid (n 53) 80–82, 93 and MC Setalvad, *The Common Law in India* (Stevens & Sons 1960) 74.

Thus, one can readily understand why, in 1906, SC Banerji thought that it was an accident of history that the 1877 Act chose to retain the basic features of the law administered by Chancery, including the rule that damages, and not performance, are the primary remedy for breach of contract.[75] In 1877, it was by no means inevitable that the Indian legislature would adopt this approach. Banerji thought that, in India,

> where courts of justice are both courts of law and equity, it would probably have been more satisfactory to frankly recognise specific performance as the primary remedy in cases of breach of contract, and not to fetter the discretion of the judge by any consideration as to the adequacy of damages.[76]

However, the shape of the law of specific relief in the 1877 Act was no surprise since

> the 1877 Act is pre-eminently an embodiment of English jurisprudence; its author was a practical English lawyer of eminence in his profession; he avowedly derived his materials from the jurisprudence in which he had been trained; and the numerous illustrations given in the Act may, with rare exceptions, be identified with actual cases recorded in the English equity reports.[77]

The 1877 Act made damages the primary remedy by dividing the subject of specific relief into contracts that may and contracts that cannot be specifically enforced. In the latter category is any contract for the non-performance of which 'compensation in money is an adequate relief'[78] and a number of other well-known bars to specific relief, such as imprecision[79] and constant supervision.[80] In the former category—contracts that may be specifically enforced—is any contract the non-performance of which cannot adequately be compensated in money.[81] The 1877 Act was reviewed by the Law Commission in 1958,[82] which led to significant amendments to what became the 1963 Act, either diluting or removing some of the bars to specific performance. The 1963 Act also omitted the many illustrations to the provisions of the 1877 Act, the Law Commission taking the view that some of them were not warranted by the language of the provision.[83]

[75] SC Banerji, *The Law of Specific Relief in British India* (2nd edn, R Cambray 1917). This work is based on the Tagore Law Lectures delivered by Banerji in 1906. The current edition is SC Banerji, *The Law of Specific Relief* (13th edn, Universal Law Publishing 2015). All references in this chapter are to the second edition unless otherwise stated.

[76] ibid 78.

[77] C Collett, *The Law of Specific Relief in India* (4th edn, Thacker Spink 1907) page v. The illustrations were drawn by Lord Hobhouse.

[78] 1877 Act, s 21(a); 1963 Act, s 14(a).

[79] 1877 Act, s 21(b) and (d); 1963 Act, s 14(b).

[80] 1877 Act, s 21(b) and (g); 1963 Act, s 14(d).

[81] The law may have come a full circle because the 2018 amendment, as explained below, makes specific performance, rather than damages, the primary remedy for breach of contract, subject to certain restrictions on its availability.

[82] Law Commission of India, 'Specific Relief Act, 1877' (Law Com No 9, 1958). The Chairman of this Law Commission was MC Setalvad, India's first Attorney General, and its members included MC Chagla, VKT Chari, and NA Palkhivala.

[83] ibid [8].

2. The Scheme of the 1963 Act Prior to 2018

Before the 2018 amendment, which is considered separately below, sections 10 and 14 of the 1963 Act divided the subject of specific relief into those contracts that the court may and those which the court cannot specifically enforce.[84] Some of the bars to specific relief in sections 14 and 20 warrant closer analysis and are considered in turn below. Constraints of space do not permit an analysis of all of them, including the important ones of partial specific performance, personal service, and undue hardship.[85]

i. The adequacy rule

Prior to its abolition in 2018, the adequacy-of-damages rule gave rise to a large body of case law. This case law demonstrates that the Indian courts departed from (or qualified) the analysis of adequacy in English law in at least two respects. First, compensation in money was said to be adequate only if it would allow the claimant to secure substantially the benefit for which he or she contracted. Second, in ascertaining whether his or her 'loss' can fully be compensated by an award of damages, what is relevant is not the loss in respect of which he or she is entitled to recover damages but actual loss.[86] Thus, if the performance of the contract would have given the promisee a benefit or advantage (or avoided a loss) for which damages would not be recoverable, it is likely that specific performance will be granted (subject to other rules).

Before turning to the cases, it is right to emphasise that they do not explicitly endorse either (especially the latter) of the two propositions set out above: instead, those propositions are advanced here as the preferable explanation of the approach to adequacy is to be found in the Indian authorities.

(a) Two tests of adequacy

Section 14(a) of the 1963 Act[87] provides that 'a contract for the non-performance of which compensation in money is an adequate relief cannot be specifically enforced'. The counterpart to this rule is section 10, which deals with contracts that may be

[84] See also 1877 Act, ss 12 and 21.

[85] Both the 1877 and 1963 Acts contain a general rule prohibiting partial specific performance. The 1877 Act provided that it could exceptionally be granted if the unperformed part was relatively small in value and 'admits of compensation in money', which the defendant would be ordered to pay. If the unperformed part—whether capable of assessment in monetary terms or not—was significant in size, specific performance would be granted only if the claimant relinquished 'all claim to further performance and all right to compensation'. The Law Commission thought that it was anomalous in the latter case to deny the claimant compensation in the form of an abatement of the purchase price; see Law Commission (n 83) [27]. The 1963 Act implemented this recommendation in s 12(3). The personal service objection is dealt with by s 14(b) of the 1963 Act; see Banerji (n 76) 161ff. Undue hardship and nominal consideration are dealt with by s 20(2) of the 1963 Act; see Banerji (n 76) 301ff.

[86] For a summary of the English position, to the contrary, see J McGhee QC and others (eds), *Snell's Equity* (34th edn, Sweet & Maxwell 2019) [17-007], but see D Friedmann, 'Economic Aspects of Damages and Specific Performance Compared' in D Saidov and R Cunnington (eds), *Contract Damages: Domestic and International Perspectives* (Hart 2008) 84–86, 90. The 1963 Act, s 16(a) does provide that specific relief shall be refused if the claimant 'would not be entitled to recover compensation for its breach'. But this probably refers to a personal bar from claiming damages: see Collett (n 78) at 211: 'under clause (a) there is nothing in the contract itself to prevent compensation being recovered, but it is some objection personal to the plaintiff'.

[87] See 1877 Act, s 12(a).

specifically enforced, notably where damages are not adequate. Section 10 identifies two such classes of contracts: 'when there exists no standard for ascertaining the actual damage caused by non-performance' (subsection (a)) and 'when . . . compensation in money would not afford adequate relief' (subsection (b)). The 1877 Act contained a third class: 'when it is probable that pecuniary compensation cannot be got' (section 12(d)). This 'doubtful doctrine',[88] based on *Watkins v Maule*,[89] was criticised by Banerji, a criticism that the Law Commission endorsed in 1958,[90] leading to its abolition in 1963.

According to Banerji, the two components of the adequacy rule that survived until 2018—no standard for ascertaining actual damage and inadequacy of monetary compensation—recognise that a thing of no or little value generally may, nonetheless, have special value for the claimant (*pretium affectionis*)[91] and that it is sometimes impossible fairly to estimate the value of a thing, usually because there is no market for it.[92] Although these provisions were undoubtedly intended to codify the circumstances in which the courts of equity in England granted specific relief,[93] there were early indications that the adequacy test would be applied less strictly in India, that is, that damages would be regarded as adequate only if the claimant thereby 'gets effectively what he bargained for'.[94] A brief analysis of the Indian decisions (below) demonstrates that this has turned out to be the case. English law also appears to have moved in this direction, since it has been said that the test is whether damages are *appropriate* (rather than simply adequate or inadequate).[95]

(b) Application of the adequacy tests

An Explanation to section 12 of the 1877 Act provided that a court 'shall presume' that a breach of a contract to transfer immovable property 'cannot be adequately relieved by compensation in money' and that a contract to transfer movable property can be. As one would expect, specific performance of a contract to purchase immovable property is readily granted.[96] However, the effect of the Explanation is only that the party able to rely on the presumption to which it gives rise need not lead evidence: it is open to the other party to do so and rebut the presumption.[97] In theory, this should mean that a contract for the purchase of land is not specifically enforceable if the land has an easily identifiable substitute or if the interest of the buyer is profit on resale rather than use.

[88] Banerji (n 76) 129, 130.
[89] *Watkins v Maule* (1820) 2 Jac &W 237, 37 ER 618.
[90] Law Commission (n 83) [9].
[91] Banerji (n 76) 87. This is dealt with mainly by s 10(a) of the 1963 Act, s 10(a) (the 1877 Act, s 12(b)). The illustration to s 12(b) (referring to an agreement to purchase two rare China vases) is based on *Falcke v Gray* (1859) 4 Drew 651; see Stokes (n 53) 953.
[92] Banerji (n 76) 87.
[93] Collett (n 78) 116.
[94] Banerji (n 76) 160 ('Where payment of money would, in effect, amount to a substantial performance of the contract, a promisee must be content with it'). This chapter does not address procedural considerations, important as they are. In practice, given the pace of commercial litigation in the Indian courts, claimants may well be unable to obtain what they bargained for, whether they sue for specific performance or damages.
[95] See eg *Rainbow Estates v Tokenhold* [1999] Ch 64, 73; *Beswick v Beswick* [1968] AC 58.
[96] See eg *Brij Ballab v Mahabir Prasad* AIR 1924 All 209; *Hukmichand v Pioneer Mills* AIR 1927 Oudh 55.
[97] *ML Devender Singh* (n 9) [21].

That is, indeed, the case in India, in contrast to what appears to be the position under English law.[98] In *Ramji Patel v Rao Kishore Singh*,[99] the claimant advanced a sum of Rs 5,000 to the defendant to enable him to pursue an appeal to the Judicial Committee against an adverse decision of the courts in India. The defendant agreed to transfer his proprietary rights in the village of Khedi should the appeal succeed and to repay the advance with interest should it fail. The appeal succeeded, but the defendant refused to transfer the property. The courts below found that the claimant did not enter into the contract in order to obtain land; his purpose was to earn profit on the money advanced.[100] On the strength of this finding, the Judicial Committee set aside the decree for specific performance granted by the courts in India, holding that compensation in money is adequate for the breach of a contract for the purchase of land if the purchaser's purpose was profit rather than use.[101]

In the converse case, where the claimant agrees to buy movable property, the presumption that compensation in money is adequate can be displaced if it is established that the claimant will be unable to obtain an exact or close substitute. Thus, the courts have readily allowed specific performance of a contract to purchase shares of a private company,[102] commodities not readily available in the market,[103] and rare articles or those with unique features.[104]

(c) *Commercial uniqueness*

A faithful application of the two tests of adequacy in section 10 would appear to leave no room for the argument that an article, although not physically unique, is of special importance to the claimant by reason of the purpose for which he or she made the contract. It may be 'commercially unique'[105] because a delay in obtaining a substitute could have an adverse impact on the claimant's business or because the substitute, although available elsewhere, is, in practice, difficult to obtain. In English law, in addition to the well-known *Sky Petroleum* case,[106] certain observations of Wright J ('the ship is of peculiar and practically unique value to the plaintiff')[107] and Sir Robert Megarry V-C ('what matters is the adequacy of damages in place of the thing that ought to have been delivered')[108] support the suggestion that what matters is the uniqueness of the thing to the claimant and not its inherent uniqueness.

[98] See A Burrows, *Remedies for Torts, Breach of Contract and Equitable Wrongs* (4th edn, OUP 2019) 403.

[99] *Ramji Patel v Rao Kishore Singh* (1929) 11 LW 443 (PC).

[100] ibid 449: 'No special damages have been proved by the plaintiff. He simply invested money, and a return of money should normally be sufficient . . . It is not shown that he had any pressing need for land.'

[101] ibid 450. The Board did not use these words, but it is implicit in the disposition of the case based on the finding of the courts below recited at 449.

[102] *Jainarain Ram Lundia v Surajmull Sagarmull* (1949–50) 11 FCR 379 (Federal Court) 395; *Bank of India v Jamsetji AH Chinoy* (1949–50) 67 IA 76 (PC) 90.

[103] *Uttar Pradesh State Electricity Board v Ram Barai Prasad* AIR 1985 All 265.

[104] Banerji (n 76) 72–73, 88–93; Collett (n 77) 115.

[105] Burrows (n 99) 405 citing GH Treitel, 'Specific Performance in the Sale of Goods' [1966] JBL 211.

[106] *Sky Petroleum Ltd v VIP Petroleum Ltd* [1974] 1 WLR 576.

[107] *Behnke v Bede Shipping Co* [1927] 1 KB 649, 661 (emphasis added). The claimant was a German ship owner, and the defendant had agreed to sell one of possibly only two steamships in the world with boilers that complied with German regulations.

[108] *Howard Perry & Co Ltd v British Railways Board* [1980] 1 WLR 1375, 1382–83 (emphasis added). Megarry V-C ordered the delivery up of 500 tons of steel because substitute steel was not easily available, potentially causing

There are few instances of a claimant successfully running a 'commercial uniqueness' case under the 1877 Act, but the picture was considerably altered by certain amendments in the 1963 Act. The background to these amendments was the Law Commission's view that the presumptions in the Explanation in the 1877 Act were misleading with respect to movable property.[109] Accordingly, the amended Explanation in the 1963 Act retained the presumption against specific relief for movable property generally but discarded it where the property (a) 'is not an ordinary article of commerce', (b) 'is of special value or interest to the plaintiff', or (c) 'consists of goods which are not easily obtainable in the market'. The Law Commissioners drew the first two exceptions from *Falcke v Gray*[110] and *Pusey v Pusey*[111] and the third from American cases ordering specific performance of a contract to supply an article that only the defendant is capable of supplying.[112] It is conceivable that the courts would have reached the same result under the 1877 Act, by accepting that special value to the claimant is relevant even under the general rule of adequacy. However, as the *Frankfinn Aviation* case illustrates,[113] the amended Explanation in the 1963 Act is a clear and unambiguous recognition of commercial uniqueness. The claimant, a cabin crew training institute, agreed to take a two-year lease of the fuselage of an Airbus 300 at the defendant's premises, renewable for two years at the claimant's option. After two years, the claimant exercised the option to renew, but the defendant purported to terminate the contract. The claimant sought an injunction-restraining breach, which may be granted only if the contract is specifically enforceable.[114] The claimant contended that the contract would be specifically enforced because the aircraft was commercially unique.[115] In a careful judgment holding that the claimant was entitled to an interim injunction, Gita Mittal J referred to the *Behnke* and *Sky Petroleum* cases with approval and found that the fuselage was not easily available in the market.[116] It was therefore not an 'ordinary article of commerce' and of 'special value and interest to the plaintiff'.

(d) *Beswick v Beswick in India: A wider approach to the adequacy rule?*

The foregoing analysis illustrates the first proposition with which this section began: damages are adequate in Indian law only if the claimant will be able to procure from the market exactly or substantially that for which he had bargained. In two cases, founded on *Beswick v Beswick*, there are suggestions of a wider approach that

a serious disruption to the claimant's business. For a complete account of the English cases, see Burrows (n 99) 458–65.

[109] Banerji (n 76) 72.

[110] *Falcke* (n 92).

[111] *Pusey v Pusey* 23 ER 465.

[112] Law Commission (n 83) [24]. The draft of the second exception proposed by the Law Commissioners read slightly differently 'or is otherwise of special value or interest to the plaintiff'. Nothing of substance turns on the omission of the word 'otherwise'. The reason for the omission is perhaps to put paid to the argument that the claimant must demonstrate that a property is not an ordinary article of commerce *and* of special value to him.

[113] *Frankfinn Aviation Services Pvt Ltd v BC Gupta* (2007) SCC Online Del 1981.

[114] 1963 Act, s 41(e).

[115] *Frankfinn* (n 114) [17].

[116] ibid [31], [37], and [52].

would make performance the primary remedy even where damages would perfectly or substantially substitute for actual performance. In *Beswick v Beswick*, the fact that the widow would get no more than nominal damages (in her capacity as the administrator of the estate) was, for Lord Hodson[117] and Lord Pearce,[118] evidence that damages were *not* an adequate remedy. This arguably means that 'loss', in the adequacy analysis, refers not to legally recoverable loss but to actual loss, whether recoverable or not.

In the first of the two Indian cases,[119] the claimant was awarded a contract to provide hospitality services to a convention centre. The convention centre purported to terminate this contract. It contended that the contract was not specifically enforceable because the loss sustained by the claimant, if any, could be recouped through an award of damages. The Delhi High Court rejected that argument on the ground that 'adequacy of damages would be relevant only if the parties are able to get immediately what they contracted for'.[120] It cited *Beswick* with approval. However, the Court's suggestion that damages are awarded as an 'incentive' for the defendant to complete the contract is erroneous, as is the observation that damages fail to incentivise performance only if the defendant expects to derive 'unusual economic benefits' from breach: that is to confuse the defendant's gain (from breach) with the claimant's loss, which is the subject matter of any damages award. The second case that appears to herald a wider approach to specific relief can be taken more shortly, for the learned judge's suggestion that specific performance should be preferred to damages since it is a 'more speedy and efficacious remedy'[121] is inconsistent with the statutory scheme as it stood prior to 2018, which anointed damages as the primary remedy.

ii. Other bars to specific performance

Two other bars to specific performance, constant supervision and imprecision, were addressed by section 21(b) and 21(g) of the 1877 Act, respectively, which provided that a contract cannot be specifically enforced if it 'involves the performance of a continuous duty extending over a longer period than three years from its date' (subsection (g)) or 'runs into such minute or numerous details . . . or otherwise from its nature is such that the court cannot enforce specific performance of its material terms' (subsection (b)).

This 'arbitrary limit' of three years was criticised: 'it may be doubted if a hard and fast rule in a matter like this can advance the purpose of a court of equity'.[122] The Law Commission agreed,[123] and section 14(d) of the 1963 Act contains the modified rule: 'a contract the performance of which involves the performance of a continuous duty which the court cannot supervise'.[124] The rationale for this rule (in the 1877 as

117 *Beswick* (n 96) 81F (Lord Hodson).
118 ibid 88G, 89A (Lord Pearce). See further Burrows (n 99) 470–71.
119 *Old World Hospitality Pvt Ltd v India Habitat Centre* (1998) 73 DLT 374.
120 ibid [161].
121 *Prithvi Raj Singh v Dalip Kulkarni* AIR 1999 Raj 201, [29].
122 Banerji (n 76) 169.
123 Law Commission (n 83) [45].
124 1963 Act, s 14(d) (emphasis added).

in the 1963 Act) is probably that the enforcement of such contracts would consume a disproportionate share of judicial resources and give rise to a risk of repeated contempt applications.[125]

By way of example, the Indian courts have refused to order the defendant to perform a contract that would involve close cooperation for a period of twenty-five years,[126] to prepare a set of account papers in accordance with a contractual specification,[127] and to apply jointly with the claimant to the government for a mining licence and thereafter cooperate in its exploitation.[128] These are uncontroversial instances of the application of the rule. The area of controversy has concerned two questions: what 'constant supervision' actually means and its application to building contracts.

(a) 'Constant supervision': Activities and results

The formulation of the constant supervision objection, in the 1877 and the 1963 Acts, refers to 'the performance of a continuous duty' that the court cannot supervise. The use of the word 'performance', in particular, suggests that there is a difference between the accomplishment of an objective by the end of a potentially long period and the performance of a particular thing over a long period. Only the latter infringes the rule. This corresponds closely to the distinction Lord Hoffmann drew, in *Argyll Stores*, between an *activity* and a *result*.[129] In that case, Lord Hoffmann was concerned with cases in which specific performance may be refused on the ground of constant supervision even though compensation in money is not an adequate remedy. His Lordship pointed out that constant supervision has mistakenly been thought to mean that a court officer must physically supervise the enforcement of the contract (a mistake that is evident in some Indian cases as well[130]), whereas what it refers to is the likelihood of repeated contempt applications for enforcement. This risk is higher if the defendant is ordered to perform a continuing activity than if he or she is ordered to procure a certain result.[131]

The Indian cases adopt a similar approach. For example, Jai Lal J observed that there is a distinction between 'agreements which contemplate the continuous performance of specific acts . . . and contracts which contemplate forbearance from the performance of certain acts'.[132] In another case, Ved Pillai J rejected the contention that the obligation to clear three encumbrances and execute a mortgage within ten years infringed the constant supervision rule: '"continuous" means "joined together without interruption" . . . and implies constant succession'.[133]

[125] Banerji (n 76) at 166.
[126] *Central Bank Yeotmal v Vyankatesh Bapuji* AIR 1949 Nag 286.
[127] *Najibulla Sardar v Harimohan Mitra* AIR 1932 Cal 481, [6].
[128] *Krishnamurthy v Sokab* (1996) 1 MLJ 218 (Madras HC).
[129] *Co-operative Insurance Society Ltd v Argyll Stores (Holdings) Ltd* [1998] AC 1.
[130] See eg *Anil Kumar v Bhagirath Lal* 14(2) [1961] ILR 737, 742.
[131] *Argyll Stores (Holdings) Ltd* (n 130) 13D (Lord Hoffmann), criticised by A Tettenborn, 'Absolving the Undeserving: Shopping Centres, Specific Performance and Law of Contract (1998) Conveyancer and Property Lawyer 23.
[132] *Nathu Lal v Muni Lal* AIR 1927 Lah 898, [5].
[133] *Lekshmikutty Amma v Govindan Nair* (1963) KLJ 752, 753.

(b) Constant supervision and imprecision in building contracts

Under the 1877 Act, the courts invariably came to the conclusion that a building contract could not be enforced specifically, either because damages were adequate (where the builder sued) or because of imprecision and constant supervision (where the owner sued).[134] This was unsurprising, since the 1877 Act was based on the view that then prevailed in England as to the specific performance of building contracts.[135] The Law Commission agreed that the specific performance of building contracts would generally infringe the constant supervision rule but considered that it should be available in 'certain exceptional circumstances'.[136] The result was section 14(3)(c) of the 1963 Act, which provided, prior to the 2018 amendment, that specific performance may be granted if three conditions there set out are satisfied. The language of section 14(3) is virtually identical to the words used by Romer LJ in *Wolverhampton Corporation v Emmons*.[137]

Three years after section 14(3) was enacted, the Madras High Court considered its effect in *Jaina Beevi v Govindasami*.[138] The claimant in that case, formerly a tenant of the defendant, had agreed to vacate the premises on the understanding that he would be given a lease after a new building was constructed in place of the existing building. The High Court observed that section 14(3) is 'modelled on the views of the Chancery in [*Carpenter Estates v Davis*[139]] and analogous cases' and would have ordered specific performance as the new building had already been constructed.[140]

One question that has troubled the courts is whether section 14(3) is confined to an action by the owner or is also available to the builder. The language used suggests it is so confined,[141] since condition (iii) refers to the builder *obtaining possession* in pursuance of the contract. The rationale for this limitation was explained by the Delhi High Court in a case in which the defendant builder agreed to demolish a dilapidated house owned by the claimant and construct a new building in its place, taking a 50 per cent share in the new property. The owner repudiated the agreement. The High Court dismissed the builder's claim for specific performance. It said that section 14(3) is confined to an action by the owner because the interest of the owner in a building contract is the acquisition of property, in contrast to the interest of the builder (profit): damages are therefore an adequate remedy for the builder but not for the owner.[142]

[134] See eg *DC Sabharwal v Union of India* AIR 1951 PH 426; *Union Construction Co Pvt Ltd v Chief Engineer, Eastern Command* AIR 1960 All 72.

[135] *Jaina Beevi v Govindaswami* (1966) 79 LW 657, citing the case that perhaps definitively established the rule in England: *Ryan v Mutual Tontine Westminster Chambers Association* [1893] Ch 116, 124 (Lord Esher MR), 125 (Lopes LJ), 128 (Kay LJ).

[136] Law Commission (n 83) [46].

[137] *Wolverhampton Corporation v Emmons* [1901] 1 QB 515, 525, noted by the Law Commission (n 82) 22 n 2.

[138] *Jaina Beevi* (n 136).

[139] *Carpenters Estates v Davis* [1940] Ch 160.

[140] The claim failed because the contract was not enforceable (for reasons that do not matter for present purposes).

[141] *Vipin Bhimani v Sunanda Das* AIR 2006 Cal 209. *Parthasarathi Ghosh v Maa Construction* AIR 2008 Cal 171 overlooks the 1963 Act, s 41(3).

[142] *Vijay Dixit v Sheila Khanna* [1996] 36 DRJ 476 (Delhi HC) [12].

While this approach is justifiable in a case in which the builder's interest in the contract is, in reality, profit (eg a quick resale), the Calcutta High Court has held that a builder is never entitled to specific performance.[143] This may be doubted. There may well be cases in which damages would not be an adequate remedy for the builder, for example, where the property that the builder proposes to construct is part of a larger complex of properties. In such cases, the general rule that specific relief will be refused if 'compensation in money is an adequate relief' (section 14(1)(a)) is not infringed, and there is no need to resort to the exception in section 14(3) that specific relief may be granted 'notwithstanding anything contained in . . . section 14(1)(a)'. Counsel's argument in that case that section 14(3) is not relevant to a builder for whom compensation is not adequate (and therefore does not infringe section 14(1)) was therefore correct, and the High Court rejected it on the erroneous assumption that section 14(3) is exhaustive of cases relating to building contracts.

(c) *Mutuality*

Stokes, being of the view that the 'English doctrine [of mutuality] found its place in the courts of equity rather from a desire for symmetry than from its inherent utility', did not include it in his draft Bill.[144] It is not to be found in the 1877 Act, and the debates in the Legislative Council demonstrate that the omission was deliberate.[145] In an early case, Muttuswami Iyer J correctly observed that 'the doctrine of mutuality has no application in this country'[146] and granted specific performance to a minor. However, the doctrine was revived by the advice of the Judicial Committee in *Mir Sarwarjan v Fakhruddin Chowdhuri*,[147] which, with respect, is difficult to reconcile with the language and legislative history of the 1877 Act. The Law Commission recommended the abolition of mutuality,[148] and section 20(4) of the 1963 Act provides that 'the court shall not refuse to any party specific performance of a contract merely on the ground that the contract is not enforceable at the instance of the other party'. There is no doubt that mutuality is no longer part of Indian law.[149] This is confirmed by the 2018 amendment, which does not include mutuality in the (exhaustive) list of grounds on which specific performance may be refused.

143 *Sushil Kumar Agarwal v Kalidas Sidhu* AIR 2009 Cal 174.
144 Stokes (n 53) 931.
145 Banerji (n 76) 351.
146 *Krishnasami v Sundarappayyar* [1895] ILR 18 Mad 415.
147 *Mir Sarwarjan v Fakhruddin Chowdhuri* (1912-13) 39 IA 1 (PC).
148 Law Commission (n 83) [51].
149 In 1993, the Law Commission accepted that the mutuality was never part of Indian law but did not think it was necessary, on this account, to delete s 20(4): see Law Commission of India, 'Specific Relief Act 1963' (Law Com R No 147, 1993) 9. All that the claimant must establish is that he or she is, and has been, '*ready and willing*' to perform: see 1963 Act, s 16(c) and Law Commission (n 83) [60], [61].

IV. The 2018 Amendment

I turn finally to the 2018 amendment.[150] Some of the changes it makes are fundamental; others less so. They may be summarised as follows.

The first and most significant change is to abolish the rule that damages represent the primary remedy for breach of contract. This is achieved by amendments to sections 10 and 14. Section 10 now provides that specific performance 'shall' be granted, 'subject to the provisions contained in' sections 11(2), 14, and 16. Section 14 contains an apparently exhaustive list of four types of 'contracts not specifically enforceable'. Three of these correspond to contracts that were not capable of being specifically enforced under the old law.[151] The fourth, which is to be found in section 14(a), is new: 'where a party to the contract has obtained substituted performance' under section 20, that contract may not be specifically enforced. The adequacy of damages rule that was previously in section 14(1)(a) has been omitted, consistently with the amendment to section 10.

The second principal change made by the 2018 amendment is the introduction in section 20 of a new remedy, substituted performance. It may respectfully be observed that the drafting of this provision is not of the standard that one would ordinarily associate with the hand of a parliamentary draftsman; but what it appears to provide is that the promisee, upon a breach of contract by the promisor, may choose to have the contract performed by a third party or by him- or herself and recover the costs of doing so from the promisor. If the promisee obtains substituted performance in this way, it cannot seek specific performance but may sue for damages: sections 20(3)–(4).

The third main change is the introduction of section 20A, which prohibits the courts from granting an injunction where to do so 'would cause impediment or delay in the progress or completion' of certain infrastructure projects identified in the Schedule to the Act.[152]

The most significant and far-reaching of these changes is the first, because it overturns the premise on which this area of the law has operated since 1877, namely that damages are the primary remedy for breach of contract. There is, it is true, a case for doing this: indeed, it is the course that Maine initially wished to take. But there are also compelling points to be made in favour of retaining damages as the primary remedy, which is not merely a quirk of history, as it is sometimes characterised. It is therefore regrettable that Parliament made so important a change to the law without any sustained analysis of these points, any consultation or, it would appear, any real debate in

[150] This section of the chapter states the law as it stood on 30 June 2020 and does not take into account cases decided after that date.

[151] Section 14(b) corresponds to s 14(1)(d) (constant supervision); s 14(c) corresponds, with some changes, to s 14(1)(b) (contract dependent on personal qualifications); and s 14(d) corresponds to s 14(1)(c) (contract by its nature determinable).

[152] There are other, less significant (albeit somewhat curious), changes: see, in particular, the changes to ss 11(1), 14A and 16(c). The 2018 amendment also requires a suit for specific performance to be decided within twelve months or (if the court so orders) eighteen months of its commencement: s 20C.

the House. So far as one can tell, the only guidance that Parliament did have came from the report of an Expert Committee constituted by the Government in 2016. But at least some of the reasons given in the report for proposing to make specific performance the primary remedy do not, with respect, withstand scrutiny. For example, it is suggested that specific performance is a preferable remedy because of the rule that damages for breach of contract must always be assessed as at the date of breach.[153] There is (or ought to be) no such rule.[154] It is also suggested that damages do not 'give to the promisee the benefit of the promise' because they are 'circumscribed by strict tests' of foreseeability and mitigation.[155] However, the Indian courts, as noted above, applied the adequacy-of-damages test by reference to the claimant's actual loss, not his or her legally recoverable loss. Specific performance would therefore have been available if damages, because of the foreseeability or any other rule, would not compensate the claimant's actual loss. Another reason given in the report is that the adequacy test produced uncertainty because its application 'depends on the individual perception of the judge'.[156] This may also be doubted. Specific performance, like any equitable remedy, is discretionary, but that discretion is not at large: it falls to be exercised in accordance with settled equitable principles. The outcome of a claim for specific performance is not any more or less difficult to predict than the outcome of a claim for common law remedy, such as damages.

There are five other criticisms that may be made of the changes introduced by the 2018 amendment.

First, the need for the new remedy of 'substituted performance' is not obvious. The costs of a substitute would be recoverable as damages under sections 73 or 75, if they are reasonably incurred and do not constitute a failure to mitigate. The Expert Committee seems to have thought that this remedy is inadequate because the foreseeability and mitigation rules produce uncertainty.[157] As to the former, it is bound to be foreseeable that the promisee may, upon a breach by the promisor, obtain a substitute. As to the latter, the law of mitigation requires only that the promisee act reasonably. If the promisee does not do so (eg by deliberately obtaining an expensive substitute, although others were available in the market), there is nothing objectionable about the fact that he or she cannot recover damages for this. One of the difficulties about the new section 20(1) is that it would appear to permit precisely this, since it does not require the 'expenses and other costs actually incurred' to be reasonably incurred. This is difficult to justify.[158]

[153] *Report of the Expert Committee Report on Specific Relief Act 1963* (Ministry of Law and Justice, Government of India 2016) [11.5.5].

[154] There are a number of recent authorities that recognise this, discussed in A Dyson and A Kramer, 'There Is No Breach Date Rule: Mitigation, Difference in Value and Date of Assessment' (2014) 130 Law Quarterly Review 259.

[155] *Report of the Expert Committee* (n 154) [11.3.1].

[156] ibid [11.5.3], [12.1.1].

[157] ibid [11.12.2].

[158] The Expert Committee appears to have been of the view that the requirement that the promisee give notice to the promisor of his intention to obtain substituted performance would ensure that the promisee does not '*abuse his right*': see ibid [11.12.5]. But there is no real justification for allowing the promisee to recover expenses unnecessarily and unreasonably incurred merely because the promisor, upon being told of his intention to incur them, did not perform the contract.

Second, section 21(1) previously permitted the claimant in a suit for specific performance to seek 'compensation for its breach either in addition to or in substitution of such performance'. The 2018 amendment deletes the words 'in substitution of'. This means that the court may grant damages in addition to, but *not* instead of, specific performance.[159] That, in turn, means that the claimant would be left with no recourse at all if specific performance is refused (eg on the ground that it would involve constant supervision), because the court no longer has power to award damages in lieu, and any fresh claim for damages for breach of contract would be barred by section 24 of the 1963 Act and Order 2, rule 2(3) of the Code of Civil Procedure 1908. Depriving the claimant of a damages remedy in this way could not be justified on any rational basis.[160] Another curious feature of the amendment is that no corresponding change has been made to section 40(1), which gives the court the power to award damages 'in addition to, or in substitution for' an injunction. The words 'in substitution of' have not been deleted from section 40(1). Nor has section 41(e), which provides that an injunction to restrain the breach of a contract may be granted only if that contract would be specifically enforced. The consequence of the 2018 amendment is therefore that a claimant who seeks an injunction to restrain the breach of a contract may be awarded damages in lieu, but a claimant who seeks specific performance of the same contract may not. This is, with respect, impossible to justify.

Third, the 2018 amendment abolishes the adequacy of damages rule but retains the constant supervision rule, which is now to be found in section 14(b). The amendment does *not*, however, retain the exception to the constant supervision rule that permitted the enforcement of building contracts in certain circumstances. This exception was to be found in what was previously section 14(3), discussed in section III above. That provision has been omitted. The consequence is that building contracts that infringe the constant supervision rule (as they usually would[161]) cannot be specifically enforced even if the requirements of the old section 14(3) are satisfied. This is unlikely to be what Parliament intended, but it is the effect of the words Parliament used.

[159] It is true that s 21(1) is concerned only with what remedy the claimant may seek, not with what remedy the court may grant. As to the latter, s 21(2) (which the 2018 amendment does not alter) provides that the court may award damages even if specific performance is refused. That would be an award of damages in lieu of specific performance. It is therefore arguable that the court's power to award damages in lieu is unaffected by the 2018 amendment. This, however, would render the amendment to s 21(1) redundant because it would have achieved nothing. It would also lead to the conclusion that the court may grant, under s 21(2), a remedy that the claimant is prohibited by s 21(1) from seeking, which is unlikely to be correct. That is reinforced by s 21(5), which provides that compensation shall not be awarded under s 21 '*unless the plaintiff has claimed such compensation in his plaint*'. The effect of the amended s 21(1) is that the plaintiff may not claim '*such compensation*' (i.e. compensation in lieu of, as opposed to in addition to, specific performance) in his plaint. To get around this difficulty, plaintiffs may argue that the words '*such compensation*' in s 21(5) refer to compensation under s 21 generally, whether instead of or in lieu of specific performance, and that it is sufficient, therefore, to claim the latter in the plaint in order to comply with s 21(5). This is wrong as a matter of language (because it is implicit in s 21(5) that it is the compensation actually awarded that must have been claimed in the plaint) but may be a route the courts are tempted to take in practice to avoid concluding that they no longer have the power to award damages instead of specific performance.

[160] The explanation for the amendment may be that Parliament thought (wrongly) that the words 'in substitution of' specific performance in the old s 21(1) were a reference to the substituted performance of the contract (the remedy now introduced by s 20) and accordingly deleted them. They were, of course, a reference to damages awarded in substitution of the *remedy* of specific performance, not to costs incurred in obtaining substituted performance of the *contract*.

[161] See eg Law Commission (n 83) [46]. It was precisely for this reason that s 14(3) was introduced in 1963.

Fourth, some of the grounds on which the court was entitled, under the old law, to refuse specific performance have been removed for no apparent reason. For example, section 20(2)(b) of the old law, which allowed the court to refuse specific performance if it would cause undue and unforeseeable hardship to the defendant, has been deleted. Section 14(1)(b), which required the court to refuse specific performance of a contract which '(i) runs into such minute or numerous details or (ii) which is so dependent on the personal qualification or volition of the parties or (iii) otherwise from its nature is such that the court cannot enforce specific performance of its material terms' has been recast so that it now contains only the second of these limbs.[162] This suggests that a contract that is unsuitable for specific performance for some reason *other* than that it is dependent on the personal qualifications or volition of the parties must, nonetheless, be specifically enforced.

Fifth, although the 2018 amendment came into force on 1 October 2018, it is unclear whether it operates retrospectively and, if so, in what sense. One possibility is that the amended Act applies to all proceedings commenced after it came into force, irrespective of when the underlying contract was entered into; another is that it only applies to contracts entered into, or perhaps causes of action arising, after 1 October 2018; and still another is that it applies even to pending proceedings irrespective of when the cause of action arose. The Act does not contain any transitional provision or savings clause or otherwise deal with its temporal application. I do not propose to consider this issue in this chapter, save to observe that it is perhaps surprising that Parliament did not deal with it by express provision, particularly because the temporal application of amending legislation has given rise to extensive litigation in the Indian courts in recent years.[163] It suffices to say that, one way or another, it is conceivable that the 1963 Act as it stood prior to the amendment will remain the law for a number of years. In view of the points made above, Indian law is perhaps none the worse for that.

V. Conclusion

If a speech that Sir Henry Maine gave in the Legislative Council on 11 November 1864 had carried the day, the Indian law of specific performance may have assumed, in 1877, the form Parliament attempted to give it in 2018. Maine proposed that the default remedy for breach of contract should be performance, not damages, because this, he thought, would generally work less injustice on the defendant: 'the more scientific instrument will inflict the less deadly wound'.[164] As it happened, the subject of specific performance was left to the authorship of Stokes in 1877, and the law since then was organised around the rule that the default remedy is damages, not performance. But the Indian courts applied the adequacy rule less strictly than they might have done,

[162] See s 14(c), as amended.

[163] See eg *Board of Control for Cricket in India v Kochi Cricket Pvt Ltd* (2018) 6 SCC 287 in relation to the applicability of the Arbitration and Conciliation (Amendment) Act 2015.

[164] Rankin (n 53) 79.

and it is not obvious that there was any substantial difference in result between Indian law and jurisdictions that adopted specific performance as their starting point. But the 2018 amendment, by making specific performance available virtually as of right, has made this question academic. It has also had various other consequences, including the seemingly inadvertent abolition of the jurisdiction to award damages in lieu of specific performance and the ability specifically to enforce building contracts in certain circumstances. It is therefore difficult to resist the conclusion that the 2018 amendment is, to put it at its lowest, a mixed bag.

The action for the agreed sum is, of course, as wide as it can be short of a rule that the claimant is *always* entitled to the agreed sum, but it is a mistake to infer that this is because Indian law intends to protect the claimant's performance interest more directly than does the common law. The more accurate, if also more prosaic, explanation is that the law took a wrong turn in the 1960s by reason of the use of a fiction and the misinterpretation of section 53 of the Contract Act. It is a matter that the Supreme Court may wish to put right when it next has the opportunity to do so.

19

Rescission of Contracts Voidable for Lack of Free Consent

*Steven Elliott KC and Divya Behl**

I. Introduction

Rescission involves a contract becoming void and the parties being restored to their original positions. The remedy is available on more than one basis. This contribution concerns rescission at the election of a party whose consent to the formation of a contract was not free because it was vitiated in one way or another, for example, by a fraudulent misrepresentation. The purpose is to expound the essential rules and principles regulating this remedy. We consider the solutions the Indian legislature and courts have found to some of the basic problems any common law system must confront in this area, and we identify important issues the Indian courts have yet to address.

This part of Indian law was largely inspired by English law. Indeed, so far as concerns rescission, it seems that the Indian Law Commissioners who prepared the original draft of the Contract Act did not think they were proposing any especially important departures from English law.[1] However, their treatment of the topic, and that more fully realised in the final text of the Contract Act and the Specific Relief Act 1877, made three major advances.

First, the legislation articulated a single remedy without reference to the jurisdictional division between the common law and equity. At that time, before even the Judicature reforms,[2] in England, Chancery and the common law courts applied somewhat different rules to the rescission of contracts.[3] At a stroke, the Contract Act spared India this fruitless complexity. Second, the grounds for rescission were organised as a list of factors vitiating free consent. This clarified and made explicit the justificatory basis of the remedy. It is easy to forget that this was an analytic novelty in its

* For taking the time to read and comment on a draft of this article, we thank KV Krishnaprasad, Dominic O'Sullivan KC, Shivprasad Swaminathan, and Niranjan Venkatesan.

[1] Third Indian Law Commission, *Second Report on the Substantive Law for India* (1868) 4–6.

[2] Supreme Court of Judicature Acts 1873 and 1875 (England).

[3] D O'Sullivan, S Elliott, and R Zakrzewski, *The Law of Rescission* (3rd edn, OUP 2023) especially chs 3 and 10. As that text indicates, the duality has never fully been resolved in England and remains a source of uncertainty.

Steven Elliott KC and Divya Behl, *Rescission of Contracts Voidable for Lack of Free Consent* In: *Foundations of Indian Contract Law.* Edited by: KV Krishnaprasad, Niranjan Venkatesan, Shivprasad Swaminathan, and Umakanth Varottil, Oxford University Press.
 DOI: 10.1093/9780191997211.003.0019

time.[4] Third, the Contract Act systematically distinguished between void agreements and voidable contracts, the latter alone being liable to rescission. English courts had, at that time, only very recently begun to organise the law in this way and to think rigorously about the status of agreements procured by fraud and the like.[5] These innovations put the remedy on a sound modern footing, which has not required fundamental revision. In part because it was pioneering, however, the Indian legislation is not as clear conceptually on all points as a more settled statement might be, and it presents a number of puzzles.

Because Indian contract law was inspired by English law, Indian courts have sometimes looked for guidance in English case law and secondary sources, whether in elucidating the legislation or in filling lacunae under the rubric of justice, equity, and good conscience.[6] One of the lessons of this study, however, is that English law can be a false friend, as a linguist would put it. Sometimes for better and sometimes for worse, Indian legislation creates a remedy whose differences from that found in English law are as pronounced as its similarities. While the Indian Supreme Court rightly emphasises the primacy of Indian legislation,[7] that court is itself sometimes guilty of disregarding it. We counsel more careful attention to the particular features of Indian legislation and greater caution about English sources.

II. Preliminary Note on the Specific Relief Act 1963

The two principal statutes regulating rescission for lack of free consent are the Contract Act and the Specific Relief Act 1963. The historical reasons why the specific performance of contracts was omitted from the Contract Act and then separately treated in the Specific Relief Act 1877 have been considered by a number of commentators.[8] There was a logic in also including rescission in the Specific Relief Act 1877 for rescission involves the specific 'unperformance' of a contract.[9] However, this introduced some difficulty because the provisions of the Specific Relief Act 1877 were adapted from a

[4] S Tofaris, 'A Historical Study of the Indian Contract Act 1872' (PhD thesis, University of Cambridge 2011) 149 and ch 4.

[5] O'Sullivan, Elliott, and Zakrzewski (n 3) [3.40]–[3.41].

[6] *Wagela Rajsanji v Sheikh Masludin* (1887) ILR 11 Bom 551 (JCPC); *Bhagwandas Goverdhandas Kedia v Girdharilal Parshottamdas and Co* AIR 1966 SC 543 (contract); *Hungerford Investment Trust v Haridas Mundhra* AIR 1972 SC 1826 (specific relief); *Cotton Corporation of India v United Industrial Bank* AIR 1983 SC 1272. But compare the more indigenous approach advocated in *Rattan Lal v Vardesh Chander* AIR 1976 SC 588.

[7] *Kapur Chand Godha v Mir Nawab Himayatalikhan Azamjah* AIR 1963 SC 250; *Cotton Corporation of India* (n 6).

[8] See amongst others GC Rankin, *Background to Indian Law* (CUP 1946) ch 5, 99 and more recently N Venkatesan, Chapter 18 of this volume. The Specific Relief Act 1963 is a modified re-enactment of the Specific Relief Act 1877. The thinking behind the modifications is set out in the Law Commission of India, *The Specific Relief Act 1877* (Law Com Report No 9, 1958).

[9] As Stokes put it, rescission is 'exactly the opposite of the specific performance of contracts': W Stokes, *The Anglo-Indian Codes*, vol i (Clarendon Press 1887) 933.

part of the draft New York Code of 1862, which contained a freestanding treatment of the remedy, whereas in India the Contract Act already contained detailed provisions adapted from the Law Commissioners' draft.[10] The result is a measure of conceptual inconsistency and substantive overlap. Notwithstanding the difficulty, it is necessary to read the provisions of the two statutes together as a unified body of law regulating the rescission of contracts, giving neither any special priority. In this unified regime, section 27 of the Specific Relief Act 1963 is the source of the court's power to rescind contracts, but exercise of this power is subject to the provisions of both statutes.[11]

III. Void Agreements and Voidable Contracts

Under the conceptual scheme of the Contract Act, agreements may be legally enforceable or else void. An agreement that is legally enforceable is said to be a contract.[12] We sometimes speak of void contracts, but that is a contradiction because a void agreement is not a contract at all. An agreement may be void from inception (so that there never is a contract), as where one or both parties lacked competency to contract or where the consideration or object was unlawful.[13] Alternatively, an agreement may be enforceable at the outset but later cease to be enforceable, as where performance becomes impossible or unlawful.[14] Here, there is a contract, but it is then wiped away. The contract is said to 'become void'.

Our concern is with agreements that are enforceable at the outset but that may become void at the option of one or more of the parties. These are known as voidable contracts.[15] Until the option is exercised, there is a contract that all parties are bound to perform and that any of them may sue to enforce. Title to assets may pass to the wrongdoer under a voidable contract,[16] albeit it is a title defeasible by rescission, and third parties who do not have notice of the vitiating factor may acquire indefeasible rights in those assets from the wrongdoer.[17] But if the contract is rescinded, it ceases to be enforceable (it becomes void), and specified consequences follow.[18]

[10] Rankin (n 8) 100–101, 938.

[11] The statutory explanation to this provision states that in relation to territories to which the Transfer of Property Act 1882 does not extend, the provision applies only to contracts in writing, but that Act has been extended to all of the territories of India.

[12] Contract Act, s 2(g) and (h).

[13] ibid s 10.

[14] ibid s 56.

[15] ibid s 2(i) and (j).

[16] *Central National Bank Ltd v United Industrial Bank Ltd* AIR 1954 SC 181. If the majority opinion in *Official Receiver, Jhansi v Jugal Kishore Lachhi Ram Jaina* AIR 1963 All 459 was that the recipient of a payment made under a voidable contract does not gain even a defeasible proprietary title, that opinion is wrong. Dwivedi J's concurring opinion should be preferred on this point.

[17] Sale of Goods Act 1930, s 29; *Ningawwa v Byrappa* AIR 1968 SC 956.

[18] *Satgur Parsad v Har Narain Das* AIR 1932 PC 89.

IV. Contracts Voidable on other Grounds

Our particular concern is with contracts that are voidable on the basis that the party entitled to avoid did not freely consent to the formation of the agreement.[19] But lack of free consent is not the only basis on which a contract may be voidable. A contract may also be voidable on the basis that one of the parties has repudiated the contract or defaulted in certain ways.[20] Section 27 of the Specific Relief Act 1963 distinguishes between contracts that are 'voidable' and those that are 'terminable', but within the scheme of the Contract Act, both are treated as voidable contracts.[21]

While the basis of rescission differs in these two cases, the nature and consequences of the restitutionary remedy are, in essence, the same. In both cases, the effect of the entitled party's election to rescind is that the contract ceases to be enforceable and becomes void. And in both cases, each party must restore or make compensation for any advantages they have received under the contract.[22] Even a party in breach is entitled to restitution of advantages it has conferred.[23] Through rescission on whichever basis, the parties are therefore returned to the positions they occupied before the contract was made.

In these respects, Indian law differs markedly from English law as it now stands.[24] Under English law, a contract terminated for repudiatory breach is only ended to the limited extent necessary to free the parties from further performance of executory obligations, and restitution of advantages already conferred is significantly confined.[25] But Indian law does not stand alone. So far as one can tell from the *Restatement (Third) of Restitution*, a similar approach is mainstream in the United States,[26] and the New Zealand Parliament has also assimilated the 'cancellation' of contracts for misrepresentation and for breach.[27]

Section 75 of the Contract Act provides that 'A person who rightfully rescinds a contract is entitled to compensation for any damage which he has sustained through the

[19] The Contract Act, s 10 should not be read as meaning that the free consent of all parties is a condition of an agreement being a contract such that without free consent the agreement is void from the outset. Consistently with the common law, the Contract Act, s 19 makes clear that agreements formed without free consent are voidable contracts.

[20] For example, ibid ss 39, 53, and 55.

[21] *Muralidhar Chatterjee v International Film Company* AIR 1943 PC 34. Rankin J seems to have had misgivings about this conclusion, describing the case extrajudicially as presenting 'grave difficulty of a practical character': Rankin (n 8) 102.

[22] Contract Act, ss 64 and 65; Specific Relief Act 1963, s 30. Moreover, the bars to rescission listed in the Specific Relief Act 1963, s 27(2) apply as much to rescission of a terminable contract as to rescission of a contract voidable for lack of free consent.

[23] *Muralidhar Chatterjee* (n 22). That case also decided that the innocent party may be entitled to set off any damages it has suffered by the breach.

[24] See *McDonald v Dennys Lascelles Limited* (1933) 48 CLR 457, 476–77, adopted in England in *Johnson v Agnew* [1980] AC 367, 396–97 and in *Hurst v Bryk* [2002] 2 AC 185, 193–94. The clarification of English law largely post-dates the Contract Act: see O'Sullivan, Elliott, and Zakrzewski (n 3) [3.30]. In *Muralidhar Chatterjee* (n 22), Rankin J said (at [23]) that 'Their Lordships are not concerned to make the Act agree in its results with English law.'

[25] Discussed in O'Sullivan, Elliott, and Zakrzewski (n 3) [1.06]–[1.34].

[26] American Law Institute, *Restatement (Third) of Restitution* (2011) §§ 37 and 54.

[27] Contract and Commercial Law Act 2017 (New Zealand), s 37.

non-fulfilment of the contract.' It is not at all clear how that relief is consistent with restoring the innocent party to its original position by way of restitution upon the avoidance of the contract.[28] In some cases, it will be logically impossible to achieve both remedial objectives for they involve placing the plaintiff in inconsistent positions.[29] However, the Contract Act does not appear to require that the innocent party elect between the two.[30] The problem does not arise in relation to rescission for lack of free consent because, the complaint being about formation rather than non-fulfilment of the contract, section 75 does not apply.[31]

V. Invalid Guarantees

Guarantees are conceived by the Contract Act as being contracts,[32] albeit with some special features.[33] Sections 142 and 143 of the Contract Act provide that guarantees are 'invalid' where they are obtained by misrepresentation concerning a material part of the transaction or by keeping silent as to material circumstances. The concept of invalidity is not used elsewhere in the legislation, and there is no explanation as to how an invalid guarantee compares to a void agreement or a voidable contract.

As we have observed, at the time of the Contract Act, the English courts had only recently focused on the status of a contract liable to be rescinded. Before that time, agreements affected by fraud or the like were often described as void, or vitiated, or invalid without regard to whether they had yet been rescinded. But by the end of the 1860s, English lawyers understood that such contracts were voidable, not void, and that this meant valid until rescinded, not void until ratified.[34] Where such agreements continued to be described as being invalid, this was properly shorthand for voidable. For example, in *Davies v London and Provincial Marine Insurance Company*, Fry J spoke of guarantees affected by misrepresentation or non-disclosure as being 'not valid' before going on to declare that the guarantee in question should be rescinded.[35]

Consistently with this, 'invalid' in sections 142 and 143 should be read as a synonym of voidable, not void. This also makes sense in the context of the statute, for misrepresentation and non-disclosure go to the freedom of the creditor's consent to the

[28] Contract Act, s 65.

[29] This inconsistency leads some writers to conclude that the Contract Act (specifically its Myanmar equivalent) cannot mean what it says when it provides that contracts terminable for repudiatory breach are voidable contracts with the same restitutionary consequences as follow the avoidance of contracts for lack of free consent: A Briggs and A Burrows, *The Law of Contract in Myanmar* (2017) 171–72.

[30] Under the *Restatement (Third) of Restitution* (n 26) §§ 37 and 54, rescission and expectation-based damages are alternative remedies for repudiation and material breach between which the plaintiff must elect.

[31] *Maharashtra State Electricity Distribution Company Ltd v Datar Switchgear Ltd* 2013 SCC Online Bom 1755; *Mirza Javed Murtaza v UP Financial Corpn* AIR 1983 All 234; *Ahmad Yarkhan v Abdul Gani Khan* AIR 1937 Nag 270.

[32] For example, the Contract Act, s 127.

[33] Substantive rules of the Indian law governing guarantees are considered in W Courtney, Chapter 20 of this volume.

[34] *Oakes v Turquand* (1867) LR 2 HL 325, 338 (argument) and 346; *Reese River Silver Mining Co Ltd v Smith* (1869) LR 4 HL 64, 73.

[35] *Davies v London and Provincial Marine Insurance Company* (1878) 8 ChD 469, 475 and 478.

formation of a contract just as coercion, undue influence, and fraud do. In general, such matters make contracts voidable, not void,[36] so that it would be anomalous if misrepresentation and non-disclosure produced a different result in relation to guarantees. Properly understood, sections 142 and 143 create special grounds on which guarantees may be rescinded, appropriate to the particular circumstances of those transactions, but they do not create an exclusive remedial response. Misrepresentation and non-disclosure under these provisions sit alongside the general grounds for rescission as additional grounds available only in respect of guarantees. Although they have some special features, guarantees are contracts like any other, and they may also be avoided on grounds of coercion, undue influence, and fraud in the usual way.

VI. Grounds

Other contributors to this volume consider the grounds for rescission in detail and so this part is limited to three generic issues: third party wrongdoing, causation, and the burden of proof.

1. Third-Party Wrongdoing

The Contract Act does not give a consistent answer to the question in what circumstances *A* can avoid a contract with *B* where *A*'s consent was caused by the wrongdoing of a third party, *C*.

Fraud is defined to include fraudulent acts 'committed by a party to a contract, or with his connivance, or by his agent'.[37] Connivance suggests some form of conspiratorial participation in the fraud. It therefore seems that a contract cannot be rescinded for the fraud of a third party, *C*, where the party benefiting from the fraud, *B*, knew the full circumstances but kept quiet provided *B* did not participate actively in the fraud. It may be that, in practice, *B*'s conduct will, in many such cases, constitute tacit connivance within the definition. It is, nonetheless, striking that the purely passive but knowing beneficiary of a fraud should be protected.

Coercion and misrepresentation are defined without a comparable limitation so that, read literally, it appears that a contract may be liable to rescission even where *B* was totally unaware of *C*'s wrongdoing.[38] It is surprising that *B*'s rights should be so fragile as to be vulnerable to avoidance for something *B* did not do or even know about. It is also surprising that contracts induced by coercion and misrepresentation should, in this way, be more vulnerable to rescission than contracts induced by fraud. These consequences suggest that this was not the legislator's intention. More likely, the legislator

[36] Contract Act, ss 19 and 19A.
[37] So far as agency is concerned, see also the Contract Act, s 238.
[38] ibid ss 15, 18, and 19.

simply did not address the consequences of third-party wrongdoing in relation to these two grounds. One solution would be to read across from the fraud provision, thus permitting avoidance in cases of connivance and agency.[39] Another solution would follow the longstanding English rule that a contract can be avoided for third-party wrongdoing only where (a) *C* acted as *B*'s authorised agent or else (b) *B* actually knew the essential facts.[40]

Undue influence is defined in a way that presupposes that it can only exist bilaterally, between the parties to a contract,[41] but tripartite scenarios are common in practice. For example, in *Tungabai v Yeshwant Dinkar Jog*, a heavily indebted husband who had mortgaged all his own property caused his submissive wife to grant a mortgage over her property to raise funds to repay some of his debts.[42] Notwithstanding the limited scope of the legislation, Indian courts have been prepared to set aside contracts in tripartite scenarios such as this. In *Poosathuri v Kannappa Chettiar*, Lord Shaw said that undue influence encompassed cases where a party to the transaction exercised influence in conspiracy with, or through the agency of, others.[43] But in *Tungabai's* case, the Board went further and held that 'when a third party who benefits by a transaction has notice of the facts which raise the presumption [of undue influence], he is in no better position than the person who exercises the influence'.[44] That covers cases of presumed undue influence. In cases of actual undue influence, the creditor will be affected if it had notice of the exercise of undue influence. This situation is governed by section 89 of the Indian Trusts Act 1882.[45]

It therefore seems that for undue influence, *B* will be fixed with the consequences of *C*'s misconduct where it had notice (ie knowledge) of the facts treated by the court as impairing *A*'s consent. This is consistent with classical English law.[46] More recently, however, in a line of cases beginning with *Barclay's Bank v O'Brien*, the House of Lords has reshaped this part of English law so far as it applies to surety transactions where the relationship between the surety and the debtor is non-commercial and the transaction is not, on its face, financially advantageous to the surety.[47] In cases of this kind, the House of Lords has held that the creditor will be fixed with *constructive* notice of any impropriety unless it takes special measures to immunise its security, which usually means ensuring that the surety obtains independent advice. The editors of *Pollock and*

[39] So far as misrepresentations by agents are concerned, see ibid s 238.
[40] O'Sullivan, Elliott, and Zakrzewski (n 3) [9.04]–[9.05].
[41] Contract Act, s 16.
[42] *Tungabai v Yeshwant Dinkar Jog* AIR 1945 PC 8.
[43] *Poosathuri v Kannappa Chettiar* AIR 1920 PC 65.
[44] *Tungabai* (n 42). Earlier cases to like effect include *Lakshmi Doss v Roop Laul* (1906) ILR 30 Mad 169, 178; *Badiatnnessa Bibee v Ambika Charan Ghosh* (1914) 18 CNW 1133 (Bengal High Court); *Narayana Doss Balakrishna Doss v Buckraj Chordia Sowcar* AIR 1928 Mad 6; *Rama Patter v Lingappa Gounder* AIR 1935 Mad 726.
[45] 'Where, by the exercise of undue influence, any advantage is gained in derogation of the interests of another, the person gaining such advantage without consideration, or with notice that such influence has been exercised, must hold the advantage for the benefit of the person whose interests have been so prejudiced': *Dubash DK Amhad Ibrahim Sahib v AKRMK Meyyappa Chettiar* AIR 1940 Mad 285. See also S Swaminathan and V Singh, Chapter 9 of this volume.
[46] See eg *Bainbridge v Browne* (1881) 18 Ch 188, 197.
[47] The main cases are *Barclay's Bank v O'Brien* [1994] 1 AC 190 and *Royal Bank of Scotland v Etridge (No 2)* [2002] AC 773, which is the primary consolidating authority.

Mulla treat these cases as representing Indian law as well,[48] but the Indian courts have yet to indicate whether they propose to follow this new path.

If the Indian courts were to follow the *O'Brien* reforms, they would create an even greater discrepancy between the rule applied where a guarantee is obtained by a third party's undue influence and the rule applied where a guarantee is obtained by a third party's misrepresentation. In that latter situation, the creditor will only be affected if the third party acted with the creditor's 'knowledge and assent'.[49] Applying different rules in these two situations may lead to anomalous results because, in the real world, those situations tend to accompany and shade into one another.

The Contract Act therefore gives a diversity of answers to the question of in what circumstances a contract will be set aside where one party's consent was vitiated by the wrongdoing of a third party. It is difficult to discern the reasons for these differences.

2. Causation

A contract will only be voidable where consent was not free in that it was caused by the vitiating factor. Section 14 of the Contract Act states that 'Consent is said to be so caused when it would not have been given but for the existence of such coercion, undue influence, fraud, misrepresentation or mistake.'[50] *Chikkam Ammiraju v Chikkam Seshamma* is a classic example.[51] A husband threatened to commit suicide if his wife and son did not sign a release deed in favour of the husband's brother. The court rescinded the deed because consent was 'caused' by the coercive threat.

Two features may be mentioned. First, by stipulating a 'but for' test for causation, the statute resolves an issue relating to fraud and misrepresentation that continues to trouble English law. A contested view of the English authorities holds that causation in the form of inducement will be made out where the representation was present before the mind of the representee without 'speculation' as to what they might otherwise have done.[52] In India, by contrast, section 14 mandates a counterfactual approach, which compares the actual events that have occurred with the hypothetical events that would have occurred if the vitiating factor had not existed.[53] Consent is only unfree if the vitiating factor made a difference to the consenting party's conduct.

[48] RY Vardhan and others (eds), *Pollock and Mulla: The Indian Contract Act, 1872* (16th edn, LexisNexis 2022) [16.8.15.2].

[49] Contract Act, s 142; see *Corporation Bank v Mohandas Baliga* ILR 1993 Kar 201; *T Raju Shetty v Bank of Baroda* AIR 1992 Kant 108; *Balkrishna YN Kirtikar v Bank of Bengal* (1891) ILR 15 Bom 585; *AR Krishnaswami Ayyar v Travancore National Bank Ltd* AIR 1940 Mad 437.

[50] See also the explanation to the Contract Act, s 19 and the discussion in Briggs and Burrows (n 29) 95–96.

[51] (1916) 3 LW 490 (Madras High Court).

[52] Authorities commonly cited in support of this view include *Edington v Fitzmaurice* (1885) 29 ChD 459 (CA) 481, 483; *Reynell v Spry* (1852) 1 De GM & G 660, 708–709; *Smith v Kay* (1859) 7 HLC 750, 759. This view of the English authorities is contested by N Venkatesan in 'Causation in Misrepresentation: Historical or Counterfactual? And "But for" What?' (2021) 137 Law Quarterly Review 503.

[53] Contract Act, s 14. This section does not tell us whether the relevant counterfactual is one in which the truth was told or one in which the representation was not made. The answer may differ depending on the particular circumstances of the case in question.

Second, section 19 of the Contract Act provides, by way of an exception applicable in a limited class of cases, that a contract will not be voidable if the party whose consent was affected had the means of discovering the truth with ordinary diligence. The limited class comprises those cases where 'consent was caused by misrepresentation or by silence, fraudulent within the meaning of section 17'. This is difficult to interpret sensibly. It would be odd if the ordinary diligence exception applied *only* in fraud cases, and indeed, it would be odd if the exception applied in fraud cases at all. One who deliberately persuades another to act on a lie can hardly defend on the basis that they should have been more careful.[54] Indian courts have managed to avoid the conclusion that the exception applies in cases of fraudulent misrepresentation on the basis that the comma should (it is said) be ignored as not forming part of the statute, with the consequence that the word 'fraudulent' only qualifies the word 'silence'.[55] Why the exception should apply in cases of fraudulent silence remains unexplained.

3. The Burden of Proof

The burden of proving a causative vitiating factor usually rests on the rescinding party.[56] However, this is modified in cases involving fiduciary relations and other relations of influence as well as impaired mental capacity.

First, section 111 of the Indian Evidence Act 1872 provides that the burden of proving the 'good faith' of a transaction will lie on a party in a position of 'active confidence'. This seems to replicate the fair dealing rule in traditional English equity.[57] The provision applies to fiduciaries of various kinds, the common characteristic of which is that they are bound to protect the interests of the other.[58] To uphold the transaction, the fiduciary must prove there was 'fair play' and that the transaction is perfectly fair, adequate, and equitable.[59] This may require a close evaluation of the circumstances, including the nature of the benefit conferred, the age and capacity of the party seeking to rescind, and whether they had competent and independent advice.[60]

Second, section 16(3) of the Contract Act provides that once it is established that a person was in a position to dominate the will of another,[61] and that the transaction

[54] English law was clear about this at the time of the Contract Act: *Directors of the Central Railway of Venezuela v Kisch* (1867) LR 2 HL 99, 120–21; and soon afterwards, *Redgrave v Hurd* (1881) 20 ChD 1 (CA) 13–14, 23.

[55] *Kopparthi Venkataratnam v Palleti Sivaramudu* AIR 1940 Mad 560 and earlier authorities cited therein. *Premchand v Ram Sahai* AIR 1932 Nag 148 is an example of a non-fraudulent misrepresentation case in which the exception has been applied.

[56] Indian Evidence Act 1872, ss 101–103.

[57] *Krishna Mohan Kul v Pratima Maity* AIR 2003 SC 4351. The English rule is identified and explained in O'Sullivan, Elliott, and Zakrzewski (n 3) ch 8.

[58] *Anil Rishi v Gurbaksh Singh* (2006) 5 SCC 558.

[59] *Krishna Mohan Kul* (n 57).

[60] ibid. In relation to independent advice, see also *Inche Noriah v Shaik Allie Bin Omar* [1929] AC 127 (JCPC); *Vasireddi Bala Chendra Sekhra Vara Prasada Bahadur Garu v Unnava Subbaya Garu* AIR 1930 Mad 317; *Ram Sumran Prasad v Govind Das* AIR 1926 Pat 582; *Kali Bakhsh Singh v Ram Gopal Singh* (1913) 41 IA 23.

[61] This may be proven or else it may be established by presumption where the rescinding party can prove one of three factual predicates, being a fiduciary relationship, a relationship of real or apparent authority, or impaired mental capacity: the Contract Act, s 16(2).

appears to be unconscionable, then the burden will fall on that dominant person to prove that the contract was not induced by undue influence, meaning that they did not use their position to obtain an unfair advantage. This usually requires proof that the vulnerable person was separately advised.[62]

Section 16(3) of the Contract Act is expressed to operate without prejudice to section 111 of the Indian Evidence Act 1872.[63] Where they both apply, which is in cases involving fiduciary relations, section 111 should predominate because its requirement is broader. Section 16(3) alone will apply in cases where there is no fiduciary relationship, being cases of impaired mental capacity and those involving relationships of influence or authority without the fiduciary element of active confidence.

VII. Election

It is essential to the idea of a voidable contract that one or more parties has the option to avoid the contract.[64] It would be wrong to read section 2(i) of the Contract Act as meaning that the option is to make the agreement enforceable by law.[65] A contract is an enforceable agreement.[66] From that starting point, the party entitled to rescind may exercise the option by electing to avoid the contract; or else it may elect to ratify the contract;[67] or finally, it may do nothing, hoping to keep its options open, but taking the risk that rescission may become barred before it comes to elect.[68]

Election is all or nothing. As Rankin J put it, 'The option which characterises a voidable contract is an option either to say "it shall not be enforceable at all" or to leave it as a good contract enforceable by any party on the usual conditions.'[69] This is an aspect of the prohibition on partial rescission:[70] a party cannot pick and choose which parts of a contract it wishes to sustain, for that would involve rewriting the parties' bargain. If the contract is properly severable, where a single instrument contains two or more independent bargains, then these may be rescinded or ratified separately.[71]

As to whether election is also final, certainly electing to ratify a contract extinguishes the right to avoid it, provided the electing party knows the material facts or is otherwise

[62] *Poosathuri* (n 43).

[63] Section 16(3) was added by amendment in 1899. This may have been a response to Pollock's concern that s 111 of the Evidence Act 1872 was liable to be overlooked: F Pollock, *The Law of Fraud, Misrepresentation and Mistake in British India* (Thacker, Spik & Co 1894) 65–66.

[64] The Contract Act, s 2(i) reads 'An agreement which is enforceable by law at the option of one or more of the parties thereto, but not at the option of the other or others, is a voidable contract.'

[65] ibid.

[66] ibid s 2(h).

[67] 'Ratify' is the term used in the Specific Relief Act 1963, s 27(2)(i), but Indian texts and judgments often prefer 'affirm': see eg the Indian Supreme Court in *Ganga Retreat & Towers Ltd v State of Rajasthan* (2003) 12 SCC 91. We use 'ratify' to be consistent with the legislation, recognising that this word is also used to mean something quite different in the context of agency: the Contract Act, ss 196–200.

[68] *Ningawwa* (n 17); *Ganga Retreat & Towers Ltd* (n 67); *Reese River Silver Mining Company Ltd* (n 34) 73; *Clough v London and North Western Railway Co* (1871) LR 7 Ex 26, 34.

[69] *Muralidhar Chatterjee* (n 21).

[70] Specific Relief Act 1963, s 27(2)(d); *Indra Nath Banerjee v Rooke* (1910) ILR 37 Cal 81, 89; *Ohid Bux v Dorshu* AIR 1926 Cal 959.

[71] Specific Relief Act 1963, s 27(2)(d).

free of the vitiating factor.[72] But if, instead, a party elects to rescind a contract, can it ever go back on that? The English Court of Exchequer gave this question a negative answer in *Clough v London and North Western Railway Co*,[73] a major decision delivered shortly before the enactment of the Contract Act. But section 66 of the Contract Act gives a different answer. It states that 'The rescission of a voidable contract may be communicated *or revoked* in the same manner, and subject to the same rules, as apply to the communication or revocation of a proposal.'[74] Those rules are contained in sections 5 and 6 of the Contract Act.

It is perplexing that the statutory rules governing communication of proposals should apply to revocation of an election to rescind. A proposal is the first step in a bilateral transaction that, to be effective, also requires an acceptance on the part of the recipient. Revocation of a proposal occurs only, according to the statute, where the proposer communicates notice of revocation before the proposal is accepted, or where no acceptance is given within the requisite time, or where the acceptor fails to fulfil a condition precedent to acceptance, or where the acceptor learns that the proposer has died or become insane.[75] These are events that interrupt a proposal that has not yet become effective. These rules cannot be applied directly to an election to rescind, for that is a unilateral act which does not require reciprocation, but instead takes effect immediately upon communication. But if those rules are incapable of applying to the revocation of an election to rescind, what limits are there on the possibility of revocation?[76]

In the absence of statutory guidance, and in circumstances where English common law took a different path, Indian courts will have to articulate rational limits to the power to revoke consistent with the essential principles of the legislation. Again, however, Indian law does not stand alone. The US *Restatement of Restitution* and *Restatement (Second) of Contract* offer a practical solution, providing that an election to rescind is revocable unless the rescinding party has also recovered what that party gave, obtained a final judgment for rescission, or become estopped from enforcing the contract.[77] Presumably, a revocation operates as a final election to ratify the contract.

A further consequence of section 66 of the Contract Act is to apply the rules concerning communications of proposals in sections 3 and 4 to an election to rescind and

[72] *Ganga Retreat & Towers Ltd* (n 67); *Ningawwa* (n 17); *Kunja Lal Bhuiya v Hara Lal Bhuiya* AIR 1943 Cal 162; *Clough* (n 68) 34, 35. There may be circumstances in which discovery of further information gives a fresh right to rescind, but no Indian case seems to illustrate this. The English cases are collected at O'Sullivan, Elliott, and Zakrzewski (n 3) [23.96]ff.

[73] *Clough* (n 68) 34, 36. English courts have treated an election to rescind as irrevocable ever since: eg *Peyman v Lanjani* [1985] Ch 457 (CA) 494, 500.

[74] This seems to have been overlooked: *Kunja Lal Bhuiya* (n 72); RY Vardhan and others (eds), *Pollock and Mulla: The Indian Contract and Specific Relief Acts* (16th edn, LexisNexis 2019) [19.3].

[75] Contract Act, ss 5, 6.

[76] Vardhan and others (n 74) [66.3] suggest that revocation is limited to circumstances where the decision to rescind has not yet been communicated to the other party. But the statute speaks of revoking the 'rescission' and, because an election to rescind does not take effect until the election has come to the knowledge of other party (see s 4 of the Contract Act), prior to communication, there is no rescission that could be revoked.

[77] *Restatement of Restitution* (1937) § 68(2) and Reporter's Note at 282; *Restatement (Second) of Contract*, vol 3 (1981) § 382 and Reporter's Note at 242–43. The point was not taken up in the *Restatement (Third) of Restitution* (n 26) § 54. The authors in O'Sullivan, Elliott, and Zakrzewski (n 3) advocate this approach where rescission is a judicial remedy. Whether rescission is a judicial remedy in India is discussed in section VIII.

to the revocation of an election. These provisions impose three requirements. First, there must be a communication from one party to the other. The communication need not take any particular form,[78] and indeed, it does not need to be verbal or even active—'any act or omission' rescinding or revoking will do. No reason need be assigned for an election to rescind, and if a reason is given, the rescinding party may, in subsequent proceedings, support the election on other grounds.[79]

Second, whether an act or omission should be taken as communicating rescission or revocation depends on subjective considerations. In particular, it is necessary that either the communicating party intends to communicate an election to rescind or a revocation *or* the act or omission has the effect of communicating one of these things. This is a little odd. Nowadays, common lawyers would usually ask whether the act or omission objectively communicated rescission or revocation, in the sense that it would be understood in this way by a reasonable person. Instead, section 3 concentrates on the subjective intentions and understandings of the parties without regard to reasonableness and without requiring a meeting of the minds. It therefore seems that a communication intended to rescind can be effective even though the recipient quite reasonably did not understand it in this way. Equally, a communication that was not intended to rescind can be effective for this purpose provided only that the recipient mistook it for an election to rescind, however unreasonably.

Third, section 4 states that 'the communication of a proposal is complete when it comes to the knowledge of the person to whom it is made'. The statute does not explain the significance of a communication being complete, but in the case of an election or revocation under section 66, this can only be that it does not take effect until the communication comes to the counterparty's knowledge. On the face of it, this rules out the result in *Caldwell's* case.[80] In that much-discussed decision, the English Court of Appeal recognised an exception to the communication requirement where the fraudster bought Mr Caldwell's automobile, giving a cheque that was dishonoured, and then absconded, thus making communication impossible. The Court held that Mr Caldwell had effectively rescinded, and so recovered title, by notifying the police and the Automobile Association three days before the rogue resold to an innocent purchaser.

Caldwell's case is now settled law in England, but the decision attracted criticism at the time on the basis that it tends to undermine the protection given to innocent purchasers by what is, in India, section 29 of the Sale of Goods Act 1930.[81] Under that provision, an innocent purchaser from a rogue is only protected where the contract by which the rogue acquired the asset has not yet been rescinded at the time of the resale.

[78] See *Official Receiver, Jhansi* (n 16). That case also illustrates that communication to an agent acting in the course of business transacted for the principal is equally effective: the Contract Act, s 229.

[79] *Blanche Fonseca v Jupiter Airways Ltd* AIR 1953 Bom 417.

[80] *Car and Universal Finance Co Ltd v Caldwell* [1965] 1 QB 525 (CA). The Vardhan and others (n 74) [66.2], as well as Briggs and Burrows (n 29) 114, suggest that the result in *Caldwell's* case would be reached under the Contract Act, but neither mentions s 4 or explains how it would be overcome.

[81] W Cornish, 'Rescission without Notice' (1964) 27 Modern Law Review 472, 478; English Law Reform Committee, *Transfer of Title to Chattels* (12th report, Cm 2958, 1966) [16]; A Turner (ed), *Turner and Spencer Bower: The Law of Actionable Misrepresentation* (3rd edn, Butterworth 1974) 261.

The possibility of an uncommunicated rescission recognised in *Caldwell's* case makes it more likely that initial contracts will have been rescinded by the time of resale in circumstances of which the innocent purchaser could not know. The Indian position is consonant with the criticisms of *Caldwell's* case and represents a sensible balancing of the interests involved.[82]

VIII. Whether a Court Order Is Necessary

An effectively communicated election is necessary to bring about rescission, but must a rescinding party also obtain an order of the court? Put differently, is rescission a self-help remedy, such that effective communication of an election itself extinguishes the contract and automatically generates rights to restitutionary relief? Or is rescission a judicial remedy, such that the election only gives a right to approach the court to ask for orders rescinding the contract where it is the court's order that extinguishes the contract and vests rights to restitution?

This is a difficult problem, which all common law systems must confront. Broadly, English common law historically treated rescission as a self-help remedy, while in equity, rescission was treated as a judicial remedy, although the cases are not always consistent. The House of Lords has twice favoured a generalised self-help model,[83] but those decisions have not succeeding in completely suppressing the judicial remedy model.[84] One English scholar has advocated the legislative abolition of self-help rescission,[85] while one has argued that rescission should always take effect by election.[86] The point bears on a range of topics, including the status of the contract following election, the operation of statutory limitations, the nature and location of property rights following election, whether developments between the dates of election and of judgment may bar rescission, and whether or how such developments should be taken into account when crafting the relief to be given upon rescission.

In *Hungerford Investment Trust v Haridas Mundra*,[87] the Indian Supreme Court unequivocally favoured the self-help model, saying this:

> A Court generally adjudicates upon the antecedent rights of the parties. When a Court adjudges rescission of a contract or a decree, it is only concerned with the question whether the person rescinding it was justified in doing so. The Court does not create any right which parties did not possess when it makes a declaration that a contract has

[82] Moreover, if we are right that rescission is, in India, an exclusively judicial remedy, it will follow that innocent purchasers are protected by the Sale of Goods Act 1930, s 29 up to the point at which court orders are made rescinding initial sales.

[83] *Reese River Silver Mining Company Ltd* (n 34); *Abram Steamship Company Limited v Westville Shipping Company Limited* [1923] AC 773.

[84] O'Sullivan, Elliott, and Zakrzewski (n 3) chs 3, 10 and especially 11.

[85] J O'Sullivan, 'Rescission as a Self Help Remedy: A Critical Analysis' [2000] Cambridge Law Review 509.

[86] S Elliott, 'The Basic Structure of Rescission' in B McFarlane and S Elliott (eds), *Equity Today* (Hart 2023).

[87] *Hungerford Investment Trust* (n 6). See also *Ganga Retreat & Towers Ltd* (n 67). This is also the view of Vardhan and others (n 74) [19.5.1.2], albeit they cite Australian authority rather than the *Hungerford* case.

> been validly rescinded. Merely because it is necessary for the Court to pass an order of rescission, when a controversy arises, it does not follow that it is the Court that rescinds the contract. The Court is only passing upon the validity of the rescission already made by the party.

Because of this, 'the rights of the parties crystallised' when the election to rescind was announced in a letter, and later events could not change that. As authority for this ruling, the Indian Supreme Court offered the decision of the House of Lords in *Abram Steamship Company Limited v Westville Shipping Company Limited*.[88]

It does not appear that, in reaching this conclusion, the Supreme Court considered legislative provisions that bear on the question or previous Indian jurisprudence. Most importantly, section 27(1) of the Specific Relief Act 1963 begins, 'Any person interested in a contract may sue to have it rescinded.' This intends that the contract will remain extant when the suit is brought and that, in consequence of the suit, the contract may be rescinded by the court. Section 27(2) puts this beyond doubt by identifying a list of circumstances in which 'the court may refuse to rescind the contract'. This power would be pointless if rescission had, in every case, already been effected by announcing an election. Absent a separate notice, the pleadings themselves would constitute sufficient notice[89] so that the very act of commencing proceedings under section 27 would make the relief sought unnecessary. The Limitation Act 1963 proceeds on the same basis. A three-year limitation period applies to suits 'for the rescission of a contract', which begins to run 'when the facts entitling the plaintiff to have . . . the contract rescinded first become known to him'.[90] This, again, envisages a proceeding in which an extant contract may be rescinded by the court, which is straightforwardly inconsistent with the ruling in the *Hungerford* case.

It is true that sections 19 and 19A of the Contract Act speak of contracts being voidable 'at the option' of the party in question, that section 19A also speaks of the party who was 'entitled' to avoid a contract, and that section 66 speaks of that party communicating '[t]he rescission of a voidable contract'. These expressions are consistent with a self-help theory of rescission,[91] but they are also consistent with the idea that an election to rescind is an essential condition to relief that is then granted by the court.

In addition, there are three substantive features of Indian law that are difficult to square with self-help rescission, each of which English law does not share. First, if it were possible to rescind by election alone, the statutory limitation period would be nugatory. In *Janki Kunwar v Ajit Singh*, the widow of a vendor of land sued more than three years after she had learnt the facts entitling her to rescind.[92] The Judicial Commissioner

[88] *Abram Steamship Company Limited* (n 83).
[89] *Indra Nath Banerjee* (n 70) 88; *Clough* (n 68) 35–36.
[90] The Limitation Act 1963, sch point 59.
[91] In relation to the Contract Act, s 19, see *Blanche Fonseca* (n 79).
[92] *Janki Kunwar v Ajit Singh* (1885) ILR 15 Cal 58. This decision was followed in *Raja Rajeswara Dorai Alias Muthu v ALARRM Arunachellam* (1915) ILR 38 Mad 321, which is more fully reasoned. Under English law, completed contracts for the sale of land cannot be rescinded by a mere election: O'Sullivan, Elliott, and Zakrzewski (n 3) [14.24]–[14.28], [15.07]–[15.10].

had treated the suit as one for possession of the land and so subject to a twelve-year limitation period, which the widow's suit fell within. The Judicial Committee reversed that order on the basis that the land could not be recovered until the deed of sale had been set aside, 'and it was necessary to bring a suit to set aside the deed'. If it were possible to rescind merely by communicating an election, it might never be necessary to bring a suit caught by the three-year limitation period.

Second, we have already observed that Indian law permits the revocation of an election to rescind. This would cause considerable difficulty and insecurity if the election itself made the contract void, automatically revested title to assets, and automatically gave the parties restitution claims, subject to possible revocation. But if rescission is a judicial remedy, then it is possible to envisage circumstances in which an election to rescind may be revoked up to the point at which the court acts on the election by extinguishing the contract. Third, section 19A of the Contract Act empowers the court, in undue influence cases where the rescinding party has received a benefit under the contract, to set aside the contract either absolutely or 'upon such terms and conditions as to the Court may seem just'. This is only consistent with judicial rescission.

Against these points may be set section 86 of the Indian Trusts Act 1882:

> Where property is transferred in pursuance of a contract which is liable to rescission or induced by fraud or mistake, the transferee must, on receiving notice to that effect,[93] hold the property for the benefit of the transferor,[94] subject to repayment by the latter of the consideration actually paid.

This may be said to envisage that rescission occurs upon communication of the election, with the immediate consequence that the rescinding party gains an equitable interest in property held by the transferee, subject only to making counter-restitution.[95] However, that interpretation of section 86 is inconsistent with the other legislative features identified in the preceding paragraphs, which indicate that rescission is a judicial remedy.

One solution may lie in section 96 of the Indian Trusts Act 1882, which provides that nothing in the relevant chapter shall 'create an obligation in evasion of any law for the time being in force'. In *Raja Rajeswara Dorai Alias Muthu v ALARRM Arunachellam*,[96] Miller J accepted that section 86 contemplates rescission taking effect by election but reasoned that rescission of this kind would evade the Limitation Act 1908 by permitting the rescinding party to sue for possession after the third year, as was tried in *Janki Kunwar v Ajit Singh*. But even if we allow that the concern of section 96 is not limited

[93] Presumably, this means a communication that satisfies the requirements of the Contract Act, s 66, as discussed above.

[94] This is an 'obligation in the nature of a trust': Indian Trusts Act 1882, s 80.

[95] English law recognises a similar interest that arises in this way where contracts are rescinded in equity for fraud: *Lonrho plc v Fayed (No 2)* [1992] 1 WLR 1, 11–12; *Shalson v Russo* [2005] Ch 281, 320–322; *Independent Trustee Services Ltd v GP Noble Trustees Ltd* [2013] Ch 91 (CA) [52]–[55].

[96] *Raja Rajeswara Dorai Alias Muthu* (n 92).

to penal and revenue laws, this is, nonetheless, an imperfect solution in that it deprives section 86 of practical effect.

A solution that better reconciles section 86 with the other legislation discussed above would be to recognise that the interest created by section 86 upon notice is contingent on the court's eventual order and counter-restitution, with the transferee retaining the residual interest. If the court refuses to rescind the contract, or the transferor does not make counter-restitution, the transferor's interest would fail, leaving the transferee with an unencumbered title. Similarly, the contingency would be frustrated if the transferor failed to sue for rescission within the limitation period, again leaving the transferee with an unencumbered title. But if the court rescinds the contract, and the transferor makes counter-restitution, the transferor's interest would be perfected, and the court would make whatever orders were needed to enforce it. On this approach, section 86 holds the position while the dispute is ventilated, including by conferring priority for the contingent interest in the transferee's insolvency. On this basis, the interest created by section 86 is similar to an equitable security interest.

Evidently, the pieces of Indian law do not fit together as neatly as they might, and it is possible that the people who drafted the various statutes did not have a uniform view of this issue. Nonetheless, the dominant provisions of Indian legislation create a judicial remedy. On one view, judicial rescission gives the court greater flexibility to do justice in the circumstances as they may have become by the time of trial, as well as greater flexibility to unravel potentially complex arrangements. The Judicial Committee recognised, in 1885, that rescission in India is a judicial remedy,[97] and the Supreme Court may wish to consider the issue more fully should an opportunity arise.

IX. Bars

Fundamental to any account of the rescission of voidable contracts are the bars that may preclude relief. While the Contract Act gives early prominence to the grounds, bars are overlooked. That omission was partially remedied by what is now section 27(2) of the Specific Relief Act 1963, which provides that 'the court may refuse to rescind the contract' in five circumstances.

Section 27(2) does not claim to be an exhaustive statement of the circumstances in which the court may refuse relief, but nor do Indian courts claim to have a free hand. The court's discretion whether to grant relief, like the discretion to order specific performance of a contract,[98] should be exercised in accordance with the legislation and with sound and reasonable judicial principles. To a significant extent, the circumstances in which it would be unjust or inequitable that a right to rescind should continue have been crystallised in the bars,[99] as defined by statute and associated jurisprudence.

[97] *Janki Kunwar* (n 92).

[98] *K Nanjappa v RA Hameed* AIR 2015 SC 3389, [21]–[26].

[99] *Ganga Retreat & Towers Ltd* (n 67). It is unfortunate that in this major statement of the bars to rescission, the Supreme Court did not mention the Specific Relief Act 1963, s 27(2).

Where none of the bars applies, rescission will usually follow as a matter of course. In one early case, the primary judge had considered that enforcing the contract as it would have been absent the fraud would give satisfactory relief, but the appellate judges held that this was beyond his powers: the plaintiff 'insists on his right to a rescission; and we must adjudge a rescission of the contract'.[100]

1. Ratification

Taking the provisions of section 27(2) of the Specific Relief Act 1963 in turn, the court may refuse to rescind a contract 'where the plaintiff has expressly or impliedly ratified the contract'. This has been touched on above under the rubric of election, noting that ratification is irrevocable. A party may only ratify where it knows the material facts or is otherwise freed from the factor that vitiated their consent.[101] Longstanding English case law indicates that there need be no intention to ratify.[102]

Ratification is often implied from conduct that manifests an intention to continue with the contract. Illustrations include a case in which a purchaser of land commenced construction knowing that the auction notice had misrepresented the applicable floor area ratio,[103] a case in which salvors continued to perform by recovering and selling a dredger under a salvage agreement said to have been procured by fraud and misrepresentation,[104] and a case in which a retired partner accepted payment under a retirement deed said to have been procured by coercion.[105] As the effect of ratification is to extinguish a right, it is not surprising that ratification will only be implied from conduct that is unequivocal.[106] Sections 3, 4, and 66 of the Contract Act, which regulate communication of an election to rescind, do not apply directly to an election to ratify. This is anomalous, and there must be a reasonable argument that those provisions reflect rules of justice, equity, and good conscience, which also apply in this cognate context.

In general, a party entitled to rescind may keep the question open so long as it does nothing to ratify the contract.[107] The dealings between the parties in a particular case may be such, however, that failure to rescind implies acquiescence.[108] In *Ganga Retreat & Towers*, the Supreme Court said that a right to rescind 'must be promptly exercised',[109] but in another case, where proof of a conspiracy emerged in bits and pieces, a judge of

[100] *Ra'vji Janaa'rdan Sa'rangpa'ni v Ganga'dharbhat* (1879) 4 Bom 29, 33.
[101] *Ningawwa* (n 17); *Ganga Retreat & Towers Ltd* (n 67).
[102] *Scarfe v Jardine* (1882) 7 App Cas 345 at 361.
[103] *Ganga Retreat & Towers Ltd* (n 67) (the court may also have considered that the construction made *restitution in integrum* impossible).
[104] *Orient Underwater Engineers (Pvt) Ltd v Cochin Port Trust* 2017 (1) KHC 833, [16].
[105] *Broadway Centre v Gopaldas Bagri* AIR 2002 Cal 78, [21].
[106] *Raja Mohan Manucha vs Manzoor Ahmad Khan* (1942) 46 BOMLR 170 (PC); *Ningawwa* (n 17).
[107] *Ningawwa* (n 17); *Clough* (n 68) 34.
[108] *Erlanger v The New Sombrero Phosphate Co* (1878) 3 App Cas 1218, 1278–79.
[109] *Ganga Retreat & Towers Ltd* (n 67).

the Bombay High Court remarked that the defrauded party was entitled carefully to review and consider the material indicating fraud before determining its election.[110]

2. Change of Circumstances

The court may also refuse to rescind a contract 'where, owing to the change of circumstances which has taken place since the making of the contract (not being due to any act of the defendant himself), the parties cannot be substantially restored to the position in which they stood when the contract was made'. This bar is often known by a partly Latin label, '*restitutio in integrum* impossible'.[111]

The statutory formulation of the bar has some notable features. First, it is not limited to the rescinding party being unable to return an asset it has received. Instead, subject to the parenthetical exception, the bar extends to any change of circumstances during the life of the contract that has the consequence that the parties cannot be restored to their original positions. Second, it seems that rescission may be barred unless *both* parties can be restored.[112] This is a departure from the English position, which is that rescission will only be barred by an inability to restore the wrongdoer to its original position.[113] Under English law, it is for the rescinding party to decide whether it is content to be restored to an inferior position as the price of rescinding in changed circumstances. Third, restoration need only be substantial. In this, Indian legislation follows the rule favoured by English equity rather than the more exacting requirement of the English common law.[114] For example, the mere fact that the rescinding party has used goods obtained under the contract will not bar rescission as it would have at common law.[115] The benefit of the use cannot be specifically restored, but substantial restoration can be achieved by a compensatory payment.

An important question on which there seems to be no Indian authority is the extent to which restitution and counter-restitution can be achieved by payment of monetary compensation where the asset itself is no longer available, perhaps because it has been sold on or consumed. Section 65 of the Contract Act appears to contemplate payment of compensation in lieu of specific restoration but does not identify the circumstances in which this is permitted. Where compensation is permitted in lieu of specific restitution or counter-restitution, it seems that the change of circumstances is effectively reversible, and rescission should not be barred.

110 *Shree Pushkar Chemicals & Fertilizers Ltd v Huntsman (International) India Pvt Ltd* 2018 (1) ABR 801 (Bom HC).

111 See eg *Ganga Retreat & Towers Ltd* (n 67).

112 See *Indra Nath Banerjee* (n 70) 89. Richardson J spoke in terms suggesting that only the position of the wrongdoer need be taken into account, but he did not mention the terms of the legislation.

113 *Western Bank of Scotland v Addie* (1867) LR 1 Sc App 145 (HL), 164–65; *Spence v Crawford* [1939] 3 All ER 271 (HL(Sc)) at 279. This also appears to be the position in the United States: *Restatement (Third) of Restitution* (n 26) § 54(3).

114 *Erlanger* (n 108) 1278–79. The common law position is exemplified by *Clarke v Dickson* (1858) El Bl & El 140, 120 ER 463.

115 *Shree Pushkar Chemicals & Fertilizers Ltd* (n 110).

3. Intervention of Third-Party Rights

The court may also refuse to rescind a contract 'where third parties have, during the subsistence of the contract, acquired rights in good faith without notice and for value'.[116] This complements section 29 of the Sale of Goods Act 1930, which provides that where the seller acquired possession under a voidable but as yet unrescinded contract, the buyer acquires good title provided the buyer buys in good faith and without notice of the seller's defect of title. The statutory bar may also encompass, perhaps unintentionally, the case of a multilateral contract with innocent parties whose rights rescission would destroy.[117]

4. Delay

The Limitation Act 1963 stipulates a three-year limitation period for any suit to rescind a contract.[118] Time begins to run when the facts entitling the plaintiff to rescind the contract first become known to it.[119] Mere suspicion is not knowledge for this purpose: the plaintiff must have had 'a substantial ground to go upon'.[120] This does not cater for coercion and undue influence cases, in which the plaintiff may remain subject to the coercion or influence even though it knows the material facts.[121]

In England, where no statutory limitation applies directly to a claim to rescind a contract, delay is partly regulated by the doctrine of laches.[122] The Indian Supreme Court has held, in the parallel case of specific performance, that limitations legislation implicitly excludes the operation of laches in India: 'If the suit is in time, delay is sanctioned by law; if it is beyond time, the suit will be dismissed as barred by time: in either case no question of equity arises.'[123] But while mere delay within the limitation period does not bar rescission, circumstances attending the delay may constitute acquiescence, and delay may give the opportunity for changes of circumstances such as engage the *restitution in integrum* impossible bar. This is the meaning of the Supreme Court's statement in *Ganga Retreat & Towers* that 'delay in election may make it unjust that the right to elect should continue'.[124]

[116] It is open to question whether it is necessary to bar rescission altogether as opposed to protecting the innocent third party's title while giving the plaintiff whatever other advantages the remedy offers against the wrongdoer. This point is developed in O'Sullivan, Elliott, and Zakrzewski (n 3) [20.21].

[117] See eg *Re Metal Constituents Limited (Lord Lurgan's Case)* [1902] 1 Ch 707, 710.

[118] Limitation Act 1963, sch point 59.

[119] Additionally, ibid section 17 provides, broadly, that where there is a fraud or concealment, time shall not run until the plaintiff has discovered the fraud or could, with reasonable diligence, have discovered it. But since time does not run until the plaintiff knows the facts entitling the plaintiff to rescind, s 17 will usually be redundant in rescission cases.

[120] *Indra Nath Banerjee* (n 70) 85.

[121] *Someshwar Dutt v Tirbhawan Dutt* (1934) 61 Ind App 224 (JCPC).

[122] See especially *Lindsay Petroleum Co v Hurd* (1874) LR 5 PC 221, 239–41; *Erlanger* (n 108) 1279.

[123] *Madamsetty Satyanarayana v G Yellogi Rao* AIR 1965 SC 1405.

[124] *Ganga Retreat & Towers Ltd* (n 67).

Somewhat anomalously, the Limitation Act 1963 applies to suits seeking rescission but does not apply directly where rescission is, instead, raised by way of defence to a claim to enforce a contract.[125] In England, there is an equitable jurisdiction to apply limitation legislation by analogy in some rescission cases.[126] Either that doctrine or else justice, equity, and good conscience may warrant a similar approach in India.

X. Effect of Rescission

1. Contract Becomes Void

The cardinal consequence of rescission is that the contract ceases to be legally enforceable and becomes void. Section 64 of the Contract Act provides that the party against whom the contract is rescinded 'need not perform any promise therein contained in which he is promisor'. It seems inherent in the idea that the contract becomes void that the rescinding party is also released from its promises.

Arbitration clauses usually survive by force of a statutory fiction that they are independent agreements.[127] In addition, *Mackender v Feldia AG*,[128] in which the English Court of Appeal decided that jurisdiction clauses also survive avoidance, has been treated as applicable in India.[129] Whilst impeccably practical, this treats a contract that has become void as having some continuing effect.

2. Restoration of Property Rights

Common law systems struggle to explain the effect of rescission on property rights.[130] In India the point is regulated by section 86 of the Indian Trusts Act 1882. We earlier argued that this creates a contingent interest in assets still held by the wrongdoer, which may be perfected by a court order. Along with declaring the contract rescinded, the court will typically make an order under section 65 of the Contract Act vindicating the proprietary interest by compelling transfer of the asset back to the rescinding party.

[125] *Rangnath Sakharam v Govind Narasinv* (1904) 28 Bom 639; *Raja Rajeswara Dorai Alias Muthu* (n 92).
[126] *Molloy v Mutual Reserve Life Insurance Co* (1906) 94 LT 756 (CA); *Oelkers v Ellis* [1914] 2 KB 139, 149–51; *Armstrong v Jackson* [1917] 2 KB 822, 830–31; *IGE USA Investments Limited v HMRC* [2021] EWCA Civ 534.
[127] Arbitration and Conciliation Act 1996, s 16(1).
[128] *Mackender v Feldia AG* [1967] 2 QB 590 (CA).
[129] See eg *General Enterprises v Jardine Henderson Ltd* AIR 1978 Cal 407; *Shree Precoated Steels Ltd v Macsteels International Far East* 2008 (2) BomCR 681. *Mackender* (n 128) is also treated as applicable by the Vardhan and others (n 74) [19.5.6].
[130] O'Sullivan, Elliott, and Zakrzewski (n 3) ch 16.

3. Consequential Claims and Adjustments

Section 65 of the Contract Act provides that upon a contract becoming void, 'any person who has received any advantage under such agreement or contract is bound to restore it, or to make compensation for it to the person from whom he received it'. This is mutual: obligations are imposed on both the rescinding party and the wrongdoer.[131] Section 65 posits two possibilities. The first is specific restoration of advantages received. This can only refer to assets transferred or money paid. The second possibility is compensation.[132] It is important to understand that this is not compensation for loss or damage in the sense used in section 73 and elsewhere in the statute.[133] Instead the compensation is a money substitute for the advantage to be restored. As such, the compensation is quantified by the value of the advantage.[134]

Advantages restored by way of a compensatory payment conventionally include the benefit derived from the use of assets; for example, notional rent may be charged in respect of the use of land or interest may be charged in respect of the use of money.[135] In a case involving a quarrying concession, compensation was calculated by reference to a reasonable royalty.[136] In some cases, a party may be required to effectively assume a burden transferred by the contract.[137] The court has an array of powers to adjust the positions of the parties.[138] More difficult is the question of whether compensation may be offered or required in lieu of specific restitution and counter-restitution. The Indian courts will need to grapple with some difficult questions. Is compensation always a possible substitute where an asset is unavailable, or does unavailability sometimes bar rescission?[139] How should an asset be valued where the market has fluctuated?[140] Can a rescinding party effectively force the other party to accept the return of a monetary substitute, keeping the asset for itself? And what about services: are executed contracts for services incapable of rescission or can services be restored by way of a compensatory payment?[141]

Section 64 of the Contract Act requires that a rescinding party restore any 'benefit' it received under the contract 'so far as may be'. It is doubtful that any difference was

131 *State of Rajasthan v Associated Stone Industries (Kotah) Ltd* AIR 1958 SC 466; *Muralidhar Chatterjee* (n 21).
132 The Specific Relief Act 1963, s 30 also empowers the court to order compensation against the rescinding party.
133 Section 73 is titled 'Compensation for loss or damages caused by breach of contract'.
134 *Govindram Seksaria v Edward Radbone* AIR 1948 PC 56.
135 ibid.
136 *Associated Stone Industries (Kotah) Ltd* (n 131).
137 *Fatick Chand Seal v State of West Bengal* (1966) ILR 2 Cal 50, citing *Adam v Newbigging* (1886) 34 ChD 682 (CA).
138 *Erlanger* (n 108) 1278.
139 The issue is also unresolved in English law, as to which see O'Sullivan, Elliott, and Zakrzewski (n 3) [18.51]–[18.75].
140 In *Govindram Seksaria* (n 134), the asset in question, certain machinery, was valued as at the date on which the contract became void.
141 There appear to be no Indian authorities. In England, services can be restored by way of a compensating payment notwithstanding earlier House of Lords authority to the contrary: compare *O'Sullivan v Management Agency and Music Ltd* [1985] QB 428 (CA) and *Guinness plc v Saunders* [1990] 2 AC 693, 698 with *Boyd & Forrest v The Glasgow Railway Company* 1915 SC (HL) 20.

intended between the concepts of a benefit under section 64 and an advantage under section 65. The obligation under section 64 therefore duplicates the rescinding party's obligation to make counter-restitution under section 65.[142] The words 'so far as may be' seem to cover the situation where the rescinding party received a performance that was not actually beneficial to them or not beneficial to the extent of its usual market value. An example might be a homeowner tricked or coerced into having their roof retiled unnecessarily. In such cases, compensation may be assessed by reference to the actual benefit to the rescinding party, if any.

4. Section 19A Adjustments

Uniquely in the case of undue influence, section 19A of the Contract Act gives the court the power to set aside the contract 'either absolutely or, if the party who was entitled to avoid it had received any benefit thereunder, upon such terms and conditions as to the Court may seem just'. This anomalous provision is considered by Shivprasad Swaminathan and Veda Singh in Chapter 9 of this volume.

XI. Alternative and Independent Claims

A person who is entitled to rescind may, instead, elect to ratify the contract and insist that it be performed. Section 19 of the Contract Act gives a ratifying party an additional right where the ground for rescission was fraud or misrepresentation. In those cases, such a person is also entitled to 'be put in the position in which he would have been if the representation made had been true'. In effect, the representation is treated as if it were a contractual warranty and the ratifying party is entitled to enforce the contract on that basis. This is objectionable in principle because the ratifying party did not negotiate or pay for a warranty.

This aspect of section 19 has no predecessor in the common law, at least in the general terms in which it is expressed, and no known kin outside those jurisdictions with the same legislation. Its consequences, if applied literally, are such that Pollock and Mulla thought section 19 'obviously' does not mean what it says.[143] A simple example makes the point. A manufacturer of mining machinery fraudulently represents to a landowner that it has discovered a vein of gold in the land worth upwards of Rs 50 crores after extraction costs and so persuades the landowner to purchase machinery for Rs 5 crores. Testing reveals the fraud before the mining starts. Clearly, the landowner may rescind, returning the machinery, and recover the Rs 5 crores it paid. Should the landowner also be entitled to insist instead that the manufacturer pay Rs 50 crores to

[142] The Specific Relief Act 1963, s 30 also duplicates the rescinding party's obligation to make counter-restitution.
[143] F Pollock and DF Mulla, *The Indian Contract Act* (2nd edn, Sweet & Maxwell 1905) 88.

put it in the position as if the representation had been true and there was gold in the land? Surely not.

Some tribunals have tried to make sense of this aspect of section 19 by reading it as a statutory equivalent of the action for deceit.[144] There may be cases in which the two result in a financially equivalent outcome, but there will be many cases in which this is not the case. The mining machinery example just given illustrates this. Section 19 results in an award of Rs 50 crores, whereas tort damages would compensate only for the loss the landowner suffered by entering the contract, which is the amount it paid for the machinery less credit for its resale value. There may, of course, be other cases in which damages in tort would exceed an award under section 19.

This raises a further question. Quite apart from section 19, where a person is entitled to rescind a contract on grounds of fraud, may they claim damages in tort on the same basis, whether instead of rescission or in addition to it?[145] Until recently, this would not have been controversial. Consistently with the common law in England,[146] Indian law recognises a tort of deceit that is independent from and cumulative with the right to rescind. Accordingly, a plaintiff who can prove fraud may sue for rescission, or damages, or both.[147] Any damages in tort must, of course, be quantified taking into account the restitution the rescinding party receives and any other consequences of rescission. Damages in tort are usually calculated to compensate the plaintiff for loss suffered in having entered the contract so that no relevant loss may remain once the contract has been unwound. But there may be cases in which extraneous loss is recoverable as damages, such as expenses incurred preparing to perform a contract.[148] If rescission is barred, damages may be the only civil remedy available to the victim of a fraud.[149]

A view has developed in the Delhi High Court, however, that section 19 of the Contract Act operates as an exclusive remedy in relation to the consequences of pre-contractual misrepresentation so that damages cannot be claimed in tort.[150] While it appears that Indian tort law does not give a damages remedy for purely innocent misrepresentations,[151] this is not because section 19 is an exclusive remedy. It is true that

[144] This appears to have been the approach of the arbitral tribunal whose award was considered by the Delhi High Court in *Daiichi Sankyo Company Limited v Malvinder Mohan Singh* 2018 (1) ARBLR 492 (Delhi), if not the Delhi High Court itself.

[145] We assume that Indian tort law does not provide a damages remedy for mere misrepresentation, coercion, or undue influence. This aspect of Indian law is surprisingly undeveloped, and the Indian Supreme Court has said that Indian courts should be guided by developments in the English courts: *Rajkot Municipal Corporation v Munjulben Jayantilal Nakum* (1997) 9 SCC 552.

[146] *Goldrei, Foucard & Son v Sinclair* [1918] 1 KB 180 (CA).

[147] *Ahmad Yarkhan* (n 31); *Chhanga Lal v Municipal Corporation of Delhi* AIR 2008 Delhi 146, [21]; *Shree Pushkar Chemicals & Fertilizers Ltd* (n 110). In England, *Adam v Newbigging* (n 137).

[148] *Sibley v Grosvenor* (1916) 21 CLR 469.

[149] *Indra Nath Banerjee* (n 70) 89.

[150] *Gaurav Monga v Premier Inn India Pvt Ltd* (Delhi HC, 6 January 2017) [23]; *Daiichi Sankyo Company Limited* (n 144).

[151] *Premchand* (n 55); *Ahmad Yarkhan* (n 31); *Goldrei* (n 146). This seems to be a better explanation for the statement in *Sorabshah Pestonji v Secretary of State for India* (1927) 29 BOMLR 1535 (Bom HC) that the only remedy in that case lay in section 19.

statutory provisions may be exhaustive of their subject matter, but section 19 does not purport to regulate all of the remedial consequences of fraud and the other grounds. It would be most surprising if it did, because it would mean that the Indian courts have been systematically wrong to award damages in deceit where the context was pre-contractual.[152]

[152] For example *Trojan & Co Ltd v RM NN Nagappa Chettiar* AIR 1953 SC 235; *S Chatterjee v KL (Dr) Bhave* AIR 1960 MP 323.

PART III
SPECIAL CONTRACTS

20

Indemnity and Guarantee

Wayne Courtney

I. Introduction

The Indian Contract Act 1872 (hereafter 'the Contract Act') contains two provisions (sections 124 and 125) defining the nature of a contract of indemnity and the rights of the promisee under it. Immediately following this are another twenty-two provisions (sections 126–47) on guarantees. A full treatment of the law in this area is impossible to achieve in a single chapter.[1] The object is to discuss some of the more controversial aspects of the Contract Act and to provide comparative insights by reference to other common law systems. I will also make some observations about the reforms proposed by the Law Commission of India in its *Thirteenth Report*.[2]

II. Indemnities

1. Nature of indemnities

The range of indemnities contemplated by section 124 is much narrower than the English common law conception of indemnity. When read in conjunction with section 125, which addresses actions against the indemnified party, it seems that the principal concern was with promises to indemnify against claims by, or liabilities to, third parties. This is, perhaps, not surprising in light of the historical development of indemnity contracts. Even in the late nineteenth century, most of the reported English cases concerned indemnities in this general form or, more specifically, indemnities against the promisor's breach of contract where such breach was likely to lead to a claim by a third party against the promisee.

The Contract Act's choice of activating events is rather puzzling. Focusing on the activity of natural or juristic persons excludes losses caused by natural events, as are often the subject of contracts of indemnity insurance. Limiting the relevant actor to the

[1] N Bhadbhade (ed), *Pollock & Mulla: The Indian Contract Act 1872* (14th updated edn, LexisNexis Butterworth Wadhwa 2013) devotes 145 pages to these topics. A typical English text would be upwards of 800 pages.

[2] Law Commission of India, *Thirteenth Report on the Contract Act 1872* (1958) <https://cdnbbsr.s3waas.gov.in/s3ca0daec69b5adc880fb464895726dbdf/uploads/2022/08/2022080532.pdf> accessed 7 June 2023 (*Thirteenth Report*).

Wayne Courtney, *Indemnity and Guarantee* In: *Foundations of Indian Contract Law*. Edited by: KV Krishnaprasad, Niranjan Venkatesan, Shivprasad Swaminathan, and Umakanth Varottil, Oxford University Press. © Oxford University Press 2024.
DOI: 10.1093/9780191997211.003.0020

promisor or third party is conceptually untidy. It is entirely possible, although perhaps not very common outside insurance, for *A* to indemnify *B* against losses caused by *B*'s own conduct. It is also possible for an indemnity from *A* to *B* to apply to losses attributable to concurrent causes, being acts or omissions of *A*, *B*, and others. The definition would lead to some difficult questions of characterisation. Fortunately, by accepting that the statute is not exhaustive, these definitional problems seem not to have posed any serious obstacles to the development of Indian law.

Another limitation that has been suggested is that section 124 of the Contract Act covers only express promises of indemnity. Whether or not that interpretative gloss is correct,[3] implied indemnities have readily been recognised under Indian law.[4] In that respect, the Law Commission's recommendation[5] to insert the words 'expressly or impliedly' after 'promises' in section 124 is sensible and consistent with the case law. Further, section 145 refers to an implied promise by a principal debtor to indemnify the surety.[6]

2. Liabilities, Costs, and Compromises

Section 125 addresses two related points. Subsection (1) establishes the conclusiveness of the liability, subject to the provisos mentioned. In a general sense this is a matter of *proof* of actual or potential loss within the scope of the indemnity. Subsection (2) deals more directly with a matter of *scope*, namely that costs incurred in proceedings should be recoverable, again subject to the provisos mentioned.[7] Subsection (3) could be read as addressing either of these matters; that is, subject to the provisos, the compromise is treated as conclusive proof of an actual liability; or the scope of the indemnity is extended to cover a compromise of an alleged liability. The opening words of section 125 and internal cross-reference in section 125(3) to 'any such suit' favour the former interpretation.[8] Strictly, section 125(3) applies only when a suit has been brought and not where a compromise is made beforehand. It has been accepted, however, that the indemnifier may still be bound in the latter situation.[9]

Indian courts, drawing upon English decisions, have endorsed a further refinement that is not explicit in section 125(3): if the indemnified party gives due notice of the claim or action and the indemnifier fails to intervene, then the indemnifier is precluded from asserting that the compromise was imprudent.[10] Some of the older English

[3] ibid [103]. The Law Commission merely indicated that the amendment to the Act should 'provide clearly' that a promise of indemnity could be implied.

[4] *Izzat-un-nisa Begam v Partab Singh* (1909) 31 All 583 (PC); *Tilak Ram v Surat Singh* AIR 1938 All 297; *Lala Shanti Swarup v Munshi Singh* [1967] 2 SCR 312. See also *Secretary of State v Bank of India Ltd* [1938] 2 All ER 797 (PC).

[5] *Thirteenth Report* (n 2) 84.

[6] See text to n 107 below.

[7] Cf *Bhawani Prasad v Gopal Singh* (1888) 10 All 531; *Raja Venkatarangayya Appa Rao v Raja Varaprasada Rao Naidu* (1920) 43 Mad 898.

[8] See also *Alla Venkataramanna v Palacherla Manqamma* AIR 1944 Mad 457, (1944) Mad 867.

[9] *Kali Charan v Durga Kunwar* (1913) 35 All 168.

[10] ibid; *Alla Venkataramanna* (n 8).

authorities support this proposition, though recent authorities are more circumspect.[11] Also, English law has so far concentrated upon indemnities against liability to third parties, where the indemnified party is the debtor/defendant vis-à-vis the third party. It remains unsettled whether the same principle would apply to indemnities in respect of third-party defaults, where the indemnified party is the creditor/plaintiff vis-à-vis the third party. Section 125 does not differentiate between situations.[12]

3. Enforcement of Indemnities

i. The two modes of enforcement

The Contract Act came into effect shortly before the administration of law and equity was unified in England. At that time, an indemnified party's action to enforce the indemnity under English law depended, in part, upon the nature of the loss.[13] The promise to indemnify was usually construed to be a promise to keep the indemnified party harmless against loss by the specified event. Enforcement at common law was generally by way of a claim for damages for breach of contract. The contract would only be broken when the indemnified party actually sustained loss; at that point, by definition, the indemnifier had not kept the indemnified party harmless against loss. The damages award corresponded to the amount of actual loss. The remedies provided by the common law courts were, therefore, inefficacious to protect the indemnified party before loss occurred. Where the loss was merely anticipated, the indemnified party had to seek relief in a court of equity. Intervention in equity was said to rest upon the power of a court of equity to compel specific performance of a contract of indemnity. It would, however, be more accurate to say that equity operated by specifically enforcing a particular term of a contract—the promise to indemnify—rather than by way of specific performance of the whole contract.[14]

ii. When does loss occur?

Identifying the point at which a potential loss crystallises into an actual loss can be critical. Before fusion, it could determine the appropriate forum—a court of law or equity—for action. It also had, and still has, consequences for the application of limitations statutes.[15] There developed a default rule on damnification that applies to indemnities against claims by, or liabilities to, third parties.[16] In general, a mere claim, demand, or action against, or liability of, the indemnified party is not an actual loss.

[11] See eg *Ben Shipping Co (Pte) Ltd v An Bord Bainne (The C Joyce)* [1986] 2 All ER 177.

[12] *Ramaswami Sastri v Kali Raghava Iyengar* (1917) 43 IC 124; *Ramchandra Loyalka v Shapurji Bhownagree* AIR 1940 Bom 315, (1940) 42 Bom 550.

[13] A fuller account is given in W Courtney, *Contractual Indemnities* (Hart 2014) [1-18]–[1-23], [7-19]. See also *Osman Jamal and Sons Ltd v Gopal Purshottam* AIR 1929 Cal 208, (1928) 56 Cal 262; *Gajanan Moreshwar Parelkar v Moreshwar Madan Mantri* AIR 1942 Bom 302, (1942) 44 Bom 703; *Alla Venkataramanna* (n 8); *Chunibhai Patel v Natha Bhai Patel* AIR 1944 Pat 185, (1944) 22 Pat 655; *Abdul Hussain Shaikh Gulamali Jambawalla v Bombay Metal Syndicate* AIR 1972 Bom 252, (1972) 74 Bom 43.

[14] Cf the Specific Relief Act 1963, s 12.

[15] See eg *Lala Shanti Swarup* (n 4); *Abdul Hussain Shaikh Gulamali Jambawalla* (n 13).

[16] Courtney, *Contractual Indemnities* (n 13) [6-23]. Authorities include *Collinge v Heywood* (1839) 9 Ad & E 634, 112 ER 1352; *Re Richardson, ex p the Governors of St Thomas's Hospital* [1911] 2 KB 705 (CA); *McIntosh*

Actual loss crystallises when the indemnified party pays money to the third party in respect of the claim or liability or, perhaps, when the indemnified party's property is seized and sold in satisfaction of a liability. Thus, in practice, unless equitable relief is available, the indemnified party must pay first and recoup later.

Indian law has adopted a substantially similar default rule on damnification.[17] In its *Thirteenth Report*, the Law Commission was concerned by the failure of the Contract Act to address the matter of enforcement of the indemnity before loss. That concern seems to have been prompted by differences of opinion among Indian courts as to whether such enforcement was possible.[18] The Law Commission accepted (correctly[19]) that it was, and recommended the addition of a new section 125A.[20] The section is directed at two distinct matters. The first is a matter of timing: at what point is the indemnified party able to enforce the indemnity? This is addressed partly in subsection (1) ('where a liability has arisen') and in subsection (2) and the explanatory comment. The second matter concerns the form of relief.

iii. Forms of relief

The two types of order mentioned in section 125A—to set apart a fund and to discharge the indemnified party's liability—are both recognised forms of *quia timet* relief,[21] though the former appears relatively rarely nowadays.[22] They perform different functions. The order to establish a fund is, in general, calculated to safeguard the indemnified party's position vis-à-vis the indemnifier. In itself, it only provides interim protection. The fund must later be applied to discharge the indemnified party's liabilities. In contrast, an order to discharge the indemnified party's liability is a final and effective order for indemnification. When executed, the order effects proper performance of the promise to indemnify in respect of the relevant liability.

An order to discharge a liability is just one form of order for indemnification; there are others. Relief is discretionary, and the particular form chosen in any case depends upon the circumstances. The most general kind of order directs the indemnifier to procure the release or discharge of the indemnified party from the liability. The method is left to the indemnifier's discretion. Section 125A(1) appears to be similar but slightly

v Dalwood (No 4) (1930) 30 SR (NSW) 415 (FC); *Firma C-Trade SA v Newcastle Protection and Indemnity Association (The Fanti) (No 2)* [1991] 2 AC 1 (HL).

[17] See eg *Bhavani Alias Rukmani Amma v Anantha Kamthi* (1916) 31 Mad 556, 35 IC 789; *Kalavakolanu Seetamma v Poduri Narayanamurthi* (1920) 43 Mad 470; *Ranganath v Pachusao* AIR 1935 Nag 147; *Tilak Ram* (n 4); *Chunibhai Patel* (n 13); *Alla Venkataramanna* (n 8); *Lala Shanti Swarup* (n 4). See generally *Gajanan Moreshwar Parelkar* (n 13).

[18] *Thirteenth Report* (n 2) 50–51. The relevant authorities are noted in Bhadbhade (n 1) 1343.

[19] *Osman Jamal and Sons Ltd* (n 13) and *Gajanan Moreshwar Parelkar* (n 13) contain useful discussions of the English authorities.

[20] *Thirteenth Report* (n 2) 84.

[21] *Re Richardson, ex p the Governors of St Thomas's Hospital* (n 16); *Firma C-Trade SA* (n 16); *Osman Jamal and Sons Ltd* (n 13); *Gajanan Moreshwar Parelkar* (n 13); *New India Assurance Co Ltd v State Trading Corp of India* AIR 2007 Guj 517; cf *Mohideen Batcha Sahib v Sheik Dawood Sahib* AIR 1926 Mad 1035, (1926) 51 Mad 203 (orders 7 and 8).

[22] Cf *Rowland v Gulfpac Ltd* [1999] 1 Lloyd's Rep Bank 86; *Papamichael v National Westminster Bank plc* [2002] 1 Lloyd's Rep 332.

narrower, as it refers only to discharge and not release. More particularly, the indemnifier may be directed to pay a specific sum to the third party so as to discharge the indemnified party from the liability. In some circumstances, the indemnified party may even be entitled to call for payment in advance to itself so that it can then use the funds to pay the third party. The exact scope of this last form of order is unsettled.[23] It is clear that such an order will not be made when the indemnifier is 'interested' in the application of the funds it pays by way of indemnity.[24] A typical instance is where the indemnifier is also liable to the third party such that it would have to pay again if the indemnified party failed to discharge the liability.[25]

iv. Timing

The timing of relief depends upon the nature of the relief sought. The position for final orders for indemnification is clearest. The circumstantial factors identified in s 125A(1) and (2) are consistent with the position already reached by Indian courts.[26] To obtain an order for indemnification, there must be a clear, definite liability that is presently accrued. It is not necessary that the liability be established by judgment, nor that proceedings be commenced against the indemnified party. More intriguing is the explanatory comment to s 125A, which *negates* a precondition that the liability can 'effectively be enforced against him'. In *Khetarpal Amarnath v Madhukar Pictures*,[27] Gajendragadkar J accepted that the right to enforce the indemnity arose once the indemnified party's liability became absolute but later added that the indemnified party had to satisfy the court of 'the existence of a clear *enforceable* claim against him'.

III. Guarantees

1. Nature and Formation

Section 126 defines a guarantee as a contract to 'perform the promise, or discharge the liability, of a third person in case of his default'. The surety's liability is, subject to the terms of the guarantee, co-extensive with the debtor's (section 128). This reflects the common law's general understanding of a guarantee as being a secondary obligation. A refinement introduced by the common law distinguishes between two types of guarantee obligation: one being to ensure that the principal debtor performs, the other being to perform if the debtor does not.[28] This distinction does not usually

[23] See Courtney, *Contractual Indemnities* (n 13) [7-43]–[7-50].

[24] *Re Law Guarantee Trust and Accident Society Ltd* [1914] 2 Ch 617 (CA); *British Union and National Insurance Co v Rawson* [1916] 2 Ch 476 (CA); *Osman Jamal and Sons Ltd* (n 13); *Khetarpal Amarnath v Madhukar Pictures* AIR 1956 Bom 106.

[25] *Rankin v Palmer* (1912) 16 CLR 285; *Osman Jamal and Sons Ltd* (n 13).

[26] *Gajanan Moreshwar* (n 13); *Khetarpal Amarnath* (n 24).

[27] *Khetarpal Amarnath* (n 24) (emphasis added).

[28] *Moschi v Lep Air Services Ltd* [1973] AC 331 (HL) 344–45; *Sunbird Plaza Pty Ltd v Maloney* (1988) 166 CLR 245; *McGuinness v Norwich and Peterborough Building Society* [2011] EWCA Civ 1286, [2012] 2 All ER (Comm) 265.

alter the extent of the surety's liability – which corresponds to the debtor's – but it can affect the nature of the creditor's claim and, in some instances, the calculation of liability in respect of obligations that were to fall due after the principal contract has been terminated. This distinction is noted in *Pollock and Mulla*[29] but it does not seem to have gained widespread acceptance in Indian law.

i. Arrangements between co-debtors

Section 132 of the Contract Act deviates from the common law. It provides that where two parties are together liable to the creditor, then the creditor is not affected by any arrangement between the two parties as to responsibility for that liability, even if the creditor is aware of it. According to normal privity rules, this must be right. But it was established in English law by the time of the Contract Act that the creditor could be affected by notice of such an arrangement between two principal debtors and that notice might come after entry into the principal transaction.[30] The creditor was obliged to treat the secondary debtor as if it were a surety, at least for the purposes of some of the standard defences, for example, discharge by giving time to the debtor. The reason for departing from the common law position is, perhaps, that the policy underpinning it is questionable.[31] The creditor might well object that its rights ought not to be unilaterally diminished by notice of events after contract.

ii. Past consideration

There is a sharp conflict of opinion over whether 'past' consideration can sustain a guarantee in Indian law. The question typically arises in a case where the surety makes an oral promise, or signs a guarantee, after the creditor has already supplied the goods, or advanced the money, to the principal debtor. Some decisions on section 127 have read the words 'anything done or any promise made' literally to include past consideration.[32] Others have adhered to the past consideration rule.[33] As a matter of authority, the question must await resolution. At the level of principle, a few points can be made.

Illustration (c) in section 127, in which the guarantee is 'void', is tautological so far as it states that the surety makes the promise 'without consideration'. The clear implication is that the consideration fails here because it was past: the creditor sold and delivered the goods before the surety's promise. So, if past consideration is always sufficient, Illustration (c) must simply have misstated the intention behind section 127. This is possible, but not a conclusion to be lightly reached.[34]

[29] Bhadbhade (n 1) 1355.

[30] *Oakeley v Pasheller* (1836) 10 Bli NS 548, 6 ER 202. See also *Overend, Gurney & Co v Oriental Financial Corp* (1874) LR 7 HL 348; *Rouse v Bradford Banking Co* [1894] AC 586 (HL); W Courtney, *The Modern Contract of Guarantee* (4th edn, Sweet & Maxwell 2020) [1-032].

[31] Note the scepticism in *Swire v Redman* (1876) 1 QBD 536, 543–545.

[32] Bhadbhade (n 1) 1380; *Ghulam Husain Khan v Faiyaz Ali Khan* AIR 1940 Oudh 346; *Y Venkatachalapathi Reddy v Bank of India* 2002 4 ALD 173, 2002 6 ALD 412; *M/S Poysha Oxygen Pvt Ltd v Sh Ashwini Suri* 2009 SCC OnLine Del 2216, [16], [21].

[33] See eg *Pestonji Meekji Mody v Meherbai* AIR 1928 Bom 53; *Paulo Varghese v Ittipe Abraham* AIR 1952 Tr & Coch 202; *Ram Narain v Hari Singh* AIR 1964 Raj 76; *Bank of Credit and Commerce v VK Abdul Rahiman* (1998) 92 Comp Cas 739 (Ker).

[34] Cf *Mahomed Syedol Ariffin v Yeoh Ooi Gark* AIR 1916 PC 242.

The use of the past tense in section 127 is itself not conclusive. The words 'anything done'[35] provide a stronger pointer in favour of past consideration. However, it is also possible to read those words as conforming to conventional principles, under which a past act can serve as valid executed consideration. At common law, a critical question would be whether there was an anterior request by the surety for the creditor to enter the principal transaction with, or to make advances or supplies to, the principal debtor. The creditor's act in response to that request can then be related to the subsequent promise of guarantee.[36] There is good consideration.

It is possible to read section 127 in this way as being entirely consistent with the common law concept of consideration. Where an explicit request by the surety is lacking, courts elsewhere in the Commonwealth have found other ways around the past consideration rule. Sometimes, the principal contract and guarantee are treated as a single, composite transaction to be effected among the parties. Provided that the agreements are executed reasonably close in time, the order of execution is immaterial.[37] Since the surety will usually be aware of, or involved in, negotiations preceding execution of the principal contract and guarantee, this conclusion could also be justified on the basis of an implied request by the surety.

Kali Charan v Abdul Rahman[38] is sometimes cited by Indian courts as authority for the proposition that past consideration is sufficient for a guarantee. The Privy Council curtly dismissed an argument that there was no consideration for a guarantee given about a month-and-a-half after the principal agreement had been executed. The reasoning is, on the whole, unsatisfying. It is not clear to what extent (if at all) the sureties were aware of, or involved with, the principal agreement. Accordingly, the case may not be explicable on the basis of a prior implied request. What is clear is that the principal agreement obliged the principal debtor to furnish 'sufficient security' for performance of the terms of the agreement. The result could then be justified on a conventional analysis: the creditor provided consideration to the sureties by accepting the proffered guarantee in discharge of the debtor's obligations to furnish security under the principal agreement.

A contrary perspective looks to harmonise section 127 with the exceptions to the consideration rule under section 25. Section 25(2) goes beyond the common law.[39] It accepts as valid consideration a promise 'to compensate' a person who 'has already voluntarily done something for the promisor'. It is debatable whether a promise of guarantee would qualify as a promise 'to compensate'. And, in some cases at least, it is hard to see how the creditor's act would be 'for' the surety rather than 'for' the debtor. So, although this section may allow past consideration, it is difficult to apply directly to guarantees. It might then be argued that section 127 is really just an extrapolation of

[35] The 1868 draft Act referred to 'anything which is done or agreed to be done'.
[36] The 1868 draft Act included the qualifier 'which is an inducement to the surety to give the guarantee'.
[37] See Courtney, *Modern Contract of Guarantee* (n 30) [2-065].
[38] AIR 1918 PC 226.
[39] *Sindha Shri Ganpat Singh v Abraham* (1896) 20 Bom 755; *Gobind Ram v Piran Ditta* (1935) 16 Lah 546; Bhadbhade (n 1) 606–608.

section 25(2) to a three-party situation: the reference to benefit to the principal debtor, rather than promisor (under section 25(2)) is necessary to address the limitation just mentioned.

iii. Parties to the guarantee

It has been suggested that there must be a contract to which the surety, principal debtor, and creditor are all 'privy';[40] or that the principal debtor must, 'by implication', be a party to the guarantee.[41] Yet, it has also been said that a simultaneous tripartite contract is not necessary.[42] The latter view is right in principle. Indeed, it is more common to find two distinct agreements, one between principal debtor and creditor and the other between creditor and surety. The references to three parties or privity in the textbooks and cases are, in substance, directed at a triangular contractual relationship among the parties: between the creditor and debtor, the creditor and surety, and the debtor and surety.

It is the request (express or implied[43]) by the debtor to the surety to undertake the guarantee that creates a promise of indemnity between them (by virtue of section 125) and so completes the triangle.[44] There is some authority to the effect that an undertaking, not given at the debtor's request, must be an indemnity rather than a guarantee.[45] The rationale seems to be that if the final side of the triangle is not completed, the arrangement between creditor and surety cannot be a guarantee. This is misconceived. The distinction between an indemnity and a guarantee lies in the nature of promise made by the promisor (surety) to the promisee (creditor). Whether the promise was given at the request of a third party can have little, if any, bearing on that point. This is reinforced by the fact that other jurisdictions also accept the converse proposition: if an indemnity is given upon request, the requesting party may be taken to have impliedly promised to indemnify the indemnifier against the liability so assumed.[46] There is no obstacle to finding, in the right circumstances, a similar indemnity from debtor to indemnifier under section 124 of the Contract Act.[47]

The objection about requests may have a deeper foundation, namely that a surety who acts without a request should not be entitled to an indemnity on any basis after it pays the creditor. Within the scheme of the Contract Act, there are several considerations. Section 145 could be construed as only applying to guarantees given upon request. This avoids the contortions of reclassifying as an indemnity what is really a guarantee.[48] Some support for this view might be drawn from Illustration (b) to the

[40] Bhadbhade (n 1) 1355.
[41] *Suresh Narain Sinha v Akhauri Balbhadra Prasad* AIR 1957 Pat 256; *Nagpur Nagarik Sahakari Bank Ltd v Union of India* AIR 1981 AP 153; *M/S Chand Chits & Finance Ltd v M/S Super Advertisers* AIR 1992 Del 85.
[42] *Prasanjit Mahtha v United Commercial Bank Ltd* AIR 1979 Pat 151.
[43] *Raja Jagannath Bakhsh Singh v Chandra Bhukhan Singh* (1936) 12 ILR 484.
[44] *Ramchandra Loyalka* (n 12).
[45] *Periyamianna Marakkayar & Sons v Banians & Co* AIR 1926 Mad 544; *Ramchandra Loyalka* (n 12); *Brahmayya & Co v K Srinivasan Thangirayar* AIR 1959 Mad 122; *Union Bank of India v Avinash Bhonsle* (1991) 93 Bom LR 282.
[46] See Courtney, *Modern Contract of Guarantee* (n 30) [12-027]–[12-029].
[47] *Thirteenth Report* (n 2) [103].
[48] See eg *Muthu Raman Chetty v Chinna Vellayan Chetty* AIR 1917 Mad 83.

section. Another, technical, argument may be that a principal debtor who never made a request is not a 'party' to the guarantee, and a surety cannot enforce an implied promise in its favour against a non-party. The scope of section 69 of the Contract Act must also be taken into account. The positions set up by sections 69 and 145 broadly correspond to the distinction between the debtor's restitutionary and contractual liability to the guarantor in English common law. It would be surprising if an officious surety were able to recover under section 145 but not under section 69. The idea that an officious surety should be denied restitution has some support in England,[49] though there are also opposing views.[50]

2. Formalities

Section 126 eschews any requirement of writing. The requirement remains in the United Kingdom[51] and in various other common law jurisdictions, where it produces a steady stream of disputes over whether a particular undertaking is a guarantee or indemnity (the latter falling outside the statute). This is an arid debate[52] and, as a matter of principle, it is difficult to see why a writing requirement should apply to one and not the other.[53]

3. Conditions Precedent

Section 144 conforms to the common law.[54] It is merely a specific application of the more general point that parties can create a condition precedent to the formation of contract or to the performance of one or more obligations in a contract. The more interesting question is when such a condition precedent will be inferred. This is a matter of construction, not law. In the United Kingdom, for example, a statement that a guarantee is 'joint' or 'joint and several'[55] is presumed to create a contractual condition that all designated sureties join the guarantee.[56]

Section 144 can be contrasted with section 138, which prevents the *release* of one co-surety from discharging the others. The two sections are not inconsistent. As Mance LJ pointed out in *Capital Bank Cashflow Finance Ltd v Southall*,[57] the surety may 'be willing to take a chance' on a subsequent deed of release being given but not the risk

[49] *Owen v Tate* [1976] 1 QB 402 (CA).
[50] See P Birks and J Beatson, 'Unrequested Payment of Another's Debt' (1976) 92 Law Quarterly Review 188; R Goff and G Jones, *The Law of Restitution* (7th edn, Sweet & Maxwell 2007) [15-011] and R Goff and G Jones, *Goff and Jones: The Law of Unjust Enrichment* (9th edn, Sweet & Maxwell 2016) [20-02].
[51] Statute of Frauds 1677, s 4.
[52] But see *Actionstrength Ltd v International Glass Engineering In.Gl.En SpA* [2003] UKHL 17, [2003] 2 AC 541.
[53] In British Columbia, for example, the writing requirement applies to both: Law and Equity Act 1996, s 59(6).
[54] See Courtney, *Modern Contract of Guarantee* (n 30) [3-087]–[3-096].
[55] Sections 43 and 44 of the Contract Act cut through many of the complications of joint liability at common law.
[56] See eg *Harvey v Dunbar Assets plc* [2013] EWCA Civ 952, [2013] BPIR 722, [23]–[25].
[57] [2004] EWCA Civ 817, [2004] 2 All ER (Comm) 675, [26].

of a co-surety failing to execute the guarantee in the first place. So, at common law, an anti-release clause to the same effect as section 138 under the Contract Act is generally not regarded as establishing a precondition that all intended sureties must sign.[58]

4. Vitiating Factors

The Contract Act contains provisions about misrepresentation (section 142) and non-disclosure (section 143) in relation to guarantees. Other vitiating factors, such as mistake, duress, and undue influence, are left to general provisions.[59] It is somewhat surprising that section 142 was considered necessary.[60] Perhaps it was intended to clarify the role of third parties or, by implication, to rule out rescission of the guarantee for misrepresentation by the debtor alone. Curiously, section 142 states that the guarantee is 'invalid', whereas the general misrepresentation provision (section 19) would render it voidable at the surety's option.[61]

i. Third parties

A guarantee is vitiated by a material misrepresentation made by the creditor or by someone else 'with his knowledge and assent'.[62] Misrepresentation by others—particularly by the principal debtor—is, in practice, often a greater concern than misrepresentation directly by the creditor. Attributing such misrepresentations to the creditor has been a source of considerable difficulty in other common law jurisdictions. One approach is to treat the representor (eg the principal debtor) as agent of the creditor for the purposes of obtaining the guarantee; the actions and knowledge of the agent are attributed to the creditor as principal.[63] But this is contrived and artificial, especially where one family member guarantees the debts of another.

English law[64] accordingly developed a more sophisticated approach, which is applied to undue influence and misrepresentation involving third parties.[65] Transactions with certain features cause the creditor to be 'put on inquiry'. A guarantee crosses this threshold if the relationship between surety and debtor is 'non-commercial', and the surety does not appear to derive any direct benefit from giving the guarantee. The creditor must then take certain steps to enable the surety to obtain advice before executing the guarantee. A creditor who fails to do so runs the risk of misrepresentation or undue influence between debtor and surety: the guarantee will be vitiated, even if the creditor

[58] Courtney, *Modern Contract of Guarantee* (n 30) [3-095].

[59] See the Contract Act, ss 14–21.

[60] Cf ibid ss 18 and 19.

[61] S Elliott KC and D Behl in Chapter 19 of this volume cogently argue that 'invalid' should be read as a synonym for 'voidable'.

[62] See also *Thirteenth Report* (n 2) [113].

[63] Courtney, *Modern Contract of Guarantee* (n 30) [4-197]. A similar route is available under the Contract Act, ss 229, 238.

[64] Australian law adopted a different solution: *Garcia v National Australia Bank Ltd* (1998) 194 CLR 395.

[65] *Royal Bank of Scotland plc v Etridge (No 2)* [2001] UKHL 44, [2002] 2 AC 773 is now the leading decision, superseding *Barclays Bank plc v O'Brien* [1994] 1 AC 180 (HL).

was unaware of the circumstances. This development was really a piece of judicial legislation to respond to an immediate and recurrent problem. It remains to be seen whether it will be regarded as suitable for local conditions and applied by Indian courts.[66]

ii. Non-disclosure

If section 143 applied to all 'material circumstances', the duty of disclosure would resemble that applied to insurance at common law. However, the section has been interpreted in light of the prevailing case law at the time of the Contract Act, which points to a narrower rule unique to guarantees. 'Material' circumstances are matters that would 'not naturally be expected to have taken place between the parties'.[67] An account of examples falling on either side of the line can be found in standard textbooks.[68] The section also sets out a causative element, namely that the guarantee be obtained *by means of* keeping silence.[69]

There are two matters of further interest. First, the duty of disclosure in some respects appears to be higher for fidelity guarantees than for commercial guarantees. The employer must disclose to the surety any prior known (or suspected) dishonesty of the employee in service.[70] Illustration (a) in section 143 is to the point. (If the 'failure to account' were due to carelessness or misfortune rather than dishonesty, the duty would be very stringent indeed.[71]) The duty is a continuing one, applying to misconduct discovered by the employer after the guarantee.[72] It is not entirely clear how this differential treatment is to be explained juristically. It may be that the same basic standard of disclosure applies in all cases but that supplementary elements can be derived from context.[73] So, by requesting a fidelity guarantee, the employer impliedly makes a further representation to the surety that the employee is believed to be honest. The ongoing duty of disclosure might be recast as a failure to mitigate by the employer or as an impairment of the surety's eventual remedy against the debtor under section 139.

Second, section 143 does not describe the state of mind of the creditor. In *Balkrishna VN Kirtikar v Bank of Bengal*,[74] it was held that the section only applies to intentional concealment as opposed to mere non-disclosure. This view has been endorsed by the Law Commission.[75] *Balkrishna* was a bold decision for its time. The authorities were

[66] See S Elliott KC and D Behl, Chapter 19 of this volume, suggesting that the language of s 142 itself may prevent adoption of this approach.

[67] *Hamilton v Watson* (1845) 12 Cl & Fin 109, 8 ER 1339. See also *Secretary of State for India v Nilamekam Pillai* (1883) 6 Mad 406; *Imperial Bank of India v VP Avanasi Chettiar* (1930) 59 MLJ 513.

[68] See Bhadbhade (n 1) 1466–70; Courtney, *Modern Contract of Guarantee* (n 30) [4-007]–[4-010], [4-019]–[4-020].

[69] *Nilamekam Pillai* (n 67).

[70] *Co-operative Commission Shop Ltd Chak Jhumra v Udham Singh* AIR 1944 Lah 424; *Radha Kanta Pal v United Bank of India Ltd* AIR 1955 Cal 217.

[71] In *Lee v Jones* (1864) 17 CBNS 482, 144 ER 194, which appears to be the basis for Illustration (a), the employers knew that the employee was substantially in arrears in accounting but did not know that he had been dishonest.

[72] *Phillips v Foxall* (1872) LR 7 QB 666; *Radha Kanta Pal* (n 70).

[73] *North Shore Ventures Ltd v Anstead Holdings Inc* [2011] EWCA Civ 230, [2012] Ch 31, [24], [29]–[30].

[74] *Balkrishna VN Kirtikar v Bank of Bengal* (1891) 15 Bom 585. See also *Imperial Bank of India* (n 67).

[75] *Thirteenth Report* (n 2) [114] (recommending substitution of 'by wilful silence' for 'by means of keeping silence'). See also Bhadbhade (n 1) 1466.

not coherent, and the Court, with little discussion, preferred dicta in the Exchequer Chamber[76] over the contrary ratio of a prior House of Lords decision.[77] Other Indian authority had been more cautious.[78] *Lee v Jones*,[79] which seems to be the basis for Illustration (a), is inconclusive. The 1868 draft of the Contract Act used the word 'concealment' rather than 'keeping silence', but it is hard to know whether this is significant. Whatever its relevance in the nineteenth century, fraud seems to play little or no part in the modern English law non-disclosure rule: the question is whether the creditor, knowing of the material factor, did or did not disclose it.[80]

5. Discharge by Notice or Death

Sections 130 and 131 apply to continuing guarantees as defined in section 129. The definition of a continuing guarantee in terms of a 'series of transactions' works well enough for a discrete sequence of principal contracts. It is more problematic when applied to a single principal contract under which a series of exchanges may occur. In one decision, the Privy Council held that a fidelity guarantee, in respect of the debtor's performance of duties as a cashier at the creditor bank, was not 'continuing'.[81] It is, then, questionable whether Illustration (a) to section 129 really is an instance of a continuing guarantee.[82]

The surety under a continuing guarantee will be discharged in respect of future transactions by a notice of revocation. Where the surety dies, by section 131, death alone discharges the surety in the future. The Contract Act here departs from the common law (which still requires notice[83]) and it is hard to see this as an improvement. A contract of guarantee is generally not a personal contract; performance does not depend upon the surety being alive. The creditor, however, faces the risk of transacting with the debtor without security in the event of an unreported death. It seems more practicable that the personal representative for the deceased surety's estate inform the creditor than that the creditor be forced to make regular enquiries about the surety's vitality.

[76] *North British Insurance Co Ltd v Lloyd* (1854) 10 Exch 523, 535; 156 ER 545, 550 (the primary ground for decision was that the fact was not material).

[77] *Railton v Matthews* (1844) 10 Cl & Fin 934, 8 ER 993. Bhadbhade (n 1) 1466 fn 79 asserts that this decision is the basis for Illustration (a); contra n 79. If Bhadbhade were right, surely this would weaken the authority of *Balkrishna*.

[78] *Nilamekam Pillai* (n 67).

[79] (1864) 17 CBNS 482, 144 ER 194.

[80] *London General Omnibus Co Ltd v Holloway* [1912] 2 KB 72 (CA) 78–79, 80–81; *North Shore Ventures Ltd* (n 73).

[81] *SN Sen v Bank of Bengal* AIR 1920 PC 35. See also *Myingyan Municipal Committee v Maung Po Nyun* AIR 1930 Rang 173.

[82] *Myingyan Municipal Committee* (n 81), 174 but contrast *Durga Priya Chowdhury v Durga Pada Roy* AIR 1928 Cal 204.

[83] *Brautbury v Morgan* (1862) 1 H & C 249, 158 ER 877; *Coulthart v Clementson* (1879) 5 QBD 42; *Re Whelan* [1897] 1 IR 575.

6. Altering or Releasing the Principal Obligations

i. Variance of principal contract

The rule is not easy to apply to a series of distinct contracts under a continuing guarantee.[84] This is because, among other reasons, there is no original principal contract specified by the guarantee to serve as a benchmark for 'variations'. It may, instead, be more fruitful to ask whether a given transaction is within the general scope of the guarantee. Thus, to modern eyes, it is doubtful that the variance rule should catch Illustration (d) in section 133. If the new supplies are regarded as being made on credit, accompanied by cash payments for debts outstanding from prior supplies, then it is not obvious that there has been a prejudicial variation of any *particular contract* nor that the new supplies are beyond the scope of the guarantee. An alternative characterisation of Illustration (d) might be that, in substance, the new supplies are really being made for cash, whereas the guarantee only covers supplies on credit. Then, the surety is not liable for those later transactions, either because (a) there is no underlying debt due, the buyer having paid in full, or (b) the new transactions fall outside the scope of the guarantee. The variance rule does not enter the picture.

Section 133 refers to 'any variance', but it has been accepted that the surety is not discharged if the creditor can show that the variation is insubstantial or can only be beneficial to the guarantor.[85] The English common law rule is the same in this respect.[86] The section provides for discharge only for 'transactions subsequent' to the variance. Illustrations (a)–(d) encompass separate dealings under a single ongoing contract and also separate contracts. The section does not easily fit a single contract with a single act of performance, as in Illustration (e).[87] 'Obligations' (not 'transactions') may come closer to what was intended in the section. The English common law rule diverges on this point: the guarantor is discharged from all outstanding obligations unless the varied part is divisible and can be severed from the rest of the contract.[88] This is not easily satisfied and so an unauthorised variation often leads to absolute discharge.

The creditor and surety can contract out of the protection provided by section 133,[89] and this is routine practice for sophisticated commercial transactions. The ambit of

[84] See Bhadbhade (n 1) 1413. Accordingly, English law distinguishes 'course-of-dealing' guarantees from 'specific-contract' guarantees; the variation rule has little or no application to the former: *National Merchant Buying Society Ltd v Bellamy* [2013] EWCA Civ 452, [2013] 2 All ER (Comm) 674, [30]–[33]; cf G Moss and D Marks, *Rowlatt on Principal and Surety* (6th edn, Sweet & Maxwell 2011) [4-77].

[85] *AKA Khan Ghuznavi v National Bank of India Ltd* (1916) 33 Ind Cas 34; *MS Anirudhan v Thomco's Bank* AIR 1963 SC 746; cf *Keshavlal Hari Lal Setalvad v Pratapsingh Moholalbhai Sheth* AIR 1932 Bom 168, (1932) 34 Bom LR 167. Illustrations on either side of the line are discussed in Bhadbhade (n 1) 1417–21.

[86] *Holme v Brunskill* (1878) 3 QBD 495 (CA).

[87] *Keshavlal Harilal Setalvad* (n 85) (section contemplates a continuing guarantee as in s 129). This point was left open on appeal: (1935) 37 Bom LR 315. Illustration (e) is loosely based on *Bonser v Cox* (1843) 6 Beav 100, 49 ER 767.

[88] See Courtney, *Modern Contract of Guarantee* (n 30) [7-007],]7-092]–[7-095]. This severance approach was applied to a 'giving time' situation in *DK Mohammad Ehiya Sahib v RMPM Valliappa Chettiar* AIR 1936 Mad 576, (1936) 163 IC 2246.

[89] This was controversial for some time, but the Supreme Court has now settled the issue for all of the surety's rights under Chapter VIII: *Basavaraj v Canara Bank* (2010) 12 SCC 458, approving *T Raju Setty v Bank of Baroda*

such anti-discharge clauses should be constrained by a process of construction. A clause will usually only preserve the surety's liability if the variation is within the 'purview' of the guarantee.[90] This is a somewhat amorphous concept, which involves considering the commercial scope of the guarantee and the nature and extent of the risk originally assumed by the surety.

ii. Giving time

A legally binding agreement[91] between creditor and debtor giving the debtor extra time to perform will discharge the surety under section 135. This rule is more stringent than the variance rule because there is no leeway allowed for unsubstantial or beneficial extensions of time.[92] The section parallels the common law, which continues to the present day. The rule is based on a concern about prejudice:[93] either the surety will be prevented from paying off the creditor and suing the debtor for indemnity at the original time or, if the surety is allowed to sue, then this will undermine the extension agreed between creditor and debtor. The rationale is unduly technical, and extensions of time are often given with the objective of benefiting the debtor. Nor is there any obvious reason for a more stringent rule to be applied to time as opposed to other kinds of variation in performance.

An agreement between the creditor and a third *party* to allow extra time to the debtor does not affect the surety: section 136. This is a corollary of the rationale given above. The creditor's rights against the debtor are not directly affected, though action by the creditor may constitute a breach of the contract with the third party. As the debtor was not a party to this arrangement, there is no prejudice in allowing the guarantor to pay at the original time and then sue the debtor.

iii. Discharge and release of the principal debtor and forbearance to sue

These matters are addressed in sections 134, 135, and 137. That release or discharge of the debtor has the same effect on the surety generally follows from the principle of co-extensiveness, recognised in section 128. If the underlying obligation goes, so too does the surety's obligation to the creditor. There are other, complementary justifications.[94] The release or discharge may occur by agreement between the parties (either as an express release or implied release by way of novation or substitution[95]) or by operation of statute or general law in the given circumstances. Some sensitivity is required to prevent the purpose of a guarantee from being undermined. It would be counterintuitive, for example, to conclude that the creditor's termination of a loan contract for breach

AIR 1992 Kant 108. See also *Sita Ram Gupta v Punjab National Bank* (2008) 5 SCC 711; *M/S HDFC v Gautam Kumar Nag* (2012) 5 SCC 604.

[90] *Trade Indemnity Co Ltd v Workington Harbour & Dock Board* [1937] AC 1 (HL); *CIMC Raffles Offshore (Singapore) Ltd v Schahin Holding SA* [2013] EWCA Civ 644, [2013] 2 All ER (Comm) 760.
[91] *Amrit Lal Goverdhan Lalan v State Bank of Travancore* AIR 1968 SC 1432.
[92] Cf *DK Mohammad Ehiya Sahib v RMPM Valliappa Chettiar* AIR 1936 Mad 576, (1936) 163 Ind Cas 2246.
[93] *Polak v Everett* (1876) 1 QBD 669, 673–74; *Rouse* (n 30) 593; *Amrit Lal Goverdhan Lalan* (n 91).
[94] *Mahant Singh v U Ba Yi* [1939] AC 601 (PC) 606–607; *Moschi* (n 28) 348.
[95] *Bishal Chand Jain v Chattur Sen* AIR 1967 All 506.

must discharge the surety from any liability to repay the sum advanced, on the basis that termination has the effect of discharging the principal debtor from future performance.[96] Likewise, the surety remains liable when the principal debtor is discharged in bankruptcy or liquidation without the debt being satisfied in full.[97]

Illustration (c) to section 134 is correct in outcome, though it is doubtful whether it reflects the concept of discharge in this section. It may simply be an example of the obligation guaranteed being dependent upon the creditor's prior performance[98] and so the obligation never arises. Illustration (b) might be the same, if the supply of water is a condition precedent to performance; more likely, it was intended to represent discharge for the creditor's repudiation or serious breach by interfering with the water supply and preventing performance.

Mere forbearance to sue the principal debtor does not release the surety (section 137). The reason is that forbearance does not discharge the underlying liability, even if the delay overruns the limitations period for the principal debt.[99] Furthermore, it is always open for the surety to claim an indemnity from the debtor after paying,[100] and for such an action, time would start to run only when the surety paid. A *promise* not to sue the principal debtor is different. Whatever may be the true position at common law,[101] section 135 makes clear that a promise not to sue will discharge the surety. In most cases (whether of release or of a promise not to sue), the real issue is whether the arrangement between creditor and debtor is absolute or whether the creditor has reserved its rights against the surety. In the latter situation, the surety is not discharged because the debtor has acknowledged the possibility that the creditor will proceed against the surety, who will, in turn, claim indemnity from the debtor.[102] Although a release with a reservation of rights sounds like a contradiction in terms, a pragmatic approach is taken to the notion of 'release'. The arrangement practically bars action between creditor and debtor without extinguishing the debtor's or surety's liability.

7. Releasing a Co-surety

Section 44 abrogates the common law rule that a release of a joint promisor discharges the others. The first part of section 138 confirms that section 44 applies to co-sureties and extends the abrogation to co-sureties whose liability is joint and several.[103] The

[96] Cf *Moschi* (n 28).
[97] *Maharashtra State Electricity Board v Official Liquidator* AIR 1982 SC 1497.
[98] Cf Illustration (c) in s 54.
[99] The time bar against the debtor is procedural, not substantive: *Mahant Singh* (n 94) 609–610; *Aziz Ahmad v Sher Ali* AIR 1956 All 8; *Bombay Dyeing & Manufacturing Co Ltd v State of Bombay* AIR 1958 SC 328. See also *Thirteenth Report* (n 2) [108].
[100] *Carter v White* (1883) 25 Ch D 666 (CA) 672; *Subramania Aiyar v Gopala Aiyar* (1910) 20 MLJ 633.
[101] See Courtney, *Modern Contract of Guarantee* (n 30) [6-059]–[6-065].
[102] *Murugappa Mudaliar v Munusami Mudali* AIR 1920 Mad 216; *Annadana Jadaya Goundar v Konammal* AIR 1933 Mad 309; *Mahant Singh* (n 94) 609; *United Bank of India v Modern Stores (India) Ltd* AIR 1988 Cal 18.
[103] Discharge of a surety who is only severally liable at common law does not affect the liability of the other co-sureties, except so far as their right of contribution is prejudiced: *Ward v Bank of New Zealand* (1883) 8 App Cas 755 (PC).

preservative effect of section 138 is, presumably, subject to contrary agreement between the parties. So, it should be possible to include a term in the guarantee making the continued liability of co-sureties a condition of the surety's liability to the creditor.

Release concerns a surety's liability to the creditor. A surety's rights against, or liabilities to, other co-sureties are a distinct matter. At common law, it is open to a surety to assert that its right to recoupment has been impaired, either by loss of a direct personal claim for contribution against the released co-surety or because it can no longer be subrogated to the creditor's rights against the released co-surety.[104] Whether there is, in fact, prejudice depends upon the circumstances. In theory, the same argument ought to be available under sections 139 and 141, which would allow discharge pro tanto.[105] However, the second part of section 138 states that the release does not affect the released co-surety's responsibility to other sureties. Thus, any contrary agreement aside, direct personal rights of contribution appear to be unaffected and so the surety will not be prejudiced on this basis. However, there might still be scope to argue for prejudice on the ground that the surety's subrogated rights have been lost.[106]

8. The Surety's Rights against Other Parties

i. Indemnity from the principal debtor

By section 145, a surety has the benefit of a promise of indemnity from the debtor in respect of whatever sum the surety has rightfully paid under the guarantee. This entitlement is only available when the surety provides the guarantee at the debtor's express or implied request.[107] The indemnity purports to have a contractual basis. It is, however, peculiar to describe the indemnity as being implied 'in' the contract of guarantee because the principal debtor is not necessarily a party to that contract. A neater solution is a separate, implied contract of indemnity between surety and debtor.[108] In any event, the purport of the section is clear enough.

The scope of the indemnity is set by the words 'rightfully paid'. As others have pointed out, the expression is inapt because there is nothing wrongful in the surety paying too much to the creditor;[109] it simply cannot recover the excess from the debtor. Closer to the mark, perhaps, is '*rightly* paid', that is, up to the amount of the surety's actual liability.[110] By the principle of co-extensiveness (section 128), this generally mirrors the actual liability of the debtor, and it seems to be the import of Illustration (c).[111] A further question is whether the debtor and surety must also have been *compellable* to pay.

[104] See generally *Re Wolmershausen* (1890) 62 LT 541, 545; *Ward v National Bank of New Zealand* (1883) 8 App Cas 755.

[105] See section III.1 below.

[106] For instance, because the creditor held securities from the co-surety or had the benefit of some priority or longer limitation period.

[107] See text to n 48 above.

[108] In English law, see *Re a Debtor* [1937] Ch 156 (CA). cf *Ramchandra Loyalka* (n 12).

[109] Bhadbhade (n 1) 1472.

[110] See *Thirteenth Report* (n 2) [116] ('sums paid were such as the creditor was *legally entitled to recover*').

[111] See also *Anand Singh v Collector of Bijnor* AIR 1932 All 610.

The English common law sometimes permits the surety to recover under a contractual indemnity even though the creditor's claim would have failed because the contract was unenforceable or the debtor or surety could have raised some other defence.[112] In Indian law, there has been some debate as to whether the surety is entitled to an indemnity if it pays a time-barred debt. It seems that the surety's payment is rightful if the debt is time-barred only against the debtor,[113] but it is not rightful if the debt is time-barred against both of them.[114]

The indemnity includes interest on the sum rightfully paid.[115] The Law Commission has stated that the section also covers special damage suffered by the surety in appropriate cases.[116] Illustrations (a) and (b) to section 145 show that the indemnity can extend to costs incurred in defending a claim brought by the creditor on the guarantee. The test, as revealed by the contrasting results in Illustration (a) and (b), is whether the surety had reasonable grounds for defending the action. It may also be relevant to consider whether the likely costs of defence are proportionate to the claim and whether the defence was only for the surety's benefit.[117] The illustrations to section 145 can be read as referring only to sums paid to the creditor for the creditor's costs and not the surety's own costs. However, so long as the defence was reasonable, these should be covered by the indemnity. Similarly, the illustrations only provide examples of an unsuccessful defence. Presumably, the surety would still be entitled to its own costs (so far as they are not recovered from the creditor) when it successfully defends the creditor's action.

At common law, the surety's right to indemnity from the debtor is enforced as and when the surety actually pays the creditor.[118] There is a distinct equitable jurisdiction to grant *quia timet* relief to the surety against the debtor before the surety pays. The jurisdiction has been long established in English law, and it is recognised also in Indian law.[119] Relief may take the form of a declaration of the surety's right to indemnity or an order that the debtor perform the principal obligation or pay the money to the creditor when due. The relief shares many of the features of specific relief to enforce contracts of indemnity against liability,[120] though it developed apart from contract and by reference to more general notions of suretyship.

[112] *Alexander v Vane* (1836) 1 M & W 511, 150 ER 537; *Re Chetwynd's Estate* [1938] Ch 13; *Argo Caribbean Group Ltd v Lewis* [1976] 2 Lloyd's Rep 289 (CA) 295–96.

[113] *Raghavendra Gururao Naik v Mahipat Krishna* (1925) 27 Bom LR 178, AIR 1926 Bom 244; *Anand Singh* (n 111). The Law Commission supported this result in its *Thirteenth Report* (n 2) [117] and recommended that a note be added to s 145.

[114] *Tarachand Lakhmichand Chuhan v Gopal Lachiramkumar* AIR 1959 MP 297; *Bihar State Co-operative Bank v Shri Nareshwar Prasad* 2004 (3) BLJR 1963. See also *Re Morris; Coneys v Morris* [1922] 1 IR 81 affd [1922] 1 IR 136.

[115] Bhadbhade (n 1) 1474. English authorities include *Re Fox, Walker & Co; ex p Bishop* (1880) 15 Ch D 400 (CA); *Re Watson* [1896] Ch 925, 937.

[116] *Thirteenth Report* (n 2) [118].

[117] See eg *Gillett v Rippon* (1829) Mood & M 406, 173 ER 1204; *Re International Contract Co; Hughes's Claim* (1872) LR 13 Eq 623.

[118] Courtney, *Modern Contract of Guarantee* (n 30) [12-015].

[119] *SK Mohideen Batcha Sahib* (n 21); *Sripatrao Sadashiv Upre v Shankarrao Sarnaik* (1930) 32 Bom LR 207, AIR 1930 Bom 331.

[120] See section II.3 above.

ii. Contribution from co-sureties

The provisions in the Contract Act for contribution resemble the common law in most respects. Section 146 acknowledges that the co-sureties may modify or exclude the default rules for contribution by a 'contract' to the contrary.[121] At common law, a common intention falling short of a legally enforceable contract is also sufficient.[122] Unlike section 43, section 146 does not expressly mention the well-known equitable principle that where some co-sureties are insolvent, the extra burden is shared among solvent co-sureties. The omission was not, presumably, intended to alter this principle.

A surety can enforce its right to contribution from another co-surety to obtain payment once the former has paid more than its fair share of the common debt. In English law, there is also a *quia timet* jurisdiction in equity. A surety can call upon co-sureties to contribute to an accrued liability even before the surety pays the creditor. The parameters of this relief are not as well defined as those for *quia timet* actions against principal debtors.[123] Nonetheless, since they rest upon similar considerations, this kind of relief should be recognised in Indian law as well.[124]

Section 147 prescribes the method for calculating the amount of contribution when the co-sureties have different limits of liability. There are several approaches to this problem in theory, and none is perfect. The Contract Act treats co-sureties as equally liable for each common 'layer' of liability, the co-sureties gradually dropping out as their limit of liability is reached. This method has much to commend it. It equalises sharing as far as possible, based on what the burden actually is rather than what it might have been. However, some might object that it does not do enough to respect the different degrees of risk taken on by the co-sureties, which are reflected in different limits of liability. The Contract Act differs from the common law, which seems to favour the 'maximum liability' method.[125] According to that method, the maximum limits of liability of each co-surety are used to prorate the actual liability, up to the cap for each co-surety. In the illustrations to section 147, *A* would be liable for 10,000/(10,000 + 20,000 + 40,000)—that is, 1/7—of the sum in each illustration, *B* for 2/7 of that sum, and *C* for 4/7 of that sum. This method has been criticised as giving undue weight to the limits of liability when the actual burden is far below them. In Illustration (a), for example, *A* gets off very lightly. Another technique used by the common law is known as the 'independent liability' method.[126] Each surety's liability is calculated as if there were no other co-sureties, and those figures are then taken as a ratio to share the amount actually due. So, in Illustration (a), the sum of 30,000 rupees is split among *A*, *B*, and *C* in the ratio 1:2:3. In Illustrations (b) and (c), the ratio becomes 1:2:4. The 'independent liability' method can be used where one or more of the sureties has unlimited liability.

[121] Cf the explanatory note to the Contract Act, s 43.

[122] Courtney, *Modern Contract of Guarantee* (n 30) [12-238].

[123] ibid [11-162]–[11-165].

[124] See eg *SK Mohideen Batcha Sahib* (n 21) (referring, with apparent approval, to *Wolmershausen v Gullick* [1893] 2 Ch 514).

[125] *Ellesmere Brewery Co v Cooper* [1896] 1 QB 75 (DC) 81–82 (though, on the facts, there was no right of contribution). See also *Ellis v Emmanuel* (1876) 1 Ex D 157, 162; *Steel v Dixon* (1881) 17 Ch D 825, 830.

[126] *Commercial Union Assurance Co Ltd v Hayden* [1977] QB 804 (CA).

iii. Subrogation

The surety's right of subrogation was established in the common law well before the Contract Act. Indeed, its deficiencies had already led English parliament to create a statutory right of subrogation.[127] The provisions in the Contract Act are briefer by comparison. Under section 140, the surety is invested with 'all the rights which the creditor had against the principal debtor' and by section 141, the surety is entitled to 'the benefit of every security which the creditor has against the principal debtor at the time when the contract of suretyship is entered into'. Unlike the English statute, the Contract Act does not refer to the creditor's rights against others. It is, however, accepted that the surety's right of subrogation encompasses such rights.[128] In enforcing the creditor's rights against co-sureties by subrogation, the surety is presumably restricted to recovering the amount of contribution actually due, not the whole debt. There is a difference between section 140 and section 141 in timing. Section 141 refers to securities held by the creditor at the time of entry into the guarantee. It has been suggested[129] that this was not a deliberate policy choice but rather it codified a view of English law that was probably already outmoded at the time of the Act.[130] In any event, this aspect of section 141 is practically subsumed by section 140, which entitles the surety to all the creditor's securities at the time of payment, whether or not they existed at the time of the guarantee.[131]

Timing is an issue in another respect, namely, the point at which the surety becomes 'invested' with the creditor's rights. Section 141 is silent on this, and section 140 refers to 'payment or performance of all that he is liable for'. In the simplest case, the surety guarantees the whole debt and pays the debt in full. In a second case, the surety guarantees the whole debt, but the liability under the guarantee is limited, and the surety pays up to the limit. Although the surety has, in a sense, paid 'all that he is liable for', the general rule is that the rights remain with the creditor until the guaranteed debt is paid in full from other sources. In a third case, the surety guarantees a distinct part of a larger debt and pays that portion in full. This situation has provoked disagreement among Indian courts. One solution is to give the surety an immediate, proportionate interest in the creditor's rights.[132] Another solution postpones the right of subrogation until the remainder of the debt is paid in full from other sources.[133] The latter solution is preferred by Pollock and Mulla and the Indian Law Commission, whereas the former is adopted in English law.[134]

[127] Mercantile Law Amendment Act 1856, s 5.
[128] *Krishnasami Pattar v Gopalakrishna Reddiar* AIR 1927 Mad 421; *Chunduri Panakala Rao v Atmuri Venkata Sarvesam* AIR 1936 Mad 342.
[129] Bhadbhade (n 1) 1456.
[130] See eg *Pearl v Deacon* (1857) 24 Beav 186, 53 ER 328; *Forbes v Jackson* (1882) 19 Ch D 615, 621; but cf *Polak* (n 93) 676. The Mercantile Law Amendment Act 1856, s 5 has no express temporal limit.
[131] *Parvateneni Bhushayya v Potluri Suryanarayana* AIR 1944 Mad 195.
[132] ibid.
[133] *Goverdhandoss Gokuldas v Bank of Bengal* (1890) 15 Bom 48.
[134] Bhadbhade (n 1) 1460–61; *Thirteenth Report* (n 2) [112]. Contrast Courtney, *Modern Contract of Guarantee* (n 30) [12-271]–[12-273].

9. Acts or Omissions by the Creditor That Prejudice the Surety

A surety has no defence at common law on the general ground that it has been prejudiced by the creditor's acts or omissions.[135] There are, instead, more specific bases, such as variation of the principal contract, impairment or release of securities held by the creditor, connivance or fraud by the creditor,[136] and so on. Some of these have already been discussed. The Contract Act sets out the surety's residuary protection, splitting it across two sections. Under section 139, the surety is discharged if the creditor acts inconsistently with the surety's rights or omits to perform a duty owed to the surety such that the surety's 'eventual remedy' against the debtor is impaired. Under section 141, the surety is discharged if the creditor loses or parts with a security for the performance of the principal contract.

The language of section 139 is somewhat oracular. One must know the content of the surety's 'rights' or the creditor's 'duty' before concluding that the section applies. The language suggests a concern with the surety's ability ultimately to recoup itself from the debtor in respect of sums paid. Illustration (b)—'wilful negligence' in liquidating a security at undervalue—is a common example. While the creditor's act does reduce the amount of the surety's initial liability (as compared to retaining the security and claiming on the guarantee in full), the surety is ultimately worse off because it could have paid the creditor and recovered a greater sum by liquidating the security itself.

The section also catches some acts and omissions that increase (a) the likelihood of default or (b) the amount of the initial liability. Illustration (a) to section 139, concerning advance payments to a shipbuilder,[137] has been thought to prejudice the surety in both ways.[138] Illustration (c) also represents an increase in the risk of default or the amount of liability, though the result could also be justified by the usual principles governing discharge for breach or repudiation of contract.

Dealings with securities can fall within section 139 or section 141. The protection under both sections starts from the time the surety enters the guarantee. However, for section 141, the protection only applies to securities that the creditor held at the time of the guarantee. As illustration (c) shows, the creditor is free to give up securities obtained afterwards. This temporal limitation is a remnant of English law predating the Contract Act, and it has been abandoned in that jurisdiction.[139] It is also hard to justify in its own terms, given the unlimited protection offered under section 139. Another distinction between the two sections is that section 141 applies to cases where the security is wholly relinquished or lost, as opposed merely to being impaired or liquidated for a diminished value. This is really a difference in extent, not kind, and it is not regarded as significant in other common law jurisdictions. Loss of or 'parting

[135] Courtney, *Modern Contract of Guarantee* (n 30) [8-106].
[136] See eg *Bank of India v Trans Commodity Merchants Ltd and Patel* [1983] 2 Lloyd's Rep 298, 302.
[137] The illustration is based on *General Steam-Navigation Co v Rolt* (1858) 6 CBNS 550, 141 ER 572.
[138] *Hackney Empire Ltd v Aviva Insurance Ltd* [2012] EWCA Civ 1716, [2013] 1 WLR 3400, [60], [70].
[139] See nn 129, 130 above.

with' the security under section 141 suggests deliberate or culpable action or a culpable omission.[140] The standard of conduct proscribed appears to be substantially the same as that under section 139.

Instances of prejudicial acts or omissions under section 139 and section 141 can be found in the cases.[141] So, for example, a creditor is not obliged at general law to acquire further securities for the guaranteed obligations. But if the creditor does obtain security, it ought to comply with any formalities necessary to perfect it.[142] The creditor is not obliged to liquidate securities promptly, or even at all, before proceeding against the guarantor.[143] Yet, if it chooses to liquidate a security, it ought to exercise reasonable care to obtain a proper price.[144]

Under both sections 139 and 141, the surety is discharged to the extent of the loss or impairment and not absolutely. Of course, if that figure exceeds the amount of the surety's liability, then the discharge is, for practical purposes, total.

[140] *State of Madhya Pradesh v Kaluram* AIR 1967 SC 1105; *State Bank of Saurashtra v Chitranjan Rangnath Raja* AIR 1980 SC 1528; *Industrial Finance Corp of India Ltd v Cannanore Spinning and Weaving Mills Ltd* AIR 2002 SC 1841. See also *Indian Bank, Sardar Patel Road v Ambika* (2001) Kar LJ 478.

[141] See Bhadbhade (n 1) 1442–45, 1457–59.

[142] *Bank of India Ltd v Rustom Fakirji Cowasjee* (1955) 57 Bom LR 850.

[143] *Bank of Bihar Ltd v Damodar Prasad* AIR 1969 SC 297; *Karnataka Bank Ltd v Gajanan Shankararao Kulkarni* AIR 1977 Kant 14; *Union Bank of India v MP Sreedharan Kartha* AIR 1993 Ker 285; *Industrial Investment Bank of India Ltd v Biswanath Jhunjhunwala* 2009 (9) SCC 478. See also *China & South Seas Bank v Tan* [1990] 1 AC 536 (PC), cited in *Industrial Finance Corp of India Ltd* (n 140).

[144] See Bhadbhade (n 1) 1444–45. In English law, the duty to take care in this respect is derived from equity and not based upon the tort of negligence.

21

Bailment and Pledge

Gail Pearson

I. Introduction

Possession without title is central to bailment.[1] Bailment underwrites rights and duties in everyday commercial and international transactions. In India, it is central to sales tax and port charges disputes. Gold loans are ubiquitous, though not evidently disputed. The bailment part of the Indian Contract Act 1872 (hereinafter 'the Contract Act') has thirty-three clauses. These include the possessory securities, liens, and pledges. The Contract Act is not a complete code.[2] Additional legislation imposes Contract Act-like bailee duties on carriers and others taking charge of goods and informs current litigation.[3] The Contract Act swept away distinctions in the bailee's degree of care.[4] Yet, additional legislation means anomalies in the expression of liability of those in possession of goods.[5]

Utilising a single concept of bailment, the Contract Act sets out obligations independent of detailed categories.[6] In this, the Contract Act departs from 19th-century

[1] 'The essence of bailment is possession and the consent of the owner of the goods is not necessary. The distinction between possession and custody of goods is also noted by jurists': *MS Rasiklal Kantilal & Co v Board of Trustee of Port of Bombay* (2017) 11 SCC 1, [38]. Possession is a common law legal concept. It may differ from physical custody and its meaning will fluctuate according to the facts. For the classic account, see F Pollock and R S Wright, *An Essay on Possession in the Common Law* (Clarendon Press 1888). For a succinct account, see M Bridge, *Personal Property Law* (OUP 2005) ch 2.

[2] *Irrawaddy Flotilla v Bugwandass* [1891] UKPC 23 (Lord McNaghten).

[3] See the Indian Railways Act 1890 (repealed), s 72. This was repealed by the Railways Act 1989, which, in s 99, preserves the responsibility of the railway for loss and non-delivery as per the duties of the bailee in the Contract Act. The Major Ports Trust Act 1963 (MTP Act), ss 42, 43, imposes bailee duties as under the Contract Act. The Court in *The Board of Trustees of the Port of Bombay v Sriyanesh Knitters* 1999 7 SCC 359 said the MTP Act was not an exhaustive code. This was affirmed in *Chairman of Board of Trustees, Cochin Port Trust v M/S Arebee Star Maritime* (2021) 11 SCC 641 (*Cochin 2*) [67]. Rules for central warehousing under the International Airports Authority Act 1971 also impose the Contract Act bailee rights and duties; see *International Airports Authority of India v M/s Grand Slam International* 1995 3 SCC 151. Relevant for capital markets, the Depositories Act 1996 does not override the Contract Act pledge provisions on mutual rights and obligations; see *PTC India Financial Services Ltd v Venkateshwarlu Kari* (Supreme Court of India, 12 May 2022) [9.5], [9.8].

[4] *Sheik Mahamad Ravuther v The British Indian Steam Navigation Co Ltd* (1909) ILR 32 Mad 95 (Sankaran Nair J), referred to in *Taj Mahal Hotel v United India Insurance Company Limited* (2020) 2 SCC 224, [24].

[5] The Carriers Act 1865 was not repealed at the time of the Contract Act. It was repealed by the Carriage by Road Act 2007. See *Cochin 2* (n 3). See *Nath Bros Exim International Ltd v Best Roadways Ltd* [2000] INSC 140. Following inconsistent High Court decisions, *Irrawaddy Flotilla* (n 2) 9, 10 held that the duties of common carriers did not come under the Contract Act. The Carriage by Road Act 2007 does not impose liability on the carrier as a bailee, as is the case for railways, ports, and airports, but imposes and caps liability on the basis of fault or neglect; see Carriage by Road Act 2007, ss 10, 15.

[6] Contract Act, s 151.

Gail Pearson, *Bailment and Pledge* In: *Foundations of Indian Contract Law*. Edited by: KV Krishnaprasad, Niranjan Venkatesan, Shivprasad Swaminathan, and Umakanth Varottil, Oxford University Press.
DOI: 10.1093/9780191997211.003.0021

British law. *Coggs v Bernard*[7] cemented the notion of gradations of responsibility according to different categories of bailment. William Jones, jurist and Indian classicist, critiqued *Coggs v Bernard*, yet restated the notion of shifting obligations dependent on the type of bailment.[8] Drawing on Halhed,[9] Jones adopted a natural law approach pointing to strong similarities between Hindu and Roman laws of contract pertinent to bailment.[10] It is notable that the innovative Contract Act categorisation of mixtures (of the bailor's goods with the bailee's own) is different from Roman law.[11]

India was not a blank canvas. Commentators argued that proposed Contract Act clauses departed from law or custom or found analogies with Hindu and Mahommedan laws and, in the north, differed on whether proposed clauses aligned with the Punjab Civil Code.[12] There were already separate statutes for carriers at the time of the Contract Act.[13] There is little in the history of British legislative reform to suggest that the Law Commissioners drafted rules generated by English concerns regarding bailment. The Commissioners referred to English, French, German, and Italian laws but not the customary laws of the country. This was noted in India. Some asked whether there was any advantage in superseding existing law with the law of other countries.[14] The most scrutinised clauses were about theft, a matter that is still of concern.[15]

The Contract Act defines bailment, bailor, and bailee.[16] A pledge is a bailment for a distinct purpose.[17] There are five elements defining bailment: delivery, of goods, on a contract, for a purpose, and return or disposition of the goods at the direction of the bailor.[18] The bailee's chief obligation is to care for the goods to the standard of a person of ordinary prudence taking care of that person's own goods under similar circumstances, the notional goods being of the same bulk, quality, and value as the bailed goods.[19] If the bailee meets this standard, the bailee is not responsible for loss of the

[7] (1703) 2 Ld Raym 909.

[8] W Jones, *An Essay on the Law of Bailments* (William Fessenden 1807 [1781]).

[9] NB Halhed, *A Code of Gentoo Laws, or, Ordinations of the Pundits, from a Persian Translation, Made from the Original, Written in the Shanscrit Language* (CUP 1776). Persian was the language of administration.

[10] Jones (n 8) 134, 136.

[11] Contract Act, ss 155, 156, 157; S Worthington, *Proprietary Interests in Commercial Transactions* (Clarendon Press 1996) 135–42; P Birks, 'Mixtures' in N Palmer and E McKendrick (eds), *Interests in Goods* (2nd edn, Lloyds of London Press 1993) 449–68. Birks argues that accession, specification, executory division (division of a mass or bulk owned by one person), and substitution are events distinct from mixing. There is a discussion of accession in the context of transfer of property in ship building in *The State of Madras v Gannon Dunkerley & Co (Madras) Ltd* 1959 SCR 379, 421, 422.

[12] This was a series of administrative rules based on a digest of Indian usage and British procedure that was never formally enacted. It was compiled by Richard Temple (later Governor of Bombay) about 1854 as instructed by John Lawrence, Chief Commissioner of Punjab, later the Governor General at the time of enacting the Contract Act; see MP Jain, *Outlines of Indian Legal History* (5th edn, Wadhwa & Company 1993) 226–27.

[13] On bailments to carriers, see the Railways Act 1854, the Carriers Act 1865, the Government Railways Act 1870, and the Railway Act Amendment Act 1871.

[14] EL Brandreth (Member of the Indian Civil Service and linguist), *Abstract of the Proceedings of the Council of the Governor General of India Assembled for the Purpose of Making Law and Regulations under the Provisions of the Act of Parliament 24 & 25 Vic cap 67*, 6 December 1867.

[15] *Karnataka Pawn Broker's Association v State of Karnataka* 1998 7 SCC 707.

[16] Contract Act, s 148.

[17] ibid s 172.

[18] ibid s 148.

[19] ibid s 151.

bailed goods.[20] The parties can alter this liability by contract.[21] The related obligation is to redeliver the goods,[22] and there are statutory provisions for mixtures.[23] If the bailee is not paid, the bailor must pay the bailee for any necessary expenses.[24] The difference between a pledge and bailment is the pledgee's right to sell bailed goods.[25]

Contested areas include whether a contractual relationship is strictly necessary, the role of the bill of lading in sub-bailments, and the relationship between deemed sales for taxation purposes and a bailment. Possession is recognised as a theory for bailment but receives limited treatment. While courts have distinguished between the contractual and tortious aspects of bailment, there is little discussion of the relationship between the statutory standard of care based on prudence or reasonableness and requirements for negligence. Litigation tends to involve arms of the state, such as customs and transport authorities. India's big commercial houses seem absent. There are absences around exclusion clauses, retention of title clauses, and share pledging for margin lending. A recent question is the relationship between bailment and consumer protection.[26]

II. Bailment

Palmer sees bailment as a circle of relationships, more important than its literal meaning.[27] The split between ownership and possession involves title to the ownership interest (general property) and title to the possessory interest (special property). Possession is challenging, and a person may have custody without possession.[28] The bailor is not necessarily the owner. Bailment fits into the law of personal property, but fitting it into the families of the common law is not straightforward. It is described as linked to trust law,[29] *sui generis*,[30] a question of contract, and as being akin to tort.

Whether or not a transaction is a bailment impacts if and how goods must be returned, the circumstances of compensation for loss regarding the goods, and other

[20] ibid s 152.
[21] ibid.
[22] ibid s 148.
[23] ibid ss 156, 157, 155.
[24] ibid s 158.
[25] ibid s 176.
[26] S Bansal, 'Taj Mahal Hotel v United India Insurance Co. Ltd.: Re-Aligning the Focus on Consumer Protection Act' (2020) 8 International Journal on Consumer Law and Practice 118.
[27] N Palmer, *Bailment* (3rd edn, Sweet & Maxwell 2009) [23-001].
[28] 'One who has custody without possession, like a servant, or a guest using his hosts goods, is not a bailee': F Pollock and D Mulla, *The Indian Contract and Specific Relief Acts* (13th edn, LexisNexis Butterworths1931) in *Rasiklal Kantilal* (n 1) [31].
[29] See *South Australian Insurance Co v Randell* (1869) LR 3 PC 101, which refers to bailment on trust but rejects the relationship as one of trustee and cestui que trust.
[30] G Paton, *Bailment in the Common Law* (Stevens 1952); see *State of Bombay (Now Gujarat) v Memon Mahomed Haji Hasam* 1967 SCR (3) 938, 944.

liabilities. A bailment is distinct from agency,[31] licence,[32] and sale.[33] In a sale but not a bailment, ownership or title passes. In a bailment, an owner has possession or immediate right to possess the goods and passes only possession to the bailee. In the classic distinction between hire arrangements with an option to purchase and an obligation to purchase,[34] the first is a bailment and the latter a sale. A series of decisions affirms this distinction.[35]

The simplicity of the distinction between sale and bailment was challenged by state sales tax legislation, replaced in 2017 by the Goods and Services Tax Act 2017. To support the state's taxing powers, in 1982, an amendment to the Constitution of India was introduced through Article 366 (29A), by which different types of transactions, including transfers of the right to use, are deemed sales.[36] The amendment was prompted by a decision that sales tax could not be levied without a sale, and a state legislature could not turn a hire purchase into a deemed sale.[37] The goods and services tax envisaged that Article 366 (29A) would be deleted; instead, it was retained. An unforeseen consequence is that a deemed sale without a transfer of ownership is not a bailment.[38]

'Sale-or-return' or 'sale-on-approval' transactions are bailments, since there is delivery of the goods but no sale until the buyer adopts the transaction.[39] Packaging may be sold as with expensive containers [40] or bailed as with recycled containers[41] or gas cylinders.[42] Storage contracts may involve a sale or the provision of services with a bailment. Cases have found a bailment preparatory to a food supply scheme[43] and no bailment in a government service to deliver mail.[44]

Meeting the five elements of the statutory definition is not straightforward.[45] The question is whether the elements of the statutory definition must be strictly met and in what circumstances.

[31] See *UCO Bank v Hem Chandra Sarkar* 1990 (3) SCC 389.

[32] *Taj Mahal Hotel* (n 4) approved *Ashby v Tolhurst* [1937] 2 KB 242 (which was distinguished in *The City of Sydney Council v West* (1966) 114 CLR 481 (Menzies and Taylor JJ) and emphasises the degree of control over the goods, distinguishing between the valet parking bailment and merely being allowed to park in a parking space.

[33] See the distinction between a sale and work and services contract in *Hindustan Aeronautics Limited v State of Karnataka* AIR 1984 SC 744.

[34] In *Lee v Butler* [1893] QB 318, there was an agreement to sell, and payment of the instalments was the condition for property to pass, and in *Helby v Matthews* [1895] AC 471, there was no agreement to buy but simply an option to do so.

[35] *Ashan Devi v Phulwasi Devi* 1961 2 SCR 522; *M/S Damodar Valley Corporation v The State of Bihar* AIR 1961 SC 440; *Itw Signode India Ltd v Collector of Central Excise* AIR 1961 SC 663; *Installment Supply (P) Ltd v Union of India* AIR 1962 SC 53; *Bharath Metha v State by Inspector of Police Chennai* [2008] INSC 498. See also Sale of Goods Act 1930, s 30(2).

[36] The Constitution of India, art 366 (29A), made to facilitate state sales taxes, also refers to right to use for a consideration. See the discussion in *20th Century Finance Corpn Ltd v State of Maharashtra* [2000] INSC 306.

[37] *KL Johar and Co v Deputy Commercial Tax Officer* (1965) 2 SCR 112.

[38] *20th Century Finance Corpn Ltd* (n 36) [35] on the transfer of a right to use goods.

[39] Sale of Goods Act 1930, s 24.

[40] *Hyderabad Deccan Cigarette Factory v State on Andhra Pradesh* (1966) 17 STC 624 (SC). Note also *State of Maharashtra, Bombay v Britannia Biscuits Co Ltd* 1995 Supp 2 SCC 72, where the tin for the tinned biscuits was considered an inexpensive item.

[41] See *United Breweries Ltd v State of AP* 1997 3 SCC 530, which affirms *Beecham Foods Ltd v North Supplies (Edmonton) Ltd* (1959) 2 All ER 336.

[42] *Sardar Carbonic Gas Co v Sher-I-Punjab Trading Co* 15 (1979) DLT 129.

[43] *Ram Padarath Mahto v Mishri Singh* 1961 2 SCR 470, 476, 477.

[44] *Satyanathan v K Subramanyan* [1955] 2 SCR 83.

[45] Contract Act, s 148.

1. A Contract

In addition to transfer of possession, classical bailment theory requires an implied or express contract between bailor and bailee.[46] Yet, Tay suggests that *Coggs v Bernard* linked possession with obligation,[47] and Palmer shows how decisions fitted gratuitous bailment into a fiction of contract.[48] Palmer emphasises the independent character of bailment, although it has been treated like tort for procedural purposes.[49] McMeel argues that there is no independent concept of bailment spanning the law of obligations and property and that the contractual element is an afterthought in the modern context.[50]

The Contract Act definition of contract includes free consent and consideration.[51] Yet, the Supreme Court of India has also highlighted possession. Without an enforceable contract and proof of consideration, when a state customs authority seized a vehicle, it was held to be the bailee.[52] The Supreme Court referenced Pollock and Wright's classic text.[53] A later decision,[54] relying on Palmer,[55] found bailment on a theory of possession. The Supreme Court said privity need not be introduced if it was unnecessary, that a bailment is not technically subject to the limitations of an agreement, and that the remedies are not in substance contractual. The Supreme Court stated, 'It is sufficient if that possession is within the knowledge of the person concerned.'[56] Statutory custody and delivery (or possession)[57] were also the basis of bailment in an airport storage case.[58]

Free consent may be necessary for a contract, but is it necessary for a bailment? Can a bailment arise without the consent or knowledge of the bailor; must the bailor have consented to the bailee's possession of the goods? The Privy Council canvassed opposing views of academic writers and concluded that the focus is on the bailee, who must have voluntarily taken the goods of another into custody and thus become the bailee.[59]

[46] On Blackstone, William Jones, and Story, see A Tay, 'The Essence of a Bailment: Contract, Agreement or Possession?' (1966) 5 Sydney Law Review 239.

[47] *Coggs* (n 7) 919 (Holt CJ); ibid 242.

[48] N Palmer, 'Gratuitous Bailment Contract or Tort?' (1975) 24 International and Comparative Law Quarterly 565.

[49] ibid 567, 572.

[50] G McMeel, 'The Redundancy of Bailment' (2003) Lloyds Maritime and Commercial Law Quarterly 169, 171, 179.

[51] Contract Act, s 10.

[52] The Court also referred to the finder: *Memon Mahomed Haji Hasam* (n 30) 943, 944. In *Morris v CW Martin & Sons Ltd* (1966) 1 QB 716 (CA), decided one year earlier, Lord Diplock, at 731–32, said that the relationship of bailor and bailee exists independently of a contract, derives from Roman law, and is an older concept than the parol contract.

[53] The extract from Pollock and Wright (n 1) draws on the English decision *R v McDonald* 1885 15 QBD 323.

[54] See *The Trustees of the Port of Bombay v The Premier Automobiles Ltd* 1981 AIR 1982 on the Bombay Port Trust Act 1879.

[55] N Palmer, *Bailment* (Law Book Company 1979) 2.

[56] *The Premier Automobiles Ltd* (n 54).

[57] Contract Act, s 149.

[58] Legislation provided that the rights and liabilities of the Central Warehousing Corporation were as per the Contract Act: *International Airports Authority of India* (n 3).

[59] *The Pioneer Container* [1994] 2 AC 324 (PC) 342 (Lord Goff).

The Supreme Court earlier recognised voluntarily taking another's goods into possession (as opposed to the owner entrusting the other with possession). The owner sent goods by rail from Quetta to New Delhi after partition and only some arrived. They travelled on the Pakistani Railways (forwarding railway), and then on the Indian Railways (receiving railway). Subba Rao J outlined the alternatives. The problem was that there was no document authorised by the forwarding railway to create the receiving railway as bailee. While finding an implied contract between the owner and the receiving railway, the decision gives support to a theory of voluntary assumption of custody as the basis of bailment. Subba Rao J referred to 'consciously' taking 'over the responsibility of the bailee' and the other accepting 'that relationship'.[60]

Bills of lading evidence a contract of carriage and are documents of title (transferable on delivery) that confer the right to possession.[61] A British case rejected the proposition that a bill of lading transfers the bailment.[62] Under the Major Ports Trust Act 1963 (MPT Act), the Port Trust assumes duties as bailee for goods of which it has taken 'charge',[63] but it is less clear where a contract of bailment lies and who is the bailor.[64] Problems arise when the port seeks to recover storage fees and whether the steamer agent or consignee is liable. An Australian case held that the stevedore at the port was a bailee, and further, by accepting the bill of lading, the consignee accepted the situation between the consignor and stevedore.[65] However, the Court in *Chairman of Board of Trustees, Cochin Port Trust v M/S Arebee Star Maritime* (*Cochin 2*) said that it was irrelevant whether the bill of lading was endorsed for delivery or to transfer title. The time of transfer of title was irrelevant; in the MPT Act scheme the steamer agent was liable until the port trust took charge of goods and the 'importer, owner, consignee or their agent' is liable for storage charges.[66]

2. Goods

Goods are generally tangible property and capable of possession. The Contract Act does not define 'goods', though they were defined as 'every kind of moveable property' when the Sale of Goods was part of the Contract Act.[67] On the principle of construing

[60] *Union of India v Amar Singh* AIR 1960 SC 233.

[61] Goods are often shipped on Sea Waybills, which are evidence of the contract of carriage but not negotiable. This has implications for the transfer of title argument that makes the consignee liable for port charges.

[62] *Future Express* [1993] 2 Lloyds Rep 542 (CA). In *Future Express*, see the discussion of the opposing view of Professor Roy Goode at 550.

[63] MTP Act, ss 42(6), 43(1)(ii).

[64] For a summary of these cases, see *Board of Trustees Cochin Port Trust v M/S Arebee Star Maritime Agencies* (2018) 4 SCC 592.

[65] *Port Jackson Stevedoring Pty Ltd v Salmond and Spraggon (Aust) Pty Ltd* [1980] UKPCHCA 1, [47] (Barwick CJ), where goods were stolen after unloading. There, the clauses in the bill of lading exempting liability extended to the stevedore.

[66] *Cochin 2* (n 3) [82]. The Court, at [71], overruled the finding in *Sriyanesh Knitters* (n 3) that there can be a bailment between the Port Trust and the consignee. The notion that any liability of the consignee rests on transfer of property in the goods to the consignee or that there is a relationship of bailor and bailee between the consignee and the Port Trust was rejected in *Rasiklal Kantilal* (n 1).

[67] Contract Act, s 76.

the statute as a whole, this would have been the meaning of goods for bailment. The Sale of Goods Act 1930 defines 'goods', and in dicta, the Supreme Court has said that this provides the meaning for bailment, and that goods should be marketable or saleable.[68] This definition excludes money.[69]

Moveable property in the goods definition may extend to property rights in water and electricity and software. The Supreme Court held that electro-magnetic waves were not goods within the meaning of Article 366(12) of the Constitution of India or in State legislation and said it was unnecessary to determine whether the telephone system is not goods but immoveable property.[70] A High Court decision said that there was no bailment of electricity or the meter box, though sale of electricity may be amenable to the Sale of Goods Act 1930.[71]

3. Delivery

The bailment definition refers to delivery, not possession.[72] Without delivery, a contract for bailment does not create the bailment.[73] The essence of delivery is transfer of possession.[74] The definition of delivery refers to 'doing anything' to put the goods in the possession of the bailee. The 'Explanation' to the definition of bailment codifies attornment so that if a person is already in possession of the goods of another person and then contracts to hold them as a bailee, the person becomes the bailee, and the owner becomes the bailor.[75] Conceptually, possession is indivisible. As Goode says, it is held and transferred entire.[76] There are no distinct possessory titles but shared possession. This raises actual possession and constructive possession.[77]

There is a distinction between actual custody and juridical possession.[78] Providing receipts (symbolic of the goods) to an agent may not relinquish their possession.[79]

[68] The Sale of Goods Act 1930, s 2 (7), adopted from the British Sale of Goods Act 1892, states, '"goods" means every kind of movable property other than actionable claims and money; and includes stock and shares, growing crops, grass, and things attached to or forming part of the land which are agreed to be severed before sale or under the contract of sale'; *RD Saxena v Balram Prasad Sharma* [2000] INSC 442. The case, concerning a lien, held that a solicitor's case file documents were not goods.

[69] *KMS Lakshmanier and Sons v Commissioner of Income Tax* 1953 AIR 145, where a security deposit for bales of cotton was not a bailment.

[70] *CTO v Young Men's Indian Assn* (1970) 1 SCC 462.

[71] *Sri Hanuman Steel Rolling Mill v CESC Ltd* AIR 1996 Cal 449, [58], [54].

[72] Contract Act, s 148.

[73] In *The Morvi Mercantile Bank Ltd v Union of India* 1965 (3) SCR 254. Ramaswami J affirmed *Dublin City Distillery (Great Brunswick Street, Dublin) Ltd v Doherty* [1914] AC 823, where there was a contract but no delivery since the whiskey held in the warehouse was deliverable but not delivered.

[74] Contract Act, s 149.

[75] ibid s 148. See further Pollock and Wright (n 1) 161.

[76] R Goode, *Commercial Law* (Harmondsworth, 1982) 62. *Midland Silicones Ltd v Scruttons Ltd* [1959] 2 QB 171, 189 said that the bailee must have exclusive possession.

[77] *Gamer's Motor Centre (Newcastle) Proprietary Limited v Natwest Wholesale Australia Proprietary Limited* (1987) 163 CLR 236 discusses the concept of constructive possession.

[78] *Official Assignee of Madras v Mercantile Bank of India Ltd* [1935] AC 53.

[79] 'The respondents did not part with the possession of the goods or receipts in the juridical sense of that word; they merely parted with the custody, by entrusting the receipts to the insolvents as their agents or mandatories for the special purpose of convenient dealing with the goods': ibid (Lord Wright).

A railway receipt can be a document of title, and under the Contract Act, such documents can be pledged.[80] When a bank returned fourteen railway receipts to the owner of goods to facilitate movement of the goods within the port, the Privy Council said the bank was still in possession of the goods. It had merely parted with custody; it had not relinquished the pledge. This was redelivery by the pledgee (bailee) for a limited purpose, to deal with goods in a way in which the banker was unable to do so.[81] A Supreme Court decision where goods were pledged to a bank by endorsing railway receipts rested on the railway receipt as a document of title. A powerful dissent found that there was no valid pledge and discussed constructive delivery, stating that actual, symbolic, or constructive delivery was necessary to complete a pledge. Examples included constructive delivery by giving the key to a store.[82] Giving a delivery order to a warehouse is insufficient as something more must be 'done under it'.[83] The something more would be attorning to the person named in the delivery order, in which case there would be constructive delivery to that person.

By contrast, a finder must take actual custody to establish bailment.[84] Aligning with free consent, finding involves a voluntary assumption of custody.

There may be change of possession without the owner intending to deliver the goods. In a unilateral bailment, a party may take possession without consultation or knowledge of the owner. An example is a bailment of necessity to protect the goods of the owner. The possessor may know the goods belong to the owner or have reasonable cause to believe the goods belonged to a third party, neither the seller nor the owner. These situations may arise, as Palmer suggests, to protect cultural property and where the state may become the possessor.[85]

We can infer that the goods do not have to be in the possession of the bailee with the consent of the owner. The Contract Act does not state that the goods must be delivered to, or in the possession of, the bailee with the consent of the bailee.

4. For a Purpose

'Purpose' is a wide notion designed to circumvent the different categories of bailment. The types of purpose canvassed in *Coggs v Bernard* and Jones in *An Essay on the Law of Bailments* included for the use of the bailor; lent for the use of the bailee; hired to the

[80] ibid. In *The Morvi Mercantile Bank Ltd* (n 73) 264 (Subba Rao J), the Court discussed *Official Assignee of Madras* (n 78) and an earlier decision, *Ramdas Vithaldas Durbar v S Amerchand & Co* (1916) LR 43 LA 164. Before the amendments to the Contract Act in 1930, there was no definition of a document of title.

[81] *Official Assignee of Madras* (n 78).

[82] *The Morvi Mercantile Bank Ltd* (n 73) 269 (Ramaswami J). Ramaswami J referred to *Ward v Turner* (1751) 2 Ves Sen 431, 443. There has been a debate as to whether this is a symbolic transfer of possession or a transfer of control in fact. See Pollock and Wright (n 1) 61.

[83] *The Morvi Mercantile Bank Ltd* (n 73) 269. This accords with *Dublin City Distillery (Great Brunswick Street, Dublin) Ltd* (n 73), where something more than receiving a delivery order from the owner was required for a constructive delivery.

[84] Contract Act, s 71.

[85] N Palmer, 'The Role of Bailment in Cultural Property Claims' (2014) 19 Art Antiquity & Law 197.

bailee; as security for a loan; and in order to do something with the goods, such as carry them from one place to another.

Purpose may prevent constructive possession that is constructive delivery. When a car park contract excluded 'safe custody', the person who paid to leave their car and did not hand over keys, had not parted with possession and was not a bailor.[86] Romer LJ said, 'if the car had been left there for any particular purpose that required that the defendants should have possession of the car delivery would rightly be inferred.'[87] By contrast, in *Taj Mahal Hotel v United India Insurance Company Limited*, valet parking met the purpose requirement for bailment.[88]

5. Return or Disposition of the Goods

This element of a bailment requires the goods to be returned to the bailor or disposed of at the direction of the bailor once the purpose of the bailment is accomplished. This restoration of possession is predicated on the proposition that the bailor must retain ownership. An inability to restore the goods may take the transaction out of the realm of bailment and into sale. Bailed goods may be restored as they stood in their original form or in an altered state. There must be some 'clear physical heredity' with the original goods.[89] Whether the parties intended a sale and resale or a bailment for the provision of services depends on the intention of the parties. The disposition of the goods is inherent in bills of lading.

The Indian position is different from the classical common law position, where the exact goods must be returned to the bailor so that if the nature of the goods or the terms of the arrangement make this impossible, it will not be a bailment. In grains storage, the return of an identical chattel or equivalent amount was not sufficient.[90] By contrast, a more recent UK case held that grain delivered by one person and mixed with that of others was a bailment.[91] This concurs with the longstanding Indian position where the provisions for mixtures, proportional ownership, separation of goods, and a bailee's liability for compensation all assume a bailment.[92]

III. Sub-bailment

There is a sub-bailment if the bailee gives possession of the goods to a third person, who holds them as the sub-bailee. To do this, the bailee must be in possession or have

[86] *Ashby* (n 32).
[87] ibid 255.
[88] *Taj Mahal Hotel* (n 4).
[89] N Palmer, *Bailment* (2nd edn, Sweet & Maxwell 1991) 135.
[90] In two Australian cases, grain delivered for storage was held to be a sale, not a bailment. *South Australian Insurance Co* (n 29); *Chapman Bros v Verco Bros & Co* (1933) 49 CLR 306.
[91] *Mercer v Craven Grain Storage* Ltd [1994] CLC 328 HL.
[92] Contract Act, ss 155, 156, 157.

an immediate right of possession. The Contract Act does not refer to sub-bailment, but it may be inherent in the definition of bailment as the requirement of 'delivery by one person to another for a purpose' would encompass delivery to another by a bailee.[93] Any contract is between the bailee (as sub-bailor) and the sub-bailee. It follows that there may be a chain of bailments. Two questions arise: identification of the relationship between owner and sub-bailee and whether the sub-bailee can invoke the terms on which the goods were sub-bailed.[94]

NR Srinivasa Iyer v New India Assurance Co, Ltd[95] affirmed two leading cases on sub-bailment and the relationship between the owner and the sub-bailee.[96] In both, the sub-bailee voluntarily took goods (a mink stole, clocks) belonging to another into the sub-bailee's possession. There was no contract between the owner and the sub-bailee, neither did the sub-bailee attorn to the owner; nevertheless, the sub-bailee was liable to the owner or bailor.

In *Srinivasa Iyer* itself, the insurer was the bailee and the car repairer the sub-bailee. The son of the owner of a damaged car took it directly to the repairer. The Court constructed a bailment to the insurer based on the contract of insurance (which required the insured to take the car straight to the nearest repairer) plus the insurer accepting the repairer and negotiated the repair. Handing the car over to the repairer was 'a delivery on behalf of the insurer who would be the bailee and the repairer would be the sub-bailee'.[97] In the mink stole and clocks cases, the bailee had actual custody prior to the sub-bailment. Here, the insurer did not have actual possession, and there is no discussion of constructive possession or constructive delivery. The Court said, 'The obligation to get the car repaired was of the Insurer. It had a right to take the car into its custody. It did formally take the car into the custody.' What can only be constructive delivery rested on a right to custody and acknowledgement of this in the dealings with the repairer, the sub-bailee who had actual possession.

Consent to the sub-bailment by voluntarily taking possession and consent to the terms of the sub-bailment intersect. At common law, the sub-bailment may require the actual or implied consent of the owner, and the sub-bailee must have sufficient notice of the interest in the goods of a person other than the bailee in order, by taking custody, to assume 'the responsibility for the goods which is characteristic of a bailee'.[98] Sub-bailment is at issue in the port charges cases. Yet, the Court in *Cochin 2* declined to make a finding on this.[99]

[93] Contract Act, s 148.
[94] *'Starsin', Owners of Cargo v 'Starsin', Owners and/or Demise Charterers of* [2003] UKHL 12, 135 (Lord Hoffmann).
[95] (1983) 3 SCC 458.
[96] *Morris* (n 52), followed in *Gilchrist Watt & Sanderson Pty Ltd v York Products Pty Ltd* [1970] 1 WLR 1262.
[97] *NR Srinivasa Iyer* (n 95) 490.
[98] *The Pioneer Container* (n 59) [342] (Lord Goff). But see *Johnson Mathey v Constantine Terminals* [1976] 2 Lloyds Rep 215; A Bell, 'Sub-Bailment on Terms' in Palmer and McKendrick (n 11) 159.
[99] *Cochin 2* (n 3) [66].

IV. Bailor's Duties and Rights

Without a possessory title, the bailor is not entitled to bail goods, is responsible for loss to the bailee, and is not permitted to receive or give directions regarding them.[100]

The bailor must disclose known faults in the goods and, if goods are bailed for hire, is strictly liable for damaged goods, irrespective of the bailor's knowledge of faults.[101] In an illustration, a person, unaware they are hiring out a damaged carriage, is liable for faults that materially interfere with the use of the goods or expose the bailee to extraordinary risk. If the bailor does disclose faults, the bailor is not responsible under this section for damage. The section does not appear to contemplate third-party risk. In a sale and lease-back, typically the financier (the new owner) does not see the goods, yet there has been a constructive delivery from the seller (old owner) to the financier, who becomes the bailor to the old owner, now bailee.[102] In a gratuitous bailment of loan for use, the bailor may have to indemnify the bailee.[103]

The bailor is obliged to repay any of the bailee's necessary expenses for the purpose of the bailment.[104] The port charge cases have wrestled with whether the consignor or consignee is the bailor. *Rasiklal Kantilal* assumed that the necessary expenses provision applies to a MPT Act situation, even though the MPT Act does not refer to this section of the Contract Act. The Court said persons claiming through the bailor (such as the consignee) were bound, unless released from the obligation by the bailee.[105] In *Cochin 2*, the question of the applicability of section 158 of the Contract Act on necessary expenses was left open.[106]

A bailor is entitled to any increase or profit from the goods when the bailee redelivers the goods to the bailor.[107] On redelivery of stocks and shares, the bailor is generally entitled to bonus shares and dividends. Any 'accretion' should be returned to the bailor, but if a pledge covers the accretions, these are retained by the bailee.[108] The bailor is entitled to terminate the bailment at any time if the bailee does anything with the goods inconsistent with the conditions of the bailment.[109]

V. Bailee's Duties and Rights

A bailee has two main duties: to meet the person of ordinary prudence standard of care,[110] and redeliver the goods at the proper time.[111] The bailee is not responsible for

[100] Contract Act, s 164.
[101] ibid s 150.
[102] See *Michael Gerson (Leasing) Ltd v Wilkinson* [2001] 1 All ER 148 (CA).
[103] Contract Act, s 159.
[104] ibid s 158.
[105] *Rasiklal Kantilal* (n 1) [43].
[106] *Cochin 2* (n 3) [79].
[107] Contract Act, s 163.
[108] *Standard Chartered Bank v Custodian* AIR 2000 SC 1488, [50].
[109] Contract Act, s 153.
[110] ibid s 151.
[111] ibid, ss 148, 160.

loss of the bailed goods if the bailee meets these obligations.[112] The parties can alter liability by contract. Unauthorised use of the goods does not meet the standard of care, and if this happens, a bailee must compensate.[113] There is an interaction between loss of goods and frustration.[114] A bailee seeking to rely on destruction of goods to argue frustration 'must show that the destruction was not due to any breach of his duty as a bailee'.[115] Other legislations impose Contract Act-like bailee obligations.[116] If a third party interferes with the bailee's rights by depriving the bailee of use, possession, or damages the goods, the bailee has the same rights against that third party as the bailor, and either the bailee or the bailor may sue the third party.[117]

1. The Standard of Care

The statute suggests a duty of 'prudence' similar to an equitable duty of care.[118] In recent decisions, the bailee's measure of care is said to be the same in English common law as applied in India and founded in negligence.[119] This predates negligence as in *Donoghue v Stevenson*.[120] The Contract Act statutory duty of prudence is assimilated to a standard of reasonable care. Courts, while referring to ordinary prudence, also discuss reasonable care or directly invoke negligence. The obligation is likely similar irrespective of its statutory genesis or categorisation as contractual or tortious. Discussion of any fault element is missing. Comments suggest that negligence is distinct from 'deficiency in service', though failure to meet the standard of prudent care amounts to such deficiency.[121]

The *Taj Mahal Hotel* case held that the required standard is one of reasonable care.[122] There, the bailee had to show 'that efforts were undertaken by it to take reasonable care of the vehicle bailed, and that the theft did not occur due to its neglect or misconduct'.[123] The Court found that five star hotels have a 'relatively higher degree of care as

[112] ibid ss 152, 161.
[113] ibid s 154.
[114] ibid s 56.
[115] *Ram Chandra Singh v Savitri Devi* [2003] INSC 510 (Sinha J). The same statement was made in *MD Army Welfare Housing Organisation v Sumangal Services Pvt Ltd* [2003] INSC 509.
[116] MPT Act, ss 42, 43; Indian Railways Act 1890, s 72; Carriers Act 1865, s 8.
[117] Contract Act, s 180. There is an apportionment provision: ibid, s 181.
[118] This could be similar to statutory duties for managed investments similar to trust duties. Traditional banker–customer relations are not usually characterised as fiduciary, and the bailee's relationship to the bailor would fall short of a fiduciary duty. There is no evidence as to why prudence rather than reasonableness was used to denote the bailee–bailor relationship.
[119] *Nath Bros Exim International Ltd* (n 5) ('If a person was negligent and did not take as much care as he would have taken of his own goods, he would be liable in damages'). See also *The Premier Automobiles Ltd* (n 54) 540 ('the law of torts is concerned with those situations where the conduct of one party causes or threatens harm to the interests of the other party').
[120] [1932] AC 562 (HL). As pointed out in S Worthington, *Personal Property Law* (Hart 2000) 78.
[121] *Nath Bros Exim International Ltd* (n 5). This was claimed in *Taj Mahal Hotel* (n 4). See Consumer Protection Act 2019, s 2 (11), which refers to fault.
[122] *Taj Mahal Hotel* (n 4) [19], [20]. See the Contract Act, ss 151, 152.
[123] *Taj Mahal Hotel* (n 4) [19].

a reasonable person would normally expect higher quality and safety of the services made available by such hotels'.[124] It found that the standard of care was the same irrespective of payment or a gratuitous bailment and affirmed a decision on Malaysian provisions similar to sections 151 and 152 of the Contract Act.[125] In *Taj Mahal Hotel*, the car keys were stolen from the desk. The Court said that the hotel was negligent.[126] It was not enough simply to provide an attendant or security guard;[127] the hotel should have taken additional measures. It had not met the required standard of care as the keys were not kept 'outside the reach of outsiders' nor cars parked 'in a safe location with adequate barriers to verify their owners'.[128]

Srinivasa Iyer refers to the standard of ordinary prudence affirmed in the obligation of 'reasonable care' and the requirement to show that the loss occurred 'without any neglect or default or misconduct of himself'.[129] In *Srinivasa Iyer* the insurance company sub-bailed the car to the repairer, where fire destroyed the car due to carelessness with flammable material. The Court assumed that the standard of reasonable care is the same as the standard of ordinary prudence and found the bailee liable.[130]

The Contract Act-like bailee obligations under other legislations have been judicially considered. Under Customs legislation, the obligation is to take 'reasonable care' and return property.[131] Where the port was treated by statute as an Contract Act bailee, a 'careless' port trust was liable in tort as there was no contract of bailment.[132] The Indian Railways Act 1989 is subject to the Contract Act regarding the bailee's responsibility for loss.[133] Railway authorities did not meet the standard of care when, knowing of the prevalence of theft, they negligently failed to eliminate such opportunities when railway police did not get down from the train at stops to check on wagons.[134] *Nath Bros* refers to the carrier's absolute liability to deliver the goods and then the carrier's liability for loss caused by negligence or any criminal act.[135] In dicta, ordinary prudence was said to be a common law rule and assimilated to negligence.[136]

[124] ibid [20.1]. The court affirmed *Hyatt Hotel Regency v Atul Virmani* III (2008) CPJ 281 (NC) and *Klaus Mittelbachert v East India Hotels Ltd* AIR 1997 Del 201 on this point.

[125] *Port Swettenham Authority v TW Wu & Co* [1979] AC 580, [20.3]. Worthington, *Personal Property Law* (n 120) 87 suggests that *Port Swettenham Authority and China-Pacific SA v Food Corporation of India and The Winson* [1982] AC 939 (HL) may establish that a lower standard of care is required of a gratuitous bailee.

[126] *Taj Mahal Hotel* (n 4) [21].

[127] ibid [20.2].

[128] ibid [21]. Further examples included well-guarded spaces if parking was in the vicinity of the hotel, CCTV cameras, or handing the car over only on receipt of a parking slip.

[129] *NR Srinivasa Iyer* (n 95) 491, affirming *Morris* (n 52) [720] (Lord Denning). In *Sanderson v Collins* [1904] 1 KB 628, 630, Collins MR said 'the bailee must use reasonable care which has been described as ordinary care'.

[130] *NR Srinivasa Iyer* (n 95) 492.

[131] *Memon Mahomed Haji Hasam* (n 30) 943.

[132] *The Premier Automobiles Ltd* (n 54) 539.

[133] *Union of India v M/S Udho Ram & Sons* 1963 (2) SCR 702, 706. The relevant provisions are Indian Railways Act, s 72 and the Contract Act, s 151.

[134] *M/S Udho Ram & Sons* (n 133) 704, 705–707.

[135] *Nath Bros Exim International Ltd* (n 5).

[136] ibid.

2. Contracting Out

If the bailee meets the standard of care, the bailee is not responsible for loss except for 'any special contract'.[137] What can be excluded? In a bill of lading case, one judge, construing the Contract Act, said parties could contract to a higher standard than that of ordinary prudence but cannot contract out of the minimum standard.[138] Two judges, without referring to the Contract Act, said negligence could be excluded if a clause referred specifically to negligence.[139] The court in *Taj Mahal Hotel* distinguished *Sheik Mahamad* on the contracting out of negligence point and affirmed *Nath Bros* (a carrier's case), which had found that an exclusion clause did not excuse liability.[140] *Taj Mahal Hotel* involved bailment of a car and the Contract Act, not carrier's liability. Shantanagoudar J said the view in *Sheik Mahamad* that it was not possible to contract out of the minimum standard of ordinary prudence should be followed, otherwise this required standard of care would become illusory.[141] His Lordship acknowledged that some liability of the bailee for third parties, such as contributory negligence or acts of God, may be excluded. In summary, as indicated in *Taj Mahal Hotel*, a hotel cannot contract out of its liability for negligence in respect of a vehicle for its guest; even if there is an exemption clause, the hotel bailee must prove that any loss was not due to its negligence or failure of care. If there is an exemption clause, the bailee must prove the loss was covered by the exemption clause.[142] Sub-bailment and exclusion of liability does not appear to have surfaced in the Indian context.[143]

3. Redelivery and Mixtures

The bailee must redeliver the goods without demand when the time of the bailment has ended or its purpose accomplished and is liable if the bailee fails to redeliver or dispose of them at the bailor's direction.[144] This raises both breach of contract and tortious

[137] Contract Act, s 152.

[138] *Sheik Mahamad Ravuther* (n 4) (Sankaran Nair J), as referred to in *Taj Mahal Hotel* (n 4) [24]. His Lordship agreed that it was possible to modify absolute liability as an insurer but not the minimum Contract Act statutory liability.

[139] *Taj Mahal Hotel* (n 4) [24]. This accords with English law at the time. This had been followed by High Courts, which held that parties can contract out of the Contract Act, s 151. See *Taj Mahal Hotel* (n 4) [25].

[140] *Taj Mahal Hotel* (n 4) [27], [28].

[141] ibid [28]:

> if the hotel is allowed to exclude its liability for negligence by way of a contract, the standard of care imposed under Section 151 will become illusory and virtually redundant, rendering consumers vulnerable without any remedy. In our view, the standard of care required to be taken by the hotel as a bailee under Section 151 is sacrosanct and cannot be contracted out of.

[142] ibid [30]. This in part accords with *Beaumont-Thomas v Blue Star Line Ltd.* (1939) 3 All ER 127, where the contractual duty had first to be established if the exemption clause were unclear. In *Sydney Corporation v West* [1965] HCA 68, a clause in a parking station contract exempted loss or damage however it may arise. The clause was ineffective as the act of allowing the car to be driven away on the basis of a stolen parking ticket was more than negligence and outside the terms of the contract.

[143] Cf eg *The Pioneer Container* (n 59); *Port Jackson Stevedoring Pty Ltd* (n 65).

[144] Contract Act, ss 160, 161, 165, 166, 167. See *St Joseph Textiles v Union of India and Another* AIR 1993 SC 1692, [5].

unlawful interference with goods.[145] At issue is the measure of damages.[146] Finders do not have to redeliver, cannot recover preservation costs, can keep goods until compensated, can sell in some circumstances, and can sue for any reward.[147] If joint owners bail goods, they can be redelivered without all of them consenting.[148]

The Contract Act scheme resolves some issues for mixture of the bailor and bailee's goods. If mixing is non-consensual and the goods can be divided, each retains ownership, and the bailee is responsible for separation, including damage.[149] If the goods cannot be separated and redelivered, the bailee must compensate the bailor.[150] In a consensual mixture, the bailor and bailee take the resulting mixture as proportional co-owners.[151] There is no provision for apportioning costs to determine the proportionate interests of the bailor and the bailee.[152] No Contract Act provisions involve a mixture with the goods of third parties, as is common in bulk storage of say, grain.[153] There is general provision for a third party to claim goods by applying to the court to resolve title.[154]

VI. Possessory Securities

The Contract Act provides for both the lien and the pledge. The common law lien gives the lien holder the right to detain possession until the underlying obligation is fulfilled, usually payment of a debt.[155] The equitable lien does not require possession.[156] A lien cannot be transferred; it is a personal right.[157] In a pledge, the pledgor or bailor transfers possession to the pledgee or bailee as security for the repayment of a debt or other obligation such as a guarantee. Tangible goods and documentary intangibles such as shares, bills of exchange, and bills of lading may be pledged. An unredeemed pledge can be sold. A pledge is distinct from a mortgage, where the mortgagee does not have possession but a property right and the right to foreclose.[158]

[145] See *Dhian Singh Sobha Singh v Union of India* AIR 1958 SC 274 on conversion and detinue and *Union of India v Salween Timber Construction (India)* AIR 1969 SC 488 on contract.

[146] See *Owners of the Steamship 'Mediana' v Owners, Master and Crew of Lightship 'Comet'* [1900] AC 113.

[147] Contract Act, ss 71, 169, 168.

[148] ibid s165.

[149] ibid s 156. See the illustration .

[150] ibid s 157. See the illustration. This is similar to the Roman approach plus compensation.

[151] ibid s 155. There is no illustration.

[152] In the consultation period, CD Field suggested that parties should 'proportionably' bear this cost: National Archives of India, Reference No 544, Legislative Department (May 1872).

[153] See the different solution of co-ownership in bulk rather than proportional ownership in *Mercer* (n 91).

[154] Contract Act, s 167.

[155] The Contract Act distinguishes between particular and general liens securing payment regarding particular goods or all indebtedness to the lien holder: ss 170, 171.

[156] An equitable lien may require a contract capable of specific performance. This was rejected in *Hewett v Court* (1983) 149 CLR 639.

[157] *Sewell v Burdick* (1884) 10 App Cas 74. For a discussion of the common law lien and pledge, see J Peden and R John, 'Lienee's Statutory Power of Sale' (1968) 6 University of Queensland Law Journal 1, 24.

[158] *Balkrishnan Gupta v Swadeshi Polytex Ltd* 1985 (2) SCC 167, [5(ii)].

The hypothecation and pledge are treated as practically the same in India.[159] In a hypothecation, the pledged goods remain in the possession of the pawnor, while in a pledge, the pledgee has possession.

1. Pledge

In a pledge, the bailor is the pawnor and the bailee the pawnee.[160] Transfer of possession may be actual or constructive and factually complex (delivery of a railway receipt is sufficient.)[161] The aeroscraps case involved a promissory note, disputed location, a watchman, plus the pawnee giving the pawnor statutory notice to pay the watchman, otherwise the pawnee would sell the aero scrap. The test was 'control and custody'.[162] In contrast with the lien's mere possessory right, the pawnee's 'special property' in the pledge[163] 'necessary to secure the debt'[164] can be transferred.[165] A limited interest in goods may be pledged, and the pledge is valid only to that extent.[166] There is conflicting authority on whether the mercantile agent can pledge to set off the agent's personal debts[167] or pledge goods of multiple owners for a fluctuating amount.[168]

A pledge, unlike a general lien, will not secure all monies owed, only the debt, performance of the promise, interest on the debt, and expenses.[169] It cannot secure past debts, but there is a statutory presumption that it secures future advances.[170]

The pledgor can redeem the property until the pawnee sells.[171] The voidable title rule[172] can apply to give the pawnee ownership. If the pawnor defaults, the pawnee

[159] 'Though such a distinction exists, yet it is an accepted legal principle that hypothecation is treated as a sub-species of pledge and virtually has the same legal effect': *Infrastructure Leasing & Fin Services Ltd v BPL Limited* [2015] INSC 19, 177. See also *Gulamhusain Lalji Sajan v Clara D'Souza* AIR 1929 Bom 471 on the relevance of the Contract Act, s 176 to hypothecation. 'Hypothecation' is defined in the Securitisation and Reconstruction of Financial Assets and Enforcement of Security Interest Act 2002, s 2(1)(n). The Depositories Act does not define 'pledge' or 'hypothecation'.

[160] Contract Act, s 172. The states have separate pawnbroker legislation regulating the business of pawnbroking that is concurrent with the Contract Act. For a detailed account of the pledge and its relationship to other possessory securities, see *PTC India Financial Services Ltd* (n 3).

[161] This is not restricted to a mercantile agent. See the Contract Act, s 178 construed in *The Morvi Mercantile Bank Ltd* (n 73) (Subba Rao J) 263, 264. See also *Official Assignee of Madras* (n 78).

[162] *Lallan Prasad v Rahmat Ali* 1967 (2) SCR 233, 238.

[163] *Karnataka Pawn Broker's Association* (n 15).

[164] *Lallan Prasad* (n 162) affirmed in *Balkrishnan Gupta* (n 158).

[165] But not ownership; see *Carter v Wake* (1877) 4 Ch D 605; *Sewell* (n 157).

[166] Contract Act, s 179.

[167] See M Bridge, *The Sale of Goods* (OUP 1997) 440, referring to *Lloyds and Scottish Finance Ltd v Williamson* [1865] 1 All E R 641; *Biggs v Evans* [1894] 1 QB 88, where the set-off was not accepted, with New Zealand cases *R and E Tingey & Co Ltd v John Chambers & Co Ltd* [1967] NZLR 785; *Ceres Orchard Partnership v Fiatagari Australia Pty Ltd* [1995] 1 NZLR 112.

[168] *Kaltenbach v Lewis* (1883) 24 Ch D 54, (1885) 10 App Cas 617; *Re Farmers & Settlers Coop Society Ltd; City Bank of Sydney v Barden* (1909) 9 S R (NSW) 41 compared with *Thoresen v Capital Credit Corporation Ltd* (1962) 37 DLR (2nd) 317.

[169] Contract Act, s 173. The pawnee can claim extraordinary expenses to preserve the pledge from the pawnor; see ibid s 175.

[170] ibid s 174.

[171] ibid s 177; *Lallan Prasad* (n 162), affirmed in *Balkrishnan Gupta* (n 158).

[172] Contract Act, s 178A.

has two courses of action—initiate recovery of the debt while retaining the goods as security or give reasonable notice to the pawnor and sell the goods,[173] giving good title.[174] The right to sell and the right to redeem are 'collateral rights and concurrent'[175] and may be waived.[176] Both refer to the stipulated time of the promise, and if there is such a stipulation, make time of the essence.[177] On a sale on default, the pledgee is entitled only to the amount to cover the loan and must restore any surplus proceeds to the pledgor. If there is a shortfall, the pawnor is still liable for the balance.[178] When shares are pledged as security for a loan, on default, the pledgee cannot appropriate the shares to oneself and must give notice of any sale to the pledgor.[179] For dematerialised securities, under the Depositories Act 1996, the mandatory recording of a pawnee who invokes a pledge as the 'beneficial owner' does not alter the pawnor's right to redeem as the Contract Act reference to an 'actual sale' is a sale to a third party.[180]

There are established propositions: a pawnee who cannot redeliver cannot sue; if there is an order to repay the debt, the pawnee must return the goods or put the proceeds of sale towards the debt; if the pawnee denies the pledge and sues on the debt, and the pledge is found to be valid, the pawnor can pay the debt and redeem the goods.[181] The pawnee is not able to recover on both the debt and pledge, obviating any unjust enrichment.[182]

The pawnee, as secured creditor, impacts insolvency law and priorities.[183] A company pledging shares in another company will still retain voting rights in that company even after that pledgor company has gone into management.[184] With exceptions,[185] no other creditor of the pawnor can take the pledge or its price if the pawnee's claim is unsatisfied.[186] The view that government debts should prevail in

[173] ibid s 176. See *Ex p Hubbard* (1886) 17 QBD 699. Note that the Securitisation and Reconstruction of Financial Assets and Enforcement of Security Interest Act 2002 does not apply to pledges and liens.

[174] *Karnataka Pawn Broker's Association* (n 15).

[175] *Infrastructure Leasing & Fin Services Ltd* (n 159) [177] construing the Contract Act, ss 176, 177. Referring to redemption of the pledge, the Delhi High Court described payment by the pawnor and return of the pledge by the pawnee as 'mutual, reciprocal, and simultaneous obligations'; see *GTL Limited v IFCI Limited* (2011) IA No.11586/2011 in CS (OS) No.1771/2011 (Delhi High Court).

[176] Contract Act, s 63. In *Infrastructure Leasing & Fin Services Ltd* (n 159) [175], the hypothecation had not been waived.

[177] Contract Act, ss 176, 177.

[178] ibid s 176.

[179] See eg *GTL Limited* (n 175). For dematerialised shares, a beneficial owner can pledge or hypothecate the shares but must gain approval from the depository and give notice to the depository: Depositories Act 1996, s 12.

[180] Contract Act, s 177; *PTC India Financial Services Ltd* (n 3) [9.11].

[181] *Infrastructure Leasing & Fin Services Ltd* (n 159) affirming *Lallan Prasad* (n 162) [17]. *Infrastructure Leasing & Fin Services Ltd* (n 159) also affirmed *Gulamhusain Lalji Sajan* (n 159), *Nim Chad Babu v Jagabandhu Ghose* [1894] 22 Ca. 221, and *Mahalinga Nadar v Ganapathi Subbien* [1902] 27 Mad 27.

[182] I have not seen any discussion of unjust enrichment.

[183] In *Infrastructure Leasing & Fin Services Ltd* (n 159), the lender remained a secured creditor. In *Bank of Bihar v State Bank of Bihar* AIR 1971 SC 1210, 'The pawnee has special property and a lien which is not of ordinary nature on the goods and so long as his claim is not satisfied no other creditor of the pawnor has any right to take away the goods or its price.'

[184] *Balkrishan Gupta* (n 158).

[185] *Central Bank of India v Siriguppa Sugars & Chemicals Ltd* [2007] INSC 806 refers to a number of cases which state that the government's right of recovery was deferred to other creditors, including a pledgee or lienee.

[186] *Bank of Bihar* (n 183) referring to *Rogers v Kennay* [1846] 9 QB 592.

priority contests is rejected.[187] However, provident fund dues rank as a first charge on assets, and a subsequent attachment for non-payment of such dues will prevail over an earlier pawnee.[188]

VII. Conclusion

The interaction between the Contract Act bailment and other legislation that imposes Contract Act statutory duties complicates the development of coherent central concepts in bailment law. There may be coalescence around the notion of the content of the standard of care of the bailee, though this requires elaboration. While there is much recital of distinctions between contract and tort and the relationship between common law and statute, there has been less attention to the fundamental concept of possession and how this might differ from 'custody' or 'taking charge of', other terms used in legislation. Some areas of modern commercial life, such as share pledging, are addressed in complementary legislation, while others, such as complex sub-bailments and goods held in bulk, may be considered for attention if the Contract Act were to be amended. As we continue to grapple with dematerialised and digitised items, and rely on e-commerce, there should be greater clarity around what may be delivered and bailed. The Contract Act led the world in codifying obligations; it should not languish in part or whole.

[187] *Union of India v Sicom Ltd* [2008] INSC 2105. Two unsecured government creditors did not prevail over the secured pawnee in *Central Bank of India* (n 185) [7], [18].

[188] *Maharashtra State Co-Op Bank Ltd v Assistant PF Commr* [2009] INSC 1636, [20], [36] also discussing constitutional rights.

22

Shareholder Agreements in India

An Unsettled Jurisprudence

Nemika Jha and Vikramaditya S. Khanna

I. Introduction

Shareholder agreements (SAs) are becoming more common around the world as the ownership of companies become more concentrated.[1] Larger investors—in particular, private equity investors—often document their understandings about their investments in increasingly sophisticated SAs. India has also witnessed a rise in SAs, usually with foreign private equity players, which reflects a level of sophistication and formality in contract negotiations that was not always present when such agreements were between family or affinity groups. This has placed increasing pressure on Indian case law to evolve in response to these agreements.

This chapter explores that response and finds that it is difficult to identify a unifying thread to the treatment of SAs in case law. Indeed, it appears that many different considerations animate the emerging case law, making it difficult for contracting parties to understand the legal terrain. The chapter then argues that greater conceptualization of the concerns at play would facilitate the development of a less confusing jurisprudence, which would inure to the benefit of all. It also begins the process of sketching out some of that conceptualization.

Section II begins by describing what SAs are and why they are important. In particular, we spend some time discussing the recent rise of SAs involving private equity, which tend to have more sophisticated provisions than agreements in the past and tend to be more carefully lawyered. Section III explores how the law in India addresses SAs

[1] For recent papers in the United States, see G Rauterberg, 'The Separation of Voting and Control: The Role of Contract in Corporate Governance' (2021) 38 Yale Journal on Regulation 1124 and JE Fisch, 'Stealth Governance: Shareholder Agreements and Private Ordering' (2022) 99 Washington University Law Review 913. For Germany, see M Roth, 'Shareholders' Agreements in Listed Companies: Germany' (16 March 2013) <https://ssrn.com/abstract=2234348> accessed 24 June 2023. For Italy, see AS Baglioni, 'Shareholders' Agreements and Voting Power: Evidence from Italian Listed Firms' (5 September 2008) <https://ssrn.com/abstract=1092864> accessed 24 June 2023. For the European Union, see Shearman & Sterling, 'Report on the Proportionality Principle in the European Union' (2007) <https://ec.europa.eu/docsroom/documents/14881/attachments/2/translations/en/renditions/pdf> accessed 24 June 2023. For India up to 2012, see V Niranjan and U Varottil, 'The Enforceability of Contractual Restrictions on the Transfer of Shares' (2012) 5 Supreme Court Cases J-1.

Nemika Jha and Vikramaditya S. Khanna, *Shareholder Agreements in India* In: *Foundations of Indian Contract Law*.
Edited by: KV Krishnaprasad, Niranjan Venkatesan, Shivprasad Swaminathan, and Umakanth Varottil, Oxford University Press.
 DOI: 10.1093/9780191997211.003.0022

and some changes in recent years. Section IV discusses the policy concerns at play. Section V concludes with observations about the state of Indian law on SAs and what steps may benefit its development and the involved parties. It also notes that the very recent proposal by the Securities and Exchange Board of India (SEBI) to require disclosure of certain agreements is a commendable first step in that direction but that some provisions in the proposal may benefit from more careful discussion attuned to the sorts of policy considerations highlighted in this chapter.

II. What Are Shareholder Agreements and Why Do They Matter?

SAs are essentially contracts between two or more shareholders to do (or not do) something.[2] At times, these contracts may also involve the company as another party to the agreement, but the quintessential SA is simply between shareholders. There is, however, considerable heterogeneity in the issues covered by SAs, what types of companies often have them, and what purposes they ostensibly serve.

For instance, SAs can address many different issues, such as shareholders agreeing on (a) voting (how to vote on an issue or series of issues), (b) governance matters (eg whether these shareholders can designate specific directors to the board or veto certain decisions), (c) restrictions on share transfers (whether shares can be freely sold or whether there are limits), (d) matters that relate to statutory corporate law rules (eg whether these shareholders get appraisal rights, inspection rights, the full extent of the duty of loyalty), and (e) perhaps more (eg how to allocate economic rights).[3] In addition, SAs typically end at some point, as may be specified in their terms, for example, when one party sells its shares, dies, or drops below some threshold level of ownership (eg 5 per cent).[4]

Also, SAs appear in many types of companies. SAs have a long historical pedigree in closely held companies as well as in family businesses, but we are increasingly seeing SAs in pre-initial public offering (IPO) companies and in some companies that have gone public. Rauterberg finds, in the United States, that in his sample, about 55 per cent of IPO companies had an SA pre-IPO and that 15 per cent of firms doing an IPO disclose they are subject to an SA post-IPO.[5] Moreover, he found that the larger and more valuable companies tended to have SAs.[6] Further, although historically SAs have been between close associates (eg founders, family), we are now witnessing them between separate and not very closely connected entities (eg private equity).[7]

[2] See Rauterberg (n 1) 1126.

[3] ibid 1129–30. Rauterberg finds in his sample of US companies that most SAs alter the default for electing the board, and many impose some obligations on the company to put up nominees of parties to the SA. He also finds that many companies have veto provisions on changes in control, the hiring or firing of the CEO, and issuing new equity, and other companies often have transfer restrictions. There did not appear to be strong industry effects except that SAs were less often seen in biological products companies; Fisch (n 1) 91.

[4] See Rauterberg (n 1) 1156.

[5] ibid 1149. See also Fisch (n 1) 917–18.

[6] See Rauterberg (n 1) 1153.

[7] For now, we abstract away from the notion that certain players in the private equity space may be repeat players so that they may be somewhat more closely connected than strangers but not as closely connected as family or

Moreover, SAs may serve multiple purposes. For example, transfer restrictions ensure that the ownership of the company changes only when existing shareholders think a potential new shareholder shares similar concerns or values.[8] This might be particularly valuable in businesses (or stages of a business) where a high level of cohesion among shareholders is important. Another common example is where certain matters of governance are thought to be better coordinated behind the scenes rather than in official board decisions (though this, of course, brings with it concerns on transparency).[9] Relatedly, sometimes, parties may want to share control amongst shareholders rather than have it dispersed, and an SA may facilitate such coordination (which, again, may come with its own costs).[10]

Although SAs may be useful in achieving these purposes, it is noteworthy that there are often alternative ways of achieving many of these purposes. For instance, if the founders are wary of new shareholders because they might not vote in ways consistent with existing shareholders, then the founders could put in place supermajority voting requirements in the memorandum or articles of association (collectively, the 'constitutional documents') that reduced those concerns or set up separate classes of stock with different rights.[11] This suggests that the contextualization achieved by SAs might also be achieved via other methods (eg amendments to constitutional documents, dual class structures, tenure voting structures) or via different SAs to the one arrived at by the parties.[12]

In light of their long history and increasing use, one might imagine that there would be a developed regulatory (or doctrinal) approach to SAs. However, there is considerable variety, both globally and over time, in how SAs are treated. Some countries (at some times) have been more willing to enforce most SAs, while others have not, though as noted, this can change over time. Indeed, as we shall see, India's position seems to have displayed some movement in the past two decades as well.

Why do SAs appear so difficult to regulate? Although there may be many explanations, one must note that SAs sit on a precarious border between contract law and corporate law.[13] SAs are frequently assessed as contracts and are thus often assumed to have limited third-party effects so that the law may tend to enforce these agreements.[14] At other times, if they are assessed under corporate law, there are concerns about notice

affinity groups. For a discussion on evolution of private equity in India, see A Afsharipour, 'Corporate Governance and the Indian Private Equity Model' (2015) 27 National Law School of India Review 17; AB Majumdar, 'The (Un)Enforceability of Investor Rights in Indian Private Equity' (2020) 41 University of Pennsylvania Journal of International Law 981.

[8] See *Salt Lake Trib Pub Co, LLC* v *AT & T Corp* 320 F 3d 1081, 1088 (US 10th Circuit Federal Court of Appeals 2003).

[9] See Fisch (n 1) 945–46.

[10] See Rauterberg (n 1) 1144–45.

[11] These alternatives may not provide all the benefits the parties may desire from an SA, but they can achieve many of those benefits (and perhaps others that the SA cannot—like binding all shareholders).

[12] To assess the complete effects of an SA, one will need to know how the SA interacts with other agreements and provisions of the articles of association (AOA) and applicable legislation.

[13] See Rauterberg (n 1) 1142–43.

[14] ibid 1174–75.

to other shareholders and the potentiality to subvert statutory law. After all, corporate law has a hierarchy to its structure[15]—there is the statutory law, the constitutional documents, and then SAs. But sometimes, the SAs are in the terrain of statutory law or the articles of association (AOA).[16] Should the law allow SAs where they run opposite to statutory law or the AOA? There has traditionally been some reticence in doing this, but in other areas of law, parties can often waive their rights as part of an agreement.[17]

Then there are broader questions with which scholars are now beginning to grapple. Should SAs that might influence how other non-party shareholders behave or how the company behaves be disclosed or policed in some way (eg some SAs may exacerbate conflicts of interest or raise transparency concerns)?[18] Should duties of some kind be attached to shareholders acting pursuant to an SA that grants them a great deal of control over the company?[19] Should shareholders voting under an SA be considered 'disinterested' shareholders for regulatory purposes or for determining which standard of review should apply to a conflicted transaction?

These difficulties become even more challenging in modern times, when SAs are often between sophisticated parties with access to top legal talent (which partially assuages concerns with waiving rights but might worsen concerns with transparency and conflicts of interest) rather than between family members or other close associates, who may not always have such legal advice or may be relying on non-legal sources to address concerns, for example, family or social norms.

These concerns tend to make the law relating to SAs fairly complex. This is no less true in India.

III. India's Experience with Shareholder Agreements

India—like many other countries—has had SAs for quite some time, and the jurisprudence is significant. This section explores that jurisprudence in some depth with a view to discerning some key themes in it. We find that the principles governing the enforceability of SAs is unsettled, and there is a lack of clarity and certainty on SAs. Supreme Court decisions have not added much clarity, and High Court decisions have often taken contradictory positions. Indeed, in our conversations with people in practice, we find that they too are concerned about what the boundaries are for the enforceability of SAs. This suggests that SAs are an area where greater synthesis of doctrine and greater understanding of the policy concerns are critical. We pursue this task in section IV, but here we begin with the Indian case law.

[15] See generally WT Allen, R Kraakman, and V Khanna, *Commentaries and Cases on the Law of Business Organizations* (6th edn, Aspen Publishing 2021) 104–106; Fisch (n 1) 935–36. For instance, while the Companies Act, 2013, s 6 establishes the superiority of statutory law, it does not deal with the issue of conflicts between constitutional documents and SAs.

[16] See Allen, Kraakman, and Khanna (n 15) 106.

[17] See Rauterberg (n 1) 1165–67.

[18] See Fisch (n 1) 946–47.

[19] See Rauterberg (n 1) 1168–69.

For the purposes of this discussion, judicial decisions on the enforceability of provisions of SAs are divided into two parts. Section III.1 deals with the judicial approach towards enforceability of restrictions on share transfers, and section III.2 deals with the enforceability of governance-related and other provisions. For expositional brevity, we have limited the analysis to the decisions of the Supreme Court and key decisions of the High Courts.

1. Restrictions on Share Transfers

Restrictions on shares transfers have occupied a great deal of space in Indian case law. We divide the discussion into share transfer restrictions in private companies and public companies.

i. Share transfer restrictions in private companies

One of the earliest landmark decisions regarding the enforceability of share transfer restrictions in the context of a private company is the Supreme Court's division bench decision in *VB Rangaraj v VB Gopalakrishnan*.[20] The main issue before the Court was whether shareholders can enter into an agreement that is contrary to the AOA of a company.

The SA in question was between two groups of shareholders who agreed that if any member of either group wished to sell his or her shares, such selling shareholder would first give an option to the members of his or her group to purchase the shares, and only if such offer was not accepted would the shares be sold to members of the other group. The plaintiffs filed a suit to declare a transfer of shares to the defendants in violation of the said agreement as void and prayed for an injunction to restrain the defendants from registering the said shares in their names. The plaintiffs contended that, even though the restrictions on transferability were not reflected in the company's articles, the two groups of shareholders were, nonetheless, bound by the contractual arrangement that was primarily designed to maintain equal ownership in the company. The defendants, on the other hand, argued that any additional restrictions on the ability to transfer shares that did not find a place in the company's articles were non-binding in nature.

After a combined reading of the provisions of the erstwhile Companies Act 1956 (hereinafter, the '1956 Act'), certain English case law[21] and its own prior ruling,[22] the

[20] *VB Rangaraj v VB Gopalakrishnan* AIR 1992 SC 453.

[21] *In Re Swaledale Cleaners Ltd* (1968) 1 All ER 1132; *Tett v Phoenix Property and Investment Co Ltd* 1986 2 BCC 99, 140. The Court relied on these judgments to reiterate that shares are freely alienable in the absence of any express restrictions in the articles.

[22] *SP Jain vs Kalinga Tubes Ltd* AIR 1965 SC 1535, where the Court held that where shareholders of a private company who had entered into a contractual agreement with a third party had caused the company to pass various resolutions to implement the terms thereof, such agreement could not be enforced against the company if the terms thereof were not incorporated in its articles.

Supreme Court concluded that any share transfer restrictions must be incorporated in the AOA.[23] Accordingly, the Court held that

> Whether under the Companies Act or Transfer of Property Act, the shares are, therefore, transferable like any other movable property. The only restriction on the transfer of the shares of a company is as laid down in its Articles, if any. A restriction which is not specified in the Articles is, therefore, not binding either on the company or on the shareholders.[24]

Given that, in this case, the company's AOA already specified certain restrictions on transferability, additional restrictions that were agreed to between the two groups of shareholders under a separate SA were disregarded as contrary to the AOA and, hence, not binding on the company and the shareholders.

The *Rangaraj* decision is, therefore, widely understood to have laid down a test of incorporation whereby contractual restrictions that are not incorporated into the AOA are non-binding and, hence, unenforceable. While the conclusion that such restrictions would not bind the company is not problematic (especially if the company is not a party to the SA) and is in accordance with a well-settled principle of English law,[25] the conclusion that such a restriction would not even be binding on the shareholders is troublesome and goes against the well-settled contract law principle that a party who has not breached the terms of a contact (in this case, an SA) can claim damages from a party who has breached the terms thereof. Put differently, the *Rangaraj* decision makes it futile to have an SA in the first place, since in order for it to be enforceable *inter se* the shareholders, every clause in the agreement would have to be incorporated in the AOA.

The issue of transfer restrictions in a family settlement (in the context of a private company) came up before the Supreme Court in the 2004 decision in *MS Madhusoodhanan v Kerala Kaumudi Pvt Ltd*.[26] The case arose out of a complex family settlement under which 50 per cent of the shares of two promoter shareholders were supposed to be transferred to the appellant upon the death of one of the said promoters. While the appellant filed for specific performance, the respondent argued that said agreement, in so far as it provided for transfer of shares to the appellant, was contrary to the provisions of the AOA of the company and hence not enforceable in accordance with the *Rangaraj* decision. The Court did not disagree with the ratio of the *Rangaraj* decision but distinguished the facts and held that, unlike a *blanket restriction* on transferability that applied to *all* shareholders (present and future) in the *Rangaraj* case,

[23] In order to arrive at the conclusion that a restriction, unless incorporated in the articles, would not be binding on the company or on the shareholders, the Court primarily relied on the 1956 Act, ss 3(1)(iii)(a) and 82. After a combined reading of the statutory provisions of the 1956 Act (in particular, s 3(1)(iii)(a), which provided that a private limited company should include provisions restricting share transfers in its articles, and s 82, which provided that shares are moveable property, transferable in a manner provided in the articles of the company), the Court concluded that any restriction, if not incorporated in the articles, would not bind the company or the shareholders.

[24] *VB Rangaraj* (n 20) [6].

[25] *Russell v Northern Bank Development Corp Ltd* [1992] 1 WLR 588.

[26] AIR 2004 SC 909.

an agreement between *certain* shareholders relating to the transfer of *certain specified* shares of a private company did not *per se* constitute a restriction on transferability. Accordingly, 'it was unnecessary for the company or the other shareholders to be a party to the agreement',[27] and the parties who had voluntarily entered into the said agreement were obliged to act in accordance with the terms thereof.

It is interesting to note that both *Rangaraj* and *Madhusoodhanan* were decisions delivered by division benches of the Supreme Court. The *Madhusoodhanan* decision did uphold the freedom of contract (albeit in a somewhat limited way) and held that the agreement between *specific* shareholders relating to the transfer of *identified* shares was specifically performable *inter se* such shareholders. However, it did not disagree with the principles laid down in the *Rangaraj* case, and hence it did not overturn the finding that a blanket restriction on all shareholders needed to be in the AOA to be enforceable.

ii. Share transfer restrictions in public companies

Although both *Rangaraj* and *Madhusoodhanan* dealt with the question of enforceability of share transfer restrictions in private companies, it was not long before the issue arose for public companies. We spend some time on these decisions and trace their judicial development to shed some light on the evolving approach.

In *Mafatlal Industries Ltd v Gujarat Gas Co Ltd*,[28] the plaintiff sold 3.87 per cent of its shareholding to the defendant (a foreign institutional investor) based on a private agreement that gave the plaintiff a right to pre-emption on the said shares. The terms of the private agreement were, however, not incorporated in the AOA of the company. The defendant further sold the said shares in the open market to several third-party purchasers. Relying on the right to pre-emption, the plaintiff sought specific performance of the agreement and also prayed for damages in the alternative. One of the key issues was whether a right to pre-emption could be enforced in view of the concept of free transferability of shares, which is one of the hallmarks of a public limited company. In holding that *Rangaraj* applied with much greater force to public companies, a single judge of the Gujarat Hight Court held that

> [W]hile V.B. Rangaraj's case was certainly concerned with a private limited company, the very distinction between a private limited company and a public limited company is, inter alia, the provision of restriction against transfer being contained in the articles of association of a private limited company whereas the articles of association of a public limited company cannot contain any such restriction. Hence, . . . the ratio in the case of V. B. Rangaraj will apply with much greater force to the case of a public limited company requires to be accepted.[29]

[27] ibid [146].
[28] 1999 97 CompCas 301 Guj.
[29] ibid [73].

The Gujarat High Court thus extended the *Rangaraj* decision to public limited companies.

However, when the enforceability of the right of first refusal in a family settlement that was agreed to between the parties, but not incorporated in the articles of a public company, came up before a single judge of the Delhi High Court in *Smt Pushpa Katoch v Manu Maharani Hotels Ltd*,[30] the Court refrained from applying the *Rangaraj* incorporation test. Instead, the Court went on to hold that, in view of the concept of free transferability of shares in public companies that is expressly provided for in section 111(A)(2) of the 1956 Act,

> there could be no fetters on the right of a shareholder to transfer his/her shares [and that] . . . even if there was such a provision in the articles of association, it would have been ultra vires the provisions of the Act, as no company can provide in the articles of association any matter which offends the specific provision of an Act.[31]

The debate on enforceability of pre-emptive rights on the shares of public limited companies was revived once again in 2010 with the decision of a single judge of the Bombay High Court in *Western Maharashtra Development Corp Ltd v Bajaj Auto Limited*.[32] The dispute arose out of a protocol agreement that was entered into between the petitioner and the respondent to set up Maharashtra Scooters Ltd (MSL), a public listed company, that would manufacture scooters utilizing the respondent's technical know-how. As per the terms of the protocol agreement, the petitioner and the respondent would hold 27 per cent and 24 per cent of the shares of MSL, respectively, and the remaining 49 per cent would be held by the public. The parties intended to control at least 51 per cent of MSL's shareholding at all times. Accordingly, clause 7 of the protocol agreement (which was incorporated in the articles of MSL) provided that in the event any party wished to sell its shareholding, such selling shareholder would first offer the shares to the other party, and any dispute in connection with the price thereof would be referred to an arbitrator. A subsequent divestment of shareholding in MSL by the petitioner resulted in a price dispute that was referred to an arbitrator. One of the key issues was whether the said restriction on the transfer of shares of MSL, a public limited company, was valid. The arbitrator relied on the decisions of the Supreme Court in the *Rangaraj* and *Madhusoodhanan* case and held that (a) clause 7 of the protocol agreement was not violative of the concept of free transferability as that said clause was binding only on two shareholders and not on all shareholders and (b) section 111(A) of the 1956 Act (which, inter alia, provided for shares of a company to be freely transferable) did not prohibit specific shareholders from entering into agreements regarding specific shares, especially when they are incorporated into the AOA.

[30] 2006 131 CompCas 42 Delhi.
[31] ibid [9].
[32] 2010 154 Comp Cases 593 Bom.

In setting aside the arbitral award, the Bombay High Court upheld the reasoning of the Delhi High Court in *Pushpa Katoch* and held that pre-emptive rights over shares of a public company are completely contrary to the substantive provisions of the law and *patently illegal*. After analysing the provisions of the 1956 Act, the Court went on to highlight that while the Act expressly permitted the AOA to impose fetters on the transfer of shares of a private company,[33] it specifically prohibited the same in the case of public companies by providing that the shares or debentures, or any interest therein, shall be freely transferable.[34] The Court, therefore, distinguished the *Rangaraj* and *Madhusoodhanan* decisions as being inapplicable to public companies. The Court further went on to hold that in view of section 9 of the 1956 Act, which provided that the provisions of the Act would prevail notwithstanding anything contrary in the AOA, the principle of free transferability enshrined in section 111(A)(2) would prevail over any agreement to the contrary (even if incorporated in the articles).

Interestingly, shortly thereafter, a division bench of the Bombay Hight Court in *Messer Holdings Limited v Shyam Madanmohan Ruia*,[35] reconsidered the validity of pre-emption rights over shares of a public limited company and overruled the decision of the single judge in the *Bajaj Auto* case by holding that voluntary private agreements imposing share transfer restrictions (in this case, a right of first refusal) would not violate the concept of free transferability provided in section 111(A) of the 1956 Act.

The Court's reasoning relied on several factors: first, that section 111A[36] was introduced to prevent *boards* from refusing to transfer shares arbitrarily, not to curtail the rights of a shareholder to deal with his or her shares as they wish. Second, being a shareholder in a public company does not undermine that shareholder's right to agree to sell his or her shares to another party on such terms and conditions that the parties may have negotiated (including a right to pre-emption) so long as the agreement is otherwise in conformity with the articles and other applicable law. Simply put, the 'freedom to purchase cannot mean obligation on the shareholder to sell his shares'.[37] Finally, the Court reasoned that *Madhusoodhanan* is an authority for the *general position* that contractual agreements voluntarily entered into by *certain* shareholders regarding *their specific* shares (in exercise of their right to free transferability) do not impose any illegal restrictions on transferability, regardless of whether the agreement relates to shares in a private or public company. Such agreements can be enforced like any other agreement, and the company or any other shareholder need not be a party to such agreement. Consequently, such agreements do not need to be incorporated in the articles.

[33] The Court referred to the 1956 Act, s 3(1)(iii).

[34] The Court referred to ibid s 111(A)(2). In the words of the Court, at *Bajaj Auto* (n 32) [61],

> The provision contained in the law for the free transferability of shares in a public Company is founded on the principle that members of the public must have the freedom to purchase and, every shareholder, the freedom to transfer. . . . Imposing restrictions on the principle of free transferability, is a legislative function, simply because the postulate of free transferability was enunciated as a matter of legislative policy when Parliament introduced Section 111A into the Companies Act, 1956.

[35] (2010) 159 Comp Cas 29 Bom.

[36] The 1956 Act, s 111A substituted the Securities Contracts (Regulation) Act 1956, s 22A.

[37] *Messer Holdings Ltd* (n 35) [51].

While *Messer Holdings* attempted to settle questions surrounding enforceability of share transfer restrictions in public companies, it did not invalidate the principles laid down in the *Rangaraj* case. Instead, the Court agreed with (and utilized) the distinction drawn by the Supreme Court in the *Madhusoodhanan* case in as much as it held that the rationale of the *Rangaraj* case (which essentially dealt with a blanket restriction on transferability for all present and future shareholders) could not be applied to a private agreement between particular shareholders for specific shares.

Both the decisions in *Bajaj Auto* and *Messer Holdings* were subject to appeal. The *Bajaj Auto* decision was appealed to a division bench of the Bombay High Court, and the *Messer Holdings* decision was appealed to the Supreme Court. During the pendency of these appeals, a three-judge bench of the Supreme Court, in January 2012, delivered a landmark decision in *Vodafone International Holdings v Union of India*,[38] which was primarily a tax dispute but also made significant observations on the nature of SAs and the view taken by the Supreme Court in the *Rangaraj* decision (without expressly overruling it). Justice Radhakrishnan, in a separate concurring opinion, indicated that the Court did not agree with the view taken in the *Rangaraj* case because it imposed restrictions on the freedom of shareholders to enter into contracts, although no such restrictions can be found in company law.[39] Indeed, the Court rejected the view of *Rangaraj* which holds that SAs are only enforceable if contained in the AOA. The Court further went on to add that nothing prohibited shareholders from entering into agreements designed towards achieving effective management of the company so long as the provisions thereof were not contrary to the AOA.[40]

An upshot of the observations in *Vodafone* is that an SA is enforceable *unless* the terms thereof are *contrary* to the AOA. By doing so, the Court did not overrule *Rangaraj*. Instead, it attempted to provide more room for interpretation of questions pertaining to the enforceability of SAs (particularly in instances where, despite the provisions of an SA not being contrary to company law or the articles, the AOA were silent in respect thereof). However, given that the *Vodafone* case was a tax dispute where the Supreme Court was not examining questions pertaining to enforceability of specific provisions of SAs, the views expressed by the Supreme Court are, at best, *obiter dicta*.

In an interesting turn of events, while the *Messer Holdings Appeal* was still pending before the Supreme Court, the division bench of the Bombay Hight Court in *Bajaj Auto Ltd v Western Maharashtra Development*[41] overturned the decision of the single

38 (2012) 6 SCC 613.

39 The Court relied on *Gherulal Parekh v Mahadeo Das Maiya* (1959) SCR Supp (2) 406 to hold that freedom of contract can be restricted only on grounds of public policy or if the company law statute expressly or impliedly prohibits shareholders from entering into such agreements.

40 From a standpoint of remedies, the Court held, at *Vodafone International Holdings* (n 38) [64],

> Of course, the manner in which such agreements are to be enforced in the case of breach is given in the general law between the company and the shareholders. A breach of shareholders' agreement which does not breach the Articles of Association is a valid corporate action but, as we have already indicated, the parties aggrieved can get remedies under the general law of the land for any breach of that agreement.

41 Appeal No 153 of 2010, Arbitration Petition No 174 of 2006, and Notice of Motion No 993 of 2010 (Bombay High Court, 08 May 2015).

judge by upholding the *Messer Holdings* decision. A large part of the division bench's decision in the *Bajaj Auto Appeal* case echoed the principles set forth in the *Messers Holdings* decision. It underscored that the legislative history behind section 111A of the 1956 Act (and its predecessor, section 22A of the Securities Contract (Regulation) Act, 1956) was to prevent boards from arbitrarily refusing to register share transfers and not to constrain shareholders from entering into agreements. Accordingly, the Court held that voluntarily negotiated restrictions on transfer (like pre-emption rights) do not violate the principle of free transferability. On the contrary, such contracts (by way of sale, pledge, or pre-emption) are a result of shareholders exercising their right to freely deal with their shares (which are essentially moveable property owned by shareholders). Bolstering its rationale, the Court held that it is settled law[42] that the legislature cannot be presumed to deprive a person of his or her right to property or interfere with such person's freedom to contract in respect thereof unless it is warranted by public policy or an express provision is made in that regard.[43]

Moreover, the Court noted that even though the SA was not incorporated in the AOA, it would still govern the rights and obligations *inter se* the parties thereto. Thus, even if MSL were not bound by the protocol agreement, the parties to the SA could still bring a suit against each other. In addition, if the SA in question here had been incorporated into the AOA, it would not violate section 111A's principle of free transferability because it is not a blanket restriction on all shareholders (a critical fact in *Rangaraj*). The Court even noted that

> we find that in today's global reality, joint ventures are extremely common and clauses similar to Clause 7 of the Protocol Agreement may become necessary to ensure that a joint promotor of a company does not sell his shareholding to a competitor who then possibly could get control of his rival. In this view of the matter and looking to the totality of the facts and circumstances of the case, we are clearly of the view that Clause 7 of the Protocol Agreement does not in any way impinge upon the principle of free transferability of shares as contemplated under section 111A of the Companies Act, 1956.[44]

Although this case involved provisions under the 1956 Act, the Court expanded its discussion to the provisions of the Companies Act, 2013 (hereinafter, the '2013 Act'), which replaced the 1956 Act. This appeared to be in recognition of both the paucity of case law on the provisions in the 2013 Act at that time and the need for having a robust contractual and enforcement framework given the existing commercial realities. The Court began by discussing section 58(2) of the 2013 Act, which specifically provides that 'without prejudice to sub-section (1), the securities or other interest of

[42] *Byram Pestonji Gariwala v Union Bank of India* (1992) 1 SCC 31; *ICICI Bank Ltd v SIDCO Leathers Ltd* (2006) 10 SCC 452.

[43] For a greater discussion on the legislative history and interpretation of the same by courts, see Niranjan and Varottil (n 1).

[44] *Bajaj Auto Appeal* (n 41) [37].

any member in a public company shall be freely transferable', and its proviso, which stipulates that 'any contract or arrangement between two or more persons in respect of transfer of securities shall be enforceable as a contract'. Thereafter, it examined its legislative history and concluded that, according to the 57th Report of the Parliamentary Standing Committee on the Companies Bill 2011, the proviso to section 58 'simply seeks to codify the pronouncements made by various Courts holding that contracts relating to transferability of shares of a company entered into by one or more shareholders of a company (which may include promoter or promoter group as a shareholder) shall be enforceable under law'.[45] It also referred to the SEBI notification dated 3 October 2013, which clarifies that SEBI's permission is not required for 'contracts for pre-emption including right of first refusal, or tag-along or drag-along rights contained in shareholders agreements or articles of association of companies or other body corporate'.[46] On a combined reading of section 58 of the 2013 Act and SEBI's notification, the Court held that the introduction of the proviso to section 58(2) of the 2013 Act not only makes what was implicit in section 111(A) of the 1956 Act explicit but also expressly resolves the larger question of enforceability of pre-emption rights. Although this was technically *obiter dicta* (as the case involved the 1956 Act), these observations highlight the considerations upon which the Court relied.[47]

It is also important to note that the division bench in the *Bajaj Auto Appeal* not only distinguished the *Rangaraj* decision on the facts on the ground that the transfer restriction being considered therein applied to *all* shareholders but also relied on the observations of the Supreme Court in the *Vodafone* case (where the apex Court hinted that the *Rangaraj* decision may have been wrongly decided without expressly overruling it) to fortify this decision.

Shortly thereafter, in early 2016, the Supreme Court was about to render its decision in the *Messer Holdings Appeal* case.[48] While this appeal could have been a golden opportunity for the Supreme Court to finally decide the much-debated issue of enforceability of share transfer restrictions in shareholders' agreements, the parties involved in the litigation entered into a settlement, thereby extinguishing the cause of action. Accordingly, the *Messer Holdings Appeal* was dismissed without deciding the issues surrounding free transferability of shares, shareholders' right to enter contractual arrangements (including transfer restrictions), and their enforceability thereof.

Nonetheless, the discussion of case law suggests an emerging jurisprudence with respect to SAs on share transfers that restricts *Rangaraj* to instances where there are blanket restrictions on all shareholders. It allows for greater enforcement, at least *inter se* the parties, of more limited SAs. This approach appears to have been extended to both private and public companies, but we are still awaiting a Supreme Court decision

[45] Standing Committee on Finance, Lok Sabha, *The Companies Bill 2011* (Fifty-Seventh Report, 2012) 104.

[46] SEBI, *Notification No LAD-NRO/GN/2013-14/26/6667*, 1.

[47] Note that the *Bajaj Auto Appeal* case (n 41) is perhaps the only case in which the Court has touched upon the changes introduced by the 2013 Act. Until the Indian courts re-examine issues pertaining to enforceability of SAs under the 2013 Act, the jurisprudence developed under the 1956 Act would continue to be relevant even under the 2013 Act.

[48] *Messer Holdings Ltd v Shyam Madanmohan Ruia* (2016) 11 SCC 484.

that directly confirms this emerging jurisprudence.[49] However, SAs relate not only to share transfers but also to governance matters. It is to that case law that we now turn.

2. Provisions Relating to Governance and Other Matters

In *IL&FS Trust Co Ltd v Birla Perucchini Ltd*,[50] the Bombay High Court had an opportunity to consider the validity of a provision that restrained a director from resigning from the board until a subscription-cum-shareholders' agreement (which was not incorporated in the articles) was completed. The question before the Court was whether the *Rangaraj* decision was limited to share transfer restrictions in SAs. Answering the question in the negative, the Bombay High Court extended the applicability of the *Rangaraj* decision to all provisions contained in an SA that relate to the management of a company and held, 'The provisions in an agreement such as the one in the present case, cannot be given effect to insofar as the management of the affairs of the company is concerned, unless those provisions have been incorporated into the articles of association.'[51] Indeed, the Court expressly rejected the contention that the *Rangaraj* ruling was confined to restrictions on share transfers. It also clarified that whether the company was a party to the subscription-cum-shareholders' agreement or not made no difference to the settled position of law that unless provisions pertaining to the management of the company are incorporated in the articles, the affairs of the company would continue to be governed by the articles. Accordingly, the Court held that 'The articles regulate the internal management of the company and define the powers of its officers. The articles also establish a contract between the company and members and between the members inter se. The contract governs the ordinary rights and obligations incidental to the membership in the company.'[52]

The extension of *Rangaraj* to general governance matters was tested just a few years later in 2007. In *Modi Rubber Ltd v Guardian International Corporation*,[53] the petitioner and the respondent entered into an SA to promote a joint venture company for the production and marketing of float glass. Clause 14 of the said agreement prohibited either of the parties from undertaking and/or participating in any similar project in India without prior consent of the other party. One of the issues was whether the respondent could undertake an additional project by setting up a wholly owned

[49] Indeed, at least the Delhi High Court has expressed some reservation about moving too far away from *Rangaraj* in *HTA Employees Union (Regd) v Hindustan Thompson Associates Ltd* 180 (2011) DLT 530, [20], noting that

> Till VB Rangaraj is not expressly overruled by the Supreme Court, this Court remains bound by the same and as aforesaid the grounds on which VB Rangaraj has been distinguished in the judgments aforesaid are not available to the appellant/plaintiff; rather the facts of the present case are akin to VB Rangaraj.

It is noteworthy that the *HTA Employees* case involved a blanket restriction on all shareholders, as in *VB Rangaraj* (n 20).

[50] (2003) 4 CompLJ 131(Bom).

[51] ibid [6].

[52] ibid [28].

[53] 2007 (2) Arb LR 133 (Del).

subsidiary without any participation of the petitioner. Relying on the *Rangaraj* and *IL&FS* decisions, the respondent argued that the said clause was non-binding as the same was not incorporated in the articles of the joint venture company. On the other hand, the petitioner placed reliance on the *Madhusoodhanan* decision rendered by the Supreme Court and argued that the said non-compete clause would continue to be applicable *inter se* the shareholders.

The Delhi High Court distinguished both the *Rangaraj* and *IL&FS* decisions on the facts by stating that the issue in the *Modi Rubber* case (which related to a restriction on entering into the same or similar business) was fundamentally different from the aforementioned decisions, where the issues related to restrictions on share transferability and management of the affairs of a company were governed by the statute and the articles of a company. Given that clause 14 was distinct and had nothing to do with share transfers and/or the management of the affairs of the joint venture, the Court held that the said clause would continue to bind the parties even if the clause was not incorporated in the articles. Accordingly, the Court held,

> So far as Clause 14 is concerned, it binds only the parties to the shareholders agreement, is unconcerned with and independent of the affairs of the joint venture. Certainly, the prohibition contained in clause 14 of the agreement is not rendered illegal or unenforceable by any provision of the Companies Act or any clause of the Articles of Association or by virtue of the principles laid down in any of the judicial pronouncements noticed hereinabove. It is also not rendered void or not binding for the reason that it is not incorporated in the Articles of Association of the joint venture.[54]

Relying on the *Modi Rubber* decision, the Delhi High Court, in *Premier Hockey Development Private Limited v Indian Hockey Federation*,[55] held that provisions of the subscription and shareholders agreement (which were neither contrary to the 1956 Act nor the AOA) were enforceable even though the same were not incorporated in the AOA of the company. The dispute in this case emanated from the respondent proposing to organize a hockey league in violation of an agreement that was entered into between the parties. The respondent, however, contended that the board resolution of the petitioner initiating the proceedings against the respondent were illegal on account of them being in violation of the notice and quorum requirements as specified in clauses 10.3.2 and 10.3.3 of the subscription and shareholders agreement between the parties. Relying on *Rangaraj*, the petitioner argued that since these clauses were not incorporated in its AOA, the same were not binding on the company.

The Delhi High Court held that, unlike *Rangaraj*, where the company was not a party to any agreement, the petitioner company in the *Premier Hockey* case was a party to the subscription and shareholders agreement, which required the company to

[54] ibid [79].
[55] (2011) 180 DLT 530.

amend its articles to reflect the terms thereof (including clauses 10.3.2 and 10.3.3). In concluding that the said agreement was not only binding (and hence enforceable) *inter se* the shareholders but also on the company (since it was a party thereto), the Court held that

> In the present case as well, there is no Article . . . in the Articles of Association of the petitioner company, which conflicts with Articles 10.3.2 and 10.3.3 of the Subscription and Shareholders Agreement. The said articles are also not in contravention of any legal provision in the Companies Act or Rules . . . Such an agreement would clearly bind not just the shareholders, but also the company, as the company is also a party to the Subscription and Shareholders Agreement.[56]

It is important to note that while the Delhi High Court in the *Hockey Premier* case distinguished the applicability of *Rangaraj* on the grounds that it related to a different set of facts (namely, restrictions on share transferability) and that the company itself was not a party to the shareholders' agreement in that case, it did not discuss or disagree with the holding of the *IL&FS* case (a case that was also decided by the Bombay High Court), where the Court had extended the applicability of the *Rangaraj* decision to all provisions contained in a shareholders' agreement in respect of the management of the affairs of a company (which would certainly include matters pertaining to the conduct of board meetings as in the *Hockey Premier* case). Therefore, while the High Court decisions in *Hockey Premier* and *Modi Rubber* upheld the parties' freedom to contract outside of the articles (subject to the terms thereof not being contrary to the statute or the AOA), the said decisions did not expressly overrule *IL&FS*.

The debate on enforceability of provisions of SAs (in particular, provisions that are neither contrary to the statute nor find a mention in the articles), once again, came up for discussion before the Delhi High Court in *World Phone India Pvt Ltd v WPI Group Inc, USA*.[57] In *World Phone*, the Delhi High Court dealt with a dispute that revolved around affirmative voting rights in a joint venture agreement. While clause 6 of the agreement provided an affirmative vote to the respondent (a minority shareholder) in the case of a rights issue, the board of directors of the petitioner (a private company) nonetheless approved a rights issue without obtaining an affirmative vote of the respondent. It is important to note that the AOA of the company were not amended to reflect the affirmative voting rights provided in clause 6 of the joint venture agreement. Therefore, the issue that arose was whether provisions of the joint venture agreement, which did not contravene the statute or the articles but on which the articles were silent, could be held to be enforceable.

In holding that the powers of the company have to be ascertained with reference to the provisions in the AOA, the Delhi High Court held,

[56] ibid [39].

[57] (2013) 178 Comp Case 173 Del.

> The question to be asked is whether the provisions of an agreement, that are not inconsistent with the Act, but are also not part of the Articles of Association, can be said to be applicable. All that Section 9 states is that clauses in the agreement that are 'repugnant' to the Act shall be 'void'. This does not mean that clauses in the agreement which are not repugnant to the Act would be enforceable, notwithstanding that they are not incorporated in the Articles of Association.[58]

Accordingly, the Court held that the affirmative vote in the joint venture agreement was not binding on the company (unless the same was incorporated in the articles). So far as the applicability of the *Rangaraj* decision was concerned, the Court relied on the rationale of *IL&FS* to hold that the *Rangaraj* decision could not be limited to the cases involving restrictions on share transfers but that it applied to all other situations that involved issues pertaining to the management of the affairs of the company.

Thus, in the *World Phone* decision, the Delhi High Court added further confusion to this area. In what would appear to be a significant constraint on the shareholders' freedom to contract outside the articles, the *World Phone* case took the applicability of the *Rangaraj* and *IL&FS* decisions further by holding that on all matters pertaining to the management of the affairs of the company, provisions in SAs would be rendered unenforceable even in instances where the said provisions were not contrary to the statute or on which the AOA were merely silent, unless the same were incorporated in the AOA.[59]

This, again, seems to resurrect a stronger version of *Rangaraj* than we had witnessed in the later cases of share transfer restrictions in SAs. Thus, although there does appear to be an emerging jurisprudential approach to SAs, that is not occurring in a linear manner as some decisions seem to harken back to the more restrictive interpretation of *Rangaraj*. Thus far, the jurisprudence is both complex and difficult to parse. Although there are certain things that seem fairly clear (such as that an SA signed by a subset of shareholders cannot be used to bind all shareholders), there are many others where the courts have adopted what look like contradictory holdings and where it is very difficult to discern what is permitted. Yet, SAs are becoming more common in India and elsewhere so that developing a more effective jurisprudence seems important. We think an early step in that direction is to discuss the policy considerations that undergird SAs and use that as the basis for thinking about SA regulation.

58 ibid [15].

59 It is also pertinent to note that the Supreme Court had delivered its decision in the *Vodafone* case in 2012 (n 38) (ie before the *World Phone* case (n 57) was decided), but the Delhi High Court took no notice of it (perhaps because it considered it *obiter dicta*). If the *Vodafone* decision (as discussed above) were to be extended to the *World Phone* case, then despite the provisions relating to the affirmative vote not being incorporated in the AOA and the board action of approving the rights issue without such affirmative vote being valid under company law, such action would still be in breach of the terms of the shareholders' agreement for which an aggrieved shareholder could pursue an action for breach of contract under contract law.

IV. Policy Considerations

The difficulty in finding a 'golden thread' for understanding the legal treatment of SAs is, in part, attributable to the sheer variety of SAs but also due to the challenging policy concerns they raise. Nonetheless, we argue that paying greater attention to those policy considerations is likely to provide greater clarity at a time when SAs are becoming increasingly common and where the policy considerations are likely to be important for efficiency and growth.

We start our analysis by noting that SAs exist because the provisions of the statutory corporate law are not thought to be meeting the needs of the shareholders who are parties to the SA. If the statutory corporate law met what the parties desired, then there would be little need to spend the time and resources to negotiate and draft an SA. However, there are multiple ways in which shareholders could change the effects of the statutory corporate law. First, they could enter an SA to effect that change among the parties or, alternatively, they could engage in an amendment of the constitutional documents which effected that change.[60] The question then becomes why prefer an SA over an amendment of constitutional documents and what policy implications does that have?

There are several central differences between amendments to constitutional documents and SAs. First, an amendment of constitutional documents, if approved by the requisite majority of shareholders, binds *all shareholders* and the company, including even those shareholders who *voted against* the amendment.[61] Generally speaking, an SA only binds those who agreed to it, so if one is not a party to the SA (ie did not agree to it), he or she is generally not bound by it.

Second, an amendment of constitutional documents must first be moved and approved by the board before it gets to a shareholder vote.[62] This provides dissenting (or minority shareholders) with some additional protection—at least in theory—against majority overreach (in the form of board oversight and approval) when they are bound by the majority vote.[63] SAs, on the other hand, have less need of board oversight because the consent of the parties to the SA is provided *explicitly* rather than implicitly via a majority of shareholders vote that compels an outcome. Moreover, SAs typically expire when one of the parties sells its shares (totally or to some extent) or dies, but charter amendments do not 'leave' when the party who proposed them leaves.[64] The relatively less permanent nature of SAs and explicit consent may suggest that board

[60] See Rauterberg (n 1) 1127–28. In theory, the company could incorporate in another jurisdiction that had laws it preferred, but we abstract away from that issue here; see Fisch (n 1) 921–22.

[61] See Allen, Kraakman, and Khanna (n 15) 104–06.

[62] ibid.

[63] This need not be the only purpose behind requiring boards to first move and approve AOA amendments. Obtaining board expertise on the substance is important too; see Allen, Kraakman & Khanna (n 15). Note also that board involvement can, in some jurisdictions, allow for consideration of non-shareholder third parties (at least in theory). See ibid.

[64] See Rauterberg (n 1) 1154, 1174–75; Fisch (n 1) 944.

oversight is not as critical as it is for charter amendments that are more permanent and where consent is implicit.

Third, amendments to a company's constitutional documents become visible to others—other shareholders, outside third parties, and so forth.[65] SAs are not part of the company's constituent documents and hence are only sometimes visible to others. This potential lack of disclosure raises its own concerns in that perhaps others are expecting the parties to the SA to do something (eg monitor management) that the SA results in them not doing. For instance, small shareholders might think a large shareholder would monitor management to some extent, but that large shareholder may not be doing this monitoring if he or she has signed an undisclosed SA where he or she agrees to vote in a particular way on certain issues. This could lead to mismatched expectations and efforts as well as exacerbating conflicts of interest.[66]

Fourth, amendments to constitutional documents cannot go beyond what statutory law permits. Thus, if there are some mandatory terms in the statutory corporate law, such amendments cannot change those terms.[67] The position in some jurisdictions with SAs seems, however, to be that an SA could go beyond the statutory corporate law, at least with respect to the shareholders who signed the SA; for example, the parties to the SA could waive their mandatory rights under statute.[68] Although this is not always clearly stated, Rauterberg argues that, at least in Delaware, it appears to be plausible.[69] This may appear troubling, but it is noteworthy that SAs that purport to avoid the mandatory terms for the parties involved essentially operate like waivers of those terms, which may appear like settlements in some sense.[70] Moreover, if the SA only applies to the contracting parties, then the waiver is limited in effect to the signing parties.

These central differences indicate what are the likely advantages and disadvantages of SAs relative to amendments to constitutional documents. One advantage of an SA is that it allows for certain sorts of minority protections (or sharing of control) that may not be easily available under the constitutional documents, [71] either because the board may not approve it, because it may not receive the requisite majority shareholder support, or because the SA may simply be cheaper to effectuate for other reasons. SAs may also permit the signing shareholders to opt out of mandatory terms that they do not consider appropriate for their situation.[72] These are private ordering benefits.

[65] See Fisch (n 1) 956.

[66] Note that because SAs may be fairly short lived (eg if a signatory sells its shares, the SA may not be binding on that signatory), that may lead to a relatively lesser need for disclosure than an AOA amendment, but this depends greatly on how long one anticipates that an SA may be in effect.

[67] See Allen, Kraakman, and Khanna (n 15) 104.

[68] See Rauterberg (n 1) 1128–29 (discussing the United States). We note that while the 2013 Act, s 6 expressly provides primacy to statutory law in cases where SAs executed by the company conflict with statutory law, it is silent on whether SAs executed solely among shareholders (without the company being a party) can go beyond statutory law.

[69] See Rauterberg (n 1) 1143, 1153.

[70] See ibid 1166–67.

[71] For sharing control, see ibid 1161 (discussing AR Gomes and W Novaes, 'Sharing of Control as a Corporate Governance Mechanism' (February 2005) <http://dx.doi.org/10.2139/ssrn.277111> accessed 25 June 2023).

[72] As mentioned in n 49 above, under Indian law, it is not clear whether SAs executed solely among shareholders can traverse beyond statutory law.

These benefits, however, must be balanced against the potential costs of SAs. One is that if there are large bargaining disparities between the parties, then we may prefer the board-mediated process[73] of amending constitutional documents. This may seem more important when the parties are not very sophisticated or do not have legal counsel but less significant when they are institutional investors such as private equity. Of course, if the board is dominated or selected by a controlling shareholder, that would weaken this argument. Another potential cost is that concerns with SAs may be largest when we think they are likely to have third-party effects (including on non-party shareholders). This is especially pronounced when SAs are not disclosed because then third parties do not know whether the SA exists and cannot take steps to reduce any negative effects on themselves. On the other hand, if SAs do not have significant third-party effects, then the lack of disclosure and lack of board involvement, compared to amendments to constitutional documents, do not appear to be of as great concern.

This suggests that SAs, relative to amendments to constitutional documents, tend to be desirable when there are few third-party effects; the signing parties are sophisticated and have access to good legal counsel (eg private equity); the SA is disclosed in some manner; and the subject matter of the SA is something that seems more difficult, costly, or unlikely to achieve via amendments to constitutional documents (or is of specific value only to the parties to the SA). Of course, not all of these need to be present, but the more of them there are, the stronger the policy case for an SA relative to such amendments.

However, this does not end the analysis because SAs can raise additional concerns that are not directly tied to a comparison with amendments to constitutional documents. For instance, Fisch has argued that SAs undermine the predictability of the corporate form because of the significant customization they permit (often outside the eyes of the other shareholders).[74] She argues that this reduces the value from standardization and potential network effects of making changes in the corporate charter.[75] This certainly seems an important consideration, but how much so is open for debate, given that many jurisdictions allow significant customization in charters and many SAs might follow the guidance provided by various venture capital associations (which cabins some of the customization).[76] In any case, this consideration appears akin to third-party effects discussed above but is not dependent on the comparison with charters, and hence we treat it somewhat separately.[77]

Rauterberg also argues that SAs have potentially cross-cutting effects on the divergence of incentives amongst shareholders.[78] For instance, an SA can bring those

[73] See Rauterberg (n 1) 1159–60; Fisch (n 1) 951–52. This may not be entirely applicable to the Indian context, where promoters/founders tend to exercise greater control over the boards of Indian companies.

[74] See Fisch (n 1) 950–51.

[75] ibid 948.

[76] See Allen, Kraakman, and Khanna (n 15) 104; See eg National Venture Capital Association, 'Model Legal Documents' (20 March 2023) <https://nvca.org/model-legal-documents> accessed 25 June 2023.

[77] See JN Gordon, 'The Mandatory Structure of Corporate Law' (1989) 89 Columbia Law Review 1549, 1565 (discussing corporate law's general problem of offering enough customization to create predictability problems).

[78] See Rauterberg (n 1) 1159–60.

shareholders signing it into a closer alignment of interests than before the SA.[79] However, it also creates potentially greater separation between the shareholders signing the SA and those shareholders who do not sign it. Whether the net divergence of interests (ie agency costs among co-owners) is greater or lesser than before is difficult to know in the abstract. Nonetheless, it is a general issue of which we should be cognizant.

There are, indeed, other issues that SAs may raise. For instance, what about an SA where some shareholders agree to vote for a merger proposed by the controlling shareholder of the target (presumably for some compensation or benefit to them)? Should the shareholders who are a party to the SA (ie those who are presumably 'interested' in the merger) and the shareholders who are not (ie those who are presumably 'disinterested') constitute two separate classes for the purposes of voting on a scheme of merger and amalgamation? Should the SA be disclosed so that shareholders who are not parties appreciate that the signatories are approving the merger not only because they think it is potentially valuable for the target but also because of the SA? Should the shareholders who sign an SA to vote the same way as certain other shareholders on most (or all) matters be treated as a 'control' group and be subject to statutory or regulatory obligations?

These questions are important and should be addressed by regulation or judicial decisions, but we do not devote much time to them because they warrant a more thorough discussion than is provided in this chapter. Suffice to say, however, that once one starts down the track of broader effects (ie beyond just comparing SAs and amendments to constitutional documents), things can quickly become complicated. Nonetheless, the comparison between SAs and amendments to constitutional documents is a useful way to begin to organize the policy responses on SAs.

One approach that seems worthy of consideration is to create a schematic that lays out some factors courts might consider when examining SAs to assess their enforceability. Surely, more adaptation will be necessary, but one must start somewhere.

A relatively simple starting point is that SAs that attempt to bind non-parties or SAs that involve all shareholders or place restrictions on the company (or the board) should merit extra scrutiny. Such SAs seem like they are mimicking charter amendments (eg trying to bind everyone) and raise questions about why the subject matter was not proposed as a charter amendment.[80] Signatories should be expected to provide significant evidence to show why an SA was thought advisable, given the availability of the charter amendment process for these sorts of matters. The *Rangaraj* decision appears to be increasingly thought of in this manner—an SA when it purports to bind all shareholders (present and future) without going through the process of amending constitutional documents is highly suspect. This raises numerous concerns—binding non-signatories, absence of disclosure, and so forth.

If an SA does not purport to bind non-parties, all shareholders, or the company (and has few other third-party effects), then one might ask whether the parties to the SA were

[79] See ibid.
[80] This is a concern animating Professor Fisch's discussion—see Fisch (n 1) 959–60.

sophisticated and received legal advice and whether the SA was disclosed. If the parties were sophisticated and the SA was disclosed, one might presume (with the opportunity to rebut given to the challenging side) that the SA is enforceable. The challenging side could then marshal whatever evidence they have to show that the SA is still harmful to third parties or otherwise leads to outcomes that are, in general terms, harmful (eg it exacerbates conflicts of interest or undermines the standardization benefits of the corporate form). If some of these features are missing (eg the SA is not disclosed), then the court can consider what weight to give to them. These factors suggest that many private-equity-induced SAs would be enforceable (especially if disclosed), while SAs between family and close associates might be more open to debate (depending on the facts).

Although such an approach does not address all issues with SAs, it does provide some structure to the inquiry based on factors that are most likely to facilitate helpful judicial decision making. Further, the case law in India is fairly amenable to this approach if *Rangaraj* is interpreted as suggested above (or if one thinks of it as being incorrectly decided).[81] Of course, with experience and regulation, such an approach might be adapted over time, but as stated earlier, a starting point based on policy considerations is likely to be useful.

We end by noting that very recently, SEBI put forward a consultation paper that suggests that agreements with key corporate players (eg promoters, top executives) and others (including third parties) that affect the management of a listed company or impose restrictions or enhance liability should be disclosed and must obtain the approvals of the board and the target company's shareholders, that is, the majority of the minority.[82] This would certainly encompass the SAs we have been discussing. While our policy analysis suggests that the recommendation to require disclosure of such SAs is a good first step, we are more reticent about the requirement for board and minority shareholder approvals. These approvals effectively turn SAs back into amendments of constitutional documents, but perhaps with a higher threshold for approval (ie because such amendments may not require a majority of the minority vote in favour). This essentially eviscerates many benefits from an SA compared to an amendment of constitutional documents and merits more careful discussion given our policy discussion in this section.

[81] For a greater discussion on the legislative history and correctness of judicial interpretation, see Niranjan and Varottil (n 1).

[82] See SEBI, 'Consultation Paper on Strengthening Corporate Governance at Listed Entities by Empowering Shareholders—Amendments to the SEBI (LODR) 2015' (21 February 2023) <www.sebi.gov.in/reports-and-statistics/reports/feb-2023/consultation-paper-on-strengthening-corporate-governance-at-listed-entities-by-empowering-shareholders-amendments-to-the-sebi-lodr-regulations-2015_68261.html> accessed 27 June 2023. This proposal would only apply to public companies listed in India, not private companies. It also does not speak specifically of enforceability of SAs but whether such agreements will be allowed for public listed entities. It is thus possible that both SEBI and the courts, under the Companies Act, could regulate SAs.

V. Conclusion

SAs are a fascinating subset of contractual agreements that have generated a great deal of case law in India and elsewhere. In spite of that, the regulation of these agreements has often defied easy categorization. An example of this can be seen in India, where the development of doctrine has meandered in somewhat confusing ways, as we describe in this chapter. After examining this development, we note that greater attention to policy considerations may be useful in engineering a more predictable and hopefully beneficial approach to SAs. We discuss how comparing SAs to amendments of constitutional documents helps to elucidate some situations where SAs may be preferable to such amendments (and vice versa). This policy analysis can then be used as a basis for developing an approach to SAs that relies on who is purportedly bound by the SA, are there significant third-party effects, whether the signatories are sophisticated players with access to good legal counsel, the level of disclosure of the SA to others, and other matters.

Although this may not resolve all concerns with SAs, it provides an approach that could be useful in providing guidance to practitioners and that might address some of the policy concerns raised by SAs. We note that just recently, SEBI has proposed a new set of rules to govern agreements with key corporate players that puts emphasis on disclosure and approvals by the board and minority shareholders. Our policy analysis suggests that disclosure is likely to be a valuable addition, but that the requirements for approvals may benefit from greater analysis and debate.

Nevertheless, what is clear is that SAs, and how they are treated under the law, are in a state of rapid evolution. In such circumstances, careful attention to policy concerns as discussed in this chapter and perhaps others, seem important and timely.

23

Contracting with the State

*Chintan Chandrachud**

I. Introduction

Governments and public authorities execute contracts all the time. That is largely a reflection upon the range and complexity of matters that the state is expected to deal with. State contracts could include everything from storing grains and potatoes, to replacing street lighting, to modernising military aircraft. The state also continues to engage in activities that—depending on one's economic world view—it may not be expected to undertake. It retains direct participation in several sectors of the economy despite nearly three decades having elapsed since the reforms of 1991. India's largest power-generation company,[1] second-largest oil exploration and production company,[2] third-largest bank,[3] and fifth largest iron and steel company[4] are all state-owned enterprises.[5]

Contracts between manifestations of the state, on the one hand, and private parties, on the other, can be conceived of through two distinct lenses.[6] The first lens considers the contract from the perspective of the *parties* to the contract. The matters relevant to the parties will not be especially different than they are for parties concluding a private contract. Do each of the parties have the requisite capacity and authority to conclude the contract? Once concluded, how is the contract likely to be construed? What remedies will be available in the event that one of the parties fails to adhere to its contractual obligations? These issues are considered in section II of the chapter.

The second lens considers the contract from the perspective of those that are *not parties* to the contract. Third parties typically have no legal interest or standing in matters of contract between private parties. However, contracts involving state authorities are different. Some third parties, such as unsuccessful bidders and competitors of the party that was awarded the contract, will have a direct legal interest in whom the state

* I am grateful to Anant Sangal and Vidisha Singh for excellent research assistance. All errors are mine.

[1] NTPC Limited.

[2] Oil and Natural Gas Corporation Limited.

[3] State Bank of India.

[4] NDMC Limited.

[5] This is based on statistics by market capitalisation, <www.moneycontrol.com> accessed 12 January 2023.

[6] In this chapter, I do not pay special attention to what scholars describe as 'internal government contracts'—namely, contracts *between* public bodies or state authorities (see ACL Davies, *Accountability: A Public Law Analysis of Government by Contract* (OUP 2012) 27). However, some of the analysis in this chapter (such as the special formation requirements described in section II below) will also apply in those circumstances.

Chintan Chandrachud, *Contracting with the State* In: *Foundations of Indian Contract Law.* Edited by: KV Krishnaprasad, Niranjan Venkatesan, Shivprasad Swaminathan, and Umakanth Varottil, Oxford University Press. © Oxford University Press 2024.
DOI: 10.1093/9780191997211.003.0023

contracted with and why they were selected. Other third parties will be concerned to ensure that public funds are not being mis-utilised or wasted. Section III accordingly focuses on judicial review of contracts upon petitions by third parties.

II. The Parties to State Contracts

Governments and public authorities are not exempted from the application of the Indian Contract Act 1872 (hereinafter 'the Contract Act'). The provisions of the Contract Act apply to agreements to which governments and public authorities are parties as they do to agreements between private parties. When governments or public authorities conclude agreements pursuant to executive powers conferred by the Constitution, or powers conferred by statute, those agreements are therefore effectively governed by (a) the Constitution or the relevant statute under which the power was exercised (or purportedly exercised) and (b) the general law of contract (the Contract Act).[7] This section focuses on (a). Reference should be made to other chapters of this volume (as appropriate) as to (b).

1. Contracts Made in the Exercise of Executive Powers

Chapter III of Part XII of the Constitution, entitled 'Property, contracts, rights, liabilities, obligations and suits', includes a series of provisions addressing agreements to which the government is a party. Article 294(b) of the Constitution effected a novation so that all contractual rights, liabilities, and obligations of the Dominion of India and the government of each province before the Constitution entered into force were transferred to the Government of India or the government of the corresponding state.[8] A similar novation was put into effect for contracts entered into by the former princely states, which would be transferred to the government of the corresponding state unless the matter fell within the legislative competence of the Government of India.[9] For the purposes of this chapter, Articles 298 and 299 are the most significant amongst those provisions in Chapter III. The first addresses governments' power to enter into contracts, while the second addresses the procedure for doing so.

i. The power to contract

In its current form, Article 298 reads as follows:

[7] The agreement will be governed by both of those sources of authority in so far as they can be interpreted consistently. To the extent of any inconsistency: (a) where the inconsistency is between the Contract Act and the Constitution, the Constitution will prevail and (b) where the inconsistency is between the Contract Act and another statute, which of those prevails is ultimately a matter of construction, although it is highly likely that the other statute, being *lex specialis*, will prevail.

[8] This was subject to any adjustments that needed to be made due to the partition of India.

[9] Constitution of India 1950, arts 295(1)(b) and 295(2).

> The executive power of the Union and of each State shall extend to the carrying on of any trade or business and to the acquisition, holding and disposal of property and the making of contracts for any purpose:
>
> Provided that—
>
> (a) the said executive power of the Union shall, in so far as such trade or business or such purpose is not one with respect to which Parliament may make laws, be subject in each State to legislation by the State; and
>
> (b) the said executive power of each State shall, in so far as such trade or business or such purpose is not one with respect to which the State Legislature may make laws, be subject to legislation by Parliament.[10]

In the early years after the Constitution was enacted, there was contestation as to whether Article 298 (in its original form) required legislation enabling the central or state governments to enter into contracts (or carry on a trade or business or deal with property). The Supreme Court of India and High Courts concluded, in several cases, that enabling legislation was at least necessary in some contexts, for example, when the government established a monopoly or 'encroach[ed] upon private rights' in order to carry out its own business.[11] Parliament attempted to put these questions to rest through the Seventh Amendment to the Constitution. Under the amended Article 298, the executive power granted to the Union and the states (including the power to conclude contracts) was no longer 'subject to any law made by the appropriate Legislature'. Rather, that power was *always* available provided that (a) if the subject matter of the contract was within the state's legislative competence, the Union's executive power would be subject to relevant state legislation and (b) if the subject matter of the contract was within the legislative competence of Parliament, the state's executive power was subject to relevant legislation enacted by Parliament.[12]

Article 298 of the Constitution in its current form bears several implications on the capacity of governments and public authorities to enter into contracts. First, Article 298 deviates from the general principle that the executive powers of the central and state governments are co-extensive with the legislative powers of Parliament and relevant

[10] In its original form, art 298 read as follows:
(1) The executive power of the Union and of each State shall extend, subject to any law made by the appropriate Legislature, to the grant, sale, disposition of mortgage of any property held for the purposes of the Union or of such State, as the case may be, and to the purchase or acquisition of property for the purposes respectively, and to the making of contracts. (2) All property acquired for the purposes of the Union or of a State shall vest in the Union or in such State, as the case may be.

[11] *Ram Jawaya Kapoor v State of Punjab* AIR 1955 SC 549; *People's Bus Service Limited v State of PEPSU* MANU/PH/0105/1955, [9]; *Pratap Chandra Biswas v Union of India* AIR 1956 Gau 85; *Maula Bux Rahim Bux and Sons v State of Vindhya Pradesh* MANU/MP/0210/1956.

[12] Such legislation, whether enacted by Parliament or the relevant state legislature, will be subject to the other provisions of the Constitution, including art 301 (which provides for the freedom of trade, commerce, and intercourse across the country).

state legislatures, respectively.[13] The default position under Article 298 is that the Central Government and each of the state governments are free to make contracts for any purpose, regardless with which entry within the three lists of the Seventh Schedule of the Constitution that purpose correlates.

Whether (and to what extent) the central or state governments retain the authority to contract after legislation has been enacted in relation to the purpose within List II or List I, respectively will depend upon the terms of the statute. However, in many cases, freedom of contract can be heavily circumscribed by the terms of the statute. For example, in one case, Parliament enacted legislation regulating mines and mineral development[14]—a matter that was within its exclusive authority. Section 4 of the said legislation prohibited the conduct of prospecting or mining operations in any area, except in accordance with the terms and conditions of a licence or lease granted under the law. The state government reserved an area of land for the exploitation of bauxite. The High Court held that it was within the state government's power under Article 298 to reserve the area, on the basis that the *owner* of land does not require a licence or lease to exploit the land. There was no inconsistency between section 4 of the statute and the state's exercise of executive power. However, if the state government wished to contract with a third party to exploit the land, its authority to contract (which was unimpeded until the statute was enacted) was now restricted by the provisions of the statute, including limitations on the size of the areas for which licences or leases could be granted, the period for which they could be granted or renewed, and the rents and royalties chargeable.[15]

Matters are more complicated when the central and state governments seek to enter into contracts for a purpose that is included in List III (the concurrent list) of the Constitution. Once again, the starting point is, first, that when there is no central or state legislation on the relevant entry within List III, the central and state governments have unimpeded authority to enter into contracts. There appears to be no direct authority as to the position when legislation has been enacted. Article 298 of the Constitution in its current form could be read as suggesting that there is an asymmetry between the contracting authority of the Central Government and the state governments. This would have the effect that when there is central legislation on the issue, the state government's contracts are subject to that legislation, whereas when there is state legislation on the issue, the Central Government's contracts are not—even in the absence of supervening central legislation—subject to that state legislation.[16] Despite

[13] This is the inevitable conclusion upon an examination of the relevant constitutional provisions. See the Constitution of India, arts 73(1) and 162, each of which applies 'subject to the [other] provisions' of the Constitution. Article 298 does not include the same qualification and, therefore, takes precedence on the subject matter to which it refers; see *H Anraj v State of Maharashtra* AIR 1984 SC 781, [12].

[14] The Mines and Minerals (Regulation and Development) Act 1957.

[15] *Amritlal Nathubhai Shah v Union of India* AIR 1973 Guj 117. An additional factual nuance, which is not strictly relevant to the point made here, is that the rules made under the law enabled the state government to refuse applications from third parties for licences or leases on the basis that the land was reserved. The High Court outlined the contractual restrictions in relation to a hypothetical licence or lease granted to a statutory corporation or an authority owned or controlled by the state government.

[16] This reading arises from the fact that the provisos to art 298 refer to purposes that are 'not' those with respect to which Parliament or the state legislature 'may' make laws. When state legislation has been enacted, Parliament may still enact legislation on the subject, owing to the provisions of art 254 of the Constitution. However, when

these indications from the text, it is likely that a court confronted with this question will adopt a more pragmatic approach, holding that a government's capacity to contract for the purposes of matters covered by List III will simply track the rules of repugnancy prescribed in the Constitution. In other words, contracts by the Central Government will be subject to relevant state legislation (unless central legislation prevails over that state legislation), and contracts by state governments will be subject to relevant central legislation (unless state legislation prevails over that central legislation).[17]

Second, there are no territorial limitations on the authority of the Central Government and state governments to engage in trade or business and enter into contracts.[18] For example, a state that puts out to tender the construction of a bridge in the state, or the redevelopment of a state museum, can market that tender and invite bids from across the country (and take all the incidental steps that it requires to do so).

Third, the provisos to Article 298 of the Constitution focus on the relationship between the centre and the states. They are ambiguous as to the relationships *amongst* state governments, where one state government seeks to do business or enter into contracts in other states. Read literally, Article 298 in its current form indicates that state governments are not subject to state legislation when doing business or entering into contracts in other states. This is because the state government's authority is subject only to 'legislation by Parliament' (in contrast with the original version of Article 298, which would have made such authority subject to 'any law made by the appropriate Legislature'). However, a literal interpretation will produce absurd consequences. For example, consider the position of the Central Government, state government *A*, and state government *B* in the following scenario. The Central Government and state government *A* wish to do business with, and enter into contracts with, the residents of state government *B*, for a purpose that is included in List II. Read literally, Article 298 would make the Central Government's exercise of executive power subject to the relevant legislation of state *B* but not impose the same limitation on state government *A*'s exercise of executive power. It is likely that the courts will avoid this asymmetry by interpreting Article 298 as requiring state government *A*'s exercise of executive power to be subject to the relevant legislation of state *B*.

Some of the issues that have been identified here arose for the Supreme Court's consideration in *Anraj v State of Maharashtra*.[19] The power to legislate in relation to lotteries organised by state governments was within Parliament's exclusive legislative competence in List I. However, Parliament had not enacted legislation regulating state lotteries. Instead, the Ministry of Home Affairs, Government of India issued a letter

central legislation has been enacted, conflicting state legislation will not (absent presidential assent under art 254(2)) prevail over central legislation.

[17] See *Kondakandla Yadaiah v State of Telangana* MANU/AP/0096/2017, where it was held that the state's power to contract on a matter within List III ('acquisition and requisition of property') is subject to legislation enacted by Parliament on the subject. This arose in the textually easier case of a state contract being subject to legislation enacted by Parliament (rather than the converse). The High Court specifically chose not to consider what the position would be if it were the other way around.

[18] *Khazan Singh v State of Uttar Pradesh* AIR 1974 SC 669, [9].

[19] *H Anraj* (n 13).

to state governments requiring the Central Government's permission to conduct lotteries. Such permission would only be granted on the condition that lottery tickets would not be sold in any other state without the consent of the government of that state. Relying on this letter, the Government of Maharashtra imposed a prohibition within the state on the sale of tickets to lotteries conducted by other states. The Government of Maharashtra's prohibition was challenged on constitutional grounds.

The Supreme Court held that since no legislation on the subject had been enacted by Parliament, state governments were free to organise lotteries in the exercise of their powers under Article 298. The Central Government could not require state governments to take its permission to organise lotteries. In any event, the Court held that it was unclear on what legislative basis a state government could enforce a breach of the condition on not selling tickets within the state without its permission. The Court therefore directed the Government of Maharashtra to forbear from giving effect to the purported ban on the sale of tickets to lotteries organised by other states. The effect of the Supreme Court's decision was that there would be a free market in state lottery tickets until Parliament enacted legislation on the subject. Although this case arose primarily in the context of governments doing business (by organising state lotteries), a subsequent Supreme Court decision observed that this could equally be conceived of as a case involving the contractual elements of Article 298.[20] A lottery ticket, the Court observed, was a contract between the seller (the state or its agent) and the purchaser of the ticket and, absent central legislation, the state had full authority to execute such contracts.

ii. The procedure for contracting

Article 299 of the Constitution of India addresses the procedure that central and state governments are required to follow when executing contracts pursuant to Article 298. All such contracts must 'be expressed to be made' by the President of India or by the Governor of the state. As HV Kamath explained during the Constituent Assembly debates, the phrase 'expressed to be made' is used in acknowledgement of the reality that the President and Governor will not actually be signing contracts.[21] Accordingly, Article 299(1) also provides that such contracts will be executed on behalf of the President or Governor 'by such persons and in such manner as he may direct or authorise'.[22] Since the President and Governor themselves act on the aid and advice of the Council of Ministers of the Central Government and state government, respectively, those governments decide who has the authority to contract under Article 299(1). At the level of the Central Government, drawing up the list of authorised signatories is a task that is

[20] *BR Enterprises v State of Uttar Pradesh* AIR 1999 SC 1867, [77].

[21] Constituent Assembly Debates, 15 June 1949 (HV Kamath). Article 299 was modelled on corresponding provisions of the Government of India Act 1935, ss 175(3) and 175(4).

[22] The text of art 299(1) suggests that, as under the Contract Act, s 186, an agent's authority to execute contracts on behalf of the President or Governor may be express (which includes written and verbal authority) or implied. In practice, the authority to contract under the Constitution of India, art 299(1) is almost inevitably express and in writing.

assigned to the Ministry of Law and Justice, Government of India.[23] The President, the Governors, and those responsible for executing contracts on their behalf are protected from personal liability in respect of such contracts.[24] This reflects the general principle (embodied in section 230 of the Contract Act) that agents acting within the scope of their authority cannot be held personally responsible for contracts executed on behalf of their principals.[25]

Unlike many other provisions of the Constitution,[26] Article 299 does not specify the effect of a failure to comply with its terms. Perhaps on account of that omission, an important question that has arisen before the courts is what the effect is of executing a contract that fails to comply with the requirements of Article 299. Early case law seemed to suggest either that Article 299(1) was not a mandatory provision or that the government could subsequently ratify a contract that was not originally executed in accordance with its terms. This issue arose in an unusual context in *Chhatturbhuj Jasani v Moreshwar Parashram*.[27] Section 7(d) of the Representation of the People Act 1951 (RPA) disqualified candidates for election to Parliament who had 'any share or interest in a contract for the supply of goods to . . . the appropriate Government'. Chatturbhuj Jasani was a partner in a firm that had entered into an agreement for the supply of *bidis* to the Central Government. However, that agreement did not comply with the requirements of Article 299(1). Jasani contended that, owing to a failure to comply with Article 299(1), there was no 'contract' at all and, therefore, section 7(d) was not engaged. In these circumstances, the Supreme Court was called upon to determine the effect of a failure to comply with Article 299(1).

During the course of its judgment, the Supreme Court laid bare the tensions underlying Article 299 of the Constitution of India. On the one hand, it was important to protect the government and the public purse from unauthorised contracts. On the other, the Central and state governments entered into hundreds of contracts every day, covering a wide range of subject matter. At one end of the spectrum would be contracts that were authorised and in proper form. At the other end would be contracts that were neither authorised nor in proper form. Between these extremes was a 'large class of contracts, probably by far the greatest in numbers which, though authorised, are for one reason or other not in proper form'.[28] For the Supreme Court, Jasani's contract fell

[23] General Financial Rules 2017, Rule 224(2), Note 1. The list of authorised signatories typically authorises bearers of office rather than individuals.

[24] Constitution of India 1950, art 299(2).

[25] Constituent Assembly Debates, 15 June 1949 (Dr Bhimrao Ambedkar).

[26] See eg the Constitution of India, art 13(2) (specifying that laws that take away or abridge fundamental rights 'shall, to the extent of the contravention, be void'); art 123(3) (specifying that ordinances made by the President that that Parliament would not have the competence to enact 'shall be void'); art 213(3) (specifying that ordinances made by Governors that would not be valid if enacted as statutes by the state legislature 'shall be void'); art 254(1) (specifying that law enacted by the legislature of a state that is repugnant to a provision of law made by Parliament that it is competent to enact, or to a provision of an existing law with respect to one of the matters in the Concurrent List, 'shall, to the extent of the repugnancy, be void').

[27] *Chatturbhuj Vithaldas Jasani v Moreshwar Parashram* 1954 SCR 817. See also *Laliteshwar Prasad Sahi v Bateshwar Prasad* AIR 1966 SC 580; *Abdul Rahiman Khan v Sadasiva Tripathi* AIR 1969 SC 302.

[28] *Chatturbhuj Vithaldas Jasani* (n 27).

within this class. The Court considered it dangerous to conclude that all these contracts were void and of no effect—not every 'petty contract' needed to be effected by a 'ponderous legal document couched in a particular form'.[29] It preferred the conclusion that such contracts were not necessarily enforceable against the government—however, the government was capable of ratifying the contract for its own benefit. Since section 7(d) did not require the existence of an *enforceable* contract, Jasani's contract fell within its four corners. Jasani was accordingly disqualified.

In reconciling the competing interests of protecting the public purse and promoting the ease of doing business, in *Chatturbhuj*, the Supreme Court veered heavily in favour of the latter. The Court correctly acknowledged that the purposes underlying Article 299 of the Constitution and section 7(d) of the RPA were quite different. Article 299 was principally meant to protect the government from unauthorised contracts, while section 7(d) of the RPA was directed towards avoiding conflicts of interest and protecting the sanctity of the electoral process. Therefore, not every 'contract' under section 7(d) was necessarily a 'contract' under Article 299. This view was also guided by hard-nosed pragmatism, because there was little preventing governments and private parties from *voluntarily complying* with agreements that did not adhere to the requirements of Article 299, and it would seem self-defeating not to impose the RPA's disqualification in that situation. However, the Supreme Court shifted the balance over time, and *Chatturbhuj* was gradually confined to its own facts.

The outcome of this rebalancing exercise was that it became the Court's settled view that an agreement not executed pursuant to the executive power of the Union or state would be void and incapable of ratification by the relevant government.[30] This is a deviation from section 196 of the Contract Act, under which an agent's unauthorised agreement may be ratified by the principal. The counterparty to an unauthorised agreement with the government would also be unable to invoke the doctrine of promissory estoppel to hold the government to its original (albeit unauthorised) promise.[31] The principle underlying promissory estoppel is that a person who, due to a representation or statement of fact, causes another person to act to their detriment to rely on that representation, should not be allowed to deny that representation, even if it is incorrect all along. If estoppel was accepted in circumstances in which an agreement did not adhere to the requirements of Article 299(1), that would, as the Supreme Court observed, virtually 'repeal'[32] Article 299(1)—or to be more precise, would very significantly limit its

[29] ibid.
[30] *Bihar Eastern Gangetic Fishermen Coop Society Ltd v Sipahi Singh* (1977) 4 SCC 145; *KP Chowdhary v State of MP* AIR 1967 SC 203, [10].
[31] *Mulamchand v State of MP* AIR 1968 SC 1218, [5]; *State of Haryana v Lal Chand* AIR 1984 SC 1326, [14]; *Jit Ram Shiv Kumar v State of Haryana* AIR 1980 SC 1285. In *Joshi Technologies International Inc v Union of India* (2015) 7 SCC 728, [53], the Supreme Court observed that the 'doctrine of promissory estoppel can still be invoked against the Government' in circumstances in which an agreement did not comply with the requirements of art 299. However, this was an *obiter* observation that goes against the grain of the authorities: W Wade and C Forsyth, *Administrative Law* (11th edn, OUP 2014) 196.
[32] *Mulamchand* (n 31).

application. As soon as each party to an unauthorised agreement detrimentally relied upon the promise of the other, the agreement could be enforced through the conduit of promissory estoppel despite the failure to comply with Article 299(1).[33]

However, there are three important respects in which courts have applied Article 299(1) in a way that promotes the ease of doing business with the government. First, courts have acknowledged that claims in restitution under section 70 of the Contract Act[34] would continue to be available to parties that performed agreements that do not adhere to the requirements of Article 299(1). In *State of West Bengal v B K Mondal and Sons*,[35] the Supreme Court considered whether the claimant, acting pursuant to an agreement that failed to comply with constitutional requirements,[36] could seek compensation under section 70 of the Contract Act for construction work undertaken for the state government. The Court concluded that section 70 applied in the circumstances. There was a difference in principle between promissory estoppel and ratification claims, on the one hand, and restitution claims, on the other. Restitution claims would not have the effect of nullifying or significantly limiting the scope of the constitutional requirements. The party invoking section 70 of the Contract Act would not be able to sue for breach of contract or specific performance but only for work already undertaken and benefits enjoyed by the counterparty. Each party would bear the risk that its counterparty could, at any time and without reason, 'pull the plug' and refuse to accept the benefits of the work performed under the agreement, thereby taking section 70 out of the picture. The Supreme Court made clear that aside from these matters of principle, promoting the ease of doing business was amongst the key drivers of its decision:

> in the functioning of the vast organisation represented by a modern state government officers have invariably to enter into a variety of contracts which are often of a petty nature ... If it was held that s. 70 was inapplicable in regard to such dealings by government officers it would lead to extremely unreasonable consequences and may even hamper, if not wholly bring to a standstill the efficient working of the Government from day to day.[37]

[33] The Contract Act, s 230(3) enables an agent to be sued personally on the contract where its principal cannot be sued. Although it is unlikely to be of much use to a private party purporting to have contracted with the government (since it is necessarily limited by the financial position of the agent purportedly representing the government), the Court has also held that this provision will not apply to contracts that fail to adhere to the requirements of art 299(1); see *State of Uttar Pradesh v Murari Lal* AIR 1971 SC 2210.

[34]

> Obligation of person enjoying benefit of non-gratuitous act.—Where a person lawfully does anything for another person, or delivers anything to him, not intending to do so gratuitously, and such other person enjoys the benefit thereof, the latter is bound to make compensation to the former in respect of, or to restore, the thing so done or delivered.

Illustrations following the section are omitted.

[35] *State of West Bengal v BK Mondal and Sons* AIR 1962 SC 779.

[36] In this instance, see the Government of India Act 1935, s 175(3) (the predecessor of the Constitution of India, art 299(1)).

[37] *BK Mondal and Sons* (n 35) [20].

Second, courts have concluded that while Article 299 of the Constitution of India requires an agreement made in the exercise of executive power of the Union or a state to be in writing,[38] the agreement need not be embodied in a *single* document or be executed as a deed. Contracts can arise through the course of correspondence so long as the requirements of Article 299 are complied with.[39] The most common example is when a public authority exercising the executive power of the state government puts out a tender notice, correspondence between a private party and the authority in relation to that tender notice ensues, and the authority ultimately communicates a notice of acceptance to the private party.[40] In such circumstances, a binding contract is concluded absent a single contractual document so long as the agreement is expressed to be made by the President or Governor, and the letter of acceptance is issued on behalf of the President or Governor by an authority that is permitted to do so.[41]

Third, had the courts remained wedded to the central logic of Article 299 as it is most commonly expressed (protecting the government from unauthorised agreements),[42] they might have arrived at the conclusion that it can only be invoked asymmetrically (ie as a shield in the hands of the government or public authority), rather than by a private party seeking to resist enforcement. However, courts have permitted private parties to invoke Article 299(1) in circumstances where a government or public authority asserts that its requirements have been complied with. This has been done by effecting adjustments to the logic of Article 299(1), including that it is also a rule of 'public policy', directed towards protecting the general public from unwittingly accepting contractual obligations to the government or public authorities. For example, in *State of Punjab v Om Parkash Baldev*,[43] a party that submitted a tender for the construction of a bridge in Punjab successfully resisted enforcement action by the government, which claimed that the parties had entered into a contract through the course of correspondence. The government's letter of acceptance was not expressed to have been accepted by the Governor of Punjab. The parties also intended to subsequently sign an agreement in proper form (which was never signed).

2. Contracts Made in the Exercise of Statutory Powers

Articles 298 and 299(1) of the Constitution of India are relevant to contracts made pursuant to executive powers of a Union or a state. They do not apply in circumstances in which governments or public authorities enter into contracts in the exercise of statutory powers.[44] Statutes (or more likely, rules and regulations made pursuant to statutes)

[38] This arises from the words 'expressed to be made' in the Constitution of India, art 299(1).
[39] HM Seervai, *Constitutional Law of India: A Critical Commentary* (Eastern Book Company 2019) 2125.
[40] See eg *Sardar Sucha Singh v Union of India* (1987) SCC (Supp) 127.
[41] *Union of India v NK Private Limited* AIR 1972 SC 915.
[42] See *Jit Ram Shiv Kumar* (n 31).
[43] *State of Punjab v Om Parkash Baldev* AIR 1988 SC 2149. See also *State of Madhya Pradesh v Ratan Lal* AIR 1994 SC 458.
[44] *Lal Chand* (n 31); *Lalji Khimji v State of Gujarat* (1993) Supp (3) SCC 567, [9].

often limit the powers of public authorities to enter into contracts, as well as prescribe the procedure for exercising those powers.[45] Indeed, the appropriate reading of Article 299(1) is that governments and public authorities cannot sidestep statutory requirements to execute contracts by relying on that provision.[46] This reading arises from the fact that Article 299(1) expressly refers to contracts 'made in the exercise of the executive power of the Union or of a State'.

Whether an authority has entered into a contract within the scope of its powers, and in compliance with required procedure, will depend upon the construction of the relevant legislation. For example, in *Orissa Industrial Infrastructure Development Corporation v Mesco*,[47] the Supreme Court held that Mesco did not have a valid lease to land belonging to a state corporation. This was because the corporation's governing statute permitted the disposal of land subject to directions issued by the state government. The state government directed that the land be leased through the execution of a lease deed, which was never ultimately executed in this case.

As with Article 299(1), a party cannot rely on promissory estoppel to seek enforcement of an agreement that has not been executed in accordance with the terms of the statute from which the public authority derived its authority to contract. However, section 70 of the Contract Act can be invoked by a party seeking compensation for performance of the agreement.[48]

3. The Status of Partially Compliant Agreements

Since agreements involving governments and public authorities may be governed by both the Contract Act and the Constitution of India or the relevant governing statute, an issue that can arise is what the status is of an agreement that is compliant with one of those sources of governing law but not the other. For instance, can an agreement that is purportedly made in pursuance of executive power conferred by the Constitution, but that fails to adhere to the requirements of Article 299, nevertheless be treated as a valid contract under the Contract Act? Conversely, can an agreement that is executed in accordance with constitutional requirements be treated as valid for some purposes but void for failing one or more requirements under the Contract Act? The authorities suggest that the courts will take a unified approach so that an agreement is either a valid contract or is void, for the purposes of both the Contract Act and the Constitution or the relevant statute.[49]

This unified approach is appropriate for two reasons. First, sections 2(g) and 2(h) of the Contract Act provide that an agreement not enforceable by law is 'said to be void'

[45] See eg Delhi Development Authority (Management and Disposal of Housing Estates) Regulations 1968, Regulations 4, 35, 36, 44.
[46] See *Jogendra Lal Saha v State of Bihar* AIR 1991 SC 1148.
[47] *Orissa Industrial Infrastructure Development Corpn v Mesco Kalinga Steel Ltd* (2017) 5 SCC 86, [17]–[18].
[48] ibid.
[49] *State of Uttar Pradesh v Mumtaz Hussain* AIR 1979 All 174, [26]; *Giridhari Lal Constructions v Union of India* (2000) 4 ALD 510, [11]–[12].

and that a 'contract' is an 'agreement enforceable by law'. Those provisions are notably not confined to the Contract Act but extend to all 'law' (including provisions of other statutes and the Constitution). This was the justification given by the Allahabad High Court in a case in which a party to an agreement with the government of Uttar Pradesh contended that title to the property under the agreement had passed even though the agreement was purportedly made pursuant to executive powers under the Constitution and failed to comply with the requirements of Article 299.[50]

It may be said that this reason is, to some extent, self-fulfilling, because it *presumes* that an agreement that is not in accordance with the provisions of the Constitution or another statute is unenforceable. The better justification for the unified approach is that it cannot have been intended that an agreement that is the culmination of an unconstitutional process would, nevertheless, in some respects, be treated as a valid contract. Indeed, as the cases that have arisen in the context of Article 299 demonstrate, that would largely defeat the purpose of provisions such as Articles 298 and 299 of the Constitution of India.[51] As to agreements that are not in accordance with other statutes, that is a matter of construction of the relevant statute—although in most cases, it would seem unlikely that the legislature could have intended for such agreements to be treated as contracts that are enforceable.[52]

Equally, it cannot have been intended that an agreement that is void under the Contract Act is to be treated as valid in some respects merely because it is concluded in accordance with constitutional and statutory requirements. For example, if an agreement made by parties under a common mistake of fact is properly executed pursuant to the exercise of executive power under the Constitution by a person authorised to do so, that agreement is, nevertheless, void in all respects by virtue of section 20 of the Contract Act. Compliance with constitutional requirements does not save the agreement.

4. Construction and Remedies

Aside from the relevant statutory provisions and rules pursuant to which governments or public authorities enter into contracts (which may inform the construction of the contract), there is no special toolkit available to the courts to interpret contracts with the state. Courts will apply the general rules of construction which apply equally to contracts between private parties.[53]

The landscape of remedies available to contracting parties is also not different. It bears mentioning that there are no general restrictions on securing injunctions or

50 *Mumtaz Hussain* (n 49).
51 See *Bikhraj Jaipuria v Union of India* AIR 1962 SC 113, [16].
52 See *Orissa Industrial Infrastructure Development Corpn* (n 47) [15].
53 See Y Goh, Chapter 3 of this volume.

orders of specific performance against governments or public authorities.[54] Unless the contract provides for a different method of settling disputes (such as through arbitration), a civil suit is the port of call for a party to a contract seeking damages for breach of contract or specific performance from a government or public authority. Although it is not strictly beyond the Supreme Court and High Courts' writ jurisdiction to entertain such claims, it is highly unlikely that they will do so. As the Supreme Court has observed,

> if the contract between private party and the State/instrumentality and/or agency of State is under the realm of a private law and there is no element of public law, the normal course for the aggrieved party, is to invoke the remedies provided under ordinary civil law rather than approaching the High Court under Article 226 of the Constitutional of India.[55]

The Supreme Court and High Courts are even less likely to adjudicate contractual breaches in the exercise of their writ jurisdiction when doing so demands detailed evidentiary inquiries and the cross-examination of witnesses.

III. State Contracts and Third Parties

Third parties will usually have no standing or direct legal interest in matters of contract between private parties.[56] A private party seeking to procure raw materials can access the market, negotiate directly with the suppliers of its choosing, and swiftly conclude a contract for the supply of those materials. In the same circumstances, a public authority would likely establish 'elaborate and time-consuming selection processes'[57] to choose its supplier, which processes would be subject to challenges by third parties, scrutiny by the courts, and requests for information under the Right to Information Act 2005.

This section considers the grounds for review available to third parties when challenging the process of contracting undertaken by public authorities[58] and the circumstances in which the courts will intervene in that process. However, a more fundamental

[54] In England, the Crown Proceedings Act 1947, s 21(1) prohibits injunctions or orders of specific performance being granted against the Crown, although the scope of that provision has been a matter of significant contestation; see H Beale (Gen ed), *Chitty on Contracts*, vol 1 (33rd edn, Sweet & Maxwell 2019) [11-016]–[11-020].

[55] *Joshi Technologies International Inc* (n 31). See also *Jagdish Mandal v State of Orissa* (2007) 14 SCC 517, [21] ('The power of judicial review will not be permitted to be invoked . . . to decide contractual disputes. The tenderer or contractor with a grievance can always seek damages in a civil court'); *State of Bihar v Jain Plastics* (2002) 1 SCC 216. Moreover, when a public law remedy is available to the contracting party, it will not really be invoking the court's writ jurisdiction in its *capacity as a contracting party*. Rather, the contractual relationship may have merely given rise to an interaction with the state that has prompted the invocation of the court's writ jurisdiction.

[56] A notable exception is the prohibition on anti-competitive agreements that cause an appreciable adverse effect on competition: see Competition Act 2002, s 3.

[57] *BSNL v Telephone Cables Limited* (2010) 5 SCC 213.

[58] These third parties will most commonly have some skin in the game—for example, parties that participated in a bidding process but whose bid was not selected. However, this will not always be the case. For example, a nongovernmental organisation or public-interest organisation may commence a public-interest litigation challenging a decision to award a contract.

question needs to be tackled before addressing those issues. What counts as the 'state' or a public authority? Although the answer to that question might seem obvious, it is often notoriously difficult. It also does not lend itself to a binary response. Some institutions and authorities are more 'public' than others, and precisely how 'public' an institution is will be relevant to the grounds of review and remedies available to third parties.

1. The Private–Public Spectrum

Consider the position of four actors or authorities along the private–public spectrum. At one end of the spectrum is a private actor (P1'). This private actor complies with relevant legal and regulatory requirements but is not owned or controlled by the Central or state governments and does not serve a public function. Consider a local coffee shop or furniture retailer that pays its taxes, complies with applicable safety standards, and has secured the licences it requires to operate. Further along the spectrum is a private actor that is not owned and controlled by the Central or state governments but performs activities that can be characterised as 'public functions' (P2). The Board of Control for Cricket in India, which regulates cricket, selects the national cricket team, supports state cricket associations, and maintains physical infrastructure and cricket academies, is a somewhat unique but accepted example in this category.[59] Other examples include a public trust managing a science college that received government funding and was subject to the rules and regulations imposed by a university established by statute.[60]

Still further along the spectrum, now much closer towards the 'public' end, is an authority that is financially, functionally, and administratively controlled by the central or state governments (P3).[61] The extent of financial, functional, and administrative control will be determined by various factors, including (a) whether the government owns part of (or the whole of) the share capital of the authority, (b) whether (and to what extent) financial assistance provided by the state meets the expenditure of the authority, (c) whether the authority enjoys a state-conferred monopoly status, and (d) whether some or all of the directors of the authority are appointed by the government.[62] This category includes several companies incorporated by statute, as well as many companies incorporated under the companies legislation that are owned by central and/or state governments, although those are by no means definitive identifiers. Finally, at the far end of the spectrum is the 'government' most narrowly defined—Parliament and the Central Government, each of the state legislatures and governments, and the constituent ministries and departments of those governments (P4).[63]

[59] *Board of Control for Cricket in India v Cricket Association of Bihar* (2015) 3 SCC 251.

[60] *Anandi Mukta Sadguru v VR Rudani* (1989) 2 SCC 691.

[61] *Pradeep Kumar Biswas v Indian Institute of Chemical Biology* (2002) 5 SCC 111; *Zee Telefilms v Union of India* AIR 2005 SC 2677.

[62] *Ajay Hasia v Khalid Mujib Sehravardi* AIR 1981 SC 487; *Ramana Dayaram Shetty v International Airport Authority of India* (1979) 3 SCC 489.

[63] This typology does not find reference in the case law and is deployed in this chapter for convenience.

A number of practical implications flow from precisely where an actor or authority lies along this spectrum. First, the opening article of the Constitution's chapter on fundamental rights defines the 'State'. Article 12 of the Constitution of India provides that the state includes 'the Government and Parliament of India and the Government and the Legislature of each of the States and all local or other authorities within the territory of India or under the control of the Government of India'. Article 12 can be unpacked into three components: (a) the Government and Parliament of India and the Government and the Legislature of each of the states, (b) all local or other authorities within the territory of India, and (c) all local or other authorities under the control of the Government of India.

It is self-evident from component (a) of this definition that P4 authorities fall within the definition of the 'State'. Component (c) was directed towards extraterritorial application to authorities that were under the *de facto* control of the Government of India, even though they were not within the territory of India.[64] The contestation within the case law has focused on the meaning of component (b) of Article 12. As it is currently interpreted by the courts,[65] P3 authorities also fall within the definition of the 'State'. This has important consequences. A number of fundamental rights apply 'vertically' (ie to relationships between state actors and private actors) rather than 'horizontally' (ie to relationships between private actors).[66] State authorities are required to comply with fundamental rights in all their interactions with private actors, including in the process of contracting. A failure to do so risks the relevant state action (including a contract) being set aside as unconstitutional by the court.

Second, Article 32 of the Constitution of India, which is itself a fundamental right, guarantees 'the right to move the Supreme Court by appropriate proceedings' for the enforcement of fundamental rights. This enables direct recourse to the Supreme Court in the exercise of its writ jurisdiction where authorities falling within the definition of the 'State' (once again, P3 and P4 authorities) violate fundamental rights, including the 'golden triangle'[67] of the right to equality (Article 14), the right to freedom (Article 19),

[64] Constituent Assembly Debates, 25 November 1948 (Dr Bhimrao Ambedkar):

> There are many cases occurring now in international affairs where territories are handed over to other countries for the purposes of administration either under a mandate or trusteeship. I think it is desirable that there ought to be no discrimination so far as the citizens of India and the residents of those mandated or trusteeship territories are concerned in fundamental rights.

[65] *Pradeep Kumar Biswas* (n 61); *Zee Telefilms* (n 61).

[66] Articles 15(2) (the prohibition of discrimination on the basis of religion, race, caste, sex or place of birth), 17 (the abolition of untouchability), 23(1) (the prohibition of traffic in human beings and forced labour) and 24 (the prohibition on employment of children under fourteen in hazardous activities) are notable exceptions. These fundamental rights apply both vertically and horizontally; see *Kaushal Kishor v State of Uttar Pradesh* (2023) 4 SCC 1. A private agreement that perpetuates untouchability or forced labour, for example, can be declared void and unenforceable without reference to the Contract Act. See *State of Kartnataka v Appa Balu Ingale* AIR 1993 SC 1126, [24] ('a contract, covenant or any private transaction tending to recognise, encourage or effectuate untouchability in any form is, therefore, void ab initio'). The Contract Act, s 24 (which makes agreements whose considerations and objects are unlawful void) provides an independent basis to declare such agreements void and unenforceable, but the availability of a constitutional remedy will have ramifications for the standing of the party that brings the claim.

[67] *Minerva Mills v Union of India* AIR 1980 SC 1789.

and the right to life and personal liberty (Article 21).[68] A third party that alleges that the tendering process conducted by a state authority violated the right to equality therefore has direct access to the Supreme Court.

Third, direct recourse is also available to the High Courts in the exercise of their writ jurisdiction, where P2, P3, and P4 actors act unlawfully or unfairly (or, in the case of the P3 and P4 authorities, violate fundamental rights).[69] Article 226(1) of the Constitution of India empowers the High Courts to exercise writ jurisdiction for the enforcement of fundamental rights and 'for any other purpose'. The language of Article 226(1) is broad and, on its face, appears to enable the exercise of writ jurisdiction against all actors and authorities (including P1 actors) and in all circumstances. In practice, however, High Courts exercise their jurisdiction under Article 226 with discretion. Writ petitions under Article 226 are usually not maintainable when an alternative remedy (eg a civil suit seeking damages for breach of contract) is available.[70] This makes it highly unlikely that High Courts will exercise writ jurisdiction where the action is against a P1 actor, in respect of which remedies in private law are likely to be available. Finally, Article 226 does not have the effect of altering the definition of the 'State' under Article 12, or otherwise extending the scope of fundamental rights. For that reason, the High Courts cannot, in the exercise of their writ jurisdiction, enforce fundamental rights against P2 actors. Even when High Courts exercise writ jurisdiction in respect of P2 actors, that jurisdiction is restricted to the public functions performed by P2 actors.[71]

For litigants, invoking the writ jurisdiction of the Supreme Court under Article 32 and the High Courts under Article 226 yields significant practical advantages. Courts exercising writ jurisdiction are saddled with less procedural and evidentiary rules. Disputed questions of fact can simply be decided by way of affidavit (although witnesses may be summoned for cross-examination where the issue cannot be decided on affidavits).[72] Writ petitions have 'consumed less time and seen higher disposal rates' than civil suits, which can remain unresolved for years at the trial level alone.[73]

[68] The narrow exception to this is if a third party alleges that a P1 or P2 actor has violated fundamental rights that have horizontal effect. For example, a third party alleging that a private agreement that perpetuates untouchability (and therefore violates art 17) has direct recourse to the Supreme Court.

[69] Only four (Bombay, Calcutta, Delhi, and Madras) of the twenty-four High Courts have original civil jurisdiction, which means that in respect of the twenty other High Courts, art 226(1) enables claimants to bypass the civil courts of first instance.

[70] *State of Madhya Pradesh v Bhailal Bhai* AIR 1964 SC 1006; *State of Himachal Pradesh v Gujarat Ambuja Cement Ltd* AIR 2005 SC 3936; *Star Paper Mills Ltd v State of Uttar Pradesh* (2006) 10 SCC 201.

[71] This leaves open a potential gap in the application of fundamental rights. The way in which the case law currently applies is that if a state withdraws from a field of activity and a private authority fills the void, that authority will be classified as P2 rather than P3; see G Bhatia, 'What Is the State—V: Zee Telefilms, the Death of the Functional Approach, and an Alternative' (Indian Constitutional Law and Philosophy, 19 August 2014) <https://indconlawphil.wordpress.com/2014/08/19/what-is-the-state-v-zee-telefilms-the-death-of-the-functional-approach-and-an-alternative> accessed 25 December 2020.

[72] *Barium Chemicals Limited v Company Law Board* AIR 1967 SC 295.

[73] A Padmanabhan, 'Rights: Breadth, Scope, and Applicability' in S Choudhry, M Khosla, and PB Mehta (eds), *The Oxford Handbook of Indian Constitution* (OUP 2016) 583.

IV. Grounds for Review

As the analysis above indicates, the appropriate forum for filing proceedings in judicial review is influenced by the nature and character of the decision-making authority. The same goes for the grounds for judicial review available to third parties. Judicial review can broadly be divided into two categories—non-rights-based review and rights-based review. When a third party alleges that a P2, P3, or P4 actor or authority has acted unlawfully or otherwise unfairly, its challenge will be subjected to a non-rights-based review. The test that will be applied to determine whether the conduct should be set aside is whether the authority acted illegally, irrationally, or based on procedural impropriety.[74] Illegality goes to whether the authority acted beyond its powers—for example, by contracting out a matter that a statute specifically prohibited it from contracting out or by failing to take account of relevant considerations identified by the statute (or conversely, taking account of considerations which the statute regards as irrelevant). Irrationality—also known as 'Wednesbury unreasonableness'[75]—goes to whether the authority took a decision that defied logic or accepted moral standards. Procedural impropriety goes to whether the authority acted with bias, adopted a flawed tendering process, or failed to adopt a tendering process at all when it ought to have done so.

When a third party alleges that a P3 or P4 authority has violated fundamental rights under the Constitution, its challenge will be subjected to a rights based review. The test to be applied in determining whether a particular fundamental right has been violated will vary from one right to another.[76] However, the rights-based review of contracts awarded by P3 and P4 authorities will almost always focus on whether the right to equality under Article 14 has been violated. The test to adjudicate an Article 14 violation will be whether the conduct of the authority was 'arbitrary'.[77] In practice, the arbitrariness ground (within rights-based review) has been treated more or less interchangeably with the irrationality ground (within non-rights based review).[78]

The practical effect of the case law is that whether a public authority's process of contracting is subjected to rights-based review or non-rights based review may have some impact on the taxonomy and the conceptual framework deployed by the parties and the court. However, the substantive distinction between rights-based review and non-rights-based review has collapsed. The nature of the inquiry undertaken by the court in either case will be almost identical: in its broadest formulation, to ascertain whether the state action has been 'fair, reasonable, non-discriminatory, transparent,

[74] *Tata Cellular v Union of India* (1994) 6 SCC 651, [94]. *Delhi Development Authority v UEE Electricals Engg (P) Ltd* (2004) 11 SCC 213, [11]–[12]; see *Council of Civil Service Unions v Minister for the Civil Service* [1985] AC 374.

[75] This is derived from the English Court of Appeal's decision in *Associated Provincial Picture Houses Ltd v Wednesbury Corporation* [1947] EWCA Civ 1.

[76] For example, it is likely that a contract that is challenged on the basis that it violates the right to privacy will be subject to proportionality review: *Justice KS Puttaswamy v Union of India* (2019) 1 SCC 1.

[77] *EP Royappa v State of Tamil Nadu* (1974) 4 SCC 3.

[78] For an analysis, see P Jalan and R Rai, 'Review of Administrative Action' in Choudhry, Khosla, and Mehta (n 73) 436–39.

non-capricious, unbiased, without favouritism or nepotism, in pursuit of promotion of healthy competition and equitable treatment'.[79]

V. Standard of Review

Barring some significant but isolated exceptions, the Supreme Court's consideration of third-party challenges to contracts with public authorities has followed a consistent trajectory. In the early years, the Court took the view that governments and public authorities had more or less unimpeded freedom to choose its contracting partners, in much the same way as private parties. This view was gradually abandoned over time, resulting in an expansion of the Court's jurisdiction to consider challenges to contracts and government authorities. Despite this widening of the Court's jurisdiction, the standard of review has remained very high—making it highly unlikely that the Court will interfere in the process of contracting.

In the 1950s, the Supreme Court took the view that public authorities were no differently positioned than private parties and were at liberty to decide whom they contracted with. Dejected third parties that were not awarded contracts could not invoke the Court's writ jurisdiction claiming that their right to equality under Article 14 had been violated because another party's bid had been selected over theirs. This is exemplified by the Court's decision in *C K Achutan v State of Kerala*,[80] which concerned the tendering process for a contract to supply milk to a government hospital. An unsuccessful bidder challenged the process on a number of grounds, including that it was discriminatory and violated Article 14. Rejecting the challenge, the Court observed that

> it is perfectly open to the Government, even as it is to a private party, to choose a person to their liking, to fulfil contracts which they wish to be performed. When one person is chosen rather than another, the aggrieved party cannot claim the protection of Article 14, because the choice of the person to fulfil a particular contract must be left to the Government.[81]

Over time, the Court began to acknowledge that public authorities were not in the same position as private parties and did not have unimpeded freedom to select their counterparties.[82] In *Ramana Dayaram Shetty v International Airports Authority*,[83] the Court held that in all their dealings with the general public (including when entering into contracts), governments and public authorities were bound to obey rational, relevant, and non-discriminatory standards. A failure to do so would violate basic norms

[79] *Special Reference No 1 of 2012* (2012) 10 SCC 1.
[80] *CK Achuthan v State of Kerala* AIR 1959 SC 490.
[81] ibid.
[82] U Varottil, 'Government Contracts' in Choudhry, Khosla, and Mehta (n 73) 976–77.
[83] *Ramana Dayaram Shetty* (n 62). See also *V Punnen Thomas v State of Kerala* AIR 1969 Ker 81; *Erusian Equipment & Chemicals Ltd v State of West Bengal* (1975) 1 SCC 70.

of fairness embodied in the common law and in Article 14 of the Constitution. The Supreme Court justified this revised approach based on the rise of the welfare state and the expansion of economic activity undertaken by the government. Governments and public authorities owned thousands of acres of land, decided who would have the authority to exploit minerals and other natural resources, and granted licences to do business in a large number of regulated industries. Governments and public authorities could therefore no longer claim to be in the same position as private actors: '[t]he Government is still the Government when it acts in the matter of granting largesse and it cannot act arbitrarily. It does not stand in the same position as a private individual.'[84]

Even as the Court became more receptive to rights-based and non-rights-based challenges to contracts executed by governments and public authorities, the standard of review remained remarkably high. The Court has consistently held that the standard should be higher in practice than it is for other challenges to administrative action. Choosing whom to contract with falls within the domain of economic policy, in respect of which governments and public authorities have been afforded a significant margin of discretion.[85] The Court has also emphasized that its review would almost always focus on the process of contracting, and it would be very unusual for the Court to take umbrage with the terms of the contract.[86]

In *Tata Cellular v Union of India*,[87] the Supreme Court set out what has been considered, over the years, the most authoritative formulation of the principles to be applied when considering challenges to contracts entered into by governments and public authorities:

(1) The modern trend points to judicial restraint in administrative action.
(2) The Court does not sit as a court of appeal but merely reviews the manner in which the decision was made.
(3) The Court does not have the expertise to correct the administrative decision. If a review of the administrative decision is permitted it will be substituting its own decision, without the necessary expertise which itself may be fallible.
(4) The terms of the invitation to tender cannot be open to judicial scrutiny because the invitation to tender is in the realm of contract. Normally speaking, the decision to accept the tender or award the contract is reached by process of negotiations through several tiers. More often than not, such decisions are made qualitatively by experts.
(5) The Government must have freedom of contract. In other words, a fairplay in the joints is a necessary concomitant for an administrative body functioning in an administrative sphere or quasi-administrative sphere. However, the decision must not

[84] *Ramana Dayaram Shetty* (n 62).
[85] *Uflex Ltd v Government of Tamil Nadu* (2022) 1 SCC 165.
[86] *Vice Chairman & Managing Director, CIDCO v Shishir Realty Pvt Ltd* (2021) SCC OnLine SC 1141, [28]; *Silppi Constructions Contractors v Union of India* (2020) 16 SCC 489, [19].
[87] *Tata Cellular* (n 74). These principles have been cited in dozens of cases. See eg *Tejas Constructions & Infrastructure (P) Ltd v Municipal Council, Sendhwa* (2012) 6 SCC 464; *Siemens Aktiengeselischaft & Siemens Ltd v DMRC Ltd* (2014) 11 SCC 288; *State of Punjab v Bandeep Singh* (2016) 1 SCC 724; *Municipal Council, Neemuch v Mahadeo Real Estate* (2019) 10 SCC 738.

only be tested by the application of Wednesbury principle of reasonableness (including its other facts pointed out above) it must be free arbitrariness not affected by bias or actuated by mala fides.

(6) Quashing decisions may impose heavy administrative burden on the administration and lead to increased and unbudgeted expenditure.

These all-weather principles apply to challenges to contracts of P2, P3, or P4 actors or authorities, whether on rights-based or non-rights-based grounds, at the High Courts and at the Supreme Court. The practical effect of these principles is that the Supreme Court and High Courts are reluctant to interfere in the process of contracting by governments and public authorities. Although a full empirical analysis is beyond the scope of this chapter, in sixty-seven cases involving the contracts of governments and public authorities considered by the Supreme Court from the years 2010 to 2022, only fourteen (or about 21 per cent) of cases resulted in the Court interfering with the process of contracting.[88] The cases where the Court intervened included a contract from the Aurangabad Municipal Corporation for the sale of advertising rights on street lamp poles (which was set aside on the basis that the Corporation awarded the contract without inviting tenders);[89] a memorandum of understanding between the State of Uttarakhand and a public-sector undertaking in relation to the provision of 'smart card' driving licences (which was set aside on the basis that the contracting process was not transparent);[90] and an auction process undertaken by the Punjab State Leather Development Corporation, which refused to accept two qualifying bids (for reasons not specified in its decision) and, instead, commenced a fresh auction process.[91]

Upon a writ petition having been filed, the court will first confront the unenviable choice of imposing a stay on performance (risking placing the project in cold storage for an extended period) or allowing performance to continue (risking the expenditure of public funds on a project that is the culmination of an unlawful tendering process). The court is more likely than not to allow performance to continue.[92] When the petition is ultimately decided, a judgment setting aside the process of contracting and ordering recommencement of the process is a disruptive event. Challenges can take months, if not years, to decide. A considerable amount of money may already have been spent on the project. Recommencing the project will almost inevitably result in an escalation in costs. The beneficiaries of the project (eg the users of a shipping port or the future passengers of a planned railway service) will remain deprived of those benefits for a longer period.[93]

[88] See Table 23.1.

[89] *Elektron Lighting Systems (P) Ltd v Shah Investments Financial Developments & Consultants (P) Ltd* (2015) 15 SCC 137.

[90] *Score Information Technologies Ltd v Sriyash Technologies Ltd* (2016) 12 SCC 417.

[91] *Bandeep Singh* (n 87).

[92] *NG Projects Ltd v Vinod Kumar* (2022) 6 SCC 127, [23].

[93] See *Sterling Computers v M&N Publication Ltd* AIR 1996 SC 51, where the Supreme Court articulated some of these concerns.

Table 23.1 Schedule: Challenges to government public authority contracts considered by the Supreme Court from 2010 to 2019

	Case	Outcome[a]
1.	*Afcons Infrastructure Ltd v Nagpur Metro Rail Corpn Ltd* (2016) 16 SCC 818	U
2.	*Agmatel India Pvt Ltd v Resoursys Telecom* (2022) 5 SCC 362	U
3.	*Akhil Bhartiya Upbhokta Congress v State of MP* (2011) 5 SCC 29	S
4.	*Alauli Anchal Boat Traffic Coop Society Ltd v State of Bihar* (2016) 6 SCC 296	U
5.	*Ambulance Access Foundation India v Union of India* Writ Petition (Civil) No. 518 of 2008	U
6.	*Association of Registration Plates v Union of India* (2005) 1 SCC 679	U
7.	*Bakshi Security & Personnel Services (P) Ltd v Devkishan Computed (P) Ltd* (2016) 8 SCC 446	U
8.	*Bhubaneswar Development Authority v Adikanda Biswal* (2012) 11 SCC 731	U
9.	*Bihar State Housing Board v Radha Ballabh Health Care & Research Institute (P) Ltd* (2019) 10 SCC 483	U
10.	*BSNL v Telephone Cables Ltd* (2010) 5 SCC 213	U
11.	*Caretel Infotech Ltd v Hindustan Petroleum Corpn Ltd* (2019) 14 SCC 81	U
12.	*Central Coalfields Ltd v SLL–SML (Joint Venture Consortium)* (2016) 8 SCC 622	U
13.	*Centre for Public Interest Litigation v Union of India* (2012) 3 SCC 1	S
14.	*Chhattisgarh State Industrial Development Corpn Ltd v Amar Infrastructure Ltd* (2017) 5 SCC 387	U
15.	*City Industrial Development Corpn v Platinum Entertainment* (2015) 1 SCC 558	S
16.	*Consortium of Titagarh Firema Adler SPA—Titagarh Wagons Ltd v Nagpur Metro Rail Corpn Ltd* (2017) 7 SCC 486	U
17.	*CRRC Corpn Ltd v Metro Link Express for Gandhinagar & Ahmedabad (Mega) Co Ltd* (2017) 8 SCC 282	U
18.	*Daulat Sitaram Kodone v State of Maharashtra* (2014) 13 SCC 341	S
19.	*Elektron Lighting Systems (P) Ltd v Shah Investments Financial Developments & Consultants (P) Ltd* (2015) 15 SCC 137	S
20.	*Essar Steel Ltd v Union of India* (2016) 11 SCC 1	U
21.	*Indian Oil Corpn Ltd v Arti Devi Dangi* (2016) 15 SCC 480	U
22.	*Indian Oil Corpn Ltd v Shashi Prabha Shukla* (2018) 12 SCC 85	U
23.	*Indian Oil Corpn Ltd v T Natarajan* (2018) 9 SCC 235	U
24.	*Indsil Hydro Power and Manganese Ltd v State of Kerala* (2020) 16 SCC 276	U
25.	*Jal Mahal Resorts (P) Ltd v KP Sharma* (2014) 8 SCC 804	U
26.	*Joshi Technologies International Inc v Union of India* (2015) 7 SCC 728	U
27.	*JSW Infrastructure Ltd v Kakinada Seaports Ltd* (2017) 4 SCC 170	U
28.	*Kulja Industries Ltd v Western Telecom Project BSNL* (2014) 14 SCC 731	S
29.	*Larsen & Toubro Ltd v Union of India* (2011) 5 SCC 430	U
30.	*Maa Binda Express Carrier v North-East Frontier Railway* (2014) 3 SCC 760	U
31.	*Manohar Lal Sharma v Narendra Damodardas Modi* (2019) 3 SCC 25	U
32.	*Michigan Rubber (India) Ltd v State of Karnataka* (2012) 8 SCC 216	U
33.	*Montecarlo Ltd v NTPC Ltd* (2016) 15 SCC 272	U

Table 23.1 Continued

	Case	Outcome[a]
34.	*Municipal Corpn Ujjain v BVG India Ltd* (2018) 5 SCC 462	U
35.	*N Ramachandra Reddy v State of Telangana* 2019 SCC OnLine SC 1112	U
36.	*NG Projects Ltd v Vinod Kumar* (2022) 6 SCC 127	U
37.	*Nagendra Rai v Om Prakash Singh* (2014) 15 SCC 463	U
38.	*Natural Resources Allocation In re Special Reference No 1 of 2012* (2012) 10 SCC 1	U
39.	*Nova Ads v Metropolitan Transport Corpn* (2015) 13 SCC 257	S
40.	*NTPC Ltd v Ansaldo Caldaie Boilers India (P) Ltd* (2012) 4 SCC 471	S
41.	*Patel Engg Ltd v Union of India* (2012) 11 SCC 257	U
42.	*Reliance Telecom Ltd v Union of India* (2017) 4 SCC 269	U
43.	*Rishi Kiran Logistics (P) Ltd v Kandla Port Trust* (2015) 13 SCC 233	U
44.	*Roots Industries India Ltd v Airports Authority of India* (2016) 3 SCC 569	U
45.	*Sam Built Well (P) Ltd v Deepak Builders* (2018) 2 SCC 176	U
46.	*Score Information Technologies Ltd v Sriyash Technologies Ltd* (2016) 12 SCC 417	S
47.	*Shagun Mahila Udyogik Sahakari Sanstha Maryadit v State of Maharashtra* (2011) 9 SCC 340	U
48.	*Shimnit Utsch India (P) Ltd v WB Transport Infrastructure Development Corpn Ltd* (2010) 6 SCC 303	U
49.	*Shobikaa Impex (P) Ltd v Central Medical Services Society* (2016) 16 SCC 233	U
50.	*Siemens Aktiengeselischaft & Siemens Ltd v DMRC Ltd* (2014) 11 SCC 288	U
51.	*Silppi Constructions Contractors v Union of India*(2020) 16 SCC 489	U
52.	*Soma Isolux NH One Tollway (P) Ltd v Harish Kumar Puri* (2014) 6 SCC 75	U
53.	*South Delhi Municipal Corpn v Ravinder Kumar* (2015) 15 SCC 545	U
54.	*State of Assam v Susrita Holdings (P) Ltd* (2014) 11 SCC 192	S
55.	*State of Jharkhand v CWE-SOMA Consortium* (2016) 14 SCC 172	U
56.	*State of Punjab v Bandeep Singh* (2016) 1 SCC 724	S
57.	*State of UP v Al Faheem Meetex (P) Ltd* (2016) 4 SCC 716	U
58.	*Sunita Gupta v Union of India* (2014) 15 SCC 601	S
59.	*Swaraj Abhiyan v Union of India* (2018) 4 SCC 300	U
60.	*Tehri Hydro Development Corpn v Alstom Hydro France* (2010) 11 SCC 612	U
61	*Tejas Constructions & Infrastructure (P) Ltd v Municipal Council Sendhwa* (2012) 6 SCC 464	U
62.	*TN Generation and Distribution Corpn Ltd v CSEPDI-Trishe Consortium* (2017) 4 SCC 318	U
63.	*Uflex Ltd v Govt of Tamil Nadu* (2022) 1 SCC 165	U
64.	*Union of India v Gurdayal Singh* (2015) 4 SCC 332	U
65.	*Usha Mehta v Govt of AP* (2012) 12 SCC 419	S
66.	*Vice Chairman & Managing Director, CIDCO v Shishir Realty Pvt Ltd*2021 SCC OnLine SC 1141	S
67.	*Yashwant Sinha v CBI* (2020) 2 SCC 338	U

[a]. In this column, 'S' denotes that the court set aside the process of contracting or some aspect of it, and 'U' denotes that the court upheld the process of contracting in its entirety.

It is unsurprising, then, that courts often find ways to soften the blow, even in those instances where they conclude that the process of contracting fails relevant constitutional standards. Consider the *Ramana Dayaram Shetty* case itself,[94] where the Supreme Court concluded that a contract in relation to a restaurant and two snack bars at Bombay's International Airport was awarded to an unqualified applicant. Despite arriving at this conclusion, the Court nevertheless chose not to set aside the contract, as over five months had passed between the acceptance of the tender and the petition challenging the process. In the interim, the successful tenderer spent a considerable amount of money towards performance of the contract and had already begun operating the snack bars.[95]

Therefore, it is very unusual to encounter cases in which courts set aside contracts of governments or public authorities in circumstances that give rise to major economic upheavals. Two Supreme Court decisions—made within a period of three years from 2012 to 2014—stand out like sore thumbs. In the '*2G Spectrum*' case,[96] the Court cancelled 122 licences to mobile telecommunications spectrum, awarded a few years earlier, on the basis that the government allotted them on an arbitrary 'first come, first served' basis. More remarkably, the Court substituted the government's decision with its own, concluding that an auction was the *only* constitutionally permissible method of allocating all natural resources.[97] In the '*Coalgate*' case,[98] the Supreme Court set aside 214 coal block allocations that were made to power, steel, and cement companies on the basis that they were arbitrary and illegal. Some of these allocations dated back to 1993, which was more than twenty years before the Court's judgment.

The way in which the *2G Spectrum* and *Coalgate* cases were heard and decided gives rise to serious questions involving due process, institutional competence, and the separation of powers.[99] However, there are good reasons to assume that those decisions will not influence the Court's (otherwise fairly consistent) approach of providing latitude to governments and public authorities on whom to contract with and on what terms to do so. Both cases involved allegations of corruption on a large scale and misuse of public office going to the highest levels of government. The Supreme Court conceived of its role as an anti-corruption crusader that was tasked with stamping out crony capitalism. That role was performed in a highly 'public' setting, even by the Court's own standards—with minute-to-minute coverage and courtrooms packed with reporters in anticipation of headline-grabbing observations. The *2G Spectrum* case, for example, was referenced no less than 477 times in a single English newspaper in one year.[100]

[94] *Ramana Dayaram Shetty* (n 62). See also *Air India Ltd v Cochin Intl Airport Ltd* (2000) 2 SCC 617, 623.

[95] *Ramana Dayaram Shetty* (n 62).

[96] *Centre for Public Interest Litigation v Union of India* (2012) 3 SCC 1.

[97] This broad conclusion was swiftly repudiated, although the Court's decision to cancel the licences remained unaffected; see *Special Reference No 1 of 2012* (n 79).

[98] *Manohar Lal Sharma v The Principal Secretary* (2014) 9 SCC 516.

[99] Varottil (n 82); S Krishnaswamy, 'The Supreme Court on 2G: Signal and Noise', Seminar 642 (20 February 2013); C Chandrachud, 'Anticorruption by Fiat: Structural Injunctions and Public Interest Litigation in the Supreme Court of India' (2018) 14 Socio-Legal Review 170.

[100] C Chandrachud, 'Measuring Constitutional Case Salience in the Indian Supreme Court' (2016) 6 Journal of Indian Law and Society 42.

These factors are alien to a vast majority of cases involving judicial review of contracts with the state on the Supreme Court's docket. Mega corruption scandals aside, the Court remains reluctant to interfere in the process of contracting.

VI. Conclusion

The principal challenge with regulating contracts with the state is to strike an appropriate balance between two competing objectives: first, to afford the parties sufficient liberty of contract and commercial autonomy; second, to ensure that the state party (or a private party exercising public functions) conducts itself transparently and fairly and can be held to account for a failure to do so. The constitutional regime that has evolved over the course of several decades strikes that balance with relative success. Three factors in particular have contributed to this success. The special formation requirements prescribed by the Constitution have been interpreted and applied quite strictly, while leaving some room for commercial flexibility and allowing parties that have supplied goods or services under unauthorised contracts to access remedies in restitution. The courts have also sustained a 'soft' rather than 'hard' public–private divide so that parties that do not fall within the constitutional definition of a 'state' but perform public functions nevertheless remain amenable to the writ jurisdiction of the High Courts when they execute contracts in the exercise of those functions. Finally, although the breadth of the courts' jurisdiction to intervene in the process of contracting has expanded over time, courts have consistently imposed a high threshold for intervention.(Table 23.1)

PART IV
CONCLUSION

24

Concluding Remarks

Hugh Beale

I. Introduction

The stated aim of the project to celebrate the 150th birthday of the Indian Contract Act 1872 (hereinafter 'the Contract Act') was

> to produce, in collaboration with academics and practitioners from around the world, an authoritative commentary on Indian contract law.

The chapters in this volume certainly do this: they contain a detailed analysis of the statute and its interpretation by the courts. Thus, readers will have an account of almost all the general part of the law of contracts, of the special contracts that are still governed by the Contract Act (indemnity and guarantee, and bailment), and of two other fields of great practical importance, shareholders' agreements and contracting with the State. The analysis is not confined to the Contract Act—for example, Goh's chapter on interpretation covers aspects of the Indian Evidence Act 1872 and Naravane's discussion of assignment has to consider sections of the Transfer of Property Act 1882, while the Contract Act has to be read alongside the Specific Relief Act 1963, as amended in 2018.[1]

The collection does much more, however, than just provide a commentary on the Act(s). The introductory chapters by Swain and by Paterson and Bant explore the origins of the Contract Act, the sources of some of its less usual provisions, and the aims of the codification. Similar themes are picked up in many of the chapters on particular subjects. Many chapters also look forward to possible reform of the Contract Act.

In this conclusion, I do not attempt to summarise the explanations of each area of law given in the individual chapters; they speak for themselves. Nor will I deal with the adoption of the Contract Act in other jurisdictions.[2] Instead, I focus on some of the general themes and explore three issues.

[1] Specific Relief (Amendment) Act 2018; see N Venkatesan, Chapter 18 of this volume, section IV. Also the Trusts Act 1882, s 4 is parallel to the Contract Act, s 23, and s 84 deals with transfers of property for an illegal purpose: see T Sebastian and A Ahluwalia, Chapter 11 of this volume, section II.

[2] See May Fong Cheong, Chapter 4 of this volume, section I.

Hugh Beale, *Concluding Remarks* In: *Foundations of Indian Contract Law*. Edited by: KV Krishnaprasad, Niranjan Venkatesan, Shivprasad Swaminathan, and Umakanth Varottil, Oxford University Press. © Oxford University Press 2024.
DOI: 10.1093/9780191997211.003.0024

The first is about the Contract Act (and the linked legislation) at the time of its enactment. There are groups of inter-linked questions about the aims of the drafters and legislators:

(1) Although as Pollock wrote, the Contract Act was 'not only the work of different hands, but work done from quite different points of view',[3] to what extent was the final result influenced by theories and ideas derived from continental European thought? Was the drafting an exercise in 'legal science' so that a basic concept such as 'agreement' should determine the concrete provisions of the Contract Act? Or were the drafters more pragmatic when it came to detailed provisions? Was the exercise really more than an attempt to state English law as it was understood at the time, with some marginal improvements? What freedom were the courts to have to develop the law?
(2) To what extent were the drafters seeking to make sure the Contract Act would be suitable for local conditions?
(3) What were their aims in terms of making the law accessible? How far did the drafting style succeed in achieving accessibility?
(4) What conception did they have of the parties and types of transaction or dispute to which the Contract Act would apply, and what was the overall philosophy in terms of, say, individualism versus welfarism (the protection of weaker parties)?

Second, we should consider what substantive reforms our commentators think are desirable—reforms that are possibly needed to make the Contract Act workable, to fill gaps, or to replace provisions that do not produce what now seems the best outcome.

The third issue is to ask questions about the Contract Act today similar to those we asked about the Act as it was passed:

(1) Are the courts still applying the traces of, for example, the Will Theory that are found in the Act, or are they interpreting it as if it were (with a few marked exceptions) a restatement of the common law as it is understood in say England, Hong Kong, Singapore or (with rather more deviations) Australia?
(2) How accessible is modern contract law in India?
(3) In so far as we may be able to generalise from the various topics within the scope of the project, what is the overall nature of contract law in India today? Who and what disputes does it govern, and what is its overall philosophy compared to that of some other legal systems?

[3] F Pollock and D Mulla, *The Indian Contract Act: With a Commentary, Critical and Explanatory* (1st edn, Sweet & Maxwell 1905) v, cited in KV Krishnaprasad, Chapter 10 of this volume, section I.

II. The Contract Act in 1872

1. Will Theory and a 'Scientific' Approach

In Chapter 1 of this volume, Swain explains the different influences on the Bill and the fate of some of the more radical proposals, such as on consideration, specific performance, and *bona fide* purchasers.[4] I will concentrate on the final Contract Act. In the various chapters, there are recurring questions over the extent to which its provisions were influenced by Will Theory and the extent to which the drafters aimed at a supposedly 'scientific' approach[5] so that the theory produced concrete provisions that differed from English law at the time—though English law was itself not always clear or wholly coherent. The work of writers such as Pothier were drawn on when the courts needed to fill gaps in the law.[6] But though the Will Theory was popular with writers and was adopted by some judges, it was, in many respects, inconsistent with the traditional common law, and at the end of the day, the civilian doctrine tended to be moulded or adapted to fit with common law traditions, even if the civilian approach had an influence on the way that home-grown doctrines were perceived.[7]

In the Contract Act, there do seem to be examples of conceptual purity leading to results that are certainly different to the position in the other common law systems, and which are sometimes questionable in practical terms. Thus, for a contract to come into existence, section 10 of the Contract Act requires 'parties competent to contract', while section 11 provides that minors and those without mental capacity lack capacity. Sections 2(g) and (h) have the effect that an agreement that is not a contract is void. As a result, an agreement by a minor is void however advantageous it is to the minor[8] and one by a person lacking mental capacity is void whether or not the other party knew, or ought to have known, of the lack of capacity. But that is a fairly isolated example. Even though Stephen's draft adopted definitions from the Civil Code prepared for New York by Field,[9] which seemed to make agreement and consent 'a central pillar of the legislation',[10] Swain notes that Stephen doubted whether substantive law could be based on abstract principle.[11]

We certainly see borrowings from Pothier and civilian thought, whether coming direct from writers or indirectly via the Field Code. Several chapters in this book refer

[4] See W Swain, Chapter 1 of this volume, section VII.

[5] See JM Paterson and E Bant, Chapter 2 of this volume, section II.1 ('an ambition was for the Act to be "scientific"'); see the sources cited in their n 32.

[6] For instance, the doctrine of offer and acceptance; see AWB Simpson, 'Innovation in Nineteenth Century Contract Law' (1975) 91 Law Quarterly Review 247.

[7] Thus Swain writes 'English law reached a compromise which saw a gradual shift in the way that consideration was perceived, and which left the doctrine looking less like an attempt to find a genuine exchange and more about whether an agreement was intended to have contractual effect': W Swain, Chapter 1 of this volume, section V.

[8] The Contract Act, s 58 provides a restitutionary claim for necessaries supplied to persons lacking capacity. For other cases of minors and persons of unsound mind, restitution may be available under the Specific Relief Act 1963, ss 65 or 33, respectively, though possibly only where neither party was aware of the problem: see N Maitra, Chapter 8 of this volume, section IV.

[9] See W Swain, Chapter 1 of this volume, section VI.

[10] See ibid, section VIII.

[11] See ibid, section VII.

to the Contract Act being based upon the Will Theory,[12] or at least being heavily influenced by it.[13] But as Swain points out,[14] the common law doctrine of consideration, which is not required under the Will Theory and does not really fit with it, was retained in the Contract Act with only very minor variations.

More usually, it seems to me that the drafters were doing little more than borrow definitions and phrases that were convenient and were altering them to fit either the common law approach or with what was thought convenient.[15] Thus, section 10, with its reference to 'free consent' by competent parties and a lawful object, does look very much like Article 1108 of the Code Napoleon,[16] save that 'cause' is replaced by consideration, or like § 745 of the Field Code, which required 'cause or consideration'. However, close examination suggests that, in fact, the Field Code and the Contract Act both vary the language from the Napoleonic model in order to fit with the common law: thus, in the Field Code, the requirement of an object becomes 'a lawful object'—in other words, 'object' is no longer a free-standing essential; the reference is now just to agreements that may have an illegal purpose. Section 10 of the Contract Act follows suit, adding that the consideration must also be lawful.

Similarly when we look at the definition of 'free consent' in section 14 and the provisions on mistake, it is seems clear that the draftsman has a common law model in mind. In French law, for example, relief is given because the claimant's consent was not wholly free or fully informed, for instance, because the claimant was mistaken as to an essential characteristic of the subject matter. In English law, in contrast, with the exception of common mistake as to the facts, which was an (unhappy) 19th-century importation, the claimant will not get relief unless the defendant has 'behaved badly' in some way—for example, inducing the contract by fraud, misrepresentation or duress. § 752 of the Field Code was on the Napoleonic lines, providing that an 'apparent consent' is not real or free when obtained by duress, menace, fraud, undue influence, or mistake, which includes a unilateral mistake as to the facts.[17] Section 14 of the Contract Act seems to be derived directly from § 752, but 'free consent' is defined in terms that represent common law. So misrepresentation is added as a ground on which consent

[12] For instance, see S Tofaris, Chapter 5 of this volume, section II.2 ('premised on the Will Theory', though noting that incompatible requirements like consideration survived and that the provisions on offer and acceptance 'were based on Stephen's assessment of the balance of convenience between the parties and contradicted the results generated by a faithful application of the Will Theory'); N Nuggehalli and R Surana, Chapter 6 of this volume, section II; S Swaminathan and V Singh, Chapter 9 of this volume, section II.1 ('arguably the Grundnorm').

[13] See N Nuggehalli and R Surana, Chapter 6 of this volume, section II.

[14] See W Swain, Chapter 1 of this volume, section VII. See also S Tofaris, Chapter 5 of this volume, section II.2.

[15] See S Tofaris, Chapter 5 of this volume, section V.4 (English postal rule not adopted).

[16] Article 1108:

> Four requisites are essential for the validity of an agreement:
> The consent of the party who binds himself;
> His capacity to contract;
> A definite object which forms the subject-matter of the undertaking;
> A lawful cause in the obligation.

See similarly the Field Code, § 745, which required 'cause or consideration'. Article 1128 of the revised Civil Code (2016–18) requires consent, capacity, and 'content which is lawful and certain'.

[17] See the Field Code, § 762. A mistake of law is relevant only if it is shared or, where the mistake is unilateral, the other party knows of it but does not rectify it: Field Code, § 763.

may not be free, but mistake is narrowed by reference to sections 20–22. The result is that the Contract Act neatly articulates the doctrine of common mistake in section 20 and explicitly departs from the French model:

> 22. Contract caused by mistake of one party as to matter of fact.—A contract is not voidable merely because it was caused by one of the parties to it being under a mistake as to a matter of fact.

On other occasions, phrases that seem very civilian are used, but the words borrowed can be given a meaning that is compatible with the common law. Section 13 of the Contract Act provides an example:

> 13. 'Consent' defined.—Two or more persons are said to consent when they agree upon the same thing in the same sense.

While section 13 seems to require a 'meeting of the minds' (which is what I assume Pothier would have said, since, in principle, this remains the position in French law)[18], its wording is sufficiently open that it can be read as compatible with the common law's traditional 'objective' approach—which is that it suffices that the parties reasonably appear to each other to have agreed on the same thing in the same terms.[19] Tofaris points out that there is no reference to the objective approach in the Contract Act and that the importation of the objective test into Indian law seems to have been the result of later judicial borrowing from English law when the objective approach became more prominent in the late 19th century; but the fact that Stephen retained section 13 in the Contract Act and did not see the need to follow the Field Code in adding that sometimes the parties might be 'deemed so to agree'[20] suggests that he considered the words of section 13 to be broad enough to cover an objective approach. Certainly, in the Indian Evidence Act 1872, which he also drafted, the approach as to when the court may look outside the words of a contract in writing is very much along common law lines.[21]

[18] See H Beale and others, *Ius Commune Casebooks for the Common Law of Europe: Cases, Materials and Text on Contract Law* (3rd edn, Hart 2019) 104–107 (hereinafter *Ius Commune Casebooks*). As Tofaris points out in Chapter 5 of this volume, section VI,

> For Will Theorists like Pothier, there was no contract where an offer was withdrawn without communication before it was accepted because the consent necessary to form an agreement was lacking. Pothier pursued the consent-based reasoning to its rational conclusion. The Contract Act did not: the refusal to rule that uncommunicated revocation was absolutely effective (binding both parties) signified the limits of any influence that the Will Theory had.

An uncommunicated revocation is still ineffective in French law (see eg Cass civ, 17 December 1958, D 1959.1.33); unless an option has been granted (Civil Code, art 1124), the offer cannot be accepted, though if the offeror had agreed to keep the offer open for a fixed period, the offeror may have to compensate the offeree for wrongful revocation: see *Ius Commune Casebook* (above) 231–32.

[19] See S Tofaris, Chapter 5 of this volume, section III.

[20] § 765: 'Consent is not mutual, unless the parties all agree upon the same thing in the same sense. But in certain cases defined by the chapter on INTERPRETATION, they are to be deemed so to agree without regard to the fact.'

[21] See G Yihan, Chapter 3 of this volume.

It is arguable that the Contract Act contains remnants of the Will Theory. Thus, Nuggehalli and Surana say that 'a commitment to the Will Theory remains in the capacious terms in which section 2(d) of the Act defines consideration'.[22] Certainly, the Contract Act adopted a less strict definition of consideration than English law, one that may be seen as subjective in the sense that it seemed to do away with any requirement that the promise or act bargained for had any objective value,[23] but whether that was under the influence of the Will Theory or just seeking to get rid of what were seen as inconvenient technicalities is hard to say.

Another possible sign of continental thinking being carried through to detailed provisions is that the definition of coercion in section 15, and likewise that of misrepresentation in section 18, does not require that the threat or misstatement must be made by the other party to the contract. Civilian codes often allow a defence of 'threat by a third person' on the ground that the claimant's consent was not free.[24] (They do not deal with misrepresentation by a third party, since relief will be available on the ground of the claimant's mistake.) However, Elliott and Behl question whether the draftsmen of the Contract Act even thought about coercion or misrepresentation by a third person.[25] None of the illustrations involve such cases.

Thus, my overall impression is that, for the most part, the impact of the Will Theory on the Contract Act is only skin deep.

We also see other deliberate departures from civilian traditions. The Code Napoleon dealt with illegality only by providing that only things that can be dealt with lawfully could be the object of a contract (Article 1128) and that an obligation with an unlawful cause may not have any effect (Article 1131). The Field Code similarly required that both the object of the contract (§ 776) and the consideration (§ 782) be lawful. The Draft Bill contained something very similar,[26] but section 23 is a much closer refection of the English doctrine.

2. Statute, Code, or Restatement?

The pressure for a code of contract law came from not just utilitarian idealists but also lawyers and officials in India.[27] It would be easier to understand and to administer a single law of contract rather than the diversity that, in principle at least, applied before 1872, with different laws applying to Muslims, Hindus, and Europeans.[28] That pressure

[22] See N Nuggehalli and Ri Surana, Chapter 6 of this volume, section I, referring to S Swaminathan, 'Eclipsed by Orthodoxy: The Vanishing Point of Consideration and the Forgotten Ingenuity of the Indian Contract Act 1872' (2017) 12 Asian Journal of Comparative Law 141, 152.

[23] See N Nuggehalli and R Surana, Chapter 6 of this volume, section I.

[24] For example, the French Civil Code, art 1142: 'Duress is a ground of nullity regardless of whether it has been applied by the other party or a third party'; see *Ius Commune Casebook* (n 18) 620–21.

[25] See S Elliott KC and D Behl, Chapter 19 of this volume, section VI.1.

[26] See T Sebastian and A Ahluwalia, Chapter 11 of this volume, section II.

[27] See W Swain, Chapter 1 of this volume, section III.

[28] See ibid, section II—though, as I understand it, appeals from those courts might well result in solutions closer to English law.

for codification did not exist in England, where, in 1830, it was said that codification was a 'dead letter', and only parts of the laws of contract were ever put into statutory form.[29]

How did the drafters envisage the courts applying the Contract Act? When parts of English law were 'codified' in the later 19th century (eg in the Sale of Goods Act 1893), the result was very much a traditional statute, and the courts have interpreted it as such (save that they sometimes have recourse to pre-Act case law even when it has supposedly been superseded by the Contract Act[30]). So the provisions of the Sale of Goods Act 1893 are applied in a rather literal fashion. In contrast, the continental understanding seems to be that a code is to provide a series of provisions on which the courts can build doctrine, often relying on general provisions such as those requiring good faith[31] but sometimes extrapolating from particular provisions.[32] What was envisaged for the Contract Act?

I do not find this easy to answer. Some of the Contract Act's provisions do look more like a code than a statute because they are so brief and lacking in detail (eg section 13 quoted earlier). The same is true of some sections in other Acts. For example, Naravane argues that section 6(e) of the Transfer of Property Act 1882, which provides that 'a mere right to sue cannot be transferred', should be interpreted as broad principle rather than literally so that it should not prevent the transfer of a right to sue if the assignee has a genuine commercial interest in enforcing the right.[33] Section 73 of the Contract Act on damages is another example of a rather brief provision that lacks detail. Quite a number of the Contract Act's provisions are, as Paterson and Bant put it, 'standards-based' rather than 'rule-based'. Arvind, in his illuminating discussion of section 74, argues that

> in structure, purpose, and intent, section 74 resembles neither an English statute nor a civilian code as much as it resembles the US Uniform Commercial Code—a law that was explicitly drafted to permit a more socially and contextually aware form of judging.[34]

Other provisions, such as sections 3–9 on the Communication, Acceptance and Revocation of Proposals, or sections 17 and 18 defining fraud and misrepresentation, respectively, seem as precise as an English statute might be. So there does not seem to be a universal pattern. In fact, most of the Contract Act seems quite detailed; and even a very broad-brush provision such as section 27, which states simply that

[29] See ibid, section III.

[30] See C Twigg-Flesner and R Canavan, *Atiyah and Adams' Sale of Goods* (14th edn, Pearson 2021) 4–5.

[31] This was particularly the case in German law: see eg the development of controls over standard terms of contract: H Kötz, *European Contract Law* (2nd edn, OUP 2017) 135.

[32] For example, the development of the *obligation de renseignement* in French law, first proposed in doctrine, then adopted in the courts and now enacted in the Civil Code, art 1112-1: see *Ius Commune Casebook* (n 18) 574–75.

[33] See S Naravane, Chapter 7 of this volume, section VI.2, citing in support *Union of India v Sri Sarada Mills* AIR 1973 SC 281.

[34] See TT Arvind, Chapter 17 of this volume, section IV.

> Every agreement by which any one is restrained from exercising a lawful profession, trade or business of any kind, is to that extent void.'

seems to have been understood at least very soon afterwards as to be interpreted literally. So in 1909, Pollock and Mulla explain the section in terms of a wish 'to make the smallest number of exceptions to the rule',[35] rather than as a broad principle that the courts should qualify as necessary—though that is what the courts have done.[36] So how far Arvind's description of section 74 can be applied to the rest of the Contract Act remains an open question.

I have pointed out that section 73 is brief, but it is supplemented by a long list of illustrations; and illustrations are used throughout the Act. Both the Transfer of Property Act 1882 and the Indian Evidence Act 1872 (which was also drafted by Stephen) also use illustrations. This use of illustrations makes one wonder whether the Contract Act was following a third model, one that we now know as a 'Restatement'. Before the Contract Act, it seems that contract law often had to be applied by judges with little or no legal training, and they would often apply what they understood was broadly English law. Something in the form of the Contract Act—broad provisions followed by examples—might have been conceived of as a general guide to contract law for such courts rather than either a statute or a civilian-type code.

This depends on what we mean by a 'Restatement'. One of the main characteristics of both the American Law Institute's Restatements and the European[37] and Latin American 'Principles'[38] (which are explicitly modelled on the American Law Institute Restatements[39]) is that they are only 'soft law', which no court is bound to follow. The Contract Act, in contrast, is clearly meant as 'hard law'. However, to some extent, the Contract Act does follow the Restatement in its use of examples so that sometimes it resembles a simple textbook rather than a statute of the more traditional kind.

I must confess to having been doubtful whether the Contract Act was meant as a Restatement even in the second sense. I understand that by 1872 there was increasing professionalisation, with many more judges who had received a training in England sitting in India. It would not seem sensible to draft a style of law more suited to a non-professional model that was on its way out. Moreover, as Barnett points out, section 73 deals only with what we would now call remoteness and does not explain the measure of damages, neither does it mention the equally important principle of mitigation, which one would think should be laid out clearly even for less skilled professionals. Rather, I suspected that section 73 and its illustrations might have just been an example part of a tendency to follow the lead of the Field Code on points that were thought to

[35] See T Zhong Xing and U Varottil, Chapter 12 of this volume, section I.

[36] See section III.1.ii below.

[37] O Lando and H Beale (eds), *Principles of European Contract Law, Parts I and II* (Kluwer 2000); O Lando and others (eds), *Principles of European Contract Law, Part III* (Kluwer 2003).

[38] 'Principles of Latin American Contract Law', <www.trans-lex.org/400750/_/principles-of-latin-american-contract-law-> accessed 3 November 2023. See also R Momberg and S Vogenauer, 'The Principles of Latin American Contract Law: Text, Translation, and Introduction' (2018) 23 Uniform Law Review 144.

[39] See Lando and Beale, *Principles of European Contract Law* (n 37) xxvi.

be less important.[40] Although § 1840 of the Field Code does not use quite the same language as section 73, it is similar in substance, and it is one of only two general provisions on damages for breach of contract;[41] the remaining eighteen sections in Article I on Damages for Breach of Contract deal with particular situations, just like the examples in the Contract Act. However, Paterson and Bant have shown that not only was there a history of using illustrations in legislation for India but also the First Law Commissioners saw the illustrations as a way of conveying the meaning of precise but 'hard and awkward expressions' and of suggesting the reasons for the choice of the expression. The illustrations also link the Act's provisions to pre-existing principles of law.[42] So I think the idea that the Contract Act was meant as a Restatement, at least in the sense of a set of rules supplemented by explanations and illustrations to make the law understandable, is plausible.

This suggests that 'accessibility' was a key concern of the drafters. But accessibility raises the question: accessibility to whom? To judges and lawyers? Or is the aim to make the law accessible at least some non-lawyers, for example, business people? The style of the Contract Act, with its relatively short sections and its examples, certainly suggests that it might have been intended for the non-lawyer.[43] But that does not seem to have been a concern at the time: the targets seem to have been lawyers and judges.

3. The Overall Pattern of the Contract Act

Overall, it is my impression that though radical changes such as creating major exceptions to the doctrine of consideration were seriously considered,[44] the Contract Act in its final version followed English common law at the time pretty closely, with only a few departures. Some of the departures were intended to clarify or improve on the position under English law: sections 62 and 63 removing the requirement of consideration when a contract is altered or one party agrees not to enforce its rights, section 25 dealing with accepting validity of past consideration, section 56 on contracts that become impossible,[45] some of the provisions on indemnities and guarantees,[46] and the decision not to have multiple categories of bailments[47] are just some examples. Other departures seem to be adaptations to suit local conditions, though it is not always easy to tell the difference. Arvind argues persuasively that at least the 1899 amendment to section 74 to cover a penal bond that would be forfeited in the event of breach (which

[40] See N Venkatesan, Chapter 18 of this volume, section III.1.

[41] The Field Code, § 1841 provides that 'No damages can be recovered for a breach, which are not clearly ascertainable in both their nature and origin'.

[42] See JM Paterson and E Bant, Chapter 2 of this volume, section III.4.

[43] See Lando and Beale, *Principles of European Contract Law* (n 37) xxvi–xxvii.

[44] I was struck by Swain's remark that 'perhaps the extraordinary thing is not that Stephen baulked at this measure but that the Commissioners contemplated it in the first place': see W Swain, Chapter 1 of this volume, section IX.

[45] See W Swain, Chapter 1 of this volume, section VIII; N Bhadbhade, Chapter 14 of this volume, section III.

[46] See W Courtney, Chapter 20 of this volume, section II.1.i (effect of arrangement between co-debtors) and section III.2 (no requirement of writing).

[47] See G Pearson, Chapter 21 of this volume, section I.

had been held not to be a clause stipulating a sum of money payable on breach) was meant to help with the social problem of oppressive agricultural lending.[48] But was a Statute of Frauds provision omitted because writing was seldom used for contracts in India or because even in England it had been found to cause more trouble than it was worth? Probably both.[49] Overall, the adaptations to local conditions seem relatively few—but I do not know enough about those conditions to be able to say what might usefully have been considered.

4. The Original 'Philosophy' of the Contract Act

I will discuss the issue of the 'philosophy' underlying the Contract Act in more detail when I come to the present-day situation, but even in 19th-century terms, it does not seem to have been the aim to give the courts extensive powers to protect unsophisticated or weak contracting parties who had entered into unfavourable contracts. The original version of section 16(2) contained a version of the English unconscionability doctrine, but it applied only to 'a person whose mind is enfeebled by old age, illness or mental or bodily distress'. Swaminathan and Singh[50] suggest that a broad doctrine of unconscionability may have been thought to be incompatible with the Will Theory.[51]

It is true that, in 1899, Chalmers proposed recasting section 16 so as to rest it on a secure 'general principle' that would empower courts to intervene in cases where parties do not 'contract with each other on a footing of equality', and consequently, the stronger imposes 'unfair terms on the other';[52] but just who was to be protected is not clear, as he also said that the Bill was not 'intended in any way to apply to, or to affect, *bona fide* business transactions'[53] or to 'interfere with freedom of contract where the parties to a contract are really free and contract with each other on a footing of equality'.[54] A 'footing of equality' can have a variety of meanings; and even if section 16(1) was intended to bring in a broad doctrine of unconscionability, both section 16(2) and the fact that Illustration (e) says that the lender who has granted a fresh loan on unconscionable terms must disprove undue influence suggest that 'domination' is to have a rather narrow meaning, as indeed the courts held subsequently.

However, it is important not to judge an enactment of 1872 by modern standards. Even laws of contract that now provide very much fuller protection for parties who get into 'contractual trouble' of one kind or another than does English law—for example,

[48] See TT Arvind, Chapter 17 of this volume, section III.2. However, it was argued that abolishing the distinction between penalties and liquidated damages would 'afford greater facilities to the grasping money lender to impose on the ignorant borrower'; see W Swain, Chapter 1 of this volume, section VII.

[49] Ibid.

[50] See S Swaminathan and V Singh, Chapter 9 of this volume, section II.1.

[51] However, the Will Theory has not prevented French law from developing the doctrine of '*violence par circonstances*', which applies when one party takes advantage of the other's predicament: see eg Cass soc 3 July 1963, Bull civ no 545 (translated in *Ius Commune Casebook* (n 18) 643) and now the Civil Code, art 1143.

[52] See S Swaminathan and V Singh, Chapter 9 of this volume, section II.2.

[53] Governor General's Council Proceedings of 17 February 1899, *Gazette of India Part VI* (Calcutta, 18 February 1899) 28.

[54] See TT Arvind, Chapter 17 of this volume, section III.2.

German law, with its doctrine of *culpa in contrahendo*, its duties of pre-contractual disclosure, its controls over unfair standard terms, and its doctrine of change of circumstances[55]—did not have these protections at the time. Though versions of some of the doctrines had been discussed in academic writing, none appeared in the *Bürgerliches Gesetzbuch* (BGB) of 1900; they were all developed by the courts during the 20th century, relying principally on the 'general clause' requiring good faith.[56] They were not incorporated into the BGB until 2002. So, we may say that, for its time, the Contract Act seems to have been intended to provide a reasonable degree of protection for weaker parties.

III. The Modern Law of Contract in India

1. Interpretation of the Contract Act: Common Law Basis/Bias?

i. Gap-filling

The Contract Act, even when read together with the Indian Evidence Act 1872, the Specific Relief Act 1963, and the Transfer of Property Act 1882, does not contain a complete statement of contract law:[57] comparing it to what we teach our students in England, there are a number of gaps. In such cases, it would be only natural for the courts to look to rules and concepts adopted in the common law generally.[58] Some of the chapters in this volume will help to fill the gap. For example, the Contract Act does not explain how contracts are to be interpreted, and the Indian Evidence Act 1872 does so only indirectly by controlling what evidence may be considered.[59] Goh's chapter is an invaluable guide to current practice, even though he cautions against departing too far from the words of the legislation.[60]

For obvious reasons, some issues not dealt with by the Act are not covered in this volume. One example is implied terms: section 9 states that a promise may be implied, but the Act says nothing more. Here, the textbooks such as *Pollock & Mulla* give a full account of the Indian decisions,[61] which seem to follow English law fairly closely, though perhaps with less emphasis on reluctance to imply terms in fact.[62] Another is the question of the incorporation of terms into a contract—in particular, the ticket cases such as *Parker v SE Railway Co.*[63] Here, the position seems less certain. The courts have adopted the English test, viz, did the party seeking to rely on the term give reasonable

[55] See section IV.2 below.
[56] § 242 BGB.
[57] See JM Paterson and E Bant, Chapter 2 of this volume, section I.
[58] See S Tofaris, Chapter 5 of this volume, section VII.1. (Tofaris gives the example of invitations to treat, which are not mentioned in the Act, see ibid, section IV.1).
[59] See G Yihan, Chapter 3 of this volume, section II.3.
[60] Ibid, section II.3.
[61] See RY Vardhan and C Narayan (eds), *Pollock & Mulla, The Indian Contract and Specific Relief Acts* (15th edn, LexisNexis 2017) 196–204.
[62] Cf *Marks and Spencer plc v BNP Paribas Securities Services Trust Co (Jersey) Ltd* [2015] UKSC 72, [2016] AC 742.
[63] (1876–77) LR 2 CPD 416 (CA).

notice of it at or before the time of contracting?[64] But it is not always clear how far Indian courts will simply follow the English rules. Would they, for instance, apply the notorious rule in *L'Estrange v F Graucob Ltd*[65] that (in the absence of a vitiating factor or similar defence) a party who has signed a document is bound by its contents even if the party had not read the document and has no idea that it contains a term to which the party would never have agreed had they known? English courts set great store by this rule,[66] which, to my mind, is wholly characteristic of English law but which, as I will explain below, may not be wholly desirable. It seems curious that though there are a few cases that adopt the rule,[67] *Pollock & Mulla* does not state it as a basic principle.[68]

A gap that is particularly worth noting is that the Contract Act does not have any provision on unfair terms, even clauses that exclude or limit liability. Arvind explains that the courts have applied the incorporation rules mentioned above and also the rules of construction developed in English law, including the fierce 'main purpose' rule:

> Looking at the whole instrument, and seeing what one must regard . . . as its main purpose, one must reject words, indeed whole provisions, if they are inconsistent with what one assumes to be the main purpose of the contract.[69]

Sometimes, they have attacked the substance of the clause by holding that the clause was unconscionable, and on one occasion, the High Court of Delhi held that section 73 created a legal right to compensation for breach which, as a matter of public policy, cannot be waived.[70]

Nor does the Contract Act cover all topics at the 'boundaries' of contract law[71]—in other words, other types of liability that may impinge on contracts. The Act does contain provisions on what we now call unjust enrichment but not, for example, on liability in damages for fraud or negligent misrepresentation. Of course, these will be damages in tort, not contract, but in England they are seen as an important part of 'the law affecting contracts' and feature prominently in both undergraduate contract courses and textbooks.

[64] See TT Arvind, Chapter 17 of this volume, section II.2; see also Vardhan and Narayan (n 61) 122–26.

[65] [1934] 2 KB 394 (KBD).

[66] See eg *Peekay Intermark Ltd v Australia & New Zealand Banking Group Ltd* [2006] EWCA Civ 386, [2006] 2 Lloyd's Rep 511, [43] (Moore-Bick LJ) ('an important principle of English law which underpins the whole of commercial life').

[67] See S Tofaris, 'The Regulation of Unfair Terms in Indian Contract Law: Past, Present, and Future' in M Chen-Wishart and S Vogenauer (eds), *Studies in the Contract Laws of Asia III: Contents of Contracts and Unfair Terms* (OUP 2020).

[68] Vardhan and Narayan (n 61) 122–23; they merely note that in *S Manuel Raj and Co v J Manilal & Co* AIR 1963 Guj 148, a party was bound by a term in a contract that it had signed; HK Saharey (ed), *Dutt on Contract* (9th edn, Eastern Law House 2000) 98 states the rule without giving any authority.

[69] *Glynn v Margetson & Co* [1893] AC 351, 357 (Lord Halsbury LC), quoted in *Skandia Insurance v Kokilaben Chandravadan* AIR 1987 SC 1184.

[70] See TT Arvind, Chapter 17 of this volume, section II.2, remarking that the last approach 'has thus far exerted a rather limited influence over subsequent cases, and it is to be hoped that it stays that way'.

[71] See JM Paterson and E Bant, Chapter 2 of this volume, section II.1.

ii. Interpretation of the Act

When we turn to the interpretation of the Contract Act itself, we seem to see it being interpreted very much as if it were a codification of common law as it is found in jurisdictions such as England, Hong Kong, or Singapore.[72] There are points on which the Contract Act departs from the common law in those jurisdictions; but in a number of these cases, the Act seems to be interpreted in such a way as to bring the results into line with the standard common law models.[73] Paterson and Bant suggest that this is only natural.[74] I am sure they must be right, at least at a time when many Indian lawyers would have studied in England and some English lawyers would have practiced in India.

This phenomenon is only to be expected when the Contract Act uses words that have a meaning in the pre-existing law without defining them,[75] or it is relatively open-textured.[76] However, in several chapters, we have seen this phenomenon even where it involves a good deal of judicial creativity, reading into the Contract Act what is not obviously there in order to cure what is seen as a gap or a shortcoming in the Act. Examples are reading economic duress into the definition of coercion in section 15 or limiting the scope of section 27, which appears to invalidate any contract term that restrains trade, so as to apply it only to restraints that operate after the main period of the contract.[77] Sometimes, the courts have adopted the 'English' rule even though that seems to fly in the face of the Contract Act. A prime example[78] is the importation of reasonableness into section 27, by stating it as a requirement of validity,[79] or by granting injunctive relief on terms,[80] or by the interpretative techniques mentioned previously.[81] Similarly, section 74 appears to abolish the distinction between penalty clauses and liquidated damages by giving the court a broad power to award a reasonable sum, not exceeding the amount agreed, in all cases.[82] However, the courts have resurrected the distinction

[72] See above in this chapter, section I. Swain remarks that 'by the mid-nineteenth century, as colonial legal systems became more legalistic, the law applied in the colonies grew closer to that which operated back in London': W Swain, Chapter 1 of this volume, section II.

[73] For example, the resort to notions of 'benefit and detriment' and 'value in the eyes of the law' for consideration, when those had been omitted from the Contract Act, see N Nuggehalli and R Surana, Chapter 6 of this volume, section I; the reading of the Contract Act, s 16 to require undue influence, see S Swaminathan and V Singh, Chapter 9 of this volume, section II.4.ii.

[74] See JM Paterson and E Bant, Chapter 2 of this volume, section II.1.

[75] See ibid, section III.2.

[76] For example, 'compensation for loss or damage' in the Contract Act, s 73.

[77] See T Zhong Xong and U Varottil, Chapter 12 of this volume, section III.3. The courts also distinguish between non-competition and other types of covenants (see ibid, section III.4) and 'read down' not only the contract terms to which it might otherwise apply (section III.6) but also the section itself so as not to include restraints that do not implicate a 'profession, trade or business' (section III.5).

[78] Another example is the dilution of the Contract Act, s 63 by holding that though the section abolishes the requirement of consideration where the party actually dispenses with performance under the original contract, it has no application where the dispensation is to happen in the future; see N Nuggehalli and R Surana, Chapter 6 of this volume, section III.4.

[79] See T Zhong Xing and U Varottil, Chapter 12 of this volume, section III.2 (though the authors note that this approach is 'somewhat more uncommon').

[80] See ibid, section IV.1.

[81] The authors conclude (section IV.1) that 'The various judicial carve-outs from the scope of section 27 have somewhat mitigated its harshness and allowed Indian courts to balance, often through proxies and rules of thumb, notions of legitimate interests and the need to protect free trade'.

[82] See TT Arvind, Chapter 17 of this volume, section II.1.

at least in part by adopting the 'genuine pre-estimate test' to determine whether the agreed amount is a reasonable sum to award when the loss is hard to determine.[83] And on the issue of the interpretation of contracts, Goh urges Indian courts to pay more attention to the provisions of the Indian Evidence Act 1872, rather than simply following the English line.[84]

iii. Advances on English law

However, the Indian courts have not just followed English law; in a number of situations, they have been more creative and have gone beyond it. An example is the doctrine of promissory estoppel. As Nugehalli and Surana explain, in England this can only be used when the promise was one to give up existing contractual or other rights. At least in a few cases of promises to charity, the Indian courts have come close to adopting the kind of reliance liability found in the US Restatement 2d of Contracts, § 90.[85] Perhaps this was forced on them because Indian law does not recognise the deed under seal,[86] and the nearest equivalent, the provision of section 25 that a promise 'expressed in writing and registered' is binding even without consideration, applies only in cases where there was natural love and affection, that is, in intra-family transactions. Initially even more interesting for anyone who believes that the more conservative common law systems should adopt 'reliance liability', the doctrine of promissory estoppel has been used to prevent the government from going back on promises of subsidies, etc that private parties have acted on.[87] However, not only has this been confined to representations made by State organs, but it also seems to have been merged with the public law doctrine of legitimate expectations.[88]

A list of liberalities would have to include the Indian Evidence Act 1872, where the courts seem largely to have overcome (or to ignore) the apparent rigidity of the Evidence Act's rules as to what evidence may be admitted and are more free to admit evidence of prior negotiations and subsequent conduct than are English courts.

The fact that India has a formal written Constitution adds an extra dimension, but the application of it to contractual disputes (via section 23) seems rather limited—as has application of the nearest equivalent in England, the Human Rights Act 1998.[89]

[83] See ibid, section II.1. Some courts have relied, instead, on principles of unconscionability, despite its apparent limit in Indian law to cases involving public bodies: ibid and S Swaminathan and V Singh, Chapter 9 of this volume, section II.4.iii.

[84] G Yihan, Chapter 3 of this volume, section V.

[85] While I agree that these cases show that the courts do not stick to a strict bargain theory, I don't think that they show that the courts are following the Will Theory. Under the Will Theory, a joint declaration of wills creates an obligation without either a bargain or reliance (though in many systems, an obligation without anything in return—a gift promise—will not be enforceable unless it was in writing and notarised). I would rather say that the Indian courts are adopting (to some extent) reliance liability as an alternative to bargained-for consideration.

[86] See Vardhan and Narayan (n 61) 592.

[87] See *Motilal Padampat v State of Uttar Pradesh* [1979] 2 SCC 40; N Nuggehalli and R Surana, Chapter 6 of this volume, section IV.

[88] Ibid.

[89] See H Beale (Gen ed), *Chitty on Contracts* (35th edn, Sweet & Maxwell 2023) [3-102]ff (hereinafter *Chitty*).

IV. Substantive Problems with the Contract Act and Other Acts

The chapters identify a number of problems of substance that seem to require legislative intervention. They include the following (which are in the order of the relevant chapters in the volume, not of importance):

(1) Privity: though it may have been the intention behind section 2(d) of the Contract Act to disapply not only privity of consideration but privity of contract as well, the courts have confirmed the common law doctrine of privity of contract.[90] Consideration should be given to enabling the parties to give third-party beneficiaries the right to enforce to sue, as recommended by the Law Commission of India,[91] at least where the contract so provides expressly or by necessary implication. The English Contracts (Rights of Third Parties) Act 1999 seems to be working reasonably well[92] and might be considered as a model.

(2) Assignment: the effect of s 6(e) of the Transfer of Property Act 1882 could be clarified.[93] The law on assignments generally, and in particular those that do not comply with the formal requirements of the Transfer of Property Act 1882, might also be put into a new statutory form.[94] But if it is safe to allow assignments of 'non-actionable claims' (without, it seems, the assignor having to be joined), is there really still a need for the more restrictive Transfer of Property Act 1882?

(3) Incapacity: the scope of application of section 11 is unclear, especially in relation to young persons not domiciled in India[95] and persons who are unable to form 'a rational judgment as to [a contract's] effect upon his interests'.[96]

(4) Contracts with persons who lack capacity should be made voidable, not void; the current law may prejudice the interests of minors and possibly those of unsound mind.[97]

(5) There is need of a clear and more coherent provision on when either party may obtain restitution of any benefits transferred under a contract affected by incapacity.[98]

[90] See S Naravane, Chapter 7 of this volume, section I.

[91] Ibid.

[92] See H Beale, 'A Review of the Contracts (Rights of Third Parties) Act 1999' in A Burrows and E Peel (eds), *Contract Formation and Parties* (OUP 2010) 225. A broadly similar measure (though with a somewhat different test of intention to confer enforceable rights on a third party in s 1) has been adopted in Scotland; see the Contracts (Third Party Rights) (Scotland) Act 2017.

[93] See S Naravane, Chapter 7 of this volume, section IV.2.

[94] See ibid, section V.

[95] See N Maitra, Chapter 8 of this volume, section II.1.

[96] See ibid, section II.2.

[97] See ibid, section II.3, noting that contracts with people who are disqualified, which has little to do with the other two types of incapacity, should remain void.

[98] See ibid, section IV.

(6) Unconscionable dealings: the narrow interpretation of section 16 of the Contract Act, which is read as applying only when the parties were in a fiduciary capacity or the weaker party had some mental incapacity,[99] merits reconsideration.[100]

(7) Possibly, section 16(3) should be reconsidered. It raises a presumption of undue influence only when the transaction was unconscionable, a much higher bar than in England (where the test is whether the transaction 'requires explanation'[101]).

(8) A general unconscionability provision, aimed at giving relief to disadvantaged parties in unconscionable transactions, should be considered, as twice recommended by Law Commission of India Reports.[102]

(9) Effect of coercion, fraud, etc: the drafting of sections 10, 14, and 19 of the Contract Act is incompatible with that of section 19 and needs correction. Section 10 provides that free consent is required for a contract so that, without it, the contract will be void, and section 14 defines consent as free when it was not caused by coercion, fraud, etc, whereas section 19 renders contracts obtained by coercion, fraud, etc voidable.[103]

(10) Section 19 second paragraph, which seems to make every representation into a contractual warranty, needs reconsideration.[104]

(11) Mistake: clarification is needed of the distinction between mistakes that prevent a contract being formed because the parties are not in agreement (eg where *A* and *B* have different intentions, each of which is as reasonable as the other,[105] or where *A* cannot accept an offer from *B* if *A* knows that *B* has made a mistake in the offer[106]—cases that now have to be slotted within section 13[107]) and mistakes as to the facts, where *A*'s mistake is irrelevant even if *B* was aware of it, unless *B* caused *A*'s mistake, as provided in section 22 of the Contract Act.

(12) It may be useful revise section 21 so as to remove the distinction between mistakes of law and mistakes of fact.[108]

[99] Except for *parda nashin* women and the illiterate, exceptional cases that merit clear legislative statement even if nothing else is changed.

[100] See S Swaminathan and V Singh, Chapter 9 of this volume, section II.4.

[101] See *Royal Bank of Scotland v Etridge* [2002] 2 AC 773 (HL) 798; S Swaminathan and V Singh, Chapter 9 of this volume, section II.4.ii.

[102] See S Swaminathan and V Singh, Chapter 9 of this volume, section II.4.i (though Illustration (c) of the Contract Act, s 16—the debtor who borrows more from the moneylender—already seems to come close). The decision in *Central Inland Water Transport v Brojonath Ganguly* (1986) 3 SCC 156 (SC) resembles a very broad doctrine of unconscionability but applies only to contracts involving the State, although it has recently been extended to consumer disputes: ibid, section II.4.iii —as Arvind notes, it has sometimes been applied to strike down 'underliquidated damages' clauses that cap the liability of the developer at a very low amount in the event of delay in a species of consumer contracts, namely, house building contracts; see TT Arvind, Chapter 17 of this volume, section II.2.

[103] See KV Krishnaprasad, Chapter 10 of this volume, section III.1.i.

[104] See ibid, section III.4.

[105] As in *Raffles v Wichelhaus* (1864) 2 Hurl & C 906 (QB), as that case is now usually interpreted, or *UP Government v Lala Gupta* AIR 1960 All 420, cited by KV Krishnaprasad, Chapter 10 of this volume, section IV.3.

[106] As in *Hartog v Colin & Shields* [1939] 3 All ER 566.

[107] This is KV Krishnaprasad's 'first stage in Chapter 10 of this volume, section II.1.ii.

[108] See ibid, section IV.4.

(13) Illegality: there are numerous difficulties with provisions of the Contract Act: for example, in knowing what sorts of illegality trigger section 23, whether a party who is unaware of the other's unlawful purpose may enforce the contract despite section 23 seeming to render the contract void, and whether (or how) an illegal act in the course of performance affects either party. Moreover, section 27 of the Specific Relief Act 1963—which allows the court to make a declaration of rescission if the contract 'is unlawful for causes not apparent on its face and the defendant is more to blame than the plaintiff'—seems hard to fit with section 23, which renders an illegal contract void. The court's decision that title may pass under an illegal contract is hard to reconcile with both section 23 and section 6(h) of the Transfer of Property Act 1882.[109] There is 'room for further development' in the area of restitutionary remedies.[110]

(14) Restraint of trade: in restraint-of-trade cases, the courts use as a considerable variety of techniques to achieve what seem to be sensible results.[111] But as Umakanth and Zhing Xing say, it would be better to amend the sections to make these 'work-arounds' unnecessary and make the law more transparent, predictable and 'upfront'.[112]

(15) Termination for breach: the use of 'voidable' and 'rescission' to describe what I would call 'termination' for breach in sections 55 and 75, when section 39 talks of putting an end to the contract, is at the least unhelpful as well as inconsistent with the Specific Relief Act 1963.[113]

(16) Actions for the price: it seems unfortunate that the Indian courts have allowed a party to claim the price for services that have not been rendered under the 'fiction of fulfilment' derived (incorrectly, it is argued) from the old case of *Mackay v Dick*.[114]

(17) Specific performance: Niranjan makes trenchant criticisms of the 2018 amendment to the Specific Relief Act 1963 for removing the 'adequacy-of-damages' requirement for specific performance[115] and for arguably removing the power to award damages in lieu of specific performance,[116] as well as of the drafting of

[109] See T Sebastian and A Ahluwalia, Chapter 11 of this volume, section V.2.

[110] See ibid, section VI. To my mind many of the difficulties with the legislation on illegality follow from (a) a rules-based approach and (b) treating an illegal contract as void (a the Contract Act, s 23 does) rather than it being unenforceable. India should consider adopting either the flexible, 'factors-based' approach of the UK Supreme Court in *Patel v Mirza* [2016] UKSC 42, [2017] AC 467, or a statutory discretionary scheme as in New Zealand. The authors reject this as unnecessary, but I submit that a 'claim-by-claim' approach (ie asking if this claim should be allowed, rather than whether the contract is void or unenforceable) is helpful—and an open discretion might be clearer than rules that may have to be qualified or 'bent' in order to reach appropriate results.

[111] See this chapter, section III.1.ii; T Zhong Xing and U Varottil, Chapter 12 of this volume, section I).

[112] See T Zhong Xing and U Varottil, Chapter 12 of this volume, section IV.1.

[113] See M Naniwadekar, Chapter 13 of this volume, section V.1; S Elliott KC and D Behl, Chapter 19 of this volume, section IV.

[114] (1880–81) LR 6 App Cas 251. See also N Venkatesan, Chapter 18 of this volume, section II.2.i.

[115] See N Venkatesan, Chapter 18 of this volume, section IV. Subject to the other bars in s 14 (such as contracts requiring personal service or a continuous duty that the court cannot supervise), the claimant can obtain specific performance unless they have obtained 'substituted performance' from a third party under s 20—a new remedy for a common law system but one that, in some civilian systems, is regarded as the primary form of specific performance, eg the German ZPO (*Zivilprocessordnung*), § 887.

[116] See N Venkatesan, Chapter 18 of this volume, section IV.

the amendment. This is obviously a matter on which views may differ, and it is unfortunate that the change does not seem to have been considered carefully in Parliament.[117]

(18) Rescission: it would be helpful to sort out whether rescission is a judicial remedy or a self-help remedy, which is uncertain despite the fact that Indian law does not have the 'fruitless complexity' of the difference between remedies at common law and in equity.[118]

(19) 'Invalidity' of guarantees: the terminology around rescission for lack of 'free consent', especially the reference to 'invalidity' of guarantees in sections 142 and 143 of the Contract Act, needs to be made consistent .[119]

(20) Sums payable on breach of contract: the provisions of section 74 of the Contract Act on sums stipulated as payable on breach of contract are, at best, confusing. Arvind sets out a series of propositions that, if adopted, would be a great improvement on the current law.[120]

But from the very careful analyses of the case law that is in the chapters, it is my impression that, on most of the topics that they consider, the courts are producing results that are considered sensible; or in some areas (like rescission for lack of free consent, where there are fewer decisions), they will be able to do so with the help of the chapters in this collection. The results generally are pretty much in line with the common law as applied in England, Hong Kong, and Singapore. My assumption is that most commentators feel that this is satisfactory. As Paterson and Bant say, 'the Contract Act itself has largely stood the test of time'.[121]

1. Accessibility

Paterson and Bant's chapter provides an excellent discussion of the general issues around accessibility, and I will not repeat their points. But what concrete lessons does it contain for Indian contract law? There are a number of issues to think about:

(1) Can the legislation on contract be found all in one place? In some countries, there has been a major effort to bring together at least consumer provisions: see the French *Code de la consommation* and the UK Consumer Rights Act 2015. The UK Act is less broad in its coverage, but it makes an attempt to integrate

[117] Ibid.
[118] S Elliott KC and D Behl, Chapter 19 of this volume, section I. This issue is debated in England (ibid section VIII) and in *IGE USA Investments Ltd v Revenue and Customs Commissioners* [2021] EWCA Civ 534, [2021] Ch 423, [91] Henderson LJ said that the authorities are in such a state of disarray that only the Supreme Court can reconcile them.
[119] See W Courtney, Chapter 20 of this volume, section III.4; S Elliott KC and D Behl, Chapter 19 of this volume, section V.
[120] See TT Arvind, Chapter 17 of this volume, section IV.
[121] See JM Paterson and E Bant, Chapter 2 of this volume, section IV.

what it does cover, which the *Code de la consommation* does not. I can see why assignment is in the Transfer of Property Act 1882 (it is, or should be, all about property rights), but having the parol evidence rule (which we all know is not, in fact, a rule of evidence—it is not about how the statement may be proved but about a question of substance, what counts as a term of the contract[122]) strikes me as unhelpful. Likewise, it might be helpful to bring the relevant provisions of the Specific Relief Act 1963 into any new Contract Act.

(2) Are there significant areas that are not covered by the Contract Act where it would be helpful to have the rules put into statutory form? Examples might be intention to create legal relations, incorporation rules, interpretation, and when terms may be implied into a contract.

(3) Does the legislation still represent what the courts are actually doing? As just two examples of the issue, (a) section 39 is read as requiring a serious breach before the innocent party can put an end to the contract—which is not obviously what the section says, and (b) when a contract has been frustrated, the courts seem to allow a party who has to restore a benefit it has received to off-set expenses it has incurred—which is not an obvious result of section 64 of the Contract Act. The recent reforms in France were, in part, an attempt to update the Code Napoleon to reflect the current understanding of the law[123]—and perhaps that was even more true of the first draft by Pierre Catala and his colleagues, which preserved more features of the law that were dropped in 2016, such as *la cause*.[124] Is something similar needed here?

(4) Is the Contract Act drafted in the best way? In the United Kingdom (and the same is true in Australia[125]), we have had a lot of discussion about making legislation easier to understand. When the Law Commissions were drafting the terms of reference for the project on unfair terms, the Law Commissions were asked:

> to consider the desirability and feasibility of
>
> ...
>
> (3) Making any replacement legislation clearer and more accessible to the reader, so far as possible without making the law significantly less certain, by using language which is non-technical with simple sentences, by setting out the law in a simple structure following a clear logic and by using a presentation that is easy to follow.[126]

[122] Neither is it only about oral evidence, nor is it a rule, only a presumption. Hence the saying (which goes back at least to L Hoffmann, *The South African Law of Evidence* (Butterworths 1970), ch 9) that 'the parol evidence rule ... shares with the Holy Roman Empire, the distinction of being misleading in all three of its component parts'. The Holy Roman Empire was (at least in the view of outsiders) neither Holy, nor Roman, nor an Empire.

[123] See S Whittaker and J Cartwright, 'Introduction' in J Cartwright and S Whittaker (eds), *The Code Napoleon Rewritten* (Hart 2017) 1, 7; S Rowan, *The New French Law of Contract* (OUP 2022) 3.

[124] On the *Avant-projet Catala*, see J Cartwright, S Vogenauer, and S Whittaker (eds), *Reforming the French Law of Obligations* (Hart 2009).

[125] See JM Paterson and E Bant, Chapter 2 of this volume, section II.4; and see eg P Butt, 'Modern Legal Drafting' (2002) 23 Statute Law Review 12.

[126] Report, *Unfair Terms in Contracts* (Law Com No 292; Scot Law Com No 199, 2005) [1.6].

The aim was to have legislation that could be readily understood, not necessarily by consumers but by consumer advisers who do not have a legal training and by business people with some experience of contracting.[127] To indicate what the Law Commissions had in mind, unusually, the Law Commissions' Consultation Paper[128] contained a partial draft Bill prepared by Parliamentary Counsel. To Parliamentary Counsels' credit, its efforts were approved by the Plain English Campaign.[129] Unfortunately, the draft Bill prepared by the Law Commissions was never adopted as such, though a few of the ideas were carried forward to the Consumer Rights Act 2015. When the Consumer Rights Bill was drafted, it was also intended to be in simpler language.[130] There is quite widespread agreement among consumer lawyers that, sadly, this aim was far from being achieved.[131] But there is no reason to stop trying to make legislation easier to understand.

(5) A particular issue is the use of illustrations or examples. I am sure that judges and practising lawyers in India no longer need illustrations to help them understand statutes, at least where the rules are, indeed, set out in the sections of the Contract Act and the illustrations are not left to do much of the work, as with the illustrations to section 73.[132] But if legislation is to be readily understandable to at least some non-lawyers, examples seem to be a useful idea. In England, unfortunately, we have lost this battle. The Consumer Credit Act 1974 (CCA) contains examples, and the Law Commission's Consultation Paper on Unfair Terms provisionally proposed including examples in the Bill. But when we came to the Report, we were told by Parliamentary Counsel that this was a complete non-starter. Why? Apparently, because one of the CCA examples is demonstrably wrong[133]—and the Office of Parliamentary Counsel had decided that never again would it allow examples to be used in legislation. So the draft Bill in the Report was without examples, and the Consumer Rights Act 2015 has none. I hope that the Indian equivalent would not be so risk averse.

But this does raise an issue that affects all the questions above: accessible to whom? If it is intended that only Indian lawyers should ever read the Act (a view that I suppose might get some support in the legal profession!), there may be little need to worry. But part of the drive behind the French reforms was to make it easier for lawyers from other legal systems to find out about (and hopefully then adopt) French law. The

[127] See Report, *Unfair Terms in Contracts*, Law Com No 292 (n 128) [2.45].

[128] *Unfair Terms in Contracts* (CP No 166; Scottish Law Commission Discussion Paper No 119, 2002).

[129] See Report, *Unfair Terms in Contracts*, Law Com No 292 (n 128) [2.47].

[130] 'There is general agreement across business and consumer groups that the existing UK consumer law is unnecessarily complex. It is fragmented and, in places, unclear, for example where the law has not kept up with technological change or lacks precision or where it is couched in legalistic language': Explanatory Notes, [5].

[131] See eg P Giliker, 'The Consumer Rights Act 2015—A Bastion of European Consumer Rights' (2017) 37 Legal Studies 78, 85–86; J Devenney, 'The Legacy of the Cameron–Clegg Coalition Programme of Reform of the Law on the Supply of Goods, Digital Content and Services to Consumers' [2018] Journal of Business Law 485.

[132] See this chapter, section II.2.

[133] Courtney identifies some similar problems in the Contract Act—and also cases in which the basis of the result stated is unclear; e.g. W Courtney, Chapter 20 of this volume, sections III.1.ii, III.5 and III.6.

Restatements of English law produced by Professor (now Lord) Burrows[134] also have this as one of their aims.[135]

2. The Nature and Philosophy of Modern Indian Contract Law

Though Arvind's chapter is directly concerned only with agreed sums and limitation clauses, in section III of his chapter entitled 'Towards a Diagnosis: Rediscovering the Social Function of Contract Law', he argues that

> A closer examination of the historical origins of the discretion conferred by section 74, and the purposes that underlay it, suggests a very different path that Indian law can and should take, which will resolve not only the problems with the current state of Indian law itself, but also problems from which the common law elsewhere continues to suffer.[136]

This suggests we should think about the social functions of the Contract Act as a whole.

Where does the Contract Act stand in comparison to other laws of contract, especially the more modern civilian systems? We can point to a number of key issues on which there are major differences between the traditional common law systems and many of the systems that have been heavily influenced by either Napoleonic law or German law.

By way of illustration, let me compare English and German contract law on a number of key issues. In brief,

(1) German law has developed a duty of disclosure under the rubric of *culpa in contrahendo* (itself adopted on the basis of the general clause requiring good faith, § 242 BGB) and, when there is such a duty, German law recognises 'fraud by silence'.[137] It also allows a contract to be avoided by a party that was mistaken about the essential nature of the subject matter.[138] English law not only has no duty of disclosure and does not recognise fraud by silence[139] but also does not allow a contract to be avoided because one party was mistaken as to the substance or essential qualities of the subject matter of the contract, unless that mistake was caused by a misrepresentation by the other party.[140]

[134] See A Burrows, *A Restatement of the English Law of Unjust Enrichment* (1st edn, OUP 2012); A Burrows, *A Restatement of the English Law of Contract* (2nd edn, OUP 2020).
[135] See Burrows, *A Restatement of the English Law of Unjust Enrichment*, 2nd edn (n 136) vii.
[136] See TT Arvind, Chapter 17 of this volume, section III.
[137] See B Markesinis, H Unberath, and A Johnston, *The German Law of Contract*, (2nd edn, Hart 2006) 305–10.
[138] § 119 II BGB.
[139] For a modern statement of the position, see *ING Bank NV v Ros Roca SA* [2011] EWCA Civ 353, [2011] All ER (D) 39 (Apr) [92] (Rix LJ, remarking that 'silence is golden').
[140] For a more detailed comparison see *Ius Commune Casebook* (n 18) ch 14.

(2) German law imposes liability for breaking off negotiations contrary to good faith; English law imposes liability for breaking off negotiations only if one party fraudulently or (possibly) negligently gave the other party incorrect factual information about whether the contract negotiations were likely to succeed.[141]

(3) As to unfair terms, German law provides that 'surprising clauses' do not form part of the contract, whether or not the document containing the clause has been signed,[142] and imposes controls over the fairness of terms that were not negotiated.[143] In English law, if the contract has been signed, the clause will form part of the contract, as we saw earlier; and only certain types of unfair term—principally, clauses that in some way exclude or restrict liability—are invalid or valid only if reasonable under the Unfair Contract Terms Act 1977.

(4) In the cases of fundamental change of circumstances, German law allows the court to adjust the contract to restore the original balance;[144] English law gives no relief unless the contract or the 'contractual venture' turns out to be substantially and permanently impossible.[145]

(5) English law has no doctrine of good faith and, though the courts have used their inherent jurisdiction to develop the law to solve some problems of unfairness that German law might deal with under the doctrine of good faith,[146] it very seldom requires more than that the parties refrain from dishonesty; with only a very few exceptions, the general English law of contract does not require either party to have a reasonable 'consideration for the interests of the other party'.[147] It is true that, recently, it has been recognised that there may be an implied duty of good faith when the contract is 'relational',[148] but the Supreme Court has not yet confirmed this development and has emphasised that there is no general duty of good faith in English contract Law.[149]

As the result of the reforms in 2016, French law is now very close to German law on all these points.

Where does the Contract Act stand? I have argued that the Contract Act as interpreted and applied today seems to place Indian contract law firmly in the common law tradition as found in England, Hong Kong, or Singapore. For example, good faith seems to have even less of a hold in Indian contract law than it does in England. Mysoor

[141] ibid ch 13. Liability for negligence in this situation was imposed in *Box v Midland Bank Ltd* [1979] 2 Lloyd's Rep 391, on appeal (as to costs only) [1981] 1 Lloyd's Rep 434.

[142] § 305c BGB.

[143] ibid §§ 303–10.

[144] ibid § 313; see Markesinis, Unberath, and Johnston (n 140) ch 7.

[145] For a comparison see *Ius Commune Casebook* (n 18) ch 29.

[146] See *Interfoto Picture Library Ltd v Stilletto Visual Programmes Ltd* [1989] 1 QB 433, 439 (Bingham LJ).

[147] This is taken from the definition of 'good faith' in the European Commission's *Proposal for a Regulation of the European Parliament and of the Council on a Common European Sales Law* (11 October 2011) COM(2011) 635 final, art 2(b).

[148] This development began with the decision in *Yam Seng Pte Ltd v International Trade Corp Ltd* [2013] EWHC 111 (QB), [2013] Lloyd's Rep 526. A full account of good faith in English law can be found in *Chitty* (n 89) [2-026]–[2-113] (S Whittaker).

[149] See *Pakistan International Airline Corp v Times Travel (UK) Ltd* [2021] UKSC 40, [2021] 3 WLR 727; *Chitty* (n 89) [2-043].

and Kumar argue that 'there is no reason to assume that no duty of good faith can be read into the interpretation of the Contract Act itself, or into Indian common law'. However, they say that the courts do not use the language of good faith or speak of how a duty of good faith might be implied.[150] A decision of the Kerala High Court has held that an arbitrator's decision that clauses permitting unilateral termination of the contract was subject to a requirement of good is not illegal under the standard of review in the section 28(3) of the Arbitration and Conciliation Act 1996, but Mysoor and Kumar have found no other cases, and there are decisions to the contrary.[151]

The only aspect in which Indian law seems to deviate at all is that the courts may be more liberal in the area of changed circumstances/impracticability—as to this, there are hints that it may suffice that a contract has become 'impracticable to perform',[152] and Bhadbhade notes a case in which a contract was held to be frustrated by a 400 per cent increase in prices.[153] That suggests a more liberal approach than at least modern English judgments,[154] which not only seem to insist on impossibility in a pretty literal sense but also, even when performance of a contract has become impossible without the fault of either party, are inclined to refuse to find frustration on the ground that the contract allocated the risk to the complaining party.[155] But the one decision is not much to go on; most Indian courts seem to reject any notion that a contract may be discharged, let alone adjusted, just because it has become excessively difficult to perform.

I have argued elsewhere that the differences reflect differing views of a contract, of what contract law is seeking to do, and of the role that the courts should play in enforcing contracts; and that, in turn, these differences in approach reflect the differing kinds of case that typically come before the courts.[156]

I think the main reason for the hard-nosed English attitude is that in the only English courts whose decisions are reported (in practice, in civil and commercial cases, the High Court, and the appellate courts—county court judgments are reported only very sporadically), the overwhelming bulk of cases are 'commercial' cases, usually involving high-value contracts between parties who are sophisticated or, at least, well advised.

[150] See M Kumar and P Mysoor, Chapter 15 of this volume, section I. Duties of good faith are recognised in specific types of contract such as insurance: ibid section IV.1.iv.

[151] Ibid, section IV.1.ii.

[152] See N Bhadbhade, Chapter 14 of this volume, section IX.5.

[153] *Easun Engg Co Ltd v Fertiliser v & Chemicals Travancore Ltd* AIR 1991 Mad 158; see N Bhadbhade, Chapter 14 of this volume, section XII.1.ii (though it appears that the increase was also held to fall within the *force majeure* clause in the contract).

[154] Some of the older English judgments seem less demanding, including *Krell v Henry* [1903] 2 KB 740 (CA) (the coronation cases seem to be almost the only examples of frustration of purpose) and *Metropolitan Water Board v Dick Kerr & Co Ltd* [1918] AC 119 (performance of construction contract disrupted by the First World War; contract frustrated because performance in economic circumstances after the war, which was still continuing at the time of judgment, would be radically different). In Chapter 14 of this volume (section III), Nilima Bhadbhade refers to GC Rankin, *Background to Indian Law* (CUP 1946). Rankin wrote (ibid, at 109) that

> If one were inclined to seek a test of Stephen's draft by asking how under it the Coronation cases, or the cases of 'frustration of adventure' arising out of the war of 1914–18 would fall to be determined, I think it might be claimed for the Indian statute that on the whole it would have provided better justice and greater certainty than have been achieved in the English decisions.

[155] See eg *Edwinton Commercial Corp v Tsavliris Russ (Worldwide Salvage & Towage) Ltd ('The Sea Angel')* [2007] EWCA Civ 547.

[156] H Beale, 'The Impact of the Decisions of the European Courts on English Contract Law: The Limits of Voluntary Harmonisation' (2010) 18 European Review of Private Law 501.

Between such parties, the old notions of freedom and sanctity of contract, and of self-reliance—'qui dit contractuel dit juste'[157]—are quite plausible. I suspect that the case loads of the courts in many countries are very different, often involving small businesses and lower-value contracts.

To this should be added two further points about English contract law. The first is that, often, the contracts being litigated (eg commodity contracts or charterparties) were made in a market that fluctuates dramatically, and the real question is whether a party that has ended up 'out of the money' can find a way to escape from the contract so as to throw the loss back onto the other party. The English courts have certainly developed the law in ways that appear to be designed to prevent a party taking opportunistic advantage, such as the doctrine laid down in the *Hong Kong Fir* case,[158] which interprets contracts so as to prevent the victim of a breach by the other party from terminating when the breach had only slight effects and the motivation appeared to be to escape what had turned out to be a bad bargain. However, in such cases, any uncertainty as to how the law will be applied is likely to encourage litigation, and the English courts have frequently preferred 'bright-line' rules that they consider will give more predictable outcomes to rules that may seem to produce 'just' results on the facts of the particular case.[159] It is interesting that it is unclear whether the *Hong Kong Fir* doctrine is part of Indian law; quite possibly, 'opportunistic termination' is not a phenomenon that often confronts an Indian court.[160]

The second point is that English law is an 'export product'. The English legal profession goes to great lengths to sell its services to businesses around the world and to encourage the use of English law as the 'law of choice' for international transactions.[161] And, rightly or wrongly, it has been assumed that international businesses are capable of looking after their own interests and that the English courts should not try to control the fairness of the terms of their contracts. When the Unfair Contract Terms Act 1977 was adopted, there was a deliberate decision that it should not apply to either international supply contracts or contracts that are subject to English law only because the parties have chosen that law to govern the contract:[162]

> The effect of imposing our proposed controls in relation to those contracts might well be to discourage foreign businessmen from agreeing to arbitrate their disputes in England.[163]

[157] A Fouillée, *La science sociale contemporaine* (2nd edn, Librairie Hachette 1885) 410; L Rolland, 'Qui dit contractuel dit juste' (2006) 51 McGill Law Journal 765, 771.

[158] *Hongkong Fir Shipping Co Ltd v Kawasaki Kisen Kaisha Ltd* [1962] 2 QB 26.

[159] See eg *Bunge Corp v Tradax SA* [1981] 1 WLR 711 (HL).

[160] See M Naniwadekar, Chapter 13 of this volume, section V.2.

[161] See H Kötz, 'The Jurisdiction of Choice: England and Wales, or Germany?' (2010) 6 European Review of Private Law 1243.

[162] Contract Act, ss 26 and 27.

[163] Law Commissions, *Exemption Clauses Second Report* (Law Com No 69, Scot Law Com No 39, 1975) [232].

So English contract law is 'law for big business'. Perhaps the same is true for Hong Kong and Singapore.

What types of cases are the Indian courts having to deal with? I have not had the opportunity to look at the detailed facts of the many cases cited in the chapters, but it is my impression that while the Indian courts are often dealing with large and sophisticated parties, the variety of parties and contracts is much greater than in England. Also, though I am sure that disputes over deals 'that have turned sour' are as common in India as anywhere else, the disputes may not often involve the kind of opportunism in the face of changed market prices that, because of the sums at stake, produce so much litigation in the Commercial Court in London. That might explain why the case law on termination under the Contract Act seems to be relatively underdeveloped—many of the English cases on the topic, including the *Hong Kong Fir* case, were driven by sudden shifts in the market.

To me, this raises a question that should be asked in an overview of the Contract Act, and it is the same question that confronted the reformers in the 19th century: to what extent is the common law model adopted in England suited to the types of case and types of litigants coming before the courts in India? Does the law fit? Perhaps colleagues who practice and teach in India can provide an answer; I know I cannot do so.

What I can say, however, is that in England, there is a group that seems to need the kind of protections that are found in, say, French and German law but are so conspicuously lacking in English law. This is small businesses. In particular, I think small businesses need protection from unfair terms in the other party's standard contract.[164] Small businesses are unlikely to read or understand the other party's standard terms, and the cost of taking legal advice will be so high relative to the value of most of the small business's transactions that they will seldom seek it.

3. Consumer Legislation and Other Regulations

Our project is about the Contract Act and general contract law. That is perfectly sensible, but it does leave me in a slight quandary if I am to try to give any evaluation of Indian contract law and its modern characteristics. In almost every legal system, general contract law has been supplemented by consumer legislation, and it is not really possible to give an accurate picture of the whole without taking the consumer legislation into account. The same can be said of employment and housing legislation. There may also be specific legislation on consumer credit.

I am not in a position to explore fully what special legislation protects contracting parties in India. Arvind tells us that, in India, employment contracts are largely governed by the ordinary law of contract. He also refers to the Consumer Protection Act 2019 and makes the interesting and important point that the definition of consumer is

[164] This was recommended by the Law Commissions' Report, *Unfair Terms in Contracts*, Law Com No 292 (n 128).

unusually wide: it includes self-employed persons in relation to contracts entered into for the purpose of their business.[165]

The Consumer Protection Act 2019 regulates a wide variety of unfair practices, including the use of unfair terms, and section 2(46) provides that a contract is unfair if it has a term that causes significant change in the rights of the consumer, giving a non-exhaustive list of such terms.[166] The use of contracts containing these terms can therefore be prohibited by the Central Consumer Protection Authority.[167]

If we are to understand the role the law of contract plays in a jurisdiction, we cannot exclude such 'public-law' measures from the picture. At least in the United Kingdom, these play an important role in protecting consumers by policing the market. The EU Directive on Unfair Terms in Consumer Contracts[168] contains a provision requiring Member States to enable a public body[169] to take steps to prevent the use of unfair terms.[170] In the United Kingdom at least, that provision has had a very significant impact. For example, terms that purported to exclude or restrict a trader's liability for death or personal injury caused by negligence had been rendered ineffective by the Unfair Contract Terms Act 1977,[171] but there was nothing to prevent a trader from using such a term. In the 1980s, it was not uncommon to find such clauses still being used by traders—presumably, either through ignorance or in the hope of deterring claims from injured consumers who did not know the law. When the Directive was implemented, the task of enforcement was given to the Office of Fair Trading.[172] Initially, I was very sceptical as to whether this would do much good.[173] I am happy to say that I was proved wrong. The Director General of Fair Trading (and after 2002, the Office of Fair Trading (OFT)[174]) was very active and achieved a great deal in terms of encouraging traders and, on occasions, sectors of industry such as mobile phone providers, to improve the terms that they offer to consumers.[175] The OFT's role has now been taken over by the Competition and Markets Authority (CMA), which also publishes a very useful guidance to traders.[176] The CMA's powers are now set out in the Consumer Rights Act 2015.[177]

165 Consumer Protection Act 2019, s 2(7)(ii)(a). Curiously, it seems that this applies to goods bought by the self-employed person but not to services.

166 It seems odd that the list does not include exclusion or limitation of liability clauses. Perhaps they were thought too obvious to be worth mentioning. That, again, prompts the question, 'Too obvious to whom?'

167 Consumer Protection Act 2019, s 18.

168 Council Directive 93/13/EEC of 5 April 1993 on unfair terms in consumer contracts.

169 It was argued that merely giving the power to the Office of Fair Trading was not adequate to implement the Directive, and powers to initiate proceedings had also to be given to the Consumers Association: see Unfair Terms in Consumer Contracts Regulations 1999, SI 1999/2083, art 12 and sch 1. Power to initiate proceedings was also given to various regulators.

170 Council Directive 93/13 (n 171) art 7.

171 Unfair Contract Terms Act 1977, s 2(1).

172 See Unfair Terms in Consumer Contracts Regulations 1994, SI 1994/3159, Reg 8.

173 See H Beale, 'Legislative Control of Fairness: The Directive on Unfair Contract Terms in Consumer Contracts' in J Beatson and D Friedmann (eds), *Good Faith and Fault in Contract Law* (OUP 1995) 231, 251–61.

174 The office of Director General of Foreign Trade was abolished by the Enterprise Act 2002.

175 See S Bright, 'Winning the Battle against Unfair Contract Terms' (2000) 20 Legal Studies 331.

176 See eg CMA37, 'Unfair Contract Terms Guidance' <www.gov.uk/government/publications/unfair-contract-terms-cma37> accessed 4 November 2023.

177 The legislation that now implements the Directive as a whole is the Consumer Rights Act 2015, Part 2 and, as regards art 7, sch 3. On public enforcement generally, see *Chitty*, vol II (n 89) [41-470]ff.

The Directive also provides that a term that is unfair within the meaning of the Directive shall not be binding on the consumer.[178] In contrast, the Indian Consumer Protection Act 2019 provides for the regulation of traders by the state and, except in the case of product liability,[179] does not grant rights or give remedies to individual consumers. So, an unfair term seems to remain enforceable in the courts. This seems unfortunate for consumers, let alone for small businesses, which may be just as much in need of protection.

From considering the extent of special measures affecting contracts in India, Arvind reaches a radical conclusion, which is worth quoting:

> The consequence is that Indian contract law operates in a very different context from English law. The steady retreat of general contract law in England from a significant number of areas of interaction means that the courts can refocus principles on the needs of commercial transactions. That option is not tenable in the Indian context, where the transactional context, and the nature of the social and economic relations to which a transaction relates, matter in a way they do not elsewhere. Whatever the desirability in purely normative terms of the positions in relation to freedom of contract that have been taken elsewhere in the common law world, in the Indian context, emphasis has to be placed on the purposes that the statutory discretion created by section 74 was intended to serve.[180]

A similar point may well apply more generally. I suspect there might be little enthusiasm in India for adopting the full panoply of protective measures found in Germany, but it is clear that some areas of contract law merit careful consideration, for example, unconscionability and exclusion and limitation of liability clauses. Both are topics on which the courts have concerns[181] and the Indian Law Commission has recommended change.[182]

V. The Future

Tofaris writes,

> The future is likely to increase the pressure on the rules in the Act. If anything, the methods of contracting and communicating will continue to change rapidly. Indian law will have to deal with difficult questions that will inevitably arise. One approach is to revisit the Act, in the light of its history, and examine afresh whether it provides

[178] Council Directive 93/13 (n 171) art 6(1).

[179] Contract Act, s 39. In Chapter 17 of this volume (section IV), TT Arvind notes that product liability may include deficient services.

[180] See TT Arvind, Chapter 17 of this volume, section IV (footnotes omitted).

[181] ibid section IV.

[182] See S Swaminathan and V Singh, Chapter 9 of this volume, section II.4.i.

> an answer. . . . A second approach is to adopt a flexible and creative reading of the Act's provisions.[183] . . . Nonetheless, there are limits to how far the Act's language can apply. A third approach, therefore, is to seek solutions outside it. This is aided by the fact that the Act was never intended to be a complete code, providing an answer to every eventuality. Solutions of this type can take the form of judicial law-making or separate legislation. . . . A fourth approach is to revise the Contract Act. This would facilitate its comprehensiveness and strengthen its position as the doctrinal pivot for the future development of Indian contract law. It would also be in line with the intention of those who drafted the Act. 'To suppose', Stephen wrote, 'that any code will go on by itself for ever is like supposing that a railway can be built which will not want repairs.'[184]

Revisiting the Contract Act is certainly worthwhile if, on a fresh reading, it yields a better solution than that currently applied, for example, if the current solution is one that has merely been borrowed from English law. But 'creative readings' and solutions outside both raise issues of accessibility. I would prefer to see a review and revision of the Contract Act as a whole. But meanwhile, we should acknowledge that the Contract Act was a great achievement and that it has stood the test of time remarkably well.

[183] A Briggs and A Burrows, *The Law of Contract in Myanmar* (OUP 2017) 44.
[184] See S Tofaris, Chapter 5 of this volume, section VIII (footnotes omitted).

Index

For the benefit of digital users, indexed terms that span two pages (e.g., 52–53) may, on occasion, appear on only one of those pages.